INTERNATIONAL SALES
LAW AND ARBITRATION

ASPEN PUBLISHERS
KLUWER LAW INTERNATIONAL

INTERNATIONAL SALES LAW AND ARBITRATION

PROBLEMS, CASES AND COMMENTARY

With an Introduction by Eric E. Bergsten

Joseph F. Morrissey
Assistant Professor of Law
Stetson University College of Law

Jack M. Graves
Assistant Professor of Law
Touro Law Center

Wolters Kluwer
Law & Business

AUSTIN   BOSTON   CHICAGO   NEW YORK   THE NETHERLANDS

ISBN 978-0-7355-7707-7

Published by:
Kluwer Law International
P.O. Box 316
2400 AH Alphen aan den Rijn
The Netherlands
sales@kluwerlaw.com
http://www.kluwerlaw.com

Sold and distributed in North, Central and South America by:
Aspen Publishers, Inc.
7201 McKinney Circle
Frederick, MD 21704
United States of America

Sold and distributed in all other countries by:
Turpin Distribution Services Ltd.
Stratton Business Park
Pegasus Drive, Biggleswade
Bedfordshire SG18 8TQ
United Kingdom

PREFACE

Transactions in goods form a substantial part of any general business law practice. Whether an attorney serves as transactional counsel in negotiating the terms of a "deal" or as an advocate when a dispute arises, a sound foundational knowledge of commercial law and dispute resolution options is a fundamental prerequisite for any business practice.

Our commercial world is shrinking every day, and the concept of an insular local practice is increasingly becoming a relic of our recent, but quickly disappearing, past. Accordingly, an international perspective on both the sale of goods and dispute resolution has become essential for all business practices.

For the prospective international business attorney—destined for practice in Beijing, Paris, or Chicago—the value of an international understanding of this area is obvious. Such attorneys will encounter cross-border transactions as a matter of course and will need to know the legal infrastructure that governs them and subsequent disputes that arise.

Perhaps less obvious is that for the prospective local attorney—destined to practice in Xian, Lyon or Omaha—an international understanding of this area is also valuable. An attorney can learn much about her own legal system by discovering and comparing other alternatives. Such a comparative perspective is particularly important in the commercial world where parties generally possess substantial autonomy in ordering their own legal affairs. Knowledge of a variety of legal systems and trade practices will help these attorneys structure the best deal for their clients. Further, clients in small towns around the world will increasingly be engaging in cross-border sales transactions. Attorneys for such clients must be equipped to handle the issues that will face them. In short, an international perspective is invaluable for any prospective commercial lawyer, and this casebook is intended to provide just such a perspective.

This casebook includes materials on both (i) the substantive contract law governing the international sale of goods and (ii) the law governing international arbitration as a means of contract dispute resolution. This integrated approach is somewhat unique, inasmuch as substantive contract law and dispute resolution are generally treated as separate and distinct subject matter areas. Traditionally, courses and casebooks have examined international sales law independently or in conjunction with domestic sales law. Similarly, international commercial arbitration has been studied in isolation, or in relation to domestic arbitration law, litigation, or other forms of alternative dispute resolution. While the two may both be included in a broad survey level course in international business transactions, this particular casebook is atypical as it narrowly focuses on the intersection between international sales law and international commercial arbitration.

One reason to present these two subjects together is that an arbitration agreement is, at its core, a contract—one that obligates the parties to settle their controversies through a private adjudicative process resulting in a final and binding resolution of the dispute. As such, the subject of international commercial arbitration can be presented very effectively in a doctrinal course covering international contracts in a way that enhances the process of learning both. Moreover, international commercial arbitration is the dominant means of resolving disputes arising out of international sales transactions. Accordingly, an arbitration agreement is an integral part of any international sales agreement and consideration of the two topics in tandem is therefore both logical and effective for promoting understanding of both.

The work of the United Nations Commission on International Trade Law (UNCITRAL) in the areas of both international sales law and international commercial arbitration also reflects this close and symbiotic relationship between international sales and arbitration. Likewise, the Willem C. Vis International Commercial Moot (the Vis Moot) has been bringing students together from all over the world on an annual basis for over 14 years to study both of these topics together. The alumni of the Vis Moot have been publishing the Vindobona Journal of International Commercial Law for over a decade to promote and publish scholarship specifically in these two areas.

We have adapted the notion of a traditional "casebook" here inasmuch as most of the substance of international law is not contained in the past cases of any one particular country, but is more centrally focused on statutory law, as further explained in international treatises and various tribunals' interpretations of the agreements of previous parties. Throughout this book we use an assortment of materials—chief among them the principal statutes governing international sales and arbitration, but also certain cases, arbitral decisions, commentary, and other sources—to illustrate the law and a variety of issues that arise under that law. In each section we also pose a series of problems intended to provide students with an opportunity to apply the law, as aided by the additional materials presented in the "casebook." Finally, we have endeavored to provoke students with questions about the policies underlying the various approaches taken by the prevailing laws.

The authors would like to acknowledge the Vis Moot as the original impetus for the ideas underlying this casebook. While the authors believe the integrated approach taken by this casebook to be an effective one, irrespective of any interest in the Vis Moot, this approach is particularly valuable when used in a course that is also intended to prepare students for possible participation in the Moot.[1]

In sum, our hope in combining the doctrinal treatment of international sales law and arbitration in a single casebook is to offer the opportunity to address these two subjects together, in a manner that leads to a deeper understanding of the individual aspects of each. Further, we hope that promoting a deep understanding· of these topics will also aid one of the central goals of UNCITRAL—the facilitation and promotion of international trade, as the students who study these topics become practitioners and business people who are better equipped to participate in and strengthen the international commercial marketplace.

December 20, 2007   *Joseph F. Morrissey*

Jack M. Graves

---

[1] *See* Jack M. Graves and Stephanie A. Vaughan, *The Willem C. Vis Int'l Commercial Arbitration Moot: Making the Most of an Extraordinary Educational Opportunity*, 10 Vindobona J. 173, 180-190 (2006) (Section 3.1, Professor Graves describing the concept of building a law school course around the annual Vis Moot problem).

ACKNOWLEDGEMENTS

The authors owe a debt of gratitude to many people for helping make this book project happen. First and foremost, thanks to Deans Darby Dickerson and Ellen Podgor at Stetson University College of Law and Dean Lawrence Raful at Touro Law Center for supporting the project. Thanks go out to Eric Bergsten for all his work with the Vis Moot and the CISG itself and his support of this book. The book could not have been written without the wonderful resources available through the PACE Law School CISG Database, maintained by Professor Albert Kritzer, Executive Secretary of the Institute of International Commercial Law at Pace University School of Law.

Thanks also to our friends who have journeyed through the challenges of much of this material in connection with the VIS Moot, including especially our good friends Dr. Eugen Salpius, of Salpius Rechtsanwalts GmbH; Professor Christiana Fountoulakis of the University of Basel; Professors Hrvoje Sikirić, Siniša Petrović, Nina Tepeš, and Davor Babić of the University of Zagreb; Kristof Cox and his colleagues at the Catholic University of Leuven; and Professors Harry Flechtner and Ronald Brand of the University of Pittsburgh. In addition, Professors Mike Allen, Brooke Bowman, Mark Bauer, Peter Fitzgerald, Jamie Fox and Brad Stone of Stetson University College of law have been incredibly supportive of this project in every way, from being sounding boards for ideas to reviewing the format of footnotes.

Special thanks go out to the students in our International Sales Law and Arbitration courses in the fall of 2007 who fought through early drafts of this book used in their classes. Their suggestions and feedback were incredibly helpful. Jared Dolan deserves special mention for his help in putting together the proposal that ultimately led to this book. Our indefatigably enthusiastic and incredibly capable research assistants, Kathleen DiSanto, Dayanna Lopez, Teresita Lopez, and Traci McKee, have likewise been fantastic throughout this process. We truly could not have accomplished this without their help.

Special thanks go out to our paralegal, Lisa Padla, for her tireless work in proofreading and formatting drafts for hours on end (though we accept any of the inevitable typos or mistakes in this text as our own). Thanks also to the entire team of faculty support at Stetson, including Louise Petren, Shannon Mullins, and Dianne Oeste.

Finally, thanks go out to the greatest friend and colleague we could have, Professor Stephanie Vaughan, of Stetson University College of Law. Her tenacity and passion for teaching advocacy is a constant inspiration; and her support for our own respective efforts in recent years has played a very substantial part in the events leading up to this book.

INTRODUCTION

By Eric E. Bergsten

Professors Graves and Morrissey have indicated that the book they have written was inspired by the Willem C. Vis International Commercial Arbitration Moot. I consider it a great honor that teaching materials have been produced for use in law school courses in which the Moot is an integral part. That signals to me that the Moot is fulfilling its educational role. This book is directed at a larger audience as well, and it is well designed for general use in a course in international commercial law in both law schools and business schools. I wish it and the readers of this introduction great success.

International commercial law is the subject matter of this book. Commercial law is an interesting subject.[1] It becomes particularly interesting when the transactions take place between individuals and commercial entities in different countries. The way in which business operates is often different in the two or more countries concerned, and the law will certainly be different. It is sometimes possible to avoid having to concern oneself with the foreign law by a choice of law clause in the contract that provides that the contract will be governed by one's own law. However, that only shifts the problem to the other party; it does not eliminate it. What I have found to be the most interesting aspect of my work in the field of international commercial law has been the contacts with foreign lawyers. We think about the same problems, but with somewhat different perspectives. What is self-evident at home may be strange abroad.

The Moot is designed to give students a glimpse of what practice in this field consists of. It involves a dispute over a contract of sale subject to the United Nations Convention on Contracts for the International Sale of Goods (CISG). The dispute is to be settled in arbitration. It has turned out that the combination of a sales dispute with international commercial arbitration as the means of dispute settlement is an excellent vehicle for introducing students to the legal rules that govern the relationships between commercial parties in different countries.

The value of the combination of CISG and arbitration was not as clear to me when the Moot began fifteen years ago in 1993. The Moot was intended to promote awareness of the work of the United Nations Commission on International Trade Law (UNCITRAL) and especially of the CISG to students

---

[1] I have to admit that not everyone finds it so, which continues to amaze me.

around the world. The organization of a moot required a forum for the settlement of the dispute, and it was natural that the forum would be an arbitral tribunal. An international moot could not be based on the sales dispute arising in a national court, even though that also happens in practice. Moreover, UNCITRAL had done important work in the field of international commercial arbitration and the Moot could bring that work to the students' attention as well. By 1993 the UNCITRAL Arbitration Rules of 1976 were being used in many *ad hoc* arbitrations and were increasingly used as institutional rules with the changes necessary to fit them into an institutional context. The UNCITRAL Model Law on International Commercial Arbitration dating from 1985 had already been incorporated into many national arbitration laws and, even where the Model Law had not been adopted as such, it had become the standard by which new and existing arbitration laws were measured. UNCITRAL was also active in promoting the adoption of the 1958 Convention on the Recognition and Enforcement of Foreign Arbitral Awards (New York Convention). In summary, the subject matter of the proposed Moot was a contract of sale subject to the CISG with arbitration being a necessary, but at the beginning a subsidiary, feature.

The original conception of the Moot as involving a contract for the sale of goods with arbitration as a clearly subsidiary feature was similar to the way in which arbitration enters into the typical contract of sale, be it domestic or international. The business parties are interested in the transaction. If they anticipated disputes that could not be settled amicably, they would not enter into the transaction. An arbitration clause in the contract probably indicates that the parties used a form widely used in the particular trade or that the clause was in the general conditions of one or the other of the parties. A negotiated dispute resolution clause in a sales contract is a less common occurrence, though it is more likely to occur if the contract is large and not of a routine nature. There are, of course, some types of business activity in which disputes are so common that a dispute resolution clause is considered to be a necessary provision. Construction contracts are the most obvious example and there have been interesting developments in recent years in devising dispute resolution clauses for large construction projects, such as airports and large dams. The reports are that the adverse consequences of the disputes that inevitably arise have been significantly reduced.

Consistent with the conception that the Moot was primarily about the CISG, the early Problems had almost no issues of arbitration law or practice. Gradually that changed so that in recent years the Moot Problem has included both sales law and arbitration issues. It has been a happy development for many reasons. The one that is most relevant to the current book is that they fit so well together for educational purposes. They can be used to demonstrate both how the lawyer drafts the contract and how the provisions interact if the transaction does not go as anticipated.

When drafting a contract of sale, or when drafting the general conditions for a client's purchase orders, sales contract forms or order confirmations, the lawyer must draft in the light of the applicable law. A provision might be drafted, for example, to specify when and where the goods must be inspected and when notice of any alleged non-conformity must be given. The applicable law would already have provisions on those matters, but they may be either more general than would be desired in the specific contract or not well suited to the nature of the transaction. A course in which the law of sales was taught through the mechanism of contract drafting would be an effective way to teach both the doctrinal law and the business context in which the legal rules are applicable. The contract drafting exercise might include a dispute resolution clause, which we can now assume would provide for arbitration. It would be appropriate at that stage to discuss those aspects of the law of arbitration that one should know before drafting the clause. That would include such matters as the relative advantages of ad hoc or institutional arbitration, how the arbitrators are chosen, the procedure that will be followed before the tribunal and enforcement of the eventual award. In regard to the relationship between the arbitration clause and the remainder of the sales contract, one might discuss the separability of the arbitration clause from the sales contract in which it is located and where to look to determine whether the formal requirements to conclude a valid arbitration agreement through the use of the arbitration clause are the same as those to conclude a valid contract of sale.

In the Moot the same or similar questions are asked, but now from the point of view of the transaction as it actually took place. Was the notice of alleged non-conformity of the goods on time and sufficiently detailed? Was the contract of sale validly concluded? Was the arbitration agreement validly concluded? Is it possible that the contract of sale was validly concluded but not the arbitration agreement even though it was a clause in the sales contract or perhaps that the arbitration agreement was validly concluded but not the contract of which it was one of the clauses? What should the arbitral tribunal do if one of the parties has challenged the jurisdiction of the tribunal in the courts? All of these questions and more can be discussed in the classroom but they can be explored in more depth in the Moot.

This is not the place to discuss the advantages of arbitration, especially those arising in an international transaction. Suffice it to say that almost everyone would much prefer arbitration to litigating in the other party's courts, which would otherwise be the only option for one of the parties.

The Moot simulates some aspects of an arbitration. It cannot simulate an entire arbitration. The Moot has no procedure for the students to gather the facts, though there is a limited substitution for it and the Moot is considerably more fact-intensive than are most moots. There is no witness examination before the tribunal. Most importantly, there is no possibility for the parties to reach a settlement. Each of them could be the subject matter of an international competition, but it is not possible to have all of them in the same competition. The consequence is that the Moot emphasizes the interpretation and application of the law to the somewhat complex facts and the contentious side of arbitration rather than its more conciliatory side.

The Moot, like any other well constructed moot, serves as a vehicle to train law students in some of the ten "fundamental lawyering skills" lawyers should be able to engage in as identified in the American Bar Association's "MacCrate Report"[2]: (1) problem solving; (2) legal analysis and reasoning; (3) legal research; (4) factual investigation; (5) communication (oral and written); (6) counseling; (7) negotiation; (8) litigation and alternative dispute resolution procedures; (9) the organization and management of legal work; and (10) recognizing and resolving ethical dilemmas. Interestingly enough, the Moot seems to have had the greatest impact in this respect among the students from civil law countries, where the law is taught in a more doctrinal fashion than it is in the United States.

Among those lawyering skills the three that were preeminent in the conception of the Moot, and that remain at the forefront today, are legal analysis and reasoning, legal research and communication. Those lawyering skills can be exercised most effectively if the students begin with at least a basic knowledge of the subject matter. We can assume that the student participants from every country will have studied the law of contracts, though many will not have studied the special case of a sale of goods. Few will have studied the different approaches to the interpretation of legal texts in other countries. However, those different approaches to textual interpretation arise in the Moot because the sales dispute involves difficult questions of interpretation of the CISG. The CISG is the law of the 70 countries that are currently party to it. It is a text that is not of the same nature as the otherwise applicable domestic law of sales, i.e. UCC Article 2 in the United States. The text is the same in all 70 countries,[3] which might lead to the idea that it is a uniform law, adopted and subject to sovereign interpretation in each of them. It would be difficult to deny that that would be an accurate positive law description as far as it goes. However, it is not the entire story. One of the provisions in the CISG is Article 7(1): "In the interpretation of this Convention, regard is to be had to its international character and to the need to promote

---

[2] Task Force on Law Schools and the Profession, American Bar Association, Legal Education and Professional Development-An Educational Continuum (July 1992).

[3] There are some differences arising from the use of the relatively few permitted derogations by means of declaration and from inconsistencies in the six official language versions. Fortunately, there are only a few such differences.

uniformity in its application ...." That provision was also adopted by each of the 70 countries, and it is therefore a direction to the courts as to how to act when interpreting the CISG. The national courts and arbitral tribunals would not be fulfilling their obligations if they were not at least aware of the interpretations offered by courts in other countries to the provision in question. It is primarily the task of the lawyers for the parties to bring those different interpretations to the attention of the court or tribunal. That may be easier for the students to recognize in the Moot than it would be in the classroom. The Moot arbitrators who do not come from the United States or Germany may not be satisfied by a citation to a decision of the Second Circuit Court of Appeals or the *Bundesgerichtshof*. They may wish argument from a wider range of perspective. That would, of course, be true in practice as well. Moreover, what is often a surprise to students from common law countries is that some of the arbitrators will be more impressed by the interpretations offered by the legal scholars who have studied the question than they are by the decisions of even the most respected courts, since those opinions are recognized as having authority in many legal systems.

The description of the Moot just given may make it seem to be both educationally worthwhile and challenging. Most of the participants have found it so. The book that Professors Graves and Morrissey have written will do much to enhance the educational value of the Moot by offering the students who use it a basic foundation of knowledge of both the CISG and international commercial arbitration. The courses in which it might be used permit an even deeper penetration into the mysteries of these two areas of international commercial law. It should not be thought that use of the book or participation in a course in which the Moot is an integral part will eliminate the challenge. It will only increase it. So much will have been learned, but all that knowledge will still have to be applied to the facts of the Moot Problem and the arguments for claimant and later for respondent will still have to be communicated in writing and orally to lawyers and law professors who come from other countries. That is a real challenge. What I hear every year from the lawyers and law professors who come to the Moot in Vienna or Hong Kong is how well the students are prepared. I am sure that the users of this book will be among those praised for their dedication and understanding of the CISG and international commercial arbitration.

TABLE OF CONTENTS

Part II: ENTER THE CISG

2 ‖ APPLICATION AND GENERAL PROVISIONS

3 | FORMING A CONTRACT UNDER THE CISG   105

4 | THE OBLIGATIONS OF THE PARTIES   147

5 ‖ REMEDIES FOR BREACH

207

6 ‖ DAMAGES
267

Part III: DISPUTE RESOLUTION
299

7 ‖ ARBITRATION AS AN ALTERNATIVE TO NATIONAL COURTS
301

9 | ARBITRATION AS A PROCEDURE TO DECIDE THE PARTIES' DISPUTE 423

10 ‖ ARBITRATION AS A FINAL AWARD: CHALLENGES AND ENFORCEMENT 459

Part I | SETTING THE STAGE

Students and attorneys reading this book hopefully find the potential to participate in international commercial transactions exciting on many levels. Indeed the globalization of business and culture is proceeding today at a pace that is unprecedented. Technology has made international communication and interaction easier and quicker than ever. A business in Tokyo can find a supplier in Mexico City through a quick series of searches on the internet. An agreement might be struck in a short period of time through the exchange of order forms through e-mail communications. Travelling might not even be necessary at all.

Businesses participate in such transactions to exchange goods with other nations and to advance their own economic interests. So too, attorneys who counsel such businesses can engage in a cultural exchange that can also be both professionally and economically rewarding. Keep in mind that engaging in such transactions involves crossing borders in a way that necessitates understanding and cooperation among the vast array of cultures that exist throughout the nations of the world.

First, however, it is important to understand the theory and the mechanics of international commercial transactions. For centuries, scholars and politicians alike have debated the value and role of international trade as a tool for economic development and increased public welfare and well being. Part I of this book will attempt to briefly cover some of this background to acquaint the reader with that theoretical context.

Part I will also provide useful background on the international organizations that have grown up to help facilitate and regulate trade. It is difficult to study international commercial transactions without at least some understanding of those organizations and the work they have done and are continuing to do. The CISG itself, the subject of Part II of this book, was the work of one such pivotal organization, the United Nations Commission on International Trade Law (UNCITRAL). UNCITRAL has also been instrumental in the development of a Model Law on International Commercial Arbitration, which will be the focus of much discussion in Part III of this book.

Part I will also focus on practical commercial and legal issues that anyone participating in an international commercial transaction should consider. Included among those topics will be international commercial arbitration. While that topic is considered at length in Part III of this book, it is introduced in this early chapter so that the examples of arbitrations encountered even in Part II might be understood more easily. Arbitration is largely a function of contract law. Accordingly, an understanding of some of the basic principles of arbitration before embarking on the contract law issues presented in Part II should prove helpful.

When considering all of these issues, it is the authors' hope that the reader will not lose sight of the practical aspects to the issues presented. Accordingly, in this Part, and throughout the book, there will be hypothetical situations raised and the reader will be challenged to apply theory to practice.

1 THE STUDY OF INTERNATIONAL COMMERCIAL LAW

> "…[B]y increasing the general mass of productions, it [international trade] diffuses general benefit, and binds together by one common tie of interest and intercourse, the universal society of nations throughout the civilized world."[1]
>
> - David Ricardo

David Ricardo wrote those words almost 200 years ago and yet globalization of trade is as important and as controversial today as it was then, perhaps more so. This chapter will present helpful background to the study of the international sale of goods, including a discussion of classical economic theorists such as Ricardo who have been advocates of trade. The views of those who are critical of trade will also be presented. In addition to that theoretical background, this chapter will outline protectionist measures designed to regulate trade, describe the international institutions that have grown up to promote trade, and survey some of the relevant legal infrastructure. Finally, the chapter will discuss contemporary commercial and legal considerations that anyone participating in an international sale of goods should take into account.

To begin with, however, consider the following hypothetical situation:

Example 1-1

Johnson & Gamble ("J&G") is a diversified multi-national consumer products company headquartered in the United States and listed on the New York Stock Exchange. J&G is represented by the company vice president who resides in central New Jersey and has had little international exposure.

NizhnyNorilskMagnetogorsk ("NNM") is a huge Russian conglomerate. It manufactures steel, aluminum and nickel. It is partly state owned (75%), and partly privatized (25%). NNM is also involved in providing consumer goods and services to people who live in the factory towns throughout Russia in which it has operations. It is represented by a team including the first

---

[1] David Ricardo, *On the Principles of Political Economy and Taxation* 7.11 (3d ed., John Murray 1821).

deputy to the general director of NNM and the first deputy to the minister of geology of Russia.

J&G wants to import Russian Steel in order to make their new MAK X disposable razor blades. Russian steel is considerably lower cost than US steel, making this deal extremely attractive to J&G. NNM is interested in expanding its sales to the United States but has also been instructed by its government ownership to encourage investment by J&G into Russia. All of the individuals involved personally want a deal to be struck because such a success would advance their careers and no doubt also result in personal financial gain.

Both parties understand that disputes might arise during the course of their dealings. However, neither party is interested in submitting any disputes to the state or national courts of their counterparty's country.

Imagine representing one of the parties above. One of the major roles of a business attorney is to identify the client's goals, foresee potential conflicts, and craft a creative business arrangement that will meet the client's goals while preventing any unforeseen problems from developing in the future.

Of course, the attorneys on the other side of the transaction will be doing the same thing for their client, and the goals of all the parties to a transaction may not coincide. Another role of the business lawyer is to attempt to create solutions and compromises when the goals of the parties to a transaction seem to conflict. It is sometimes in the best interests of the client to compromise on various points if it means being able to reach an agreement with the counterparty. Sometimes, however, the best business decision for a client is not to compromise but simply to walk away from a deal. As a word of caution, business lawyers should be careful not to obstruct a deal by fighting for points that a client (after being educated about the point) really does not consider a concern. Do not let "winning" in negotiations stand in the way of making a deal that works for a client.

There are many basic business and legal issues that should be considered when contemplating this type of transaction. The fact that this transaction involves the international sale of goods complicates matters considerably. While reading the following pages, try to contemplate *ex ante* what the true goals of each of the parties to this potential transaction are and attempt to structure an arrangement to meet those goals. Anticipate all of the possible pitfalls that might hinder a successful business venture. This scenario will be re-visited toward the end of this chapter and throughout this book.

I.   INTERNATIONAL TRADE: THE THEORY, THE INSTITUTIONS,
        AND THE LAW

Before going into the commercial and legal considerations that any advocate
involved in international commercial transactions must face, it is important to
understand some basic background on international trade. This beginning section
will focus on: (A) the theoretical arguments for and against international trade,
(B) an overview of protectionist measures, (C) a survey of the international
organizations that support international trade generally, and (D) the sources of
law that relate to international commercial transactions.

A.   TRADE THEORY

Economists and politicians throughout the world continue to debate whether
international trade is positive or negative. Economists have long argued that
international trade can increase the overall wealth of all the countries involved in
the trading. Economists such as Adam Smith and David Ricardo in the 18th and
19th centuries based this conclusion on theories of *absolute advantage* and
comparative advantage. Such theories have received wide acclaim for
illustrating, through models, that trade can improve the wealth of all trading
nations instead of enriching one at the expense of the other.[2] Nonetheless, other
economists and politicians continue to insist that international trade can harm
nations, citing phenomena such as unemployment and industry decline as a result
of cheap imports being brought into a country.[3] Another common argument is
that modern free trade advocates are simply attempting to promote the economies
of the developed world, at the expense of lesser developed nations. These
theorists argue that some level of protectionism is in a country's best interest. As
you think about international trade, consider for yourself which arguments
persuade you.

Economists' explanations of why international trade is beneficial dates back to
Adam Smith and his seminal work, *The Wealth of Nations*, published in 1776,[4]

---

[2] Consider, for example, the following statement of noted economist John Maynard Keynes: "I was
brought up, like most Englishmen, to respect free trade not only as an economic doctrine which a
rational and instructed person could not doubt but almost as a part of the moral law." John Maynard
Keynes, *National Self-Sufficiency*, in *The Collected Writings of John Maynard Keynes* vol. XXI,
233 (1933).

[3] *See e.g.* Charles Schumer & Paul Craig Roberts, *Exporting Jobs Is Not Free Trade: Rethinking
Protectionism*, Intl. Herald Trib. Op. 6 (Jan. 7, 2004) (identifying a New York securities firm that
planned to replace its team of 800 American software engineers, who each made approximately
$150,000 per year, with a team of software engineers from India, who would each make
approximately $20,000 per year).

[4] Adam Smith, *An Inquiry into the Nature and Causes of the Wealth of Nations* (Edwin Cannan ed.,
Random House 1937).

and to David Ricardo and his work, *The Principles of Political Economy and Taxation*, published in 1817.[5] To illustrate their theories, these economists simplified the complex world in which we live by using models that involved a world with two countries that make two products. After analyzing their models, Smith and Ricardo each came to the clear conclusion that international trade was a benefit to both of the trading nations.

1.   Absolute Advantage

Smith offered the intuitive reasoning that if each of the two countries makes one of the two products more efficiently than the other, then each country should specialize in making the product that it makes more efficiently and trade with the other country to get the other product. The situation Smith was describing involves the concept of absolute advantage. When one country can produce something more efficiently than another country it is said to have an absolute advantage over the other country with respect to that good. In Smith's example, each of the two countries has an absolute advantage over the other country with respect to one of the goods. Accordingly, trade should ensue because it will result in both countries enjoying more products than would otherwise be the case.

Smith's concept can be understood more easily with an example. Keep in mind that the example has to be set in a simplified world consisting of two countries and two goods that are identical whether made in one country or the other. The only input needed is labor, which is freely transferable to production of either good, and trade between the countries (including transport of goods) is free. Admittedly, that is a lot to assume. Nonetheless, with those assumptions, imagine that the two countries, A and B, each make both shirts and shoes.

In a pre-trade world, Countries A and B are capable of producing the following units per 100 hours of labor:

Country	Shirts		Shoes
A	50	*or*	50
B	30	*or*	100

Here Country A has an absolute advantage in producing shirts. It is more efficient for Country A to produce shirts because 100 units of labor will produce more shirts in Country A than it will in Country B. Likewise, Country B has an

---

[5] Ricardo, *supra* n. 1.

absolute advantage in producing shoes since it can produce more pairs of shoes than Country A with the same amount of labor. In this scenario, the two countries should engage in trade and specialize in the product in which they have an absolute advantage – Country A specializing in shirts and Country B specializing in shoes.

For example, before trading, each country may decide to produce the following units per 100 hours of labor:

Country	Shirts		Shoes
A	25	*and*	25
B	15	*and*	50
Totals	40		75

However, if each country specializes in producing the good in which it has an absolute advantage, then (with the same 100 hours of labor) each country can produce the following units:

Country	Shirts	Shoes
A	50	–
B	–	100
Totals	50	100

This result yields more units of both shirts and shoes than existed before specialization and overall global wealth has been maximized. The countries should trade shirts for shoes until each country has reached its optimal level of consumption. For example, Country A could trade 20 shirts for 40 pairs of shoes. In the end, Country A would have 30 shirts and 40 pairs of shoes (much better than in the pre-trade world). Country B would have 20 shirts and 60 pairs of shoes (also much better off than in the pre-trade world).

2.   Comparative Advantage

David Ricardo expanded on the concept of absolute advantage by imagining a world with two countries that produce two goods where one of the countries was more efficient than the other at producing both goods. In other words, one country had an absolute advantage over the other country with respect to both goods. In this world, it is not so intuitive that the countries should trade. It is not clear that the more efficient country would gain anything from trade. Similarly, it is not so clear that the less efficient country could effectively afford to trade with the more efficient country.

Despite being less efficient than the first country at producing both goods, the second country would still likely be relatively better at producing one of the two goods when compared to the other country. Ricardo called this that country's comparative advantage.

Ricardo argued that each country should specialize and produce that good for which it has a comparative advantage and should then trade that good with the other country to get the product which it does not produce itself. The result, he argued, should increase wealth for both countries. In that way, global wealth will be maximized. The following example should make this complex notion easier to grasp:

In a pre-trade world, Countries A and B are capable of producing the following units per 100 hours of labor:

Country	Shirts		Shoes
A	100	*or*	200
B	25	*or*	100

Here, Country A has an absolute advantage over Country B in shirts since it can produce more shirts than Country B with the same inputs (4 times as many). Likewise, Country A has an absolute advantage over Country B in shoes since it can produce more shoes than Country B with the same inputs (2 times as many). Country B does not have an absolute advantage over Country A in either shirts or shoes since it cannot produce either more efficiently than Country A.

However, according to Ricardo, trade should occur because, when compared with Country A, Country B is better at producing shoes than it is at producing shirts. Country A is four times as efficient as Country B in shirts (100 units versus 25 units); but only two times as efficient as Country B in shoes (200 units versus 100 units). According to this analysis, Country A has a comparative advantage in producing shirts; shirts production is its strongest production capability when compared with Country B. Similarly, Country B has a comparative advantage in producing shoes; shoes production is its strongest production capability when compared with Country A. This is true even though

Country A generally is more efficient than Country B at producing both shirts and shoes.

If that is not entirely clear, one can also use relative opportunity cost to analyze the situation. Opportunity cost in the simplified world under consideration (where there are just the two countries that produce the two goods) means the quantity of one good that the country has to give up in order to produce the other good. It would cost Country A two pairs of shoes to produce one shirt. (Each hour of labor in Country A could produce two pairs of shoes or one shirt.) By contrast, it would cost Country B four pairs of shoes to produce one shirt. (Four hours of labor would yield either four pairs of shoes or one shirt.) So the opportunity cost for Country A to produce shirts is lower than for Country B (two pairs of shoes versus four). Thus, with this opportunity cost analysis, Country A again is shown to have a comparative advantage in producing shirts.

Conversely, it would cost Country A half of a shirt to produce one pair of shoes. (In Country A one half of an hour of labor would produce one pair of shoes or half of a shirt). It would cost Country B one-fourth of a shirt for one pair of shoes. (One hour of labor would produce one pair of shoes or one-fourth of a shirt). So, the opportunity cost for Country B of producing shoes is lower (one-fourth of a shirt) than the opportunity cost for Country A of producing shoes (half of a shirt). Accordingly, with this opportunity cost analysis, Country B has a comparative advantage in producing shoes.

For example, before trading, each country may decide to produce the following units per 100 hours of labor:

Country	Shirts		Shoes
A	70	*and*	60
B	20	*and*	20
Totals	90		80

However, if each country specializes in producing the good in which it has a comparative advantage, then (with the same 100 hours of labor) each country can produce the following units:

Country	Shirts	Shoes
A	100	–
B	–	100
Totals	100	100

This result yields more shirts and shoes production than in the pre-trade world. Again, overall global wealth has been maximized. The countries should trade shirts for shoes until each country has reached its optimal level of consumption. For example, Country A could trade 25 shirts for 65 pairs of shoes. After trading, Country A would have 75 shirts and 65 pairs of shoes (better than in the pre-trade world). Country B would have 25 shirts and 35 pairs of shoes (also better off than in the pre-trade world).

Based at least in part on this Ricardian model showing the wealth gains resulting from international trade, international trade and development organizations, including the World Trade Organization and the World Bank, have pursued free trade among nations as an ideal. In fact, the World Trade Organization even discusses the principle of comparative advantage on its web site.[6] It goes on to describe empirical results from global trade in the 25 years after the end of World War II and concludes that as trade among nations increased, so too did wealth.[7]

3.   The Critics of Free Trade

The push for free trade, however, has not been universally well received. In fact, there are many scholars, politicians, and social activists who fiercely fight against the idea of attempting to move toward more free trade. From some scholars' perspectives, the absolute and comparative advantage models are plagued with too many assumptions that are simply unworkable in the complex modern world.[8] The models make many assumptions. A few of those assumptions were described above: that the world is a simple one that consists of two nations, with two products, that the products are interchangeable no matter where produced, that labor is the only input needed, that labor is freely transferable from one production good to another, and that trade is costless. These conditions simply do not exist in the world today, and some of these critics would hold that the

---

[6] World Trade Org., *Understanding the WTO* 13-14 (3d ed. 2007) (available at http://www.wto .org/english/thewto_e/whatis_e/tif_e/understanding_e.pdf).
[7] *Id.*
[8] *See* James M. Cypher & James L. Dietz, *The Process of Economic Development* (Routledge 1997); Paul R. Krugman, *Rethinking International Trade* 118–122 (MIT Press 1990).

results for the Ricardian model breaks down in light of true market imperfections.[9]

Some critics argue that increased trade often means factory closings and lay-offs in jurisdictions where production is shifting as a result of increased trade.[10] Environmentalists argue that freer trade potentially means environmental standards being ignored by countries attempting to produce goods more cheaply and gain a comparative advantage. Health advocates worry that the health and safety standards of products are similarly overlooked by countries seeking to manufacturer products or supply foodstuffs at comparatively cheap prices.

Perhaps more cutting is the argument of many developmentalists that a free trade agenda, which is being pushed primarily by developed economies, is disingenuous. These critics point out that the developed economies built most of their industry in an environment that was indeed protectionist and may have benefited from the exploitation of colonial holdings.[11] To insist that developing countries today proceed without those same benefits is to lock those countries into their status of being lesser developed.[12]

---

[9] See, for example, Sir James Goldsmith, who wrote on the movement toward more free trade, "it will impoverish and destabilize the industrialized world while at the same time cruelly ravaging the third world." Sir James Goldsmith, *The Trap* 25 (Fixot 1993). Later in that same book, Goldsmith insists, provocatively, that "[i]t must surely be a mistake to adopt an economic policy which makes you rich if you eliminate your national work force and transfer your production abroad, and which bankrupts you if you continue to employ your own people." *Id.* at 28; *see also* James Fallows, *Looking at the Sun* (Vintage 1994) (focusing on the growth of Asian economies and differences in cultural norms as complicating factors that challenge traditional economic thinking).

[10] International meetings of international trade organizations like the World Trade Organization (WTO) have become extraordinarily controversial. In 1999, a WTO ministerial meeting in Seattle, Washington was met with loud protests and meeting participants were unable to come to any agreements regarding crucial issues affecting trade. Since then, meetings in Doha, Qatar in 2001, Cancun, Mexico in 2003, and Hong Kong, China in 2005 all resulted in controversy between developed and developing countries over who is gaining from the development of trade. Much of the developing world took a position that it is not gaining from trade, and new policies must be put in place to redress that situation. This controversy continues, although it is principally concerned with how to structure trading rules to make the benefits of trade available to all parties involved.

[11] *See e.g.* Carmen G. Gonzalez, *Deconstructing the Mythology of Free Trade: Critical Reflections on Comparative Advantage*, 17 Berkeley La Raza L.J. 65 (2006).

[12] Along these lines, it is interesting to note the view of a few influential politicians from developing countries. Discussing agricultural trade subsidies granted by many developed countries, Colombian President Andres Pastrana posed the following question:

> How is it possible that the most powerful countries of the world, with most of the resources on the planet, may channel these to their agricultural sectors not fully understanding, it would appear, that in doing so they close the doors to the growth and the livelihoods of those subsisting on farming in the rest of the world?

As recently as 2005, the United States met intense opposition as it attempted to promote the Free Trade Area of the Americas (FTAA). That arrangement would have allowed for the free flow of goods between the countries of the Americas, while at the same time restricting the flow of labor. At a meeting in Argentina to discuss the FTAA, thousands protested against the FTAA.[13]

B.   PROTECTIONIST MEASURES

In addition to theoretical commentaries critical of free trade, all one has to do is observe the breadth of protectionist measures that have been adopted by countries all over the world to understand that, despite the rhetoric of free trade employed by many, the reality is that countries do not always believe that unfettered free trade is truly in their best interest. A protectionist measure is one that helps any particular nation or state to protect its industry from the competition that results from free trade. There are many reasons why nations might employ protectionist measures and many types of measures that can be used.

First and probably foremost among the reasons why a country might be protectionist is the notion that countries do not want to disadvantage or abandon entire industries (and the workers and owners of those industries), regardless of whether that country's comparative advantages might lie elsewhere. An example of this is the agricultural industries of developed economies. Despite the fact that lesser developed economies might have comparative advantages in agriculture, protectionist measures such as government subsidies still support the agricultural industries of those countries.[14]

Nicole Winfield, *Developing Countries Tell the US, EU to Stop Subsidies, Open Markets*, Associated Press Worldstream (June 11, 2002). Also reflecting on the difficult situation for the agricultural sector in his country, Jamaican Agriculture Minister Roger Clarke complained:

> Already, we're reeling under the effects of dumped cheap goods on us, and this puts us in a terrible position, because were not even in a position to subsidize. In countries like Jamaica, cheap imported foodstuffs have exacted a heavy toll on local farmers unable to compete with the low-cost subsidized produce… We have to rethink our strategy because we were going along a road which they called free trade… This is really flying in the face of whatever we're talking about at the WTO, and it is going to be for us now to rethink. We have to find a way because it cannot go like this, our people are going to be totally wiped out.

Dionne Jackson Miller, *US Farm Bill Prompts Regional Rethink*, SUNS—South-North Dev. Monitor No. 5120 (May 17, 2002) (available at http://www.sunsonline.org/results.php).
[13] *See Bush Fails to Revive Free Trade Talks in Latin America Amid Mass Protest*s, Democracy Now! (Nov. 7, 2005) (TN broad., transcr. available at http://www.democracynow.org/article .pl?sid=05/11/07/1438223).
[14] Developed countries' use of government subsidies for the agricultural industry is a topic of heated debate. In 2003 at the 5th Meeting of the WTO in Cancun, Mexico, delegates from Asia,

A second motivation for adopting protectionist measures is the strategic notion that a country does not want to rely on other nations for basic necessities. An example of this phenomenon might be found in the oil and gas industry. Some countries have kept those industries largely regulated or even owned by government in an attempt to make sure that the domestic supply of those strategic goods is not threatened.[15]

1.   Dumping

Yet another reason why countries adopt protectionist measures is to counter-act dumping. Dumping occurs when one country decides to sell a particular product to a foreign market at prices that are below the prices paid for that product in its own country, or below production costs. Countries or industries that engage in dumping are attempting to lock in a share of the market for the particular good in the foreign country. In the extreme, those engaging in dumping would like to run the local industry out of business in the foreign country, and then later raise prices to capture greater profits.[16] Anti-dumping efforts are a country's measures designed to combat this predatory practice and might include any or a combination of protectionist measures.[17] In fact, the World Trade Organization, discussed below, adopted an Anti-Dumping Agreement pursuant to which countries are authorized to take anti-dumping measures when there is material injury to the relevant domestic industry.[18]

Africa, Latin America, and the Caribbean walked out of negotiations due to the United States' and the European Union's refusal to cut back on the $300 billion in governmental subsidies given to farmers in their countries. Elizabeth Becker, *Poorer Countries Pull out of Talks over World Trade*, N.Y. Times A1 (Sept. 15, 2003).

[15] For example, until 2005, Gazprom, the Russian oil and gas monopoly, could not be owned by persons not residing in the Russian Federation. Gazprom.com, *Investors, Shares*, http://www.gazprom.com/eng/articles/article21713.shtml (accessed Oct. 1, 2007).

[16] See James Fellows, *Looking at the Sun*, where the author quotes Peter Drucker and describes a phenomenon he calls "adversarial trade" where the aim is "to drive the competitor out of the market altogether rather than to let the competitor survive." Fallows, *supra* n. 9 (quoting Peter Drucker, *The New Realities* (Harper & Rowe 1989)).

[17] For example, the United States Department of Commerce utilizes a controversial methodology called "zeroing" to calculate antidumping duties on a foreign producer's imports. Dan Ikenson, *Zeroing in: Antidumping's Flawed Methodology under Fire*, Free Trade Bull. No. 11, Ctr. for Trade Policy Stud. (Apr. 27, 2004) (available at http://www.freetrade.org/pubs/FTBs/FTB-011.pdf). Using this methodology, sales made by the foreign producer at or above fair market value are all treated as having a zero dumping margin (rather than a negative margin), while sales from the same foreign producer made below fair market value are treated as having a positive dumping margin. *Id.* Thus, when combined together, the foreign producer's overall margin of dumping is significantly higher and higher anti-dumping duties can be imposed. *Id.*

[18] *Uruguay Round Agreement: Agreement on Implementation of Article VI of the General Agreement on Tariffs & Trade 1994*, http://www.wto.org/english/docs_e/legal_e/19-adp.pdf (Apr. 15, 1994).

2. Tariffs, Licenses, Quotas, and Subsidies

Among protectionist measures a nation might employ are tariffs, licenses, quotas, and government subsidies. Tariffs are customs duties that are imposed by a country on certain imported goods to make those imported goods less competitive on that country's domestic market.[19] Tariffs are one of the easiest ways to restrict the access of a country's markets to foreign imports.

Licenses are similar to tariffs in that they typically simply make the imported product more expensive. Where an import license is required, anyone importing a foreign good must apply for such a license and pay any related fee.[20] This process, like tariffs, raises the price of the imported good and makes that good less competitive on the domestic market. To the extent granting licenses is discretionary and not automatic, countries exert even more control over imported goods. With discretionary licensing, a country might exclude an import altogether by not granting an import license.

Quotas are a direct restriction on imports. Import quotas restrict the amount of foreign imports of any particular good to a certain quantity.[21] Quotas can be designed to apply specifically to imports from a particular country or to all imports of a particular good.

Government subsidies are a less obvious protectionist measure and may be more difficult to readily recognize. When a government subsidizes domestic production of any particular product or industry, it makes those products cheaper for the domestic market to produce and therefore makes competition from foreign products more difficult.[22] Subsidies can take many different forms, making them potentially difficult to identify. Subsidies frequently take the form of direct payments from government to the selected industry, or might exist in the form of reduced taxes for the selected industry.

---

[19] Interestingly, most countries apply a significantly higher than average tariff to imported alcohol and tobacco products. To see a comprehensive list of countries with links to each country's import tariff schedule, see Export.gov, *International Logistics, Tariff/Import Fees, Country Specific Tariff and Tax Information,* http://www.export.gov/logistics/country_tariff_info.asp#P505_22515 (accessed Sept. 15, 2007).

[20] For example, Thailand allows most goods to be imported into the country without a license, with the exception of certain textiles and food-processing products. On the other hand, Saudi Arabia only allows Saudi Arabian companies, which are 100% owned by Saudi Arabians, to import goods into the country; these importers must be granted a license from the government. To review the import regulations of numerous countries, see http://country.alibaba.com/profiles/index.htm, *select* [desired country], *select* Market Access.

[21] For example, the European Union maintains a trade quota on Australian imported meat, limiting the amount of beef imported from Australia to approximately seven tons per year. *See* Belinda Tasker, *British Meats Ban Unlikely to Help Australian Farmers*, Austrl. Associated Press Pty. Ltd. Intl. News (Aug. 7, 2007).

[22] As discussed *supra* n. 14, government subsidies for the agricultural sector are common for developed countries but garner significant resistance and criticism from developing countries.

3.   Prohibitions on Trade

Of course the most dramatic example of a protectionist measure is an outright *prohibition on trade* from any particular industry or country. While this may seem extreme, it was generally the position of the former Soviet Union to prohibit trade with foreign nations, with certain exceptions. Further, politically motivated embargoes have the same result. Proponents of free trade argue that politically motivated embargoes, such as the United States' embargo of Cuban products, fail to change the behavior of targeted regimes but rather inflict additional suffering on the citizens of those countries.[23]

4.   Non-Tariff Barriers

There are also other *non-tariff barriers* to trade, including government requirements about the quality, labeling, or production standards for certain products. An example is provided by the labeling requirements for bottles of wine in the United States. It is possible that small wineries in South Africa may not want to spend the additional money required to investigate those requirements and comply with them in order to export their wines to the United States markets. In that sense, the labeling requirement acts as a barrier to trade. Another example of this is the quality of food items. Where a government, for example Germany, requires that its seafood have no more than a certain level of cadmium, then other jurisdictions will have to be certain that their products comply with that requirement if they want to export their seafood into Germany.[24] This quality standard acts as a kind of barrier to trade.

It is not at all clear that these types of measures are undertaken by countries as protectionism. It is likely that many of these standards and requirements are genuinely adopted in the best interests of consumers, their health, and perhaps the environment. However, the true purpose of a non-tariff barrier to trade may be difficult to ascertain in any specific case.

---

[23] Daniel T. Griswold, *The Embargo Harms Cubans and Gives Castro an Excuse for the Policy Failures of His Regime*, Insight on the News (May 27, 2002) (available at http://www.freetrade.org /node/330) (identifying that economic sanctions against the countries of North Korea, Iran, Iraq, and Burma have failed to change the behavior of the regimes); *see also* Peter Fitzgerald, *The Cuban Thistle Crisis: Why the Rest of the World Will Never Understand the United States Sanction Policy*, Commentary & Analysis, SanctionsWatch.com October 15, 2004 (available at http://www.law .stetson.edu/fitz/fitzstuff/Cuba%20Thistle%20Crisis.pdf) (arguing that the United States embargo against Cuban products has failed to lead to political change for over forty years).

[24] *See Swiss Seller v. German Buyer (New Zealand Mussels Case),* Bundesgerichtshof case VIII ZR 159/94, Germany, Mar. 8, 1995 (available at http://cisgw3.law.pace.edu/cases/950308g3.html). This decision of the German Supreme Court is further explained in Chapter 4.

C. INTERNATIONAL ORGANIZATIONS

Because international trade, whether entirely free or not, is of such importance to the stability and operation of the global economy, many international organizations have emerged to support and facilitate trade among nations. Among the most important of these organizations are: (1) the World Trade Organization, (2) the World Bank, (3) the International Monetary Fund, (4) the International Institute for the Unification of Private International Law (UNIDROIT), and (5) the United National Committee on International Trade (UNCITRAL).

1. The World Trade Organization[25]

The World Trade Organization (WTO) is an international organization that promotes and facilitates trade between nations. The WTO grew out of the General Agreement on Tariffs and Trade (GATT). The GATT was created in 1947 and adopted by 23 nations in 1948.[26] That agreement represented a multilateral attempt by nations to reduce tariffs and thereby promote international trade. At the time it was created, the GATT was intended only to be provisional. It was originally hoped that an International Trade Organization (ITO) would be created to oversee and facilitate the growth of international trade; however, an ITO never materialized. Nonetheless, the signatory nations to the GATT met periodically at "rounds" of discussions to continue negotiations concerning the regulation and promotion of international trade. Through those years the provisions of the GATT, along with the number of its signatories, increased dramatically.

At the eighth round of negotiations, the Uruguay Round (1986–1994), 123 country participants agreed to replace the GATT with a much more expansive set of provisions that would constitute and be administered by the WTO.[27] Beginning in 1995, the WTO substantially expanded on the terms of the GATT and included provisions regarding services and intellectual property rights – subjects that were previously not included in the GATT. As of January 2007, the WTO had 150 member nations from across the globe. In its current state, the WTO's main functions are to administer WTO trade agreements, provide a forum for trade negotiations, handle trade disputes, monitor national trade policies,

---

[25] *See generally* World Trade Org., http://www.wto.org (last accessed Aug. 10, 2007).
[26] The twenty-three founding members were: Australia, Belgium, Brazil, Burma, Canada, Ceylon, Chile, China, Cuba, Czechoslovakia, France, India, Lebanon, Luxembourg, Netherlands, New Zealand, Norway, Pakistan, Southern Rhodesia, Syria, South Africa, United Kingdom, and the United States. World Trade Org., *Before 1995: GATT Signatories Before the WTO Came into Being*, http://www.wto.org/english/thewto_e/gattmem_e.htm (last accessed Nov. 10, 2007).
[27] World Trade Org., *supra* n. 6, at 18–22 (available at http://www.wto.org/english/thewto_e/whatis_e/tif_e/understanding_e.pdf).

provide technical assistance and training for developing countries, and cooperate with other international organizations.[28]

Moving toward freer trade is a clear and focused goal of the WTO.[29] As a result of the WTO's predecessor, the GATT, tariffs on industrial goods across the globe had fallen to less than 4% on average by the mid 1990s.[30] The WTO has continued to work to lower trade barriers; as a result, merchandise exports have grown approximately 6% annually over the past 50 years.[31] However, the WTO is not blindly devoted to the pursuit of free trade. The WTO officially acknowledges in its constituent agreements that in certain circumstances trade barriers are appropriate if in the best interests of consumers, developing countries, health, or environmental welfare.[32] Thus, the WTO attempts to take a somewhat balanced position between free trade and restricted trade. Nonetheless, the WTO has been frequently criticized for serving the agendas of developed countries while sacrificing the welfare of the developing world.

The chief guiding principle of the WTO is the most favored nation principle.[33] Although the name implies favorable or preferential treatment for a country, the principle actually means that there can be no favored nation.[34] The best treatment a member nation accords another member nation in terms of free trade and access to markets must be applied to all member nations.

---

[28] World Trade Org., *The WTO in Brief* 8 (2007) (available at http://www.wto.org/english/res_e/doload_e/inbr_e.pdf). For additional information pertaining to the WTO, including *The 10 Benefits of the WTO Trading System* and *The 10 Common Misunderstandings of the WTO*, see http://www.wto.org/english/thewto_e/whatis_e/whatis_e.htm.

[29] *Id.* at 1 (highlighting that the WTO's "main function is to ensure that trade flows as smoothly, predictably and freely as possible").

[30] World Trade Org., *supra* n. 6, at 11.

[31] World Trade Org., *supra* n. 28, at 3.

[32] For example, the WTO Agreement on the Application of Sanitary and Phytosanitary Measures specifically allows countries to adopt rules that protect the health of its citizens and makes special additional rules for developing countries. *Agreement on the Application of Sanitary and Phytosanitary Measures* (Apr. 15, 1994) (available at http://www.wto.org/English/docs_e/legal_e/15-sps.pdf). In addition, the Fourth Ministerial Conference held in Doha, Quatar in 2001 resulted in a Ministerial Declaration that focuses work of the WTO on the needs and interests of developing nations. *See* Doha WTO Ministerial Declaration of November 14, 2001 (available at http://www.wto.org/english/thewto_e/minist_e/min01_e/mindecl_e.htm).

[33] This principle is so important that it is set forth in Article 1 of the 1947 General Agreements on Tariffs and Trade.

[34] As with most legal principles, however, there are exceptions. For instance, countries can set up free trade agreements that apply to goods traded only within those countries—therefore discriminating against countries that are not parties to the free trade agreement. World Trade Org., *supra* n. 6, at 11.

2. The World Bank[35]

The World Bank is an international organization dedicated to the reduction of global poverty. Like the WTO, the World Bank also dates back to the post World War II years. It was founded at the Bretton Woods Conference in 1944 as the International Bank for Reconstruction and Development (the IBRD) and was dedicated to post-war reconstruction efforts in Europe. Today, the World Bank continues to provide assistance for reconstruction efforts following natural disasters and conflicts, but has expanded its scope dramatically to include the alleviation of poverty around the world.[36]

To facilitate its mission, the World Bank is currently made up of 2 organizations —the IBRD, which focuses on middle income developing countries, and the International Development Agency (IDA), which focuses its efforts on the world's poorest nations. Through these two organizations, the World Bank makes loans to developing countries and their businesses. It also makes grants to nations to help promote economic environments where development can flourish.[37]

The IBRD is made up of 185 nations that all fund the IBRD in proportion to their subscription for shares in the IBRD. As of November 2007, the United States has the largest stake in the IBRD, holding more than 16% of the shares of the IBRD, and Japan has the second-largest stake in the IBRD with slightly over 8% of the shares.[38] As of November 2007, the IDA has 166 member nations with the United States again holding the largest stake at just over 12% of the shares.[39]

3. The International Monetary Fund[40]

The International Monetary Fund (IMF) was also established in the post World War II era. It was founded in 1945 with the goal, among other things, of helping

---

[35] *See generally* The World Bank, http://www.worldbank.org (last accessed Nov. 11, 2007).

[36] The slogan of the World Bank is "working for a world free of poverty." *Id.*

[37] One of the current projects of the World Bank, among many others, is the Bangladesh Central Bank Strengthening Project, which will cost approximately $46.13 million. The goal for this project is to "achieve a strong, and effective regulatory, and supervisory system for Bangladesh's banking sector." To review the database of over 10,000 projects from 1947 until the current date, listed according to location, goal, theme, or sector, visit The World Bank, *supra* n. 35, *select* Projects & Operations, *select* Project Database.

[38] The World Bank, *IBRD: Votes and Subscriptions* (July 24, 2007) (available at http://www.worldbank.org, *select* About, *select* Organization, *select* Boards of Directors, *select* Member Countries, *select* Voting Power, *select* IBRD).

[39] The World Bank, *IDA: Votes and Subscriptions* (July 24, 2007) (available at http://www.worldbank.org, *select* About, *select* Organization, *select* Boards of Directors, *select* Member Countries, *select* Voting Power, *select* IDA).

[40] Intl. Monetary Fund, http://www.imf.org (last accessed Nov. 11, 2007).

to promote the growth and development of balanced international trade.[41] To accomplish this, the IMF also attempts to address balance of payment problems that member nations may have, and facilitate economic development generally in order to promote trade.[42]

The IMF is funded by contributions from its member nations, and as of November 2007, the IMF had 185 member nations. The contribution amounts are based upon the size of a member's economy. Consequently, more developed nations contribute more to the IMF but also have a corresponding amount of voting power within the organization. Similar to the IBRD and the IDA, the United States is the largest stakeholder with more than 16% of the voting power at the IMF.

The IMF uses its contributions to make loans and financial assistance available to member nations in need.[43] It frequently attaches conditions to its loans, attempting to encourage countries in need to reform their economies to prevent any future financial crises.[44]

4.   International Institute for the Unification of Private Law[45]

Situated in Rome, the International Institute for the Unification of Private International Law (UNIDROIT) is a private institution created as part of the League of Nations in 1926. After the demise of the League of Nations, UNIDROIT was re-constituted in 1940 with the goal of unifying private commercial law around the globe. Currently, UNIDROIT is made up of 61 member states, all of which contribute financially to the organization. Over the years UNIDROIT has been responsible for drafting many international conventions and model laws relating to private commercial transactions.[46]

---

[41] *See generally* Intl. Monetary Fund, *Articles of Agreement*, art. 1 (available at http://www.imf .org/external/pubs/ft/aa/aa01.htm).

[42] *Id.*

[43] For example, in 2002, the IMF Executive Board approved a $16 billion loan to Turkey in order for the country to continue implementing its comprehensive economic reform policy. Intl. Monerary Fund, *supra* n. 40, at http://www.imf.org/external/np/sec/pr/2002/pr0207.htm.

[44] However, the "conditionality" of the IMF loans is highly criticized by developing countries. *See* Anthony Rowley, *Winds of Change Poised to Sweep IMF, World Bank*, Bus. Times Singapore World (Sept. 29, 2005).

[45] Intl. Inst. for the Unification of Priv. L. (UNIDROIT), http://www.unidroit.org (last accessed Nov. 11, 2007).

[46] For example, UNIDROIT is responsible for the Convention relating to a Uniform Law on the International Sale of Goods (The Hague 1964), available at http://www.unidroit.org/english/conventions/c-ulis.htm, and The Convention on Agency in the International Sale of Goods (Geneva 1983), http://www.unidroit.org/english/conventions/ 1983agency/1983agency-e.htm.

The most relevant UNIDROIT text for our study of the sales of international goods is the UNIDROIT Principles of International Commercial Contracts (the UNIDROIT Principles), drafted in 1994 and then expanded upon in 2004. The UNIDROIT Principles were designed to reflect general principles of contract law prevailing internationally. The members of the working group who drafted the UNIDROIT Principles envisioned a multitude of situations in which the UNIDROIT Principles would apply.[47] In fact, the Preamble to the UNIDROIT Principles states that they will apply when: (i) the parties so choose; or (ii) the parties agree to be governed by general principles of law or the *lex mercatoria*; or (iii) the parties have neglected to choose a governing law.[48] Further, the UNIDROIT Principles may supplement or help interpret international or domestic law.[49] Finally, the UNIDROIT Principles may serve as a model for national or international legislators.[50] The UNIDROIT Principles are reflective of international norms that tend to prevail in international commercial transactions. As a result, the UNIDROIT Principles can be used as persuasive authority for tribunals to consider, even when they do not apply directly.[51]

5.   The United Nations Commission on International Trade Law[52]

The United Nations Commission on International Trade Law (UNCITRAL) was formed in 1966 by the General Assembly of the United Nations. Its mandate is to facilitate international trade by harmonizing the diverse bodies of international trade law that exist in nations around the world. It is now the United Nations' principal legal body that deals with international trade.[53] UNCITRAL is currently made up of 60 member nations, all of which are elected by the General Assembly and are representative of all the world's regions and economic systems.[54]

---

[47] UNIDROIT Principles Preamble (2004) (available at http://www.unidroit.org/english/principles/contracts/principles2004/blackletter2004.pdf).

[48] *Id.*

[49] *Id.*

[50] *Id.*

[51] *See id.* at Preamble (providing that the UNIDROIT Principles "may be used to interpret or supplement international uniform law instruments"); Michael Joachim Bonell, *The UNIDROIT Principles of International Contracts and CISG: Alternative or Complementary Instrument?* 26 Unif. L. Rev. 26, 33 (1996) ("[B]esides clarifying unclear language, the UNIDROIT Principles may also be used to fill veritable gaps found in CISG.").

[52] *See generally* UN Commn. on Intl. Trade L., http://www.uncitral.org (last accessed Nov. 11, 2007) [hereinafter UNCITRAL].

[53] For a history of the development of UNCITRAL, see *id.* at http://www.uncitral.org/uncitral/en/about/origin.html. In addition, to review a manual providing the basic facts on the UNCITRAL, see UNCITRAL, *Basic Facts about the United Nations Commission on International Trade Law* (2007) (available at http://www.uncitral.org/pdf/english/texts/general/V0650941.pdf).

[54] In May 2007, the UNCITRAL General Assembly elected the following thirty nations to serve: Armenia, Bahrain, Benin, Bolivia, Bulgaria, Cameroon, Canada, Chile, China, Egypt, El Salvador,

Over the years, UNCITRAL has drafted many different influential texts to harmonize and facilitate international trade. Three of those texts are fundamental to the study of international sales and arbitration. First, is the Convention on Contracts for the International Sale of Goods (the CISG) that was finalized in 1980 and became effective in 1988. The CISG provides a uniform law to govern international sales contracts and will, of course, be the focus of Part II of this casebook. Second, UNCITRAL has also adopted a Model Law on International Commercial Arbitration (the UNCITRAL Model Law). The Model Law has been adopted by many countries around the world and therefore generally governs arbitrations in all of those jurisdictions. The Model Law will be the subject of much of Part III of this book. [55] Third, UNCITRAL is now responsible for promotion of the 1958 Convention on the Recognition and Enforcement of Foreign Arbitral Awards (the New York Convention).[56] The New York Convention is one of the key reasons why arbitral awards in international cases are enforceable around the world. Enforceability of arbitral awards is one of the main reasons why international arbitration is a viable and attractive option for the resolution of international disputes. The New York Convention will also be the subject of further study in Part III of this book.

UNCITRAL has also developed a reporting system named Case Law on UNCITRAL Texts (CLOUT).[57] Through the CLOUT system, researchers can find case law and arbitration decisions from around the globe that relate to UNCITRAL's principal texts. Selected CLOUT cases and arbitrations are referenced, summarized, or reprinted in this book to illustrate how the CISG has been interpreted by various jurisdictions across the world.

France, Germany, Greece, Honduras, Japan, Latvia, Malaysia, Malta, Mexico, Morocco, Namibia, Norway, Republic of Korea, Russian Federation, Senegal, Singapore, South Africa, Sri Lanka, and United Kingdom. *Id.* at http://www.un.org/News/Press/docs//2007/ga10596.doc.htm.

[55] UNCITRAL Model L. on Intl. Com. Arb. (1985, amended in 2006) (available at http://www.uncitral.org/pdf/english/texts/arbitration/ml-arb/MLARB-english_revised%2006.pdf). The UNCITRAL Model Law is discussed in detail in Part 3. UNCITRAL has also adopted a set of arbitration rules, which will also be considered in Part 3 of this book. UNCITRAL Arb. R. (1976) (available at http://www.uncitral.org/pdf/english/texts/arbitration/arb-rules/arb-rules.pdf).

[56] The New York Convention was adopted by the United Nations before the formation of UNCITRAL. It entered into force in June 1959, and as of November 2007, 142 countries are signatories to the Convention. The text of the New York Convention, along with the list of signatory countries, is available at http://www.uncitral.org/uncitral/en/uncitral_texts/arbitration/NYConvention.html.

[57] The CLOUT system is located at http://www.uncitral.org/uncitral/en/case_law.html.

6. The International Chamber of Commerce[58]

The International Chamber of Commerce (ICC) is a non-governmental organization made up of businesses and associations from approximately 130 nations.[59] It was founded in 1919 to facilitate and promote open trade and engages in a wide variety of activities and functions to further that goal.

The ICC has adopted international commercial terms (Incoterms), terms that represent a set of pre-defined conditions relating to the risks involved with international commercial transactions. The first set of these terms was published in 1936. The most recent definitions were published in 2000. Incoterms facilitate transactions between trading parties because they allow those parties to adopt the well known Incoterms into their contract and not spend time negotiating all of the more specific provisions incorporated thereby. Incoterms will be discussed briefly in Section II. D. below and more fully in Chapter 4.

The ICC also contributes to trade finance. The ICC promulgated the Uniform Customs and Practice for Documentary Credits (UCP) in 1933. The UCP contains a set of standards used by banks to govern the terms of trade finance transactions. The UCP's current version became effective in 2007.

The ICC also established the International Court of Arbitration (ICA) in 1923 and thereby paved the way for popularizing arbitration as a forum for international dispute resolution. The ICA is now one of the world's leading body for organizing and overseeing international arbitrations.

D. SOURCES OF LAW RELATING TO INTERNATIONAL SALES OF GOODS

To understand the sources of law relating to international sales of goods, it is crucial to understand first how different legal systems approach the law and what sources of law exist in those different legal systems. This section will address those issues and then go into a discussion about the sources of international law that may be applicable in any given international sale of goods.

1. Civil Law versus Common Law

Any attorney engaged in an international transaction must consider the differences that exist between the jurisdictions of the counterparties to any given transaction. Not only will the actual rules of law in each jurisdiction potentially be different, but the entire system too could be different. The most basic distinction among the legal systems of the world is whether a particular nation

---

[58] Intl. Chamber of Com., http://www.iccwbo.org/ (last accessed Nov. 11, 2007).

[59] *Id.* at http://www.iccwbo.org/id93/index.html.

has a civil law system or a common law system.[60] Attorneys from either system must understand how their counterparts from a different system find, understand, and interpret the law.[61]

Civil law systems trace their roots back to Rome and the codified law of Roman Emperor Justinian, the *Corpus Juris Civilis*, that dates back to the sixth century A.D.[62] Indeed, most of continental Europe, including, France and Germany, inherited this civil law tradition and promoted it throughout the world where those countries exercised a significant amount of influence.[63] Common law systems, by contrast, are based on the English jurisprudential system. It is principally England, Ireland, Scotland, and nations that came under the influence of England that inherited this tradition. Included among those countries are England's former colonies, including Australia and the United States.

In a civil law system, the law is primarily found in written legislation enacted by the government. Frequently that legislation will be in the form of a written codification of the law that represents the entire body of law on a particular topic in that jurisdiction. Perhaps the most influential of the civil law codes that exist are the French Napoleonic *Code Civil* (adopted in 1804) and the German *Bürgerliches Gesetzbuch* (enacted in 1900).[64] However, not all civil law countries have enacted comprehensive codes. Nevertheless, all civil law countries do give primacy to written enactments of law. Courts and other adjudicatory bodies must look to the appropriate enactments for guidance in any particular dispute and resolve the dispute solely with reference to that written

---

[60] For additional scholarly commentary on the legal systems of the world, see R. David & J. Brierly, *Major Legal Systems in the World Today* (3d rev. ed., Stevens Publg. 1985), and Rudolf Schlesinger, *Comparative Law: Cases, Text, Materials* (6th ed., Found. Press 1998).

[61] In relation to "gaps" not explicitly stated in the CISG, Professor Honnold discussed a distinction between civil and common law systems: "If judges simply follow habit, common law courts will be less inclined than civil law courts to extract 'general principles' from the Convention and, conversely, will be more likely than civil law courts to see a 'gap' in the statute that requires the use of domestic law." John Honnold, *The Sales Convention in Action—Uniform International Words: Uniform Application?* 8 J.L. & Com. 207, 209–210 (1988).

[62] Peter Stein, *Justinian's Compilation: Classical Legacy and Legal Source*, 8 Tul. Eur. & Civ. L. Forum 1 (1993).

[63] For example, China's Civil Code, inherited from Japan, is based on the German model. *See* Edward J. Epstein, *The Theoretical System of Property Rights in China's General Principles of Civil Law: Theoretical Controversy in The Drafting Process and Beyond*, 52 L. & Contemp. Probs. 177, 183 (1989); Xu Guodong, *Structures of Three Major Civil Code Projects in Today's China,* 19 Tul. Eur. & Civ. L. Forum 37, 54 (2004).

[64] *See* John Merryman, *The Civil Law Tradition: An Introduction to the Legal Systems of Western Europe and Latin America* 26–33 (Stanford U. Press 1985) (providing an excellent discussion of the difference between the French Code Napoleon (the *Code Civil*), based upon divination of the "natural order" of things (the pronouncement of which would abolish all that had come before), as compared to the German approach, wherein the drafters engaged in a "scientific" study of the pre-existing legal norms and attempted to incorporate them into the *Bürgerliches Gesetzbuch*, along with the essential elements of Roman law).

law. In a civil law system, previous case law does not constitute a source of law, though it might be somewhat persuasive in attempting to argue for an outcome that is consistent with the majority of previous cases. In fact, and by way of example, the French *Code Civil* specifically states that judges may not make general or normative pronouncements.[65] On the contrary, in such civil law jurisdictions the written law is supreme.

By legislating basic principles, civil law countries seek to ensure consistency in judicial proceedings through uniform adherence to those written enactments. Accordingly, the rule of law – the primacy of those legal principles – will always be carried out in practice. In civil law systems, scholarly commentary on the written enactments of law is particularly persuasive in aiding adjudicators as they attempt to apply the enactments to a variety of factual circumstances.[66]

By contrast, in a common law system, case law forms binding precedent that subsequent courts must follow. In this way, common law jurisdictions seek to ensure that the rule of law is carried out and that the law is consistently applied from case to case, with subsequent cases always following similar cases that were decided in the past.

Of course, the common law system is not as clear cut as it may seem. Because so many factual distinctions exist in any given situation, it is often difficult to find a previous case where the exact same facts exist as those in the principle case under consideration.[67] Where any differences do exist, advocates have leeway to argue to a tribunal that the new factual circumstance must be governed by a new rule of law and that such a result would still be consistent with previous case law. The potential for such arguments, critics claim, actually destabilizes the law and leads citizens and advocates to believe that they can frequently achieve the results they desire in a particular dispute, no matter what binding precedent exists.

Common law systems also generally have written enactments of law in addition to binding case law. For example, the United States Constitution is in fact a written enactment of law that provides the supreme law of the nation.[68] In addition to the Constitution, in the United States, statutes govern specific subject

---

[65] French Civ. Code, Prelim. Title of the Publication, Operation and Application of Stats. in Gen., art. 5 (translation available at http://195.83.177.9/upl/pdf/code_22.pdf).

[66] *See* Honnold, *supra* n. 61, at 207 (highlighting the importance of scholarly writing in the civil law world).

[67] In the United States, lawyers state that a case "is on all fours" if he or she finds a previous case with the same circumstances as the case at hand. Very seldom, however, does this occur.

[68] In fact, Article VI of the United States Constitution states, "This Constitution, and the Laws of the United States which shall be made in pursuance thereof; and all Treaties made, or which shall be made, under the Authority of the United States, shall be the supreme Law of the Land; and the Judges in every State shall be bound thereby, any thing in the Constitution or Laws of any state to the contrary notwithstanding."

areas. Most relevant to sales law is the Uniform Commercial Code (UCC), which governs commercial transactions, including the sale of goods. Some version of the UCC exists in almost every state in the United States.[69] Statutory law in common law jurisdictions, such as the UCC in the United States, differs from the codified law found in many civil law countries in that statutes in common law jurisdictions do not purport to represent the entire body of law on a given subject.[70] In common law systems, a statute is a specific pronouncement of law that is supplemented by the body of case law that existed on topic prior to the statute becoming effective. In addition, subsequent cases also interpret and apply statutes. Those cases then become binding sources of law and therefore must be consulted even if a statute exists on a particular topic.

When comparing a civil law jurisdiction to a common law jurisdiction, other subtle differences become apparent. Because civil law jurisdictions do not have the multitude of cases that form sources of law in common law jurisdictions, the sources of law in civil law jurisdictions are necessarily less detail oriented. In a common law system, it is possible to find hundreds or possibly thousands of cases that describe a specific rule of law and apply that rule in many different circumstances. That amount of specificity is simply not possible in a civil law jurisdiction where broader principles of law are set forth in written enactments of law, leaving adjudicators to apply those principles as they see fit in each case.

For example, in a civil law jurisdiction, a civil code might state that one must not misrepresent any material fact in connection with a contract for that contract to be valid. That general principle would need to be applied to every case where misrepresentation in a contract matter was alleged, and a tribunal would need to use its best judgment to carry out the principle. The tribunal might consider the results of previous cases and scholarly commentary on the topic, but the tribunal can only base its decision on the written code. In these systems, tribunals are entrusted with carrying out the basic guiding principles set forth in the code.

By contrast, in a common law jurisdiction, there might be thousands of cases where courts have held, over hundreds of years, that misrepresenting material facts in connection with a contract invalidates the contract. However, all of those cases set forth specific circumstances providing more guidance on what might be a material fact in any given matter. Moreover, the cases themselves might address what constitutes a misrepresentation. Further, materiality and misrepresentation might change depending on the type of transaction involved. In small transactions, the level of materiality might be different than in larger

---

[69] *E.g.* Fla. Stat. §672 (2007); Ill. Compiled Stat. 810 Ill. Comp. Stat. §5 (2007).

[70] Honnold, *supra* n. 61, at 210 (arguing that the UCC is not a "code" in the civil law sense because "[t]he UCC does not lay out the basic rules of contracts and torts ("obligations") and generally applicable remedial principles that are needed to solve problems that arise beyond the borders of the specific rules").

transactions. There might also be a statute that applies and prohibits fraud in connection with contract formation. That statute would also need to be considered as would any cases that had interpreted that statute. In a common law world, advocates would research existing statutes and case law, searching for cases that closely resemble their fact pattern to determine the law governing the outcome of their case.[71]

2. Sources of International Law

Perhaps a discussion about the sources of international law should start with the fact that most laws are not specifically international in scope. Most laws around the world are designed to apply to the jurisdiction in which they exist. However, it is also possible that domestic laws can be applied internationally. For example, a United States company doing business with a Russian company might opt to have Russian law govern their relationship. Even if parties from two countries do not agree to have any particular law govern their relationship, a conflict of laws analysis will likely lead to the laws of one of the two countries involved applying. Thus, even domestic laws have an international aspect. However, the sources of commercial law that are truly international are very limited, consisting of treaties on the one hand, and the *lex mercatoria* on the other.[72]

a. Treaties

A treaty is a written document that has been agreed to by the nations that have ratified it. Typically a treaty is first signed on behalf of a country by someone vested with appropriate authority. Nonetheless, a treaty must then be ratified by the government of the signatory nation in order to become binding on that nation.

Treaties are essentially contracts whereby the ratifying nations agree to be bound by the provisions of the treaty. However, treaties typically also become law in the ratifying nations. For example, Article VI of the United States Constitution provides that "all Treaties made, or which shall be made, under the Authority of the United States, shall be the supreme Law of the Land.[73] Other countries,

---

[71] For further discussion on the differences between civil and common law systems, see John Spanogle, Jr., *The Arrival of International Private Law*, 25 Geo. Wash. J. Intl. L. & Econ. 477 (1991).
[72] The 1946 Statute constituting the International Court of Justice (the United Nations' primary court) defined the sources of international law that that court should consider to include international treaties and customary sources of international law (i.e. *lex mercatoria*).
[73] For example, Article VI of the United States Constitution provides that "all Treaties made, or which shall be made, under the Authority of the United States, shall be the supreme Law of the Land."

which do not have such a provision automatically making treaties law, can choose to implement any given treaty through the adoption of a domestic statute.

The existence of international sources of law is juxtaposed to the concept of national sovereignty. At the heart of sovereignty is the notion that every nation has the right to exercise jurisdiction over its own people and territory and should not have to submit to any external source of authority, most particularly to any foreign nation. In this way, nations maintain their own independence and control over their own citizenry.[74] Treaties interfere with the sovereignty of nations and are therefore often difficult to enact. Through a treaty, ratifying nations agree to cede some of their sovereignty and willingly agree to be governed by an external instrument. The tension that exists when nations contemplate entering into treaties is always based on this dynamic – giving up a country's own sovereignty over a particular matter and submitting to some external source of authority.[75]

Treaties may or may not include dispute resolution provisions for occasions when conflicts arise. Further, just as a contract may or may not be formally called a contract, a treaty may or may not be formally called a treaty. Treaties might also be referred to as conventions, protocols, and agreements. Of course, the most significant treaty for international commercial transactions, and the focus of the next five chapters of this book, is the CISG. Likewise, the most significant treaty for international commercial arbitration is the New York Convention (discussed further in Part III of this book).

b.   *Lex Mercatoria*

While treaties contain specific written provisions that can be interpreted like a statute or code, the *lex mercatoria*, or the law merchant, has no specific codification and very little clarity. *Lex mercatoria* is the phrase used to describe international customs and norms that are so deeply entrenched in the international community that they can be said to be international laws. While

---

[74] However, national sovereignty has its limits. The United Nations (UN) Charter permits the UN to intervene in Member States for humanitarian purposes, such as the UN's intervention in Bosnia and Herzegovina in 1995 to provide UN assistance related to humanitarian relief and refugees, demining, human rights, elections, and rehabilitation of the infrastructure and economic reconstruction. UN, Dept. of Peacekeeping Operations, *UN Mission in Bosnia & Herzegovinia*, http://www.un.org/Depts/dpko/missions/unmibh/ (updated Sept. 16, 2007). To see a listing of the UN's current and past projects, see http://www.un.org/Depts/dpko/dpko/index.asp.

[75] The concern over national sovereignty was present in the creation of the CISG. In the Sixth Meeting of the General Assembly of the United Nations on the establishment of a New International Economic Order, the delegate from Russia stated, "it was necessary to establish rules that would facilitate commercial transactions on the basis of respect for sovereignty and national independence, non-intervention in the domestic affairs of States and mutual benefit." Bruno Zeller, *International Trade Law—Problems of Language and Concepts?* 23 J.L. & Com. 39, 39 (2005).

conceptualizing the *lex mercatoria* may be easy, identifying what constitutes the *lex mercatoria* is extremely difficult. The very definition of the *lex mercatoria* suggests the question of what customs and norms are so entrenched and so widespread internationally as to be included. In fact, critics of the notion argue that the vagueness of the *lex mercatoria* allows advocates to advance arguments on behalf of clients that are well beyond the scope of any relevant written identifiable law.

Despite the critics' perspective, some certainty exists with the *lex mercatoria* in the area of international commercial transactions. As mentioned earlier, UNIDROIT adopted a document called the Principles of International Commercial Contracts (the UNIDROIT Principles) to reflect the fundamental principles of international commercial law that are applied around the world. Because such a well-respected organization has reflected on those principles and spent many years creating this document, it is arguably a very valuable source of the *lex mercatoria*.[76] As discussed above, the Preamble to the UNIDROIT Principles states that they shall apply to a transaction when parties have agreed that "their contract be governed by general principles of law, the *lex mercatoria* or the like."[77] The UNIDROIT Principles are particularly useful when the law designated by the parties to govern their transaction is silent on a particular topic that is addressed by the UNIDROIT Principles.[78]

Similarly, the Principles of European Contract Law (PECL) were drafted and designed to reflect fundamental principles of contract law that exist throughout the European Union.[79] PECL is the work product of a commission of experts from countries throughout the European Union, the Commission on European Contract Law working under the European Commission. A first draft of PECL was adopted in 1995, with subsequent revisions and additions in 1998 and 2003. Similar to the UNIDROIT Principles, the preamble to the PECL states that if parties agree that their contract should be governed by general principles of

---

[76] *Costa Rican Co. v. French Co., Ad Hoc* Arbitration, Cost Rica, Apr. 30, 2004 (available at http://www.unilex.info/case.cfm?pid=2&do=case&id=1100&step=FullText) (applying the UNIDROIT Principles when the parties' contract simply stated that disputes should be resolved "on the basis of good faith and fair usages and with regard to the most sound commercial practices and friendly terms").

[77] UNIDROIT Principles Preamble.

[78] *See Swiss Buyer v. Austrian Seller (Chemical Fertilizer Case)*, ICC Arbitration no. 8128, Switzerland, 1995 (available at http://cisgw3.law.pace.edu/cases/958128i1.html). After finding that the CISG was silent as to the applicable rate of interest, the arbitral tribunal applied the solution that was adopted by the UNIDROIT Principles. Relying upon Article 7(2) CISG, discussed further in Chapter 2, the tribunal reasoned that the UNIDROIT Principles were applicable because they are considered general principles on which CISG is based.

[79] *See generally* Principles of European Contract L. (Commn. European Contract L. 1995) (available at http://frontpage.cbs.dk/law/commission_on_european_contract_law/) [hereinafter PECL].

international law or the *lex mercatoria*, then PECL shall apply.[80] However, the PECL has not been as well-received as the UNIDROIT Principles in this regard.[81]

It is important to note that the *lex mercatoria* should not be viewed as being mutually exclusive with other sources of law. In fact, tribunals often rely on both the *lex mercatoria* and codified sources of law, such as the CISG, in conjunction with each other.[82] Furthermore, when the parties in a dispute have not expressly chosen a governing law, tribunals have applied codified sources of law such as the CISG as representative of the *lex mercatoria*.[83]

II.   COMMERCIAL AND LEGAL CONSIDERATIONS

Part I of this chapter just described why countries trade with each other, what institutions exist to support free trade, and what laws may apply to an international commercial transaction. Part II will present a variety of commercial and legal issues that parties to an international sale of goods should consider when structuring a transaction or participating in the resolution of a dispute. The issues that will be presented include: (A) managing applicable laws; (B) considering international arbitration; (C) limiting financial risk; (D) allocating shipping risks; (E) hedging currency risk; and (F) navigating cultural differences.

---

[80] PECL art. 1:101(3)(a).

[81] *See Natl. Bank of Country X v. Defendant Y (Printed Banknotes Case)*, ICC Arbitration no. 9474, France, Feb. 1999 (available at http://cisgw3.law.pace.edu/cases/999474i1.html) (describing the UNIDROIT Principles and the PECL as "other recent documents that express the general standards and rules of commercial law").

[82] Specifically, Article 9 of the CISG provides that international trade usages impliedly apply to the parties' contract, unless the parties have expressly agreed otherwise. This provision, therefore, illustrates the point that the *lex mercatoria* does not compete with codified bodies of law, but rather that the two sources complement each other. Bernard Audit, *The Vienna Sales Convention and the Lex Mercatoria*, in *Lex Mercatoria and Arbitration* 174 (Thomas E. Carbonneau ed., rev. ed. Juris Publg. 1998) (reprint of a chapter of the 1990 edition of this text).

[83] *See Turkish Seller v. Swiss Buyer*, ICC Arbitration no. 5713, France, 1989 (available at http://cisgw3.law.pace.edu/cases/895713i1.html) (finding that the CISG applied in absence of the parties' choice because the Convention "may be fairly taken to reflect the generally recognized usages regarding the matter of the non-conformity of goods in international sales"). It is interesting to note that at the time of this arbitral decision, only seventeen nations were signatories to the CISG. *See also Yugoslavian Seller v. Italian Buyer (Cowhides Case)*, ICC Arbitration no. 7331, Paris, 1994 (available at http://www.unilex.info/case.cfm?pid=1&do=case&id=140&step =FullText) (applying the CISG in the absence of express choice by the parties because the Convention embodies "general principles of international commercial practice").

A.   MANAGING APPLICABLE LAWS

Parties should generally attempt to include a governing law provision in their contract to avoid the confusion that ensues without one. If parties do not specify a governing law in their contract, then conflict of laws rules will determine the applicable law with the result not always being what one or the other party would have wanted or anticipated when entering the transaction.[84] In most of the world, parties are given the autonomy to choose the law that they want to govern their transaction. However, that is not always true. In the United States, for example, that autonomy might be circumscribed by the UCC's choice of law provisions.[85] A very common version of that provision insists that the choice of law must be from a state that "bear[s] a reasonable relation" to the transaction. Even with this provision governing, however, an attorney structuring a transaction should be sure to include a choice of law provision in the agreement. The choice should simply be one with a reasonable relation to the transaction.

In certain cases, the CISG will govern international sales of goods transactions where a law to govern an international commercial transaction has not been chosen by the parties. As will be discussed in Chapter 2, the CISG will apply by default if both parties are from countries that are contracting states to the CISG, or if the rules of private international law[86] lead to the law of a country that is a contracting state.[87]

---

[84] Parties might even agree that sources of *lex mercatoria* govern their contract, such as the UNIDROIT Principles. However, as the UNIDROIT Principles themselves explain, if the parties desire such a choice they should also opt for arbitration since arbitrators are more likely to honor that choice while state or national tribunals may feel confined to apply state or national laws. UNIDROIT Principles off. comment 4(a) (2004).

[85] The UCC in §1-105 limits the applicability of the UCC to transactions that "bear a reasonable relation" to the state. Interestingly, the UCC was revised in 2001, and revised Article 1-301 gives parties greater freedom to choose to apply the UCC by limiting the reasonable relation requirement to consumer transactions. While revised Article 1 has now been adopted by many states, the states that have adopted the revisions have failed to adopt the revised §1-301. Ronald Mann, Elizabeth Warren & Jay Lawrence Westbrook, *2006 Comprehensive Commercial Law Statutory Supplement* xi. (Aspen 2006); *see also* Jack M. Graves, *Party Autonomy in Choice of Commercial Law: The Failure of Revised UCC*, 36 Seton Hall L. Rev. 59 (2005).

[86] In the United States, the rules of private international law generally refer to any law that governs relationships between private parties from different countries. By contrast, in many civil law countries, the rules of private international law refer more specifically to conflict of laws rules that apply to situations involving parties from different countries. Commentators generally agree that the phrase, as it is used in the CISG, has the narrower meaning of choice of law or conflict of laws rules in the forum court. *See* Joseph Lookofsky, *The United Nations Convention on Contracts for the International Sale of Goods*, in *International Encyclopaedia of Laws—Contracts, Supplement* 29, 33 (J. Herbots & R. Blanpain eds., Kluwer L. Intl. 2000). For additional discussion pertaining to the applicability of the CISG to a dispute, see Chapter 2.

[87] *See* CISG art. 1(1)(a)-(b), discussed in detail in Chapter 2.

If the parties have not chosen a governing law and the CISG does not apply to the transaction, then conflict of laws rules become relevant. It is not always clear which conflict of laws rules will apply to a given transaction. In fact, many rules of arbitration specify that the arbitrators should use whatever conflict of laws rules they deem applicable.[88] Even if the appropriate conflict of laws rules are clear, the results that follow from those rules are not always clear. Frequently, conflict of laws rules specify that the applicable law should be the law of the country with the closest relation to the contract.[89] When a contract has been signed in one country, negotiated in another, and the goods are produced in a third country and delivered in a fourth, it becomes very difficult to apply the closest connection standard. The unexpected result from a conflict of laws analysis may not be desirable for either of the parties to the transaction. Once again, this underscores the desirability of choosing a governing law in the first place. Applicable laws will be discussed in more detail in Chapter 2.

B.   CONSIDERING ARBITRATION FOR DISPUTE RESOLUTION

A detailed study of arbitration is presented in Part III (Chapters 7 – 10) of this book. However, it is important to address arbitration even at this early stage as one of the issues to consider when engaging in an international sale of goods. This section will briefly address: (1) the pros and cons of arbitration; (2) the basic nature of an arbitration agreement; and (3) the private rules and governing law applicable to arbitration.

1.   The Pros and Cons of Arbitration

For parties to an international sale of goods, arbitration provides an alternative to dispute resolution in national courts. Arbitration is a private means for resolving legal disputes in which the parties ask one or more arbitrators to decide their dispute and agree to be bound by that decision. Arbitration is especially attractive in international commercial transactions for its perceived neutrality.

---

[88] *See e.g.* UNCITRAL R. of Arb. art. 33(1); *but see* Arb. R. of the Intl. Chamber of Com. art. 17(1) (allowing arbitrators to make a direct choice of substantive law without reference to any conflict of laws rules).

[89] If the parties have not expressly or impliedly determined the law to govern a parties' contract, many national courts apply the law of the court with the closest connection to the transaction. *See e.g. Mansonville Plastics Ltd. [Canada] v. Kurtz GmbH [Austria/Germany]*, 2003 BCSC 1298, Canada, 2003 (available at http://www.yorku.ca/osgoode/cisg/cases/masonville.htm) (finding that the transaction had its "closest and most substantial connection with Toronto and thus the law that should apply is the Law of Ontario"). In addition, Article 5 of The Federal Economic Contract Law of the People's Republic of China, adopted by the National People's Congress in 1985, also provides that the law of the country having the closest connection with the contract applies in the absence of an express choice by the parties.

Using arbitration avoids any perception of bias that might exist if one of the parties is subjected to the national courts of the other party's country. Unlike national courts, the members of an arbitral panel do not necessarily have ties to any particular country, and a panel of three arbitrators from multiple countries is often chosen by the parties.

Arbitration is also favored because arbitration awards are generally much easier than national court decisions to enforce outside of the country in which they are rendered. As a result of the wide acceptance of the New York Convention, an award made by a tribunal in one country, perhaps chosen for convenience or neutrality, can easily be enforced in almost any country in which either party may have financial assets. The subject of enforcement of awards is explored further in Chapter 10.

Arbitration in International Commercial Transactions

– The Two Most Important Factors –

(1) Neutral Decision Makers

(2) Internationally Enforceable Awards

There are a variety of additional reasons why parties might choose arbitration, including the confidentiality and expeditiousness of the arbitral process, as well as the expertise of available decision makers.

While there are many benefits to arbitration, especially in the international context, there are also potential detriments that should not be overlooked. The parties to an arbitration agreement will sometimes be unable to join additional claims, and third parties cannot be required to participate in arbitration without express consent. Court involvement may be required during the arbitral process, perhaps adding additional disputes on top of those arising from the parties' commercial agreement. Lastly, an erroneous decision by the arbitrators is not generally subject to appeal. All of these factors must be considered by the parties in deciding whether or not arbitration is appropriate for any given transaction.

Finally, the cost of arbitration should be mentioned. In terms of the cost of the tribunal itself, arbitration will almost always be more expensive because the parties must pay the arbitrators and, perhaps, pay for the services of an arbitral institution. Arbitration, however, will very often result in other cost savings that will more than offset the additional costs of the tribunal. The expedited and simplified nature of arbitration will typically reduce other associated costs, such as the cost of legal counsel. Moreover, for most businesses, "time is money," and each of the parties may realize substantial savings in terms of the reduced time spent by their employees involved in dispute resolution.

In deciding whether arbitration is appropriate for any particular transaction, the parties and their counsel will need to consider all of these issues, as there is no single correct answer for all commercial disputes. This subject is explored further in Chapter 7.

2.   The Arbitration Agreement

Arbitration is primarily a matter of contract between the parties. The jurisdiction of an arbitral tribunal is grounded entirely in the consent of the parties. In contrast, the jurisdiction of national courts is typically based on some combination of governmental power and implied party consent—the latter arising from relevant contacts of the parties with the place whose courts are seeking to assert jurisdiction. Accordingly, contract law principles often come into play in the interpretation and performance of an arbitration agreement.

The parties' arbitration agreement may be contained within the broader contract at issue in the parties' dispute or in a separate agreement. It may relate to a range of possible future disputes or to a pre-existing dispute the parties subsequently decide to submit to arbitration. The terms of the agreement may be extensive or may be quite brief. Under virtually all current national laws, the primary requirement is that the arbitration agreement be evidenced by a signed writing.[90]

Whatever form it may take, an arbitration agreement is generally treated as autonomous or separable from the main contract governing the transaction subject to dispute—even if the arbitration agreement is contained in a clause within that main contract. This concept of "separability" is of great importance to the effectiveness of any arbitration regime, as it may, in certain circumstances, preserve the jurisdiction of the tribunal—even if the main contract containing the arbitration clause is deemed invalid by that tribunal. The subject of separability is explored in considerable detail in Chapter 8.

As indicated above, arbitration is largely a matter of contract. However, the parties' autonomy in this regard is not unlimited. An arbitration agreement is

---

[90] *See* New York Convention Article II (June 10, 1958), http:// http://www.uncitral.org/pdf/english/texts/arbitration/NY-conv/XXII_1_e.pdf; UNCITRAL Model Law Article 7(2); *but see* UNCITRAL Model Law Article 7 (*Option II*) (as revised in 2006, which provides an alternative version of Article 7 requiring only "agreement by the parties" and eliminating any writing requirement). From a practical perspective, an award rendered pursuant to such an oral arbitration agreement would present enforceability issues. This issue is discussed further in Chapter 8. However, the inclusion of such an option in the current version of the Model Law may be indicative of an increasing pre-enforcement trend where the parties have agreed on arbitration—whatever the means of that agreement.

governed by a variety of laws—most importantly the law of the place of arbitration and the law of any potential place of enforcement of an award made by the arbitrators.[91] For example, any governing law will protect the basic "due process" rights of the parties, irrespective of any agreement between them to the contrary.[92] The parties' right to arbitrate certain disputes may also be subject to certain limitations based on public policy of a relevant jurisdiction. These limits are explored further in Chapter 8.

For the most part, however, the law governing the arbitration will consist of various "default legal rules," which are fully subordinate to the parties' right to choose different rules, as a matter of contract. This interplay between the default legal regime and any contractually agreed upon rules is explored further in Chapter 7 and developed throughout Part III of this book. However, a brief introduction is provided below.

3.   The Rules and Law Governing Arbitration

Parties will often choose a specific set of arbitration rules to govern the resolution of their dispute. In addition, however, the place of arbitration will provide a governing arbitration law, the *lex arbitri*, that will often supply a substantial body of default legal rules. The UNCITRAL Model Law is a prime example of such a law. It has been adopted in over 50 countries and seven states of the United States, and it is exemplary of modern commercial arbitration law.[93]

The default legal rules within the Model Law are provided in order to answer basic questions regarding the arbitral process in the event the parties fail to do so. However, if the parties expressly answer these questions themselves, then the default legal rule yields to the parties' agreement. The parties may provide for their own rules in either of two ways. They may do so through the express terms within their arbitration agreement, itself, or they may do so through the "incorporation" of a pre-drafted set of arbitration rules into that agreement.

---

[91] This book will focus primarily on the UNCITRAL Model Law and the New York Convention.

[92] *See e.g.* UNCITRAL Model Law Article 18; New York Convention Article V.1.(b).

[93] *See* Appendix A (listing Model Law jurisdictions). The UNCITRAL Model Law can be viewed at http://www.uncitral.org/uncitral/en/uncitral_texts/arbitration/1985Model_arbitration.html. Many of the specific details of United States federal arbitration law, as well as conflicts between United States state and United States federal arbitration law are well beyond the scope of this course. We will make occasional references to a few basic United States cases and the influence of United States practitioners on international commercial arbitration; however, United States arbitration law is in many ways inconsistent with mainstream, modern international commercial arbitration law, as found in most other sophisticated states involved in international trade. These latter nuances and anomalies of United States law are better left to a course that focuses specifically on arbitration under United States federal and state law.

Most arbitration rules are drafted and supplied by private institutions that provide administrative services to assist the parties in facilitating the arbitration of their dispute. For example, the International Chamber of Commerce (ICC), arguably the world's leading organization in the field of international commercial dispute resolution, provides its own set of rules and recommends that parties adopt these rules in their arbitration agreement. Like many arbitration institutions, the ICC has a model clause that it recommends parties use in their agreements if they wish to resolve their disputes with arbitration administered by the ICC.

ICC Model Clause

All disputes arising out of or in connection with the present contract shall be finally settled under the Rules of Arbitration of the International Chamber of Commerce by one or more arbitrators appointed in accordance with the said Rules.[94]

In this model clause, the ICC Arbitration Rules are incorporated into the parties' agreement by reference. The rules then essentially become additional express terms of the parties' arbitration agreement. Of course, any conflict between the precise terms written within the contract itself and the incorporated terms referenced should be resolved in favor of the specific contract terms. However, the parties' express terms, whether specifically stated in the agreement, or incorporated by reference, will take precedence over any default legal rules of the place of arbitration. All of these concepts are developed further in Chapter 7.[95]

In addition to institutional rules, the parties may also choose to use the UNCITRAL Arbitration Rules.[96] Many institutions allow the parties to choose these rules instead of the institution's own rules. They may also be used if the parties choose to submit their dispute to arbitration without any institutional assistance—a process called *ad hoc* arbitration. This distinction between institutional and *ad hoc* arbitration will be developed further in Chapter 7.

---

[94] Int'l Chamber Com., *International Court of Arbitration, ICC Standard and Suggested Clauses for Dispute Resolution Services*, http://www.iccwbo.org/court/arbitration/id4114/index.html (accessed Oct. 1, 2007).

[95] *See also* app B.

[96] One other point about "rules" is worth mentioning here at the outset in hopes of avoiding confusion later. UNCITRAL, the same body that is responsible for the UNCITRAL Model Law originally promulgated in 1985 and recently revised in 2006, also promulgated the UNCITRAL Arbitration Rules in 1976. Each of these will be discussed thoroughly in Part III. However, it is important at the outset to distinguish between the UNCITRAL Model Law, which is positive law (once adopted by a sovereign) and the UNCITRAL Rules, which are only relevant if expressly adopted by the parties in the same manner as any other set of private rules.

When considering the relationship between "rules" and "law," one must, however, remember to distinguish between mandatory legal rules and default legal rules. The parties' agreement, including any private arbitration rules, is given priority over any default legal rules. However, the parties may not, under any circumstances, change or negate a mandatory legal rule, such as the requirement that each party be afforded basic due process. This distinction between mandatory and default rules of law is important in both the CISG and in the law of arbitration and will be discussed throughout this book. That distinction is also illustrated by the chart set forth in Appendix B.

C.   LIMITING FINANCIAL RISK

For any seller in a commercial transaction, the largest risk may be the financial risk of delivering goods, but not getting paid. For any buyer, the largest risk may be the financial risk of paying for goods, but not receiving them. These risks are greatly magnified in an international commercial transaction, as the parties are located across national borders and possibly across the globe. In a domestic transaction, a party is likely to be more comfortable attempting to enforce payment or delivery from another party in the same country. However, attempting to use courts or enforcement mechanisms across national borders is much more daunting.

To manage these financial risks, many transactions are structured through the use of commercial *letters of credit*. Letters of credit represent promises made by banks that essentially guarantee payment on a sales contract, provided that the seller submits the appropriate documents. Such an exchange of documents for payment is called a *documentary sale*. The required documents typically include the following.

Letter of Credit Transactions
Typical Required Documents
(1) Commercial invoice
(2) Packing list
(3) Certificate of Origin
(4) Negotiable bill of lading
(5) Insurance certificate
(6) Certificate of inspection

The commercial invoice includes the basic contract terms, including a description of the goods, the quantity, and the price, as well as the carriage and delivery terms. In essence, the commercial invoice represents a "bill" to be paid by the buyer pursuant to the letter of credit. The packing list provides the details of packing the goods for transport (often in a sealed "container"), and the certificate of origin provides information required for import/export controls.

The bill of lading is particularly important in a documentary sale, because this is the document that actually controls title to the goods. A documentary sale requires a *negotiable* bill of lading. This negotiability is what allows one party to transfer title to the goods by transferring (*negotiating*) a negotiable bill of lading. In contrast, a straight bill of lading is not negotiable. Because the documents, including the bill of lading, are to be exchanged for payment, negotiability is crucial.

The seller will also typically be required to insure the goods and provide a certificate of such insurance, thus protecting the insurable interest of each party throughout the process of carriage, irrespective of when title actual passes between the parties. The buyer will often require a certificate of inspection. In view of the fact that the buyer is actually paying for the goods before seeing them (documents and payment are usually exchanged while the goods are in route), the buyer will often arrange for inspection of the goods prior to shipment from the port of embarkation. The inspectors will be employed by the buyer, who will provide the appropriate instructions regarding inspection of the goods, but will then provide a certificate to seller, which the seller can then include with the documents to be presented for payment.

By using banks and letters of credit, sellers are guaranteed to be paid if they submit the appropriate documents. Likewise, buyers are guaranteed that they will only pay only if they receive the appropriate documents allowing them to take title to the goods. The banks and their agents act as middlemen to ensure that the documents provided by the seller conform to the letter of credit agreement and only allow payment when they do. Of course, the parties to the transaction pay the banks a fee for their involvement, but that fee reduces the risk the parties undertake. Once trading partners establish a certain amount of confidence with each other, they often choose to reduce transaction costs by eliminating the letter of credit arrangement and taking upon themselves the risk of non-payment or non-delivery.

In a letter of credit transaction governed by United States law, UCC Article 5 will provide the applicable law. However, Article 5 largely consists of default rules, which may be varied by agreement of the parties. In an effort to promote the application of uniform rules to letter of credit transactions, the International Chamber of Commerce (ICC) issues a set of Uniform Customs and Practice for Documentary Credits (UCP), which are incorporated in most letter of credit agreements. The current version of these terms is contained in UCP 600, which became effective on 1 July 2007.

Letter of Credit Transactions

-The Two Most Important Principles-

(each reflected in UCC Article 5 and UCP 600)

(1) *The Independence Principle.* Under the *Independence Principle*, the issuing bank's promise to pay against documents is entirely independent of underlying contract for the sale of goods, and the bank's obligation (and thereby buyer's obligation) is not subject to any defenses arising out of that underlying contract.

(2) *Perfect Tender.* Payment pursuant to a letter of credit obligation requires *"perfect tender"* or *"strict compliance"* by the seller in the submission of the required documents.

When one considers the effect of the independence principle, the significance of the list of required documents, including any inspection certificate, becomes clearer. The buyer cannot rely on a breach of the contract for sale to avoid payment. The only basis for refusing payment under the letter of credit is seller's failure to submit the appropriate documents. Of course the buyer can still bring an action for damages arising out of the contract of sale, but this is one of the risks a buyer hopes to avoid through the use of a letter of credit. In recognition, however, of buyer's risk, seller is required to tender documents that perfectly comply with the requirements specified in the letter of credit. Again, we find a balanced approach in an effort to protect the interests of both seller and buyer.

The specifics of a documentary sales transaction are somewhat complex and certainly vary from deal to deal. However, the basic documentary sales transaction generally involves the same basic steps.

The Letter of Credit Transaction

(1) In the first step of a typical transaction, the buyer and the seller enter into a sales contract that specifies the goods to be tendered and the method of shipment.

(2) In the second step, the buyer of goods establishes an arrangement with its bank in its country whereby that bank

agrees to issue a letter of credit in favor of the seller, also known as the beneficiary of the letter of credit. That document will commit the issuing bank to make payment on buyer's behalf when the bank receives the required documents (showing that the seller has shipped the goods).

(3) In a possible third step, the seller might set up an arrangement with a bank or banks in its own country to interact with the issuing bank (buyer's bank). One possibility is that seller may ask its own bank to serve as a "confirming" bank, thereby, independently promising to pay seller in exchange for submission of the required documents. Alternatively, the seller may use an "advising" bank, which will serve as an intermediary between seller and the issuing bank, but will not independently guarantee payment to seller. Confirming and advising banks may also be used in combination. While the seller could forgo the use of any additional bank and interact with the issuing bank itself (thereby saving some expense) this option may introduce increased risk as the seller must rely entirely on the letter of credit agreement with a bank in a foreign country. For the remainder of this sample transaction, seller's use of a confirming bank is assumed.

(4) In the fourth step, the seller arranges for any required inspection and actually ships the goods. When seller does so, it will receive any inspection certificate from the party designated by buyer and will receive the negotiable bill of lading from the carrier. Seller will also prepare or obtain the additional required documents.

(5) In the fifth step, the seller delivers the required documents to its bank (the confirming bank) in return for payment. If for any reason the shipping documents do not conform to the requirements of the letter of credit, the bank will refuse payment. Assuming, however, the seller has provided conforming documents, the bank must pay the seller.

(6) In the sixth step, the confirming bank (the seller's bank) will present the documents to the issuing bank (the buyer's bank) in exchange for payment of the promised price for the goods. Again, the issuing bank is obligated to pay the confirming bank, as long as the documents precisely conform to the requirements of the letter of credit.

(7) In the seventh step, the issuing bank provides the documents to the buyer in exchange for the buyer's payment of the price. The buyer then has paid for the goods and has the documents necessary to retrieve the goods.

(8) In the eighth and final step, the buyer picks up the goods at the port of delivery with the documents it received from its bank. The most crucial document at this step is of course the negotiable bill of lading, which controls title to the goods.

Notice how the financial risk of this transaction has been minimized. When the seller ships goods, it is confident that it will be paid for the goods, as long as it presents conforming documents (which are within its control to generate or obtain). If the seller's bank does not pay as it should, the seller has familiar channels of dispute resolution available in its own country. From the buyer's perspective, the buyer only pays its bank in exchange for documents showing that seller has actually shipped the goods (conforming goods if an inspection certificate is also required) and that buyer will acquire title to the goods and can thereby retrieve them. If for some reason the buyer's bank does not follow through with its obligations on behalf of the buyer, the buyer can bring an action against its own bank in its own jurisdiction. The diagram below helps to illustrate this transaction.

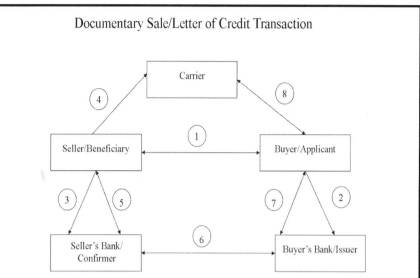

Documentary Sale/Letter of Credit Transaction

1. Parties form a contract for the sale of goods that also establishes the documents required by the letter of credit.
2. Buyer applies for a letter of credit in favor of the seller from its bank. Buyer's bank agrees to issue the letter of credit.
3. Seller may also approach its bank. Seller's bank becomes the confirmer if it agrees to accept the letter of credit from buyer's bank.
4. Seller ships goods.
5. Seller presents bill of lading and other documents to its bank and receives payment.
6. Seller's bank transmits the bill of lading and other documents to buyer's bank in exchange for reimbursement.
7. Buyer makes payment to its bank in exchange for the bill of lading and other documents.
8. Carrier releases goods to buyer when proper documents including the bill of lading are produced.

D.   ALLOCATING THE COSTS AND RISKS OF CARRIAGE

In every sale of goods transaction there are risks and responsibilities related to the shipping or "carriage" of the goods involved. The goods could be lost in a storm at sea, stolen by the carrier, or may have appeared to conform at the time of they were dispatched by the seller but not conform by the time they reach their point of delivery to the buyer. Someone must arrange and pay for carriage of the goods from seller to buyer. Someone must also pay for any insurance against casualty to the goods during transit. Every contract for a sale of goods must allocate these costs, as well as the risk of loss. These are typically the three most significant issues that arise in the carriage of goods: (1) who will be responsible to arrange and pay for carriage; (2) who will be responsible to arrange and pay for any insurance against loss or casualty to the goods during transit; and (3) when does the risk of loss or casualty to the goods transfer from seller to buyer?

Each of these three issues might involve substantial negotiations in efforts to reach mutually agreeable solutions as to the broad variety details arising with respect to the transfer of goods from buyer to seller. Alternatively, the parties could simply incorporate, as part of their agreement, a set of pre-defined terms commonly used and understood in international commercial transactions that describe how each of these three issues will be addressed. These terms are called Incoterms. Like the UCP terms addressed in the previous section, Incoterms are issued by the ICC.

Incoterms are acronyms (like FOB or CIF) that stand for a comprehensive set of delivery terms defined in advance by the ICC. Incoterms describe who bears which of the burdens and risks associated with carriage of the goods.[97] Incoterms can be incorporated into a sales contract explicitly, avoiding the need for lengthy negotiations concerning these shipping terms. Incoterms also have become accepted as international trade usages and are therefore sometimes even implied into contracts governed by the CISG.[98] When the terms are explicitly used in a contract, it is helpful to indicate that the ICC definitions are being contemplated and the year of the edition referenced (the ICC revises Incoterms periodically). For example, the delivery term in a contract for the sale of goods by a New York seller might read "delivery FOB, New York (Incoterms 2000)."[99]

The use of a particular set of Incoterms is also important in the documentary sales transaction explained in the previous section.

For example, the CIF term specifically requires a negotiable bill of lading, unless otherwise agreed by the parties. This negotiable bill of lading allows a current holder of the bill of lading to sell or transfer the goods in transit by transferring (negotiating) the bill of lading in exchange for payment. Incoterms and their use will be discussed at greater length in Chapter 4 in relation to the obligations of the seller and buyer under a sales contract.

---

[97] For a listing of all Incoterms and their respective definitions, see http://www.iccwbo.org/Incoterms/id3040/index.html. Incoterms are discussed in more detail in Chapter 4.

[98] *See* Marc Rich & Co. A.G. [Switzerland] v. Iritecna S.p.A. [Italy], Corte di Appello di Genova no. 211, Italy, Mar. 24, 1995 (available at http://cisgw3.law.pace.edu/cases/950324i3.html) (ruling that the term F.O.B, Free on Board, was binding on the parties as an international trade usage pursuant to Article 9(2) CISG); *BP Oil Intl., Ltd. [U.S.] v. Empresa Estatal Petroleos de Ecuador* (PetroEcuador) [Equador], 332 F.3d 333, 337–338 (5th Cir. 2003) (available at http://cisgw3.law. pace.edu/cases/030611u1.html) ("Even if the usage of Incoterms is not global, the fact that they are well-known in international trade means that they are incorporated through article 9(2).").

[99] The list of Incoterms has been updated most recently in 2000.

Example 1-2

In a documentary sale transaction supported by a letter of credit, the seller will almost always specify "C" terms (e.g., CIF), which place a greater burden on seller than "F" terms (e.g., FOB), but give seller considerably more control over the goods until the seller has negotiated the bill of lading and turned over the required documents in exchange for payment, thereby allowing buyer to take delivery of the goods. In contrast, a seller will typically specify the less burdensome (to seller) "F" terms when selling to an established customer on open account (i.e., trusting the buyer to pay the price when due, but leaving it to buyer to arrange and pay the cost of carriage).

E.   HEDGING CURRENCY RISK

Another risk that is only present in an international commercial transaction is the risk of currency fluctuations. In our hypothetical sale between a United States Company and a Russian company, the currency risk would involve fluctuations in the value of the Russian ruble against the United States dollar. Currency fluctuations can be magnified by political considerations and, generally speaking, developing countries have much wider fluctuations in the value of their currencies than developed countries.

Again, careful planning of a transaction *ex ante* can minimize the risk posed by currency fluctuations. One way that companies protect against currency fluctuations is to enter into a currency hedge transaction in addition to the sale of goods transaction. For example, if the United States – Russian contract is priced in Russian rubles, the Russian company might feel comfortable but the United States company may want to enter into a futures contract to lock in a certain exchange rate between the ruble and the dollar to hedge against any harmful currency fluctuations.

A creative way to avoid currency risk is to structure a barter transaction. In a barter transaction, companies exchange products and never exchange money. A classic example of a barter transaction dates back to 1972 when PepsiCo agreed to exchange its Pepsi syrup to the Soviet Union in exchange for Stolichnaya Vodka. By 1988 one billion Pepsis per year were sold in the Soviet Union, and 676,000 cases of Stolichnaya were sold to the United States.[100] This barter transaction avoided any currency issues that Pepsi would have had in attempting to trade with the Soviet Union. This was especially important since the ruble at

---

[100] William F. Buckley, Jr., *Pepsi at the Summit*, Natl. Rev. (June 24, 1988).

the time was not a freely convertible currency. Barter is also referred to as counter trade.

F.   NAVIGATING CULTURAL DIFFERENCES

Cultural differences can make counterparties to trade suspicious of each other. Cultural and linguistic differences may also stand in the way of parties actually understanding what their counterpart wants and needs. Because of these potential problems that are unique in international transactions, it is imperative for parties to account for cultural differences when forming and developing a relationship and the contracts that govern any particular transaction. Focus should be placed on cultivating a relationship by getting to know trading partners, their traditions, their language, and their expectations.[101]

Cultural differences can also become an impediment to trade based on the notion that certain developed nations are engaging in cultural imperialism. Cultural imperialism is the practice of pushing one's cultures, values, and institutions onto other cultures in a way that diminishes the cultural identity of those cultures. While it is not clear to what extent cultural imperialism actually exists (many theorists argue that this phenomenon is more of a specter than a reality), the fear of cultural imperialism can cause some nations to erect barriers to trade, in the interest of preserving a national culture or identity.[102]

In fact, on October 20, 2005, the United Nations Education, Scientific and Cultural Organization (UNESCO) adopted the Convention on the Protection and Promotion of the Diversity of Cultural Expressions (the Culture Convention). The Culture Convention came into effect on March 18, 2007 with the goal of promoting and preserving the cultural institutions and identities of the countries that have ratified it. In pursuit of that goal, the Culture Convention specifically authorizes sovereign nations to take measures designed to promote those goals, including trade protection. The Culture Convention was adopted by an

---

[101] It is important for each party to research the business and social etiquette of its counterparty because there are cultural differences that could make the difference in closing a deal with a foreign party. Export America, the monthly publication of the U.S. Department of Commerce's International Trade Administration, published an article cautioning United States exporters of the importance of learning the cultures of prospective international business partners. *See* Margaret Kammeyer, *The Other Customs Barrier: Cultural Research Avoids Business Blunders*, 2 Export Ame. 32 (Apr. 2001) ("Savvy exporters are now not only expected to be familiar with country marketing reports but should also conduct research on their clients' culture and regional etiquette when preparing to enter new markets."). For example, in India, the significance of a business deal is often determined by the amount of time spent in negotiations. *Id.* In Germany, only for family members and close friends should refer to persons by their first names. *Id.*

[102] *See* David Rothkop, *In Praise of Cultural Imperialism, Effects on Global Culture*, For. Policy (June 22, 1997).

overwhelming majority of the countries participating in the General Conference, with 148 countries approving and only two, the United States and Israel, opposing it.[103]

On a transactional basis, overcoming cultural resistance to trade may involve making a counterparty understand that it and its country will benefit by going forward with a particular transaction. It may also involve adjusting the ways in which a particular client produces or markets its products to take into account the cultural sensitivities of its counterparty.

PROBLEMS

Problem 1-1: Re-Considering the International Commercial Transaction. As you contemplate representing the United States or the Russian company in the example presented at the beginning of this chapter, you probably will not be considering the comparative advantages that are motivating the trade, though they are surely present. What do you need to consider? This chapter has given you an overview of many of the legal and commercial considerations that are important in structuring an international commercial sale. How do those considerations apply here? What do you perceive to be the biggest risk of the transaction? What might you include in your contract to minimize the risk of this transaction and the likelihood that your parties will end up in a dispute? Will you opt for arbitration as your dispute resolution mechanism? Is it possible or advisable to manage the parties' relationship in stages and structure this first transaction in a certain way with expectations that future transactions might be structured differently? What other questions about the situation might bear on how you would structure the deal? Again, imagine you were representing the United States party, how would you advise it? What if you represented the Russian party? How might your advice differ? Remember as an attorney working in international sales, you will not always be representing parties from your own country, perhaps not even often.

---

[103] It is unclear at this time how the Culture Convention will affect trade among nations. For a thoughtful discussion of the Culture Convention, see Christopher M. Bruner, *Culture, Sovereignty and Hollywood: UNESCO and the Future of Trade in Cultural Products* (Bepress Leg. Series Working Paper no. 1972, Feb. 1, 2007) (available at http://law.bepress.com/expresso/eps/1972).

Part II | ENTER THE CISG

The Convention on Contracts for the International Sale of Goods (CISG) was enacted by UNCITRAL at an international diplomatic conference in Vienna, Austria on April 11, 1980. Accordingly, it is sometimes referred to as the 1980 Vienna Convention. This casebook will refer to this convention simply as the CISG. The CISG came into effect on January 1, 1988 and as of December 1, 2007, 71 countries have become parties to the CISG.[1] The United States ratified the CISG on December 11, 1986. Countries continue to become signatories to the CISG, with Paraguay becoming a party in early 2007.

The overarching goal of the CISG is to facilitate international trade by providing a set of uniform rules to govern contracts for the international sale of goods. By providing a uniform set of rules, parties from different countries will all understand the sales law to which their transaction will be subject, thereby reducing at least one large barrier to trade that has traditionally existed.[2] The preamble to the CISG itself sets this principle forth, clearly stating one of the goals of the CISG as the:

> adoption of uniform rules which govern contracts for the international sale of goods and take into account the different social, economic and legal systems would contribute to the removal of legal barriers in international trade and promote the development of international trade.[3]

---

[1] *See* Unilex's website listing the Contracting States to the CISG (available at http://www.unilex.info/dynasite.cfm?dssid=2376&dsmid=13351&x=1).

[2] Consider, for example, the remarks of Japanese Professor Kazuaki Sono of Hokkaido University regarding the introduction of the CISG, "With bright prospects for the entry into force of the [CISG], unification at a global scale is finally in sight in this field after over half a century of efforts. The Vienna Sales Convention now enjoys praise throughout the world as a workmanlike attempt to devise legal rules and practical procedures for international sales transactions. Once the Vienna Sales Convention enters into force, it will assist to smooth the process of international sales." Kazuaki Sono, *The Vienna Sales Convention: History and Perspective*, in *International Sale of Goods: Dubrovnik Lectures* 1, 1 (Petar Sarcevic & Paul Volken eds., Oceana: 1986).

[3] CISG Preamble (Apr. 11, 1980). It is interesting to note that legal scholars differ as to the importance of the CISG Preamble. *Compare* 1969 Vienna Convention on the Law of Treaties § 31(2) (providing that the preamble to a treaty can be relevant to the interpretation of that treaty); Fritz Enderlein & Dietrich Maskow, *International Sales Law* 19-20 (Oceana 1992) ("The principles [the Preamble] contains can be referred to in interpreting terms or rules of the Convention."); *with* Peter Schlechtriem, *Uniform Sales Law The UN Convention on Contracts for the International Sale of Goods* 38 n. 11 (Manz 1986) ("[The] preamble . . . refers to the public international law obligations and goals of the signatory states and may not be used for the interpretation and gap-filling of the substantive legal provisions"). Most of the scholars that dismiss the importance of the

The CISG reduces barriers to trade by minimizing or reducing the need to consider different legal systems that might be relevant in any particular transaction.[4] Uniform law eliminates that problem. As Australian scholar, Professor Bruno Zeller of Victoria University expressed:

> The adoption of uniform rules has been achieved by introducing the same rules into various domestic systems replacing domestic rules. ... The CISG promises to take into consideration the variances and differences encountered through different social, economic and legal systems which would as a result advance different solutions to potentially the same problems. With such a system in place the legal barriers to international trade would be removed hence reducing or managing cross border legal risks.[5]

The CISG is a treaty but has also become law in the countries that have adopted it (whether automatically, as is the case in countries where a treaty becomes law, or by an enacting statute, as is the case in countries where treaties do not automatically become law). Accordingly, it is critical for attorneys in these jurisdictions to be familiar with the CISG.

Unfortunately, as is illustrated below, attorneys in the United States are not always as familiar with the CISG as they should be—a mistake that can result in significant costs and negative results for both the attorneys involved and their clients.[6]

Example II-1

A Canadian group of companies alleged that it had agreed with a buyer from Oregon to sell certain truckloads of cedar wood shakes. The buyer contested the sale in an action in a U.S. federal court relying on the argument, among others, that there was no contract in writing and thus the applicable statute of

---

Preamble, do so by identifying that the ideals set forth in the Preamble are embodied in CISG Article 7(1).

[4] *E.g.* John O. Honnold, *Uniform Law for International Sales under the 1980 United Nations Convention* 34 (3rd ed., Kluwer Law International 1999); Peter Schlechtriem, *Requirements of Application and Sphere of Applicability of the CISG,* Victoria U. of Wellington L. Rev. 781, 781-782 (2005/4).

[5] Bruno Zeller, *The CISG – Getting Off the Fence,* 74(9) The Law Inst. J., Victoria 73-74 (2000).

[6] In the United States, if an attorney assumes that the U.C.C. applies in a contract dispute, when in reality the CISG should apply, that attorney would be in violation of Model Rule of Professional Conduct 1.1, the attorney's duty of competence. Further, the attorney could be subject to a legal malpractice lawsuit if the client is unsuccessful in litigation due to such mistake. *See* Ronald A. Brand, *Professional Responsibility in a Transnational Transactions Practice,* 17 J. L. & Commerce 301, 337 (1998).

> frauds contained in Oregon's U.C.C. was not satisfied. The case
> went to the appellate level on the issue, which was finally
> resolved in favor of finding the statute of frauds satisfied and a
> contract to exist. Ironically, the appropriate governing law was
> actually the CISG, which states clearly that there is no writing
> requirement to prove a contract. Thus, had the CISG been
> applied, this issue would have been resolved quickly and easily.[7]

The foregoing example is just one case where attorneys were unfamiliar with the
CISG and its applicability to transactions and disputes. A 2006 survey conducted
by Professor Peter Fitzgerald of Stetson University College of Law confirmed
that many practitioners and judges in the United States are not familiar with the
CISG.[8] According to the survey, only ten percent of United States practitioners
surveyed were thoroughly familiar with the CISG, while forty-four percent were
not at all familiar. Only four percent of judges surveyed in the United States
were thoroughly familiar with the CISG, while eighty-two percent were not at all
familiar. These statistics are alarming, especially when one considers that the
CISG has been the law in the United States for almost two decades.

Part II of this book seeks to redress this situation and make the CISG accessible
for the reader. The authors' goal is for the reader to be able to understand the
CISG, apply it correctly, and take it into consideration when planning an
international sales transaction. Part II is roughly organized in accordance with
the way the CISG is organized. Chapter 2 will address when the CISG is applied
as well as its opening provisions that are of general application. Chapter 4 will
then move to formation of a contract under the CISG. Chapter 4 will cover the
obligations of both the buyer and the seller in an international sale of goods.
Chapter 5 will turn to remedies for breach of any of those obligations. Finally,
Chapter 6 will discuss damages available under the CISG as well as some
exemptions to liability.

Throughout Part II examples are used. Most are from actual court cases or
arbitrations. Where that is the case, the examples are footnoted with reference to
the court case or arbitration. In addition, scholars are cited both in the text and in

---

[7] *See GPL Treatment, Ltd. v. Louisiana-Pacific Corp.,* 894 P.2d 470 (Or. App. 1995), aff'd 914
P.2d 682 (Or. 1996). In response to the *GPL Treatment* case, Professor Harry Flechtner commented
that, "The [*GPL Treatment*] case thus stands as a stark warning that all practitioners whose practice
encompasses commercial matters should be familiar with the Convention. . . . Attorneys who fail to
familiarize themselves with CISG and the crucial changes it makes risk both their clients' rights and
their own professional reputation." Harry M. Flechtner, *Another CISG Case in the U.S. Courts:
Pitfalls for the Practitioner and the Potential for Regionalized Interpretations,* 15 J. L. &
Commerce 127, 131–132 (1995).

[8] Peter L. Fitzgerald, *The International Contracting Practices Survey Project,* 27 J. LAW &
COMMERCE ___ (*Forthcoming* 2008).

the footnotes so that the reader can turn to outside sources for more discussion of each topic, as needed or desired.

2

APPLICATION AND GENERAL PROVISIONS

The First Three Rules of Statutory Construction:

    (1)   Read the Statute;

    (2)   Read the Statute;

    (3)   Read the Statute.[1]

The CISG is a statute. As such it is critical that each provision of the CISG be scrutinized so that its meaning can be discerned, considered and applied. This chapter will begin coverage of the CISG by: (I) making some introductory remarks about interpretation, before addressing (II) the scope of the CISG's coverage and (III) its general prefatory provisions.

I.   INTERPRETING THE CISG

The CISG has become law in both common law and civil law systems. Students of law and practicing attorneys from civil law countries will be familiar with interpreting and analyzing written codes like the CISG since their system is based on such written enactments of law. However, students of law and attorneys from common law countries will have less familiarity with interpreting codes since their system is based on the analysis of case law as precedent. However, even common law students and attorneys have some familiarity with written enactments of law based on statutory law in their own countries. For example, the CISG is similar in some ways to the UCC in the United States. This section will discuss interpretation of the CISG, regardless of what background the student or practitioner comes from.[2] Part A will discuss general interpretive issues, while Part B will focus on the CISG's own dictates for how it should be interpreted.

A.   General Principles of Interpretation

Regardless of whether one is coming from a common law or civil law background, as with any statute or code, one must first look to the exact written language of the statute in order to interpret its meaning. For this reason, it cannot

---

[1] Professor Morrissey's admonition to all law students working with any statutory text.

[2] For a guide to statutory interpretation generally, see Linda D. Jellum and David Charles Hricik, *Modern Statutory Interpretation: Problems, Theories, and Lawyering Strategies* (Carolina Academic Press 2006).

be stressed enough that students and attorneys must scrutinize the words of the CISG when attempting to interpret and apply it. As set forth above, it is helpful to read, re-read, and read again the words in order to glean their nuances.

Nonetheless, as with any statutory or code-based law, there are often gaps or ambiguities that become apparent as parties attempt to apply the statutory language of the CISG. Disputes subject to the CISG have been brought before courts and arbitral tribunals across the world, and the outcomes of those disputes add to an understanding of how the CISG might be interpreted and applied.

In civil law countries, cases and arbitrations are not binding on any subsequent tribunal of any sort. Under the law of these countries, the opinions are simply persuasive evidence of how the CISG may be interpreted and applied. Of course, in common law countries, previous court cases (but not arbitrations) must be considered as they are indeed a source of law in those countries. However, courts in common law jurisdictions are placed in a precarious situation when it comes to using previous cases from their jurisdiction to help interpret and apply the CISG.

Article 7(1) of the CISG, which will be discussed at greater length later in this chapter, states that the CISG should be interpreted and applied with due regard to its international character and the need to promote uniformity in its application in international trade. Following Article 7 in this regard seems at odds with strict adherence to any one jurisdiction's previous case law.[3] Nonetheless, common law courts are bound to look to precedent as a binding source of law and must then also pay due regard to attempting to reach decisions that will indeed promote a uniform application of the CISG internationally.[4]

As the various sections of the CISG are considered in this casebook, therefore, decisions of courts and arbitral tribunals will also be considered to illustrate how tribunals have interpreted the CISG. Keep in mind the different significance those cases and arbitrations have in the common law and civil law systems.

In addition to cases and arbitrations, there are other sources that provide guidance on how to interpret and apply the CISG. First, there is the diplomatic history of

---

[3] Professor Graves, for example, asserts that if a common law court is faced with domestic case law precedent that is at odds with the clear trend of foreign cases, the common law court should actually defer to the international cases and reject its own prior holding.

[4] *See e.g. Genpharm Inc. v. Pliva-Lachema A.S., Pliva d.d.*, 361 F. Supp. 2d 49 (E.D.N.Y. 2005) (identifying first that there were "only a handful of American cases" interpreting the CISG, and then looking to Article 7 CISG to apply the principles upon which the CISG is based). On the contrary, a civil law country will likely look to international case law for interpretations of the CISG. *See Ostroznik Savo v. La Faraona soc. coop. a r.l.,* Tribunale [District Court] di Padova Sez. Este, Italy, Jan. 11, 2005 (available at http://www.unilex.info/case.cfm?pid=1&do=case&id= 1005&step=Keywords) (relying upon international case law interpreting the CISG to ensure "autonomous interpretation and uniform application").

the CISG. There are many documents illustrating the debates that occurred when the CISG was drafted and that help explain why certain choices were made in that convention.[5] Among those documents is the Secretariat Commentary on the draft of the CISG that was presented to UNCITRAL in 1978, just a few years before final adoption of the official text.[6] The legislative history can be very persuasive when attempting to urge one interpretation of the CISG over another.[7]

Second, many scholars have commented on the CISG over the years.[8] That scholarly commentary is also very helpful when trying to make sense of any ambiguities in the Convention.[9] Of course it is often possible to find scholarly commentary that supports alternative views of any one provision. Excerpts and references to both the legislative history of the CISG and scholarly commentary on the CISG will also be included throughout this book.

In addition to general scholarly commentary there are also now opinions of the CISG Advisory Committee on various issues covered by the CISG. This Advisory Committee is an independent private body made up of leading scholars on the CISG with the goal of promoting a uniform international interpretation of the CISG.[10] Accordingly, its opinions reflect a consensus among leading scholars

---

[5] For committee reports from the UNCITRAL drafting committees, see http://www.cisg.law.pace.edu/cisg/conference.html. *See also* John O. Honnold, *Documentary History of the Uniform Law for International Sales: The Studies, Deliberations and Decisions That Led to the 1988 United Nations Convention* (1989).

[6] Secretariat Commentary on the 1978 Draft, *Guide to CISG Article 1* (available at http://cisgw3 .law.pace.edu/cisg/text/secomm/secomm-01.html).

[7] *See Austrian Seller v. German Buyer (Vine Wax Case)*, Bundesgerichtshof [Federal Supreme Court] no. VIII ZR 121/98, Germany, Mar. 24, 1999 (available at http://cisgw3.law.pace.edu/ cases/990324g1.html) (utilizing the legislative history of the CISG to support its interpretation of Article 35).

[8] Two of the leading treatises interpreting the CISG are *Commentary on the UN Convention on the International Sale of Goods* (Peter Schlechtriem & Ingeborg Schwenzer eds., 2d ed., Oxford U. Press 2005) [hereinafter *Commentary on CISG*], and Honnold, *supra* n. 5. In addition, see *International Sales Law* (Ingeborg Schwenzer & Christiana Fountoulakis eds., Routledge-Cavendish 2007), Joseph Lookofsky, *Understanding the CISG in the USA* (2d ed., Kluwer L. Intl. 2004), and Peter Huber and Alistair Mullis, *CISG: A New Textbook for Students and Practitioners* (Sellier 2007).

[9] *See Dutch Seller v. English Buyer*, Netherlands Arbitration no. 2319, Netherlands, Oct. 15, 2002 (available at http://cisgw3.law.pace.edu/cases/021015n1.html) (relying heavily upon the writings of international scholars such as Professors Schlechtriem, Bianca, Bonell, and Lookofsky).

[10] *See* Dr. Loukas Mistelis, *CISG-AC Publishes First Opinion*, http://cisgw3.law.pace.edu/ cisg/CISG-AC.html, last updated Feb. 1, 2007. "The founding members of the CISG-AC are *Professor Dr. Eric E. Bergsten*, Emeritus of Pace University, formerly Secretary General of UNCITRAL, *Professor Dr. Michael Joachim Bonell*, University of Rome La Sapienza, formerly Secretary General of UNIDROIT, *Professor E. Allan Farnsworth*, Columbia University, New York, *Professor Dr. Alejandro Garro*, Columbia University, *Professor Sir Roy Goode*, University of Oxford, *Professor Dr. Sergei N. Lebedev*, Moscow Institute of International Relations, *Professor Dr. Jan Ramberg*, Emeritus, Stockholm University, *Professor Dr. Dr. h.c. Peter Schlechtriem*, Emeritus, University of Freiburg, *Professor Hiroo Sono*, Hokkaido University and *Professor Dr.*

of the CISG and are therefore extremely persuasive. CISG Advisory Council Opinions will also be referenced throughout this text.

Unlike case law, which is binding legal authority under the law of common law countries, neither legislative history nor scholarly commentary, even that contained in Advisory Council opinions, is ever a binding source of law. Nonetheless, such sources can be extremely persuasive in convincing a tribunal of your client's position.

B. THE INTERPRETIVE GUIDANCE OF CISG ARTICLE 7

Perhaps most important to the interpretation of the CISG, however, is the guidance the CISG itself provides. Article 7 specifically addresses how the CISG should be interpreted. Accordingly, Article 7 is actually the first provision of the CISG that this book will address.

Article 7

(1) In the interpretation of this Convention, regard is to be had to its international character and to the need to promote uniformity in its application and the observance of good faith in international trade.

(2) Questions concerning matters governed by this Convention which are not expressly settled in it are to be settled in conformity with the general principles on which it is based or, in the absence of such principles, in conformity with the law applicable by virtue of the rules of private international law.

Article 7(1) mandates that when interpreting the CISG, regard should be had for three main goals: (i) the international character of the CISG; (ii) the need to promote uniformity in its application; and (iii) the observance of good faith in international trade. These broad mandates supplement every article of the CISG and may help resolve close questions of interpretation. For example, if a party is attempting to stress a particular interpretation of any specific provision of the CISG because it is a common understanding in that party's country, a tribunal

---

Claude Witz, Universität des Saarlandes and Université Robert Schuman, Strasbourg . . . . Three more members were invited to join the Council in 2003 and 2004, *Professor Dr. Mª del Pilar Perales Viscasillas*, Universidad Carlos III, Madrid, *Professsor Dr. Ingeborg Schwenzer*, University of Basel, and *Professor John Y. Gotanda*, Villanova University. *Id.*

might focus on the mandate of 7(1) and reject the argument. Instead, the tribunal should focus on the international consensus regarding the issue and not on any particular domestic laws or norms.[11]

Further, the tribunal may consider that the CISG seeks to promote uniformity in international sales transactions and not defer to the differences that exist from country to country. This method of interpretation was explained in depth by Professor Peter Huber of Johannes Gutenburg Universitat Mainz:

> the Convention has to be interpreted autonomously. This means that the terms of the CISG should not simply be regarded as having the same meaning as identical terms that may exist in the domestic legal system. They should rather be given a "CISG-meaning", based on the structure and the underlying policies of the Convention as well as on its drafting and negotiating history. Of course, this autonomous interpretation may lead to the result that the CISG-term actually has the same meaning as a corresponding domestic term. One should, however, not jump to that conclusion too easily, but only after a careful analysis.[12]

Note that Article 7(1) is the only provision in the CISG that references good faith, and that it does not establish an affirmative duty of good faith. It only requires that the interpretation of the CISG should consider good faith. This is in contrast to many countries, including the United States, Germany, and China, where a duty of good faith in commercial transactions is mandated.[13] Nonetheless, a party's failure to act in good faith could work to the benefit of its counterparty in a dispute since questions of interpretation of the CISG invariably arise. If indeed some degree of bad faith is evident on the part of one party to a transaction, then close calls on interpretation of any provision of the CISG should normally favor the other party.

---

[11] *See* Franco Ferrari, *Tribunale di Vigevano: Specific Aspects of the CISG Uniformly Dealt with,* 20 J. L. & Com. 225, 228–230 (2001) (quoting a Swiss court as stating that "[t]he starting point of any interpretation must be the Convention itself not domestic law").

[12] Peter Huber, *Some Introductory Remarks on the CISG* 228 (Sellier, European L. Publishers 2006).

[13] *See* UCC §1-203 ("Every contract or duty within this Act imposes an obligation of good faith in its performance or enforcement"); German Civil Code § 242 ("The obligor must perform in a manner consistent with good faith taking into account accepted practice."); Contract Law of the People's Republic of China art. 6 ("The parties must act in accordance with the principle of good faith, no matter in exercising rights or in performing obligations.").

Example 2-1

A German buyer engaged in negotiations for the sale of sour pitted cherries from a Belgian seller. The seller argued a contract had been formed through the exchange of communications including the seller's confirmation form. Standard terms, one of which indicated Belgian law was to govern the contract, were printed on the back of the seller's confirmation form. The German court decided that enforcing the standard terms amounted to a violation of the good faith principle embodied by Article 7(1) of the CISG because the standard terms would likely favor the drafter and the counterparty may be unaware of the content of such standard terms due to different nations' practices.[14]

Compare: Good Faith

According to a strict interpretation of Article 7 of the CISG, good faith is merely a general principle for interpreting provisions of the CISG. The CISG fails to indicate whether good faith should be considered when assessing party conduct or whether good faith incorporates fair dealing. The CISG does not provide a definition of good faith. The CISG also allows parties to derogate from any provision, including Article 7.

Unlike the CISG, the UNIDROIT principles do not include good faith as an interpretative principle. Rather, Article 1.7 of the UNIDROIT Principles imposes a non-waivable duty on parties to act in good faith and engage in fair dealing.

The Restatement (Second) of Contracts in the United States is similar to the UNDROIT Principles with respect to good faith. §205 of the Restatement establishes the duties of good faith and fair dealing, instead of simply utilizing good faith as a principle of interpretation.

The UCC in the United States also imposes a duty of good faith on every commercial transaction. Where the party to a transaction is a merchant, that duty includes "honesty in fact and the observance of reasonable commercial standards of fair dealing in the trade" (UCC §2-103).

---

[14] *German Buyer v. Belgian Seller (Pitted Sour Cherries Case),* Landgericht [District Court] Neubrandenburg no. 10 O 74/04, Germany, Aug. 3, 2005 (available at http://cisgw3.law.pace.edu/cases/050803g1.html). See also Example 3-1 in Chapter 3 for more discussion of this case.

> PECL represents a combination of the CISG, on the one hand, and the UNIDROIT principles, the Restatement, and the UCC on the other hand. Under PECL, good faith should be applied as an interpretive principle (Article 1 §106); but is also imposed as a duty upon the parties conduct (Article 1 §201). Similar to the UNIDROIT Principles and the Restatement, PECL also includes an obligation of fair dealing upon the parties conduct (Article 1 §201).

Article 7(2) is frequently referred to as the gap-filling provision. It states that questions governed by the CISG that are not settled by it should be settled as follows: first, in conformity with the general principles on which it is based; or second, if (and only if) no such principles apply to the situation, in conformity with the law applicable by virtue of the rules of private international law. In Article 7(2), focus is placed on issues that are governed by the CISG but not resolved by it. This creates the potential for controversy to arise. For example, someone may argue that good faith is covered by the CISG—although not described as a *duty* of good faith—so that an issue concerning good faith might fairly be resolved in accordance with the general principles upon which the CISG is based.[15] A counter argument would be simply that there is no duty of good faith governed by the CISG, and therefore, such questions are outside of its scope. Article 7(2) creates some uncertainty in this regard but also provides flexibility for parties to argue for outcomes that are in line with the general principles upon which the CISG was founded.

Article 7(1) clearly delineates certain principles upon which the CISG is based (international character, promotion of uniformity in application, and the observance of good faith), but Article 7(2) is not limited to those. Commentators have suggested that principles found outside of Article 7, but within the CISG, should be included here as well.[16] Examples of this include: (i) estoppel principles like those contained in Article 29; (ii) encouraging communication between the parties as illustrated in Articles 19, 21, 39, 47, 48 and elsewhere, and (iii) taking steps to minimize loss, like the mitigation principle contained in Article 77 and the preservation of goods principle contained in Articles 85-88.[17] Additionally, principles that are not clearly identified within the CISG may

---

[15] *See e.g. Kunsthaus Math. Lempertz OHG [Dutch] v. Wilhelmina van der Geld [German]*, Arrondissementsrechtbank [District Court] Arnhem, Netherlands, July 17, 1997 (abstract available at http://www.unilex.info/case.cfm?pid=1&do=case&id=355&step=Keywords) (ruling that the application of the principle of good faith in international trade, which is a general principle underlying CISG, confirmed the decision that the buyer's claim was time-barred).
[16] Honnold, *supra* n. 5, at 104–110.
[17] *Id.*

nonetheless be general principles embodied in the CISG, and courts and tribunals have accordingly applied such principles to disputes.[18] Furthermore, the principles set forth in both the UNIDROIT Principles and the PECL are also potentially general principles upon which the CISG was founded and have been successfully argued to be included in Article 7(2).[19]

If it is not possible to find general principles upon which the CISG is based to resolve issues that are governed by the CISG but not addressed within it, then resort should be made to the domestic law that is applicable to the matter by virtue of the appropriate conflict of laws rules. This is a last resort because of Article 7(1)'s mandate that due regard be had for the international character of the CISG and the uniformity of its application world-wide. Resort to any particular domestic law runs counter to that mandate.

II.   SCOPE OF APPLICATION

The first chapter of the CISG covers the CISG's applicability to a sales transaction. That question turns on: (A) the parties to the transaction; (B) the rules of private international law; (C) the types of sales transaction; and (D) the legal issues presented.

A.   THE CISG GOVERNS SALES BETWEEN PARTIES FROM DIFFERENT CONTRACTING STATES

Article 1 of the CISG explains when the CISG will apply. According to Article 1, the CISG only applies when there is a "sale of goods between parties whose places of business are in different States." Therefore, there must be an international sales transaction to trigger the CISG. Further, either Article 1(1)(a) or Article 1(1)(b) must be satisfied. Article 1(1)(a) is sometimes referred to as the direct applicability provision, and it is satisfied if both of the countries where the parties are located are parties to the CISG (Contracting States).[20] Article

---

[18] *See e.g. Colombian Case*, Corte Constitucional no. 529/00, Colombia, May 10, 2005 (available at http://cisgw3.law.pace.edu/cases/000510c7.html) (determining that the CISG recognizes the general principle of party autonomy); *Conservas la Costena S.A. de C.V. v. Lanis San Luis S.A. & Agro- industrial Santa Adela S.A.*, COMPROMEX, Comisión para la Protección del Comercio Exterior de Mexico [Mexican Commission for the Protection of Foreign Trade] no. M/21/95, Mexico, Apr. 29, 1996 (available at http://cisgw3.law.pace.edu/cases/960429m1.html) (finding that the general principles of the CISG allow for informal contracting).
[19] *See Holzimpex Inc: v. Republican Agricultural Unitary Enterprise,* Supreme Economic Court of the Republic of Belarus no. 8-5/2003, Belarus, May 20, 2003 (available at http://cisgw3.law.pace.edu/cases/030520b5.html) (applying the rate of interest pursuant to Article 7.4.9(2) of the UNIDROIT Principles because the CISG is silent on the calculation of interest).
[20] *See United States Seller v. Mexican Buyer (Wood Case)*, Sixth Civil Court of First Instance no. 868/99, Mexico, July 14, 2000 (available at http://cisgw3.law.pace.edu/cases/000714m1.html)

1(1)(b) is sometimes referred to as the indirect applicability provision, and it is satisfied when the "rules of private international law lead to the application of the law" of a Contracting State.[21]

Article 1

(1) This Convention applies to contracts of sale of goods between parties whose places of business are in different States:

(a) when the States are Contracting States; or

(b) when the rules of private international law lead to the application of the law of a Contracting State.

(2) The fact that the parties have their places of business in different States is to be disregarded whenever this fact does not appear either from the contract or from any dealings between, or from information disclosed by, the parties at any time before or at the conclusion of the contract.

(3) Neither the nationality of the parties nor the civil or commercial character of the parties or of the contract is to be taken into consideration in determining the application of this Convention.

Article 1(1)(a) is relatively straightforward. An attorney need only check to see if the parties to the transaction have places of business in a country that is a party to the CISG. See Appendix A for a listing of Contracting States.[22]

(applying the CISG to the parties' dispute because both parties had their places of business in Contracting States—the United States and Mexico). See Appendix A for a listing of all countries that are parties to the CISG, the dates the CISG entered into force in all countries, and any applicable declarations and reservations.

[21] *See e.g.* Franco Ferrari, *Pace Law School, Cross References and Editorial Analysis*, Art. 1, http://cisgw3.law.pace.edu/cisg/text/cross/cross-1.html.

[22] Article 99 of the CISG provides the precise time when the CISG takes effect in a Contracting State.

Example 2-2

An Italian innkeeper orders porcelain from a French manufacturer and a dispute arises. The parties had a written contract but did not specify what law would govern. The CISG governs the transaction as both parties have their place of business in Contracting States.[23]

Then again, determining where a party has its place of business for purposes of the CISG is not always so simple. Many of the parties to international sales transactions are multi-national corporations that have many places of business and manufacturing around the world. Article 10 of the CISG provides guidance on this point.

Article 10

For the purposes of this Convention:

(a) if a party has more than one place of business, the place of business is that which has the closest relationship to the contract and its performance, having regard to the circumstances known to or contemplated by the parties at any time before or at the conclusion of the contract;

(b) if a party does not have a place of business, reference is to be made to his habitual residence.

Article 10 of the CISG dictates that "if a party has more than one place of business, the place of business … which has the closest relationship to the contract and its performance" should be considered its place of business for purposes of the CISG. It is important to note the qualifying language of Article 10 as well: when determining which office has the closest relation to the transaction, only what was "known to or contemplated by" both the parties at or before the conclusion of the contract may be considered. Thus, if a counterparty to a transaction does not know or has not contemplated that the other counter party has more than one place of business, those other places of business may not be considered.[24]

---

[23] Based on *Al Palazzo S.r.l v. Bernardaud di Limoges S.A.*, Tribunale [District Court] di Rimini no. 3095, Italy, Nov. 26, 2002 (available at http://cisgw3.law.pace.edu/cases/021126i3.html).

[24] Circumstances that may be relevant to the knowledge of the parties includes the addresses used in communications, the location where goods were inspected, visits to a party's office, etc.

Example 2-3

In the same example as the previous case, assume that the French manufacturer has a manufacturing facility and sales office in England. Further, the Italian innkeeper orders porcelain from a sales representative in England and the porcelain is shipped from there. In that case, a tribunal could find that the French party's place of business for purposes of this transaction is England. England is not a Contracting State to the CISG so Article 1(1)(a) would not be satisfied.

B.   THE CISG CAN APPLY THROUGH THE RULES OF PRIVATE INTERNATIONAL LAW

Article 1(1)(b) is more complicated than Article 1(1)(a) and must be considered at some length. Article 1(1)(b) indicates that the CISG will apply "when the rules of private international law lead to the application of the law of a Contracting State." As was mentioned in Chapter 1, "the rules of private international law" for many European countries is synonymous with conflict of laws rules, and that meaning seems to be what was intended in the CISG. Article 1(1)(b) is not a conflict of laws rule itself; rather, it implicates whatever conflict of laws rules that are applicable in any given transaction.[25]

There are several important sources for conflict of laws rules in private international law. There are international conventions addressing conflict of laws. There are also national statutes addressing conflict of laws, like the UCC in the United States. Further, there are conflicts-of-laws provisions in arbitration laws and rules. Before discussing Article 1(1)(b) further, it is helpful to survey a selection of these rules.

Commentary on the CISG, supra n. 8, at 157. In addition to utilizing Article 10 to supplement Article 1(1)(a), Article 10 may also be used to determine whether a transaction is "international" in scope, as required for the CISG to apply when the rules of private international law lead to the implication of the CISG pursuant to Article 1(1)(b). *See S.a.r.l. Pelliculest /S.A. Rhin et Moseille v. Morton International GmbH / Société Zurich Assurances S.A.*, Cour d'Appel de Colmar, France, Oct. 24, 2000 (available at http://cisgw3.law.pace.edu/cases/001024f1.html) (applying the CISG to the parties' dispute pursuant to Article 1(1)(b) after finding the parties' contract to be international is scope, despite the fact that seller's agent was located in the same country as the buyer).

[25] Joseph Lookofsky, *The 1980 United Nations Convention on Contracts for the International Sale of Goods,* in *International Encyclopaedia of Laws— Contracts,* Suppl. 29, 1-192 at 33 (J. Herbots & R. Blanpain eds., Kluwer L. Intl. 2000); Michael Joachim Bonell & Fabio Liguori, *The U.N. Convention on the International Sale of Goods: A Critical Analysis of Current International Case Law—1997 (Part 1),* Unif. L. Rev. 385 (1997) ("[C]onflict of laws is not a matter governed by [the CISG].").

The 1955 Hague Convention on the Law Applicable to the International Sale of Goods (the 1955 Hague Convention) is one such international convention.[26] It was signed by one African and eight European countries.[27] This convention was an attempt to unify the conflict of laws rules that existed among countries at the time in order to make conducting an international sales transaction more predictable in terms of what law would ultimately govern the transaction.[28] Article 2 of the 1955 Hague Convention specifies that the parties to a transaction may specifically choose the law to govern their transaction. This focus on party autonomy is common throughout conflict of laws rules. Absent the parties' choice, however, Article 3 provides that the law of the seller's "habitual residence" should apply. Although the 1955 Hague Convention does not define "habitual residence," it is typically understood to be the seller's primary place of business.[29] Using the law of the seller's primary place of business has commonly been used by conflict of laws rules as the default rule because the seller typically has the bulk of the responsibilities in a sales transaction (i.e. manufacturing goods in accordance with the contract specifications, and delivering goods to a particular place). However, Article 3 qualifies the default rule by providing that if the seller took the buyer's order in the buyer's country, or availed itself of the buyer's territory, then the laws of the buyer's country should prevail. Finally, if the sale took place at an exchange, then the laws of the country where the exchange is located would prevail.

The 1980 Rome EC Convention on the Law Applicable to Contractual Obligations (the 1980 Rome Convention) is another such convention.[30] It was negotiated among and for the countries of the European Economic Community and was signed by 15 European countries,[31] becoming effective in 1991. Like

---

[26] For information regarding the 1955 Hague Convention, including the full text of the convention, see Hague Conference on Private International Law, http://www.hcch.net (English translation of the 1955 Hague Convention available at 74 Yale L.J. 463 (1965)).

[27] The nine parties to the 1955 Hague Convention include: Belgium, Denmark, Finland, France, Italy, Niger, Norway, Sweden, and Switzerland. *Id.*

[28] The introduction to the 1955 Hague Convention states that the signatory nations desired to "establish common provisions concerning the law applicable to sales of goods." *Id.*

[29] *See* Joseph Lookofsky, *Alive and Well in Scandinavia: CISG Part II*, 18 J. L. & Com. 289, 297 (1999) (available at http://www.cisg.law.pace.edu/cisg/biblio/lookofsky1.html) (noting that Article 3 of the 1955 Hague Convention points to the law of the country of the seller's residence); *Italdecor s.a.s. v. Yiu's Industries (H.K.) Limited*, Corte di Appello [Court of Appeals] Milano, Italy, Mar. 10, 1998 (available at http://cisgw3.law.pace.edu/cases/980320i3.html) (explaining that when the parties have not chosen a governing law, under Article 3 of the 1955 Hague Convention the transaction will be governed by the "domestic law of the country of the residence of the seller").

[30] For a full text of the 1980 Rome Convention, *see* RomeConvention.org, *Instruments*, *Text of the Convention*, http://www.rome-convention.org/instruments/i_conv_orig_en.htm.

[31] The original ten parties to the 1980 Rome Convention include: Belgium, Denmark, France, Germany, Greece, Ireland, Italy, Luxembourg, the Netherlands, and the United Kingdom. Spain and Portugal acceded to the 1980 Rome Convention in 1992; and Austria, Finland, and Sweden followed in 1997. *Id.* at http://www.rome-convention.org/instruments/implementation.htm.

the 1955 Hague Convention, the 1980 Rome Convention attempted to make conflict of laws rules uniform and predictable.[32] Again, like the 1955 Hague Convention, Article 3 of the 1980 Rome Convention defers to the parties' choice to select the governing law for a contract. However, absent such choice, the 1980 Rome Convention in Article 4(1) states that the governing law should be the law of the country that is "most closely connected" to the contract. Article 4(2) further states that the country most closely connected is typically the country where the party who is to carry out the "characteristic performance" has its habitual residence. Generally, in a sales contract, the party carrying out characteristic performance has been understood to be the seller.[33] Another important aspect of this convention is Article 21, which holds that if a party to the 1980 Rome Convention is also a party to the 1955 Hague Convention, then the earlier convention, the 1955 Hague Convention, will prevail.

The European Community is considering a proposal to replace the 1980 Rome Convention with the *Regulation of the European Parliament and the Council on the Law Applicable to Contractual Obligations (Rome I)*. The proposed regulation is designed to modernize and clarify the conflict of laws principles of the 1980 Rome Convention.[34] Under Rome I's new formulation of conflict of law principles, parties are still able to choose the law to govern their transaction in Article 3, but Article 3(2) clarifies that parties may also choose to be governed by general principles of law that are recognized internationally. This is a clear departure from the 1980 Rome Convention, as well as the 1955 Hague Convention, and would allow parties to have their agreement governed by "the UNIDROIT principles, the Principles of European Contract Law or a possible future optional Community instrument."[35]

---

[32] The Preamble to the 1980 Rome Convention states that the Contracting Parties were "ANXIOUS to continue in the field of private international law the work of unification of law which has already been done within the Community, in particular in the field of jurisdiction and enforcement of judgments, [and] WISHING to establish uniform rules concerning the law applicable to contractual obligations. *Id.* at http://www.rome-convention.org/instruments/i_conv_orig_en.htm.

[33] According to the Giuliano-Lagarde Report on the Convention on the Law Applicable to Contractual Obligations, "[I]n bilateral (reciprocal) contracts whereby the parties undertake mutual reciprocal performance, the counter-performance by one of the parties in a modern economy usually takes the form of money. This is not, of course, the characteristic performance of the contract. It is the performance for which the payment is due, i.e. depending on the type of contract, the delivery of goods, the granting of the right to make use of an item of property, the provision of a service, transport, insurance, banking operations, security, etc., which usually constitutes the centre of gravity and the socio-economic function of the contractual transaction." Mario Giuliano & Paul Lagarde, Report on the Convention on the Law Applicable to Contractual Obligations ("Giuliano-Lagarde Report"), J. Officiel C 282, 1 (1980).

[34] *See* European Commision, Explanatory Memorandum on the Rome I Regulation, Sec. 2, http://europa.eu.int/eur-lex/lex/LexUriServ/site/en/com/2005/com2005_0650en01.pdf (Dec. 15, 2005).

[35] Rome I, art. 3(2).

Rome I also streamlines the conflict of laws rules from the 1980 Rome Convention. Article 4 of Rome I sets forth different types of contractual obligations and specifies what law will apply in each case. For sales of goods, the law that will apply is the law of the seller's habitual residence.[36] This new regulation was designed to convert the presumption from the 1980 Rome Convention that in a sale of goods, the law of the seller's habitual residence will apply into a fixed rule. The new regulation has also eliminated any exception to that rule.[37] Finally, Rome I specifies that it takes precedence over the 1955 Hague Convention and other bilateral international conventions if they concern matters governed by this Regulation.[38]

The 1986 Hague Convention on the Law Applicable to the International Sale of Goods (the 1986 Hague Convention) was an attempt to revise the 1955 Hague Convention and bring it into sync with the CISG.[39] However, the 1986 Hague Convention has never actually come into force. Nonetheless, it is informative as a more modern approach to conflicts than the 1955 Hague Convention and is more consonant with the CISG. Like the 1955 Hague Convention, Article 7 of the 1986 Hague Convention promotes autonomy by allowing parties to choose whatever law they would like to govern their transaction. In the absence of choice, however, Article 8 of the 1986 Hague Convention defaults to the law of the country where the seller has its habitual place of business—similar to the 1955 Hague Convention. However, the 1986 Hague Convention has more exceptions that may alter the default conclusion that the law of seller's place of business governs the contract. In fact, Article 8(2) provides three specific situations that call for the laws of the buyer's place of business to control: (1) if negotiations and the contract's conclusion occurred in the buyer's country; (2) if the seller must perform its obligations of delivery in the buyer's country; and (3) if the buyer dictates the principal terms of the deal as a result of a call for bids initiated by the buyer. In addition to thee three specific exceptions to the default rule, Article 8(3) provides a general exception to the default rule: in any event, if the transaction is more closely connected with a law that is different than the law

---

[36] Rome I, art. 4(1)(a).

[37] *See* European Commission, Explanatory Memorandum on the Rome I Regulation, Sec. 4.2, http://europa.eu.int/eur-lex/lex/LexUriServ/site/en/com/2005/com2005_0650en01.pdf (Dec.15, 2005). Two years after its initial proposal, Rome I still struggles to come into force mainly because of Article 5 and 8 concerning the application of consumer law and jurisdictional discretion. Lorraine Mallinder, *EU Split over 'Rome I' Contracts Rules*, http://www.europeanvoice.com/ archive/article.asp?id=28090 (posted May 16, 2007). The burdens Article 5 imposes on online businesses by potentially subjecting them to 27 different sets of consumer law due to country-of-destination rules are the primary source of disagreement. *Id.* Article 8 is also controversial because it allows EU judges to choose the applicable law in contractual disputes. *Id.*

[38] Rome I, art. 23(2).

[39] Hague Conference on Private International Law, *Convention on the Law Applicable to Contracts for the International Sale of Goods*, http://www.hcch.net/index_en.php?act=conventions .pdf&cid=61 (Dec. 22, 1986).

that might prevail in accordance with the foregoing rules, then the law of that country should be applied.

In the Americas, one treaty pertaining to conflict of laws rules has been promulgated—*the 1994 Inter-American Convention on the Law Applicable to International Contracts* (the 1994 Inter-American Convention).[40] Five Latin American countries are parties to the 1994 Inter-American Convention: Bolivia, Brazil, Mexico, Uruguay, and Venezuela; however only two countries (Mexico and Venezuela) have actually ratified it.[41] It is interesting to note that the United States has not signed this convention. Like the European conventions on conflict of laws, the 1994 Inter-American Convention also allows parties to choose the law to govern their transaction (see Article 7).[42] Article 9 goes on to specify that if the parties do not make such a choice, the law of the country with the "closest ties" will govern.[43]

The UCC is a legislative enactment providing conflict of laws rules in the United States. The UCC is different from the conventions described above because it is a domestic model law, binding only when adopted by states in the United States. Unlike the conventions, the UCC does not attempt to provide uniformity among nations in its approach to conflict of laws and is not quite as permissive as any of the previously described conventions. Although the UCC takes on a slightly different form in each state where it has been adopted, the most common iteration of the UCC's conflict of laws provision is found in §1-105. §1-105 allows parties to choose a law to govern their transaction but restricts that choice to a law that bears a "reasonable relation" to the transaction. Absent an express choice by the parties, the UCC will apply to transactions with an "appropriate relation" to that UCC's state.[44] This specific language has allowed courts in the United States to

[40] For a full text of the 1994 Inter-American Convention, see Office of International Law, *Inter-American Convention on the Law Applicable to International Contracts*, http://www.oas.org /juridico/English/treaties/b-56.html (Mar. 17, 1994).
[41] *Id.* at http://www.oas.org/juridico/English/sigs/b-56.html.
[42] For a discussion of the significance of the conflict of laws provision in the Inter-American Convention see Jack M. Graves, *Party Autonomy in Choice of Commercial Law: The Failure of Revised UCC §1-301 and a Proposal for Broader Reform*, 36 Seton Hall L. Rev. 59, 102–103 (2005). Professor Graves argues that the broad language used in the Inter-American Convention allows parties to choose any body of law to govern their relationship, even a-national laws like the UNIDROIT Principles. *Id.* at 102.
[43] For a thoughtful discussion of the Inter-American Convention and a comparison of its principle features to the 1980 Rome Convention, see Friedrich K. Juenger, *The Inter-American Convention on the Law Applicable to International Contracts: Some Highlights and Comparisons,* 42 Am. J. Comp. L. 381 (1994).
[44] The UCC was revised in 2001 and revised Article 1 gives parties greater freedom to choose to apply the UCC by limiting the reasonable relation requirement to consumer transactions and states that "an agreement by parties to an international transaction that any or all of their rights and obligations are to be determined by the law of this State or of another State or country is effective, whether or not the transaction bears a relation to the State or country designated." UCC §1-

apply a law that actually might not have the "closest" relation to the transaction, providing that the court found that law to be more "appropriate."[45]

In private international commercial arbitration, the law governing the arbitration frequently directs the arbitral panel to simply apply whatever conflict of laws rules the arbitrators deem appropriate. Article 28 of the UNCITRAL Model Law on Commercial Arbitration (UNCITRAL Model Law), for example, provides that the parties may choose a rule of law to govern their transaction. However, in the absence of such a choice, the arbitrators shall "apply the law determined by the conflict of laws rules which it considers applicable."[46]

As was discussed in Chapter 1, parties to an arbitration might also choose to have a certain set of rules govern their arbitration proceedings. Many institutional rules contain provisions similar to the one just described in the UNCITRAL Model Law. Article 33 of the UNCITRAL Arbitration Rules (UNCITRAL Rules), for example, has essentially the same formulation as Article 28 of the UNCITRAL Model Law.[47] However, the UNCITRAL Rules do not use the formulation "rules of law" but instead just specifies that the parties might designate a "law" to govern their transaction. This distinction is an important one. The use of the word "law" alone is frequently narrowly construed to mean only national laws, whereas use of the phrase "rules of law" could include generally accepted principles of law, such as the UNIDROIT Principles.

The *International Chamber of Commerce Rules of Arbitration* (ICC Rules) are perhaps even more permissive than either the UNCITRAL Model Law or Rules. In Article 17, the ICC Rules allow the arbitral tribunal to simply apply whatever rules of law it deems applicable—implying that the tribunal is free to choose a law in any way it deems proper.[48]

301(c)(2). While revised Article 1 has now been adopted by many states, the states that have adopted the revisions have failed to adopt the revised Article 1-301. *See* Jack M. Graves, *Party Autonomy in Choice of Commercial Law: The Failure of Revised UCC §1-301 and a Proposal for Broader Reform*, 36 Seton Hall L. Rev. 59, 102–103 (2005).

[45] "Where a transaction has significant contacts with a state which has enacted the Act and also with other jurisdictions, the question what relation is 'appropriate' is left to judicial decision." UCC §1-105 cmt. 3. Note also that other courts of the United States have interpreted UCC §1-105 in accordance with the *Restatement (Second) of Conflict of Laws*, which states in Section 188 that the applicable law should be the law with the "most significant relationship" to the issue being considered. *See In re Merritt Dredging Co.,* 839 F.2d 203 (4th Cir. 1988); *Morris v. SSE, Inc.,* 912 F.2d 1392 (11th Cir. 1990).

[46] UNCITRAL Model Law Art. 28, discussed in detail, *infra* in Chapter 7.

[47] The UNCITRAL Rules are considered at length in Part II of this book. Generally speaking, they are model rules that UNCITRAL has developed to aid parties wanting to engage in commercial arbitration. For a full text of the UNCITRAL rules, see http://www.uncitral.org/pdf/english/texts/arbitration/arb-rules/arb-rules.pdf.

[48] For a full text of the ICC Rules of Arbitration, see International Court of Arbitration, International Dispute Resolution Services, *Rules of Arbitration*, http://www.iccwbo.org/

The chart on the following pages gives an overview of the rules that have just been described. After a quick survey of the provisions of the leading rules in this area, it should be clear that determining what laws to apply in the absence of a law being designated by the parties is frequently very difficult. The analysis typically depends on the interpreter's understanding of which jurisdiction has the closest connection to the transaction (though it is sometimes described differently). Regardless, the precise statutory language of the applicable conflict of laws rules must be followed in order to arrive at the substantive law that will apply to the transaction. If you spend some time with the different formulations of conflict of laws rules, you will soon realize that the different conflict of laws rules can very readily lead to the application of different substantive laws.

Selected Conflict of Laws Rules
1955 Hague Convention
• Article 2: uses law agreed upon by the parties;
• Article 3(1): where no choice, then apply law of seller's "habitual residence" or its branch if a branch was involved;
• But 3(2): if seller gets order in buyer's country, apply buyer's country's rules;
• But 3(3): if goods bought on an exchange, apply the law of exchange's country.
1980 Rome Convention
• Article 3: uses law agreed upon by the parties;
• Article 4: where no choice, apply law of the forum of "characteristic performance;"
• Shipping of goods usually considered characteristic performance.
Proposed Rome I Regulation
• Article 3: uses law agreed upon by the parties;
• Article 4: where no choice, apply law of seller's "habitual residence."

1986 Hague Convention
• never signed, but instructive as a modern source of conflicts analysis; • Article 7: uses law agreed upon by the parties; • Article 8(1): where no choice, apply law of seller's residence at time of formation; • Article 8(2): but apply Buyer's law if: (i) negotiations and formation in Buyer's country, (ii) delivery in Buyer's country, or (iii) Buyer conducted a bidding process; • Article 8(3): but apply other law if it is manifestly more connected to the contract.
1994 Inter-American Convention
• Article 7: uses law agreed upon by the parties; • Article 9: where no choice, apply law of the forum "with the closest ties."
UCC
• Section 1-105: parties can choose the law of a state that has "reasonable relation" to the transaction; • Where no choice, then UCC will apply to transactions with an "appropriate relation" to the state of the UCC
UNCITRAL Model Law on Arbitration
• Article 28(1): use choice of rules of law designated by parties; • Article 28(2): where no choice, apply the law determined by the conflict of laws rules that arbitrators consider applicable.
UNCITRAL Rules of Arbitration
• Article 33: use choice of law designated by parties; • Article 33: where no choice, apply the law determined by the conflict of laws rules that arbitrators consider applicable.
ICC Rules of Arbitration
• Article 17: uses choice of law designated by the parties; • Article 17: where no choice, apply the law that the arbitrators deem applicable, without reference to any conflict of laws rules.

Example 2-4

In Example 2-3, the French manufacturer had a manufacturing facility and sales office in England and dealt with the Italian Innkeeper from that place of business. As discussed in that example, Article 1(1)(a) might not lead to the application of the CISG since the place of business relevant for seller is England.

Turning then to Article 1(1)(b) the rules of private international law must be consulted. In this case, a tribunal could find that the rules of private international law applicable are found in the 1980 Rome Convention. (Italy, France and the United Kingdom are all parties to that convention.) Under the 1980 Rome Convention, the laws of the country where characteristic performance occurred would govern. Since the seller shipped the goods from England, a tribunal might find that English law would apply. Since England is not a Contracting State to the CISG, the CISG would not apply by virtue of CISG Article 1(1)(b).

Example 2-5

A German seller formed a contract for the sale of food with a buyer from Lichtenstein. Germany is a Contracting State, but Lichtenstein is not. Thus Article 1(1)(a) does not lead to application of the CISG. Turning to Article 1(1)(b), the tribunal applied the rules of private international law. It used the closest connection test to determine that the contract had the closest connection to Germany (since the seller was German) and that therefore the laws of Germany should apply. Since Germany is a Contracting State to the CISG, according to Article 1(1)(b), the CISG was found to apply to the transaction.[49]

Having just described how Article 1(1)(b) might lead to the application of the law of a Contracting State and therefore trigger the CISG, it is important to note that the CISG also contains an exception to the application of this provision. In fact, Article 95 of the CISG allows any Contracting State to specifically opt out of Article 1(1)(b). Notably, the United States and China have made an Article 95 declaration.

---

[49] Based on *Liechtenstein Buyer v. German Seller (Foodstuff Case)*, Arbitral Tribunal Hamburg, Germany, Sept. 4, 1996 (available at http://cisgw3.law.pace.edu/cases/960904g1.html).

Consider how the Article 95 declaration operates. In a transaction between two parties, one a Contracting State and the other not a Contracting State. Without an Article 95 declaration, if the rules of private international law lead to the application of the law of the Contracting State, then the CISG will apply. If the rules of private international law lead to the application of the law of the other state, then the substantive contract law of that other state will apply. In this situation, Article 1(1)(b) dictates that the Contracting State give up the use of its own domestic contract law and be bound by an international law—the CISG. However, the counterparty that is not a Contracting State will never have to compromise in this way. By not becoming a Contracting State, it has refused to ever give up its own domestic law in favor of the CISG. When the Contracting State has made the Article 95 declaration, then if the rules of private international law point to the application of its law, its domestic law of contracts will be implicated. By making the Article 95 declaration, the country has avoided giving up its own domestic contract law where counterparty would not do the same.

Example 2-6

A United States corporation entered a contract with a seller from England for computer equipment. A United States court determined that Article 1(1)(a) of the CISG was not applicable because England is not a Contracting Party. Further, because the United States has made an Article 95 declaration, the sale would not be governed by Article 1(1)(b). Therefore, the CISG is not applicable.[50]

In this example, the seller is from England. In most of the conflict of laws rules we surveyed, the law of the seller's jurisdiction typically applies. Accordingly, even if Article 1(1)(b) could have been applied, the CISG still would not likely apply since the conflict of laws rules would have likely led to the law of England, a country not a party to the CISG. Had the seller been from the United States, then the conflict of laws rules would have likely led to the law of the United States, a Contracting State to the CISG. In this scenario, without the Article 95 declaration, the CISG would have applied.

Even if the rules of Article 1(1)(a) or Article 1(1)(b) would normally lead to the application of the CISG, the CISG recognizes the autonomy of the parties in a transaction to choose some other law to govern their relationship. Article 6 of

---

[50] Based on *Impuls I.D. Intern., S.L. v. Psion-Teklogix, Inc.*, 234 F. Supp. 2d 1267 (S.D. Fla. 2002).

the CISG specifically states that the parties can opt out of the CISG where it might otherwise apply.

> ### Article 6
>
> The parties may exclude the application of this Convention or, subject to article 12, derogate from or vary the effect of any of its provisions.

In addition, even if the parties do not wish to opt out of the entire CISG, the parties can derogate from any particular provision. This is a powerful right that any party structuring a transaction that will be governed by the CISG might consider.[51]

One begins to see that it is difficult to consider even the first article of the CISG without being familiar with other articles of the CISG as well. This holds true throughout the CISG. It will rarely be sufficient to focus solely on one provision, even if that provision is central to a question being asked. Accordingly, one must be aware of all of the provisions of the CISG to thoroughly handle any issues that may arise.

> ### Example 2-7
>
> The Italian innkeeper orders porcelain from the French manufacturer, but the parties specify that the "laws of Italy" should govern the transaction. In this scenario, some cases and tribunals have ruled that when parties specify the law of a particular nation they are specifically opting out of the CISG, an international source of law, as authorized by Article 6.[52] According to this logic, a tribunal faced with this situation will apply the domestic sales law of Italy and not the CISG. However, the better analysis is that the CISG, as a treaty that has

---

[51] Professor John O. Honnold describes the notion of party autonomy and the primary role that the contract plays under the CISG: "The Convention in two fundamental ways responds to the power of agreement. The Convention itself was produced by agreement. States from all parts of the world, through collaboration sustained for over a decade, reached consensus on a Convention of over a hundred articles. . . . Consistent with these origins, the Convention does not interfere with the freedom of sellers and buyers to shape the terms of their transactions." Honnold, *supra* n. 5, at 3.

[52] *See also Società X[Italy] v. Società Y [Japan],* Ad hoc Arbitral Tribunal – Florence, Italy, Apr. 19, 1994 (available at http://cisgw3.law.pace.edu/cases/940419i3.html). In *that case,* the parties from Italy and Japan opted for the contract to be governed by Italian law. The tribunal determined that the parties must have meant Italian domestic contract law rather than the CISG.

> become the law of Italy, is the proper law implicated by the
> contract, and therefore the CISG should apply.

Example 2-7 illustrates the potential for confusion when parties simply specify
that the law of a particular country should govern and that country is a
Contracting State. On the one hand, as pointed out in the example, the law of the
country is indeed the CISG so a logical interpretation of the clause leads to the
CISG. On the other hand, had the parties intended the CISG to apply, they could
have certainly specified it by name; thus, a tribunal may determine that the
parties intended to exclude the CISG in favor of the domestic law.

Either way, this confusion can be avoided with careful drafting of the choice of
law provision. Whether the parties want to implicate the CISG, or the domestic
law of a particular country, the parties should clearly and unequivocally state
their choice of law in the agreement. Consider the following choice of law
provision: "This agreement shall not be governed by the CISG, but shall be
governed by the Italian law that governs domestic contracts in Italy." Of course
not all choice of law provisions are drafted so clearly.

C.   THE CISG APPLIES ONLY TO SALES OF GOODS

Article 1 specifies that the CISG will apply only to a sale of goods. Although the
term "goods" is not defined in the CISG, Professors Peter Schlechtriem and
Ingeborg Schwenzer have maintained that the term should be interpreted as
widely as possible to cover all objects that are the subject matter of commercial
sales contracts.[53] Nevertheless, questions arise concerning a vast array of items,
including intangibles, such as computer software,[54] or products that are attached
to the ground, such as plants or trees.

---

[53] *Commentary on the CISG, supra* n. 8, at 28.
[54] See Professor Joseph Lookofsky on this point, arguing strongly that intangible items are within
the CISG's scope. Regarding computer programs specifically, Professor Lookofsky gives four
reasons why they should be considered goods: (i) the CISG is not expressly limited to tangible
property, (ii) the essential nature of software is that of a functional machine, which would be
considered a good, (iii) CISG can well regulate functional items like software, and (iv) any
copyright in software does not change its functional nature. *See* Joseph Lookofsky, *Understanding
the CISG in the USA* 20–21 (2d ed., Aspen 2004).

> **Example 2-8**
> A German court was faced with the question of whether to classify strawberry plants as goods. It did so, placing the transaction within the scope of the CISG.[55]

While the CISG never affirmatively defines what a good is, Article 2 does provide a list of what is not considered a good under the CISG.

> **Article 2**
>
> This Convention does not apply to sales:
>
> (a) of goods bought for personal, family or household use, unless the seller, at any time before or at the conclusion of the contract, neither knew nor ought to have known that the goods were bought for any such use;
>
> (b) by auction;
>
> (c) on execution or otherwise by authority of law;
>
> (d) of stocks, shares, investment securities, negotiable instruments or money;
>
> (e) of ships, vessels, hovercraft or aircraft;
>
> (f) of electricity.

Consideration of these categories shows that they include areas of particular domestic sensitivity that the drafters of the CISG did not want to attempt to govern with the CISG. For example, goods purchased for personal use by consumers are generally transactions that are the subject of domestic consumer protection laws. Such laws differ from country to country and even within the states of the United States. The CISG did not hope or even attempt to try to unify the laws governing such protection. Additionally, goods purchased at auction present unique issues of contract formation.[56] All of the categories of sales of

---

[55]*Dutch Seller v. German Buyer (Strawberry Plants Case),* Oberlandesgericht Köln, Germany, Apr. 3, 2006 (available at http://cisgw3.law.pace.edu/cases/060403g1.html).

[56] Honnold, *supra* n. 5, at 47.

goods excluded under Article 2 of the CISG represent transactions that are better-suited to be regulated by domestic laws.[57]

Assuming a transaction involves goods that are not excluded by Article 2 (and assuming Article 1 has been satisfied), then the CISG will normally apply. However, many transactions are made more complicated because they involve the buyer supplying certain inputs for the goods to be purchased or because the transaction involves both goods and services. Article 3 describes these types of transactions and provides guidelines for when they fall within the CISG.

Article 3

(1) Contracts for the supply of goods to be manufactured or produced are to be considered sales unless the party who orders the goods undertakes to supply a substantial part of the materials necessary for such manufacture or production.

(2) This Convention does not apply to contracts in which the preponderant part of the obligations of the party who furnishes the goods consists in the supply of labour or other services.

Article 3(1) contemplates a manufacturing order and concludes that such order should be considered a sale of goods, unless the buyer supplies a "substantial part" of the production materials.[58] CISG Advisory Council Opinion Number 4 states that "substantial part" in this context should typically be assessed by an economic criterion.[59] This Advisory Council Opinion advises that determination should be made on a case-by-case basis, and that no fixed percentage will always be applicable to determine what is a "substantial part." Nonetheless, the opinion cautions that any percentage below 50% should be considered too low.[60]

---

[57] *See Commentary on the CISG, supra* n. 8, at 41 (stating that the Article 2 exclusions were included in the CISG based upon fears that the CISG would extend to contract of sales that were "merely of local importance in economic terms").

[58] Based upon the language of Article 3(1), it is clear that the CISG is presumed to apply. Thus, the burden of proof lies with the party opposing the applicability of the CISG. *Commentary on the CISG, supra* n. 8, at 58.

[59] CISG-AC Opinion no. 4, *Contracts for the Sale of Goods to Be Manufactured or Produced and Mixed Contracts (Article 3 CISG)*, paras. 2.8–2.10, Oct. 24, 2004 (available at http://cisgw3.law .pace.edu/cisg/CISG-AC-op4.html).

[60] The Advisory Council bases this reasoning upon the preference to apply the CISG, as well as the need for uniform interpretation and application of the CISG. *Id.* at 2.10.

Article 3(2) explains that when a contract is for goods and services, the CISG will only apply when the "preponderant part of the obligations" is for goods, not services. Generally speaking, the CISG attempts to regulate transactions that may be a hybrid of goods and services, so long as the transaction is primarily a sale of goods. The CISG Advisory Council Opinion Number 4 also addresses this issue. Similar to Article 3(1), the Council states that an economic value criterion should be used to evaluate what constitutes the "preponderant part" of a contract.[61] However, no pre-established percentage should be applied to assess whether the "preponderant part" requirement has been satisfied. Instead, the "preponderant part" should be evaluated with reference to the entire transaction, taking into account factors such as the content of the contract, the structure of the price, and the weight given to different obligations.[62] However, the Advisory Council did suggest that where at least 50% of the contract is for goods, the CISG could still apply.[63]

Example 2-9

A Portuguese buyer purchases a portable warehouse shed from a French seller for 500,000 francs, such price to include dismantling of the warehouse and re-assembly at the buyer's location. The price of the warehouse was 381,200 francs, while dismantling and delivery costs were 118,800 francs. The court determined the hybrid transaction was covered by the CISG because the preponderant part in terms of value represented the sale price of the warehouse (the goods), not the cost of dismantling and delivery services (the services).[64]

Despite the guidance given by Articles 2 and 3 on what constitutes a sale of goods covered by the CISG, questions may still arise in this area. Consider the following case discussing distributor and related agreements.

---

[61] *Id.* at para 3.3.

[62] *Id.* at para 3.4.

[63] *Id.* Defining "preponderant part" to mean more that 50% is also a consensus among scholars. *E.g. Commentary on the CISG, supra* n. 8, at 60; Fritz Enderlein & Dietrich Maskow, *International Sales Law* 36 (Oceana 1992).

[64] *M. Marques Roque Joachim [France] v. La Sarl Holding Manin Rivière [Portugal]*, Cour d'appel [Court of Appeal] Grenoble no. 93/4879, France, Apr. 26, 1995 (available at http://cisgw3 .law.pace.edu/cases/950426f2.html).

Viva Vino Import Corporation v. Farnese Vini S.r.l.

CIV.A. 99-6384

United States District Court, Eastern District of Pennsylvania

29 August 2000

Jan E. Dubois, J.

I.   Introduction

This case arises out of three alleged agreements between plaintiff, Viva Vino Import Corporation, a Pennsylvania corporation and defendant, Farnese Vini S.r.l., an Italian company. The agreements provided, in essence, for distribution of defendant's wines in Pennsylvania and other parts of the United States by plaintiff.

The Complaint contains four counts –

(1) breach of contract;

(2) promissory estoppel;

(3) unjust enrichment; and,

(4) tortious interference with business relations.

Defendant's Counterclaim is based on breach of contract.

Plaintiff argues that the United Nations Convention on Contracts for the International Sale of Goods, codified at 15 U.S.C.A. App. 1998 (the "CISG"), and/or Pennsylvania law should apply to all of plaintiff's claims and the Counterclaim. Defendant contends that Italian law should apply to all such claims.

II.   Discussion

A.   The CISG

The CISG does not apply to tort claims. Consequently, it is inapplicable to plaintiff's claim of tortious interference with business relations.

There is no dispute that both the United States and Italy are signatories to the CISG. When two foreign nations are signatories to the CISG, that Treaty governs contracts for the sale of goods between parties whose places of business are in such nations unless the contract contains a choice of law provision to the contrary. *See* 15 U.S.C. App. at Art. 1(1)(a); *See also Filanto, S.p.A. v. Chilewich Int'l Corp.*, 789 F.Supp. 1229, 1237 (S.D.N.Y.1992). The agreements at issue do not contain a choice of law provision.

Defendant challenges the application of the CISG to this case on the ground that none of the agreements at issue had as the subject a particular sale of goods, and none had definite terms regarding quantity and price. *See Helen Kaminski Pty. Ltd. v. Marketing Australian Prods.*, 1997 WL 414137, at *2-3 (S.D.N.Y. July 23, 1997) (refusing to apply the CISG to a distributorship agreement because it did not contain definite terms regarding the price or types of goods to be sold); *see also* 15 U.S.C.A.App. at Art. 14.

The three agreements between plaintiff and defendant were

> (1) an exclusive distributorship agreement;
>
> (2) an agreement granting plaintiff a 25% interest in defendant; and,
>
> (3) a sales commission agreement.

None of these agreements were for a specific sale of goods, and none had specific terms as to price and quantity. Although exclusive distributorship agreements are considered contracts for the sale of goods under the Uniform Commercial Code adopted in Pennsylvania, this approach has been rejected in connection with the CISG. *See Helen Kaminski*, 1997 WL 414137, at *2.

This Court agrees with the rationale adopted by the court in *Kaminski* and concludes that the CISG does not apply to distributorship contracts that do not cover the sale of specific goods and contain definite terms regarding quantity and price. Because the agreements at issue in this case do not cover the sale of specific goods and set forth definite terms regarding quantity and price, the CISG is inapplicable.

Accordingly, the Court will turn to whether Pennsylvania or Italian law should apply to the case.

* * * * *

Notes and Commentary

Note 1: This court denied application of the CISG on the basis that the contracts involved here were not for the sale of specific goods or for a specific quantity. Is there any support in the CISG for that approach? Article 1 does state that the CISG applies to sales of goods. Isn't that what was contemplated by the distributorship agreement? By extension, might the other agreements (related to the distributorship) be said to be a part of the same transaction such that the CISG should govern all three agreements? Would it make a difference if the terms of all three agreements had been placed in one document? If they had been, would CISG Article 3(2) be implicated? If so, what analysis?

Note 2: Chapter 3 will discuss the CISG's provisions on formation of a contract. Among those provisions is Article 14. That article states that for an offer to be valid, there must be reference to price and quantity. However, Article 14 goes on to state that the offer may expressly or implicitly fix or make provision for determining the quantity and the price. Given that this court was troubled by the lack of express specificity of goods and quantity, does Article 14 help allay those concerns?

Note 3: Other cases decided under the CISG make a distinction that the CISG should govern the sale of specific goods under a distributorship arrangement but not the distributorship framework arrangement itself.[65]

Note 4: By comparison, a United States court applying the UCC to the facts of the *Viva Vino* case may have determined that the distribution agreement constituted a sale of goods, reaching a different result than the *Viva Vino* court's analysis under the CISG. The *Viva Vino* court specifically acknowledges that the Pennsylvania UCC had been applied to distributorship agreements. In addition, the court in *Warrick Beverage Corp. v. Miller Brewing Co.* held that a distribution agreement between a beer manufacturer and distributor fell within the scope of Article 2 of the UCC because the transaction involved the sale of beer products.[66] Likewise, the court in *Leibel v. Raynor Manufacturing Co.*, specifically considered whether distributorships fell under the UCC as a sale of goods and concluded that it did.[67] That court reasoned that distributorships ultimately involve the sale of goods from the manufacturer to the distributor and therefore fall within the UCC.[68]

---

[65] *See e.g. French Seller v. German Buyer (Computer Chip Case),* Oberlandesgericht [Provincial Court of Appeal] Koblenz, Germany, Sept. 17, 1993, UNCITRAL CLOUT Case 281 (available at http://cisgw3.law.pace.edu/cases/930917g1.html).

[66] 352 N.E. 2d 496 (Ind. Ct. App. 1976).

[67] 571 S.W.2d 640 (Ky. App. 1978).

[68] *Id.* at 643.

Note 5: Despite the fact that a United States court applying the UCC might have come to a different result, this court certainly seems to be respecting and following the precedent set in the *Helen Kaminski* case. Given the tension, mentioned earlier, between following domestic precedent in common law countries and attempting to apply the CISG in a way that promotes international uniformity (in accord with CISG Article 7), might this court have done something differently? Could it or should it have considered commentary like that of Schlechtriem and Schwenzer suggesting that the CISG should be interpreted as widely as possible to find transactions within its scope.[69] Consider whether scholarly commentary regarding the international application of the CISG should be taken into account generally by tribunals even in common law jurisdictions.

D.   THE CISG GENERALLY EXCLUDES ISSUES OF: VALIDITY, PROPERTY
      INTERESTS, OR PERSONAL INJURY

Articles 4 and 5 of the CISG set forth additional provisions regarding the scope of the CISG's application. In accordance with those articles, unless the CISG expressly provides otherwise, the CISG does not address issues concerning: (1) validity, (2) property interests, or (3) personal injury.

Article 4

This Convention governs only the formation of the contract of sale and the rights and obligations of the seller and the buyer arising from such a contract. In particular, except as otherwise expressly provided in this Convention, it is not concerned with:

(a) the validity of the contract or of any of its provisions or of any usage;

(b) the effect which the contract may have on the property in the goods sold.

---

1.   Validity

Article 4 more narrowly defines the scope of the CISG's application. Article 4(a) states that the CISG "governs only the formation of the contract of sale and the rights and obligations of the seller and the buyer arising from such a contract." Specifically, Article 4(a) states that, unless the CISG expressly provides

---

[69] *See supra* n. 54.

otherwise, the CISG does not cover issues related to the validity of the contract. Instead, such issues must be determined with reference to domestic law. Validity issues encompass any issue that would make a contract invalid under the relevant domestic laws. Common validity issues include fraud, incapacity, duress, and a subject matter of the transaction that is illegal. Validity issues can, as indicated by the term used to describe them, make a contract invalid under the domestic rules related to those issues.

Professors Schlechtriem and Schwenzer have argued that if the matter is governed by the CISG then even if the matter might lead to a contract being invalid under the relevant domestic law, the CISG should govern. They provide as an example the concept of impossibility that might indeed make a contract invalid under a relevant domestic law. However, Schlechtriem and Schwenzer argue that issues based on impossibility should be determined based upon the provisions of the CISG, since the CISG does contain provisions on impediments that address that notion.[70]

There is some controversy over what issues are truly matters of validity that are to be excluded from the CISG. For example, courts in the United States have taken the position that the theory of unconscionability is a validity issue outside the scope of the CISG.[71] On the other hand, Professor Schlechtriem has written that the concept of "unconscionability" should be determined based upon the provisions of the CISG.[72]

Even though the CISG relegates validity issues to domestic law, another article of the CISG provides additional clarification, further demonstrating the interrelated nature of the CISG's provisions. As has been mentioned earlier in this chapter, Article 7 of the CISG gives a general statement about how the CISG itself should be interpreted. Article 7(1) states that when interpreting the CISG, regard should be given for its international character, the need to promote uniformity in its application, and the observance of good faith in international trade. Accordingly, Schlechtriem and Schwenzer suggest that when looking to domestic law for validity standards, one should look to any domestic laws that

---

[70] *Commentary on the CISG, supra* n. 8, at 68.

[71] *See Barbara Berry, S.A. de C.V. v. Ken M. Spooner Farms, Inc.*, 2006 U.S. Dist. LEXIS 31262 (W.D. Wash. Apr. 13, 2006). In *Barbara Berry*, a United States District Court relied upon domestic law in ruling that a warranty disclaimer in a contract between a Mexican buyer and an American seller was valid. In doing so, the court relied upon domestic law, reasoning that "[w]hether a clause in a contract is valid and enforceable is decided under domestic law, not the CISG." *Id.* at *4. The court then went on to analyze the clause based upon the UCC 's unconscionability standards. *Id.* at **5–11.

[72] "If, however, domestic provisions use 'indefinite concepts' such as 'unconscionable' or 'treuwidrig' [unconscionability in German], the contractual clause should be measured by the CISG and not by domestic law." Peter Schlechtriem, *Uniform Sales Law—The U.N. Convention on Contracts for the International Sale of Goods* 32 n. 83(b) (Manz 1986).

would invalidate a contract, regardless of the whether the term "validity" itself is used in that domestic legal system.[73] In this way, a uniform international application of the term "validity" can be achieved. Note, however, that this should not be read as undermining Schlechtriem and Schwenzer's general proposition that issues covered by the CISG should be handled by it, even if the relevant domestic law treats the issue as one regarding validity.

Example 2-10

An Australian electronics company contracted to purchase DVD players from a Chinese electrical equipment company. The parties' contract included a penalty clause requiring the seller to pay penalties if the goods were delivered late. After repeated delayed deliveries, the Australian buyer commenced arbitration proceedings seeking damages, including penalties pursuant to the penalty clause of the contract. After determining that the CISG governed the parties' contract but did not govern the validity of penalty clauses, the tribunal applied Chinese domestic law to determine that the penalty clauses were permissible.[74]

Note that the UNIDROIT Principles do contain a provision allowing parties to agree upon reasonable payments for non-performance. A different tribunal might have claimed that the UNIDROIT Principles contain general principles upon which the CISG is based and, in accordance with Article 7, might have looked there to resolve this dispute, instead of resorting to Chinese domestic law.

---

2. Property Issues

Again, "except as otherwise expressly provided," Article 4(b) excludes from the CISG's coverage "the effect which the contract may have on the property in the goods sold." During the preparatory stages of the CISG, it was recognized that it

---

[73] *Commentary on the CISG, supra* n. 8, at 65–66. Here Schlechtriem and Schwenzer are striving to apply the international standard to make sure that all countries are able to supplant the CISG with the same types of domestic law. So, on the one hand if a country doesn't use the term validity but has a law that makes a contract void in certain circumstances, that law would be applicable. On the other hand, if a country has a law that uses the term validity but it does not render the contract void, then such a law would not be applicable under the CISG.

[74] Based on *Australian Buyer v. Chinese Seller*, China Intl. Economic & Trade Arbitration Commn. [CIETAC] (PRC) Arbitration no. CISG/2005/04, China, Nov. 9, 2005.

was too difficult to unify international laws on property rights.[75] Thus, those issues remain the province of domestic law and will be resolved in accordance with the application of the domestic law applicable to the contract.[76] However, the CISG does contain provisions that govern the allocation of risk in the parties' contract (i.e. when risk regarding the goods passes from the seller to the buyer), which will be discussed in detail in Chapter 4.[77]

Article 4(b) also underscores the concept that the CISG deals with the rights of the parties to the transaction, i.e. the buyer and the seller, and not any third parties which may have a property interest (for example, a security interest) in the goods being sold. While the CISG does not determine the property rights such a third party might have in the goods, the CISG does dictate the rights and obligations of the buyer and seller with respect to the sale of the goods under consideration. Consequently, the CISG may also affect the goods subject to the third party's property claim by determining the remedies available to the buyer and seller under the sale agreement. When this situation arises, domestic law will dictate whether the third party creditor's rights to goods prevail over the rights of either the seller or the buyer in the sales transaction.[78]

Example 2-11

A German corporation purchased a yacht from a Dutch seller. Under the parties' contract, the seller retained title to the yacht. The German company then transferred the yacht to a silent partner of the company. When the German company went bankrupt, the Dutch seller claimed it had the right to repossess the yacht pursuant to the retention-of-title clause in the contract. The court held that the CISG did not apply to a dispute over the validity of a retention-of-title clause.[79]

Note that this court did not address the threshold question of whether the CISG would have applied to this transaction at all

---

[75] Consider in this regard, the text of the Secretariat Commentary, "In some legal systems property passes at the time of the conclusion of the contract. In other legal systems property passes at some later time such as the time at which the goods are delivered to the buyer. It was not regarded possible to unify the rule on this point nor was it regarded necessary to do so . . . ." Secretariat Commentary on the 1978 Draft, *Guide to CISG Article 4,* para. 4 (available at http://cisgw3.law .pace.edu/cisg/text/secomm/secomm-04.html).

[76] *Commentary on the CISG, supra* n. 8, at 69–70.

[77] Loss of the goods or damage to the goods are presumed to be the main risks involved in this transfer. Schlechtriem, *supra* n. 72, at 87.

[78] Honnold, *supra* n. 5 at 70.

[79] Based on *Dutch Seller v. German Buyer*, Oberlandesgericht [Provincial Court of Appeal] Koblenz no. 5 U 534/91, Germany, Jan. 16, 1992 (abstract available at http://www.unilex.info/ case.cfm?pid=1&do=case&id=30&step=Keywords).

> based on Article 2's exclusion of vessels from the scope of the CISG.

3.   Personal Injury

Article 5 of the CISG states that the CISG excludes any liability of the seller for "death or personal injury caused by the goods" that are subject to a sales transaction.

> **Article 5**
>
> This Convention does not apply to the liability of the seller for death or personal injury caused by the goods to any person.

Similar to validity issues, personal injury caused by products is treated differently around the world – in some countries it is based on the law of torts, in others it is based on the law of contracts, and in other countries it is based on a combination of both.[80] Additionally, products liability is considered an area of special concern because many jurisdictions provide consumers with special protections against manufacturers and sellers of defective goods. For these reasons, the relevant domestic law was left to govern products liability claims.[81]

III.   GENERAL PROVISIONS

We have already encountered several of the General Provisions from the second chapter of the CISG, including Article 7 on interpretation and Article 10, which defines a party's place of business. This section will discuss in detail the remaining articles of the General Provisions including: (A) the principles of contract interpretation, set out in Article 8, (B) the significance of past practices and trade usages, described in Article 9, and (C) the absence of a writing requirement, contained in Article 11.

A.   PRINCIPLES OF CONTRACTUAL INTENT

While Article 7 describes broadly how the CISG should be interpreted, Article 8 focuses more narrowly on how to interpret the intent of the parties to the sales transaction. In preparing Article 8, the delegates were faced with the task of

---

[80] Enderlein & Maskow, *supra* n. 63, at 45; *Commentary on the CISG, supra* n. 8, at 76.
[81] *Commentary on the CISG, supra* n. 8, at 77.

reconciling different theories regarding the basics of contract formation.[82] Some theories focus on subjective intent of the parties, a "meeting of the minds," while others focus on external indicia of intent.[83] As a result of these difficulties, Article 8 contains both a subjective and an objective approach.[84]

Article 8

(1) For the purposes of this Convention statements made by and other conduct of a party are to be interpreted according to his intent where the other party knew or could not have been unaware what that intent was.

(2) If the preceding paragraph is not applicable, statements made by and other conduct of a party are to be interpreted according to the understanding that a reasonable person of the same kind as the other party would have had in the same circumstances.

(3) In determining the intent of a party or the understanding a reasonable person would have had, due consideration is to be given to all relevant circumstances of the case including the negotiations, any practices which the parties have established between themselves, usages and any subsequent conduct of the parties.

Article 8(1) explains that statements and conduct of a person should be interpreted according to that party's subjective intent—making the subjective intent of that party paramount. The focus of inquiry under Article 8(1) is therefore begins with the party making the statement. However, the remaining part of Article 8(1) explains that subjective intent should apply only "where the other party knew or could not have been unaware what that intent was." This represents a subjective standard of interpretation. The focus becomes what the other party actually knew. However, there is an objective component to this section as well. The standard employed includes using a party's subjective intent where the other party could not have been unaware of that intent. This is an objective manner of measuring subjective intent. It will capture a situation where

---

[82] Honnold, *supra* n. 5, at 117.

[83] *Id.*

[84] For general discussion of the interaction between the subjective and objective components of Article 8, see E. Allen Farnsworth, *Article 8*, in *Bianca-Bonell Commentary on the International Sales Law* 95–102 (Giuffre 1987) (available at: http://cisgw3.law.pace.edu/cisg/biblio/farnsworth-bb8.html).

a party claims not to have known of the other party's subjective intent but that is simply not a possibility.[85] By objective measurement that party must have known of the other's intent. By including this objective standard in Article 8(1), proving knowledge of subjective intent becomes easier.[86]

Where subjective intent cannot be discerned, Article 8(2) contains a completely objective standard. Under Article 8(2), the focus of the inquiry shifts from the party making the statement to the listener. This section indicates that statements and conduct of a party should be interpreted the way "a reasonable person of the same kind as the other party" would have interpreted them. Article 8(3) goes on to explain that when determining what the understanding of a reasonable person would be, one should take into account "*all* the relevant circumstances of the case (emphasis added)." When read in conjunction with each other, the standard for interpretation is: the understanding that a reasonable person of the same kind as the other party would have had in the same circumstances. This is a very expansive approach to interpretation. In evaluating the relevant circumstances, Article 8(3) specifically states that the relevant circumstances to be considered include, but are not limited to, negotiations, business practices of the parties, usages, and subsequent conduct.

Example 2-12

A Chinese buyer purchased heating units from a German seller. The parties had different interpretations of contractual terms that determined the refund price of returned heating units. The term stated, "If the goods purchased by the buyer have not been sold or are still remaining, the seller should allow the buyer to return them at the contract price unconditionally." The tribunal determined that "when two parties interpret the 'contract price' differently, all relevant circumstances of the case should be considered to determine the intent of the party or the understanding a reasonable person would have had (Article 8). Accordingly, the tribunal determined a refund of the contract price to represent the unit price of the heating unit, not the total contract price.[87]

---

[85] The degree of knowledge used in Article 8(1), "could not have been unaware," is also used in Article 35(3) discussed in Chapter 4 (Section I.B.). Professor Honnold defines the phrase as "facts that are before the eyes of one who can see." Honnold, *supra* n. 5, at 259.

[86] Enderlein & Maskow, *supra* n, 63, at 62.

[87] *Chinese Buyer v. German Seller (Heaters Case),* CIETAC, China, Dec. 7, 2005 (available at http://cisgw3.law.pace.edu/cases/051207c1.html).

This expansive approach is in stark contrast to the parol evidence rule of law still in effect in the United States.[88] The parol evidence rule, if it applies, has the effect of preventing one party from introducing extrinsic evidence of matters not contained in the written agreement between the parties, where that evidence is offered to contradict, or even supplement in certain cases, the written agreement.[89] While there are exceptions to the parol evidence rule as it is in effect in the United States, the basic rule prohibits the extrinsic evidence unless some specified exception would apply. The policy underlying the parol evidence rule is that evidence outside the written contract is inherently untrustworthy. Further, the rule contemplates parties' negotiations evolving so that prior arrangements or statements would be overridden by the final written agreement of the parties and are, therefore, irrelevant to explain the intent of the parties as expressed in the final contract. In Article 8(3), the CISG has taken the opposite approach and allows all evidence to be introduced and evaluated by a tribunal.

This does not preclude parties from opting for their own version of the parol evidence rule in conformity with the general principle of party autonomy. Recall that Article 6 allows parties to opt out of any of the provisions of the CISG. Therefore, parties may include a provision in their contract that states that only the written contract itself should be considered in the event of any dispute. This would, in effect, be a private parol evidence rule, permissible under Article 6.[90] In fact, the CISG Advisory Council has issued an opinion on this issue and concluded that indeed such a clause could be effective to bar evidence of intent outside of the actual written contract, provided that the clause (frequently called a merger clause) clearly evidences the intent of the parties to derogate from the CISG.[91] However, the advisory opinion goes on to indicate that when considering the intent behind the merger clause itself, evidence outside of the written contract should be allowed.[92]

---

[88] While the parol evidence rule was a creation of English law, there were many exceptions adopted by the courts over time. The exceptions have caused the parol evidence rule to become so ambiguous that the English Law Commission supports its abolition. Law Commission, Working Paper No. 70, *Law of Contract, The Parol Evidence Rule* (1976); Honnold, *supra n. 5,* at 121, n. 14.

[89] For a more complete description of the parol evidence rule, see *Restatement (Second) of Contracts* § 209–217.

[90] Huber, *supra* n. 12, at 235.

[91] CISG-AC Opinion no. 3, *Parol Evidence Rule, Plain Meaning Rule, Contractual Merger Clause and the CISG*, para. 4.1–4.6 (Oct. 24, 2004) (available at http://cisgw3.law.pace.edu/cisg/CISG-AC-op3.html).

[92] *Id.* at para 4.5

Example 2-13

A Florida tile importer (the buyer) attended a trade fair in Italy where it signed a contract to purchase tiles with an Italian manufacturer of tiles (the seller). The contract was in Italian and when the Italian seller attempted to enforce some of its provisions, the Florida buyer objected on several grounds. Its primary ground was that neither of the parties to the transaction had intended the general contract terms in the Italian contract to be binding. In fact, the Florida buyer produced affidavits from parties on both sides of the transaction supporting that contention. When the United States court was asked to consider those affidavits, it considered whether the parol evidence rule would exclude them. It concluded that the affidavits should be considered. It reasoned that since the CISG governed, Article 8 specifically allows consideration of all evidence, including evidence of negotiations prior to executing a contract.[93]

Another basis upon which the Florida buyer attempted to resist the enforcement of the contract as that the contract was written in Italian and the buyer's agent who signed the contract neither spoke, nor read Italian. In footnote 9 to the courts opinion in this case, the court expressed its strong opinion on this argument, "We find it nothing short of astounding that an individual, purportedly experienced in commercial matters, would sign a contract in a foreign language and expect not to be bound simply because he could not comprehend its terms. We find nothing in the CISG that might counsel this type of reckless behavior and nothing that signals any retreat from the proposition that parties who sign contracts will be bound by them regardless of whether they have read them or understood them."

B.   TRADE USAGE AND PARTIES' PRACTICES

Article 9 expands on the interpretive provision of Article 8 by explaining the significance of trade usage and the parties' practices in trying to ascertain intent. Article 9(1) explains that parties are bound by: (i) the usages to which they have agreed, and (ii) the practices that they have established themselves. Trade usages are well-known customary practices that exist in any particular industry, while practices are methods that particular parties typically follow.

---

[93] *See MCC Marble Ceramic Center, Inc. v. Ceramica Nuova D'Agostino, S.P.A.*, 144 F.3d 1384 (11th Cir. 1998).

Article 9

(1) The parties are bound by any usage to which they have agreed and by any practices which they have established between themselves.

(2) The parties are considered, unless otherwise agreed, to have impliedly made applicable to their contract or its formation a usage of which the parties knew or ought to have known and which in international trade is widely known to, and regularly observed by, parties to contracts of the type involved in the particular trade concerned.

Disputes that involve usages will likely hinge on whether and when behavior rises to the level of a trade usage or party practice. There are no bright-line answers to those questions. Generally, a trade usage must be a custom that is well-known and well-followed in any particular industry. Article 9 itself makes this clear in part (2) stating that the trade usage must be widely known in international trade and widely followed in transactions like the one in question. For a behavior to become a practice between parties, there should be a reasonable expectation that the behavior will continue. If one party to a transaction does not want to create that expectation in the other party, the first party should make its intentions clear that no pattern of behavior is being established. Here we see an early example of the CISG attempting to encourage communication between parties. Under Article 9, where parties do not clearly communicate, conduct may take on unwanted significance.

Example 2-14

A Dutch oil company had been selling petroleum products in Hawaii and over a period of years twice gave the Hawaiian purchaser a price reduction in an effort to help the struggling company deal with adverse market condition. Later, the buyer brought suit insisting that the Dutch oil company accept reduced payment for its products. The purchaser based its claim on two related arguments, in addition to others. First, the purchaser argued that it was common trade usage to price protect during adverse market conditions and therefore such trade usages should be implied into the parties' contract. Second, the fact that the Dutch oil company had actually twice engaged in price protection with this particular purchaser in respect to the contract

> under consideration was evidence of the trade usage being well-known and being implied into the parties' contract in this case.[94]
>
> While this case was argued under the UCC in the United States, those same arguments might be made under the CISG. The argument regarding trade usages would be grounded in Article 9; while the argument about the parties conduct subsequent to entering into the contract being indicative of intent at the time of contracting would be grounded in Article 8(3).

Again, Article 9(2) states that, unless they agree otherwise, the parties are considered to have impliedly made a part of their contract international trade usages, provided that: (i) such trade usages are widely known and observed in similar transactions; and (ii) that the parties knew or ought to have known about those usages. Here again, the CISG is taking a flexible approach to include as much evidence as possible in an attempt to ascertain the true intent of the parties. Further, the CISG is attempting to promote uniformity in international sales transactions, incorporating into contracts practices that are widely known and consistently followed internationally. Finally, by including the phrase "unless otherwise agreed," we see a specific reference to the idea that the parties are free to agree otherwise and, in fact, are encouraged to do so if they do not want particular trade usages to be implied into their relationship.

Note again the specific qualifying language used here—that for the international trade usages to be implied into the parties' contract, those parties must either have known about the practices, or they *ought to have known* about them. The latter qualification adds an objective element to prevent parties from simply denying knowledge of a common practice. This reflects the similar language used in Article 8(1). In fact, if the trade usages are widely known and followed generally, it will be difficult for a party to argue that it neither knew nor ought to have known about the practice.

> **Example 2-15**
>
> An Austrian buyer entered a contract for the sale of wood with a German seller. The German seller argued that regional trade usages specific to the wood industry were applicable to the sales contract even though not specifically mentioned in the parties' contract. These trade usages were enshrined in the customs section of the Austrian commercial code and were commonly

---

[94] See *Nanakuli Paving & Rock Co. v. Shell Oil Co.*, 664 F.2d 772 (9th Cir. 1981) for a case with essentially this description that was decided under the UCC.

> acknowledged by wood industry contracts between German and Austrian parties. The regional trade usages imposed more stringent inspection requirements than the CISG on the buyer. The court found the regional trade usages were applicable terms of the contract under Article 9, based on the parties' course of dealing in prior transactions and common use of the terms in the wood industry.[95]

The following fictitious arbitration award is based on *Frigaliment Importing Co., Ltd. v. B.N.S. International Sales Corp.*, 190 F. Supp. 116 (S.D.N.Y. 1960), a classic contract interpretation case found in many American casebooks on Contracts. After a trial to the court, Judge Friendly wrote an opinion considered by many as a Contracts "classic." This 1960 opinion pre-dated the CISG (as well as UCC Article 2) and was actually decided on common law contracts grounds. However, Judge Friendly's factual account and legal analysis seem almost equally at home under the CISG—the law that would govern this same case if it arose today. Interestingly, the parties' contract also provided for arbitration by the New York Produce Exchange. However, neither of the parties raised the issue, and the court deemed their failure a waiver of their right to arbitration. Thus, it seems fitting in this fictional decision not only to add 40 years to the dates in order to bring the case within the purview of the CISG, but also to shift the forum to arbitration in fictional Vindobona, Danubia (a useful place for fictional arbitration disputes inasmuch as it has adopted the UNCITRAL Model Law, verbatim). While the dates, forum, and applicable law have been changed, Judge Friendly's classic prose is, to the greatest extent possible, left as originally written.[96]

---

[95] *German Seller v. Austrian Buyer (Wood Case)*, Oberster Gerichtshof, Austria, Mar. 21, 2000, UNCITRAL CLOUT Case 425 (available at http://daccessdds.un.org/doc/UNDOC/GEN/V03/846/28/PDF/V0384628.pdf?OpenElement).

[96] The authors have made every effort to limit additions, changes, and deletions to those necessary to accomplish the pedagogical goals of the case.

Claimant, "F" v. Respondent, "B"

Final Award

Issued 27 December, 2000, Vindobona, Danubia

By an Arbitral Panel constituted under the Rules of the
Vindobona Arbitration Association

The issue is: "what is chicken?" Claimant says "chicken" means a young chicken, suitable for broiling and frying. Respondent says "chicken" means any bird of that genus that meets contract specifications on weight and quality, including what it calls "stewing chicken" and Claimant pejoratively terms "fowl." Dictionaries give both meanings, as well as some others not relevant here. To support its assertion, Claimant sends a number of volleys over the net; Respondent essays to return them and adds a few serves of its own. Assuming that neither party can show that the other knew—or could not have been unaware of— the first party's own subjective intent, the case nicely illustrates the need to focus on the parties' externally manifested signals as viewed through the lens of a reasonable person, rather than any secret or unexpressed intent.

In this matter, Claimant, a Swiss corporation, has brought claims against, Respondent, a New York corporation, arising out of two contracts between the parties. Each of the contracts included a written, signed provision calling for arbitration in Vindobona, Danubia, under the Rules of the Vindobona Arbitration Association. The arbitration agreement is governed by the arbitration law of Danubia,[97] as the place of arbitration. *See* Model Law Art. 20. An arbitral panel has been duly constituted and has provided each of the parties with a full and equal opportunity to present its case. *See* Model Law 18. Having considered the submissions of each of the parties, the panel of arbitrators has concluded that Claimant has not sustained its burden of persuasion that the contract used "chicken" in the narrower sense and therefore takes nothing from Respondent. Our reasoning in reaching this decision, see Model Law Art. 31(2), as well as our ultimate disposition of the matter are provided below.

---

[97] Danubia has adopted in its entirety the UNCITRAL Model Law on International Commercial Arbitration (1985), which, for ease of reference, will be cited as the "Model Law" throughout this Award.

The two parties have their places of business in different contracting states, each of which is a contracting state with respect to the United Nations Convention on the International Sale of Goods (the "CISG"). The contracts in question do not contain any choice of law provisions. The parties' contracts are, therefore, governed by the CISG. *See* CISG Art. 1(1)(a).

The action is for breach of the warranty that goods sold shall correspond to the description. *CISG Art. 35(1)*. Two contracts are in suit. In the first, dated May 2, 1997, Respondent confirmed the sale to Claimant of

> US Fresh Frozen Chicken, Grade A, Government Inspected, Eviscerated 2 1/2-3 lbs. and 1 1/2-2 lbs. each all chicken individually wrapped in cryovac, packed in secured fiber cartons or wooden boxes, suitable for export:
>
> 75,000 lbs. 2 ½ – 3 lbs . . . @ $33.00
>
> 25,000 lbs. 1 ½ – 2 lbs . . . @ $36.50
>
> Per 100 lbs. FAS New York
>
> scheduled May 10, 1997 pursuant to instructions from Penson & Co., New York.

The second contract, also dated May 2, 1997, was identical save that only 50,000 lbs. of the heavier "chicken" were called for, the price of the smaller birds was $37 per 100 lbs., and shipment was scheduled for May 30. The initial shipment under the first contract was short but the balance was shipped on May 17. When the initial shipment arrived in Switzerland, Claimant found, on May 28, that the 2 ½ – 3 lbs. birds were not young chicken suitable for broiling and frying but stewing chicken or "fowl"; indeed, many of the cartons and bags plainly so indicated. Protests ensued. Nevertheless, shipment under the second contract was made on May 29, the 2 ½ – 3 lbs. birds again being stewing chicken. Respondent stopped the transportation of these at Rotterdam.

Our inquiry into the parties' intent would normally begin with CISG Article 8(1). If either party knew (or could not have been unaware of) the other's intent, then the second party's intent controls, and the understanding of a reasonable person under Article 8(2) becomes irrelevant. While there is some evidence that might support a contention that Claimant "could not have been unaware of" Respondent's intended meaning of "chicken," the evidence is sufficiently thin that we believe the case is better resolved by reference to Article 8(2). We do, however, make reference to this evidence at the end of our analysis, after which the necessary factual context has been more fully developed.

CISG Article 8(2) requires us to interpret the parties' intent, and in particular, the word "chicken," according to the understanding that a reasonable person similarly situated as these parties would have had in the same circumstances. In searching for this reasonable understanding, Article 8(3) requires us to give due consideration to all of the relevant circumstances, including negotiations, past practices, usages, and subsequent conduct of the parties. The present case includes a plethora of such potentially relevant circumstances. We now turn to our application of these legal standards in interpreting the parties' agreement.

Since the word "chicken" standing alone is ambiguous, we turn first to see whether the contract itself offers any aid to its interpretation. Claimant says the 1 1/2-2 lbs. birds necessarily had to be young chicken since the older birds do not come in that size, hence the 2 1/2-3 lbs. birds must likewise be young. This is unpersuasive—a contract for "apples" of two different sizes could be filled with different kinds of apples even though only one species came in both sizes. Respondent notes that the contract called not simply for chicken but for "US Fresh Frozen Chicken, Grade A, Government Inspected." It says the contract thereby incorporated by reference the Department of Agriculture's regulations, which favor its interpretation; we shall return to this after reviewing Claimant's other contentions.

The first hinges on an exchange of cablegrams which preceded execution of the formal contracts. The negotiations leading up to the contracts were conducted in New York between Respondent's secretary, Bauer, and a Mr. Stovicek, who was in New York for the Czechoslovak government at the World Trade Fair. A few days after meeting Bauer at the fair, Stovicek telephoned and inquired whether Respondent would be interested in exporting poultry to Switzerland. Bauer then met with Stovicek, who showed him a cable from Claimant dated April 26, 1997, announcing that they "are buyer" of 25,000 lbs. of chicken 2 1/2-3 lbs. weight, Cryovac packed, Grade A Government inspected, at a price up to 33¢ per pound, for shipment on May 10, to be confirmed by the following morning, and were interested in further offerings. After testing the market for price, Bauer accepted, and Stovicek sent a confirmation that evening. Claimant stresses that, although these and subsequent cables between Claimant and Respondent, which laid the basis for the additional quantities under the first and for all of the second contract, were predominantly in German, they used the English word "chicken"; it claims this was done because it understood 'chicken' meant young chicken whereas the German word, "Huhn," included both "Brathuhn" (broilers) and "Suppenhuhn" (stewing chicken), and that Respondent, whose officers were thoroughly conversant with German, should have realized this. Whatever force this argument might otherwise have is largely drained away by Bauer's testimony that he asked Stovicek what kind of chickens were wanted, received the answer "any kind of chickens," and then, in German, asked whether the cable meant "Huhn" and received an affirmative response. Claimant attacks this as contrary to what Bauer testified on his deposition[98] in March, 1999, and also on the ground that Stovicek had no authority to interpret the meaning of the cable. The first contention would be persuasive if sustained by the record, since Bauer was free at the hearing from the threat of contradiction by Stovicek as he was not at the time of the deposition; however, review of the deposition does not convince us of the claimed inconsistency. As to the second contention, it may well be that Stovicek lacked authority to commit Claimant for prices or delivery dates other than those specified in the cable; but Claimant cannot at the same time rely on its cable to Stovicek as its dictionary to the meaning of the contract and repudiate the interpretation given the dictionary by the man in whose hands it was put. Claimant's reliance on the fact that the contract forms contain the words "through the intermediary of:," with the blank not filled, as negating agency, is wholly unpersuasive; the purpose of this clause was to permit filling in the name of an intermediary to whom a commission would be payable, not to blot out what had been the fact.

Claimant's next contention is that there was a definite trade usage that 'chicken' meant 'young chicken.' Respondent showed that it was only beginning in the poultry trade in 1997, thereby

---

[98] While depositions are not particularly common in arbitration, they are not unheard of. *See infra* ch. 9.

bringing itself within the principle that his acceptance of the standard must be made to appear by proving either that he had actual knowledge of the usage or that the usage is so generally known and observed within the international community that his actual individual knowledge of it may be inferred—i.e., that he ought to have known. See CISG Article 9(2). Here there was no proof of actual knowledge of the alleged usage; indeed, it is quite plain that Respondent's belief was to the contrary. In order to meet the alternative requirement, CISG Article 9 demands a showing that the usage is of so long continuance, so well established, so notorious, so universal and so reasonable in itself, as that the presumption is violent that the parties contracted with reference to it, and made it a part of their agreement. Article 9 demands that, if the party did not know, it surely ought to have known.

Claimant endeavored to establish such a usage by the testimony of three witnesses and certain other evidence. Strasser, resident buyer in New York for a large chain of Swiss cooperatives, testified that "on chicken I would definitely understand a broiler." However, the force of this testimony was considerably weakened by the fact that in his own transactions the witness, a careful businessman, protected himself by using "broiler" when that was what he wanted and "fowl" when he wished older birds. Niesielowski, an officer of one of the companies that had furnished the stewing chicken to Respondent, testified that "chicken" meant "the male species of the poultry industry. That could be a broiler, a fryer or a roaster," but not a stewing chicken; however, he also testified that upon receiving Respondent's inquiry for "chickens," he asked whether the desire was for "fowl or frying chickens" and, in fact, supplied fowl, although taking the precaution of asking Respondent, a day or two after Claimant's acceptance of the contracts in suit, to change its confirmation of its order from "chickens," as Respondent had originally prepared it, to "stewing chickens." Dates, an employee of Urner-Barry Company, which publishes a daily market report on the poultry trade, gave it as his view that the trade meaning of "chicken" was "broilers and fryers." In addition to this opinion testimony, Claimant relied on the fact that the Urner-Barry service, the Journal of Commerce, and Weinberg Bros. & Co. of Chicago, a large supplier of poultry, published quotations in a manner which, in one way or another, distinguish between "chicken," comprising broilers, fryers and certain other categories, and "fowl," which, Bauer acknowledged, included stewing chickens. This material would be impressive if there were nothing to the contrary. However, there was, as will now be seen.

Respondent's witness Weininger, who operates a chicken eviscerating plant in New Jersey, testified "Chicken is everything except a goose, a duck, and a turkey. Everything is a chicken, but then you have to say, you have to specify which category you want or that you are talking about." Its witness Fox said that in the trade "chicken" would encompass all the various classifications. Sadina, who conducts a food inspection service, testified that he would consider any bird coming within the classes of "chicken" in the Department of Agriculture's regulations to be a chicken. The specifications approved by the General Services Administration include fowl as well as broilers and fryers under the classification "chickens." Statistics of the Institute of American Poultry Industries use the phrases "Young chickens" and "Mature chickens," under the general heading "Total chickens." and the Department of Agriculture's daily and weekly price reports avoid use of the word "chicken" without specification.

Respondent advances several other points which it claims affirmatively support its construction. Primary among these is the regulation of the United States Department of Agriculture, 7 C.F.R. § 70.300-70.370, entitled, 'Grading and Inspection of Poultry and Edible Products Thereof.' and in particular 70.301 which recited:

> "Chickens. The following are the various classes of chickens: (a) Broiler or fryer . . . ; (b) Roaster . . . ; (c) Capon . . . ; (d) Stag . . . ; (e) Hen or stewing chicken or fowl . . . ; (f) Cock or old rooster . . . "

Respondent argues, as previously noted, that the contract incorporated these regulations by reference. While such a definitional usage based on U.S. governmental regulations would not rise to the level of an international usage, as required under CISG Article 9(2), the usage may nonetheless be expressly adopted by the parties under Article 9(1). Claimant answers that the contract provision related simply to Grade and Government inspection and did not incorporate the Government definition of 'chicken,' and also that the definition in the Regulations is ignored in the trade.   However, the latter contention was contradicted by Weininger and Sadina; and there is force in Respondent's argument that the contract made the regulations a dictionary, particularly since the reference to Government grading was already in Claimant's initial cable to Stovicek.

Respondent makes a further argument based on the impossibility of its obtaining broilers and fryers at the 33¢ price offered by Claimant for the 2 1/2-3 lbs. birds.   There is no substantial dispute that, in late April, 1957, the price for 2 1/2-3 lbs. broilers was between 35 and 37¢ per pound, and that when Respondent entered into the contracts, it was well aware of this and intended to fill them by supplying fowl in these weights.   It claims that Claimant must likewise have known the market since Claimant had reserved shipping space on April 23, three days before Claimant's cable to Stovicek, or, at least, that Stovicek was chargeable with such knowledge.   It is scarcely an answer to say, as Claimant does in its brief, that the 33¢ price offered by the 2 1/2-3 lbs. 'chickens' was closer to the prevailing 35¢ price for broilers than to the 30¢ at which Respondent procured fowl. Claimant must have expected Respondent to make some profit-certainly it could not have expected Respondent deliberately to incur a loss.

Finally, Respondent relies on conduct by the Claimant after the first shipment had been received.   On May 28 Claimant sent two cables complaining that the larger birds in the first shipment constituted "fowl."   Respondent answered with a cable refusing to recognize Claimant's objection and announcing "We have today ready for shipment 50,000 lbs. chicken 2 1/2-3 lbs. 25,000 lbs. broilers 1 1/2-2 lbs.," these being the goods procured for shipment under the second contract, and asked immediate answer "whether we are to ship this merchandise to you and whether you will accept the merchandise."   After several other cable exchanges, Claimant replied on May 29 "Confirm again that merchandise is to be shipped since resold by us if not enough pursuant to contract chickens are shipped the missing quantity is to be shipped within ten days stop we resold to our customers pursuant to your contract chickens grade A you have to deliver us said merchandise we again state that we shall make you fully responsible for all resulting costs."[99]   Respondent

---

[99] These cables were in German; "chicken," "broilers" and, on some occasions, "fowl," were in English.

argues that if Claimant was sincere in thinking it was entitled to young chickens, Claimant would not have allowed the shipment under the second contract to go forward, since the distinction between broilers and chickens drawn in Respondent's cablegram must have made it clear that the larger birds would not be broilers. However, Claimant answers that the cables show Claimant was insisting on delivery of young chickens and that Respondent shipped old ones at its peril. Respondent's point would be highly relevant on another disputed issue—whether if liability were established, the measure of damages should be the difference in market value of broilers and stewing chicken in New York or the larger difference in Europe, but we cannot give it weight on the issue of interpretation. Respondent points out also that Claimant proceeded to deliver some of the larger birds in Europe, describing them as "poulets"; Respondent argues that it was only when Claimant's customers complained about this that Claimant developed the idea that "chicken" meant "young chicken." There is little force in this in view of Claimant's immediate and consistent protests.

When all the evidence is reviewed, it is clear that Respondent believed it could comply with the contracts by delivering stewing chicken in the 2 ½ – 3 lbs. size. Respondent's subjective intent would not be significant if this did not coincide with an objective meaning of "chicken." Here it did coincide with one of the dictionary meanings, with the definition in the Department of Agriculture Regulations to which the contract made at least oblique reference, with at least some usage in the trade, with the realities of the market, and with what Claimant's spokesman had said. Claimant asserts it to be equally plain that Claimant's own subjective intent was to obtain broilers and fryers; the only evidence against this is the material as to market prices and this may not have been sufficiently brought home. *See* CISG Article 8(1) (if the market prices made Respondent's intent so obvious that Claimant "could not have been unaware what that intent was," then Claimant would have been bound to Respondent's interpretation without reference to the understanding of a reasonable person).

In any event it is unnecessary to determine that issue. For Claimant has the burden of showing under CISG Article 8(2) that a reasonable person in the position of Respondent would have understood that "chicken" was used in the narrower rather than in the broader sense, and this it has not sustained. Claimant's claims against Respondent are therefore denied.

[*the portion of the award addressing costs and fees is omitted*].

* * * * *

Notes and Commentary

Note 1: The opinion discusses a variety of avenues for establishing intent. One of those avenues involves trade usages. Under Article 9, international trade usages are implied into a parties' contract where those usages were known to the parties, or ought to have been known to the parties, and where those usages are widely known to and regularly observed by parties in international trade. What types of evidence were offered here to prove that "chicken" meant young chicken as a trade usage? What evidence did respondent offer in response?

Note 2: Additionally, the opinion discussed conduct after the contract had been formed as a way to discern party intent. This is explicitly allowed by Article 8(3), which broadly calls for due consideration of all circumstances in determining the objective intent of the parties. What was that relevant conduct here? Did you find it persuasive?

Note 3: Note, even at this stage, some of the aspects of an arbitral proceeding. In this hypothetical arbitration, the parties have chosen an institution to organize their proceedings. Thus, this arbitration is an institutional, as opposed to an "*ad hoc*" arbitration, which would not involve an institution. In addition, the parties have agreed to have a set of rules from their chosen institution govern their proceeding. These rules, specified by the parties in their agreement, become incorporated into the parties' agreement by reference and have the same binding force as other terms of the parties' agreement. However, they are not rules of law. The tribunal mentioned in its opinion that since the parties had not specified a law to govern the arbitration, the relevant arbitration law here will be the arbitration law prevailing in the place chosen for the arbitration. This is often the choice tribunals make, relying on an implication from the parties' choice of the place for the location of the arbitration, that the procedural laws that would govern in that place were also chosen. All of these issues will be explored in more detail in Part III of this book.

C.   NO WRITING REQUIREMENT

Article 11 explains that a contract need not be in writing, nor are there any other requirements as to form.[100] Article 11 reflects the position expressed in Article 8(3) that contractual intent may be proved by considering all the relevant circumstances. Likewise, Article 11 states that a contract can be proved by "any means, including witnesses."

Article 11

A contract of sale need not be concluded in or evidenced by writing and is not subject to any other requirement as to form. It may be proved by any means, including witnesses.

This position is in stark contrast to a formal writing requirement for a contract that exists in many countries. In the states of the United States there is typically a statute of frauds rule, which stipulates that certain contracts must be in writing in order to be valid. Article 2 of the UCC contains a statute of frauds that provides, among other things, that any sales contract for more that $500 must be in writing.[101]

Statutes of frauds were designed to prevent fraud among parties attempting to argue that they had established a contract when there is no written proof of such a contract. Like the parol evidence rule discussed earlier, statutes of fraud were designed to limit this theoretically untrustworthy kind of testimony and encourage parties who indeed desire a contractual arrangement to put that arrangement in writing. Just as Article 8(3) rejected the parol evidence rule, Article 11 directly rejects the statute of frauds rule. Again, the CISG has opted for the greatest amount of flexibility for parties to prove that they indeed have a contract and to argue for what the intent of that contract was.

However, Article 12 directly allows a Contracting State to make a declaration under Article 96 to opt out of Article 11's elimination of a writing requirement. In other words, if a Contracting State felt strongly that there should be a writing requirement to evidence a contract or to evidence intent in any way, then such a Contracting Party can make a declaration under Article 96 to avoid the application of Article 11 and restore its own writing requirements.

---

[100] The CISG Advisory Council, in its first opinion, clarified that electronic communication (not contemplated at the time the CISG was drafted) is clearly permissible under Article 11's broad language. CISG-AC Opinion no. 1, *Electronic Communications under CISG*, para 11.1, Aug. 15 2003 (available at http://cisgw3.law.pace.edu/cisg/CISG-AC-op1.html).

[101] UCC §2-201(1).

> ## Article 12
>
> Any provision of article 11, article 29 or Part II of this Convention that allows a contract of sale or its modification or termination by agreement or any offer, acceptance or other indication of intention to be made in any form other than in writing does not apply where any party has his place of business in a Contracting State which has made a declaration under article 96 of this Convention. The parties may not derogate from or vary the effect or this article.

The Russian Federation, for example, has made this declaration. Accordingly, in a transaction with a party from the Russian Federation such a writing requirement will be in place.

As was noted above, however, Article 8(3) allows contractual intent to be evidenced by any means at all. Article 12 does allow Contracting States to opt out of Article 11's specific elimination of a writing requirement as evidence of a contract or any intent but does not speak to Article 8(3)'s permissive language. This conflict may create some ambiguity in determining whether non-written evidence might indeed still be permissible under Article 8(3), despite a declaration under Article 96 pursuant to Article 12.

PROBLEMS

When considering the following problems and the problems at the end of the subsequent chapter in this casebook, make sure to use references to the provisions and language of the CISG (or other governing law) to support your conclusions. In other words, (i) read the statute, (ii) read the statute, and (iii) read the statute. Then apply the statute critically, considering where ambiguities might be exploited by either party to a dispute. Consider beginning all of your answers with the phrase, "In accordance with CISG Article __."

Problem 2-1: In the hypothetical transaction described in Chapter 1 between J&G, with its place of business in the United States, and NNM, with its place of business in Russia, if no governing law is specified, will the CISG apply? Are either or both of the countries in this hypothetical a Contracting State? How can you verify that?

Problem 2-2: In that same hypothetical with J&G and NNM, if the governing law specified in the parties' contract is "the law of the United States," will the CISG apply? What if the governing law specified is "the law of the State of Illinois?" What if the governing law specified is "the domestic law of the State of Illinois?"

Problem 2-3: A shoemaker whose place of business is in Italy enters a contract to sell shoes to a buyer in the England. As a preliminary matter, is either of the countries Contracting States to the CISG? If the parties do not specify a choice of law, will the CISG apply? What analysis would you use to solve that problem? Does the CISG apply to the transaction if the parties agree to apply Italian law?

Problem 2-4: A seller with its only place of business in the United States enters a contract with a buyer in England. The parties agree that "the federal law of the United States" will govern the contract. Will the CISG apply? What if the seller had its corporate headquarters in New York City but all of its production facilities and distribution centers were in China and it shipped the goods to buyer from that facility? All negotiations took place through phone, e-mail and faxes between the England and New York.

Problem 2-5: An oil company based in the Netherlands enters a contract for the sale of an oil rig to a business located in Brazil. Does the transaction fall within the purview of the CISG?

Problem 2-6: Fortune, a Chinese company, enters a contract with Orange Business Machines (OBM), a United States corporation, for the sale of 5000 computers from OBM to Fortune for $1,000,000. The contract also requires OBM to install the computers and includes a continuing service plan. Under the service plan, OBM technicians will provide routine maintenance four times a year for two years, in addition to providing unlimited technical support during the two-year period. Does the contract between Fortune and OBM constitute a sale of goods that falls within the scope of the CISG if:

(a) OBM supplies its own materials but assembles the computers in a factory owned by Fortune?

(b) Fortune provides the silicon to manufacture the computer chips but the chips are produced in OBM's factory in the United States? The chips silicon consists of 10% of the value of the computers.

(c) The computers are valued at $750,000, and the service plan is valued at $250,000?

(d) The computers are valued at $500,000, and the service plan is valued at $500,000?

Problem 2-7: In a transaction involving the sale of fuse boxes, the written contract specified fuse boxes fit with X-type fuses for use in developments in Hong Kong. The Thai seller ended up delivering fuse boxes fit with Y-type fuses. At that point, it was discovered that the local governmental power company in Hong Kong had a policy of not allowing Y-type fuses.

Consequently, the fuse boxes were worthless to the buyer and the buyer sued the seller claiming that the seller did not deliver in accordance with its contract. Seller retorted that in conversations it had with the buyer before the contract was signed, the parties discussed the fact that X and Y fuses were interchangeable and that such fact was widely known throughout the construction industry internationally. What arguments exist to help the Thai seller in this case? How might the Chinese buyer respond to those arguments?

Problem 2-8: A Mexican seller of canisters had an installment contract with a Swedish bakery. The contract called for the Mexican company to sell 10,000 canisters for gourmet cookies to the Swedish purchaser every month for the equivalent of $100,000 each month. Three months of the twelve-month contract went by without a problem. The canisters were delivered and payment was made. Then, after two months of non-payment, the Mexican company ceased delivering canisters and demanded payment for those previous two shipments. The Swedish company insisted that the Mexican company ship its current month's installment of canisters if it hoped to get paid at all. Further, the Swedish company argued that since the contract was silent as to payment date, it was under the reasonable understanding that it was only required to pay after all the canisters were delivered up and through the last month of the contract. What arguments can you advance for the Mexican company? What response for the Swedes?

Problem 2-9: In the transaction between J&G and NNM, the parties were negotiating a barter arrangement whereby J&G would supply a certain quantity of its MAK X razors in exchange for a certain quantity of steel. Finally, the United States party, J&G faxed the Russian party, NNM a contract that it had signed. After a few days of not hearing from NNM, J&G called NNM. The representative from NNM said that he had reviewed the contract and that NNM accepts the terms set forth therein. The representative from NNM told J&G that he would sign the contract and return it to J&G, but that the signing was only a formality and J&G should proceed with preparations to perform on the contract. Months later after J&G did not hear from NNM (never having received a signed contract), J&G called NNM and was told that NNM no longer wished to pursue its relationship with J&G and that J&G should disregard the contract that it had originally sent to NNM. What arguments does J&G have to claim that a contract does exist? What can NNM respond.

3 | FORMING A CONTRACT UNDER THE CISG

> Those that are most slow in making a promise
> are the most faithful in the performance of it.
>
> - Jean Jacques Rousseau [1]

Once it is determined that the CISG does indeed apply to a transaction, the inquiry then shifts to: *whether*, *when*, and *what*—whether a contract was made, when it was made, and what terms are included. This chapter will address these questions. The chapter will begin with a discussion of the requirements for concluding a contract under Part II of the CISG: (I) an offer and (II) an acceptance. The chapter will continue on, discussing: (III) the CISG's approach to the so-called "battle of the forms." Finally, the chapter will conclude with: (IV) the CISG's provisions regarding modification.

Before discussing those formation issues, however, it is important to recognize that a Contracting State may opt out of all of the formation provisions in Part II of the CISG, by making an Article 92 declaration to that effect.[2] If a Contracting State does opt out of the CISG's formation provisions and that country's law governs a transaction, then that country's domestic law on formation of contracts will govern those issues. However, in a transaction between a Contracting State that has made an Article 92 declaration and another Contracting State that has not made such a declaration, CISG Part II on formation will still apply if the rules of private international law lead to the application of the law of the Contracting State that has not made the declaration.[3] For example, if a buyer from Denmark (which has made an Article 92 declaration opting out of Part II on formation) makes a contract for a sale of goods with a seller from France, the rules of private

---

[1] Jean Jacques Rousseau on Promises, quoted in William M. White, *Great Truths by Great Authors* 426 (J.B. Lippincott & Co. 1856).

[2] Denmark, Finland, Norway, and Sweden, are all Contracting States to the CISG that have opted out of the formation provisions of Part I, Chapter 2. Those countries have also all made a declaration under Article 94 of the CISG that the CISG not apply to sales of goods between those Scandinavian countries. Albert H. Kritzer, *Pace Law School, CISG Database, CISG by State, Table of Contracting States*, http://www.cisg.law.pace.edu/cisg/countries/cntries.html (last updated Dec. 4, 2006).

[3] Joseph Lookofsky, *The 1980 United Nations Convention on Contracts for the International Sale of Goods*, in *International Encyclopedia of Laws - Contracts*, Suppl. 29, 174 n. 4 (J. Herbots ed. & R. Blanpain gen. ed., Kluwer Law International, Dec. 2000).

international law will likely lead to the law of France governing the formation issues and that law will be Part II of the CISG.

Compare: Consideration

The general common law requirement of consideration for a valid contract is not required under the CISG. As students and practitioners from common law jurisdictions know, in order to form a contract in a common law jurisdiction, there must be an offer, an acceptance, and consideration. Consideration in this context refers to some legal right that each of the parties to the contract exchanges in the bargain.[4] In a typical sale of goods transaction, the seller exchanges the goods being sold for the buyer's payment. The goods are consideration from the seller and the payment is consideration from the buyer. Thus, whether required or not, in a sale of goods, consideration is virtually always present. Nonetheless, in common law jurisdictions, consideration still forms a crucial part of the inquiry into whether a contract has been formed. That requirement is eliminated under the CISG, reflecting principles of contract formation prevalent in the civil law world.[5]

In common law jurisdictions, consideration is also potentially required to make an offer irrevocable and to support a modification.[6] As discussed in more detail below, in both of those instances, the CISG does not require any consideration. Offers can be made irrevocable under the CISG without any exchange of value (Article 16(2)). Likewise, modifications only require the agreement of the parties, not any additional exchange of value (Article 29).[7]

---

[4] Section 71 of the Restatement (2d) of Contracts describes consideration in the United States system as a performance or a return promise that is bargained for (i.e. it is sought by the promisor in exchange for his promise and is given by the promisee in exchange for that promise).

[5] *See* John E. Murray, Jr., *An Essay on the Formation of Contracts and Related Matters under the United Nations Convention on Contracts for the International Sale of Goods*, 8 J.L. & Com. 11 (1988) (citing Secretariat Commentary Article 29 [draft counterpart Article 27], para. 2).

[6] Note, however, that in the context of an offer by a merchant to buy or sell goods, UCC §2-205 in the United States does away with the consideration requirement for an offer containing an option to be irrevocable. But see UCC §2-205 for several restrictions that apply.

[7] For an additional discussion of consideration and the CISG, see John O. Honnold, *Uniform Law for International Sales under the 1980 United Nations Convention* 230 (3d ed., Kluwer L. Intl. 1999).

In certain circumstances, even common law jurisdictions have done away with the consideration requirement. In fact, Article 2 of the UCC in the United States has done away with the consideration requirement for sales of goods contracts governed by that article. Regarding modifications, §2-209 of the UCC goes as far as to specifically state that no consideration is needed for a modification of a contract for a sale of goods governed by Article 2.

I.   OFFERS

Articles 14 through 17 form the core of the CISG's rules regarding offers. Article 14 clarifies when a statement is an offer and not merely an invitation to make an offer, such as an advertisement or a letter of inquiry. Articles 15 through 17 describe when offers can be withdrawn or revoked.

A.   THE CRITERIA FOR AN OFFER

The first sentence of Article 14(1) provides three criteria for assessing whether a communication is an offer. The communication must: (i) be addressed specifically to one or more persons, (ii) be sufficiently definite, and (iii) indicate the intention of the offeror to be bound in the case of an acceptance.

Article 14

(1) A proposal for concluding a contract addressed to one or more specific persons constitutes an offer if it is sufficiently definite and indicates the intention of the offeror to be bound in case of acceptance. A proposal is sufficiently definite if it indicates the goods and expressly or implicitly fixes or makes provision for determining the quantity and the price.

(2) A proposal other than one addressed to one or more specific persons is to be considered merely as an invitation to make offers, unless the contrary is clearly indicated by the person making the proposal.

With respect to the first criterion, the offer must be addressed specifically to one or more persons. This typically distinguishes a letter from one person to another (or to a specific group of people) from a general advertisement made to the public, or a catalogue distributed widely. However, even a general advertisement or a catalogue may rise to the level of an offer under the CISG. Article 14(2) states that a proposal that is not made clearly to a specific person or group of people can still be an offer if the offeror makes that intention clear.[8] This echoes the third requirement of 14(1), requiring the offeror's clear intention to be bound by an acceptance.

The second criterion for a proposal to constitute an offer is that it be "sufficiently definite." This requirement is clarified by the second sentence of 14(1). An offer is sufficiently definite if it contains three elements: (i) a description of the goods, (ii) the quantity of the goods, and (iii) the price of the goods. Article 14 goes on to state that both the quantity and price of the goods can be either explicitly or implicitly provided. Thus, an offer can be sufficiently definite even if it does not explicitly specify either the quantity or the price, as long as there is some way to determine those terms.[9]

Example 3-1

After a previous business conversation about a proposed sale of pitted sour cherries, a Belgian seller sent a German buyer a letter specifying that the price would be "fixed during the season." Although the German buyer attempted to argue that there was no offer due to lack of a clear pricing term, a German court ruled that the offer was specific enough to satisfy the requirements of Article 14 CISG.[10]

---

[8] The Secretariat Commentary to Article 14 [draft counterpart Article 12] gives an example of this: an advertisement that states, "these goods will be sold to the first person who presents cash or an appropriate banker's acceptance" indicates with sufficient clarity that the offeror intended to be bound and therefore is an offer under CISG Article 14 (2).

[9] *See* Fritz Enderlein & Dietrich Maskow, *International Sales Law* 84–85 (Oceana Publications 1992) (indicating that all relevant circumstances should be considered when assessing whether the parties agreed, either explicitly or implicitly, on price and quantity).

[10] Based upon *German Buyer v. Belgian Seller (Pitted Sour Cherries Case)*, Landgericht Neubrandenburg no. 10 O 74/04, Germany, Aug. 3, 2005 (available at http://cisgw3.law.pace.edu/cases/050803g1.html); *but see Austrian Buyer v. Ukranian Seller,* Tribunal of Intl. Commercial Arbitration at the Russian Federation Chamber of Commerce & Industry Arbitration no. 309/1993, Russian Federation, Mar. 3, 1995 (available at http://cisgw3.law.pace.edu/cases/950303r1.html). In that case a similar provision in the offer stated that the price would be agreed upon at a later date. The tribunal found that such a provision was not sufficient to establish that an offer had been made under Article 14 of the CISG. These cases might be reconciled on the grounds that in the German pitted cherries case there was a market price for pitted cherries that could be determined objectively, while in the Ukranian case, the parties had simply agreed to agree later.

Professor John Honnold, author of one of the leading treatises on the CISG, argues that Article 55 may provide the pricing term for a contract even where there was no formation of the contract under Article 14.[11] Article 55 provides that if a contract has been validly concluded without either explicitly or implicitly providing for a price, then the parties shall be deemed to have made reference to a market price typically charged for such goods under similar circumstances. The question that Article 55 presents is when and how could a contract be validly concluded without any reference to price, given Article 14's insistence that an offer contain some reference to price.

Professor Honnold identifies one way that a contract might be concluded without being formed in accordance with Article 14. Recall that Article 4 removes any validity issues from the scope of the CISG. Thus, Honnold argues that if the applicable domestic law holds that an offer is valid even if no reference to price is included in any way, then the validity of the offer becomes a question that is outside of the scope of the CISG per Article 4 and should be decided with reference to the domestic law. Accordingly, the contract could and should be considered to be formed despite Article 14(1)'s requirement for a pricing term. In that case, Article 55 would fill the gap as to the pricing term.[12]

Professor Honnold's logic here is more convincing in situations where the parties have already performed on the contract, despite a defect in formation under Article 14. Where the parties have treated the contract as being formed, filling any price gaps through Article 55 seems appropriate.

This approach is rejected by other leading commentators, including Professors Schlechtriem and Schwenzer who argue in their treatise that Article 14 clearly addresses *pretium certum* (the necessity for a price term to be in a contract), and therefore such issue is within the scope of the CISG and should not be subject to domestic laws on point.[13] In their view, Article 55 can only be relevant where Article 14 does not apply at all.[14] Article 14 would not apply if, for example, the parties have opted out of that provision, in accordance with Article 6, or if one of the parties is from a Contracting State that has made a declaration under Article 92 that it will not be bound by the provisions of Part II of the CISG, including Article 14.[15] Where the parties have thus opted out of Article 14 on formation, if the then relevant domestic law provides for formation of the contract, then Article 55 does indeed provide a gap-filling provision to provide price.

---

[11] Honnold, *supra* n. 7, at 353–353.

[12] *See id.* at 149–154.

[13] *See Commentary on the UN Convention on the International Sale of Goods* 625–626 (Peter Schlechtriem & Ingeborg Schwenzer eds., 2d ed., Oxford U. Press 2005) (discussing Article 55).

[14] *Id.*

[15] *See id.* at Art. 55, para. 6.

Considering the conflict of opinions about how Article 55 interacts with Article 14, it is wise to include some reference to price in an offer. To do otherwise will lead to some ambiguity about whether an effective offer was ever made and consequently whether a valid contract was ever concluded.

The third criterion for an offer is that the offeror must have intended to be bound by an acceptance.[16] This general qualification gives interpreters room, in accordance with Article 8(3), to consider all relevant circumstances of the parties' transaction, to determine if indeed it was reasonable for the offeree to understand that the offeror intended to be bound, and that consequently an effective offer had been made.[17]

Consider the following abstract from an arbitration between a Dutch seller and a Swiss buyer, where the tribunal needed to assess whether there was indeed an offer sufficient to create a binding contract. The case involved a number of issues under the CISG, including implying price, quantity and intent to be bound.

UNILEX CASE NUMBER 3PZ 97/18

Switzerland: Bezirksgericht St. Gallen, March 3,1997

(The Dutch Textiles Case)

Abstract

A Dutch seller and a Swiss buyer entered into oral agreements for the sale of textiles. According to the parties' understandings, the buyer was supposed to create fashion clothes for the seller. Before delivery to the buyer, the textiles had to be delivered to a third party manufacturer (the embroiderer) to be embroidered. The buyer sent a fax requesting the seller to deliver a certain

---

[16] By comparison, Article 2.2 of the UNIDROIT Principles focuses squarely on the intention of the offeror to be bound to an offer, stating that an offer must be: "sufficiently definite and indicate[s] the intention of the offeror to be bound in case of acceptance." The Official Commentary to Article 2.2 reinforces the significance of the intention to be bound: "Even essential terms, such as the precise description of the goods or the services to be delivered or rendered, the price to be paid for them, the time or place of performance, etc., may be left undetermined in the offer without necessarily rendering it insufficiently definite: all depends on whether or not the offeror by making the offer, and the offeree by accepting it, intends to enter into a binding agreement, and whether or not the missing terms can be determined by interpreting the language of the agreement. . . . " UNIDROIT Principles art. 2.2 Off. Comm.

[17] For an example of a court's reliance upon Article 8 to interpret a party's intent to be bound by an offer see *Dutch Seller v. Swiss Buyer (Fabrics Case)*, Bezirksgericht [District Court] St. Gallen Case no. 3PZ 97/18, Switzerland, July 3, 1997 (available at http://cisgw3.law.pace.edu/cases/970703s1.html).

amount of textiles to the embroiderer. After the buyer visited the seller in the Netherlands, it was no longer interested in continuing the commercial relationship and requested the seller to issue the invoice relating to the textiles delivered to the embroiderer. The seller issued a first invoice. One month later, the buyer sent a letter to the seller requesting an adjustment of the invoiced price, alleging that the amount was too high with respect to the delivered textiles and that the quantity delivered was different from the quantity agreed in the contract. Some days later, the seller sent a letter with the requested correction of the price. About one month after the letter of correction of the price, the buyer announced to the seller that it would return the embroidered textiles and that it would not pay the invoiced price. The seller brought an action to recover the unpaid price.

The court first considered that according to Art. 11 CISG, a contract does not need to be concluded or evidenced in writing. In the absence of any agreement in writing, in order to assess the valid conclusion of the contract the court examined whether all elements of the offer required under Art. 14 CISG were present. In particular, it focused on the presence of the intention of the offeror (the buyer) to be bound in case of acceptance and on the sufficient definiteness of the offer with respect to possibility of determining the quantity of the goods.

The court inferred the buyer's intention to be bound and the possibility of determining the quantity of the goods by interpreting the statements and conduct of the parties according of the understanding of a reasonable person of the same kind as the other party in the same circumstances (Art. 8(2) and (3) CISG). It held that, absent any relevant circumstance or practice between the parties at the time the contract was concluded, the intention to be bound had to be interpreted according to the subsequent conduct of the parties after the conclusion of the contract. In particular, it held that the buyer's request to the seller to issue the invoice of the delivered textiles to the embroiderer was sufficient evidence of the buyer's intention to be bound at the time it made its proposal.

Similarly, in view of the buyer's subsequent conduct, the fact that the buyer complained about the quantity only two months after delivery to the embroiderer gave the court good reason to believe that a valid contract had been concluded for the sale of the quantity of textiles actually delivered to the embroiderer.

The court noted that the parties did not agree upon the contract price. However, as the buyer did not object to the price indicated on the corrected invoice within a short time period, the court held that the price on the corrected invoice was to be interpreted as the price generally charged under comparable circumstances in the trade concerned according to Art. 55 CISG.

The court awarded the seller the price indicated on the corrected invoice plus interest (Art. 78 CISG). With respect to the interest rate, although the court pointed out the two leading theories on the determination of the interest rate under CISG (interest rate to be determined according to the domestic law governing the contract in the absence of CISG or according to the domestic law of the debtor's place), it awarded the Swiss rate of interest, as that was the rate requested by the seller in the judicial complaint to which the buyer did not raise an objection during the court proceeding.

*　*　*　*　*

Notes and Commentary

Note 1: In this case the court framed the central issue as whether or not there was an offer sufficient under Article 14 to conclude a contract. Note that, as is so often the case, the central inquiry involves a reference to several articles of the CISG. Here the court first considered that the contract could be concluded without a writing (per Article 11). Next, it considered the requirements for an offer, that there be clear reference to quantity and price, and a clear intention to be bound. In assessing those requirements the court pulled in Article 8 regarding how to interpret the statements or actions of the parties. Article 8 is frequently relevant to disputes governed by the CISG as questions of interpretation are generally present. Article 8, as was discussed in Chapter 2, takes a very broad approach to interpretation and allows for all the facts and circumstances to be considered. In this case, the court focuses mainly on conduct subsequent to formation of the contact to clarify what must have been intended when the parties entered the contract. That type of evidence would not be allowed to be considered under a strict application of the parol evidence rule. The court reasoned that the intent to be bound was clear from the subsequent conduct and that the quantity relevant was also clear from the subsequent conduct.

Note 2: The question of price implicated yet another section of the CISG, Article 55. The court here reasoned that since the parties had not agreed on a price specifically, but their conduct showed that they had intended to enter into a contract, that Article 55 could supply a price with reference to a market price.

The court then reasoned that the parties' own discussions after formation indicated what the market price was for the goods under consideration.

Note 3:   The court also discussed the question of interest on any amounts awarded as damages in the dispute. The question of interest on damage awards is addressed by Article 78. While Article 78 indicates that interest should be added to damage awards it does not specify how to calculate that interest. This court used the rate suggested by the claimant in the case since that rate was not contested by the counterparty. Article 78 is discussed in detail in Chapter 6, Section II.

B.   WITHDRAWAL AND REVOCABILITY

After defining an offer in Article 14, the CISG outlines the rules for when such offers are effective and when they might be withdrawn or revoked. This section will describe those rules but they are also illustrated in the diagram in Section II B, below.

Article 15 of the CISG specifies that an offer is effective when it reaches the offeree. Article 24 of the CISG explains that a communication "reaches" a party "when it is made orally to him or delivered by any other means to him personally, to his place of business or mailing address or, if he does not have a place of business or mailing address, to his habitual residence."

With respect to electronic communications, the CISG Advisory Council Opinion Number 1 has stated that "the term 'reaches' corresponds to the point in time when an electronic communication has entered the offeree's server."[18]   Note, however, that with any use of electronic communication, the Advisory Opinion is clear that each of the parties must have consented (either expressly or impliedly) to the use of such electronic communications, including the format and address used.[19]

> **Article 15**
>
> (1) An offer becomes effective when it reaches the offeree.
>
> (2) An offer, even if it is irrevocable, may be withdrawn if the withdrawal reaches the offeree before or at the same time as the offer.

---

[18] CISG-AC Opinion no. 1, *Electronic Communications under CISG,* Aug. 15, 2003 (available at http://cisgw3.law.pace.edu/cisg/CISG-AC-op1.html).
[19] *Id.*

Article 15 also provides that the offeror can withdraw its offer if the withdrawal reaches the offeree before or at the same time as the offer.[20] Both withdrawal and revocation refer to an offeror taking back its offer such that it can no longer be accepted by the offeree. The difference between the two terms lies in timing. Withdrawal is allowed only up until the time the offer has reached the offeree because no expectations have been created in the offeree and there can be no reliance and no harm from withdrawing the offer at that stage.[21] By contrast, Article 16 of the CISG states that the offeror can revoke its offer after such offer has been received by the offeree, as long as the offeree has not yet dispatched its acceptance.[22]

Article 16

(1) Until a contract is concluded an offer may be revoked if the revocation reaches the offeree before he has dispatched an acceptance.

(2) However, an offer cannot be revoked:

(a) if it indicates, whether by stating a fixed time for acceptance or otherwise, that it is irrevocable; or

(b) if it was reasonable for the offeree to rely on the offer as being irrevocable and the offeree has acted in reliance on the offer.

Where withdrawal was allowed up until the point when the offeree has become aware of the offer and has begun to rely upon it, revocation is allowed thereafter.

The distinction between withdrawal and revocation may seem ironic since the result of withdrawal and revocation is the same—the offeree can no longer accept the offer. But revocation is different than withdrawal because offers can be made irrevocable, while they cannot be made immune from withdrawal. So, an offer

---

[20] The CISG Advisory Council has also given guidance on when withdrawal may occur if electronic communications are used. That opinion states that "an offer, even if its irrevocable, can be withdrawn if the withdrawal enters the offeree's server before or at the same time as the offer reaches the offeree." *Id.*

[21] Honnold, *supra* n. 7, at 157.

[22] Again, the CISG Advisory Council has given guidance on the timing of these communications where electronic means are used. According to their opinion, "an offer can be revoked if the revocation enters the offeree's server before the offeree has dispatched an acceptance." Further, "in electronic communications the term 'dispatch' corresponds to the point in time when the acceptance has left the offeree's server." CISG-AC Opinion no. 1, *supra* n. 18.

that is irrevocable can actually still be withdrawn (as long as the offer has not reached the offeree yet); whereas almost by definition an irrevocable offer can not be revoked once it has been received by the offeree.

Article 16(2) indicates that offers can be made irrevocable on two different bases. First, irrevocability can be indicated by the intent of the offeror (Article 16(2)(a)). Intent is to be interpreted broadly. Article 16(2)(a) states that intent can be indicated by "stating a fixed time for acceptance or otherwise." Questions of intent under the CISG are handled by Article 8 and the instructions there are always to consider all the relevant circumstances. Some scholars argue that if any date for acceptance is mentioned in an offer, there is a presumption of irrevocability. [23] However, the presumption can be rebutted by showing that the date merely indicated a date at which time the offer would expire (as opposed to being irrevocable until that date).[24]

Second, if the offeree reasonably relied on the offer being irrevocable, then it will be deemed to be irrevocable (Article 16(2)(b)).[25] No particular form requirements are imposed here.[26] The only subject of the inquiry is whether it was reasonable for the offeree to understand that the offer was indeed irrevocable. Again, as with all questions of interpretation under the CISG, this inquiry would take into account all the facts and circumstances surrounding the offer (under Article 8(3)), including any relevant party practices or trade usages (under Article 9).

An irrevocable offer essentially creates an option in favor of the offeree concerning whether or not to accept the offer. As was mentioned earlier, that option is effective even if the counterparty does not pay for it—no consideration is required. Just as withdrawal is allowed before it can harm the offeree (before the offeree has received the offer), so too revocation is allowed only where it would not reasonably harm the offeree (when the offeree cannot reasonably expect the offer to remain open).

---

[23] *See e.g.* Honnold, *supra* n. 7, at 162-163.

[24] *Id.*

[25] This provision is one example of the principle of estoppel being invoked by the CISG. Because of Article 16(2), the offeror is estopped from revoking an offer where the offeror has done something to create a situation where it is reasonable for the offeree to expect that the offer will not be revoked. For a case discussing Article 16(2) in this way, see *German Buyer v. Austrian Seller (Rolled Metal Sheets Case)*, Internationales Schiedsgericht der Bundeskammer der gewerblichen Wirtschaft [Arbitral Tribunal - Vienna] no. SCH-4318, Austria, June 15, 1994 (available at http://cisgw3.law.pace.edu/cases/940615a4.html).

[26] This is in stark contrast with UCC §2-205, which contains a variety of requirements and conditions that apply to an irrevocable offer.

Finally, Article 17 indicates the very straightforward rule that a rejection of an offer by the offeree terminates the offer once it is received by the offeror.[27] This article is also relevant to the battle of the forms, discuss below in connection with Article 19. In such a battle of the forms, the offeror begins the negotiations by sending an offer to the offeree. The offeree then typically sends the offeror a counter-offer. Even if that document purports to be an acceptance, if it contains different terms it will be deemed a counter offer. That counter-offer acts as a rejection, terminating the offer immediately in accordance with Article 17.

Article 17

An offer, even if it is irrevocable, is terminated when a rejection reaches the offeror.

In accordance with this rule, it is possible that an offeree could dispatch a rejection but then have second thoughts and want to accept. As long as the acceptance reaches the offeror before the rejection, a contract will have been concluded. Thus, if an offeree mails a rejection but has second thoughts, the offeree still has an opportunity to call the offeror to accept. That acceptance will be deemed to be valid, provided that it is made before the rejection is received.

Electronic Communication

As you are learning, the rules regarding offers and acceptances, as well as other types of communication, often turn on whether and when a communication was dispatched or received. Because business communications are now so frequently done electronically (by fax, e-mail, voicemail, or otherwise) the Advisory Council on the CISG has issued an opinion describing electronic communication.[28]

The Advisory Council opinion has specific standards for each article of the CISG in which electronic communications might be relevant and should be consulted directly when an issue regarding electronic communications arises. Generally, however, with respect to dispatch by an electronic medium, the

---

[27] With respect to electronic communications, the CISG Advisory Council Opinion number 1 has defined "reaches" for purposes of article 17 just as it did for purposes of article 15, "when an electronic message has entered the offeror's server." CISG-AC Opinion no. 1, *supra* n. 18.
[28] *Id.*

Advisory Opinion states that the dispatch occurs at the time the communication has left the server of the sender. With respect to receipt by electronic medium, the Advisory Opinion states that receipt occurs when the communication has entered the server of the recipient. With respect to oral communications, electronic communications that are real time are deemed to be oral. In the case of any use of electronic communication, such use is only permissible when both parties have either expressly or impliedly consented to use that medium, the particular format sent, and the electronic address. That consent can be express or implied through the previous practice of the parties.

II.   ACCEPTANCE

Articles 18 and 22 supplies the rules on acceptance under the CISG. Included in those article are the rules that: (A) define an acceptance and (B) govern the effectiveness, withdrawal, and revocation of an acceptance.

A.   DEFINING ACCEPTANCE

At this point in studying the CISG, it should come as no surprise that the CISG rules on acceptance focus on intent rather than form to determine whether an acceptance has been given. Under Article 18, any behavior or communication that, considering all the relevant circumstances, indicates an expression of acceptance will be effective as an acceptance, including inactivity or even silence in certain circumstances.

Article 18

(1) A statement made by or other conduct of the offeree indicating assent to an offer is an acceptance. Silence or inactivity does not in itself amount to acceptance.

(2) An acceptance of an offer becomes effective at the moment the indication of assent reaches the offeror. An acceptance is not effective if the indication of assent does not reach the offeror within the time he has fixed or, if no time is fixed, within a reasonable time, due account being taken of the circumstances of the transaction, including the rapidity of the means of communication employed by the offeror. An oral

> offer must be accepted immediately unless the circumstances
> indicate otherwise.
>
> (3) However, if, by virtue of the offer or as a result of practices
> which the parties have established between themselves or of
> usage, the offeree may indicate assent by performing an act,
> such as one relating to the dispatch of the goods or payment
> of the price, without notice to the offeror, the acceptance is
> effective at the moment the act is performed, provided that
> the act is performed within the period of time laid down in
> the preceding paragraph.

Recall Articles 7 & 8 here. The broad-based interpretation called for by Article 18 echoes the rules of contractual interpretation set forth in Article 8. Because the CISG calls for a broad-based approach to interpretation in both Articles 8 and 18, this broad approach to interpretation can be said to be a general principle upon which the CISG is based for purposes of Article 7. This is not to say that the CISG rules favor finding acceptance in close cases, but merely that the CISG mandates a consideration of all relevant circumstances when looking for the intent of the parties.

Article 18(1) states that "silence or inactivity does not in itself" amount to an acceptance. That language indicates that silence or inactivity, when coupled with other behavior, may indeed be indicative of an acceptance. This is often the case, especially in a "battle of the forms" situation, as described in Part III below.[29]

B.   EFFECTIVENESS, WITHDRAWAL, AND REVOCATION

Article 18(2) explains that an acceptance is effective upon receipt. At that point a contract is created, or, to use the CISG's language, concluded.[30] Of course, the acceptance must be communicated in accordance with the terms of the offer,

---

[29] *See e.g. Sté Calzados Magnanni [Spanish Seller] v. SARL Shoes General International [French Buyer]*, Cour d'appel Grenoble, France, Oct. 21, 1999 (available at http://cisgw3.law.pace.edu/cases/991021f1.html). In that case the French court considered all of the circumstances of the case (under Article 8), including the parties' past practices (under Article 9) to conclude that the seller did not need to expressly accept the buyer's offer to purchase. Instead, silence regarding the offer coupled with performance in providing the goods ordered, was sufficient to constitute an acceptance.

[30] Regarding electronic communications, the CISG Advisory Council Opinion number 1 has defined "reaches" for purposes of article 18(2) just as it did for purposes of articles 15 and 17, "when an electronic message has entered the offeror's server." CISG-AC Opinion no. 1, *supra* n. 18.

including within any time frame established, or, if a time frame has not been established, within a reasonable period of time.

Compare: The Common Law Mailbox Rule

Pursuant to the common law "mailbox rule," unless otherwise specified in the terms of the offer, acceptances are typically effective upon dispatch, i.e. the moment they are dropped into the mailbox.[31] Of course acceptances are now likely to be dispatched by fax, e-mail, or other electronic communication and such forms of dispatch are picked up by the mailbox rule. Regardless, once the acceptance is dispatched, it is effective and the related offer can no longer be revoked by the offeror.

Article 16(1) of the CISG contains this same rule on revocation—that, unless the offer specifies otherwise, offers cannot be revoked once an acceptance has been dispatched. However, under Article 18(2) of the CISG, the acceptance is still not effective until it reaches the offeror. This creates the time period—after dispatch of the acceptance but prior to its receipt by the offeror—during which the offeror can do nothing, but the offeree might still withdraw the acceptance. This provides the offeree with an advantage that does not exist under the common law.[32]

Further, under the mailbox rule, with the acceptance effective upon dispatch, the risk of loss of the acceptance lies with the offeror. The contract will be formed regardless of whether the acceptance actually reaches the offeror, a strange but true result of the mailbox rule. In contrast, under the CISG rule, the risk of loss of the acceptance lies with the offeree since a contract will never be formed unless the offeror actually receives that acceptance.[33]

---

[31] This rule is nuanced for options, the acceptance of which is effective upon receipt by the offeror. *See Restatement (Second) of Contracts* § 63. Further, for the mailbox rule to apply in the United States, it is typically the case that the offeree must use means of communication that are "equal or better" than the means employed by the offeror in making its offer. *Id.* at § 65.

[32] It is interesting to note that the UNIDROIT Principles and the PECL adopt similar positions as the CISG on these timing rules for offers and acceptances. *See UNIDROIT Principles*, Arts. 2.1.2– 2.1.10; *PECL* Arts. 2:202, 2:205.

[33] *See* E. Allan Farnsworth, *Formation of Contract*, in *International Sales: The United Nations Convention on Contracts for the International Sale of Goods*, 3-11–3-13 (Galston & Smit eds., Juris Publg. 1984). The default risk of loss rules of the CISG are discussed further in Chapter 4.

As was discussed above, Article 16(1) provides that an offer can not be revoked once the related acceptance has been dispatched. This creates a time period after the acceptance is dispatched during which a contract does not exist, but the offer cannot be revoked. All that might happen during this period is that the offeree could withdraw its acceptance. This effectively creates an option for the offeree where the offeree can either accept the offer by allowing its acceptance to reach the offeror, or withdraw its acceptance by getting a withdrawal notice to the offeror at or before the time when the acceptance is received by the offeror. Article 22 specifically authorizes that withdrawal.

Article 22

An acceptance may be withdrawn if the withdrawal reaches the offeror before or at the same time as the acceptance would have become effective.

Article 18(2) also contains a default rule for oral offers. Any oral offer must be accepted immediately, unless the circumstances indicate otherwise.[34] Thus, an oral offer will not remain open (and therefore need not be formally revoked) unless special circumstances are present. An example of such circumstances is where the offeror specifically states that the oral offer will remain open for a period of time and may be accepted within that time frame. Any indication by the offeror that acceptance could occur other than immediately will likely be sufficient to allow the acceptance to be made at a later point in time.

Having discussed the default rules that exist under the CISG for whether and when a contract has been formed, it is important to point out that the offeror is truly the "master of the offer." In other words, if the offeror does not want the default rules on offer and acceptance and the related timing rules to apply, the offeror can simply specify particular terms in its offer.[35]

---

[34] The CISG Advisory Council Opinion number 1 has stated that oral communications include "electronically transmitted sound in real time and electronic communications in real time." As with all electronic communications, however, the parties must either expressly or impliedly consent to the form, format and address of the electronic communication. CISG-AC Opinion no. 1, *supra* n. 18.

[35] Lookofsky, *supra* n. 3, at 62 ("The CISG offeror is properly regarded as the 'master' of his offer, in that the offer is to be interpreted according to the *offeror's* intent, at least in cases where the offeree knew or could not have been unaware what that intent was."); *see also* Murray, *supra* n. 5 (arguing that under the CISG the offeror is the master of the offer since the offeror can set a time period for acceptance under Article 18(2)).

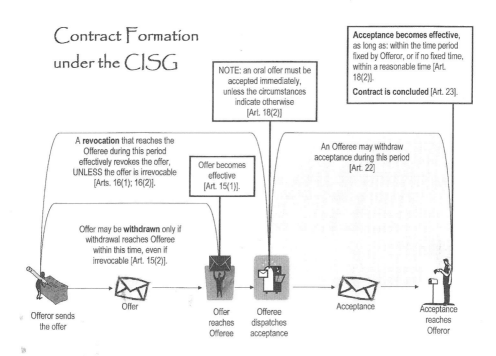

Contract Formation under the CISG

NOTE: an oral offer must be accepted immediately, unless the circumstances indicate otherwise [Art. 18(2)]

Acceptance becomes effective, as long as: within the time period fixed by Offeror, or if no fixed time, within a reasonable time [Art. 18(2)].

Contract is concluded [Art. 23].

A **revocation** that reaches the Offeree during this period effectively revokes the offer, UNLESS the offer is irrevocable [Arts. 16(1); 16(2)].

Offer becomes effective [Art. 15(1)].

An Offeree may withdraw acceptance during this period [Art. 22]

Offer may be **withdrawn** only if withdrawal reaches Offeree within this time, even if irrevocable [Art. 15(2)].

Offeror sends the offer

Offer

Offer reaches Offeree

Offeree dispatches acceptance

Acceptance

Acceptance reaches Offeror

III.   BATTLE OF THE FORMS

A typical conundrum with sales of goods transactions is the battle of the forms. Sales transactions often happen with form documents. A seller typically has its own form of purchase agreement, and a buyer typically has its own form of sales agreement. Each party will include provisions in its form agreement that are to its advantage. When a seller and a buyer exchange their respective forms in any given transaction, it is not always clear that a contract has actually been formed as each document likely contains different terms. Further, even if a contract has been formed, the question becomes which terms will be included in that contract. Article 19 of the CISG addresses these problems inherent in the battle of the forms situation.

Article 19
(1) A reply to an offer which purports to be an acceptance but contains additions, limitations or other modifications is a rejection of the offer and constitutes a counter-offer.
(2) However, a reply to an offer which purports to be an acceptance but contains additional or different terms which

> do not materially alter the terms of the offer constitutes an acceptance, unless the offeror, without undue delay, objects orally to the discrepancy or dispatches a notice to that effect. If he does not so object, the terms of the contract are the terms of the offer with the modifications contained in the acceptance.
>
> (3) Additional or different terms relating, among other things, to the price, payment, quality and quantity of the goods, place and time of delivery, extent of one party's liability to the other or the settlement of disputes are considered to alter the terms of the offer materially.

In a battle of the forms situation, the terms of the reply to an offer do not match the terms of that offer. How to treat the reply under the CISG turns on whether the additional or different terms in the reply materially alter the offer. If the additional or different terms are not material, then Article 19(2) explains that the reply is an acceptance. Therefore, a contract is concluded under Article 23 (unless the offeror objects in a timely fashion). Further, the non-material additional or different terms will become a part of the contract. Article 19(3) explains what kinds of terms are considered to materially alter an offer. Among the rather exhaustive list of terms that may be considered to materially alter an offer are those relating to pricing, quality, quantity, liability, and dispute resolution.[36]

Given the breadth of topics identified as being material, one wonders what would ever be immaterial. On the other hand, one of the authors believes that even if a topic is listed in Article 19(3), it does not necessarily make every change related to that topic material. For example, imagine a purchase of goods at $1000 per unit. Would a change of $1 per unit be deemed material? What about a change of $.01 per unit? In accordance with the strict language of 19(3) any different term is considered material. So, an approach that argues that a slight change in price (or quantity or anything else) is not material must argue that such a change simply does not represent an appreciable difference. This approach could also be supported by trade norms, which often suggest that certain variations are within acceptable limits.

---

[36] Despite the language of Article 19(3), the Austrian Supreme Court has ruled that the terms listed there need not necessarily be material if the parties do not treat them that way. *See Russian Buyer v. Austrian Seller (Mono Ammonium Phosphate Case)*, Oberster Gerichtshof [Supreme Court] case no. 2 Ob 58/97m, Austria, Mar. 20, 1997 (available at http://cisgw3.law.pace.edu/cases/970320a3.html). So, for example, if the parties have discussed that a particular delivery term is not important, then those parties should not be able to argue later that those delivery terms are material for purposes of Article 19.

If the additional or different terms are material, then Article 19(1) indicates that the reply is a rejection and a counter-offer.[37] The process then begins anew with an acceptance of that counter-offer necessary for a contract to be concluded.

Since battle of the forms situations rarely conclude with a reply that does match the offer (or counter-offer), the typical acceptance actually occurs either through conduct or silence indicating acceptance.[38] Recall that Article 18(1) allows acceptances to be made through conduct indicating a party's intent to accept the terms of the transaction. Article 18(1) also specified that even silence or inactivity (though not alone) might amount to an acceptance. In a battle of the forms situation, the parties may not focus on the differences in the forms they used to undertake the transaction. If the last counter-offer was made by the buyer, and the seller proceeds to ship the goods, then the seller's conduct in shipping the goods would likely rise to the level of an acceptance and the buyer's last counter-offer will dictate the terms of the contract. If the last counter-offer was made by the seller, and the buyer takes delivery and/or makes payment, then the buyer's conduct would also likely rise to the level of an acceptance, in which case the seller's last counter-offer will dictate the terms of the contract. Notice that in either one of these scenarios a plain reading of Article 19 indicates that the terms of the final counter-offer, including those that are additional or different and that materially alter the previous offer, will be included in the final contract.

Article 19, as it was just explained, actually represents a traditional approach to the battle of the forms that has been rejected in many jurisdictions. Not all commentators agree on this interpretation of Article 19. Some have interpreted Article 19 to represent the more modern approach. For more on this alternative, consider the "Compare" box that follows.

> ### Compare: Battle of the Forms
>
> Interestingly, in accordance with a plain reading of Article 19, the CISG takes the very same approach to the battle of the forms that the common law traditionally did. Under both the CISG and the common law, where there are materially different or additional terms in a reply to an offer that purports to be an

---

[37] Article 19(1) in fact states that all replies that contain additional or different terms are counter-offers. However, Article 19(2) provides that replies that do not materially alter the offer are acceptances.

[38] *See e.g. Dutch Buyer v. German Seller (Powdered Milk Case)*, Bundesgerichtshof [Federal Supreme Court] no. VIII ZR 304/00, Germany, Jan. 9, 2002 (available at http://cisgw3.law.pace.edu/cases/020109g1.html) (where the court found that performance of the contract indicated acceptance even though the forms used by the parties contained materially different terms).

acceptance, then that reply will be deemed to be a counter-offer. That counter-offer will govern the terms of the transaction where the counter-offer is the last offer to be made before the sale of goods goes forward. The acceptance is deemed to be the conduct of the party in engaging in the transaction. This approach is known as the *last shot doctrine*.

However, in many common law jurisdictions the last shot doctrine was abandoned. Allowing the terms of the last reply to govern the transaction was considered arbitrary and therefore unfair and inappropriate. In the United States, for example, UCC §2-207 dictates that, as between merchants, a reply to an offer that contains additional material terms is not a counter-offer, as it would be under the CISG or would have been under the common law. Instead, the reply is deemed to be an acceptance but the additional material terms simply are not included in the terms of the final contract. Any additional terms that are immaterial do become a part of the contract. This newer approach to the battle of the forms is known as the *knock-out doctrine* because additional terms that are material are "knocked-out" of the final contract.[39]

Many commentators have expressed surprise that the CISG adopted the older common law rule and not the more recently adopted rule based on the knock-out doctrine.[40] Professor Honnold, for example, goes so far as to say, "'[l]ast Shot' theories have been rightly criticized as casuistic and unfair. They do not reflect international consensus that justifies importing them into the Convention."[41]

---

[39] In addition to the UCC, the UNIDROIT Principles and the PECL utilize the more modern knock-out doctrine. *UNIDROIT Principles* art. 2.22; *PECL* art. 2:209(1). For an in-depth discussion of the battle of the forms under the CISG, the UCC, and the UNIDROIT Principles, see Maria del Pilar Perales Viscasillas, *"Battle of the Forms" Under the 1980 United Nations Convention on Contracts for the International Sale of Goods: A Comparison with Section 2-207 UCC and the UNIDROIT Principles*, 10 Pace Intl. L. Rev. 97 (1998).

[40] *See e.g.* Honnold, *supra* n. 7, at 190-191.

[41] *Id.*

> Some commentators have construed Article 19 differently to represent the more modern knock out doctrine.[42] This appears to be a somewhat strained interpretation of Article 19. However, the argument is that in a battle of the forms, the parties cannot fairly be said to have agreed on terms that are included in boilerplate in a response to an offer that purports to be an acceptance. These commentators suggest that such terms would simply not be a part of the agreement, i.e. they would be knocked out. Instead, issues governed by those terms that are then not to be included in the agreement of the parties should be addressed with reference to the CISG's gap-filling provisions.[43]

The following case from a United States Federal Court was one of the first cases in the United States to interpret and apply the CISG. In this opinion, among other issues, the court considered how contracts are interpreted under the CISG, how and when they are formed, and how to assess a battle of the forms. Coincidentally, the case involves whether or not the sale of goods contract between the parties included an arbitration clause. Thus, at this early stage in examining the CISG, this case provides some overview and discussion of arbitration principles as well. The case, and the arbitration principles discussed within it, will be re-visited in Chapter 8.

---

[42] *See* Michael P. Van Alstine, *Consensus, Dissensus, and Contractual Obligation Through the Prism of Uniform International Sales Law,* 37 Va. J. Intl. L. 1 (1996). This interpretation has also been followed by several courts. On page 91 of his article, Van Alstine cites to *Italian Seller v. German Buyer*, Amtsgericht Kehl Case no. 3 C 925/93, Germany, Oct. 6, 1995 (available at http://cisgw3.law.pace.edu/cases/951006g1.html). *See also, Dutch Buyer v. German Seller (Powdered Milk Case)*, Bundesgerichtshof [Federal Supreme Court] no. VIII ZR 304/00, Germany, Jan. 9, 2002 (available at http://cisgw3.law.pace.edu/cases/020109g1.html) (where the court also interpreted Article 19 to represent the knock-out rule).

[43] *See* Honnold, *supra* n.7, at para 170.4; Van Alstine, *supra* n. 42, at 80–91.

    Chapter 3 – Forming a Contract under the CISG

United States District Court

for the Southern District of New York

Filanto, S.p.A. v. Chilewich International Corp.

789 F.Supp. 1229

Decided April 14, 1992

[Footnotes omitted]

Opinion by Judge Brieant

By motion fully submitted on December 11, 1991, defendant Chilewich International Corp. moves to stay this action pending arbitration in Moscow. Plaintiff Filanto has moved to enjoin arbitration or to order arbitration in this federal district.

This case is a striking example of how a lawsuit involving a relatively straightforward international commercial transaction can raise an array of complex questions. Accordingly, the Court will recount the factual background of the case…

Plaintiff Filanto is an Italian corporation engaged in the manufacture and sale of footwear. Defendant Chilewich is an export-import firm incorporated in the state of New York with its principal place of business in White Plains. On February 28, 1989, Chilewich's agent in the United Kingdom, Byerly Johnson, Ltd., signed a contract with Raznoexport, the Soviet Foreign Economic Association, which obligated Byerly Johnson to supply footwear to Raznoexport. Section 10 of this contract -- the "Russian Contract" -- is an arbitration clause, which reads in pertinent part as follows:

> "All disputes or differences which may arise out of or in connection with the present Contract are to be settled, jurisdiction of ordinary courts being excluded, by the Arbitration at the USSR Chamber of Commerce and Industry, Moscow, in accordance with the Regulations of the said Arbitration." [sic]

…

The first exchange of correspondence between the parties to this lawsuit is a letter dated July 27, 1989 from Mr. Melvin Chilewich of Chilewich International to Mr. Antonio Filograna, chief executive officer of Filanto. This letter refers to a recent visit by Chilewich and Byerly Johnson personnel to Filanto's factories in Italy, presumably to negotiate a purchase to fulfill the Russian Contract, and then states as follows:

> "Attached please find our contract to cover our purchase from you. Same is governed by the conditions which are enumerated in the standard contract in effect with the Soviet buyers [the Russian contract], copy of which is also enclosed."

…The next item in the record is a letter from Filanto to Chilewich dated September 2, 1989. …This letter refers to a letter from Filanto to Chilewich of August 11, 1989, which "you [Chilewich] sent me with the contracts n 10001-10002-10003." These numbers do not correspond to the contract sued on here, but refer instead to other, similar contracts between the parties. None of these contracts, or their terms, are in the record, both parties having been afforded ample opportunity to submit whatever they wished.

The last paragraph of the September 2, 1989 letter from Filanto to Chilewich states as follows:

"Returning back the enclosed contracts n 10001-10002-10003 signed for acceptance, we communicate, if we do not misunderstood, the Soviet's contract that you sent us together with your above mentioned contract, that of this contract we have to respect only the following points of it:

> -n 5 Packing and marking
> -n 6 Way of Shipment
> -n 7 Delivery - Acceptance of Goods

> "We ask for your acceptance by return of post." [sic]

… The intent of this paragraph, clearly, was to exclude from incorporation by reference *inter alia* section 10 of the Russian contract, which provides for arbitration. Chilewich, for its part, claims never to have received this September 2 letter. In any event, it relates only to prior course of conduct.

It is apparent from the record that further negotiations occurred in early 1990, but the content of those negotiations is unclear; it is, however, clear that deliveries of boots from Filanto to Chilewich were occurring at this time, pursuant to other contracts, since there is a reference to a shipment occurring between April 23, 1990 and June 11, 1990. ...

The next document in this case, and the focal point of the parties' dispute regarding whether an arbitration agreement exists, is a Memorandum Agreement dated March 13, 1990. This Memorandum Agreement, number 9003002, is a standard merchant's memo prepared by Chilewich for signature by both parties confirming that Filanto will deliver 100,000 pairs of boots to Chilewich at the Italian/Yugoslav border on September 15, 1990, with the balance of 150,000 pairs to be delivered on November 1, 1990. Chilewich's obligations were to open a Letter of Credit in Filanto's favor prior to the September 15 delivery, and another letter prior to the November delivery. This Memorandum includes the following provision:

"It is understood between Buyer and Seller that USSR Contract No. 32-03/93085 [the Russian Contract] is hereby incorporated in this contract as far as practicable, and specifically that any arbitration shall be in accordance with that Contract."

...Chilewich signed this Memorandum Agreement, and sent it to Filanto. Filanto at that time did not sign or return the document. Nevertheless, on May 7, 1990, Chilewich opened a Letter of Credit in Filanto's favor in the sum of $ 2,595,600.00. The Letter of Credit itself mentions the Russian Contract, but only insofar as concerns packing and labeling. ...

Again, on July 23, 1990, Filanto sent another letter to Chilewich, Ex. D. to October 23 Filograna Affidavit, which reads in relevant parts as follows:

"We refer to Point 3, Special Conditions, to point out that: returning back the above-mentioned contract, signed for acceptance, from Soviet Contract 32-03/93085 we have to respect only the following points of it:

- No. 5 - Packing and Marking
- No. 6 - Way of Shipment
- No. 7 - Delivery Acceptance of Goods".

It should be noted that the contract referred to in this letter is apparently another contract between the parties, as the letter refers to "Sub. Contract No. 32-03/03122", while the contract sued on in the present action is No. 32-03/03123.

This letter caused some concern on the part of Chilewich and its agents: a July 30, 1990 fax from Byerly Johnson, Chilewich's agent, to Chilewich, mentions Filanto's July 23 letter, asserts that it "very neatly dodges" certain issues, other than arbitration, covered by the Russian Contract, and states that Johnson would "take it up" with Filanto during a visit to Filanto's offices the next week. ...

Then, on August 7, 1990, Filanto returned the Memorandum Agreement, sued on here, that Chilewich had signed and sent to it in March; though Filanto had signed the Memorandum Agreement, it once again appended a covering letter, purporting to exclude all but three sections of the Russian Contract. ...

There is also in the record an August 7, 1990 telex from Chilewich to Byerly Johnson, stating that Chilewich would not open the second Letter of Credit unless it received from Filanto a signed copy of the contract without any exclusions. ... In order to resolve this issue, Byerly Johnson on August 29, 1990 sent a fax to Italian Trading SRL, an intermediary, reading in relevant part:

> "We have checked back through our records for last year, and can find no exclusions by Filanto from the Soviet Master Contract and, in the event, we do not believe that this has caused any difficulties between us.

> "We would, therefore, ask you to amend your letters of the 23rd July 1990 and the 7th August 1990, so that you accept all points of the Soviet Master Contract No. 32-03/93085 as far as practicable. You will note that this is specified in our Special Condition No. 3 of our contracts Nos. 9003001 and 9003 [illegible]". ...

As the date specified in the Memorandum Agreement for delivery of the first shipment of boots--September 15, 1990--was approaching, the parties evidently decided to make further efforts to resolve this issue: what actually happened, though, is a matter of some dispute. Mr. Filograna, the CEO of Filanto, asserts that the following occurred:

> "Moreover, when I was in Moscow from September 2 through September 5, 1990, to inspect Soviet factories on an unrelated business matter, I met with

> Simon Chilewich. Simon Chilewich, then and there, abandoned his request of August 29, 1990, and agreed with me that the Filanto-Chilewich Contract would incorporate only the packing, shipment and delivery terms of the Anglo-Soviet Contract. Also present at this meeting were Sergio Squilloni of Italian Trading (Chilewich's agent), Kathy Farley, and Max Flaxman of Chilewich and Antonio Sergio of Filanto."

...

Mr. Simon Chilewich, in his sworn affidavit, does not refer to this incident, but does state the following:

> "In fact, subsequent to the communications and correspondence described above, I met with Mr. Filograna face to face in Paris during the weekend of September 14, 1990. During that meeting, I expressly stated to him that we would have no deal if Filanto now insisted on deleting provisions of the Russian Contract from our agreement. Mr. Filograna, on behalf of Filanto, stated that he would accede to our position, in order to keep Chilewich's business."

...

Plaintiff does not address or deny defendant's version of the Paris meeting. Filanto's Complaint in this action alleges that it delivered the first shipment of boots on September 15, and drew down on the Letter of Credit. ...

On September 27, 1990, Mr. Filograna faxed a letter to Chilewich. This letter refers to "assurances during our meeting in Paris", and complains that Chilewich had not yet opened the second Letter of Credit for the second delivery, which it had supposedly promised to do by September 25. ... Mr. Chilewich responded by fax on the same day; his fax states that he is "totally cognizant of the contractual obligations which exist", but goes on to say that Chilewich had encountered difficulties with the Russian buyers, that Chilewich needed to "reduce the rate of shipments", and denies that Chilewich promised to open the Letter of Credit by September 25. ...

According to the Complaint, what ultimately happened was that Chilewich bought and paid for 60,000 pairs of boots in January 1991, but never purchased the 90,000 pairs of boots that comprise the balance of Chilewich's original order. ... It is Chilewich's failure to do so that forms the basis of this lawsuit, commenced by Filanto on May 14, 1991.

There is in the record, however, one document that post-dates the filing of the Complaint: a letter from Filanto to Chilewich dated June 21, 1991. This letter is in response to claims by Byerly Johnson that some of the boots that had been supplied by Filanto were defective. The letter expressly relies on a section of the Russian contract which Filanto had earlier purported to exclude-- Section 9 regarding claims procedures--and states that "The April Shipment and the September Shipment are governed by the Master Purchase Contract of February 28, 1989, n 32-03/93085 (the "Master Purchase Contract")." ...

This letter must be regarded as an admission in law by Filanto, the party to be charged. A litigant may not blow hot and cold in a lawsuit. The letter of June 21, 1991 clearly shows that when Filanto thought it desirable to do so, it recognized that it was bound by the incorporation by reference of portions of the Russian Contract, which, prior to the Paris meeting, it had purported to exclude. This letter shows that Filanto regarded itself as the beneficiary of the claims adjustment provisions of the Russian Contract. This legal position is entirely inconsistent with the position which Filanto had professed prior to the Paris meeting, and is inconsistent with its present position. Consistent with the position of the defendant in this action, Filanto admits that the other relevant clauses of the Russian Contract were incorporated by agreement of the parties, and made a part of the bargain. Of necessity, this must include the agreement to arbitrate in Moscow. In the June 21, 1991 letter, Mr. Filograna writes:

"The April Shipment and the September Shipment are governed by the Master Purchase Contract of February 28, 1989 N. 32-03-93085 (the "Master Purchase Contract") The Master Purchase Contract provides that claims for inferior quality must be made within six months of the arrival of the goods at the USSR port".

...

Against this background based almost entirely on documents, defendant Chilewich on July 24, 1991 moved to stay this action pending arbitration, while plaintiff Filanto on August 22, 1992 moved to enjoin arbitration, or, alternatively, for an order directing that arbitration be held in the Southern District of New York rather than Moscow, because of unsettled political conditions in Russia.

Jurisdiction/Applicable Law …

The Arbitration Convention specifically requires courts to recognize any "agreement in writing under which the parties undertake to submit to arbitration …." Convention on the Recognition and Enforcement of Foreign Arbitral Awards Article II(1). The term "agreement in writing" is defined as "an arbitral clause in a contract or an arbitration agreement, signed by the parties or contained in an exchange of letters or telegrams". Convention on the Recognition and Enforcement Of Foreign Arbitral Awards Article II(2).

…

However, the focus of this dispute, apparent from the parties' submissions, is not on the scope of the arbitration provision included in the Russian contract; rather, the threshold question is whether these parties actually agreed to arbitrate their disputes at all. …

…

This Court concludes that the question of whether these parties agreed to arbitrate their disputes is governed by the Arbitration Convention and its implementing legislation. That Convention, as a treaty, is the supreme law of the land, U.S. Const. art. VI cl. 2, and controls any case in any American court falling within its sphere of application. Thus, any dispute involving international commercial arbitration which meets the Convention's jurisdictional requirements, whether brought in state or federal court, must be resolved with reference to that instrument. …

Accordingly, the Court will apply federal law to the issue of whether an "agreement in writing" to arbitrate disputes exists between these parties.

…

Courts interpreting this "agreement in writing" requirement have generally started their analysis with the plain language of the Convention, which requires "an arbitral clause in a contract or an arbitration agreement, signed by the parties or contained in an exchange of letters or telegrams", Article I(1), and have then applied that language in light of federal law, which consists of generally accepted principles of contract law, including the Uniform Commercial Code. …

However, as plaintiff correctly notes, the "general principles of contract law" relevant to this action, do not include the Uniform Commercial Code; rather, the "federal law of contracts" to be applied in this case is found in the United Nations Convention on Contracts for the International Sale of Goods (the "Sale of Goods Convention"), codified at 15 U.S.C. Appendix (West Supp. 1991). … Although there is as yet virtually no U.S. case law interpreting the Sale of Goods Convention, …it may safely be predicted that this will change: absent a choice-of-law provision, and with certain exclusions not here relevant, the Convention governs all contracts between parties with places of business in different nations, so long as both nations are signatories to the Convention. Sale of Goods Convention Article 1 (1)(a). Since … both the United States and Italy are signatories to the Convention, the Court will interpret the "agreement in writing" requirement of the Arbitration Convention in light of, and with reference to, the substantive international law of contracts embodied in the Sale of Goods Convention.

Not surprisingly, the parties offer varying interpretations of the numerous letters and documents exchanged between them. The Court will briefly summarize their respective contentions.

Defendant Chilewich contends that the Memorandum Agreement dated March 13 which it signed and sent to Filanto was an offer. It then argues that Filanto's retention of the letter, along with its subsequent acceptance of Chilewich's performance under the Agreement--the furnishing of the May 11 letter of credit--estops it from denying its acceptance of the contract. Although phrased as an estoppel argument, this contention is better viewed as an acceptance by conduct argument, e.g., that in light of the parties' course of dealing, Filanto had a duty timely to inform Chilewich that it objected to the incorporation by reference of all the terms of the Russian contract. Under this view, the return of the Memorandum Agreement, signed by Filanto, on August 7, 1990, along with the covering letter purporting to exclude parts of the Russian Contract, was ineffective as a matter of law as a rejection of the March 13 offer, because this occurred some five months after Filanto received the Memorandum Agreement and two months after Chilewich furnished the Letter of Credit. Instead, in Chilewich's view, this action was a proposal for modification of the March 13 Agreement. Chilewich rejected this proposal, by its letter of August 7 to Byerly Johnson, and the August 9 fax by Johnson to Italian Trading SRL, which communication Filanto acknowledges receiving. Accordingly, Filanto under this interpretation is bound by the written terms of the March 13 Memorandum Agreement; since that agreement incorporates by reference the Russian Contract containing the arbitration provision, Filanto is bound to arbitrate.

Plaintiff Filanto's interpretation of the evidence is rather different. ...While Filanto apparently agrees that the March 13 Memorandum Agreement was indeed an offer, it characterizes its August 7 return of the signed Memorandum Agreement with the covering letter as a counter-offer. While defendant contends that under Uniform Commercial Code § 2-207 this action would be viewed as an acceptance with a proposal for a material modification, the Uniform Commercial Code, as previously noted does not apply to this case, because the State Department undertook to fix something that was not broken by helping to create the Sale of Goods Convention which varies from the Uniform Commercial Code in many significant ways. Instead, under this analysis, Article 19(1) of the Sale of Goods Convention would apply. That section, as the Commentary to the Sale of Goods Convention notes, reverses the rule of Uniform Commercial Code § 2-207, and reverts to the common law rule that "A reply to an offer which purports to be an acceptance but contains additions, limitations or other modifications is a rejection of the offer and constitutes a counter-offer". Sale of Goods Convention Article 19(1). Although the Convention, like the Uniform Commercial Code, does state that non-material terms do become part of the contract unless objected to, Sale of Goods Convention Article 19(2), the Convention treats inclusion (or deletion) of an arbitration provision as "material", Sale of Goods Convention Article 19(3). The August 7 letter, therefore, was a counter-offer which, according to Filanto, Chilewich accepted by its letter dated September 27, 1990. Though that letter refers to and acknowledges the "contractual obligations" between the parties, it is doubtful whether it can be characterized as an acceptance.

More generally, both parties seem to have lost sight of the narrow scope of the inquiry required by the Arbitration Convention. *Ledee, supra,* at 186. All that this Court need do is to determine if a sufficient "agreement in writing" to arbitrate disputes exists between these parties. Cf. *United Steelworkers of America v. Warrior & Gulf Co.,* 363 U.S. 574, 582, 4 L. Ed. 2d 1409, 80 S. Ct. 1347 (1960) (party cannot be required to submit to arbitration absent agreement). Although that inquiry is informed by the provisions of the Sale of Goods Convention, the Court lacks the authority on this motion to resolve all outstanding issues between the parties. Indeed, contracts and the arbitration clauses included therein are considered to be "severable", a rule that the Sale of Goods Convention itself adopts with respect to avoidance of contracts generally. Sale of Goods Convention Article 81(l). …

… the Court will direct its analysis to whether there was objective conduct evidencing an intent to be bound with respect to the arbitration provision. Cf. *Matterhorn v. NCR Corp.,* 763 F.2d 866, 871-73 (7th Cir. 1985*)* (Posner, J.) (discussing cases). See also *Teledyne, Inc. v. Kone Corp.,* 892 F.2d 1404, 1410 (9th Cir. 1990) (arbitration clause enforceable despite later finding by arbitrator that contract itself invalid).

The Court is satisfied on this record that there *was* indeed an agreement to arbitrate between these parties.

There is simply no satisfactory explanation as to why Filanto failed to object to the incorporation by reference of the Russian Contract in a timely fashion. As noted above, Chilewich had in the meantime commenced its performance under the Agreement, and the Letter of Credit it furnished Filanto on May 11 itself mentioned the Russian Contract. An offeree who, knowing that the offeror has commenced performance, fails to notify the offeror of its objection to the terms of the contract within a reasonable time will, under certain circumstances, be deemed to have assented to those terms. Restatement (Second) of Contracts § 69 (1981); … The Sale of Goods Convention itself recognizes this rule: Article 18(l), provides that "A statement made by or other conduct of the offeree indicating assent to an offer is an acceptance". Although mere "silence or inactivity" does not constitute acceptance, Sale of Goods Convention Article 18(l), the Court may consider previous relations between the parties in assessing whether a party's conduct constituted acceptance, Sale of Goods Convention Article 8(3). In this case, in light of the extensive course of prior dealing between these parties, Filanto was certainly under a duty to alert Chilewich in timely fashion to its objections to the terms of the March 13 Memorandum Agreement--particularly since Chilewich had repeatedly referred it to the Russian Contract and Filanto had had a copy of that document for some time.

There are three other convincing manifestations of Filanto's true understanding of the terms of this agreement. First, Filanto's Complaint in this action, as well as affidavits subsequently submitted to the Court by Mr. Filograna, refer to the March 13 contract: the Complaint, for example, states that "On or about March 13, 1990, Filanto entered into a contract with Chilewich. . . ". ... These statements clearly belie Filanto's post hoc assertion that the contract was actually formed at some point after that date. Indeed, Filanto finds itself in an awkward position: it has sued on a contract whose terms it must now question, in light of the defendant's assertion that the contract contains an arbitration provision. This situation is hardly unknown in the context of arbitration agreements. See *Tepper Realtv Co. v. Mosaic Tile Co.,* 259 F. Supp. 688, 692 (S.D.N.Y. 1966) ("In short, the plaintiffs cannot have it both ways. They cannot relay [sic] on the contract, when it works to their advantage, and repudiate it when it works to their disadvantage").

Second, Filanto did sign the March 13 Memorandum Agreement. That Agreement, as noted above, specifically referred to the incorporation by reference of the arbitration provision in the Russian Contract; although Filanto, in its August 7 letter, did purport to "have to respect" only a small part of the Russian Contract, Filanto in that very letter noted that it was returning the March 13 Memorandum Agreement "signed for acceptance". Exhibit A to November 28 Filograna Affidavit (emphasis added). In light of Filanto's knowledge that Chilewich had already performed its part of the bargain by furnishing it the Letter of Credit, Filanto's characterization of this action as a rejection and a counter-offer is almost frivolous.

Third, and most important, Filanto, in a letter to Byerly Johnson dated June 21, 1991, explicitly stated that "the April Shipment and the September shipment are governed by the Master

Purchase Contract of February 28, 1989 [the Russian Contract]".
Exhibit H to December 4 Simon Chilewich Affidavit.
Furthermore, the letter, which responds to claims by Johnson
that some of the boots that were supplied were defective,
expressly relies on section 9 of the Russian Contract--another
section which Filanto had in its earlier correspondence purported
to exclude. The Sale of Goods Convention specifically directs
that "in determining the intent of a party. . . due consideration is
to be given to . . . any subsequent conduct of the parties", Sale of
Goods Convention Article 8(3). In this case, as the letter post-
dates the partial performance of the contract, it is particularly
strong evidence that Filanto recognized itself to be bound by all
the terms of the Russian Contract.

In light of these factors, and heeding the presumption in favor of arbitration,
Moses H. Cone, supra, at 24-26, which is even stronger in the context of
international commercial transactions, *Mitsubishi Motors Corp. v. Soler
Chrysler-Plymouth, Inc.,* 473 U.S. 614, 631, 87 L. Ed. 2d 444, 105 S. Ct. 3346
(1985), the Court holds that Filanto is bound by the terms of the March 13
Memorandum Agreement, and so must arbitrate its dispute in Moscow. ...

* * * * *

Notes and Commentary

Note 1: The Filanto case illustrates a wide range of issues related to contract
formation under the CISG and also arbitration. First and foremost, however,
footnote 5 in the opinion (which was omitted) underscored the fact that the CISG
as a treaty is indeed a federal law of the United States. Despite this affirmation,
however, the Filanto court at one point makes the shocking statement that the
CISG is the law in the United States because "the State Department undertook to
fix something that was not broken by helping to create the Sale of Goods
Convention." This remarkable statement highlights some of the resistance that
exists with respect to replacing domestic legal rules with international ones.

Note 2: The court goes to great efforts to summarize the arguments of both
buyer and seller under Article 19. The contrasting analyses of the buyer and
seller based on the same facts both seem plausible under the CISG's terms.
Which party has the better argument?

Note 3: The court seemed persuaded by the buyer's analysis of the transaction,
but then concludes that the only relevant inquiry is whether there is a written
agreement to arbitrate. The court finds such an agreement. What is the
governing law the court applied to that inquiry and was it correct to do so?

Note 4: The arbitration clause itself did not contain a choice of a body of contract law to govern its formation and interpretation. In the absence of such a specific choice, should the CISG apply as the substantive contract law that would govern the entire contract? Recall that the CISG governs the sale of goods, not specifically dispute resolution. Perhaps dispute resolution is so integrally a part of a contract for the sale of goods that the CISG still should govern. Alternatively, might the substantive contract law of the forum of the arbitration apply? The issue of what law governs the interpretation of an arbitration provision is a complex one that will be discussed in more detail in Chapter 7.

Note 5: The governing law questions bring up another issue—the separability of the arbitration clause. This issue will also be explored in more depth in Chapter 8, but for now it is important to understand that arbitration clauses are evaluated separately from the underlying contract. Without this separability principle, a tribunal would need to assess whether the overall contract was valid in order to validate the arbitration clause. The problem with this is that the tribunal considering the question may not have jurisdiction to make that ruling, depending on whether or not the arbitration clause is valid. Thus, its validity is evaluated separately.

Note 6: For a thoughtful discussion of some of these issues, see Ronald Brand and Harry Flechtner, *Arbitration and Contract Formation in International Trade: First Interpretations of the U.N. Sales Convention*, 12 J.L. & Commerce 239 (1993).

IV.   MODIFICATION

As was briefly mentioned above in connection with the discussion of consideration, Article 29(1) establishes that all that is required for a contract to be modified or terminated is "the mere agreement of the parties." The text of the CISG, in particular the use of the phrase "mere agreement," belies the complexity that frequently exists when attempting to establish whether indeed an agreement to modify or terminate exists. However, it is clear from reading Article 29(1) that no consideration is required,[44] nor are any other formal requirements, unless the parties have specifically provided for such requirements through their own previous agreement. All that is required is an agreement. Figuring out whether an agreement exists implicates all the rules of interpretation found in Articles 8 and 9, as well as the rules on formation of an agreement, discussed earlier.[45]

---

[44] Note that UCC §2-209(1) expressly did away with the requirement of consideration for a modification to be valid in a sale of goods transaction governed by Article 2 of the UCC.
[45] *See e.g. NV A.R. [Belgian Seller] v. NV I [French Buyer]*, Hof van Beroep Gent no. 2001/AR/0180, Belgium, May 15, 2002 (available at http://cisgw3.law.pace.edu/cases/

> ### Article 29
>
> (1) A contract may be modified or terminated by the mere agreement of the parties.
>
> (2) A contract in writing which contains a provision requiring any modification or termination by agreement to be in writing may not be otherwise modified or terminated by agreement. However, a party may be precluded by his conduct from asserting such a provision to the extent that the other party has relied on that conduct.

While article 29 itself does not require a writing for a modification, there is an exception to this rule. Recall that Article 12, discussed above, provides that a Contracting State can make an Article 96 declaration. Article 96 allows a Contracting State to adopt the CISG but still require a writing for certain aspects of a contract to be effective, including a modification.[46] Thus, an Article 96 declaration might indeed indicate that no modification may be made without the written agreement of the parties.[47]

In contrast to action taken by Contracting States through an Article 96 declaration, the parties themselves in any particular transaction can always agree that any modification must be in writing. As has already been discussed, the CISG defers to the autonomy of the parties in any transaction to structure their transaction as they see fit. In accordance with this general principle, Article 29(2) provides that the parties can agree that any modification to their contract must be in writing, i.e. a "no oral modifications clause." This seemingly simple provision has actually proven to be quite problematic. The problem is best illustrated in the following example:

020515b1.html). In that case the Belgian court found that a modification was made when one of the parties sent its counterparty a confirmation of a modification and the counterparty was silent.

[46] Argentina, Armenia, Belarus, Chile, Estonia, Hungary, Latvia, Lithuania, Paraguay, Russian Federation, and Ukraine have all made an Article 96 Declaration. In addition, China has made a declaration similar in form to Article 96 but worded differently: "The People's Republic of China does not consider itself bound by . . . article 11 as well as the provision of the Convention relating to the content of article 11."

[47] For a listing of declarations and reservations that apply to Contracting States see the UNCITRAL website that relates to the status of the CISG (available at http://www.uncitral.org/uncitral/en/uncitral_texts/sale_goods/1980CISG_status.html).

Example 3-2

A Swiss Seller and a Brazilian Buyer of custom clocks enter a contract including a term requiring any modification to be in writing. Later, as the Swiss seller attempts to fulfill the contract for the Brazilian buyer, the seller calls the buyer and asks if the buyer will accept goods that are somewhat different from those specified in the contract. The buyer, deferring to the seller, agrees over the phone. Later, of course, the clocks that were supplied prove unsatisfactory to the buyer. The buyer brings an action against seller claiming that the goods do not conform to the original contract and that no modification occurred since the original contract called for any modification to be in writing. What would result from the claim?[48]

Because the CISG typically defers to the agreement of the parties, this example presents difficulty. The parties orally agreed to the modification even though they had previously agreed only to modify in writing. In effect, it seems that the parties, in their later oral agreement, are agreeing to waive the writing requirement and, considering all the circumstances, as Article 8 insists, are agreeing to the oral modification. The problem with this analysis is that any agreement that a modification be in writing would be undermined by any subsequent oral agreement. This analysis would make superfluous the CISG's explicit provision that the parties can agree that modifications must be in writing. Such an interpretation—one that would render a part of the CISG essentially meaningless—is not favored.

However, the CISG itself, in the second sentence of Article 29(2) states that a party may be precluded from asserting a writing requirement if that party has done something that has induced the other party to rely on an oral modification. In the hypothetical above, when the buyer agreed over the phone to accept the modified clocks, it can be argued that it also induced the seller's reliance on the oral modification and thus would be precluded from asserting the writing requirement.[49]

In the end, a middle ground for interpretation of this provision likely exists. One possibility would hold that a writing requirement for modifications be upheld

---

[48] The issue in this example is based loosely on the problem used in the 14th annual Willem C. Vis International Commercial Arbitration Moot (http://www.cisg.law.pace.edu/cisg/moot/moot14.pdf).
[49] In fact, the majority of commentators assert that a subsequent oral modification can override a no oral modifications clause. *E.g.* Secretariat Commentary on the 1978 Draft, *Guide to CISG Article 29* (available at http://cisgw3.law.pace.edu/cisg/text/secomm/secomm-29.html); Honnold, *supra* n. 7, at 231.

except in unusual circumstances where there is clearly conduct by one party in accepting an oral modification that should preclude that party from asserting the defense.[50]

Consider the following case as an example of the CISG's rules on formation of a contract, battle of the forms, and modification. Note that it was decided almost 10 years after the *Filanto v. Chilewich* decision.

United States Court of Appeals, Ninth Circuit

Chateau des Charmes Wines Ltd.

v.

Sabaté USA Inc., Sabaté S.A.

328 F.3d 528 (2003)

Filed May 5, 2003

Before Betty B. Fletcher, Alex Kozinsk, and

Stephen S. Trott, Circuit Judges.

OPINION

Per Curiam

Chateau des Charmes Wines, Ltd. ("Chateau des Charmes"), a Canadian company, appeals the dismissal of its action for breach of contract and related claims arising out of its purchase of wine corks from Sabaté, S.A. ("Sabaté France"), a French company, and Sabaté USA, Inc. ("Sabaté USA"), a wholly owned California subsidiary. The district court held that forum selection clauses in the invoices that Sabaté France sent to Chateau des Charmes were part of the contract between the parties and dismissed the case in favor of adjudication in France. Because we conclude that the forum selection clauses in question were not part of any agreement between the parties, we reverse.

---

[50] In their treatise, *supra* n. 9, at 124, Enderlein and Maskow argue that an oral agreement itself should not trump a no oral modifications clause. However, they maintain that an oral agreement coupled with some other evidence showing that reliance on the oral agreement was reasonable should be sufficient.

Factual Background and Procedural History

The material facts pertinent to this appeal are not disputed. ... Sabaté France manufactures and sells special wine corks that it claims will not cause wines to be spoiled by "cork taint," a distasteful flavor that some corks produce. It sells these corks through a wholly owned California subsidiary, Sabaté USA.

In February 2000, after some preliminary discussions about the characteristics of Sabaté's corks, Chateau des Charmes, a winery from Ontario, Canada, agreed by telephone with Sabaté USA to purchase a certain number of corks at a specific price. The parties agreed on payment and shipping terms. No other terms were discussed, nor did the parties have any history of prior dealings. Later that year, Chateau des Charmes placed a second telephone order for corks on the same terms. In total, Chateau des Charmes ordered 1.2 million corks.

Sabaté France shipped the corks to Canada in eleven shipments. For each shipment, Sabaté France also sent an invoice. Some of the invoices arrived before the shipments, some with the shipments, and some after the shipments. On the face of each invoice was a paragraph in French that specified that "Any dispute arising under the present contract is under the sole jurisdiction of the Court of Commerce of the City of Perpignan." On the back of each invoice a number of provisions were printed in French, including a clause that specified that "any disputes arising out of this agreement shall be brought before the court with jurisidiction to try the matter in the judicial district where Seller's registered office is located." Chateau des Charmes duly took delivery and paid for each shipment of corks. The corks were then used to bottle Chateau des Charmes' wines.

Chateau des Charmes claims that, in 2001, it noticed that the wine bottled with Sabaté's corks was tainted by cork flavors. Chateau des Charmes filed suit in federal district court in California against Sabaté France and Sabaté USA alleging claims for breach of contract, strict liability, breach of warranty, false advertising, and unfair competition. Sabaté France and Sabaté USA filed a motion to dismiss based on the forum selection clauses. The district court held that the forum selection clauses were valid and enforceable and dismissed the action. This appeal ensued.

Discussion

...

The question before us is whether the forum selection clauses in Sabaté France's invoices were part of any agreement between the parties. The disputes in this case arise out of an agreement for a sale of goods from a French party and a United States party to a Canadian party. Such international sales contracts are ordinarily governed by a multilateral treaty, the United Nations Convention on Contracts for the International Sale of Goods ("C.I.S.G."), which applies to "contracts of sale of goods between parties whose places of business are in different States ... when the States are Contracting States." C.I.S.G., art. 1(1)(a), 15 U.S.C.App., 52 Fed.Reg. 6262 (March 2, 1987). The United States, Canada, and France are all contracting states to the C.I.S.G. 15 U.S.C.App. (Parties to the Convention). And none has acceded to the Convention subject to reservations that would affect its applicability in this case. Moreover, because the President submitted the Convention to the Senate, which ratified it, *see* Public Notice 1004, U.S. Ratification of 1980 United Nations Convention on Contracts for the International Sale of Goods: Official English Text, reprinted in 15 U.S.C.App.; Letter of Transmittal from President Reagan to the Senate of the United States (Sept. 21, 1983), reprinted in 15 U.S.C.App., there is no doubt that the Convention is valid and binding federal law. Accordingly, the Convention governs the substantive question of contract formation as to the forum selection clauses.

Our conclusion that the C.I.S.G. governs the issues in this appeal is not in conflict with authority from our sister circuits that have applied state law. Both the Second Circuit and the First Circuit have confronted the question of what law governs issues of contract formation that are antecedent to determining the validity of and enforcing forum selection clauses. In *Evolution Online Sys. Inc. v. Koninklijke Nederland N.V., KPN,* 145 F.3d 505, 509 (2d Cir.1998), the Second Circuit applied New York law to a dispute between a Dutch company and a New York corporation regarding the production of computer software and the provision of technical services presumably because the Convention does not apply "to contracts in which the preponderant part of the obligations of the party who furnishes the goods consists in the supply of labor or other services." C.I.S.G., art. 3(2). The First Circuit's decision in *Lambert v. Kysar,* 983 F.2d 1110, 1119 (1st

Cir.1993), involved the resolution of an interstate dispute that had no international dimension.

II. Under the C.I.S.G., it is plain that the forum selection clauses were not part of any agreement between the parties. The Convention sets out a clear regime for analyzing international contracts for the sale of goods: "A contract of sale need not be concluded in or evidenced by writing and is not subject to any other requirement as to form." C.I.S.G., art. 11. A proposal is an offer if it is sufficiently definite to "indicate[ ] the goods and expressly or implicitly fix[ ] or make[ ] provision for determining the quantity and the price," *id.,* art. 14, and it demonstrates an intention by the offeror to be bound if the proposal is accepted. *Id.* In turn, an offer is accepted if the offeree makes a "statement ... or other conduct ... indicating assent to an offer." *Id.,* art. 18. Further, "A contract is concluded at the moment when an acceptance of an offer becomes effective." *Id.,* art. 23. Within such a framework, the oral agreements between Sabaté USA and Chateau des Charmes as to the kind of cork, the quantity, and the price were sufficient to create complete and binding contracts.

The terms of those agreements did not include any forum selection clause. Indeed, Sabaté France and Sabaté USA do not contend that a forum selection clause was part of their oral agreements, but merely that the clauses in the invoices became part of a binding agreement. The logic of this contention is defective. Under the Convention, a "contract may be modified or terminated by the mere agreement of the parties." *Id.,* art. 29(1). However, the Convention clearly states that "[a]dditional or different terms relating, among other things, to ... the settlement of disputes are considered to alter the terms of the offer materially." *Id.,* art. 19(3). There is no indication that Chateau des Charmes conducted itself in a manner that evidenced any affirmative assent to the forum selection clauses in the invoices. Rather, Chateau des Charmes merely performed its obligations under the oral contract.

Nothing in the Convention suggests that the failure to object to a party's unilateral attempt to alter materially the terms of an otherwise valid agreement is an "agreement" within the terms of Article 29. *Cf.* C.I.S.G., art. 8(3) ("In determining the intent of a party or the understanding a reasonable person would have had, due consideration is to be given to all relevant circumstances of the case including the negotiations, any practices which the parties have established between themselves, usages and any subsequent conduct of the parties."). Here, no circumstances exist to conclude that Chateau des Charmes' conduct evidenced an "agreement." We reject the contention that because Sabaté France sent multiple invoices it created an agreement as to the proper forum with Chateau des Charmes. The parties agreed in two telephone calls to a purchase of corks to be shipped in eleven batches. In such circumstances, a party's multiple attempts to alter an agreement unilaterally do not so effect. *See In re CFLC, Inc.,* 166 F.3d 1012, 1019 (9th Cir.1999).

Conclusion

Because the contract for the sale of corks did not contain the forum selection clauses in Sybaté France's invoices, there was nothing for the district court to enforce, and its dismissal of this action was an abuse of discretion. The action is reinstated.

REVERSED and **REMANDED**.

* * * * *

Notes and Commentary

Note 1: Again, this case was decided almost 10 years after the *Filanto v. Chilewich* decision. Antipathy towards the CISG in the United States courts seems to have subsided. In *Filanto*, the court reasoned that silence, coupled with performance, was an acceptance of the terms proposed by the counter party. In this case, this court also does not seem willing to take that position. Are the two cases reconcilable on that point? More specifically, might the buyer's acceptance of all the shipments, despite having received invoices specifying the additional terms, be deemed to be an acceptance of those new terms? Is it relevant that an oral agreement was already made? What provisions of the CISG are critical to this analysis?

Note 2: Indeed both parties seem to agree that their original contract was made through their oral agreement over the telephone. Note that such an oral agreement could not be made but for the CISG's flexibility that a contract need not be evidenced by a writing. Nonetheless, recall that any Contracting State that has made an Article 96 declaration will not be bound by this permissive formation rule and may indeed still require a writing. Neither of the Contracting States in this case has made such a declaration.

Note 3: Even if the original contract was made by way of the oral telephone conversation and therefore a battle of the forms situation is not present, might there have been a valid modification? The court does not discuss this possibility at much length, but Article 29 is very permissive in that it will find a modification as long as there is an agreement between the parties. So, regardless of the formation of an initial contract, might the invoices and the subsequent silence and acceptance of shipments by the buyer represent an agreement to modify? How does Article 8 affect your answer?

PROBLEMS

Problem 3-1: In the J&G transaction with NNM, NNM sends J&G a letter stating that it can supply all the steel J&G needs for a year and will do so at its costs plus a 10% mark-up for profit. Has NNM made an offer that J&G can accept?

Problem 3-2: In response to the letter just described, J&G sends a letter to NNM in which it states that it is ready and willing to go forward with a transaction to purchase all of its steel that it will need in the coming year from NNM. Under the CISG, is that an acceptance, a counter-offer, or neither?

Problem 3-3: Assume that NNM did make an offer to J&G, and that J&G mailed back its acceptance to NNM. Before that acceptance reaches NNM, J&G faxes NNM a letter stating that it reconsidered and would only accept on terms of cost plus 5%. Is there a contract under the CISG?

Problem 3-4: Assume NNM did make an offer to J&G, but that J&G replied with a form document that included a boilerplate clause subjecting all disputes to the federal courts in New York. NNM goes forward with the transaction, shipping the first installment of steel to J&G. Is the dispute resolution provision binding? What if the front of J&G's form document was filled out in Russian to accommodate the Russian party, but the boilerplate provisions, including the one about dispute resolution, was in English. Any difference?

Problem 3-5: Assume that J&G and NNM signed a written contract governing the sale of steel from NNM to J&G in monthly installments. After the third monthly installment, J&G realized that the parties had not agreed to a dispute resolution mechanism. J&G called NNM and suggested that any disputes be handled through arbitration organized by the ICC in Paris under the ICC arbitration rules and French law. The Russians agreed but later wanted to back out of that agreement. Is the modification binding?

4 THE OBLIGATIONS OF THE PARTIES

But I have promises to keep,
And miles to go before I sleep,
And miles to go before I sleep.[1]

- Robert Frost

Once it is determined that an agreement for a sale of goods has been formed under the CISG, the next area of inquiry involves understanding the obligations of the parties. This chapter will focus on those obligations, discussing first the obligations of the seller, and second, the obligations of the buyer. Issues regarding breach of those obligations, including remedies, will be covered in Chapter 5.

I.   THE OBLIGATIONS OF THE SELLER

Article 30 of the CISG sets forth the general mandate that the seller must fulfill its obligations required by both the parties' contract and the CISG. Article 8, discussed in Chapter 2, illustrates that the CISG focuses on enforcing the intent of the parties. Therefore, requiring a seller to fulfill its obligations under its contract with buyer should come as no surprise. Beyond the express agreement of the parties, however, the CISG imposes certain additional default obligations. More specifically, this section will consider the seller's obligations regarding: (A) delivery terms, (B) conformity of the goods, and (C) third party claims.

A.   DELIVERY TERMS

The parties to an international sale of goods are obligated under the CISG to follow the terms of their express agreement regarding the specifics of delivery. However, if the parties have not explicitly agreed on specific delivery terms, the CISG will supply those terms by default. Among the crucial questions that the CISG will address in the absence of the parties' choice are: where the goods are to be delivered, who is responsible for the delivery, when will the delivery occur, and who will bear the risk associated with delivery?

---

[1] Robert Frost, *Stopping by Woods on a Snowy Evening,* Lines 14–16.

This Section will first discuss Incoterms as a convenient method through which parties often expressly agree upon a set of commercial delivery terms that answer those questions. It will then describe the CISG's default provisions regarding delivery terms that apply by default in the absence of such agreement.

1. Incoterms as Express Term

Parties can and frequently do specify the shipping terms that they want to apply to their transaction. Chapter 1 introduced the notion of Incoterms. As was explained there, Incoterms are international commercial terms that represent a set of agreements regarding the place of delivery, responsibility for carriage and insurance, and the transfer of risk of goods subject to an international sale. Incoterms are defined in detail in a publication of the International Chamber of Commerce (ICC).[2] Examples of Incoterms are: "CIF" and "FOB." A complete set of Incoterms is set forth in the chart below.

However, some of the same acronyms used by the ICC in its Incoterms are also used by other sources. For example, many states in the United States still have commercial shipping acronyms defined in their version of the UCC.[3] Thus, "CIF" or "FOB" could possibly refer to the UCC's definition of those terms. Accordingly, parties should explicitly reference the source for their commercial shipping acronym in their agreement to avoid confusion. If no reference is made to where the term is more fully defined, then a discrepancy might occur later when, for example, one party claims to have intended the UCC's definition to apply and the other party claims to have intended the ICC's definition to apply. This problem can be solved easily by reference in the contract to what source the parties are, in fact, intending to use. In addition, if the parties intend to have the ICC definition apply, the ICC recommends referencing the version of their definitions, also to avoid confusion. The most recent version of the ICC Incoterm definitions was published in 2000.[4]

---

[2] The ICC's 2000 version of its Incoterms has been endorsed by UNICITRAL. ICC, *UN Body Commends Incoterms 2000,* http://www.iccwbo.org/iccbhgg/index.html (July 18, 2000).

[3] The definitions of commercial term acronyms under the UCC are less frequently used in international sales, as the section that references and defines those terms (§2-319 to §2-324) have been eliminated from the 2001 revisions to the official UCC. A legislative note indicates the UCC terms are "inconsistent with modern commercial practices." UCC §2-319, Legislative Note. Further, the Official Comment to §2-319 suggests that, absent any express agreement by the parties, the term "must be interpreted in light of any applicable usage of trade and any course of performance or course of dealing between the parties," which often will result in the ICC definitions governing. The UCC can be found online at: http://www.law.cornell.edu/UCC/UCC.table.art2.html.

[4] For advice that use of an Incoterm should directly reference Incoterms and the year of the definition desired, see, Albert H. Kritzer, Inst. of Intl. Commercial L., Pace L. Lib., *Roadmap to*

There are two principle benefits from the use of Incoterms. First, at a micro-level, the use of Incoterms is efficient for the parties involved in any particular transaction because such use avoids the transaction costs of negotiating and agreeing upon provisions covering the issues addressed by the Incoterm. Second, at a macro-level, the use of Incoterms also promotes uniformity in international commercial transactions by establishing certain familiar norms for shipping arrangements.

The ICC groups its thirteen Incoterms into four categories based on the place of shipment of the goods in question: (1) E-term, (2) F-terms, (3) C-terms, and (4) D-terms. Notice that the Incoterms also need to be followed by a named place or port in order for the delivery term to make sense. The terms typically dictate that delivery is to be effected by the seller at the place or port specified in the parenthetical after the Incoterm itself.[5]

	Delivery	Transfer of Risk	Carriage & Insurance	Transport
E-TERM: Goods are made available at seller's place of business; minimal risk to seller.				
EXW (named place) *Ex Works*	Seller delivers by making goods available at seller's specified place of business.	Risk passes to buyer when buyer picks up the goods.	Buyer arranges and pays for further transport costs and any desired insurance.	Any

---

Incoterms (2000), http://www.cisg.law.pace.edu/cisg/Incoterms2000.html (Dec. 12, 2005). So, for example, a term in a contract might read: "delivery CIF (Shanghai) (Incoterms 2000)."
[5] The preambles to the Incoterms provide a useful summary of the terms. The preambles can be found on the ICC's website at: http://www.iccwbo.org/Incoterms/id3040/index.html. In addition, another helpful chart of Incoterms can be found on the ICC's site at: http://www.iccwbo.org/Incoterms/wallchart/wallchart.pdf.

F-TERMS: Goods are made available to buyer's carrier.				
FAC (named place) *Free Carrier*	Seller must deliver goods cleared for export to buyer's carrier at specified place.	Risk passes to buyer at delivery.	Buyer arranges and pays for further transport[6] costs and any desired insurance.	Any
FAS (named port of shipment) *Free Alongside Ship*	Seller must deliver goods cleared for export alongside ship at specific port.	Risk passes to buyer at delivery.	Buyer arranges and pays for further transport costs and any desired insurance.	Water only

---

[6] In all of the F-terms, the seller is not obligated in any way to arrange or pay for carriage. However, in practice it may be more convenient for the seller to arrange for carriage at the buyer's expense and that is often the case. See comment to FCA, term A-3 in Jan Ramberg, *ICC Guide to Incoterms 2000,* at 78 (ICC Publg. S.A. 1999).

FOB (named port of shipment) *Free on Board*	Seller must deliver goods cleared for export across the ship's rail at specified port.	Risk passes to buyer at delivery.	Buyer arranges and pays for further transport costs and any desired insurance.	Water only

C-TERMS: Seller pays for shipping to destination, but delivers to carrier and does not bear risks of transport.

CFR (Named port of destination) *Cost and Freight*	Seller must deliver goods cleared for export across the ship's rail.	Risk passes to buyer at delivery.	Seller arranges and pays costs and freight to destination; buyer arranges and pays for any desired insurance.	Water only

CIF (Named port of destination) *Cost, Insurance and Freight*	Seller must deliver goods cleared for export across the ship's rail.	Risk passes to buyer at delivery.	Seller arranges and pays costs and freight to destination; seller arranges and pays for insurance.	Water only
CPT (Named place of destination) *Carriage Paid To*	Seller must deliver goods cleared for export to carrier.	Risk passes to buyer at delivery.	Seller arranges and pays costs and freight to destination; buyer arranges and pays for any desired insurance.	Any
CIP (Named place of destination) *Carriage and Insurance Paid To*	Seller must deliver goods cleared for export to carrier.	Risk passes to buyer at delivery.	Seller arranges and pays costs and freight to destination; seller arranges and pays for insurance.	Any

D-TERMS: Seller pays for shipping to destination, delivers to destination, and bears risks throughout.

DAF (Named place) *Delivered at Frontier*	Seller must deliver goods cleared for export to frontier specified.	Risk passes to buyer at delivery.	Seller arranges and pays costs and freight.	Any
DES (Named port of destination) *Delivered Ex Ship*	Seller must deliver goods cleared for export on the ship at port specified.	Risk passes to buyer at delivery.	Seller arranges and pays costs and freight.	Water
DEQ (Named port of destination) *Delivered Ex Quay* *(Duty Paid)*	Seller must deliver goods cleared for export on the wharf (quay) at the port specified.	Risk passes to buyer at delivery.	Seller arranges and pays costs and freight.	Water

DDU (Named place of destination) *Delivered Duty Unpaid*	Seller must deliver goods at place specified.	Risk passes to buyer at delivery.	Seller arranges and pays costs and freight, but no import duties.	Any
DDP (Named place of destination) *Delivered Duty Paid*	Seller must deliver goods cleared for import at place specified.	Risk passes to buyer at delivery.	Seller arranges and pays costs and freight, including any import duties.	Any

Of course, an attorney representing a party to an international sale of goods must be able to use and understand Incoterms completely. Having the basic idea of what any particular Incoterm means is only the beginning. Reference should be made to the ICC definition that more completely defines the Incoterm in order to understand exactly what the parties to the sales agreement are undertaking. Likewise, if the UCC was referenced as the source for the commercial term used, then the attorney should consult the UCC for the exact definition of that term. Not having read and understood the full text of the applicable term is similar to not having read or understood several pages of the sales contract.

As an example, consider the following full definition of CIF from the ICC Incoterms (2000).[7]

> **COST, INSURANCE AND FREIGHT** (…named port of destination)
>
> Cost, Insurance and Freight" means that the seller delivers when the goods pass the ship's rail in the port of shipment.
>
> The seller must pay the costs and freight necessary to bring the goods to the named port of destination BUT the risk of loss of or damage to the goods, as well as any additional costs due to

---

[7] Intl. Chamber Commerce, *Incoterms 2000: CIF,* http://www.iccwbo.org/Incoterms/id3040/index.html.

events occurring after the time of delivery, are transferred from the seller to the buyer. However, in CIF the seller also has to procure marine insurance against the buyer's risk of loss of or damage to the goods during the carriage.

Consequently, the seller contracts for insurance and pays the insurance premium. The buyer should note that under the CIF term the seller is required to obtain insurance only on minimum cover. Should the buyer wish to have the protection of greater cover, he would either need to agree as much expressly with the seller or to make his own extra insurance arrangements.

The CIF term requires the seller to clear the goods for export.

This term can be used only for sea and inland waterway transport. If the parties do not intend to deliver the goods across the ship's rail, the CIP term should be used.

A.   THE SELLER'S OBLIGATIONS

A1   Provision of goods in conformity with the contract

The seller must provide the goods and the commercial invoice, or its equivalent electronic message, in conformity with the contract of sale and any other evidence of conformity which may be required by the contract.

A2   Licenses, authorizations and formalities

The seller must obtain at his own risk and expense any export license or other official authorization and carry out, where applicable, all customs formalities necessary for the export of the goods.

A3   Contracts of carriage and insurance

a) Contract of carriage

The seller must contract on usual terms at his own expense for the carriage of the goods to the named port of destination by the usual route in a seagoing vessel (or inland waterway vessel as the case may be) of the type normally used for the transport of goods of the contract description.

b) Contract of insurance

The seller must obtain at his own expense cargo insurance as agreed in the contract, such as the buyer, or any other person having an insurable interest in the goods, shall be entitled to claim directly from the insurer and provide the buyer with the insurance policy or other evidence of insurance cover.

The insurance shall be contracted with underwriters or an insurance company of good repute and, failing express agreement to the contrary, be in accordance with minimum cover of the Institute Cargo Clauses (Institute of London Underwriters) or any similar set of clauses. The duration of insurance cover shall be in accordance with B5 and B4. When required by the buyer, the seller shall provide at the buyer's expense war, strikes, riots and civil commotion risk insurances if procurable. The minimum insurance shall cover the price provided in the contract plus ten per cent (i.e. 110%) and shall be provided in the currency of the contract.

A4   Delivery

The seller must deliver the goods on board the vessel at the port of shipment on the date or within the agreed period.

A5   Transfer of risks

The seller must, subject to the provisions of B5, bear all risks of loss of or damage to the goods until such time as they have passed the ship's rail at the port of shipment.

A6   Division of costs

The seller must, subject to the provisions of B6, pay

• all costs relating to the goods until such time as they have been delivered in accordance with A4; and

• the freight and all other costs resulting from A3 a), including the costs of loading the goods on board and any charges for unloading at the agreed port of discharge which were for the seller's account under the contract of carriage;

• where applicable, the costs of customs formalities necessary for export as well as all duties, taxes and other charges payable upon export, and for their transit through any country if they were for the seller's account under the contract of carriage.

A7   Notice to the buyer

The seller must give the buyer sufficient notice that the goods have been delivered in accordance with A4 as well as any other notice required in order to allow the buyer to take measures which are normally necessary to enable him to take the goods.

A8   Proof of delivery, transport document or equivalent electronic message

The seller must, at his own expense, provide the buyer without delay with, the usual transport document for the agreed port of destination.

This document (for example a negotiable bill of lading, a nonnegotiable sea waybill or an inland waterway document) must cover the contract goods, be dated within the period agreed for shipment, enable the buyer to claim the goods from the carrier at the port of destination and, unless otherwise agreed, enable the buyer to sell the goods in transit by the transfer of the document to a subsequent buyer (the negotiable bill of lading) or by notification to the carrier.

When such a transport document is issued in several originals, a full set of originals must be presented to the buyer.

Where the seller and the buyer have agreed to communicate electronically, the document referred to in the preceding paragraphs may be replaced by an equivalent electronic data interchange (EDI) message.

A9   Checking—packaging—marking

The seller must pay the costs of those checking operations (such as checking quality, measuring, weighing, and counting) which are necessary for the purpose of delivering the goods in accordance with A4.

The seller must provide at his own expense packaging (unless it is usual for the particular trade to ship the goads of the contract description unpacked) which is required for the transport of the goods arranged by him.   Packaging is to be marked appropriately.

A10   Other obligations

The seller must render the buyer at the latter's request, risk and expense, every assistance in obtaining any documents or equivalent electronic messages (other than those mentioned in A8) issued or transmitted in the country of shipment and/or of origin which the buyer may require for the import of the goods and, where necessary, for their transit through any country.

The seller must provide the buyer, upon request, with the necessary information for procuring insurance.

B. THE BUYER'S OBLIGATIONS

B1   Payment of the price

The buyer must pay the price as provided in the contract of sale.

B2   Licenses, authorizations and formalities

The buyer must obtain at his own risk and expense any import license or other official authorization and carry out, where applicable, all customs formalities for the import of the goods and for their transit through any country.

B3   Contracts of carriage and insurance

a) Contract of carriage

No obligation.

b) Contract of insurance

No obligation.

B4   Taking delivery

The buyer must accept delivery of the goods when they have been delivered in accordance with A4 and receive them from the carrier at the named port of destination.

B5   Transfer of risks

The buyer must bear all risks of loss of or damage to the goods from the time they have passed the ship s rail at the port of shipment.

The buyer must, should he fail to give notice in accordance with B7, bear all risks of loss of or damage to the goods from the agreed date or the expiry date of the period fixed for shipment provided, however, that the goods have been duly appropriated to the contract, that is to say, clearly set aside or otherwise identified as the contract goods.

B6   Division of costs

The buyer must, subject to the provisions of A3, pay

• all costs relating to the goods from the time they have been delivered in accordance with A4; and

• all costs and charges relating to the goods whilst in transit until their arrival at the port of destination, unless such costs and charges were for the seller's account under the contract of carriage; and

• unloading costs including lighterage and wharfage charges, unless such costs and charges were for the seller's account under the contract of carriage; and

• all additional costs incurred if he fails to give notice in accordance with B7, for the goods from the agreed date or the expiry date of the period fixed for shipment, provided, however, that the goods have been duly appropriated to the contract, that is to say, clearly set aside or otherwise identified as the contract goods; and

• where applicable, all duties, taxes and other charges as well as the costs of carrying out customs formalities payable upon import of the goods and, where necessary, for their transit through any country unless included within the cost of the contract of carriage.

B7   Notice to the seller

The buyer must, whenever he is entitled to determine the time for shipping the goods and/or the port of destination, give the seller sufficient notice thereof.

B8   Proof of delivery, transport document or equivalent electronic message

The buyer must accept the transport document in accordance with A8 if it is in conformity with the contract.

B9   Inspection of goods

The buyer must pay the costs of any pre-shipment inspection except when such inspection is mandated by the country of export.

B10   Other obligations

The buyer must pay all costs and charges incurred in obtaining the documents or equivalent electronic messages mentioned in A10 and reimburse those incurred by the seller in rendering his assistance in accordance therewith.

The buyer must provide the seller, upon request, with the necessary information for procuring insurance.

As one can see from the definition of CIF, an Incoterm represents a detailed set of agreements that will be binding upon parties that use that term in a contract. Accordingly, any attorney dealing with a contract that incorporates such a term, must understand that term and its implications fully. Consider the following example of the implications of an Incoterm.

Example 4-1

A German manufacturer sold an American medical devices company an MRI machine. The machine was damaged in transit. The contract contained a CIF term, but also stipulated that title to the property did not transfer until full payment was made on the machine. The insurance company arguing the case on behalf of the American buyer, asserted that the loss should remain with the German seller since title was retained by it until full payment, which had not been made when the loss occurred. Notwithstanding that argument, the United States federal court determined that the CIF term governed the passing of risk. Accordingly, the court ruled that the risk of damage in transit transferred to the buyer after the seller delivered the MRI machine to the specified carrier.[8]

---

2.   Default Delivery Terms

As was just described, parties often agree, through Incoterms or otherwise, on the specifics of their delivery terms. Where the parties do not agree, the CISG provides for default delivery terms related to: (a) place of the delivery, (b) carriage and insurance, (c) timing of delivery, (d) delivery of required documents, and (e) transfer of risk.

---

[8] *St. Paul Guardian Ins. Co., et al. v. Neuromed Med. Sys. & Support, et al.,* 2002 WL 465312 (S.D.N.Y. Mar. 26, 2002). This case is also interesting because the CIF term was used without any reference to the ICC or any particular version of the ICC Incoterm definition. The court ultimately used CISG Article 9(2) to argue that Incoterms are usages of trade and the ICC definitions can fairly be implied into the parties' contract when the parties use such terms. *Id.* at *4.

a.   *Place of Delivery*

If the parties do not include any particular shipping term in their agreement, through use of an Incoterm or otherwise, the CISG's default terms will apply. Article 31 specifies that the agreement of the parties will govern where the goods are to be delivered. However, in the absence of agreement, if the contract involves shipment, then the seller must deliver the goods to the first carrier (Article 31(a)). If the contract does not involve shipment, and the goods are known to be at or to be produced at a particular place, then delivery is to occur at that place (Article 31(b)). In all other cases, the delivery is to occur at the place of seller's business at the time when the contract was concluded (Article 31(c)).

Article 31

If the seller is not bound to deliver the goods at any other particular place, his obligation to deliver consists:

(a) if the contract of sale involves carriage of the goods - in handing the goods over to the first carrier for transmission to the buyer;

(b) if, in cases not within the preceding subparagraph, the contract relates to specific goods, or unidentified goods to be drawn from a specific stock or to be manufactured or produced, and at the time of the conclusion of the contract the parties knew that the goods were at, or were to be manufactured or produced at, a particular place - in placing the goods at the buyer's disposal at that place;

(c) in other cases - in placing the goods at the buyer's disposal at the place where the seller had his place of business at the time of the conclusion of the contract.

The place of delivery of the goods is relevant not only for the obligations of the seller, but also may be relevant for a national court considering whether it has jurisdiction over the parties to the transaction. Where the parties have agreed, either expressly in their contract, or by default through the provisions of the CISG, that delivery will occur in a particular place, the courts of that place might well be justified in taking jurisdiction over the parties.[9]

---

[9] For an in-depth discussion of the role of Article 31 in determining a court's jurisdiction, see Ronald A. Brand, *CISG Article 31: When Substantive Law Rules Affect Jurisdictional Results*, 25 J. L. & Com. 181 (2005).

Example 4-2

A French shoe manufacturer sold a shipment of shoes to a Belgian buyer. The Belgian buyer complained to a Belgian court that the shoes delivered were not in conformity with the contract. In accordance with the then relevant European convention on jurisdiction,[10] jurisdiction is proper in the European country where performance occurs under the relevant substantive contract law. In a sale of goods transaction governed by the CISG, the court reasoned that performance occurs at the place of delivery. The court then applied Article 31(a) to determine that delivery in this case, where carriage of the goods was a part of the transaction, consisted of delivery to the carrier in France. Accordingly, the Belgian court held that it did not have jurisdiction to hear the case.[11]

---

b. Carriage and Insurance

Article 32 addresses the carriage of goods and their insurance. Article 32(1) provides that if the seller is to deliver goods to a carrier and the goods cannot be identified to the contract, then the seller must notify the buyer of the shipment, specifying the goods so that the buyer can claim them upon delivery. Article 32(2) states that if the seller is to arrange for carriage, then it is to undertake any contracts necessary for that carriage and must undertake carriage in a manner that is "appropriate in the circumstances and according to the terms usual for such transport" (Article 32(2)). This provision reflects the CISG's general deference to international norms, reflected in Article 9. Finally, if the seller is not to provide insurance, it must cooperate with the buyer so that the buyer can purchase insurance (Article 32(3)). This principle of cooperation is another

---

[10] The European Community Convention on Jurisdiction and the Enforcement of Judgments in Civil and Commercial Matters (Brussels Convention 1968), Note that the Brussels Convention of 1968 has been superseded in large part by the Brussels 1 Regulation (the Council Regulation (EC) No 44/2001 of 22 December 2000 on Jurisdiction and the Recognition and Enforcement of Judgments in Civil and Commercial Matters). For a case analyzing jurisdiction under the Brussels 1 Regulation using Article 31 of the CISG, see *German Buyer v. Belgian Seller (Pitted Sour Cherries Case)*, Landgericht Neubrandenburg no. 10 O 74/04, Germany, Aug. 3, 2005 (available at http://cisgw3.law.pace.edu/cases/050803g1.html).

[11] *See e.g. B.V.B.A. Vano v. S.A. Manufactures de chaussures Jean Cabireau*, Rechtbank van koophandel Kortrijk no. A.R. 3247/96, Belgium, Jan. 6, 1997 (abstract available at http://www.unilex.info/case.cfm?pid=1&do=case&id=334&step=Abstract). For a similar case, see *Tissage Impression Mecanique J.J.M. S.A. v. M.J.H.M. Foppen*, Gerechtshof Hertogenbosch no. 334/95/MA, Netherlands, Oct. 9, 1995 (abstract available at http://www.unilex.info/case.cfm?pid=1&do=case&id=144&step=Abstract); and *Société Franco-Africaine de distribution textile v. More and More Textilfabrik GmbH*, Cour d'Appel de Paris, France, Mar. 18, 1998 (abstract available at http://www.unilex.info/case.cfm?pid=1&do=case&id=342&step=Abstract).

general principle underlying the CISG and will be evident in provisions about notice, cure, and mitigation, addressed later in the CISG.[12]

Article 32

(1) If the seller, in accordance with the contract or this Convention, hands the goods over to a carrier and if the goods are not clearly identified to the contract by markings on the goods, by shipping documents or otherwise, the seller must give the buyer notice of the consignment specifying the goods.

(2) If the seller is bound to arrange for carriage of the goods, he must make such contracts as are necessary for carriage to the place fixed by means of transportation appropriate in the circumstances and according to the usual terms for such transportation.

(3) If the seller is not bound to effect insurance in respect of the carriage of the goods, he must, at the buyer's request, provide him with all available information necessary to enable him to effect such insurance.

Example 4-3

An Austrian buyer had contracted with a Swiss seller for the sale of a certain quantity of alcohol for resale. A dispute between the parties broke out regarding several of the basic terms of the contract. The Austrian buyer alleged, among other things, that the Swiss seller had used a train for transport of the goods in contravention of the agreement of the parties to use trucks for the delivery.

The Swiss court ruled that there was insufficient evidence to prove that the parties had agreed upon delivery by truck. The court then went on to rely on Article 32(2) of the CISG to hold that since the Swiss seller was expected to arrange for delivery, in the absence of an agreement otherwise, it was able to use whatever reasonable means it deemed appropriate for that delivery. Since the Swiss seller had used train transport in the

---

[12] *See e.g.* CISG arts. 26, 34, 39, 60, 46–48, 77, 85, 86.

> past for the delivery of alcohol, train transport was acceptable in this case too.[13]

c.   *Timing of Delivery*

Article 33 also specifies that the agreement of the parties governs the timing of the delivery (Article 33(a) and (b)). However, in the absence of agreement, the goods are to be delivered "within a reasonable time after the conclusion of the contract" (Article 33(c)).

Article 33

The seller must deliver the goods:

(a) if a date is fixed by or determinable from the contract, on that date;

(b) if a period of time is fixed by or determinable from the contract, at any time within that period unless circumstances indicate that the buyer is to choose a date; or

(c) in any other case, within a reasonable time after the conclusion of the contract.

Of course what is reasonable in a particular circumstance will not always be easy to determine. Articles 7, 8, and 9 lend some help in this inquiry. Recall here the instructions of Article 7 that when interpreting the CISG due regard is to be had for its international character and the need to promote uniformity in its application. When considering Article 7, what is a reasonable time period will likely be established with reference to international norms for transactions that are similar to the one in question. Article 8(3) states that when interpreting the intent of the parties (here the parties' intent regarding when delivery should be made) all of the relevant circumstances should be considered. Further, Article 9 indicates that party practices and accepted international trade norms can be implied into the agreement of the parties. In accordance with these sections, the Secretariat Commentary to Article 33 instructs that, "What is a reasonable time depends on what constitutes acceptable commercial conduct in the circumstances of the case."

---

[13] *See Austrian Buyer v. Swiss Seller (Spirits Case),* Bezirksgericht [District Court] der Saane no. 171/95, Switzerland, Feb. 20, 1997 (available at http://cisgw3.law.pace.edu/cases/970220s1.html).

> **Example 4-4**
>
> A German buyer contracted to buy a used business machine from a Swiss seller. The contract did not specify a delivery date. The Swiss court ruled that in accordance with Article 33 of the CISG, the machine had to be delivered within a reasonable time after conclusion of the contract. An earlier e-mail between the parties indicated that the machine was still going to be in use for about one and a half months after the contract was concluded, implying that the machine would be available for delivery at some time shortly thereafter. Accordingly, the court ruled that any delivery three months or more after the contract date would not be reasonable given these circumstances.[14]

d.   *Delivery of Relevant Documents*

Article 34 outlines the requirements for delivery of documents related to a sale of goods transaction. The delivery must be in accordance with the terms agreed upon by the parties. In addition, though, Article 34 specifies that if the seller delivers documents that do not conform to the contract, the seller may cure the defect as long as two criteria are met: (i) the cure occurs before the date required for the delivery, and (ii) the cure does not cause the buyer any unreasonable inconvenience or expense.[15] This ability to cure is yet another principle echoed throughout the CISG. Rights to cure are specifically addressed later in Chapter 5. The seller is generally allowed to cure any defects in its delivery of goods as long as there is no undue prejudice to buyer. While Article 34 specifically provides the seller with the right to cure, it also specifically preserves the buyer's right to any damages caused by the seller's delivery of non-conforming documents. Note that as described in Chapter 1, in a documentary transaction delivery of the appropriate shipping documents can be critical for a buyer's ability to actually take delivery of the goods at their final port of destination.

---

[14] *See German Buyer v. Swiss Seller (Machines Case)*, Kantonsgericht [Cantonal Court] Appenzell Ausserrhoden no. Proz, Nr. 433/02, Switzerland, Mar. 10, 2003 (available at http://cisgw3.law.pace.edu/cases/030310s1.html)

[15] This portion of Article 34, allowing for a party to cure defects in the documents is analogous to the cure provision in Article 37, discussed in Chapter 5. John O. Honnold, *Uniform Law for International Sales under the 1980 United Nations Convention* 249 (3d ed., Kluwer L. Intl. 999).

> ### Article 34
>
> If the seller is bound to hand over documents relating to the goods, he must hand them over at the time and place and in the form required by the contract. If the seller has handed over documents before that time, he may, up to that time, cure any lack of conformity in the documents, if the exercise of this right does not cause the buyer unreasonable inconvenience or unreasonable expense. However, the buyer retains any right to claim damages as provided for in this Convention.

e.   *Transfer of Risk*

Article 36 explains that the seller is liable for any non-conformity of the goods that exists before it transfers the risk concerning the goods to the buyer (Article 36(1)). In addition, the seller is liable for any non-conformity of the goods that develops after the transfer of risk to the buyer if the seller was the cause of the non-conformity (Article 36(2)).

> ### Article 36
>
> (1) The seller is liable in accordance with the contract and this Convention for any lack of conformity which exists at the time when the risk passes to the buyer, even though the lack of conformity becomes apparent only after that time.
>
> (2) The seller is also liable for any lack of conformity which occurs after the time indicated in the preceding paragraph and which is due to a breach of any of his obligations, including a breach of any guarantee that for a period of time the goods will remain fit for their ordinary purpose or for some particular purpose or will retain specified qualities or characteristics.

Because liability often turns on when the transfer of risk occurs, it is important to consider that question here. The CISG contains several default provisions with respect to when the transfer of risk occurs in an international sale of goods transaction. These provisions are not included in the section of the CISG describing the obligations of the seller. Instead, they are set forth in their own chapter on Passing of Risk, CISG Chapter IV.

Article 66 begins the CISG's treatment on transfer of risk by stating that once the risk has been transferred from the seller to the buyer, then the buyer is obligated to pay the price for the goods whether or not there is subsequent loss or damage (provided that the damage not be caused by the seller). This provision is crucial to the entire transfer of risk concept. Without the buyer's continued responsibility to pay for the goods, the risk of loss or damage would not be meaningful to buyer. It could simply not pay for the goods and have lost nothing.

Article 66

Loss of or damage to the goods after the risk has passed to the buyer does not discharge him from his obligation to pay the price, unless the loss or damage is due to an act or omission of the seller.

Notwithstanding Article 66, the Seller will still be liable for any loss or damage to the goods under Article 36(2) if the loss is due to any breach of seller's obligations. Further, even if the buyer is liable under Article 66, it is typically the case that the parties would have procured insurance to cover risk of loss or damage during transit. In such a case, even though the buyer is still obligated to pay the purchase price, the buyer should be able to seek reimbursement for its losses from the insurer.

Example 4-5

A United States buyer of jasmine aldehyde instructed the Chinese seller that the chemical could not be subjected to high temperatures during transit. The Chinese seller assured the United States buyer that the temperatures during transit would not be dangerously high. When the chemical arrived in New York it had melted.

The parties had agreed to shipment CIF and thus ordinarily the buyer would bear the risk of any loss during transit. However, in this case the tribunal found the seller to be liable for the damage since it had specifically assured the buyer that the temperature during transit would not damage the goods. Thus, the buyer was relieved of its responsibility for payment of the goods.[16]

Article 67 provides the first of the CISG's default rules regarding when the risk transfers. As with the default rules cited above, it also starts out with a statement indicating that the agreement of the parties is determinative, but in the absence of any such agreement, the default rule will apply. Remember that the inclusion of an Incoterm will incorporate a provision on when risk transfers. Thus, if an Incoterm has been used, these default provisions will not apply. The default rule in Article 67 applies where there is a sale of goods that involves carriage. In that type of transaction, if the parties have not agreed on when risk transfers, it will transfer when the seller has delivered the goods to the first carrier.

Article 67

(1) If the contract of sale involves carriage of the goods and the seller is not bound to hand them over at a particular place, the risk passes to the buyer when the goods are handed over to the first carrier for transmission to the buyer in accordance with the contract of sale. If the seller is bound to hand the goods over to a carrier at a particular place, the risk does not pass to the buyer until the goods are handed over to the carrier at that place. The fact that the seller is authorized to retain documents controlling the disposition of the goods does not affect the passage of the risk.

(2) Nevertheless, the risk does not pass to the buyer until the goods are clearly identified to the contract, whether by markings on the goods, by shipping documents, by notice given to the buyer or otherwise.

This transfer of risk is independent of other issues. For example, the seller might still be obligated under the contract to pay for the carriage of the goods, or to pay for insurance related to the goods. Regardless, if the contract does not specify when the transfer of risk occurs, in a sale that includes carriage, the risk will transfer at the moment the seller delivers to that first carrier. This means that the

---

[16] *United States Buyer v. Chinese Seller (Jasmine Aldehyde Case)*, CIETAC Arbitration no. CISG/1995/01, China, Feb. 23, 1995) (available at http://cisgw3.law.pace.edu/cases/ 950223c1.html).

buyer will then be responsible for any loss or damage to the goods that occurs in transit.

Even if the contract specified that the seller is to procure insurance for the goods while they are in transit, the default rule contained in Article 67 makes the buyer the ultimate beneficiary of the insurance. Accordingly, the buyer may have more of an interest in getting the insurance itself or in being very clear with the seller as to what level and type of insurance must be procured.

Note also that Article 67(2) states that, notwithstanding the default rule just described, the risk will not transfer until the goods to be shipped are clearly identified to the contract.[17] Making this clear identification is an obligation of the seller under Article 32(1), described above. If that obligation is not satisfied, then the risk of loss or damage remains with the seller until either the seller identifies the goods being shipped to the contract or, in the absence of such identification, the buyer actually takes delivery of the goods or breaches by failing to do so (Article 69(1)).

Article 68 specifically addresses a sale of goods that are already in transit. In this case, the transfer of the risk occurs at the conclusion of the contract, when the goods are mid-transit. Still, Article 68 adds some qualifications. First, reminiscent of Article 8's mandate that all circumstances be considered in questions of interpretation, if the circumstances indicate that the transfer of risk was assumed by the buyer starting at the moment when the goods were first delivered to the carrier, then the transfer of risk will occur at that point.[18] In no event, however, will the buyer be responsible for any loss or damage to the goods that occurred before the contract was made if the seller "knew or ought to have known" about such loss or damage and did not disclose that information to the buyer. Here, the CISG is again allowing for a broader knowledge standard than simply actual knowledge, in an effort to protect buyers from situations where the seller denies knowledge, but it is clear that the seller should have known.

---

[17] The rationale behind Article 67(2) is to prevent a seller from "abusing the lacking *identification to the contract* in order to put the blame for losses or damages on a certain buyer." Fritz Enderlein & Dietrich Maskow, *International Sales Law* 267 (Oceana Publications 1992).

[18] Several commentators argue that this exception should actually be the default rule—in other words, that the risk should always transfer at the point when the goods were first handed over to the carrier. The rationale for this is that the timing of damage during transit is difficult to determine so that a bright line rule transferring risk at the moment when transit begins is a more manageable rule. *See e.g.* Honnold, *supra* n. 15, at 409; Joseph Lookofsky, *The 1980 United Nations Convention on Contracts for the International Sale of Goods*, in *International Encyclopaedia of Laws—Contracts*, Suppl. 29, 144-145 (J. Herbots & R. Blanpain eds., Kluwer L. Intl. 2000).

> ## Article 68
>
> The risk in respect of goods sold in transit passes to the buyer from the time of the conclusion of the contract. However, if the circumstances so indicate, the risk is assumed by the buyer from the time the goods were handed over to the carrier who issued the documents embodying the contract of carriage. Nevertheless, if at the time of the conclusion of the contract of sale the seller knew or ought to have known that the goods had been lost or damaged and did not disclose this to the buyer, the loss or damage is at the risk of the seller.

Article 69 serves as a catch-all provision, applying in cases not covered by Articles 67 or 68. Article 69 differentiates between two scenarios. In the first scenario, the goods are made available to the buyer at the seller's place of business. In that case, the transfer of risk occurs at the moment the buyer either: (i) has taken the goods, or (ii) has been so late in taking the goods as to have committed a breach (Article 69(1)). In the second scenario, the seller must make the goods available for buyer at someplace other than its own place of business. In that case, the transfer of risk occurs when the goods are due at that other place, and the buyer has been notified that they are at its disposal, whether or not the buyer has actually taken the goods (Article 69(2)). Finally, Article 69(3) specifies that the transfer of risk will not occur even if the goods have been put at the buyer's disposal, if the goods have not been clearly identified to the contract.

> ## Article 69
>
> (1) In cases not within articles 67 and 68, the risk passes to the buyer when he takes over the goods or, if he does not do so in due time, from the time when the goods are placed at his disposal and he commits a breach of contract by failing to take delivery.
>
> (2) However, if the buyer is bound to take over the goods at a place other than a place of business of the seller, the risk passes when delivery is due and the buyer is aware of the fact that the goods are placed at his disposal at that place.
>
> (3) If the contract relates to goods not then identified, the goods are considered not to be placed at the disposal of the buyer until they are clearly identified to the contract.

B.   CONFORMITY OF THE GOODS

As was mentioned, Article 30 states generally that a seller must deliver goods as required by the parties' contract and the CISG.

Article 30

The seller must deliver the goods, hand over any documents relating to them and transfer the property in the goods, as required by the contract and this Convention.

Article 35 then goes on to detail the standards for conformity applied by the CISG. Article 35 is a critical one to understand since it is so often at the heart of disputes under the CISG. If a buyer is unsatisfied with the goods that have been delivered, the buyer is likely to bring an action under this Article.

Article 35

(1) The seller must deliver goods which are of the quantity, quality and description required by the contract and which are contained or packaged in the manner required by the contract.

(2) Except where the parties have agreed otherwise, the goods do not conform with the contract unless they:

(a) are fit for the purposes for which goods of the same description would ordinarily be used;

(b) are fit for any particular purpose expressly or impliedly made known to the seller at the time of the conclusion of   the contract, except where the circumstances show that   the buyer did not rely, or that it was unreasonable for   him   to rely, on the seller's skill and judgment;

(c) possess the qualities of goods which the seller has held out to the buyer as a sample or model;

(d) are contained or packaged in the manner usual for such goods or, where there is no such manner, in a manner adequate to preserve and protect the goods.

(3) The seller is not liable under subparagraphs (a) to (d) of the preceding paragraph for any lack of conformity of the goods

> if at the time of the conclusion of the contract the buyer knew or could not have been unaware of such lack of conformity.

1. Goods Must Be of the Quantity, Quality, and Description Required by the Contract

Article 35(1) states the general proposition that the seller must deliver goods of the quantity, quality, and description set forth in the contract. This general proposition is the basis for a suit by buyer that the goods received are not the goods that were ordered. Further, this provision also mandates that the goods be packaged in accordance with specifications set forth in the contract.

Example 4-6

A German car dealer bought a used car from an Italian car dealer. After the buyer took delivery of the car, it discovered that the odometer had been tampered with to show lower mileage than was actually the case. Under Article 35(1), the German buyer prevailed on a claim against the Italian seller for the delivery of non-conforming goods.[19]

---

2. Goods Must Conform

Article 35(2) describes four conditions that must be satisfied in order for goods to conform under the CISG. In particular, those conditions are: (a) conforming to the ordinary purpose of the goods, (b) conforming to any particular purpose made known to the seller, (c) conforming to any samples or models made available to the buyer before the contract for sale was concluded, and (d) being packaged in a manner appropriate to preserving and protecting the goods.

a. Goods Must Conform to their Ordinary Purpose

First, the goods must be fit for their ordinary purpose (Article 35(2)(a)). In other words, the buyer must get what a reasonable person would expect to get when ordering the goods involved. If buyer purchases computer printers, the printers

---

[19] Based on *German Buyer v. Italian Seller (Used Car Case)*, Oberlandesgericht Köln no. 22 U 4/96, Germany, May 21, 1996 (available at http://cisgw3.law.pace.edu/cases/960521g1.html).

should be able to print. Any special qualities of the printer, however, would be beyond the scope of the ordinary purpose of a computer printer.[20]

Consider the following abstract from the famous New Zealand Mussels case that discusses when a good is fit for its ordinary purpose.

The New Zealand Mussels Case

Bundesgerichtshof (German Supreme Court)

8 March 1995

Case Number VIII ZR 159/94

UNILEX Case Abstract[21]

A Swiss seller and a German buyer concluded a contract for the sale of New Zealand mussels. The buyer refused to pay the purchase price after the mussels were declared 'not completely safe' because of the quantity of cadmium they contained, which quantity was significantly greater than the advised cadmium levels published by the German Federal Health Department. The buyer gave notice to the seller of the contamination and asked it to take back the mussels. Six or eight weeks after the delivery of the mussels, the buyer complained about defects of the packaging. The seller commenced an action claiming payment and interest. At first instance the Court decided in favor of the seller, and the buyer's subsequent appeals were unsuccessful.

The Supreme Court confirmed the decisions of the lower courts, stating that the contract between the parties was governed by CISG according to Art. 1(1)(a) CISG.

The Court held that the buyer had to pay the purchase price. It was not entitled to declare the contract avoided under Arts. 25 and 49(1)(a) CISG, since the seller did not commit a

---

[20] The Secretariat Commentary explains Article 35(2)(a) as follows:

> The scope of the seller's obligation under this subparagraph is not determined by whether the seller could expect the buyer himself to use the goods in one of the ways in which such goods are ordinarily used. In particular, the obligation to furnish goods which are fit for all the purposes for which goods of the contract description are ordinarily used also covers a buyer who has purchased the goods for resale rather than use. For goods to be fit for ordinary purposes, they must be honestly resalable in the ordinary course of business….

[21] This abstract is available at http://www.unilex.info/case.cfm?pid=1&do=case&id=108&step=Abstract.

fundamental breach of the contract. The Court confirmed the findings of the lower courts, according to which the mussels were conforming to the contract since they were fit for the purposes for which goods of the same description would ordinarily be used (Art. 35(2)(a) CISG). The Court did find that the fact that the mussels contained a greater quantity of cadmium than the advised cadmium levels could well affect the merchantability of the goods, provided that the corresponding public law requirements were relevant. However, like the lower courts, the Supreme Court excluded that the seller can generally be expected to observe special public law requirements of the buyer's state; it could only be expected to do so: (1) where the same rules also exist in the seller's country; (2) where the buyer draws the seller's attention to their existence; (3) or, possibly, where the seller knows or should know of those rules due to "special circumstances", such as (i) when the seller has a branch in the buyer's country, (ii) when the parties are in a longstanding business relationship, (iii) when the seller regularly exports in the buyer's country, or (iv) when the seller advertises its own products in the buyer's country. ...

* * * * *

Notes and Commentary

Note 1: It is not as easy as it may seem to evaluate when goods are fit for their ordinary purpose. In this case, the German court considered whether a seller should know the local requirements for its goods in the jurisdiction of the buyer. The court came up with a test that is now much cited. The general rule from this case is that the seller should not ordinarily be expected to observe special public law requirements in the buyer's state. However, the court then sets forth three exceptions to that general rule. If any of those exceptions apply, then the seller could be expected to know and observe the public law requirements of buyer's jurisdiction.

Note 2: Of course the case is not a binding precedent as it might be in a common law jurisdiction. Nonetheless, the logic is persuasive. Nonetheless, might a different rule have been just as persuasively advanced? One might argue that a seller doing business with any particular buyer is obligated to provide the buyer with goods that are fit for the ordinary purposes in buyer's jurisdiction. Might that standard be fairly implied into Article 35(2)(a)? Viewed from this perspective, to rule otherwise seems inappropriate. What use are goods to the buyer if they are fit for ordinary purposes in seller's jurisdiction but not where they will ultimately be used?

Note 3: The ruling seems to build off a law and economics approach that attempts to leave the risk of any particular factor with the party who is best able to bear that risk. In this case the risk of knowing about and conforming with particular regulations in buyer's jurisdictions seems better placed on buyer. The buyer can reasonably be expected to understand the requirements that it faces in its own jurisdiction. The buyer then need only communicate those particular requirements to seller in order to bind the seller to deliver goods that conform to those requirements. From this law and economics perspective it would be inefficient to place the risk of investigating the requirements of buyer's jurisdiction on the seller.

b.   *Goods Must Conform to Particular Purpose Known to the Seller*

Second, the goods must be fit for any particular purpose that was either expressly or impliedly made known to the seller at or before the time of contracting. Here, the buyer must in some way communicate its particular purpose to the seller.[22] The CISG allows the communication to be either express or implied. So, where a contract merely specifies computer printers, if the computer printers must be able to print color photographs at a high quality, the buyer must make that particular purpose known to the seller either expressly or impliedly. In its conversations leading up to the purchase of the machines, the buyer might have mentioned to the seller its need for machines that can print high quality color photos. In this scenario, the buyer expressly made the seller aware of its particular purpose. Alternatively, the buyer may have explained that it was re-selling the machines to a chain of photography studios. In this scenario, the buyer has likely impliedly made the seller aware of its particular purpose in purchasing the machines.

Example 4-7

In comparison to the German Mussels case, there is the Spanish Paprika case. In that case, a Spanish seller supplied paprika to a German buyer. The paprika had 150% of the ethyl oxide permissible in Germany. In this case the German party proved that the parties had agreed that the pepper had to be of a quality that was consumable in Germany. Accordingly, the German

---

[22] The Secretariat Commentary to Article 35(2) states that
> The seller is not obligated to deliver goods which are fit for some special purpose which is not a purpose "for which goods of the same description would ordinarily be used" unless the buyer has "expressly or impliedly made known to the sell at the time of the conclusion of the contract" such intended use.

> court ruled that the seller breached by supplying goods that did not conform to the particular purpose made known to it.[23]

In addition to the foregoing example, consider this abstract to get a better understanding of what is meant by conforming to buyer's particular purpose and the complexity of the disputes that might arise under this Article.

Marques Roque Joachim v. La Sarl Holding Manin Rivièr

Cour d'Appel de Grenoble, Chambre Commerciale

(French Appeal Court)

26 April 1995

(The Hangar Assembly Case)

Case Number RG 93/4879

UNILEX Case Abstract[24]

A French seller and a Portuguese buyer concluded a contract for the sale and dismantlement of a second-hand hangar. The price had to be paid in three installments. The buyer paid the first two installments but refused to pay the balance, alleging the non-conformity of some metallic elements, which could not be used for the reassembling of the hangar. The seller repaired the defective elements; the buyer did not take delivery of the repaired elements, alleging that the seller had engaged to supply new metallic elements [sic]. The seller commenced an action to recover the balance of the price. The buyer in turn claimed for avoidance of the contract, refund of the price paid and damages. The Court of first instance decided in favor of the seller.

The appellate Court held that the contract was governed by CISG, as the French rules of private international law (in this case the Hague Convention of 15 June 1955 on the law

---

[23] *Spanish Seller v. German Buyer (Spanish Paprika Case),* Landgericht [District Court] Ellwangen, Germany, Aug. 21, 1995 (available at http://cisgw3.law.pace.edu/cases/950821g2.html).
[24] This abstract is available at http://www.unilex.info/case.cfm?pid=1&do=case&id=109&step=Abstract.

applicable to international sale of goods) led to the application of the law of France, a contracting State (Art. 1(1)(b) CISG).

The contract was considered to be a sales contract in accordance with Art. 3(2) CISG since the dismantlement of the hangar by the seller was not a preponderant part of its obligations (the price charged for this service amounted to approximately 25% of the total contract price).

The Court held that the seller had actually breached the contract in delivering non-conforming metallic elements: as a matter of fact, the defective elements were not fit for the particular purpose made known to the seller (reassembling of the hangar the same way as it was originally) (Art. 35(2)(b) CISG).

However, since the non-conformity related only to a part of the hangar and the seller had been able to repair the defective elements, the lack of conformity did not constitute a fundamental breach of contract: the buyer had not been deprived of what it was entitled to expect under the contract (Art. 25 CISG). Accordingly, the breach did not justify avoidance of the contract (Art. 49 CISG).

The Court held that the seller had effectively cured the lack of conformity by repair of the metallic elements in compliance with Art. 46(3) CISG. In the Court's opinion, the buyer had not given evidence of the fact that the defective elements, even after repair, could not be used for the reassembling of the hangar.

* * * * *

Notes and Commentary

Note 1: As even this abstract points out, in every case concerning an international sale of goods, the threshold inquiry is whether the CISG governs. Why did this court need to rely on **Article 1(1)(b)** to establish the application of the CISG?

Note 2: Not only is the application of the CISG a jurisdictional matter, but the CISG only governs certain types of transactions. Here, the court applies Article 3 to determine if this hybrid sale of goods and services is under the CISG's purview. Article 3 was discussed in Chapter 2, above. Recall that the Advisory Council Opinion on **Article 3** suggested that economic criteria might be used to assess whether services constitute the preponderant part of the sale. This court does just that, basing its conclusion that the CISG applies on the fact that the services constituted only 25% of the entire contract price.

Note 3: Might the court have analyzed the situation under 35(2)(a) and argued that the hanger would not be fit for its ordinary purpose if it was constructed defectively? This argument may not be successful if indeed the non-conforming metal component did not prevent the hanger from being used.

Note 4: The court ruled that delivery of the hanger did not, in fact, conform to the particular purpose known to the seller—i.e. reconstruction of the hanger as it had been constructed in France. Accordingly, the seller had breached its contract with the buyer. Regardless of this breach, the court went on to rule that the breach was not fundamental under Article 25 of the CISG and therefore the buyer did not have the right to avoid its obligations under Article 49 of the CISG. Breach, fundamental breach, and avoidance will be discussed at length in Chapter 5. At this stage, it is sufficient to recognize that not all breaches allow a counterparty to avoid its own obligations.

Note 5: In addition to the particular purpose analysis, the court also discusses the seller's ability to cure. As Chapter 5 will discuss, the CISG, through its cure provisions, encourages parties to resolve disputes themselves by giving the seller the opportunity to correct any non-conformities as long as it does not cause the buyer any unreasonable inconvenience or expense.[25] In fact, as Chapter 5 will explain, the ability of a seller to cure a defect impacts the assessment of whether a breach is fundamental or not; and therefore whether buyer can avoid its own obligations as a result of the breach. That analysis turned out to be exactly what happened in this case where the court reasoned that since the seller could cure the defect it was not fundamental and therefore buyer could not avoid its own obligations.

c.   *Goods Must Conform to Any Samples*

Article 35(2)(c) provides that the goods must conform to any sample or model that was held out to the buyer. So, if the printer dealer illustrates the printing quality of a printer using a sample machine and the sample machine prints color pictures of high quality, then the buyer has a right to assume that the machines it purchases will be capable of printing color pictures of high quality as well.

Example 4-8
An Italian buyer contracted with a United States seller for the sale of compressors. The United States company supplied the Italian manufacturer with a sample compressor and specifications. When the United States manufacturer delivered

---

[25] See CISG arts. 34, 37, and 48 for Seller's rights regarding cure.

> compressors that did not perform as efficiently as the sample, the Italian buyer brought suit alleging non-conformity under Article 35(2)(c) of the CISG. The United States federal court ruled that the goods did not conform to the sample and therefore awarded the Italian buyer damages.[26]

d.   *Goods Must Be Packaged for Preservation*

Fourth, in order to be conforming, **Article 35(2)(d)** states that the goods must be packaged in a manner that is usual in the trade of such goods, underscoring the general principle of promoting uniformity in international sales transactions in accordance with internationally accepted trade usages, as set out in Article 9. If there are no such norms, then the goods should be packaged so that the goods are adequately preserved.

Example 4-9

An Argentine seller of fruit sold a shipment of over 8000 boxes of canned fruit to a Mexican buyer. The Argentinean seller subcontracted the packaging and shipping to a Chilean supplier. When the Mexican buyer received the goods, they were damaged and the Mexican buyer brought suit. The tribunal found that the Argentinean seller had failed to package the fruit in a manner sufficient to protect and preserve the fruit as dictated by Article 35(2)(d).[27]

The following diagram makes it clear that when it comes to a claim under **Article 35**, the claim can exist under any of the four sections just described, **Article 35(2)(a), (b), (c), or (d).** However, a claim might lie at the intersection of any two or more of those sections. Thus, a claim might be possible under both **35(2)(a) and 35(2)(b);** or any other combination of the sections, including a possible claim under all four of the sections. Pinpointing where your claim lies in the diagram will help make absolutely clear the range of arguments that should be made under **Article 35(2)** in any particular situation.

---

[26] *See Rotorex Corp. v. Delchi Carrier S.p.A.*, 71 F.3d 1024 (2d Cir. 1995).

[27] *See Conservas La Costeña S.A. de C.V. v. Lanín San Luis S.A. & Agroindustrial Santa Adela S.A,.* Comisión pare la Protección del Comercio Exterior de México [Mexican Comisión for the Protection of Foreign Trade] Arbitration no. M/21/95, Mexico, Apr. 29, 1996 (available at http://cisgw3.law.pace.edu/cases/960429m1.html).

**Conformity
Under 35(2)**

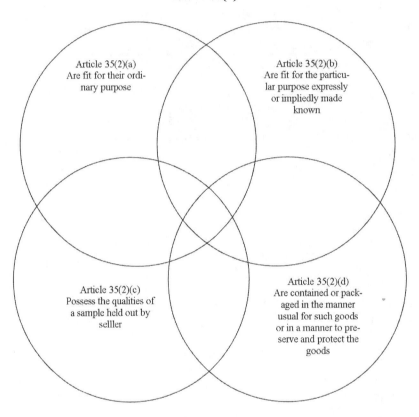

Article 35(2)(a)
Are fit for their ordinary purpose

Article 35(2)(b)
Are fit for the particular purpose expressly or impliedly made known

Article 35(2)(c)
Possess the qualities of a sample held out by selller

Article 35(2)(d)
Are contained or packaged in the manner usual for such goods or in a manner to preserve and protect the goods

e.   The Seller's Defenses

The seller has two main defenses built into Article 35. The first of the two seller's defenses is embedded in Article 35(2)(b) and therefore that defense applies only to that particular purpose clause. The second relates to any of the claims for conformity under Article 35(2).

Recall that Article 35(2)(b) establishes that goods must conform to any particular purpose made known to the seller "except where the circumstances show that the buyer did not rely, or that it was unreasonable for him to rely, on the seller's skill and judgment. Herein lies the seller's first defense. The buyer's non-conformity claim under Article 35(2)(b) will fail if the seller can show either (i) that the buyer did not actually rely on the seller's skill and judgment in selecting the goods, or (ii) that it was unreasonable for the buyer to rely on seller's skill and judgment. With respect to the first prong, it would be inappropriate to hold the seller responsible for the quality of the goods if indeed the buyer itself was an expert regarding the goods or if the buyer relied on a third party in choosing the goods.[28]   With respect to the second prong, if it was unreasonable for the buyer to rely on the seller in selecting the goods, then, even if the buyer did in fact rely on the seller, the buyer would not be able to recover.[29] This puts an affirmative burden on the buyer to do its own assessment of the goods and to conduct at least some level of analysis of whether it should rely on the seller in the given situation.   The buyer cannot blindly rely on the seller where it would be unreasonable to do so. If it was unreasonable for the buyer to rely on the seller, then it would be inappropriate to hold the seller responsible for the goods not meeting the buyer's particular purpose.

The second seller's defense is contained in Article 35(3). There, the seller is protected against any liability for non-conformity under any of the provisions of Article 35(2), including (a) fitness for the ordinary purpose, (b) fitness for a particular purpose, (c) conformity to a sample, or (d) adequate packaging. The seller's defense in Article 35(3) protects the seller against any liability under those provisions if the buyer knew or "could not have been unaware" of the alleged non-conformity at the time the contract was made. As with the seller's defense contained in 35(2)(b), here too it would be inappropriate to hold seller responsible for delivery of goods that are unsatisfactory to the buyer, if the buyer knew about the lack of conformity when it entered into the contract.[30] The CISG provides for actual knowledge of the buyer in this defense, but also provides a fall-back standard, in the event the buyer denies that it actually knew of the non-conformity but must have known. The fall-back standard is satisfied where it would be virtually impossible for the buyer not to have known of the non-conformity at the time of contracting. Thus, the buyer cannot make a claim for

---

[28] The Secretariat Commentary on Article 35 gives some examples of what kind of circumstances might indicate that the buyer did not rely on the seller, "The circumstances may show, for example, that the buyer selected the goods by brand name or that he described the goods desired in terms of highly technical specifications. In such a situation it may be held that the buyer had not relied on the seller's skill and judgment in making the purchase." *See also Commentary on the UN Convention on the International Sale of Goods* 422 (Peter Schlechtriem & Ingeborg Schwenzer eds., 2d ed., Oxford U. Press 2005) [hereinafter *Commentary on CISG*].

[29] The Secretariat Commentary on Article 35 provides that it would be unreasonable to rely on a seller if "the seller did not purport to have any special knowledge in respect of the goods in question." As with so many determinations under the CISG, commentators have argued that the determination of what is reasonable under this article will require consideration of all the relevant facts and circumstances surrounding the transaction. Cesare Massimo Bianca, *Article 35*, in *Bianca-Bonnell Commentary on the International Sales Law* 275–276 (Giuffrè 1987).

[30] For example, when the buyer of a second-hand bulldozer was expressly informed by the seller about the condition of the bulldozer and the buyer tested it before making purchasing the bulldozer, the seller was not found liable for any non-conformity pursuant to Article 35(3) CISG. *Italian Seller v. Swiss Buyer*, Tribunal Cantonal Valais no. C1 97 167, Switzerland, Oct. 28, 1997 (abstract available at http://www.unilex.info/case.cfm?pid=1&do=case&id=311&step=Abstract).

non-conformity if indeed it knew or "could not have been unaware" of the non-conformity at the time the contract was concluded.[31]

> ### Compare: Conformity v. Warranties
>
> While Article 35 of the CISG describes the seller's obligations concerning quality in terms of conformity, the UCC in the United States contains warranties of quality, including express and implied warranties. Similarly, the United Kingdom's Sale of Goods Act (SGA) also contains warranties of quality and fitness.
>
> Conformity and warranty paradigms are both directed at the same goal, ensuring the buyer that it gets what it expected to get, including receipt of goods that are fit for their ordinary purpose and any particular purpose buyer may have made known to the seller. Indeed the CISG's conformity provisions are, in many respects, similar to the UCC and the SGA's warranty provisions. Direct relationships can be seen between CISG Article 35(b)(1) on fitness for ordinary purpose and UCC §2-314, which contains an implied warranty of merchantability. Likewise, CISG 35(b)(2) on particular purpose, is analogous to UCC §2-315, which contains an implied warranty of fitness for a particular purpose.
>
> Nonetheless, differences between the two paradigms make it crucial to keep the two distinct. When applying the CISG, one must focus solely on its language and paradigm. To do otherwise is to risk applying principles that are not actually found in the CISG. For example, warranties under the UCC also generally provide that they might be excluded. In that regard, UCC §2-316 has specific language authorizing exclusion of warranties and sale of goods "as is." That concept is not explicitly present in the CISG's conformity analysis (although Article 35 does allow the parties to "agree otherwise" and Article 6 allows parties to "opt out" of any provisions of the CISG). Further, the UCC describes certain warranties as implied and others as express. Again, the CISG contains neither of those distinctions. Finally, reliance standards and other qualifications

---

[31] Professor Honnold describes this standard of "could not have been unaware" as not imposing any duty to investigate but is satisfied where the facts in questions are "the facts that are before the eyes of one who can see." Honnold, *supra* n. 15, at 259.

of the conformity standards in the CISG are also different and therefore must be applied meticulously.

Consider the following arbitration ruling as an illustration of a tribunal grappling with the standards of Article 35.

The Rijn Blend Condensate Case

Netherlands Arbitration Institute

15 October, 2002

Case Number 2319[32]

...

2. Brief Summary of the Facts

36. The following sets forth the facts as they are understood by the Arbitral Tribunal.

37. Claimants [Dutch sellers] are all active in the exploration of offshore gas fields in the Netherlands continental shelf. They have been granted production licenses for certain blocks. ...

38. Respondent [English buyer] is a major international player in the field of exploration, production and refining of crude oil and distribution of oil products and gas.

39. Condensate is an associated liquid product derived from the exploration of gas fields after separation from the gas stream by the producer. Condensate from the fields operated by Claimants and subject of the dispute is referred to as "Rijn Blend".

40. In 1993 and 1994, Claimants (or their predecessors) concluded twelve sales contracts with Respondent in relation to the abovementioned Rijn Blend....

....

47. The disputes between Claimants and Respondent relate to deliveries as of June 1998. On June 11, 1998, Claimants were informed...that Respondent had indicated that it would not take

---

[32] The full text of the case is available at http://cisgw3.law.pace.edu/cases/021015n1.html.

the next lifting of the Rijn Blend because of levels of mercury in the Rijn Blend, which made it unacceptable for further processing or sales.

48. Because of alleged lack of storage facilities, the Rijn Blend - on June 13, 1998….was transported to the United States where it was sold to LL. Petroleum Corp. at a price substantially lower than the price under the contract. In this respect, Claimants allege that they suffered losses of US $ 1.100.000.

49. On June 16, 1998, Respondent informed Claimants that it would suspend taking delivery of the Rijn Blend until a solution for the mercury problem had been found.

50. Since a solution was not found regarding the mercury problem, Respondent terminated the contracts or led the contracts to expire in accordance with the contract termination provisions or the contract provisions regarding renewal. In the intermediate period, Claimants sold the condensate not taken by Respondent to third parties…at an alleged loss as compared to the contract price. On top of the US $ 1.100.000 on the June 1998 cover sale, the Arbitral Tribunal gathers from the information provided by Claimants that other cover sales caused losses alleged to be in excess of US $ 5 million resulting in an alleged overall loss of US $ 6.333.178,58.

3. Arguments of Claimants

51. Claimants argue that the Rijn Blend delivered over the life span of the contracts was in accordance with the contracts since no specific quality requirements had been agreed upon. Furthermore, Claimants contest that they should be involved in downstream problems and that Respondent should have dealt with these problems in its contracts with a downstream customer. Also, they claim that they could not be aware of the purpose for which the Rijn Blend was used by Respondent and, therefore, had no obligations whatsoever in meeting product requirements further downstream.

52. Claimants also contest that the Rijn Blend would have shown increased levels of mercury since the contracts were concluded or that the problems downstream might have been attributable to the Rijn Blend. Furthermore, they claim that

Respondent was or should have been aware of mercury content in condensate.....

54. On the basis of these submissions, Claimants argue that the goods were conforming and that there had been a breach of contract by Respondent in refusing delivery and suspending its obligations under the contracts. Thus, Claimants requested the Arbitral Tribunal to condemn Respondent to pay damages including internal costs related to the dispute, costs of legal assistance and representation and interest.

4. Arguments of Respondent

55. Respondent declined any liability. In its opinion, the goods were not conforming and it was, therefore, entitled to refuse delivery and suspend its obligations. Respondent in this respect argued that there were increased levels of mercury in the recent past and that Claimants knew or should have known that - since Rijn Blend is used in the refinery process - it might cause damages downstream....

5. Position of the Arbitral Tribunal...

60. ....the parties agree on the following issues: 1) the application of the Convention on International Sale of Goods concluded in Vienna on April 11, 1980 (hereinafter referred to as "CISG") to the respective contracts ....

5.1 Issue 1: Conformity of the Rijn Blend

62. Article 35 (1) CISG provides that the seller should deliver goods, which are of the quantity, quality and description required by the contract. All twelve contracts do not contain quality specifications but only define Rijn Blend as a "Mix of ... condensates and/or crude oil ...", "... condensates and crude oil" or "condensates" and refer to the blocks from where the Rijn Blend originate. ... Consequently, article 35 (1) CISG is not applicable to the conformity issue.

63. Article 35 (2) CISG provides in relevant parts that the goods do not conform with the contract unless they: (a) are fit for the purposes for which goods of the same description would

ordinarily be used; or (b) are fit for any particular purpose expressly or impliedly made known to the seller at the time of the conclusion of the contract, except where the circumstances show that the buyer did not rely, or that it was unreasonable for him to rely, on the seller's skill and judgment....

67. As to Article 35 (2) b) CISG, the Arbitral Tribunal notes that the particular purpose of the goods must have been made known to the seller at the time of the conclusion of the contract. The question then arises whether Respondent, at that time (i.e., 1993 and 1994) expressly or impliedly indicated to the respective Claimants the use it intended to make of the Rijn Blend. The Arbitral Tribunal is of the opinion that it did not. First, the sale contracts do not contain a product quality specification. Absent such a specification, Respondent did not indicate expressly the particular purpose it had in mind for the Rijn Blend. Secondly, an implied indication as to a particular purpose made in 1993 and 1994 also has not been proven. There are no elements of evidence that the parties implicitly agreed upon particular requirements for the Rijn Blend. Neither is there evidence that such an implied indication—in accordance with Article 8 CISG - is to be inferred from statements, intentions or conduct of either party. Furthermore, the nature of the product leads more to the opposite conclusion. The Arbitral Tribunal understands that blended condensate such as Rijn Blend is a commodity that can be used in different capacities in refining processes and thus that various refiners may use it in varying degrees and for different purposes. Also, a buyer not necessarily should use all condensate but may resell all or parts of it.

...

Consequently, the Arbitral Tribunal rules that, absent contract quality specifications, Article 35 (2) b) CISG is not the proper basis to assess non-conformity issues in international sales of commodities such as Rijn Blend.

68. The Arbitral Tribunal, thus, finds that the dispute between the parties is to be analysed under Article 35 (2) a) CISG which requires that the goods are fit for the purposes for which goods of the same description would ordinarily be used. In this respect, three interpretations exist. According to a first line of thought, Article 35 (2) a) requires that the seller delivers goods which are of a merchantable quality. This interpretation goes back to the drafting history of CISG. ...At that time, it became clear that the

English common law countries favoured merchantable quality whereas the civil law continental European rule was to the effect that average quality is required. …

69. The second view is that the average quality rule is to be adopted in relation to CISG cases (for one such instance, see without further references, Landesgericht Berlin, September 15, 1994, Unilex database, unpublished in hard copy).

70. Scholarly writings…even among civil law scholars, are divided between merchantable and average quality (for references, see Schwenzer, I., in Schlechtriem, P., Commentary on the UN Convention on the International Sale of Goods (CISG), Oxford, Clarendon Press, 1998, Art. 35, fn. 46 and Schwenzer, I., in Schlechtriem, P., Kommentar zum Einheitlichen UN-Kaufrecht, third edition, Munich, Beck, 2000, Art. 35, No. 15 and fn. 46) with a majority of Germanic writers endorsing the average quality rule based upon similar rules in the German, Austrian and Swiss civil codes. …Finally, some French authors have specifically stated that the average quality rule of the French Civil Code is not applicable to CISG cases (Heuzé, V., o.c., 219, Audit, B., La vente internationale de marchandises, Paris, LGDJ, 1990, 96).

71. Finally, a third theory rejects both opinions mentioned above and states that neither merchantability nor average quality fit within the CISG system. This theory rather suggests a reasonable quality (Bernstein, H., and Lookofsky, J., Understanding the CISG in Europe, The Hague, Kluwer Law International, 1997, 59-60). One case has endorsed this theory in holding that the buyer's reasonable expectations are to be taken into account (Arbitral Award, June 5, 1998, Arbitration Institute, Stockholm Chamber of Commerce, Unilex database, unpublished in hard copy).

72. Contrary to Article 35 (2) b) CISG, Article 35 (2) a) does not require that quality requirements are determined at the time of the conclusion of the contract. Thus, factual elements occurring after the conclusion of the contract may be taken into account to determine quality standards….

80. The Arbitral Tribunal therefore proceeds on the basis that the Rijn Blend contained increased levels of mercury and, thus, must answer the question whether Rijn Blend with increased levels of mercury still meets the standard of Article 35 (2) a)

CISG requiring products to fit ordinary purposes of goods of the same description. The Arbitral Tribunal is thus facing the question mentioned above whether merchantable, average or reasonable quality is required.

81. As a starting point of the analysis, it should be noted that condensate is a commodity with multiple purposes. It can be used in the refining process but it may also be used by chemical and other companies (see … Report, Claimant's Exhibit No. 3, p. 1; … report, Respondent's Exhibit No. 16)….

82. The question then arises whether Rijn Blend is also a multi-purpose commodity. The evidence of all expert reports seems to be in agreement that Rijn Blend is a "full range condensate"….

85. Respondent has not adduced evidence to demonstrate that Rijn Blend was also used or could have been used in the petrochemical industry. Furthermore, Claimants did not contribute elements to indicate that Rijn Blend was used for purposes other than refining.

86. On the basis of the foregoing, the Arbitral Tribunal characterizes Rijn Blend as a single purpose commodity for the refining industry.

87. The Arbitral Tribunal now proceeds with the application to Rijn Blend of the three quality standards under Article 35 (2) a) CISG.

88. As to the standard of merchantability, … As to commodities, the English common law developed the rule that goods conform if a reasonable buyer would have concluded the contract if he had known the quality of the goods without bargaining for a price reduction (Henry Kendall & Sons v. William Lillico & Sons Ltd, [1969] 2 AC 31)….

89. Thus, a merchantability test under CISG based on English common law, if any, would raise the question whether a reasonable buyer would have concluded contracts for Rijn Blend at similar prices if such a buyer had been aware of the mercury concentrations. In this respect, the substitute cover sales made to LL. Petroleum Corp., M. International AG and H. BV are relevant. Claimants have argued that these cover sales have been contracted on an arm's length basis. From Claimants' Exhibit 5a to the Statement of Claim, it appears that the cover sale to LL. Petroleum was made at a 31% discount (US$ 9 as compared to

the price of US$ 13.04 under the contracts). Although the first sale might have been a distress sale, the subsequent 15 sales were made at discount within a range of 14% (October 1998) to 44% (February 1999). It is conjectural to what extent these discounts may be attributed to the mercury levels of the Rijn Blend but, in the opinion of the Tribunal, Claimants sufficiently have established that these cover sales were made at discounts and on an arm's length basis without that evidence being rebutted by Respondent. For that reason, the Arbitral Tribunal is ready to accept that Claimants have met their burden of proof that these ranges indicate that there was no market for Rijn Blend with increased mercury levels at prices comparable to the sales contracts when the increased levels were disclosed to prospective alternate buyers.

90. From this evidence, the Arbitral Tribunal accepts that the goods were not merchantable as this concept is generally used in common law countries having a law based on English common law. Apparently, other buyers in the market for Rijn Blend were – at times comparable to the June 1998 contemplated lifting - unwilling to pay the price Claimants had agreed with Respondent.

91. Consequently, if a merchantability test (as understood in the common law) were to be used for interpreting article 35 (2) a) CISG, it would lead to the conclusion that the delivery of Rijn Blend with increased mercury levels did not conform to the sales contracts.

92. As to average quality, ….

99. Respondent, thus, under the average quality standard, has the burden of proof to establish that the goods in June 1998 were likely to be below average quality.

100. In the opinion of the Arbitral Tribunal, Respondent has failed to meet that burden of proof. From the evidence, it is unclear whether there is a common understanding in the refining industry what average quality for blended condensates (such as Rijn Blend) should have been and what levels of mercury are tolerable. Also, it has not been proven what margins from an average standard, if any, are permissible….

102. Not having met its burden of proof, Respondent, under an average quality standard, were to be held liable for not accepting delivery of the Rijn Blend in June 1998, provided the Arbitral

Tribunal would accept such an average quality standard under Article 35 (2) a) CISG.

103. The Arbitral Tribunal is thus faced with a choice between merchantable quality and average quality since both tests lead to different conclusions. However, the Tribunal is of the opinion that neither test is to be applied in CISG cases.

104. First, the interpretation of Article 35 (2) a) CISG is to be guided by Article 7 (1) CISG which suggests that the international character of the convention and the need to promote uniformity in its application and the observance of good faith in international trade are to be taken into account in the interpretation process.

105. The need to ensure uniformity would indicate that, since there are no clear-cut cases or uniform scholarly opinions, neither standard at first sight should prevail.

106. Thus, Article 7 (2) CISG may be invoked. Article 7 (2) provides that matters governed by CISG but not expressly settled in it, are to be solved in conformity with the general principles on which CISG is based or, in the absence of such principles, in conformity with the law applicable by virtue of the rules of private international law.

107. This provision imposes first an intro-interpretation with respect to interpretation issues or gaps (i.e., solutions are first to be sought within the CISG system itself). Absent general principles on which CISG is based, recourse may be had to domestic law indicated by virtue of principles of private international law.

108. This provision would seem to exclude the average quality rule. Although it is embodied in the law of both Germanic and Romanistic legal systems, Heuzé - as referred to above - has rightly indicated that national notions regarding quality of goods are not controlling in CISG cases. For that reason, the average quality standard cannot be accepted. It is a theory, which imports a domestic notion, which is not sufficiently universal into the CISG system in violation of Article 7 (2) CISG. Furthermore, recent codifications in civil law countries such as in The Netherlands have abolished the average quality rule of Article 1428 old Civil Code in favour of a reliance standard (see Article 7:17 Dutch Civil Code).

109. The same argument against domestic conformity notions, of course, must be used in relation to the merchantability standard of the English common law. Thus, English common law based jurisdictions such as Canada, Australia, New Zealand or Singapore cannot use their merchantability criteria ne varietur in CISG cases.

110. In solving this interpretation issue, attention is also to be paid to Articles 31 and 32 of the Vienna Convention on the Law of Treaties dated May 23, 1969.

111. Article 32 of the 1969 Vienna Treaty permits to resort to the travaux préparatoires of treaties to explain ambiguous or unclear treaty provisions. Article 35 (2) a) CISG may thus be interpreted on the basis of the preparatory work during the negotiations leading to CISG.

...Thus, the drafting history of CISG does not permit to draw a clear conclusion regarding the intentions of the drafters and, consequently, it does not help to explain the ambiguity of Article 35 (2) a) CISG (Ziegel, J., Report to the Uniform Law Conference of Canada on Convention on Contracts for the International Sale of Goods, Article 35 under (3), available at www.cisg.law.pace.edu).

117. On the basis of the arguments above, the Tribunal holds that neither the merchantability test nor the average quality test are to be used in CISG cases and that the reasonable quality standard referred to above (see No. 71) is to be preferred.

118. The choice in favour of a test of reasonable quality is supported by the authors and the case cited above in No. 71 as well as by those scholarly writings that have rejected the average quality test. .... Also, any such interpretation complies with article 7(1) CISG imposing to take into account the international character of CISG and its reluctance to rely immediately on notions based on domestic law. Furthermore, the interpretation preferred by the Arbitral Tribunal is consistent with article 7 (2) CISG, which primarily refers to the general principles of CISG as possible gap fillers. In this respect, it may be noted that CISG often uses open-textured provisions referring to reasonableness (e.g., articles 8, 18, 25, 33, 34, 37, 38, 39, 43, 44, 46, 48, 49, 65, 72, 75, 77, 79, 86, 87 and 88). Finally, even if one were to rely on domestic law by virtue of article 7 (2) CISG, Dutch law

would be applicable and would also impose a standard of reasonable quality.

119. The question then arises whether the Rijn Blend delivered in 1998 did meet the reasonable quality requirement. The Arbitral Tribunal is of the opinion that it did not for at least two reasons: price and the long-term nature of the sales contracts.

120. As to price, it has been sufficiently proven (see No. 89) that the price as determined by the price formula agreed upon by the parties in all likelihood - even taking into account transportation costs - could not been obtained for cover transactions when the mercury levels were disclosed to alternate prospective buyers. This is an objective element to be taken into account when determining the quality of the Rijn Blend. Apparently, Rijn Blend with increased mercury levels has a significant lower value than Rijn Blend without increased mercury levels and a discount is to be paid for the buyer's costs in removing the mercury or a buyer's alternate use.... it is the opinion of the Arbitral Tribunal that Respondent, based on the price to be paid under the contracts, could insist upon removal of the mercury or price reduction and alternatively could refuse delivery of the Rijn Blend.

121. The long-term nature of the sales relationships between the parties corroborates the findings of the Arbitral Tribunal set forth in the preceding paragraph. Apparently, there have been no quality problems related to the levels of mercury in the Rijn Blend in the initial years of the Contracts as of 1993/1994.... Over that sufficiently long period, a pattern had developed under which - in the opinion of the Arbitral Tribunal - Respondent could expect that the Rijn Blend met the quality requirements it was or had become used to over the years. In this respect, the Arbitral Tribunal finds that the Respondent has sufficiently proven...that the Rijn Blend delivered to it had sudden increased mercury levels. The Arbitral Tribunal has not read in the evidence submitted by Claimants that there were increased mercury levels well before 1998. Consequently, the Tribunal holds that Respondent was entitled under the contracts to a constant quality level of the Rijn Blend corresponding to the quality levels that had been obtained during the abovementioned initial period of the Contracts and on which Respondent and its customers could reasonably rely....

123. On the basis of the contract price and the nature of the relationship between the parties, the Tribunal finds that the risks associated with changing compositions of the Rijn Blend thus laid with Claimants who should have monitored that composition or should have agreed to removal of the mercury or to price reduction. ….

124. Consequently, the Arbitral Tribunal holds that Claimants did not comply with their obligations to deliver Rijn Blend conforming to the contract under article 35 (2) a) CISG as of and including the June 1998 lifting….

* * * * *

Notes and Commentary

Note 1: In this case, an English long term buyer of the Rijn Blend condensate was shocked when the Rijn Blend suddenly contained what the buyer thought to be high levels of mercury. The buyer then refused to take delivery and refused to honor its obligations under subsequent contracts for the condensate. It justified its actions by claiming that the goods no longer conformed to its contracts. However, the contracts did not contain any specification for the condensate. Of course the dispute would never have arisen if the parties had indeed included product specifications in their contract. Nonetheless, even if product specifications had been included, they might not have specified the desired amount of mercury and the dispute might still have occurred.

Note 2: The tribunal assessed the claimant's arguments under the conformity provisions of Article 35, specifically the requirements that the goods conform to the particular purpose made known to the seller (Article 35(2)(b)) or the ordinary purposes of such goods (Article 35(2)(a)). The tribunal quickly dismissed the particular purpose argument and then rested its decision on fitness for an ordinary purpose. Note, though, that there is some overlap between these two standards. Indeed, a buyer's particular purpose in purchasing goods might coincide with the goods ordinary function. Was that the case here? Could the case have been decided under the particular purpose provisions of Article 35(2)(b)? Would the seller's defense in Article 35(2)(b) have gotten in the way of buyer's claim on that point? How would that defense have applied?

Note 3: The arbitral tribunal discussed at some length (and ultimately dismissed) various national law approaches to fitness for a good's ordinary purpose. That discussion should underscore the complexity of applying the standard. In fact, the tribunal concluded that under the different approaches a different result might occur. How, in the tribunal's opinion, is it possible for a good to be merchantable, but not be of average quality? Do you agree that the approaches yield different results?

Note 4: Finally, the tribunal cited to Article 7 and explained that the CISG itself instructs interpreters to consider its international character and the need to promote uniformity in its application. Accordingly, the tribunal rejected the national approaches endorsed by common law countries, on the one hand, and certain civil law countries, on the other hand. Instead, it concluded that the standard must be a-national and should be based on the CISG or its underlying principles (again in accordance with Article 7). It then chose a "reasonableness" approach, reasoning that the CISG itself uses reasonableness standards throughout.

Note 5: This excerpt provides an example of a decision issued by an arbitral tribunal. As was discussed in Chapter 1 and as will be developed in detail later in this book, there are many reasons why parties opt for arbitration. One of the important reasons is the confidentiality of the process. Notice that the names of the parties in this case have been redacted out of the opinion. Another important reason why parties choose arbitration is the neutrality of the arbitral tribunal. Another way of expressing that neutrality is the absence of national bias. In this particular case, the tribunal rejected national approaches to "ordinary purpose" from various countries. Would a national court have been as likely to do that or might it have embraced what it views as the understanding of "ordinary purpose"? Might a national court in continental Europe or England have indeed reached a different result? Indeed, the very fact that the CISG dictates that it should be interpreted with due regard to its international nature might indicate that an a-national body, like an international arbitral tribunal, might indeed be better situated to interpret and apply the CISG.

C.   THIRD PARTY CLAIMS

In Chapter 1 it was noted that the CISG does not govern property rights in the goods being sold. However, that exclusion is distinct from the seller's obligation to convey goods that are free from third party claims. Article 41 makes this generally clear, while Article 42 focuses on third party claims based on intellectual property rights in the goods sold.

1.   Goods Must be Free of Third Party Claims Generally

Article 41 states specifically that the seller must convey goods free of third party rights, unless, of course, the buyer agrees to accept goods that are subject to such rights. Here, again, the CISG defers to the intent of the parties in accordance with Article 8. If a buyer is willing to accept goods that are encumbered with the rights of another party, it may agree to do so.

Article 41

The seller must deliver goods which are free from any right or claim of a third party, unless the buyer agreed to take the goods subject to that right or claim. However, if such right or claim is based on industrial property or other intellectual property, the seller's obligation is governed by article 42.

Example 4-10

A German buyer contracted to buy natural gas from an Austrian seller. The German buyer had contemplated resale of the natural gas to Belgium. However, the Austrian seller had agreed with its supplier that none of the natural gas it sold would be resold into any of the Benelux countries, including Belgium. The Austrian Supreme Court held that sale of the natural gas by the Austrian seller to the German buyer without disclosing the restrictions on resale was a sale of goods subject to third party rights in violation of Article 41. Further, the court ruled that, absent an agreement to the contrary, the buyer had a right to expect the unencumbered ability to resell the goods.[33]

---

2.   Goods Must be Free of Third Party Intellectual Property Claims

Article 41 goes on to defer to Article 42 for more detailed provisions regarding the seller's obligation to convey goods that are free from the intellectual property rights of a third party. Because intellectual property rights are not always clearly understood by the seller, Article 42 is more generous to the seller than Article 41 by including a knowledge qualifier. The seller is only liable for selling goods that are subject to such intellectual property rights if seller knew or "could not have been unaware" of such right (Article 42(1)). This knowledge standard mirrors the language of the seller's defense in Article 35(3). It is broader than actual knowledge and allows the buyer to argue that the seller must have known of the third party right, even if seller denies actual knowledge.

---

[33] *Austrian Seller v. German Buyer (Propane Case),* Oberster Gerichtshof [Supreme Court] no. 10 Ob 518/95, Austria, Feb. 6, 1996 (available at http://cisgw3.law.pace.edu/cases/960206a3.html).

In addition, the intellectual property right that the seller knows about (or "could not have been unaware" of) must exist under the law of one of two relevant jurisdictions: (i) the jurisdiction where the goods are to be re-sold or used by the buyer, providing the parties contemplated such re-sale or use; or (ii) the jurisdiction where the buyer has its place of business (Article 42(1)(a) and (b)). This is helpful to the seller because the seller may in fact not know about intellectual property rights of a jurisdiction other than its own. While the "could not have been unaware" language provides some help to the buyer in arguing that the seller must have known of the right, it is not clear that, without special facts or circumstances, the seller would or should know of intellectual property claims that exist under the laws of other jurisdictions.

Article 42

(1) The seller must deliver goods which are free from any right or claim of a third party based on industrial property or other intellectual property, of which at the time of the conclusion of the contract the seller knew or could not have been unaware, provided that the right or claim is based on industrial property or other intellectual property:

(a) under the law of the State where the goods will be resold or otherwise used, if it was contemplated by the parties at the time of the conclusion of the contract that the goods would be resold or otherwise used in that State; or

(b) in any other case, under the law of the State where the buyer has his place of business.

(2) The obligation of the seller under the preceding paragraph does not extend to cases where:

(a) at the time of the conclusion of the contract the buyer knew or could not have been unaware of the right or claim; or

(b) the right or claim results from the seller's compliance with technical drawings, designs, formulae or other such specifications furnished by the buyer.

> **Example 4-11**
>
> A French buyer of clothing that operated retail stores purchased shirts from a German seller. The shirts infringed on the copyright of a third party because the fabrics were copies of a particular type of textile produced by a third party. The third party sued the buyer and recovered damages for the intellectual property infringement. The French buyer made a claim for indemnification from the German seller. The tribunal of first instance in France allowed the indemnification based on Article 42 (ruling that the goods were sold in violation of Article 42(1) since they were subject to a third party intellectual property right).[34]

3. Seller's Defenses to Third Party Intellectual Property Claims

Article 42 provides Seller with two explicit defenses to a claim against it for conveying goods subject to third party intellectual property rights. These defenses again are reminiscent of the seller's defenses to conformity claims under Article 35. The first defense relates to buyer's knowledge of the third party right at the time of making the contract. The seller will not be liable for its obligation under Article 42(1) if buyer knew about "or could not have been unaware of" the third party intellectual property right at the time of making the contract (Article 42(2)(a)). Again, the CISG uses this expansive language to include cases where one party, here the buyer, might argue that it did not, in fact, have knowledge but the circumstances show that it must have. This defense is premised on the notion that it would be inappropriate to hold seller responsible for delivery of goods subject to a third party intellectual property right, if the buyer knew about the third party right when it entered into the contract.

The second seller's defense applies where buyer itself was the cause of the third party intellectual property claim. For that defense to apply, the buyer must have supplied the seller with "technical drawings, designs, formulae or other specifications" that caused the resulting goods to be subject to the intellectual property right or claim (Article 42(2)(b)). This second defense underscores a principle found elsewhere in the CISG, that a party "may not rely on a failure of

---

[34] *See German Seller v. French Buyer (Printed Textile Fabric Case),* Appellate Court Colmar, France, Nov. 13, 2002 (available at http://cisgw3.law.pace.edu/cases/021113f1.html). Note that the case was ultimately appealed and reversed based on the knowledge of the buyer regarding the intellectual property claim. See example 4-12.

the other party to perform, to the extent that such failure was caused by [its own] act or omission" (Article 80).[35]

> **Example 4-12**
>
> In the case described in the preceding example, the French buyer of textiles sued the German seller due to an intellectual property claim on the goods. The court of first instance had ruled that the seller indemnify the buyer, based on the seller's breach of Article 41 in having sold goods subject to an intellectual property claim. However, the appellate court reversed, reasoning that in the circumstances present there was no way that the French buyer could have been unaware of the infringement and therefore, under Article 42(2) the German seller was no longer obligated to sell the goods free from the intellectual property interests.[36]

II. THE OBLIGATIONS OF THE BUYER

By comparison to the obligations of the seller, the obligations of the buyer are quite simple. This reflects the complex nature of the seller's role in a sale of goods when compared to the buyer's role. The seller must actually manufacture or procure and then deliver goods that conform under the contract and the CISG. The buyer, on the other hand, takes delivery of the goods and makes payment. Article 53 of the CISG sets forth these basic obligations. Neither of these obligations is particularly complicated and there are relatively few rules in the CISG that govern those actions.

A. PAYMENT

Article 53 sets forth the basic obligation of buyer to pay the purchase price in accordance with the contract and the CISG.

---

[35] If buyer does provide technical specifications for the manufacture of particular goods, then the buyer is also presumed to know about any intellectual property issues related to those goods in its own country. Enderlein & Maskow, *supra* n. 17, at 169.

[36] *See German Seller v. French Buyer (Printed Textile Fabric Case),* Appellate Court Colmar, France, Nov. 13, 2002 (available at http://cisgw3.law.pace.edu/cases/021113f1.html).

> **Article 53**
>
> The buyer must pay the price for the goods and take delivery of them as required by the contract and this Convention.

In accordance with the general principles of the CISG on the primacy of party autonomy, payment of the purchase price under the CISG should be made in accordance with the agreement of the parties (Article 54). Article 54 also indicates that any laws or regulations that apply to payment should also be followed.

> **Article 54**
>
> The buyer's obligation to pay the price includes taking such steps and complying with such formalities as may be required under the contract or any laws and regulations to enable payment to be made.

> **Example 4-13**
>
> As in example 4-3, a Swiss seller was in a contract with an Austrian buyer for a shipment of alcohol. When the Austrian buyer did not open a letter of credit to initiate payment, as the parties' contract dictated, the Swiss seller ultimately declared the contract avoided. The Austrian Supreme Court ruled that the Swiss seller was justified in its avoidance based on Article 54's requirement that the buyer pay the price as required by the parties' contract.[37]

1. Price

Just as with the seller's obligations, however, where the parties' agreement is silent regarding the buyer's obligations, the CISG will supply default terms. Articles 55 and 56 contain certain default provisions with respect to determination of purchase price.

---

[37] *See Austrian Buyer v. Swiss Seller (Spirits Case),* Bezirksgericht [District Court] der Saane no. 171/95, Switzerland, Feb. 20, 1997 (available at http://cisgw3.law.pace.edu/cases/970220s1.html) (finding that the buyer failed to fulfill its contractual duty to open a letter of credit by the specified date).

> **Article 55**
>
> Where a contract has been validly concluded but does not expressly or implicitly fix or make provision for determining the price, the parties are considered, in the absence of any indication to the contrary, to have impliedly made reference to the price generally charged at the time of the conclusion of the contract for such goods sold under comparable circumstances in the trade concerned.

Article 55 was referenced earlier in connection with Article 14.[38] Article 55 states that if a contract has been validly concluded but does not reference a price in any way, then the parties are impliedly considered to have referred to the market price generally charged for similar goods under similar circumstances at the time the contract was made. This article will not be commonly invoked, however, since under Article 14, an offer under the CISG must expressly or impliedly refer to a price.

One way a contract may be validly concluded without reference to a price is if one of the parties to the transaction has opted out of the formation rules of the CISG (either via a specific Article 6 opt-out or via an Article 92 declaration) and then is able to conclude or make a contract without an offer that references a price in some way. In that situation, Article 55 will supply the price with reference to an implied market price.

Alternatively, as was noted in Chapter 2's discussion on Article 14, Professor Honnold suggests that if a Contracting State's domestic law would allow for an effective offer that contains no reference to price, then under Article 4's exclusion of validity issues, the contract could be valid notwithstanding Article 14.[39] In that case, Article 55 might be applicable in establishing the price by reference to an implied market price. This would be all the more likely to be the case if the parties had already performed on the contract (indicating that they understood a contract to be formed). In such a case, Article 55 would be a gap-filling provision that would simply fill the gap left by the omission of a reference to price. The alternative would be to undue the transaction and allow the parties

---

[38] *See* ch. 3, pt. I(A).

[39] As was mentioned in Chapter 3, Honnold's view is a minority view. *See* Honnold, *supra* n. 15, at 150–155 (on Article 14 cross-referenced in his discussion of Article 55). Honnold's logic is far more compelling in the case in which parties have already performed (thus leaving the tribunal with a choice of restitution in the absence of contract or finding a contract based on completed performance and filling the price gap via Article 55) than in the case of a contract that remains fully executory. *Compare Commentary on CISG*, *supra* n. 28, *with* Chapter 3, n. 13.

to seek restitution from their counterpart for any performance already rendered. Restitution is discussed in more detail in Chapter 5

Article 56 presents a more straightforward default term. In accordance with Article 56 if the parties have fixed price in accordance with weight but have not agreed upon how to measure weight, then the parties should use the net weight of the goods. Net weight here means weight net of (i.e. excluding) packaging.[40]

Article 56

If the price is fixed according to the weight of the goods, in case of doubt it is to be determined by the net weight.

---

2.   Place of Payment

As with so many of the provisions regarding the obligations of the parties, Article 57 begins with deference to the agreement of the parties. Article 57's default provisions apply when the buyer is not bound by the agreement of the parties, or otherwise, to make payment at a particular place. In that case, Article 57 demands that buyer pay seller at either: (i) the seller's place of business, or (ii) if payment is to be made in exchange for the goods or documents, then the payment should be made wherever the exchange takes place.

Article 57

(1) If the buyer is not bound to pay the price at any other particular place, he must pay it to the seller:

(a) at the seller's place of business; or

(b) if the payment is to be made against the handing over of the goods or of documents, at the place where the handing over takes place.

(2) The seller must bear any increase in the expenses incidental to payment which is caused by a change in his place of business subsequent to the conclusion of the contract.

---

[40] Further, if there is a change in the net weight of the goods during shipment, the weight of the goods when they arrive at the place of delivery should be determinative. *See* Enderlein & Maskow, *supra* n. 17, at 213.

The place of payment can have other implications. At least one court has determined that the proper currency for payment was determined by the place of payment pursuant to Article 57.[41] Other courts have used the place of payment as the characteristic performance of the contract and have therefore based jurisdiction on where payment occurs.

Example 4-14

A Danish factoring company sued a German buyer on several contracts for the sale of goods. The court in Denmark ruled, in accordance with the prevailing law on jurisdiction, that it would have jurisdiction if performance of the obligation in question occurred in Denmark. The court reasoned that the performance consisted of payment for the goods. In this case the contract had not specified where payment was to be made, and, therefore under Article 57, payment was required at the Seller's place of business, which was in Denmark. Therefore, the court took jurisdiction.[42]

---

3.   Time of Payment

With respect to the timing of payment, the CISG again defers to the agreement of the parties. If the buyer is not bound to pay at a particular time by that agreement or otherwise, then the default provisions of Article 58 apply. Article 58 contains three default provisions regarding price. The default rule states that ordinarily the buyer must pay the seller at the time the seller makes the goods available to the buyer (or the documents controlling the goods).[43] However, the seller may make delivery of the goods contingent on the payment (Articles 58(1) and (2)). On the other hand, the buyer may insist upon inspection of the goods before making payment, unless inspection is inconsistent with the delivery procedures agreed upon by the parties (Article 58(3)).

---

[41] *Italian Seller v. German Buyer (Wine Case)*, Kammergericht [Upper Court] Berlin no. 2 U 7418/92, Germany, Jan. 24, 1994 (available at http://cisgw3.law.pace.edu/cases/940124g1.html).

[42] *Dänisches Bettenlager v. Forenede Factors,* Eastern Appellate Court Copenhagen, Denmark, Jan. 22, 1996 (available at http://cisgw3.law.pace.edu/cases/960122d1.html).

[43] As explained by the Secretariat Commentary, this provision stands for the proposition that the seller is not required to extend credit to the buyer. Secretariat Commentary on the 1978 Draft, *Guide to CISG Article 54,* para. 2 (available at http://cisgw3.law.pace.edu/cisg/text/secomm/ secomm-54.html).

> **Article 58**
>
> (1) If the buyer is not bound to pay the price at any other specific time, he must pay it when the seller places either the goods or documents controlling their disposition at the buyer's disposal in accordance with the contract and this Convention. The seller may make such payment a condition for handing over the goods or documents.
>
> (2) If the contract involves carriage of the goods, the seller may dispatch the goods on terms whereby the goods, or documents controlling their disposition, will not be handed over to the buyer except against payment of the price.
>
> (3) The buyer is not bound to pay the price until he has had an opportunity to examine the goods, unless the procedures for delivery or payment agreed upon by the parties are inconsistent with his having such an opportunity.

B.   TAKING DELIVERY

In accordance with Article 60 of the CISG, the buyer is obligated to do everything reasonable to facilitate seller's delivery of the goods.[44]   This underscores the CISG's general principle of encouraging cooperation between the parties.[45]   Further, Article 60(b) insists that the buyer is obligated to take delivery. This also reflects a principle of the CISG, the principle of preservation of the goods.[46] If the buyer were to deny delivery, the goods may deteriorate or waste as the seller may not be in a position to recover goods that have already been shipped to the buyer's jurisdiction.

---

[44] For example, if the contract requires the buyer to arrange for carriage of the goods, the buyer must take the necessary steps to enable the seller to hand over the goods to the carrier. Secretariat Commentary on the 1978 Draft, *Guide to CISG Article 58,* para. 2 (available at http://cisgw3.law. pace.edu/cisg/text/secomm/secomm-58.html). This provision could also require that the buyer comply with administrative regulations, such as obtaining an import license. Denis Tallon, *The Buyer's Obligations under the Convention on Contracts for the International Sale of Goods*, in *International Sales: The United Nations Convention on Contracts for the International Sale of Goods* 7-7 (Galston & Smit ed., Matthew Bender 1984).

[45] Obligations regarding cooperation can be found in Articles 19(2), 21(2), 32, 48(2), 58(3), 60(a), 65, 71, 73(2), 79(4) and 85-88. *See* Honnold, *supra* n. 15, at 342 n. 2.

[46] Obligations specifically regarding preservation of the goods are in Articles 85–88.

> **Article 60**
>
> The buyer's obligation to take delivery consists:
>
> (a) in doing all the acts which could reasonably be expected of him in order to enable the seller to make delivery; and
>
> (b) in taking over the goods.

PROBLEMS

Problem 4-1: NNM and J&G enter a contract for the sale of steel. They fail to specify where delivery is to take place or when the risk of loss will pass. Absent the parties' agreement, what default terms will the CISG provide? How would your answer change if the parties agreed to ship the goods FOB St. Petersburg, Russia (Incoterms 2000)?

Problem 4-2: A contract between an Italian suit wholesaler and a Paris department store calls for 1500 Armani designer suits. The Italian wholesaler delivers 1500 Armani Exchange suits. Under Article 35, has the Italian wholesaler delivered conforming goods? (Armani Exchange is the more reasonably priced popular version of the Armani line). What if under the terms of the same language in previous contracts, the Italian wholesaler had always delivered Armani Couture suits and not Armani Exchange?

Problem 4-3: A contract between a confectionary company and a second-hand machine resale shop called for delivery of a used printing machine that could print on foils used to wrap chocolates in the confectionary industry.[47] The seller located such a used machine and sent the buyer the machine's manual to review. The seller also invited the buyer to visit the factory where the machine was located. The seller viewed the machine, finalized the contract, and took delivery. It turned out that the printing machine could not print on the 8 mm thick foils that the confectionary company used for its chocolates without ripping the foil. However, it could print on foil that was 10 mm or thicker, and such foils were commonly used in the confectionary industry. Can the buyer make a claim under Article 35? What if page 35 of the manual that the seller provided to the buyer had specified that the machine could print on foils of 10 mm or greater thickness?

Problem 4-4: Sunshine CDs, a Chinese company, sells music CDs to J-Mart. J-Mart suspects that Sunshine does not have rights to the songs on its CDs when artists threaten to sue J-Mart if it continues to sell Sunshine's CDs. Under what

---

[47] This problem is based on the problem used in the 13th Annual Willem C. Vis International Commercial Arbitration Moot.

circumstances would J-Mart have a cause of action against Sunshine? Does the CISG require J-Mart to notify Sunshine of the third party claim?

5 | REMEDIES FOR BREACH

If you wish to be a success in the world,
promise everything, deliver nothing.[1]

- Napoleon Bonaparte

This chapter turns to the question of what recourse a party has when its counterparty makes promises that it does not keep, either intentionally or unintentionally. The CISG devotes a section to the buyer's remedies for seller's breach (Articles 45–52) and a section to seller's remedies for buyer's breach (Articles 61–65). Each of these sections is analogous to the other and each outlines the spectrum of remedies available to the aggrieved party. Needless to say, those remedies are filled with qualifications, requirements, and exceptions. In addition, the CISG encourages parties to exercise self-help, setting forth inspection, notice, and cure provisions that allow a party who might otherwise breach to remedy the situation before the parties resort to a formal dispute resolution process.

This chapter will first discuss inspection, notice, and cure provisions in Part I before turning to a discussion of the buyer's remedies in Part II and the seller's remedies in Part III. Part IV will present issues common to both the buyer's and seller's remedies, including anticipatory breach and installment contracts. Finally, regardless of which party to the transaction breaches, the CISG imposes requirements regarding preservation of goods that are involved to minimize the extent of losses that result from the dispute. Part V will outline those requirements.

I.   INSPECTION, NOTICE, AND CURE PROVISIONS

Before the buyer can claim remedies related to either non-conformity of the goods or third party claims, the buyer must generally notify the seller of such issues in a timely manner. In connection with the cure provisions of the CISG, early notice of any problem allows the seller an opportunity to address the issue and cure the problem. This section first will discuss the CISG's inspection and notice requirements regarding conformity of the goods, then will address the

---

[1] Napoleon Bonaparte, quoted in H. Paul Jeffers, *The 100 Greatest Heroes* 30 (Citadell 2003).

CISG's notice provisions regarding third party claims, and finally will describe the CISG's cure provisions.

A.   BUYER'S OBLIGATIONS TO INSPECT AND NOTIFY

Articles 38 through 40 contain the provisions relating to the buyer's inspection of the goods and notice to the seller of any non-conformity. Article 38 mandates a timely inspection of the goods delivered pursuant to the sales contract. Building off of Article 38, Article 39 requires timely notice to the seller of any non-conformity of the goods delivered. Through both of these Articles, the CISG is attempting to ensure that any claims for non-conformity are made within a reasonable period of time after the buyer gains access to the goods. However, Article 40 eliminates the requirements imposed on the buyer by Articles 38 and 39 in cases where it appears that the seller knew of the non-conformity, did not tell the buyer about it, and delivered the goods anyway.

1.   Inspection of Goods

Article 38 insists that the buyer inspect the goods in a timely fashion and therefore places the buyer in a position to observe any non-conformities sooner rather than later.

Article 38

(1) The buyer must examine the goods, or cause them to be examined, within as short a period as is practicable in the circumstances.

(2) If the contract involves carriage of the goods, examination may be deferred until after the goods have arrived at their destination.

(3) If the goods are redirected in transit or redispatched by the buyer without a reasonable opportunity for examination by him and at the time of the conclusion of the contract the seller knew or ought to have known of the possibility of such redirection or redispatch, examination may be deferred until after the goods have arrived at the new destination.

Example 5-1

An Australian buyer purchased food stuffs from an Italian seller. The Australian buyer brought a claim against the Italian seller for non-conformity of the goods. However, the Australian buyer never made any inspection, erroneously believing that it was not obligated to do so. Noting the lack of an inspection, no timely notice of any defects in the goods, as well as other factors, the Australian court refused to find the Italian seller liable for any non-conformity.[2]

Article 38 mandates that the buyer inspect the goods not only in a timely manner, but in "as short a period as is practicable in the circumstances." This standard is more specific and more demanding than merely a "reasonable period" but still will present some difficulties in its application since it does not contain any bright-line standard.[3] The CISG Advisory Council has issued an opinion on this provision stating that such a determination should take into account all the relevant circumstances.[4] So, for example, it should be practicable to inspect perishables almost immediately upon receipt, while complicated machinery may not be truly capable of being inspected until it is installed and put into use.[5]

Article 38 further explains that if the contract requires the goods to be shipped, the buyer's obligation to inspect the goods is deferred until the goods reach their destination, even if the shipping involves the buyer redirecting the goods (provided that the seller knew or ought to have known about the possibility for such redirection) (Articles 38(2) and (3)).

While Article 38 says nothing explicitly about the kind of inspection required, commentators and courts have both reasoned that Article 38 implies that a reasonable inspection must be conducted.[6] In determining whether the quality of

---

[2] *See Italian Imported Foods Pty. Ltd.[Australia] v. Pucci S.r.l. [Italy],* Supreme Court of New South Wales no. 15801/2005, Australia, Oct. 13, 2006 (available at http://cisgw3.law.pace.edu/cases/061013a2.html).

[3] John O. Honnold, *Uniform Law for International Sales under the 1980 United Nations Convention* 272 (3rd ed., Kluwer L. Intl. 1999).

[4] CISG-AC Opinion no. 2, *Examination of the Goods and Notice of Non-Conformity: Articles 38 and 39,* para. 1-2, June 7, 2004 (available at http://cisgw3.law.pace.edu/cisg/CISG-AC-op2.html).

[5] *Id.* at para. 2.

[6] *See* Secretariat Commentary on the 1978 Draft, *Guide to CISG Article 38,* para. 3 (available at http://cisgw3.law.pace.edu/cisg/text/secomm/secomm-38.html); Joseph Lookofsky, *The 1980 United Nations Convention on Contracts for the International Sale of Goods,* in *International Encyclopaedia of Laws—Contracts,* Supp. 29, 103 (J. Herbots & R. Blanpain eds., Kluwer L. Intl. 2000); Fritz Enderlein & Dietrich Maskow, *International Sales Law* 154 (Oceana Publications 1992); *Italian Seller v. Austrian Buyer (Trekking Shoes Case),* Oberster Gerichtshof [Supreme Court] no. 1 Ob 223/99x, Austria, Aug. 27, 1999 (available at http://cisgw3.law.pace.edu/cases/

any particular inspection is reasonable for purposes of Article 38, courts have considered all of the particular circumstances of the situation, including any relevant trade norms for inspections of similar types of goods.[7]

2.   Notice of Non-conformity

While Article 38 explains that an inspection to determine whether the goods conform must occur quickly after delivery of the goods is made, Article 39 contains the requirement that the buyer then timely notify the seller if it has received non-conforming goods.

Article 39

(1) The buyer loses the right to rely on a lack of conformity of the goods if he does not give notice to the seller specifying the nature of the lack of conformity within a reasonable time after he has discovered it or ought to have discovered it.

(2) In any event, the buyer loses the right to rely on a lack of conformity of the goods if he does not give the seller notice thereof at the latest within a period of two years from the date on which the goods were actually handed over to the buyer, unless this time-limit is inconsistent with a contractual period of guarantee.

Article 39(1) specifically strips the buyer of its right to claim any remedies based on non-conformity of the goods unless the buyer gives timely notice to the seller explaining the non-conformity. Such notice must be given within a reasonable time after the buyer either: (i) discovered the non-conformity, or (ii) ought to have discovered the non-conformity (Article 39(1)). Again, by utilizing the standard "ought to have discovered," the CISG provides a secondary criterion for satisfaction of the knowledge standard required of the buyer here. If the buyer claims not to have noticed the defect, the seller can argue that the buyer ought to have known of the defect.

The notice should explain the non-conformity with sufficient specificity to allow the seller to cure the defect. At least one court has denied a claim for non-

---

990827a3.html).

[7] *See* Secretariat Commentary on the 1978 Draft, *Guide to CISG Article 36,* para. 3 (available at http://cisgw3.law.pace.edu/cisg/text/secomm/secomm-36.html); Lookofsky, *supra* n. 6, at 102.

conformity even when the buyer had given the seller notice, where the notice did not explain the non-conformity with sufficient specificity.

Example 5-2

A German buyer purchased a shipment of various blankets from a Dutch seller. The German buyer notified the Dutch seller that its shipment was deficient in both quality and quantity. The Germany court rejected the claim, stating that the notification from the German buyer was insufficient since it did not adequately describe the non-conformity of the delivery so that the seller could take action to remedy the non-conformity. More specifically, the notice did not explain which type of blankets were missing in the delivery.[8]

However, there is also some ambiguity for the parties trying to determine what a reasonable time period is under **Article 39.** The CISG Advisory Council issued an opinion on the precise issue of what time frame is reasonable under **Article 39** and stated that no one time frame can be suitable for all cases.[9] Rather, all of the circumstances of each case should be considered, including the nature of the goods and the nature of the defect.[10] In addition, whether and when an inspection was held under **Article 38** should be considered. Since Article 38 insists that the buyer inspect the goods as soon as is practicable after receiving them, it would seem that at least a patent non-conformity would typically be detected at that stage and then notice of that non-conformity would need to be sent out to the seller soon after that. Indeed the CISG Advisory Council stated that, based on **Article 38,** even if an inspection was not made, Article 39's time frame for when a buyer "ought to have discovered" any defects should run from the time the inspection could have been made.[11]

Of course there may be latent non-conformities that an initial inspection of the goods fails to detect.[12] In that event, **Article 39(2)** sets forth a maximum allowed time period for notices of non-conformity of two years from the date when the goods were handed over to the buyer. However, there is also an exception to that

---

[8] *Dutch Seller v. German Buyer (Acrylic Blankets Case)*, Oberlandesgericht Koblenz no. 2 U 31/96, Germany, Jan. 31, 1997 (available at http://cisgw3.law.pace.edu/cases/970131g1.html).
[9] CISG-AC Opinion no. 2, *supra* n. 4, at para. 3.3.
[10] *Id.*
[11] *Id.* at para. 4.1.
[12] For a discussion of how Articles 38 and 39 interact with patent versus latent defects, see Lookofsky, *supra* n. 6, at 106–107.

rule for situations where a contractual guarantee would make that period longer (Article 39(2)).

Example 5-3

An Austrian buyer of installments of hiking shoes from an Italian seller brought a complaint based on defects with the hiking shoes. The Austrian buyer had notified the seller of the non-conformity three weeks after the last installment was delivered and claimed that the defects were not apparent after its initial inspection.

The Austrian Supreme Court reasoned that in accordance with Article 38, under ordinary circumstances, a thorough and professional inspection should be made within about fourteen days of delivery. The court also stated that all of the circumstances of each case should be considered in arriving at an appropriate time period.

The Court further mentioned that in the absence of an agreement as to how an inspection should proceed, trade norms should be considered. The Court ruled that, in this case, the lack of a thorough inspection within that short period of time and the consequent lack of timely notice of the defects under Article 39 precluded the buyer from bringing a claim for non-conformity under the CISG.[13]

---

3.   Seller's Knowledge of Non-Conformity

Article 40 complicates the analysis, as it is designed to prevent the injustice of seller knowingly delivering non-conforming goods to an unsuspecting buyer. In that scenario, Article 40 forgives the buyer its obligation to inspect the goods and notify the seller of the non-conformity. Further, the seller does not in fact need the buyer to notify it of the non-conformity since it already has that knowledge. Thus, Article 40 essentially eliminates the requirements of Articles 38 and 39 regarding inspection and notice of non-conformity in cases where the seller knew or could not have been unaware of the non-conformity and still did not disclose that knowledge to buyer.

---

[13] *Italian Seller v. Austrian Buyer*, Oberster Gerichtshof [Supreme Court] no. 1 Ob 223/99x, Austria, Aug. 27, 1999 (available at http://cisgw3.law.pace.edu/cases/990827a3.html).

> ### Article 40
>
> The seller is not entitled to rely on the provisions of Articles 38 and 39 if the lack of conformity relates to facts of which he knew or could not have been unaware and which he did not disclose to the buyer.

Again, the CISG provides a secondary criterion for actual knowledge—here, "could not have been unaware." This language will allow the buyer to argue that the seller must have known of the non-conformity even if seller denies actual knowledge. This is the same criterion used in **Article 35(3)**, discussed in Chapter 4. As was mentioned there, Professor Honnold describes this strict standard of "knew or could not have been unaware" as being met when a particular fact is "before the eyes of one who can see."[14]

While **Article 40** complicates the analysis, it is designed to prevent the injustice of the seller knowingly delivering non-conforming goods to an unsuspecting buyer. Underlying this notion is the **principle of good faith** and commentators have noted that the CISG is essentially requiring good faith in this provision.[15] The seller is expected to deliver conforming goods. To the extent the goods do not conform, the seller is expected to communicate that fact to the buyer. Where the seller does knowingly deliver non-conforming goods, the buyer is forgiven of its obligation to inspect the goods and notify the seller of the non-conformity. Further, the seller does not in fact need the buyer to notify it of the non-conformity since it already has that knowledge.

> ### Example 5-4
>
> A United States manufacturer sold an industrial press to a Chinese buyer with specifications that the machine be of the highest quality. The United States seller ended up delivering the press to the Chinese buyer knowing that it contained a different component than one that had been described to the buyer. The United States seller gave the Chinese buyer no notice to that effect. Four years after delivery, the machine broke down as a

---

[14] Honnold, *supra* n. 3, at 260

[15] Professor Lookofsky describes Article 40 as "an expression of the 'general principle' which requires both CISG parties to act in good faith." *supra* n. 6, at 108; *see also* Jacob S. Ziegel, *Report to the Uniform Law Conference of Canada on Convention on Contracts for the International Sale of Goods*, art. 40 (July 1981) (available at http://cisgw3.law.pace.edu/cisg/ wais/db/Articles/english2.html) ("Article 40 is an excellent example of bad faith depriving the seller of a defence to which he would otherwise be entitled.").

> result of the substitute component being used and not explained to the Chinese buyer. The Chinese buyer then brought a claim in arbitration against the United States seller for delivery of non-conforming goods. The tribunal found that Articles 38 and 39 did not bar recovery in this case since, in accordance with Article 40, those time constraints do not apply when the seller knows of the facts related to the non-conformity at the time of the delivery and does not inform the buyer.[16]

4.   Notice of Third Party Claims

Articles 41 and 42, discussed in Chapter 4 above, mandate that the seller provide the buyer with goods that are free from third party claims (Article 42 applying specifically to intellectual property claims). The buyer's right to rely on those provisions and to claim a remedy based upon a violation of those obligations is subject to the notice requirements of Article 43.

> **Article 43**
>
> (1) The buyer loses the right to rely on the provisions of Article 41 or Article 42 if he does not give notice to the seller specifying the nature of the right or claim of the third party within a reasonable time after he has become aware or ought to have become aware of the right or claim.
>
> (2) The seller is not entitled to rely on the provisions of the preceding paragraph if he knew of the right or claim of the third party and the nature of it.

Article 43 insists that, in order to prevail on a claim under Articles 41 or 42, the buyer notify the seller "within a reasonable time" after it either became aware or "ought to have become aware" of the third party claim. Again, what is meant by a "reasonable time" will be arguable, but reference can be made to international norms for claims in such circumstances. Further, when a buyer "ought to have become aware" of a claim will be difficult to determine.[17] Nonetheless, this

---

[16] *Beijing Light Automobile Co., Ltd [China] v. Connell Limited Partnership [United States]*, Arbitration Institute of the Stockholm Chamber of Commerce, Sweden June 5, 1998 (available at http://cisgw3.law.pace.edu/cases/980605s5.html).

[17] Article 43 does not create a duty to investigate possible third party claims. However, scholars argue that Article 43 does not allow the buyer to "carelessly neglect rights or claims of third parties of which he becomes aware." Enderlein & Maskow, *supra* n. 6, at 171.

Article instructs the parties to communicate their claims to each other in a timely fashion, reflecting the CISG's encouragement of communication between the parties generally. This principle may have the effect of helping to mitigate any damages by alerting the breaching party to problems sooner rather than later, allowing the party more time to potentially remedy the situation.[18]

Having set forth the requirement that the buyer must timely notify seller of third party claims, Article 43(2) then limits the principle. Article 43(2) states that the seller may not rely on that notice requirement if seller knew of the third party claim. This is analogous to Article 40, described above. This limitation appears both logical and understandable in connection with Article 41. If the seller knew of the third party claim, then timely notification of the claim to the seller by the buyer would not be necessary. Just as with Article 40, Article 43(2) seems to reflect the principle of good faith. The seller is expected not to deliver goods that it knows are encumbered by a third party claim without disclosing such fact to the buyer.

However, Article 43(2) has a questionable application to claims under Article 42 concerning third party intellectual property claims. On the one hand, since Article 42 insists that the seller have some sort of knowledge (under the standard that the seller either "knew or could not have been unaware" of the claim), then the limitation of Article 43(2) may always apply to claims under Article 42. Therefore, the buyer may not ever need to timely notify the seller under Article 43(1) of claims it may have under Article 42. On the other hand, a possible interpretation of these provisions might lead one to the conclusion that Article 43(2) would not apply to a claim under Article 42 where the seller denied actual knowledge but it was deemed that seller "could not have been unaware" of the claim. This interpretation might carry some weight since Article 43(2) did not reference a seller who "could not have been unaware" of the claim, but only one who actually "knew" of the claim.[19]

---

[18] *See Id.* ("*The buyer* not only has an obligation to give notice, he also *has to specify the nature of the right or claim*, the steps that the third party has undertaken etc., so as to enable the seller to *take immediate measures defending his rights.*" (Emphasis in original)).

[19] *See* Lookofsky, *supra* n. 6, at 112 (emphasizing that Article 43(2) only precludes a seller from relying on the buyer's failure to provide notice when the seller actually *knew* of the third party's right) (emphasis added); *see also* Enderlein & Maskow, *supra* n. 6, at 170 (explaining that the seller must have "definite knowledge" of the third party rights under Article 43(2) whereas, in regard to non-conformity under Article 40, it is sufficient that the seller "could not have been unaware" of the non-conformity).

Example 5-5

A Dutch buyer purchased a used car from a German seller in April of 1999. On August 23, 1999, the buyer learned that the car was allegedly stolen and therefore subject to a claim by the insurance company of the original owner. On October 26, 1999, the Dutch buyer notified the German seller of the alleged claim and demanded that it be reimbursed for the purchase price of the car. The German Supreme Court ruled that the buyer had not given timely notice of the third party claim to the seller under Article 43 of the CISG. The court went as far as to say that notice should have been given within one month, barring any unusual circumstances. Further, there was no evidence that the seller had known of the third party claim. Thus, the exception contained in Article 43(2) was also not applicable. Accordingly, the buyer's claim against the seller was dismissed.[20]

---

5.   Excuse for Failure to Notify

Article 39 mandates that a party give notice of any non-conformity within a short time period in order to be able to rely on a claim for the non-conformity. Article 43 is a similar provision with respect to third party claims on the goods delivered. If the buyer does not notify the seller of the existence of the third party claim, then the buyer loses the right to rely on the third party claim in an action against the seller. Notwithstanding a buyer's breach of Articles 39 and 43, Article 44 still provides that buyer with some limited remedies if the buyer had a reasonable excuse for failing to notify the seller in accordance with those sections. Article 44 allows such a buyer to reduce the price it pays or claim damages (excluding lost profits) where there is a non-conformity or a third party claim if the buyer has a reasonable excuse for not giving the required notice.[21]

---

[20] *Dutch Buyer v. German Seller (Automobile Case),* Bundesgerichtshof [Federal Supreme Court] no. VIII ZR 268/04, Germany, Jan. 11, 2006 (available at http://cisgw3.law.pace.edu/cases/060111g1.html).

[21] However, national courts that have interpreted Article 44 have been reluctant to excuse a party's failure to comply with the notice requirements of Article 39. *See* Larry DiMatteo et al., *The Interpretive Turn in International Sales Law: An Analysis of Fifteen Years of CISG Jurisprudence,* 34 Nw. J. Intl. L. & Bus. (Winter 2004) (citing multiple decisions where national courts have rejected a buyer's attempt to rely on Article 44).

> ### Article 44
>
> Notwithstanding the provisions of paragraph (1) of Article 39 and paragraph (1) of Article 43, the buyer may reduce the price in accordance with Article 50 or claim damages, except for loss of profit, if he has a reasonable excuse for his failure to give the required notice.

savior clause,, reasonable excuse

B. ALLOWING THE SELLER TO CURE

The CISG encourages the parties to remedy any problems with their transaction themselves. It does this by specifically allowing the seller to cure any defects in its performance before the defects become the subject of a larger dispute. While the CISG allows the seller to cure, it also attempts to protect the buyer from any unreasonable hardship based on that right by attaching certain conditions to the seller's right to cure.

Articles 34 and 37 allow the seller to cure defects in its performance, in cases where the due date for delivery has not yet passed, provided that certain conditions are met. Further, Article 48 allows the seller to fix a cure period where the due date for delivery has passed even if the buyer has not done so, again, provided that certain conditions are met.

1. The Seller May Cure Before the Delivery Date Has Passed

Articles 34 and 37 both address a scenario in which there is some defect in the seller's performance, but the due date for delivery of the goods under the contract has not yet arrived. Article 34 relates to the seller's delivery of non-conforming documents under the terms of the contract, whereas Article 37 relates to the seller's delivery of non-conforming goods under the terms of the contract.

a. *Delivery of Non-Conforming Documents*

Article 34 allows a seller to cure any delivery of non-conforming documents when there is still time before the due date for delivery of those documents has passed.[22]

---

[22] The types of documents contemplated in this provision include bills of lading, dock receipts, warehouse receipts, certificates of insurance, commercial or consular invoices, and certificates of origin, weight or quality. Secretariat Commentary on the 1978 Draft, *Guide to CISG Article 32,* para. 2 (available at http://cisgw3.law.pace.edu/cisg/text/secomm/secomm-32.html)

> **Article 34**
>
> If the seller is bound to hand over documents relating to the goods, he must hand them over at the time and place and in the form required by the contract. If the seller has handed over documents before that time, he may, up to that time, cure any lack of conformity in the documents, if the exercise of this right does not cause the buyer unreasonable inconvenience or unreasonable expense. However, the buyer retains any right to claim damages as provided for in this Convention.

This right to cure is subject to two restrictions. First, the seller must cure by the original due date for the documents. Second, allowing the seller to cure cannot cause the buyer any unreasonable inconvenience or expense. Of course, what is meant by unreasonable is difficult to ascertain and will likely be different depending on the circumstances of each case. A $1,000 expense might be unreasonable in small transactions but perfectly reasonable in larger ones. Article 34 also provides that allowing the seller to cure does not prevent the buyer from claiming damages for any losses caused by the seller's original non-conformity. Some scholars have suggested that an inconvenience or expense is unreasonable only if it can not be compensated for by a damage award. The right to claim damages is preserved in the last sentence of Article 34.

b.   Delivery of Non-Conforming Goods

Article 37 similarly allows the seller to cure any delivery of non-conforming goods when there is still time before the due date for the delivery has passed.

> **Article 37**
>
> If the seller has delivered goods before the date for delivery, he may, up to that date, deliver any missing part or make up any deficiency in the quantity of the goods delivered, or deliver goods in replacement of any non-conforming goods delivered or remedy any lack of conformity in the goods delivered, provided that the exercise of this right does not cause the buyer unreasonable inconvenience or unreasonable expense. However, the buyer retains any right to claim damages as provided for in this Convention.

Again, the seller's right to cure its performance during this period is subject to conditions. First, the seller must cure by the original due date for delivery. Second, allowing the seller to cure in this way cannot cause the buyer any unreasonable inconvenience or expense. Similar to Article 34, what is meant by unreasonable inconvenience or expense may not always be clear in any given transaction. However, what is clear is that these requirements are designed to protect the buyer against any hardships created by the seller's defective performance. In addition to these reasonability requirements, Article 37 (like Article 34) preserves the buyer's right to claim damages for any losses it may suffer as a result of seller's original defective performance, even where the seller later cures those defects.

2.   Seller May Set a Cure Period after the Delivery is Due

Where Article 37 allows the seller to cure any defects in its performance before the performance has become due, Article 48 allows the seller to cure defects in its performance after the performance has become due. In that case, where the seller is therefore already in breach for not having performed by the due date, Article 48 allows the seller to set its own additional time period during which it may still perform, as long as certain conditions are satisfied.

Article 48

(1) Subject to article 49, the seller may, even after the date for delivery, remedy at his own expense any failure to perform his obligations, if he can do so without unreasonable delay and without causing the buyer unreasonable inconvenience or uncertainty of reimbursement by the seller of expenses advanced by the buyer. However, the buyer retains any right to claim damages as provided for in this Convention.

(2) If the seller requests the buyer to make known whether he will accept performance and the buyer does not comply with the request within a reasonable time, the seller may perform within the time indicated in his request. The buyer may not, during that period of time, resort to any remedy which is inconsistent with performance by the seller.

(3) A notice by the seller that he will perform within a specified period of time is assumed to include a request, under the preceding paragraph, that the buyer make known his decision.

> **(4) A request or notice by the seller under paragraph (2) or (3) of this article is not effective unless received by the buyer.**

First and foremost, notice that **Article 48** is qualified and made subject to **Article 49** on avoidance. Thus, the seller's ability to set its own additional time period is also contingent upon whether or not the buyer has taken action to declare the contract avoided. The seller attempting to remedy any deficiency in its performance under **Article 48** is incompatible with the buyer pursuing avoidance under **Article 49**. Such action by the buyer is indication that it is not willing to allow the seller additional time within which to rectify its breach.

Conversely, though, as will be seen below in the discussion on avoidance, the buyer's ability to avoid may also be contingent upon Article 48 and the seller's willingness or attempt to cure any non-conformity. If the buyer does not allow the seller an opportunity to cure, the buyer may not be successful in persuading a tribunal that the non-conformity was so substantial (i.e. fundamental) that it should allow the buyer to avoid the contract and its obligations altogether.[23]

Example 5-6

A Singapore seller shipped computer hardware to a Polish buyer. An ICC tribunal found that the Polish buyer's claim of avoidance for a fundamental breach was improper where the Polish buyer denied the Singapore seller the opportunity under Article 48 to cure the defect, which could have been easily repaired at a minimal cost.[24]

Article 48(2) is at the heart of Article 48. In accordance with that section, the seller may make a request to the buyer that the seller be allowed to cure its defective performance by a certain date. The buyer can then affirmatively accept

---

[23] See *Dutch Seller v. German Buyer (Acrylic Blankets Case)*, Oberlandesgericht Koblenz no. 2 U 31/96, Germany Jan. 31, 1997 (available at http://cisgw3.law.pace.edu/cases/970131g1.html). In that case the court ruled that a particular breach was not fundamental because the seller offered to cure the defect under Article 48 and the seller refused the offer. The court stated that whether a breach is fundamental "depends not only on the gravity of the defect, but also on the seller's willingness to remedy the defect without causing unreasonable delay or inconvenience to the buyer. Even a severe defect may not constitute a fundamental breach of contract in the sense of Art. 49 CISG, if the seller is able and willing to remedy without causing unreasonable inconvenience to the buyer." *Id.*

[24] See Honnold, *supra* n. 3, at 319–321; *see also Singaporean Seller v. Polish Buyer*, ICC Court of Arbitration no. 7754, Jan. 1995 (available at http://www.unilex.info/case.cfm?pid=1&do=case&id=519&step=FullText).

or reject that proposal. However, if the buyer does not respond "within a reasonable time," then the buyer will be deemed to have accepted the proposal and the seller will be allowed its cure period (Article 48(2)). Article 48(3) states that a notice from the seller to the buyer that it intends to cure by a certain date qualifies as a request for purposes of Article 48(2). Thus, either a request or a notice from the seller to the buyer regarding the seller curing by a certain date triggers the seller's right to so cure, unless the buyer affirmatively rejects the request or notice. Upon acceptance of the proposal (either affirmatively or by silence), the buyer cannot then resort to any remedy during that period that is inconsistent with the seller performing (Article 48(2)).

Still, Article 48(1) sets forth some limits on the seller's ability to cure in accordance with this Article. First, the seller's remedy must be at its own expense. Second, the seller must remedy the situation without causing the buyer any unreasonable delay. Third, the cure must not cause the buyer any unreasonable inconvenience. Fourth, the cure must not cause the buyer any unreasonable uncertainty regarding reimbursement from the seller for any expenses the buyer might have to incur in order for seller to cure. The last three of these limitations may be difficult to apply due to the problem of assessing when delay, inconvenience, or uncertainty are unreasonable.[25] Nonetheless, the limitations reflect the CISG's attempt to balance the interests of the seller in being able to cure with the interests of the buyer in not suffering any undue hardship as a result of seller's defective performance. As was mentioned with respect to Article 34, above, some scholars have suggested that delay, inconvenience or uncertainty are only unreasonable if they can not be compensated for through damages. Article 48(1) stipulates that the buyer can always claim damages for any losses it suffers as a result of seller's original delivery of non-conforming goods.

Example 5-7

A German buyer contracted with an Italian seller for a certain quantity of tetracycline HCL in accordance with particular specifications. When the Italian seller delivered goods that did not conform to the specifications, it argued that it should be given extra time to fulfill the contract in accordance with Article 48. The German court found that the buyer was not required to

---

[25] *See Italian Buyer v. Swiss Seller (Art Books Case)*, Handelsgericht [Commercial Court] Zürich no. HG 970238.1, Switzerland, Feb. 10, 1999 (available at http://cisgw3.law.pace.edu/cases/990210s1.html) (stating that "[a]n unreasonable delay will generally be caused if a failure to keep to the delivery date already constituted a fundamental breach of contract or if the further delay led to a fundamental breach").

> give the seller additional time to cure pursuant to Article 48 because the seller could not cure its defects within the time period required by the buyer's customers and any further delay would have led to considerable damages.[26]

II.   BUYER'S REMEDIES FOR SELLER'S BREACH

Article 45 provides an outline of remedies available to the buyer following the seller's breach. Article 45 explains that if the seller fails to perform any of its obligations (described in Chapter 4 of this casebook), then the buyer can exercise any of its rights set forth in Articles 46 through 52. Those provisions include rights regarding: (A) avoidance, (B) specific performance, (C) paying a reduced price, (D) partial performance, and (E) early or excess delivery. As will soon be clear, it is necessary to refer to provisions throughout the CISG when analyzing these alternatives. Note that regardless of which remedy the buyer chooses to pursue, Article 45(2) always preserves the buyer's right to claim damages for any losses suffered.[27]

A.   AVOIDING THE CONTRACT

Among the most sought after remedies is the buyer's right to declare the contract avoided. Avoidance relieves the buyer of its obligations under the contract but still allows the buyer to seek any damages for its losses suffered (Article 81(1)). Article 49 governs the buyer's right to declare a contract avoided.

Article 49

(1) The buyer may declare the contract avoided:

(a) if the failure by the seller to perform any of his obligations under the contract or this Convention amounts to a fundamental breach of contract; or

(b) in case of non-delivery, if the seller does not deliver the goods within the additional period of time fixed by the buyer

---

[26] *See Italian Seller v. German Buyer (Tetracycline Case)*, Amtsgericht [Petty District Court] München no. 271 C 18968/94, Germany, June 12, 1995 (available at http://cisgw3.law.pace.edu/cases/950623g1.html).

[27] The buyer's right to damages is therefore cumulative of any other remedies sought and not exclusive. Harry M. Flechtner, *Buyers' Remedies in General and Buyers' Performance-Oriented Remedies* 25 J.L. & Com. 339, 341 (2005).

> in accordance with paragraph (1) of Article 47 or declares that he will not deliver within the period so fixed.
>
> (2) However, in cases where the seller has delivered the goods, the buyer loses the right to declare the contract avoided unless he does so:
>
> (a) in respect of late delivery, within a reasonable time after he has become aware that delivery has been made;
>
> (b) in respect of any breach other than late delivery, within a reasonable time:
>
> (i) after he knew or ought to have known of the breach;
>
> (ii) after the expiration of any additional period of time fixed by the buyer in accordance with paragraph (1) of Article 47, or after the seller has declared that he will not perform his obligations within such an additional period; or
>
> (iii) after the expiration of any additional period of time indicated by the seller in accordance with paragraph
>
> (2) of Article 48, or after the buyer has declared that he will not accept performance.

Article 49(1) outlines two scenarios in which the buyer can declare the contract avoided: (i) when the seller has committed a fundamental breach; or (ii) in the case of non-delivery, when the buyer has fixed an extended period for performance under Article 47, and the seller still does not deliver by the end of that period. In addition, Article 49(2) contains requirements that certain declarations of avoidance be made in a timely manner.

1.   Avoidance Based on Fundamental Breach by Seller

The buyer can declare the contract avoided if the seller has committed a fundamental breach of its obligations (Article 49(1)(a)). Fundamental breach is defined in Article 25.

> **Article 25**
>
> A breach of contract committed by one of the parties is fundamental if it results in such detriment to the other party as

> substantially to deprive him of what he is entitled to expect under the contract, unless the party in breach did not foresee and a reasonable person of the same kind in the same circumstances would not have foreseen such a result.

This definition contains two primary components: (a) the magnitude of the harm caused, and (b) the foreseeability of the harm.

a.   *The Magnitude of the Harm*

Any breach allows a party to claim damages for losses from the other party. A fundamental breach, however, allows the injured party to declare the contract avoided and its obligations eliminated. This more dramatic remedy is reserved for breaches that cross over some threshold level of detriment caused to the injured party.[28] The language of Article 25 focuses on the detriment caused by the breach as the defining characteristic for a fundamental breach. The detriment must be so grave as to "substantially deprive" the injured party of what it expected to receive under the contract.

The CISG Advisory Council issued an opinion in which it enumerated criteria for how to assess whether a breach is fundamental.[29] In its opinion, the Advisory Council indicated that tribunals should take into account the circumstances surrounding the transaction in its deliberation.[30] The Advisory Council enumerated that the following factors, among others, should be considered: (i) the terms of the contract, (ii) the purpose for which the goods were bought, and (iii) whether any non-conformity could be cured.[31] A defect that could be cured in accordance with the provisions of Article 48 is likely not to be fundamental.

b.   *Foreseeability of the Harm*

A breach is not fundamental if the breaching party did not foresee the fundamental nature of the result that would occur from its breach. As with the knowledge standards that exist throughout the CISG, this foreseeability standard

---

[28] The determination of whether a breach is fundamental is of "cardinal importance for the system of remedies, because it can determine the life or death of the contract." Michael Will, *Article 25*, in *Bianca-Bonell Commentary on the International Sales Law* 205 (Giuffrè 1987).

[29] CISG-AC Opinion no. 5, *The buyer's right to avoid the contract in case of non-conforming goods or documents,* May 7, 2005 (available at http://cisgw3.law.pace.edu/cisg/CISG-AC-op5.html).

[30] *Id.*

[31] *Id.*

also has a reasonable person criterion that can be satisfied. Thus, a breach is fundamental if either the breaching party foresaw the nature of the result or a reasonable person in similar circumstances would foresee the result. Again, this avoids the problem created when a party simply claims that it did not actually foresee the harm that would be caused. If a reasonable person in similar circumstances would have foreseen the magnitude of the harm, then the breach is fundamental.[32]

In accordance with the definition of fundamental breach found in Article 25, Article 49(1)(a) allows a buyer to avoid the contract if the seller's breach has substantially deprived the buyer of what the buyer expected to get, and the seller knew or ought to have known that its breach would cause such harm. This is a situation where the breach is of such a magnitude that the buyer should be released from its obligations under the contract. The CISG allows for just that in this situation by allowing the buyer to declare the contract avoided.

One difficulty with proceeding under Article 49(1) for the buyer is in being confident that the seller's breach amounts to a fundamental breach. If the buyer proceeds on the assumption that the breach is fundamental and then ignores any obligations it had under the contract or the CISG, then the buyer runs a risk that the seller will bring a claim against it for breach. In fact, if a tribunal then deems the seller's original breach not to be fundamental, then the buyer will indeed have breached and may be held liable for damages.

> ### Compare: Fundamental Breach vs. Perfect Tender
>
> The CISG's concept of fundamental breach is a flexible one, and one that focuses on an objectively foreseeable detriment that must substantially deprive the buyer of what it expected to get. By contrast, the perfect tender rule of UCC §2-601 provides that the buyer may reject the goods subject to the contract if "the goods or the tender of delivery fail *in any respect* to conform to the contract."[33] [emphasis added]

---

[32] While the statutory language is not clear as to when the party in breach should have foreseen the harm its breach would cause, the legislative history supports a flexible interpretation. In fact, proposals to include language in Article 25 stating that foreseeability should be determined at the time of contracting were rejected. A logical interpretation, then, consistent with that legislative history is that the foreseeability requirement should be satisfied if the breaching party could have foreseen the harm at any time before it undertook conduct that led to its breach. *See* Honnold, *supra* n. 3, at 207–209.

[33] However, in §2-612, the UCC sets up a more flexible standard for breach of installment contracts. Under that section the perfect tender rule is rejected for a standard for breach that is more like the standard under Article 25 of the CISG. UCC §2-612 states, subject to certain

2.   Avoidance Based on Non-delivery by the End of the *Nachfrist* Period

The second part of Article 49(1) provides for a clearer situation where buyer can be confident that it can declare the contract avoided. Article 49(1)(b) covers situations where the seller has not delivered the goods at all. In such a case, if the buyer follows Article 47 and fixes an additional time period for the seller to perform its obligations and the seller does not so perform or states that it will not perform, then the buyer can declare the contract avoided without having to argue that the breach was fundamental.

Article 47 applies in cases where the seller has already breached by not performing by its due date. In such cases, buyer may fix an additional period of time for the seller to cure any defects in its performance (Article 47(1)). This notice providing for an additional period of time during which the seller can deliver conforming goods is frequently referred to as a *Nachfrist* notice.[34] If the buyer chooses to deliver a *Nachfrist* notice (providing for the extension of time), then the buyer cannot resort to any other remedy during the extended period, unless the seller has notified the buyer that it will not perform even by the end of the extended period (Article 47(2)). In any event, the buyer can always claim any damages for losses it suffers as a result of the seller's original non-conformity (Article 47(2)).

> **Article 47**
>
> (1) The buyer may fix an additional period of time of reasonable length for performance by the seller of his obligations.
>
> (2) Unless the buyer has received notice from the seller that he will not perform within the period so fixed, the buyer may not, during that period, resort to any remedy for breach of contract. However, the buyer is not deprived thereby of any right he may have to claim damages for delay in performance.

If the seller does deliver during the extended period of time provided by the *Nachfrist* notice, then the buyer can not avoid the contract under Article 49.

---

qualifications, that a breach of any installment occurs if there is a non-conformity in that installment that "substantially impairs the value of that installment." UCC §2-612.

[34] The Nachfrist procedure outlined in Article 47 is similar to the mechanism found in the Section 326 of the German Civil Code. Maryellen DiPalma, *Nachfrist under National Law, the CISG, and the UNIDROIT and European Principles: A Comparison*, Intl. Contract Adviser 28 (Kluwer Winter 1999).

However, Article 47 still allows the buyer to claim any damages for the seller's delay in performance.

If, however, the seller does not deliver during the extended period then Article 49(1)(b) allows the buyer to avoid the contract on that sole basis alone. Buyer need not prove that the breach was fundamental. Further, there can be no doubt that avoidance is proper since non-delivery by the extended date will be clear (whereas proving fundamental breach generally is not as clear cut). If the buyer does not provide the *Nachfrist* notice under Article 47, then in order to avoid the contract the buyer must prove that the seller committed a fundamental breach in accordance with Article 25.

Note that Article 47 only interacts with the avoidance mechanism of Article 49(1)(b) in cases of non-delivery.[35] In such case, the seller might have chosen to deliver conforming goods late. Late delivery may not amount to a fundamental breach. In fact, it often does not.[36] Accordingly, a late delivery would not typically allow the buyer to declare the contract avoided under Article 49(1)(a) for fundamental breach. Article 47 actually provides a mechanism for the buyer to limit the seller's ability to make a late delivery. By sending a *Nachfrist* notice, the buyer sets a final time period, after which the buyer may indeed declare the contract avoided and its obligations terminated.

3.   Avoidance Must be Timely

Article 26 specifies that in any event for avoidance to be effective, notice must always be given to the breaching party. In addition to that general mandate, however, Article 49(2) specifies certain time periods when a declaration of avoidance must be made in certain circumstances. If there has been a late delivery, a claim must be brought within a reasonable time after the buyer has been made aware of the delivery (Article 49(2)(a)). In cases of any other breach where the goods have been delivered, then a declaration of avoidance must be made: (i) if no cure period has been set, within a reasonable time after the buyer knew or ought to have known about the breach; (ii) if the buyer set an additional time period pursuant to Article 47, after the expiration of that period or after the seller has stated that it will not perform; or (iii) if the seller has proposed a cure

---

[35] *See* Honnold, *supra* n. 3, at 313–314 (stating that "the only teeth" in Article 47 are in cases of non-delivery).

[36] *E.g. German Seller v. Finnish Buyer*, Turku Court of Appeal no. S 95/1023, Finland, Feb. 18, 1997 (in which late delivery did not amount to a fundamental breach); *but see Swiss Buyer v. Austrian Seller*, Court of Arbitration of the International Chamber of Commerce no. 8128, Basel, 1995 (abstract available at http://www.unilex.info/case.cfm?pid=1&do=case&id =207&step=Abstract) (in which late delivery did amount to a fundamental breach because of the added circumstance that seller knew of the importance of a timely delivery).

period in accordance with Article 48(2), after the expiration of that cure period or after the buyer has affirmatively rejected the seller's proposal (Article 49(2)(b)).

Example 5-8

In the case referenced in example 5-2, the German buyer of Dutch blankets also brought a claim regarding the Dutch seller's alleged breach of a condition of the sales contract (the condition being that buyer was to have an exclusive distributorship). The court denied the buyer's claim for avoidance since it had waited 8 weeks after it discovered the alleged breach to notify its counterparty that it was going to seek avoidance of the contract. While the court did not specify what would have been an appropriate time period, it did rule that the 8 weeks violated the timing provisions of Article 49(2)(b)(i).[37]

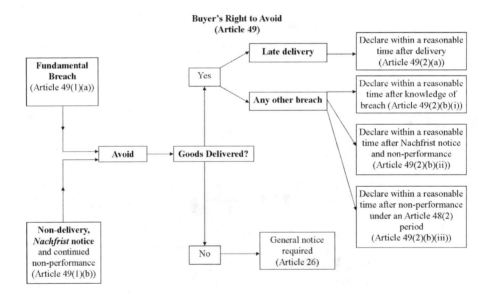

Consider the following recent case from a federal district court in New York. The case confronts issues of fundamental breach and avoidance, among other things.

---

[37] *Dutch Seller v. German Buyer (Acrylic Blankets Case)*, Oberlandesgericht Koblenz no. 2 U 31/96, Germany, Jan. 31, 1997 (available at http://cisgw3.law.pace.edu/cases/970131g1.html).

United States District Court for New Jersey

Valero Marketing & Supply Company v. Green Oy and Greeni Trading Oy

No. Civ. 01-5254 (DRD)

4 April 2006

[...]

OPINION

Debevoise, Senior District Judge

[Author's note: This case involved a contract for the sale of naptha, a petroleum product, from Greeni Trading Oy ("Greeni"), a Finnish supplier, to Valero Marketing & Supply Company ("Valero"), a United States purchaser. The parties originally agreed that Greeni would deliver 25,000 metric tons of naptha to Valero between September 10 - 20, 2001. Further, the naptha was to be shipped from various points in Europe, through Hamburg and on to New York Harbor.

The contract included a provision allowing the buyer, Valero, to approve of the vessel used by the seller, Greeni, to deliver the naptha although such approval was not "to be unreasonably withheld." Lawrence Smith, an employee of Valero, rejected the vessel Greeni had selected, a vessel referred to as the Bear G., primarily because it was 20 years old.

Due to difficulties in loading the required naptha on a vessel in Europe for delivery under the contract, it became clear that Greeni would not be able to deliver by the end of the September 10 - 20 window. Valero then agreed that it would accept delivery up until September 24th but that any naptha delivered after September 20th would be purchased at a slight discount to the original price agreed. Valero continued to state that it did not want the naptha delivered on the Bear G.

Nonetheless Greeni did deliver the naptha on the Bear G. to the New York harbor on September 22 and Valero refused to accept the delivery. Valero alleged that Greeni breached its contract and claimed damages for its losses related to that breach. Greeni counterclaimed that Valero had breached by not taking delivery of the naptha and making payment under the contract.]

…

II. Jurisdiction and Applicable Law

…

In its opinion addressing Valero's motion for summary judgment, the court held that the rights and obligations of Valero and Greeni arising under the contact are governed by the United Nations Convention on Contracts for the International Sale of Goods ("CISG"), 15 U.S.C.App., *Valero Marketing & Supply Company v. Greeni Oy & Greeni Trading Oy,* 373 F.Supp.2d 475 (D.N.J.2005).

III. Discussion

A. Reasonableness of Rejection of Bear G

The original agreement between Valero and Greeni provided that the vessel selected by Greeni "is subject to Buyer's acceptance …. Such acceptance shall not be unreasonably withheld." The reasonableness of Valero's rejection of Bear G is a factual question. Weighing the evidence, the court concludes that Valero's rejection of Bear G was unreasonable.

While Smith was a completely truthful and knowledgeable witness, he and Valero proceeded as if they could reject a vessel casually and for almost any articulated reason without seriously examining the facts as they existed at the time of the decision. Valero had no systematic criteria by which to make a judgment other than the general rule that it would not accept …vessels that were more than fifteen years old. Even that was a rule that was observed only on occasion and dispensed with on other occasions. Valero had within the past month accepted Bear G itself for a VGO shipment and had accepted it on a prior occasion. It had accepted other vessels that were more than fifteen years old, two of them, Regents Park and Teekay Fair, to transport and discharge naptha cargoes at Stolthaven Terminal in September 2001.

…

Valero undertook not to unreasonably withhold acceptance of the vessel that Greeni nominated. This obligation requires more than applying internal rules, such as age, which are sometimes applied and sometimes not applied. It requires some effort to ascertain the current condition of the nominated vessel, an effort that was not made here. In view of the fact that there has not been established a valid reason to distinguish between the transportation of naptha and VGO, Valero's acceptance of Bear G in early August and its rejection of Bear G on August 30 cannot be found to be reasonable.

The rejection of Bear G was in violation of the contract between the parties.

B. Late Delivery

Article 30 of the CISG provides that "[t]he seller must deliver the goods --- as required by the contract" and in circumstances where a period of time for delivery is fixed in the contract, Article 33(b) further mandates that "[t]he seller must deliver the goods --- at any time during that period." Bear G arrived in New York Harbor at 3:30 a.m. on September 22, 2001, and would have been ready to commence discharging its cargo at 2:00 or 3:00 p.m. the afternoon of the 22nd. Thus even if Valero had accepted Bear G and allowed it to discharge its cargo at the Stolthaven terminal, delivery would have been outside the September 10-20 contractual window.

The naptha to have been delivered during the window period was to have been blended with other components at Stolthaven. Specifically, Valero intended to use this naptha and other components on hand in its leased storage tanks, such as MTBE, to blend approximately 550,000 barrels of 87 octane reformulated gasoline ("A4" or "87 RFG") and sell it on the cash market prior to September 30, 2001.

Valero claims that as a result of Greeni's failure to perform, it was unable to blend the naptha and deliver any 87 RFG to the cash market prior to the end of September as it had planned. Valero asserts that it would have been able to sell the blended 87 RFG into the cash market prior to September 30, 2001, and that, as a result of Greeni's failure to perform within the contractual windows of either the original agreement or the modified agreement, it was deprived of the opportunity to sell 87 RFG into the cash market.

The fact that Valero breached the contract when it rejected Bear G had no effect upon the timing of Bear G's arrival in New York harbor, because Greeni proceeded just as it would have proceeded had Valero accepted Bear G. Bear G arrived outside the window for three reasons: i) it lost two days because it had to transfer loading operations to a different terminal in Hamburg; ii) it lost two days because it had to obtain additional hoses and nozzles in order to load onto Bear G the fuel being sold to Northville and Tosco; and iii) the hurricane encountered in the Atlantic delayed Bear G an additional day.

If Valero had accepted Bear G, the vessel could have proceeded directly to the Stolthaven terminal on September 22 and commenced unloading. The question must be addressed whether under the CISG this delivery outside the window would have constituted a breach of the contract. If the late delivery would not have been a breach of the contract, then Valero would have had no basis to demand new terms from Greeni, and it would have been obligated to receive the naptha and pay Greeni damages for its failure to do so. The damages would be computed on the basis of the price specified in the original agreement.

If the late delivery was a breach of the contract, then it must be determined what remedies were available to Valero under the CISG.

Although there are scholarly works that discuss the CISG, there is a paucity of case law in the United States courts. Consequently resort must be had primarily to the language of the CISG itself.

Chapter II governs the obligations of the seller. In general "[t]he seller must deliver the goods, hand over any documents relating to them and transfer the property in the goods, as required by the contract and this convention." As to the time of delivery, Article 33 provides: "The seller must deliver the goods: (a) If a date is fixed by or determinable from the contract on that date." In the present case the delivery date was "fixed by" the contract-- September 10-20, 2001. Article 47(1) provides that "[t]he buyer may fix an additional period of time of reasonable length for performance by the seller of his obligation." This is what Valero purported to do by means of the second agreement.

The fact that Greeni did not deliver (and even if Bear G had been accepted, would not have delivered) the naptha by the agreed upon date, does not end the inquiry. Article 49 sets forth the circumstances when a buyer may declare the contract "avoided."

Article 49

(1) The buyer may declare the contract avoided:

(a) If the failure by the seller to perform any of his obligations under the contract or this Convention amounts to a fundamental breach of contract; or

(b) In the case of non-delivery, if the seller does not deliver the goods within the additional period of time fixed by the buyer in accordance with paragraph (1) of article 47 or declares that he will not deliver within the period so fixed.

In the present case Article 49(1)(b) would not have provided grounds for Valero to avoid the contract, because, except for Valero's wrongful rejection of Bear G, Greeni could have, and undoubtedly would have, delivered the naptha within the additional period of time (September 24) fixed by Valero. Valero was entitled to avoid the contract for failure to deliver within the September 10- 20 window only if the failure to do so amounted "to a fundamental breach of contract."

A "fundamental breach of contract" is defined in Article 25 of the CISG:

> *A breach of contract committed by one of the parties is fundamental if it results in such detriment to the other party as substantially to deprive him of what he is entitled to expect under the contract, unless the party in breach did not foresee and a reasonable person of the same kind in the same circumstances would not have foreseen such a result.*

Valero introduced evidence concerning the volatility of petroleum product prices. Stuart Burt described the complex calculations which he undertakes to establish the price he will pay for the various components of the blend that he proposes to prepare from the various component products. Valero produced evidence supporting its contention that Greeni's failure to deliver naptha either within the original window or by September 24 caused Valero to sell 87 RFG into the cash market. Valero faced a falling price, and the delay pushed its sale of the mix from the September market into the October market resulting in a heavy loss. If that were all that there were to the scenario, that is, that Greeni's non-delivery caused these loses, Greeni's breach would be deemed fundamental. It would have resulted in such detriment to Valero as to deprive it of what it was entitled to expect under the contract, and Greeni and a reasonable person in the petroleum industry would have foreseen such a result.

But the foregoing does not reflect what actually happened in this case. The delay attributable to Greeni did not stretch on into September and October. Rather, the delay attributable to Greeni is at most a two day delay. It was ready and able to effect delivery of the naptha on September 22 and would have done so had not Valero prevented delivery by wrongful rejection of Bear G. Had delivery been effected on September 22 the litany of horrors Valero described in its post trial brief would not have taken place. Valero could have commenced mixing and using the supplies of naptha it already had on hand; the naptha on Bear G would have been available almost immediately thereafter; and Valero could have comfortably introduced its 87 RFG into the September market. Confirmation of this conclusion is found in the fact that Valero was willing to take delivery as late as September 24, albeit at a somewhat reduced price. Mr. Burt testified had such a delivery been made, he could have fully met his plan:

"Q. And based upon your experience in the blending operation, are you confident that [if] the cargo arrived by the 24th [of September] you would have been able to blend and deliver by the end of the month?

"Mr. Burt: In my experience, in this case, it was six days. In my experience, six days is plenty of time to finish a gasoline blend and make delivery, yes." (Tr. 79; *see also* Tr. 139-140).

Thus Greeni's two-day delay in delivering the naptha was not a fundamental breach and did not give Valero the right to avoid the contract under Article 49(1)(a). Further, under Article 49(2)(b) of the CISG, the buyer may declare the contract avoided "If the seller does not deliver the goods within the additional period of time fixed by the buyer in accordance with paragraph (1) of Article 47 or declares that he will not deliver within the period is fixed." Paragraph (1) of Article 47 permits the buyer to "fix an additional period of time of reasonable length for performance by the seller of his obligations."

However, when granting the extension of time, the buyer "is precluded not only from avoiding the contract but also from resorting to such remedies as demanding a price reduction ..." *Nachfrist was ist? Thinking Globally and Acting Socially; Considering Time Extension Principles of the U.N. Convention on Contracts for the International Sale of Goods in Revising the Uniform Commercial Code,* John C. Duncan, Jr., Brigham Young University Law Review (2000) 1363-1411, at 1384. Further, "[t]he buyer may not claim avoidance or price reduction as long as the additional period of time lasts ..." UNCITRAL Digest, Art. 49, ¶ 8.

In summation, Valero breached the contract by unreasonably rejecting Bear G. As a consequence Greeni is deemed to have been ready, able and willing to deliver the naptha when Bear G arrived in New York Harbor on September 22, 2001. Greeni was in breach of the contract by failing to effect delivery within the September 10-20 window. The breach, however, was not fundamental and did not enable Valero to avoid the contract. Valero did not have the right to demand that Greeni enter into a new contract. The second contract is of no effect and the parties are bound by the original contract. Valero is entitled to recover any damages it would have suffered from a two day delivery delay (and none have been shown), and Greeni is entitled to recover damages it incurred as a result of Valero's failure to accept and pay for the naptha in accordance with the contract and any other damages it suffered by reason of Valero's wrongful failure to accept Bear G.

* * * * *

Notes and Commentary

Note 1: In what way did Valero breach? The court reasons that the contract provision allowing Valero to approve of the vessel to be used to ship the petroleum product, with such approval not to be unreasonably withheld, was violated by Valero. However, Valero did have some reason why it did not approve of use of the vessel—its age. There seems to be some logic associated with not using a vessel that might be more likely to have problems, especially when the vessel is transporting a large cargo of petroleum products across the breadth of the Atlantic Ocean. Still, the court did not find this to be sufficient.

Are there other provisions in the CISG that support the court's reasoning here? What about provisions of the CISG that cut against the court's decision?

Note 2: Article 7 mandates that when interpreting the convention, regard is to be had to, among other things, the observance of good faith. Did Greeni act in good faith when it used the vessel that Valero had repeatedly rejected? If not, should that affect the analysis of whether Valero breached the contract?

Note 3: The court makes short shrift of the argument that Greeni may have fundamentally breached. The court discusses Greeni's delivery being late by two days and views that breach as not being fundamental, especially where Valero had specifically discussed allowing Greeni four extra days. However, the court does not go into Greeni's decision to use the Bear G. vessel over Valero's repeated objections. Might the use of that vessel have been a fundamental breach? Does the CISG Advisory Opinion on fundamental breach help your analysis?

Note 4: The District Court interpreted the further agreement of the parties allowing for delivery by September 24 and a price reduction to be an extension of time under Article 47, which does not permit resort to other remedies, like the price reduction. Accordingly, the District Court did not make any allowance for the price reduction agreed to by the parties. Interestingly, this case was appealed and the appellate court found the extension of time and the price reduction agreement to be a valid modification of the original agreement of the parties (under Article 29 of the CISG) and not an extension of time under Article 47. The appellate court then remanded the decision back to the district court level for further proceedings. See *Valero Marketing & Supply Company v. Greeni Oy*, 2007 WL 2064219. How might the appellate court's finding affect the ultimate outcome of the case?

4.   The Effects of Avoidance

The effects of avoidance are set forth in Articles 81 and 84. Article 81, referenced above in regards to the avoidance provision of Article 49, provides that avoidance relieves all the parties of their obligations to perform under the contract. It essentially "unmakes" the contract. Thus, the seller is relieved of its obligation to deliver goods and the buyer is relieved of its obligation to take delivery and pay for the goods. [38]   However, the parties still are bound to certain obligations.

---

[38] Secretariat Commentary on the 1978 Draft, *Guide to CISG Article 66*, paras. 2-3 (available at http://cisgw3.law.pace.edu/cisg/text/secomm/secomm-66.html).

> ## Article 81
>
> (1) Avoidance of the contract releases both parties from their obligations under it, subject to any damages which may be due. Avoidance does not affect any provision of the contract for the settlement of disputes or any other provision of the contract governing the rights and obligations of the parties consequent upon the avoidance of the contract.
>
> (2) A party who has performed the contract either wholly or in part may claim restitution from the other party of whatever the first party has supplied or paid under the contract. If both parties are bound to make restitution, they must do so concurrently.

a.   *Dispute Resolution Obligations Survive*

First, the parties still are bound to any dispute resolution provision in their contract. Even though avoidance "undoes" the contract, the survival of the dispute resolution provision is essential to effect an orderly resolution of disputes in accordance with the original intent of the parties. This provision reflects and supports the notion of the separability of an arbitration clause—the idea that an arbitration clause is separate from the contract within which it is contained and thus such a clause might be valid and effective even where the container contract is not.[39]

b.   *Other Post Avoidance Obligations Survive*

Second, the parties are still bound to any other provision that by design would survive avoidance. An example of this is a provision pursuant to which the parties agree that upon avoidance of the contract, if the purchase price has been paid, it will be returned to the buyer with interest, calculated at 8% annually. While Article 84 provides for interest on any amounts due to a counterparty after avoidance, it does not provide for a particular interest rate.[40] Thus, a provision like this in a contract must survive avoidance in order to effectuate the original intent of the parties in this regard.

---

[39] The separability of an arbitration clause is discussed at length in Chapter 8, below. It was also touched on in Chapter 1, above, in the introduction to arbitration.

[40] Just as with interest calculations under Article 78, however, what rate to use for the interest is left an open question. Interest on damages will be discussed at length in Chapter 6, Section II.

c. *Restitution*

Third, in the wake of avoidance, the parties each may make a claim for restitution from their counterparty for any value that has been transferred to their counterparty (Article 81(2)). Thus, in situations where a party has performed in whole or in part, that party may claim restitution from the other party. If the parties are bound to effect a restitution, then the parties must each transfer back to their counterparty any value that it received (Article 81(2)).

Example 5-9

A German buyer purchased sunflower oil from a French seller. Pursuant to the agreement, two to four million liters of the oil were to be delivered to a specific party in Romania each month. When the first shipment was not made, the buyer sought to avoid the contract and further sought rescission so that it could get back the purchase price that it had already paid. The Swiss court agreed with plaintiff and granted rescission under Article 81(2).[41]

Article 84 sets forth certain rights and obligations of the buyer and seller in cases where restitution is owed. In accordance with Article 84, if the seller is bound to pay back all or any portion of the purchase price that had been paid, then the seller must also pay interest on that amount. However, as was mentioned above, like interest described in Article 78, Article 84 leaves open the question of interest rate. Further, Article 84 states that the buyer must "account" for any benefit it derived from taking the goods if indeed the buyer must make restitution (or more generally where the buyer avoided the contract or insisted that the seller deliver substitute goods).

Article 84

(1) If the seller is bound to refund the price, he must also pay interest on it, from the date on which the price was paid.

(2) The buyer must account to the seller for all benefits which he has derived from the goods or part of them:

(a) if he must make restitution of the goods or part of them; or

---

[41] Based on *German Buyer v. French Seller (Sunflower Oil Case)*, Handelsgericht [Commercial Court] Zürich no. HG 95 0347, Switzerland, Feb. 5, 1997 (available at http://cisgw3.law.pace.edu/cases/970205s1.html).

> (b) if it is impossible for him to make restitution of all or part of
> the goods or to make restitution of all or part of the goods
> substantially in the condition in which he received them, but
> he has nevertheless declared the contract avoided or required
> the seller to deliver substitute goods.

5. Limits on Avoidance

Articles 82 and 83 limit a party's ability to declare a contract avoided. Article 82
places a limitation on the buyer's right to declare a contract avoided (or to require
substitute goods) in situations where it is impossible for the buyer to make
restitution of the goods substantially in the condition in which the buyer received
them. Article 82 provides three exceptions to this general rule. The rule will not
apply if: (a) the buyer is not responsible for its inability to make restitution, (b)
restitution is impossible as a result of deterioration of the goods during a proper
examination under Article 38, or (c) the buyer disposed of the goods before the
moment when it discovered (or should have discovered) the non-conformity.

Article 82

(1) The buyer loses the right to declare the contract avoided or to
require the seller to deliver substitute goods if it is
impossible for him to make restitution of the goods
substantially in the condition in which he received them.

(2) The preceding paragraph does not apply:

(a) if the impossibility of making restitution of the goods or of
making restitution of the goods substantially in the condition
in which the buyer received them is not due to his act or
omission;

(b) if the goods or part of the goods have perished or
deteriorated as a result of the examination provided for in
Article 38; or

(c) if the goods or part of the goods have been sold in the
normal course of business or have been consumed or
transformed by the buyer in the course of normal use before
he discovered or ought to have discovered the lack of
conformity.

Example 5–10

A Dutch buyer purchased flowers from a Belgian seller. The Dutch buyer later claimed that the flowers were not of a sufficient quality to meet the terms of the contract. The Dutch court determined that the Dutch buyer had lost its right to declare a contract avoided for several reasons. First, it had not notified the seller of the non-conformity within a reasonable time under Article 39. It waited four months before notifying the seller of the non-conformity. Second, it did not notify the seller that it would seek avoidance within a reasonable time under Article 49(2). Finally, the court ruled that avoidance could not be granted because the buyer could no longer make restitution of the flowers as required by Article 82(1) because the buyer had disposed of some of the goods and resold the remainder.[42]

Nevertheless, in accordance with Article 83, even when a buyer loses its right to declare a contract avoided or to require substitute goods, the buyer still retains all other remedies available under the contract and the CISG. Among those remedies is always the right to seek damages under Article 45(2).

Article 83

A buyer who has lost the right to declare the contract avoided or to require the seller to deliver substitute goods in accordance with Article 82 retains all other remedies under the contract and this Convention.

---

[42] *Biesbrouck v. Huizer Export BV*, Arrondissementsrechtbank Rotterdam no. 95-3590, Netherlands, Nov. 21, 1996 (abstract available at http://www.unilex.info/case.cfm?pid=1&do =case&id=318&step=Abstract). For a case where avoidance was allowed despite buyer's inability to return certain perishable goods, See *Spanish Seller v. German Buyer (Spanish Paprika Case)*, Landgericht [District Court] Ellwangen no. 1 KfH O 32/95, Germany, Aug. 21, 1995 (available at http://cisgw3.law.pace.edu/cases/950821g2.html).

B.   SEEKING SPECIFIC PERFORMANCE

Article 46 generally provides the buyer with remedies that require the seller to perform in order to fulfill its obligations under the contract and the CISG. Article 46(1) sets forth a general rule that the buyer may require such specific performance remedies. Articles 46(2) and 46(3) then specify particular types of performance that may be required of a seller who has delivered non-conforming goods. Specifically, Article 46(2) allows the buyer to request substitute goods, while Article 46(3) allows the buyer to request repair of the non-conforming goods.

Article 46

(1) The buyer may require performance by the seller of his obligations unless the buyer has resorted to a remedy which is inconsistent with this requirement.

(2) If the goods do not conform with the contract, the buyer may require delivery of substitute goods only if the lack of conformity constitutes a fundamental breach of contract and a request for substitute goods is made either in conjunction with notice given under Article 39 or within a reasonable time thereafter.

(3) If the goods do not conform with the contract, the buyer may require the seller to remedy the lack of conformity by repair, unless this is unreasonable having regard to all the circumstances. A request for repair must be made either in conjunction with notice given under Article 39 or within a reasonable time thereafter.

---

1.   Specific Performance Generally

Article 46(1) authorizes a buyer to require a seller to specifically perform its obligations under the contract. Specific performance is only available where the buyer is not pursuing another inconsistent remedy (Article 46(1)). Therefore, if the buyer is attempting to compel a seller to deliver the goods described in the contract, the buyer cannot also demand its payment to be returned. Again, though, Article 45(2) does allow the buyer to claim damages even if specific performance is requested. While it would be inconsistent to request a full refund of payment while also demanding delivery of conforming goods, it would not be inconsistent to claim damages for any losses related to seller's breach of its obligations, such as losses that may have been caused by the delivery being late.

Article 28 limits the availability of specific performance under Article 46 with reference to domestic law of the court hearing the claim. Article 28 explains that a court is not bound to enter a specific performance judgment under the provisions of the CISG unless such a court would do so under its own law.[43] This provision illustrates once again the deference the CISG gives to domestic law in certain areas that might be of special domestic concern. It was already seen during the discussion of Article 2 that the CISG carved out various types of transactions from its coverage. Those transactions involved a variety of areas that were deemed to be of particular national interest and thus would remain subject to domestic laws. Recall, for example, that consumer contracts fell into those exceptions. In Article 28, the CISG acknowledges that specific performance is a particular kind of remedy that is unique and also potentially of special domestic interest. Specific performance remedies require a court to compel a party to act in certain situations. Article 28 defers to a nation's domestic law with respect to whether or not such compulsion should be allowed.[44]

Compare: Specific Performance

Different legal systems, and different countries within those legal systems, have different approaches to requiring performance from a defendant.

Common law jurisdictions have been reticent to require performance and have limited such a remedy to extraordinary situations in which monetary damages would not be sufficient for some reason. So, for example, if the goods that were the subject of the contract were unique, a common law jurisdiction may indeed provide for specific performance as a remedy. However, if the goods were commodity products that are easily purchased elsewhere, then specific performance is not likely.

---

[43] Article 28 states, "If, in accordance with the provisions of this Convention, one party is entitled to require performance of any obligation by the other party, a court is not bound to enter a judgment for specific performance unless the court would do so under its own law in respect of similar contracts of sale not governed by this Convention."

[44] On this point, Eric E. Bergsten, has stated,

> The balance between Article 28 on the one hand and Articles 46 and 62 on the other is not, therefore, a compromise only between the civil law recognition of the principle that a party has the right to require the other party to perform the contract and the common law restriction on that right. It is also a recognition that in many legal system the courts will use discretion in enforcing the right and that such discretion is to be preserved by the Convention.

Les Ventes Internationales de Marchandises (Problèmes juridiques d'actualité)", Paris Economica 11–14 (1981).

> On the other hand, generally speaking, civil law jurisdictions
> have embraced the principle of specific performance. Thus, in a
> civil law jurisdiction specific performance will likely be an
> available remedy, whether the goods subject to the transaction
> are unique or not.[45]

> **Example 5-11**
> A United States buyer purchased Ukrainian steel through a
> German seller. When the German seller refused to deliver, the
> United States buyer sought specific performance of the contract.
> In accordance with Article 28 of the CISG, the United States
> federal court considered whether specific performance was
> appropriate under United States domestic law on point, Illinois'
> version of the UCC. The American court ultimately determined
> that specific performance was consistent with both the Illinois
> UCC and Article 46 of the CISG.[46]

2.   Replacement of Non-Conforming Goods

Article 46(2) provides the buyer with the right to demand delivery of substitute
goods where the buyer has delivered non-conforming goods. However, this right
is subject to two conditions: (i) the breach must be fundamental, and (ii) the
buyer must notify the seller of its demand for substitute goods in a timely
manner. Recall also that in order for the buyer to make any claim regarding non-
conforming goods, Article 39 mandates that the buyer must have notified the
seller in a timely fashion of its receipt of non-conforming goods.

a.   Fundamental Breach

Article 46(2) only allows the buyer to demand substitute goods where the non-
conformity amounts to a fundamental breach under Article 25. In other words,
the buyer may only demand substitute goods where the goods it received
substantially deprive it of what it expected to get under the contract and the seller
either knew or ought to have foreseen that result.[47] A minor defect may not
amount to a fundamental breach and therefore would not allow the buyer to

---

[45] *See* Honnold, *supra* n. 3, at 305–306; Lookofsky, *supra* n. 6, at 81; Ole Lando, *Article 28*, in
Bianca-Bonnell Commentary on the International Sales Law, para. 1.1 (Giuffrè 1987).
[46] *Magellan Intl. Corp. v. Salzgitter Handel GmbH,* 76 F. Supp. 2d 919 (N.D. Ill. 1999).
[47] Fundamental breach is described in Part II(A)(1), *supra.*

demand substitute goods.[48]   That is not to say that the buyer may not claim damages for the minor non-conformity.   Damages are always available under Article 45.   However, delivery of a new shipment of substitute goods, a fairly drastic remedy, is limited to situations where the buyer was substantially deprived of what it expected to get.   Of course, the nature of what will be a fundamental breach will change depending on the circumstances.   If the parties agree that the goods must be absolutely perfect, without any blemishes, then the slightest non-conformity might indeed be fundamental.   The standard for what is fundamental in any particular situation does not provide a bright line rule but does provide the parties, and later tribunals, discretion to determine case by case whether indeed a non-conformity amounts to a fundamental breach.

b.   *Timely Notice for the Seller*

The buyer's right to demand substitute goods is also contingent upon the buyer giving the seller timely notice of its claim (Article 46(2)).   This requirement provides some certainty to both the buyer and the seller that after a reasonable amount of time has passed, no such claims can be raised.   Timely notice of a claim for substitute goods is described in Article 46(2) as occurring either: (i) at or about the same time when the buyer notifies the seller that it received non-conforming goods (i.e. "in conjunction with notice given under Article 39"); or (ii) in any event, within a reasonable time thereafter.

Having already considered Article 39 in Part I of this chapter, the timing of a claim under Article 46(2) becomes somewhat clearer.   Notice of the non-conformity under Article 39 should occur within a reasonable amount of time after the buyer discovers or ought to have discovered the defect, but in most cases, within two years of the buyer actually receiving the goods.   Thus, notice of the claim should happen at about the same time or within a reasonable time thereafter.   What is a reasonable amount of time after the notice of non-conformity has been given is still not so clear.   As is always the case with the "reasonableness" standard, it will differ from case to case, depending on the circumstances.

Recall, though, the mandate of Article 39 that the buyer notify the seller of its receipt of non-conforming goods is eliminated pursuant to Article 40 where the

---

[48] Professors Enderlein and Maskow explain the significance of requiring substitute goods as being akin to avoidance and therefore it is logical to require a fundamental breach: "the economic consequences of a delivery of substitute goods may be the same for the seller as in the case of an avoided contract." Enderlein & Maskow, *supra* n. 6, at 179.   Similarly, Professor Honnold claims that the burden on the seller of providing substitute goods "could even surpass those of an avoidance of contract because the additional expenses incurred and the risks involved in transporting substitute goods are to be born by the seller." Honnold, *supra* n. 3, at 296.

seller knew or ought to have known about the non-conformity and did not tell the buyer about it. However, the buyer still is not exempted from its obligation to notify the seller of its demand for substitute goods. Although Article 46(2) describes the time period for such a notice by reference to Article 39, commentators have agreed that where Article 39 is not triggered (because Article 40 is applicable) then notice of the claim should be given within a reasonable period of time after the discovery by buyer of the non-conformity.[49]

3.   Repair of Non-Conforming Goods

Where the seller delivers non-conforming goods, the buyer can demand substitute goods, as was just discussed (Article 46(2)). Alternatively, however, the buyer may require the seller to repair the non-conforming goods under Article 46(3). This option does not require that the non-conformity constitute a fundamental breach. It is, however, also subject to two conditions: (i) the reasonability of the request, and (ii) the buyer must notify the seller of its demand for repair in a timely manner.

a.   *Reasonable Request*

First, the demand for repair must be reasonable considering all the circumstances. One can imagine a scenario in which the cost of repair exceeds the losses that the buyer would sustain as a result of the non-conformity. In that scenario, it may not be reasonable to demand repair. Instead, the buyer could simply seek damages under Article 45 for its losses.

b.   *Timely Notice for the Seller*

Second, Article 46(3) insists that the buyer notify the seller of its demand for repair under the same time constraints that exist under Article 46(2) relating to a demand for substitute goods, described above. Under that time constraint, the buyer must deliver notify the seller of its claim either: (i) at or around the time it notifies the seller of the non-conformity under Article 39 ("in conjunction with notice given under Article 39"), or (ii) within a reasonable time thereafter. The same complications and concerns with assessing this time period that were discussed above exist here as well. Those complications include understanding Article 39's applicability and its interaction with Article 40.

---

[49] *See Commentary on the UN Convention on the International Sale of Goods* (Peter Schlechtriem & Ingeborg Schwenzer eds., 2d ed., Oxford U. Press 2005) (citing others in their commentary on Article 46, at paragraph 33, note 74, page 547).

C.   PAYING A REDUCED PRICE ✳

Article 50 sets forth yet another remedy for the buyer. Under Article 50, if the seller delivers non-conforming goods, then the buyer can reduce the purchase price in accordance with the diminished value of the goods it received.[50]

Article 50

If the goods do not conform with the contract and whether or not the price has already been paid, the buyer may reduce the price in the same proportion as the value that the goods actually delivered had at the time of the delivery bears to the value that conforming goods would have had at that time. However, if the seller remedies any failure to perform his obligations in accordance with Article 37 or Article 48 or if the buyer refuses to accept performance by the seller in accordance with those Articles, the buyer may not reduce the price.

Once again, though, the CISG also illustrates its preference for allowing the seller to cure. If the seller does cure in accordance with Articles 37 or 48, or if the buyer refuses to accept performance under those cure provisions, then the buyer cannot invoke this provision to reduce its payment. Interestingly, the *Nachfrist* notice provision of Article 47 (where buyer allows seller an extended period of time within which to perform under the contract) is not mentioned here. That may be because such provision is invoked at the discretion of the buyer, while Articles 37 and 48 might be invoked by the seller without the buyer's express approval. It also may be because Article 47's primary concern, when read in connection with the avoidance mechanism of Article 49(1)(b), is with cases where there has been no delivery at all.

---

[50] "The remedy of reduction of price for the purchaser of defective goods derives from the *actio quanti minoris* in Roman Law. . . . If a buyer became aware, after delivery, of certain specified defects which the vendor did not declare and which, had the buyer been aware of them at the time of sale would have led him to pay a lesser price, he could bring an action for reduction of price or for rescission of contract. Defects which were evident at the time of conclusion of the contract were excluded from this remedy since the buyer should have taken them into account when calculating the price he was willing to pay." Eric E. Bergsten & Anthony J. Miller, *The Remedy of Reduction of Price* 27 American J. Comparative L. 255 (1979) (internal citations omitted).

> ### Example 5-12
> A German buyer purchased bottles from an Italian seller. Due to
> improper packaging the German buyer claimed a price reduction
> for the bottles that it actually received. The court held the buyer
> was still entitled to a price reduction even though the buyer had
> failed to avoid the contract under Article 49 due to failure to
> meet the timely notice provisions of that Article.[51]

It is critical to understand Article 50 in connection with Article 79. Article 79
will be discussed at length in Chapter 6, but it generally exempts a party's non-
performance from liability for damages if the non-performance was caused by an
unforeseeable impediment beyond the control of the breaching party (like an
earthquake or a strike). Notice that the exemption contained in Article 79 for
such impediments applies only to an Article 74 claim for damages. Accordingly,
an injured party might still seek a price reduction remedy under Article 50 even if
an Article 79 impediment excuses a claim for damages. This topic will be
revisited in connection with the discussion of Article 79 in Chapter 6.

D.   CONFRONTING PARTIAL PERFORMANCE

Article 51 provides the buyer with options when faced with a situation where the
seller only partially performs.

> ### Article 51
> (1) If the seller delivers only a part of the goods or if only a part
> of the goods delivered is in conformity with the contract,
> Articles 46 to 50 apply in respect of the part which is
> missing or which does not conform.
>
> (2) The buyer may declare the contract avoided in its entirety
> only if the failure to make delivery completely or in
> conformity with the contract amounts to a fundamental
> breach of the contract.

In cases of partial performance by the seller, the buyer's remedy provisions
contained in Articles 46 through 50, just discussed above, only apply to the part

---

of the contract that was not performed. The buyer may select from any of those remedies that may apply, including the right to avoid (Article 51(1)). However, if the seller's failure to fulfill all of its obligations under the contract amounts to a fundamental breach of the contract as a whole, then the buyer can declare the entire contract avoided (Article 51(2)).

Example 5-13

A German buyer contracted to buy 11 computer components from a United States seller. Because the buyer only received 5 of the 11 components, it brought a claim for avoidance under Article 51(2) arguing that there was a fundamental breach as to the whole contract. The German court considered the fact that the buyer had in fact purchased the other missing components before the actual delivery due date had passed and therefore found that the seller's breach was not fundamental. The court stated that when assessing whether a breach is fundamental, consideration should be made of whether a substitute transaction is possible and whether damages for the breach would be sufficient. In this case, the court ruled that since substitute purchases had already been made, avoidance under 51(2) was inappropriate and that damages for the missing components would be sufficient.[52]

E.   ADDRESSING EARLY OR EXCESS DELIVERY

Article 52 addresses situations in which the seller either delivers earlier than the contract contemplated or delivers more than the contract contemplated. In either case, Article 52 provides the buyer with options for how it may proceed.

Article 52

(1) If the seller delivers the goods before the date fixed, the buyer may take delivery or refuse to take delivery.

(2) If the seller delivers a quantity of goods greater than that provided for in the contract, the buyer may take delivery or refuse to take delivery of the excess quantity. If the buyer

---

[52] *See United States Seller v. German Buyer (Comouter Components Case)*, Landgericht [District Court] Heidelberg no. O 42/92 KfH I, Germany July 3, 1992 (available at http://cisgw3.law.pace.edu/cases/920703g1.html).

> takes delivery of all or part of the excess quantity, he must
> pay for it at the contract rate.

Pursuant to Article 52(1), if the seller delivers prior to the date specified in the contract for delivery, then the buyer may opt to reject delivery of the goods. This may be necessary, for example, if the buyer did not have warehouse space available for the goods until the delivery date specified in the contract. In that case it would be a hardship for buyer to take delivery before such date.

Pursuant to Article 52(2), if the seller delivers a greater quantity of goods than the quantity specified in the contract, then the buyer can either: (i) accept and pay for the excess at the contract rate; or (ii) reject the excess. However, even if the buyer rightfully rejects the excess delivery, the buyer still has obligations regarding the preservation of the excess goods.[53] Obligations regarding preservation are set forth in Articles 85 through 88 of the CISG, discussed in part V, below.

III.   SELLER'S REMEDIES FOR BUYER'S BREACH

Just as the buyer's remedies for the seller's breach were outlined in Article 45, the seller's remedies for buyer's breach are outlined in Article 61. And similar to Article 45, Article 61 basically states that the seller can choose any of the remedies set forth in Articles 62 through 65. There are fewer remedy rights and options for the seller when compared to the buyer because the obligations of the buyer in a sale of goods transactions are generally not as many or as complex as those of the seller. The seller's remedies include rights regarding: (A) avoidance, (B) specific performance, and (C) providing the specification of the goods to be delivered. Further, just like Article 45(2) for the seller, Article 61(2) makes clear that regardless of the remedy chosen by the seller, the seller can always claim damages for the losses.

A.   AVOIDING THE CONTRACT

Again, Article 64 on avoidance for the seller is very similar to Article 49 on avoidance for the buyer. Article 64 allows the seller to declare the contract avoided in two circumstances: (i) where the buyer has fundamentally breached the contract, or (ii) where the seller has fixed an extended (*Nachfrist*) period for the buyer under Article 63, and the buyer will not perform by the date fixed as

---

[53] Enderlein & Maskow, *supra* n. 6, at 201.

the end of the extended period. In addition, Article 64 (like Article 49) requires that certain declarations of avoidance be made in a timely manner.

> ## Article 64
>
> (1) The seller may declare the contract avoided:
>
> (a) if the failure by the buyer to perform any of his obligations under the contract or this Convention amounts to a fundamental breach of contract; or
>
> (b) if the buyer does not, within the additional period of time fixed by the seller in accordance with paragraph (1) of Article 63, perform his obligation to pay the price or take delivery of the goods, or if he declares that he will not do so within the period so fixed.
>
> (2) However, in cases where the buyer has paid the price, the seller loses the right to declare the contract avoided unless he does so:
>
> (a) in respect of late performance by the buyer, before the seller has become aware that performance has been rendered; or
>
> (b) in respect of any breach other than late performance by the buyer, within a reasonable time:
>
> (i) after the seller knew or ought to have known of the breach; or
>
> (ii) after the expiration of any additional period of time fixed by the seller in accordance with paragraph (1) of Article 63, or after the buyer has declared that he will not perform his obligations within such an additional period.

1.   Fundamental Breach by the Buyer

The seller can declare the contract avoided if the buyer has committed a fundamental breach of its obligations. In accordance with the definition of fundamental breach found in Article 25, and discussed above in Part II A, Article 64(1)(a) allows a seller to avoid the contract if the buyer's breach has substantially deprived the seller of what the seller expected to get and the buyer knew or ought to have known that its breach would cause such harm. This is a situation where the breach is of such a magnitude that the seller should be released from its obligations under the contract.

As was described in Article 49(1)(a) in connection with buyer's right to declare the contract avoided, it is sometimes difficult to be sure that the other party has indeed breached in a way that crosses the threshold and can be characterized as fundamental. Where seller proceeds under this section and does not fulfill its own obligations under the contract or the CISG, it risks a later judgment that the buyer's breach was not fundamental and that therefore the seller itself is in breach.

With regard to the buyer's obligations—principally paying the purchase price and taking delivery of the goods—the determination of a fundamental breach will likely be easier than it is when the seller, for example, supplies non-conforming goods or delivers late. Nonetheless, the construct for avoidance by the seller is the same as it is for the buyer under Article 46 and turns on whether the breach is fundamental. If so, the seller can declare the contract avoided.

Example 5-14

A United States company sold a machine to manufacture plastic gardening pots to a Greek buyer. The Greek buyer brought a claim that, among other things, the United States seller had delivered non-conforming goods in a fundamental breach of contract. Therefore, the buyer argued that it was justified in declaring the contract avoided under Article 49(1)(a) and not paying for the goods.

The United States federal court found that the United States seller's breach was not fundamental under Article 25 since the goods were actually in use by the Greek buyer. Further, since the seller had not fundamentally breached, the buyer had no right to avoid and withhold payment under Article 49(a)(1). Therefore, the buyer actually had committed a fundamental breach by not paying, which gave the seller the right under Article 64(1)(a) to avoid its obligations under the contract.[54]

---

[54] *Shuttle Packaging Systems, L.L.C. v. Jacob Tsonakis, INA S.A and INA Plastics Corporation,* 2001 WL 34046276 (W.D. Mich. Dec. 17, 2001) (available at http://cisgw3.law.pace.edu/cases/011217u1.html).

2.   Non-performance by the End of the *Nachfrist* Period

The second part of Article 64(1) is analogous to the second part of Article 49(1) and provides for a clearer situation where the seller can be confident that it can declare the contract avoided. Article 64(1)(b) covers situations where the buyer has not performed all of its obligations to pay for the goods or take delivery of them. In such cases, if the seller follows Article 63 and fixes an additional time period during which the buyer can perform its obligations and the buyer does not so perform or states that it will not perform, then the seller can declare the contract avoided. Similar to the notice described in Article 47, this notice providing for an additional time during which performance may occur is also frequently referred to as a *Nachfrist* notice.[55]

Article 63

(1) The seller may fix an additional period of time of reasonable length for performance by the buyer of his obligations.

(2) Unless the seller has received notice from the buyer that he will not perform within the period so fixed, the seller may not, during that period, resort to any remedy for breach of contract. However, the seller is not deprived thereby of any right he may have to claim damages for delay in performance.

If the seller chooses to follow Article 63, then the seller cannot resort to any other remedy during the additional period of time, unless the buyer has notified the seller that it will not perform by the end of the new time period. Article 63(2) provides that in any event, the seller can always claim any damages for losses it suffers as a result of buyer's original breach.

Just as with the *Nachfrist* notice outlined in Article 47 and discussed above, here too the CISG motivates the seller to provide the buyer with this additional time period during which the buyer may fulfill its obligations. It does this by allowing the seller to avoid its obligations without having to determine whether the buyer's breach has been fundamental, if the seller provides this extended time period and the buyer has not performed and cannot or does not perform by the end of the cure period.

With respect to the buyer's breach, frequently it will be clear that there is a fundamental breach. A likely breach by the buyer is non-payment for the goods

---

[55] *See* n. 34 and accompanying text.

or not accepting the goods that have been delivered by the seller. Such easy cases might well fall within the fundamental breach provision of Article 64(1)(a) and allow the seller to comfortably declare the contract avoided. However, other situations can occur that are not so clearly a fundamental breach. For example, the buyer might be late in setting up a letter of credit called for by the contract, or the buyer might pay in a currency that the seller does not believe was provided for by the contract. In those tougher cases, the mechanism provided in Article 64(1)(b) can give the seller assurance that it can declare the contract avoided.

Example 5-15

A French buyer purchased printing equipment from an Italian seller. The French buyer had made a down payment. However, later the buyer refused delivery on the basis that the equipment was meant for a building that was subject to construction delays and therefore delivery was impossible. Accordingly, the buyer never paid the balance of the amounts owed under the contract. The Italian seller brought a claim for the balance and other damages suffered as a result of buyer's breach.

The Italian court dismissed the French buyer's argument about its facilities not being available to accept delivery. Further, the court found evidence that the Italian seller had actually provided notice to the buyer under Article 63, giving the buyer 2 and ½ months of additional time within which to accept the goods and make payment. The court ruled that when buyer did not perform by the end of that extended period, the Italian seller had the right to avoid the contract under Article 64(1)(b).[56]

---

3.   Avoidance Must be Timely

As was mentioned in respect to the buyer declaring a contract avoided, Article 26 mandates that any party declaring a contract avoided must so notify its counterparty. Accordingly, if the seller wants to pursue avoidance as a remedy it must notify its counterparty of that decision. However, Article 64 adds additional qualifications to the notification required by the seller seeking avoidance. In cases where the breach is something other than payment of the

---

[56] *Bielloni Castello S.p.A. [Italy] v. EGO S.A. [France]*, Corte di Appello di Milano, Italy, Dec. 11, 1998 (available at http://cisgw3.law.pace.edu/cases/981211i3.html). Note that this case was heard by the Italian Court of Appeals for Milan. The lower court had originally mistakenly applied Italian domestic law and reached the opposite result.

purchase price, Article 64(2) specifies certain time periods when a declaration of avoidance must be made. If there has been late performance, a claim must be brought within a reasonable time after the seller has been made aware of the performance occurring (Article 64(2)(a)). In cases of any other breach where the purchase price has been paid, then a declaration of avoidance must be made either: (i) if no cure period has been set, within a reasonable time after the buyer knew or ought to have known about the breach; or (ii) if the seller sets an additional time period pursuant to Article 63, after the expiration of that period or after the buyer has stated that it will not perform.

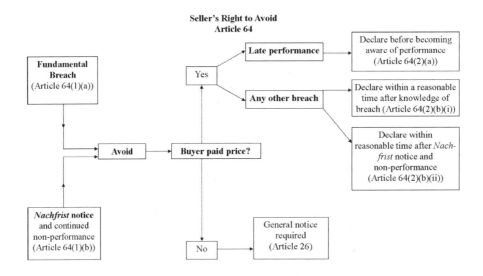

4.   Effects of Avoidance

Just as was described under the Effects of Avoidance with respect to the buyer's avoidance above, Articles 81 and 84 apply to seller's avoidance as well. Recall that avoidance means that generally the seller and the buyer are both released from their contractual obligations, except obligations regarding dispute resolution or other obligations that specifically are designed to survive avoidance (Article 81). Further, either party may make a claim for restitution after avoidance is declared. If restitution is granted to a party, the counterparty must transfer back to it any value that it received as a result of any performance that had been rendered under the contract. Recall also that interest is to be included in any return of purchase money (Article 84(1)).

B.   SPECIFIC PERFORMANCE

Article 62 is the seller's analogue to the buyer's specific performance provision in Article 46(1). Article 62 authorizes a seller to require a buyer to specifically perform its obligations under the contract. Specific performance is only available where the seller is not pursuing another inconsistent remedy (Article 62). Therefore, if the seller is demanding the buyer to return its goods, it cannot also demand that payment be made in accordance with the contract. Article 61(2) does allow the buyer to claim damages even if specific performance is requested. For example, if seller is demanding that the buyer take delivery and pay for the goods, it still might make further claims for any damages it suffered as a result of the buyer's breach (for example, there might be losses associated with late performance).

Note that payment of the purchase price will often be the remedy sought by the seller. Such payment is not ordinarily thought of as specific performance, though it is exactly the performance the seller might want.[57] Monetary remedies are not typically regarded as falling into the category of specific performance.[58]

> **Article 62**
>
> The seller may require the buyer to pay the price, take delivery or perform his other obligations, unless the seller has resorted to a remedy which is inconsistent with this requirement.

Article 28 must be considered here again, just as it was in connection with Article 46(1) with respect to the buyer's specific performance remedies. Recall that with respect to specific performance as a remedy under the CISG, Article 28

---

[57] Earlier in this chapter a discussion was presented comparing specific performance in common law jurisdictions with specific performance in civil law jurisdictions. It was pointed out there that common law jurisdictions do not typically favor specific performance remedies. However, when the performance sought it payment of the purchase price, such a remedy is commonplace. *See e.g.* UCC 2-709 specifically providing for an action pursuant to which the seller would recover the purchase price for goods from a breaching buyer.

[58] "[T]he words 'judgment for specific performance' suggest that the provision does not apply to a suit in which the seller tenders the goods to the recalcitrant buyer and claims the price. Such a suit, traditionally one at law rather than in equity, is not commonly thought of as one for 'specific performance', even though it gives the seller relief that might accurately be described as 'specific.'" E. Allan Farnsworth, *Damages and Specific Relief,* 27 Am. J. Comp. L. 247, 249–250 (1979). "Whether an action by the seller for the price is a form of specific performance is controversial. In the end, it is merely a problem of denomination, because no one doubts that the action is enforceable against the buyer." Peter Schlechtriem, *Uniform Sales Law the UN Convention on Contracts for the International Sale of Goods* 84 n. 333 (Manz 1986)

explains that a court is not bound to enter a specific performance judgment under the provisions of the CISG unless the court would do so under its own law.[59]

C.   PROVIDING SPECIFICATIONS

There is no analogue for Article 65 among the buyer's remedies. It is unique to the seller's remedies and addresses a scenario in which the seller requires specifications for the goods but has been unable to obtain them from the buyer. In that scenario, Article 65 authorizes the seller to essentially use its best judgment in trying to determine the appropriate specifications for the buyer's goods.

> **Article 65**
>
> (1) If under the contract the buyer is to specify the form, measurement or other features of the goods and he fails to make such specification either on the date agreed upon or within a reasonable time after receipt of a request from the seller, the seller may, without prejudice to any other rights he may have, make the specification himself in accordance with the requirements of the buyer that may be known to him.
>
> (2) If the seller makes the specification himself, he must inform the buyer of the details thereof and must fix a reasonable time within which the buyer may make a different specification. If, after receipt of such a communication, the buyer fails to do so within the time so fixed, the specification made by the seller is binding.

If indeed the seller chooses to proceed according to this option, it must notify the buyer of the specifications it intends to use, giving the buyer an opportunity to either accept or reject those specifications and communicate different ones. If the buyer does not reject the seller's specifications in any way, then the seller is authorized to proceed on the basis of its specifications.[60]

---

[59] See Section II(B)(1), earlier in this chapter for a more detailed discussion of Article 28.

[60] "Article 65 was designed to prevent a buyer from escaping its obligations by refusing to supply necessary specifications." Honnold, *supra* n. 3, at 391.

IV.   ANTICIPATORY BREACH AND INSTALLMENT CONTRACTS

This section will round out the discussion of remedies by describing the remedies that are equally applicable to both the seller and the buyer. In particular, those remedies involve: (A) anticipatory breach, and (B) avoidance of installment contracts.

A.   ANTICIPATORY BREACH

Articles 71 and 72 address anticipatory breach. Article 71 describes the circumstances under which a party may suspend performance, while Article 72 describes the circumstances under which a party may declare a contract avoided.

1.   **Suspension of Performance**

Pursuant to Article 71, either party may suspend its performance under a contract for the sale of goods if it becomes "apparent" that the other party is not likely to perform "a substantial part" of its obligations.

Article 71

(1) A party may suspend the performance of his obligations if, after the conclusion of the contract, it becomes apparent that the other party will not perform a substantial part of his obligations as a result of:

(a) a serious deficiency in his ability to perform or in his creditworthiness; or

(b) his conduct in preparing to perform or in performing the contract.

(2) If the seller has already dispatched the goods before the grounds described in the preceding paragraph become evident, he may prevent the handing over of the goods to the buyer even though the buyer holds a document which entitles him to obtain them. The present paragraph relates only to the rights in the goods as between the buyer and the seller.

(3) A party suspending performance, whether before or after dispatch of the goods, must immediately give notice of the suspension to the other party and must continue with

> performance if the other party provides adequate assurance
> of his performance.

This unwillingness or inability to perform a substantial part of one's obligations must become apparent only after the conclusion of the contract and must be evident from either: (a) the creditworthiness of the party, or (b) the conduct of the party in its performance on the contract up until that time. If indeed a party decides to suspend its performance under this provision, it must notify its counterparty immediately (Article 71(3)). If the counterparty provides adequate assurances of performance, then the first party must continue with its own performance (Article 71(3)). If it is the seller that is suspending performance and the goods have already been dispatched, the seller may prevent the buyer from taking delivery of the goods (Article 71(2)).

Example 5-16

A German seller delivered Styrofoam blocks to a Canadian purchaser eight weeks late. The seller alleged that it had suspended its own performance based on the buyer's failure to timely provide a letter of credit. The court found that the delay in opening the letter of credit lasted for only two weeks. Therefore, the court concluded that the German seller could have only appropriately suspended for those two weeks under Article 71(3). Since the seller delivered eight weeks late, it was still in breach for a six week delay (the delay that was not due to buyer's own delay in opening the letter of credit).[61]

---

2.   Avoiding the Contract

On the other hand, if it becomes clear to one party that the other party will commit a fundamental breach, then the first party can declare the contract avoided (Article 72(1)). Note that when comparing Article 72 to Article 71, the standards for avoidance under Article 72 are stricter than the standards for suspension under Article 71. Under Article 72 the fundamental breach of the counterparty must be clear. Under Article 71 the breach need not be fundamental, but can be a failure "to perform a substantial part" of the party's

---

[61] *Mansonville Plastics (B.C.) Ltd. [Canada] v. Kurtz GmbH [Austria/Germany]*, Supreme Court, British Columbia no. C993594, Canada, Aug. 21, 2003, UNCITRAL CLOUT Case no. 532 (available at http://cisgw3.law.pace.edu/cases/030821c4.html).

obligations. Further, under Article 71, such failure to perform need only be "apparent" and need not be absolutely "clear" as required by Article 72.[62]

> **Article 72**
>
> (1) If prior to the date for performance of the contract it is clear that one of the parties will commit a fundamental breach of contract, the other party may declare the contract avoided.
>
> (2) If time allows, the party intending to declare the contract avoided must give reasonable notice to the other party in order to permit him to provide adequate assurance of his performance.
>
> (3) The requirements of the preceding paragraph do not apply if the other party has declared that he will not perform his obligations.

In Article 72(2), the CISG makes some effort to prevent the transaction from being avoided by mandating that if the party wanting to declare the contract avoided has time, it must notify its counterparty of its intentions and allow the counterparty to provide adequate assurances that it will perform. However, this notice is not necessary where the counterparty declared that it would not perform under the contract (Article 72(3)).

> **Example 5-17**
> An Australian seller entered a contract to sell fertilizer to a Chinese buyer. The Australian seller ultimately could not perform its obligations to deliver under the contract since its supplier had not delivered the goods that were to be sold on to the Chinese buyer. Two weeks before the due date for delivery, the Australian seller notified the Chinese buyer that it would be unable to perform and stated that buyer should make arrangements accordingly. In this case, the arbitral tribunal ruled that the buyer could avoid under 72(2) without notifying the seller.[63]

---

[62] Lookofsky, *supra* n. 6, at 148.

[63] *Chinese Buyer v. Australian Seller*, China International Economic & Trade Arbitration Commission Arbitration no. CISG/1996/05, China, Jan. 30, 1996 (available at http://cisgw3.law

B.   AVOIDING INSTALLMENT CONTRACTS

Article 73 outlines a party's recourse in installment contracts where some installments have been made in accordance with the contract while others have not.

> **Article 73[64]**
>
> (1) In the case of a contract for delivery of goods by instalments, if the failure of one party to perform any of his obligations in respect of any instalment constitutes a fundamental breach of contract with respect to that instalment, the other party may declare the contract avoided with respect to that instalment.
>
> (2) If one party's failure to perform any of his obligations in respect of any instalment gives the other party good grounds to conclude that a fundamental breach of contract will occur with respect to future instalments, he may declare the contract avoided for the future, provided that he does so within a reasonable time.
>
> (3) A buyer who declares the contract avoided in respect of any delivery may, at the same time, declare it avoided in respect of deliveries already made or of future deliveries if, by reason of their interdependence, those deliveries could not be used for the purpose contemplated by the parties at the time of the conclusion of the contract.

Article 73 is very similar to Article 51. Recall that under Article 51 if the seller only partially delivers under a contract, then the buyer can pursue a remedy with respect to that part of the contract. However, if the partial delivery amounts to a fundamental breach of the entire contract, then the buyer can avoid the entire contract. Under Article 73, installments are essentially treated as parts of the overall contract.

If a party commits a fundamental breach with respect to any particular installment, then that installment can be declared avoided by the other party

---

.pace.edu/cases/960130c1.html). For a similar case where the buyer declared that it would not be able to open a letter of credit in accordance with the contract and the seller then avoided the contract under Article 72, see *Downs Investments Pty Ltd [Australia] v. Perwaja Steel [Malaysia]*, Supreme Court of Queensland Civil Jurisdiction No. 10680 of 1996, Australia, Nov. 17, 2000 (available at http://cisgw3.law.pace.edu/cases/001117a2.html).

[64] Notice that the text of the CISG uses the English spelling of the word "installment."

(Article 73(1)). Further, if the fundamental breach of one party on any one installment gives the other party "good grounds" for believing that the party will commit a fundamental breach with respect to future installments, then the non-breaching party can declare the future installments under the contract avoided (Article 73(2)).

Example 5-18

Recall Example 4-7 regarding the sale large quantities of paprika from a Spanish seller to a German buyer. The sale was to proceed in installments. The paprika in particular installments was found to contain levels of ethyl oxide that far exceeded the limit permissible in Germany. Since the contract had specified that the paprika needed to be suitable for consumption in Germany, the goods were found to be non-conforming and to represent a fundamental breach of the contract with respect to those installments. On the basis of Article 73(2), the court ruled that it was reasonable to conclude that future installments would be non-conforming as well. Therefore, the buyer was justified in avoiding the entire contract.[65]

As usual, the CISG mandates that declaration regarding avoidance be made within a reasonable time (Article 73(2)). Of course, what is reasonable will depend on the facts and circumstances surrounding each case.

Example 5-19

A Spanish buyer and a German seller entered into a contract for a sale of 10,000 springs by installments. The German seller was late with its first three installments and delivered only 1000 springs when it had been obligated to deliver 6000 by that time. Shortly after the latest installment was delivered, the buyer sent the seller a notice under Article 73(2) stating that it wanted to avoid any future installments. The Court ruled that the Spanish buyer's notice as to avoidance of the future installment was effective since sufficient grounds existed to conclude that the seller would not be able to deliver the future installments in accordance with the contract. Moreover, the court ruled that the

---

[65] *Spanish Seller v. German Buyer (Spanish Paprika Case)*, Landgericht Ellwangen no. 1 KfH O 32/95, Germany, Aug. 21, 1995 (available at http://cisgw3.law.pace.edu/cases/950821g2.html).

> notice was given within a reasonable time for purposes of Article 73(2) since it was made within 48 hours of receipt of the most recent installment.[66]

In addition, if any of the installments involved a fundamental breach and that breach made other installments not useful for their intended purposes, then all of those installments can be declared avoided (Article 73(3)). This provision depends on the interdependence of the installments to the overall contract. Thus, if a seller is shipping components of a machine to a buyer in installments, if the inability of the seller to deliver any one of the components makes the other components useless, then the buyer will have the right to declare the entire contract avoided.[67]

V.   PRESERVATION OF THE GOODS

Regardless of whether any of the parties involved in an international sale of goods transaction are ultimately responsible for damages, the CISG requires the parties to preserve the goods to the best of their ability even in situations where a dispute has arisen. The obligation of preservation typically is put upon the party in the best position to bear the burden. Thus, if the buyer does not take delivery of goods or is late in paying and the seller can still control the goods, then the seller must actually take "such steps as are reasonable" to preserve the goods (Article 85). This is the case even if the risk related to the goods has officially transferred.[68]

---

[66] *T. [German Seller] v. E. [Spanish Buyer]*, Audiencia Provincial de Barcelona, sección 16ª no. 729/96-B, Spain, Nov. 3, 1997 (abstract available at http://www.unilex.info/case.cfm?pid =1&do=case&id=313&step=Abstract).

[67] Professor Honnold sets forth the following example for Article 73(3):

> *A sales contract called for Seller to deliver one machine in January, a second in February, and a third in March. The three were designed to perform a series of interrelated production operations; none of the machines was compatible with machines made by other manufacturers. In January, Seller delivered a machine that conformed with the contract but the machine delivered in February was so defective that the Seller could not cure the defect. Replacement with a second machine was not possible.*

Because of the interdependence of the installments in this example, breach of the second installment gives the buyer the right to avoid the entire contract, including the installment already made that was in accordance with the contract. Honnold, *supra* n. 3, at 444 ex. 73A; *see also* Lookofsky, *supra* n. 6, at 151.

[68] Honnold, *supra* n. 3, at 520–522; Lookofsky, *supra* n. 6, at 171.

> ### Article 85
>
> If the buyer is in delay in taking delivery of the goods or, where payment of the price and delivery of the goods are to be made concurrently, if he fails to pay the price, and the seller is either in possession of the goods or otherwise able to control their disposition, the seller must take such steps as are reasonable in the circumstances to preserve them. He is entitled to retain them until he has been reimbursed his reasonable expenses by the buyer.

Similarly, if the buyer does take control of the goods, even if the buyer expects to make a claim against the seller concerning the goods, the buyer must "take such steps to preserve them as are reasonable" (Article 86(1)). Even if the buyer ultimately expects to reject the goods, if the goods are at buyer's disposal and no one is available to represent the seller, then the buyer still must take possession of the goods and preserve them (Article 86(2)). However, this later requirement is subject to the qualification that such an obligation cannot cause the buyer any unreasonable inconvenience or expense (Article 86(2)).

> ### Article 86
>
> (1) If the buyer has received the goods and intends to exercise any right under the contract or this Convention to reject them, he must take such steps to preserve them as are reasonable in the circumstances. He is entitled to retain them until he has been reimbursed his reasonable expenses by the seller.
>
> (2) If goods dispatched to the buyer have been placed at his disposal at their destination and he exercises the right to reject them, he must take possession of them on behalf of the seller, provided that this can be done without payment of the price and without unreasonable inconvenience or unreasonable expense. This provision does not apply if the seller or a person authorized to take charge of the goods on his behalf is present at the destination. If the buyer takes possession of the goods under this paragraph, his rights and obligations are governed by the preceding paragraph.

The provisions on preservation of the goods further specify that the party obliged to preserve the goods can warehouse them with a third party at the counterparty's expense (Article 87). However, this right is subject to the charge for the warehousing being reasonable (Article 87).

> **Article 87**
>
> A party who is bound to take steps to preserve the goods may deposit them in a warehouse of a third person at the expense of the other party provided that the expense incurred is not unreasonable.

Finally, if the goods are perishable, the party charged with preserving them may sell them to ensure that the goods are not wasted some economic value is derived from them (Article 88(2)). Even if the goods are not perishable, if the counterparty is delinquent in either picking up the goods, or taking responsibility for their storage by paying the relevant bills, then the party preserving the goods can sell them, subject to reasonable notice of the sale (Article 88(1)). If there is any cost associated with preserving the goods, the party selling them is entitled to retain an amount equal to those costs, provided that such amount was reasonable (Article 88(3)).

> **Article 88**
>
> (1) A party who is bound to preserve the goods in accordance with Article 85 or 86 may sell them by any appropriate means if there has been an unreasonable delay by the other party in taking possession of the goods or in taking them back or in paying the price or the cost of preservation, provided that reasonable notice of the intention to sell has been given to the other party.
>
> (2) If the goods are subject to rapid deterioration or their preservation would involve unreasonable expense, a party who is bound to preserve the goods in accordance with Article 85 or 86 must take reasonable measures to sell them. To the extent possible he must give notice to the other party of his intention to sell.
>
> (3) A party selling the goods has the right to retain out of the proceeds of sale an amount equal to the reasonable expenses

> of preserving the goods and of selling them. He must
> account to the other party for the balance.

Example 5–20

An Austrian buyer purchased scaffolding components from a
Chinese seller. After delivery of the goods, the buyer brought a
claim for non-conformity of the goods. Among other rulings the
arbitral tribunal stated that "Under Article 86 the buyer is
entitled to have his reasonable expenses for preservation of the
goods reimbursed by the seller; he may deposit the goods in a
warehouse at the expense of the seller if the expense is not
unreasonable (Article 87); and he may sell the goods by
appropriate means if there has been an unreasonable delay by the
seller in taking possession of the goods (Article 88.1)."[69]

PROBLEMS

Problem 5-1: Suppose NNM enters into a contract to purchase razors from J&G.
The contract calls for 10,000 men's MAK V razors to be delivered F.O.B.
Moscow on or before December 31, 2007 for a total price of $5,000 US dollars.
Which of the following would likely be considered a fundamental breach?

    a.   J&G delivers women's razors.

    b.   J&G delivers on January 1, 2008.

    c.   J&G delivers the razors to St. Petersburg.

    d.   J&G delivers its newest and most innovative razors, the MAK VI.

Problem 5-2: The MAK V razor is designed with a lubricating strip to prevent
cuts and nicks when shaving. The razors J&G ships to NNM are missing the
strip. J&G was aware of the defect before shipping the razors, but NNM fails to
inspect them upon delivery and does not realize the lubricating strip is missing
until it begins receiving customer complaints. Are there any remedies available
to NNM?

---

[69] *Austrian Buyer v. Chinese Seller*, Court of Arbitration of the International Chamber of
Commerce Arbitration no. 7531, Paris, 1994 (available at http://www.unilex.info/case.cfm?pid
=1&do=case&id=139&step=FullText). For another case discussing the parties' duties of
preservation see *Buyer [Country Unknown] v. Chinese Seller*, China Intl. Economic & Trade
Arbitration Commission (PRC)-Shenzhen Commission Case no. CISG/1991/03, China, June 6,
1991 (available at http://cisgw3.law.pace.edu/cases/910606c1.html).

Problem 5-3: J&G delivers the razors 2 weeks early. Is NNM required to take delivery? Suppose NNM takes delivery 2 weeks early, but the razors are not in conformity with the contract. Can J&G cure the non-conformity? Does your answer change if the date of delivery has passed?

Problem 5-4: Pursuant to the terms of the contract, NNM agrees to open a letter of credit for the first few transactions until the parties have established a business relationship. NNM fails to open the letter of credit within the time period agreed to by the parties. Is J&G obligated to ship the goods? If you were J&G's counsel, how would you advise J&G to proceed?

Problem 5-5: In an entirely different transaction, a Romanian seller delivered steel wire to a Croatian buyer. Upon receipt of the goods, the buyer notified the seller that the goods were substandard and then made the goods available for the seller to recover. The seller refused to recover the wire, and the buyer went to great expense to correct the defects with the wire. The seller sued for payment on the wire, stating that since buyer accepted and used the wire, it should pay for them. What result? What other steps might the buyer have taken to protect its position?

6 | DAMAGES

According to the law of nature it is only
fair that no one should become richer through
damages and injuries suffered by another.

- Marcus Tullius Cicero[1]

As suggested throughout the previous chapter, regardless of the remedy that a party seeks for an alleged breach under the CISG, the party can always seek money damages from its counterparty for any losses suffered. Having said that, the CISG also imposes a strict requirement that the injured party take steps to mitigate the damages and minimize the losses involved in the dispute. In addition to damages, there is also the question of whether and when interest on any amounts owed is due, in order to fully compensate the injured party. While that notion might seem straightforward, arriving at the appropriate interest rate has proven problematic. In addition, there are some circumstances that will exempt a party from paying any damages even if the party did not perform or performed inadequately under the contract. This chapter will look at each of these issues in turn: (I) damages, (II) interest, and (III) exemptions.

I.   DAMAGES

As the CISG repeatedly makes clear, an injured party can always seek damages from its counterparty for any injury it suffers as a result of the counterparty's breach. Article 45(2) makes that clear for the buyer, while Article 61(2) makes that clear for the seller. Article 74 sets forth the general rule governing damages. In cases of avoidance, Articles 75 and 76 provide possible methods parties may employ for calculating damages whether a party has either entered into a substitute transaction (Article 75) or not (Article 76). Importantly, Article 77 describes the breaching party's obligation to mitigate the damages it causes to minimize the losses involved in any dispute.

---

[1]Marcus Tullius Cicero, quoted in Norbert Guterman, *The Anchor Book of Latin Quotations: With English Translations* 393 (Anchor Bks. 1990).

A.   DAMAGES GENERALLY

Article 74 defines damages generally as the losses suffered by one party as a result of a breach by its counterparty. An injured party may seek damages whether or not the counterparty's breach is fundamental and whether or not the injured party has declared the contract avoided. As such, damages are the cornerstone of remedies under the CISG.[2]

Article 74

Damages for breach of contract by one party consist of a sum equal to the loss, including loss of profit, suffered by the other party as a consequence of the breach. Such damages may not exceed the loss which the party in breach foresaw or ought to have foreseen at the time of the conclusion of the contract, in the light of the facts and matters of which he then knew or ought to have known, as a possible consequence of the breach of contract.

Article 74's damage description has been understood to reflect an expectation measure of damages. The injured party has a right, under Article 74, to recover what it had expected to gain from the contract but did not due to its counterparty's breach.

Article 74 does not contain many details and the gaps that are left have been the subject of many cases and controversies. For example, there is no explicit reference to certainty as a limiting principle on damages in Article 74. In addition, it has been unclear whether or not attorney and other costs related to dispute resolution were recoverable as damages.

However, in 2006 the CISG Advisory Council issued an opinion addressing many of those issues and attempting to explain how damages are calculated under the CISG.[3] Recall that the Advisory Council opinions are not part of the CISG itself, but are commentary on the CISG. As such, the opinions are not binding, but they are extremely persuasive authority.

---

[2] For a very recent analysis of damages under the CISG, see John Y. Gotanda, "Damages in Lieu of Performance because of Breach of Contract" (July 2006). *Villanova University Legal Working Paper Series. Villanova University School of Law Working Paper Series.* Working Paper 53. at http://law.bepress.com/villanovalwps/papers/art53. In addition, a slightly earlier article by Professor Gotanda provides an excellent overview of some of the issues that the CISG left unanswered in its formulation of damages. John Y. Gotanda, *Awarding Damages under the United Nations Convention on the International Sale of Goods: A Matter of Interpretation*, 37 Geo. J. Intl. Law 95 (2005).

[3] CISG-AC Opinion No. 6, *Calculation of Damages under CISG Article 74* (2006).

CISG Advisory Council Opinion No. 6[4]

Calculation of Damages under CISG Article 74

OPINION

1. Article 74 reflects the general principle of full compensation.

2. The aggrieved party has the burden to prove, with reasonable certainty, that it suffered loss. The aggrieved party also has the burden to prove the extent of the loss, but need not do so with mathematical precision.

3. The aggrieved party is entitled to non-performance damages, which is typically measured by the market value of the benefit of which the aggrieved party has been deprived through the breach, or the costs of reasonable measures to bring about the situation that would have existed had the contract been properly performed.

> A. The aggrieved party is entitled to any net gains prevented as a result of the breach.
>
> B. Lost profits recoverable under Article 74 may include loss of profits that are expected to be incurred after the time damages are assessed by a tribunal.
>
> C. Lost profits include those arising from lost volume sales.

4. The aggrieved party is entitled to additional costs reasonably incurred as a result of the breach and of measures taken to mitigate the loss.

5. Under Article 74, the aggrieved party cannot recover expenses associated with litigation of the breach.

6. The aggrieved party is entitled to damages for pecuniary loss resulting from claims by third parties as a result of the breach of contract.

7. The aggrieved party is entitled to damages for loss of goodwill as a consequence of the breach.

---

[4] The comments on the opinion can be found at http://cisgw3.law.pace.edu/cisg/CISG-AC-op6.html.

8. If there has been a breach of contract and then the aggrieved party enters into a reasonable substitute transaction without first having avoided the contract, the aggrieved party may recover damages under Article 74, that is, the difference between the contract price and the substitute transaction.

9. Damages must not place the aggrieved party in a better position than it would have enjoyed if the contract had been properly performed.

  A. In calculating the amount of damages owed to the aggrieved party, the loss to the aggrieved party resulting from the breach is to be offset, in principle, by any gains to the aggrieved party resulting from the non-performance of the contract.

  B. Punitive damages may not be awarded under Article 74 of the Convention.

* * * * *

As one can see, the Opinion states that damages under the CISG reflect "the principle of full compensation."[5] Generally, damages are calculated as the market value of the benefit that the injured party lost as a result of the breach, or the costs involved with putting the injured party back where it expected to be if there had not been a breach.[6] Article 74 specifically states that lost profits may be included in damages. But, the Opinion goes beyond the text of Article 74 and specifies other types of losses that may be included in damages, including: losses for goodwill, net gains that were prevented by the breach, profits that might have occurred even after the tribunal renders its decision, lost profits arising from volume sales, losses from third party claims resulting from the breach, and any other costs borne by the injured party as a result of the breach and of that party's efforts to mitigate the losses. However, the Opinion makes clear that neither the costs associated with the litigation of the breach nor punitive damages are

---

[5] *Id.* For an overview of damages under the CISG, also see Liu Chengwei, *Remedies for Non-performance: Perspectives from CISG, UNIDROIT Principles & PECL*, para. 13.1 (available at http://www.cisg.law.pace.edu/cisg/biblio/chengwei-74.html#*).

[6] *Id.*; *see also* Joseph Lookofsky, *The 1980 United Nations Convention on Contracts for the International Sales of Goods*, in *International Encyclopedia of Laws—Contracts*, Supp. 29, 152–153 (J. Herbots & R. Blanpain eds., Kluwer L. Intl. 2000) ("[T]he Convention scheme seeks to place the injured party in the position he would have enjoyed 'but for' the breach.").

recoverable under Article 74.[7] Finally, any losses must be offset by any gains that may have occurred as a result of the breach.

Example 6-1

The Commentary to Advisory Opinion No. 6 sets forth the following example to explain lost volume sales:

"If a private party agrees to sell his automobile to a buyer for $2,000, a breach by the buyer would cause the seller no loss (except incidental damages, that is, the expense of a new sale) if the seller was able to sell the automobile to another buyer for $2,000. But the situation is different with dealers having an unlimited supply of standard-priced goods. Thus, if an automobile dealer agrees to sell a car to a buyer at the standard price of $2,000, a breach by the buyer injures the dealer, even though he is able to sell the automobile to another for $2,000. If the dealer has an inexhaustible supply of cars, the resale to replace the breaching buyer costs the dealer a sale, because, if the breaching buyer had performed, the dealer would have made two sales instead of one. The buyer's breach, in such a case, depletes the dealer's sales to the extent of one, and the measure of damages should be the dealer's profit on one sale."[8]

Having described the kinds of losses that might be included in a claim for damages under the CISG, it is important to note that there are three general limiting factors built into Article 74's general description of damages: foreseeability, causation, and certainty. Article 74 specifically limits damages to those that are either subjectively or objectively foreseeable by the party in breach. Article 74 uses what is by now a familiar formulation, "the loss which the party in breach foresaw or ought to have foreseen."[9] So, the breaching party cannot merely claim not to have foreseen the harm. If it should have foreseen the harm, then the foreseeability standard is satisfied.

---

[7] This is in contrast to the position taken by a United States federal court in *Zapata Hermanos Sucesores, S.A. v. Hearthsie Baking Co.*, 2001 WL 1000927 (N.D. Ill. Aug. 29, 2001), in which the court ruled that under the CISG, attorney's fees can be recovered in a claim for damages.
[8] CISG Advisory Council, *Comments to CISG Advisory Council Opinion No. 6*, para. 3.21 (available at http://www.cisg.law.pace.edu/cisg/CISG-AC-op6.html).
[9] Foreseeability as a limiting principle on damages allows both parties to assess the risks of the transaction before entering into it. Lookofsky, *supra* n. 6, at 154.

Regarding causation, Article 74 states that an injured party can recover losses suffered "as a consequence of the breach." Thus, only those losses that are caused by the breach are recoverable.

The CISG does not specifically contain language limiting damages to those which are reasonably certain. This is in contrast to other formulations of damages, such as the one contained in the UNIDROIT Principles. Article 7.4.3 of the UNIDROIT Principles states that "compensation is due only for harm . . . that is established with a reasonable degree of certainty."[10] However, the CISG Advisory Council Opinion has taken the position that damages under Article 74 must be ascertainable with a reasonable degree of certainty.[11] This limitation seems crucial to avoid over-compensating the aggrieved party.[12] Speculative damages are not awarded. Rather, only damages that can be established with a reasonable degree of certainty are recoverable. Still, the damages need not be proven with mathematical precision.

Consider the following case where the court considered whether various expenses were damages under Article 74.

United States Court of Appeals for the Second Circuit

Delchi Carrier SpA v. Rotorex Corporation

71 F.3d 1024

Decided: December 6, 1995

WINTER, Circuit Judge:

Rotorex Corporation, a New York corporation, appeals from a judgment of $1,785,772.44 in damages for lost profits and other consequential damages awarded to Delchi Carrier SpA following a bench trial before Judge Munson. The basis for the award was Rotorex's delivery of nonconforming compressors to Delchi, an Italian manufacturer of air conditioners. Delchi cross-appeals from the denial of certain incidental and consequential damages.

---

[10] The PECL limit the amount of "future losses" recoverable by a party to those losses that are "reasonably likely to occur." PECL Article 9:501(2)(b).

[11] CISG-AC Opinion No. 6, *Calculation of Damages under CISG Article 74*.

[12] Indeed, avoiding over-compensation is a goal of the CISG's damage provisions. CISG-AC Opinion No. 6, *Calculation of Damages under CISG Article 74*, § 9.

We affirm the award of damages; we reverse in part on Delchi's cross-appeal and remand for further proceedings.

BACKGROUND

In January 1988, Rotorex agreed to sell 10,800 compressors to Delchi for use in Delchi's "Ariele" line of portable room air conditioners. The air conditioners were scheduled to go on sale in the spring and summer of 1988. Prior to executing the contract, Rotorex sent Delchi a sample compressor and accompanying written performance specifications. The compressors were scheduled to be delivered in three shipments before May 15, 1988.

Rotorex sent the first shipment by sea on March 26. Delchi paid for this shipment, which arrived at its Italian factory on April 20, by letter of credit. Rotorex sent a second shipment of compressors on or about May 9. Delchi also remitted payment for this shipment by letter of credit. While the second shipment was en route, Delchi discovered that the first lot of compressors did not conform to the sample model and accompanying specifications. On May 13, after a Rotorex representative visited the Delchi factory in Italy, Delchi informed Rotorex that 93 percent of the compressors were rejected in quality control checks because they had lower cooling capacity and consumed more power than the sample model and specifications. After several unsuccessful attempts to cure the defects in the compressors, Delchi asked Rotorex to supply new compressors conforming to the original sample and specifications. Rotorex refused, claiming that the performance specifications were "inadvertently communicated" to Delchi.

In a faxed letter dated May 23, 1988, Delchi cancelled the contract. Although it was able to expedite a previously planned order of suitable compressors from Sanyo, another supplier, Delchi was unable to obtain in a timely fashion substitute compressors from other sources and thus suffered a loss in its sales volume of Arieles during the 1988 selling season. Delchi filed the instant action under the United Nations Convention on Contracts for the International Sale of Goods ("CISG" or "the Convention") for breach of contract and failure to deliver conforming goods. On January 10, 1991, Judge Cholakis granted

Delchi's motion for partial summary judgment, holding Rotorex liable for breach of contract.

After three years of discovery and a bench trial on the issue of damages, Judge Munson, to whom the case had been transferred, held Rotorex liable to Delchi for $1,248,331.87. This amount included consequential damages for: (i) lost profits resulting from a diminished sales level of Ariele units, (ii) expenses that Delchi incurred in attempting to remedy the nonconformity of the compressors, (iii) the cost of expediting shipment of previously ordered Sanyo compressors after Delchi rejected the Rotorex compressors, and (iv) costs of handling and storing the rejected compressors. The district court also awarded prejudgment interest under CISG art. 78.

The court denied Delchi's claim for damages based on other expenses, including: (i) shipping, customs, and incidentals relating to the two shipments of Rotorex compressors; (ii) the cost of obsolete insulation and tubing that Delchi purchased only for use with Rotorex compressors; (iii) the cost of obsolete tooling purchased only for production of units with Rotorex compressors; and (iv) labor costs for four days when Delchi's production line was idle because it had no compressors to install in the air conditioning units. The court denied an award for these items on the ground that it would lead to a double recovery because "those costs are accounted for in Delchi's recovery on its lost profits claim." It also denied an award for the cost of modification of electrical panels for use with substitute Sanyo compressors on the ground that the cost was not attributable to the breach. Finally, the court denied recovery on Delchi's claim of 4000 additional lost sales in Italy.

On appeal, Rotorex argues that it did not breach the agreement, that Delchi is not entitled to lost profits because it maintained inventory levels in excess of the maximum number of possible lost sales, that the calculation of the number of lost sales was improper, and that the district court improperly excluded fixed costs and depreciation from the manufacturing cost in calculating lost profits. Delchi cross-appeals, claiming that it is entitled to the additional out-of-pocket expenses and the lost profits on additional sales denied by Judge Munson.

DISCUSSION

The district court held, and the parties agree, that the instant matter is governed by the CISG, reprinted at 15 U.S.C.A. Appendix (West Supp. 1995), a self-executing agreement between the United States and other signatories, including Italy. Because there is virtually no case law under the Convention, we look to its language and to "the general principles" upon which it is based. See CISG art. 7(2). The Convention directs that its interpretation be informed by its "international character and . . . the need to promote uniformity in its application and the observance of good faith in international trade." See CISG art. 7(1); see generally John Honnold, Uniform Law for International Sales Under the 1980 United Nations Convention 60- 62 (2d ed. 1991) (addressing principles for interpretation of CISG). Case law interpreting analogous provisions of Article 2 of the Uniform Commercial Code ("UCC"), may also inform a court where the language of the relevant CISG provisions tracks that of the UCC. However, UCC case law "is not per se applicable." Orbisphere Corp. v. United States, 726 F. Supp. 1344, 1355 (Ct. Int'l Trade 1989).

We first address the liability issue. ...

Under the CISG, "[t]he seller must deliver goods which are of the quantity, quality and description required by the contract," and "the goods do not conform with the contract unless they . . . [p]ossess the qualities of goods which the seller has held out to the buyer as a sample or model." CISG art. 35. The CISG further states that "[t]he seller is liable in accordance with the contract and this Convention for any lack of conformity." CISG art. 36.

Judge Cholakis held that "there is no question that [Rotorex's] compressors did not conform to the terms of the contract between the parties" and noted that "[t]here are ample admissions [by Rotorex] to that effect." We agree. ...

Under the CISG, if the breach is "fundamental" the buyer may either require delivery of substitute goods, CISG art. 46, or declare the contract void, CISG art. 49, and seek damages. With regard to what kind of breach is fundamental, Article 25 provides:

A breach of contract committed by one of the parties is fundamental if it results in such detriment to the other party as substantially to deprive him of what he is entitled to expect under the contract, unless the party in breach did not foresee and a reasonable person of the same kind in the same circumstances would not have foreseen such a result.

CISG art. 25. ... Because the cooling power and energy consumption of an air conditioner compressor are important determinants of the product's value, the district court's conclusion that Rotorex was liable for a fundamental breach of contract under the Convention was proper.

We turn now to the district court's award of damages....

The CISG provides:

Damages for breach of contract by one party consist of a sum equal to the loss, including loss of profit, suffered by the other party as a consequence of the breach. Such damages may not exceed the loss which the party in breach foresaw or ought to have foreseen at the time of the conclusion of the contract, in the light of the facts and matters of which he then knew or ought to have known, as a possible consequence of the breach of contract.

CISG art. 74. This provision is "designed to place the aggrieved party in as good a position as if the other party had properly performed the contract." Honnold, supra, at 503.

Rotorex argues that Delchi is not entitled to lost profits because it was able to maintain inventory levels of Ariele air conditioning units in excess of the maximum number of possible lost sales. In Rotorex's view, therefore, there was no actual shortfall of Ariele units available for sale because of Rotorex's delivery of nonconforming compressors. Rotorex's argument goes as follows. The end of the air conditioner selling season is August 1. If one totals the number of units available to Delchi from March to August 1, the sum is enough to fill all sales. We may assume that the evidence in the record supports the factual premise. Nevertheless, the argument is fallacious. Because of Rotorex's breach, Delchi had to shut down its manufacturing operation for a few days in May, and the date on which particular units were available for sale was substantially delayed. For example, units available in late July could not be used to meet orders in the spring. As a result, Delchi lost sales in the spring and early summer. We therefore conclude that the district court's findings regarding lost sales are not clearly erroneous. A detailed discussion of the precise number of lost sales is unnecessary because the district court's findings were, if anything, conservative.

Rotorex contends, in the alternative, that the district court improperly awarded lost profits for unfilled orders from Delchi affiliates in Europe and from sales agents within Italy. We disagree. The CISG requires that damages be limited by the familiar principle of foreseeability established in *Hadley v. Baxendale*, 156 Eng. Rep. 145 (1854). CISG art. 74. However, it was objectively foreseeable that Delchi would take orders for Ariele sales based on the number of compressors it had ordered and expected to have ready for the season. The district court was entitled to rely upon the documents and testimony regarding these lost sales and was well within its authority in deciding which orders were proven with sufficient certainty.

Rotorex also challenges the district court's exclusion of fixed costs and depreciation from the manufacturing cost used to calculate lost profits. The trial judge calculated lost profits by subtracting the 478,783 lire "manufacturing cost" -- the total variable cost -- of an Ariele unit from the 654,644 lire average sale price. The CISG does not explicitly state whether only variable expenses, or both fixed and variable expenses, should be subtracted from sales revenue in calculating lost profits. However, courts generally do not include fixed costs in the calculation of lost profits. See Indu Craft, Inc. v. Bank of Baroda, 47 F.3d 490, 495 (2d Cir. 1995) (only when the breach ends an ongoing business should fixed costs be subtracted along with variable costs); Adams v. Lindblad Travel, Inc., 730 F.2d 89, 92-93 (2d Cir. 1984) (fixed costs should not be included in lost profits equation when the plaintiff is an ongoing business whose fixed costs are not affected by the breach). This is, of course, because the fixed costs would have been encountered whether or not the breach occurred. In the absence of a specific provision in the CISG for calculating lost profits, the district court was correct to use the standard formula employed by most American courts and to deduct only variable costs from sales revenue to arrive at a figure for lost profits.

In its cross-appeal, Delchi challenges the district court's denial of various consequential and incidental damages, including reimbursement for: (i) shipping, customs, and incidentals relating to the first and second shipments -- rejected and returned -- of Rotorex compressors; (ii) obsolete insulation materials and tubing purchased for use only with Rotorex compressors; (iii) obsolete tooling purchased exclusively for production of units with Rotorex compressors; and (iv) labor costs for the period of May 16-19, 1988, when the Delchi production line was idle due to a lack of compressors to install in Ariele air conditioning units. The district court denied damages for these items on the ground that they "are accounted for in Delchi's recovery on its lost profits claim," and, therefore, an award would constitute a double recovery for Delchi. We disagree.

The Convention provides that a contract plaintiff may collect damages to compensate for the full loss. This includes, but is not limited to, lost profits, subject only to the familiar limitation that the breaching party must have foreseen, or should have foreseen, the loss as a probable consequence. CISG art. 74; *see Hadley v. Baxendale, supra.*

An award for lost profits will not compensate Delchi for the expenses in question. Delchi's lost profits are determined by calculating the hypothetical revenues to be derived from unmade sales less the hypothetical variable costs that would have been, but were not, incurred. This figure, however, does not compensate for costs actually incurred that led to no sales. Thus, to award damages for costs actually incurred in no way creates a double recovery and instead furthers the purpose of giving the injured party damages "equal to the loss." CISG art. 74.

The only remaining inquiries, therefore, are whether the expenses were reasonably foreseeable and legitimate incidental or consequential damages. The expenses incurred by Delchi for shipping, customs, and related matters for the two returned shipments of Rotorex compressors, including storage expenses for the second shipment at Genoa, were clearly foreseeable and recoverable incidental expenses. These are up-front expenses that had to be paid to get the goods to the manufacturing plant for inspection and were thus incurred largely before the nonconformities were detected. To deny reimbursement to Delchi for these incidental damages would effectively cut into the lost profits award. The same is true of unreimbursed tooling expenses and the cost of the useless insulation and tubing materials. These are legitimate consequential damages that in no way duplicate lost profits damages.

The labor expense incurred as a result of the production line shutdown of May 16-19, 1988 is also a reasonably foreseeable result of delivering nonconforming compressors for installation in air conditioners. However, Rotorex argues that the labor costs in question were fixed costs that would have been incurred whether or not there was a breach. The district court labeled the labor costs "fixed costs," but did not explore whether Delchi would have paid these wages regardless of how much it produced. Variable costs are generally those costs that "fluctuate with a firm's output," and typically include labor (but not management) costs. Northeastern Tel. Co. v. AT&T, 651 F.2d 76, 86 (2d Cir. 1981). Whether Delchi's labor costs during this four-day period are variable or fixed costs is in large measure a fact question that we cannot answer because we lack factual findings by the district court. We therefore remand to the district court on this issue.

The district court also denied an award for the modification of electrical panels for use with substitute Sanyo compressors. It denied damages on the ground that Delchi failed to show that the modifications were not part of the regular cost of production of units with Sanyo compressors and were therefore attributable to Rotorex's breach. This appears to have been a credibility determination that was within the court's authority to make. We therefore affirm on the ground that this finding is not clearly erroneous.

Finally, Delchi cross-appeals from the denial of its claimed 4000 additional lost sales in Italy. The district court held that Delchi did not prove these orders with sufficient certainty. The trial court was in the best position to evaluate the testimony of the Italian sales agents who stated that they would have ordered more Arieles if they had been available. It found the agents' claims to be too speculative, and this conclusion is not clearly erroneous.

CONCLUSION

We affirm the award of damages. We reverse in part the denial of incidental and consequential damages. We remand for further proceedings in accord with this opinion.

* * * * *

Notes and Commentary

Note 1: The case assesses many different kinds of losses to determine whether they are properly included in a claim for damages under Article 74. The claimant in this case seemed to be quite complete in its request for damages. Notice that the court characterizes the damages as consequential or incidental. This distinction is typical of common law jurisdictions. The CISG actually does not use this terminology or distinction but merely states that the injured party may seek damages suffered as a consequence of the breach. This language seems very inclusive but also does not give much guidance on some of the specific issues confronted by this court. For example, the court struggled with what to do about fixed costs when calculating lost profits. In a common law jurisdiction, there would likely be cases that would serve as precedent on that point. Indeed, this United States court defers to cases in its own jurisdiction for guidance. Is deference to local cases an appropriate, or at least adequate, way of filling the gaps that the CISG leaves? In addition, local statutes might be in point. In the United States, UCC §2-708(2) speaks of including reasonable overhead in the calculation of lost profits. Is deference to domestic statutes on point more or less appropriate than deference to local cases?

Note 2: On a related note, the court references the *Hadley v. Baxendale* case from 19th century England. That case is a landmark case from English common law in which the principle of foreseeability was affirmed as a limitation on damages. The case has formed the cornerstone for the foreseeability principle in the United States as well. The case involved a mill that needed a replacement crank shaft in order to operate. The mill's representative contracted with a delivery company to deliver the broken shaft to the manufacturer for repair. When there were delays with the delivery, the mill sued the delivery company for damages for lost profits resulting from the fact that the mill could not operate without the crank shaft. The court ruled that the lost profits claimed in this case were not reasonably foreseeable to the delivery company based on the facts presented. If, however, the delivery company had been made aware of the special circumstances at the time of contracting, then the delivery company would have been liable for the damages that then would have been foreseeable. *Hadley v. Baxendale,* 156 Eng. Rep. 145 (1854). More specifically, Baron Alderson wrote the opinion for the court ruling that for damages to be recoverable, the losses involved must be "in the contemplation of both parties at the time they made the contract, as the probable result of the breach." *Id.* This principle of foreseeability is certainly echoed in CISG Article 74. Nonetheless, is it appropriate for the court to reference this case?

In fact, scholars have actually pointed out that the foreseeability standard set forth in *Hadley v. Baxendale* is a very different and more limited standard than the standard set forth in the CISG.[13]   Where Baron Alderson spoke of losses being the "contemplation of both parties... as the probable result of the breach," Article 74 clearly states that the losses merely should be foreseeable as a "possible consequence" of the breach. Accordingly, Article 74 seems to be much broader than the common law rule enunciated in *Hadley v. Baxendale.* Did this distinction get lost when the court defaulted to its own familiar notions of foreseeability with a reliance on the *Hadley* case? Is that a typical danger of deference to any particular nation's own historical iteration of principles that have been set forth in the CISG?

* * * * *

Before leaving Article 74, it is also important to consider Article 50 and the interplay between those two sections. Recall that Article 50 specifically allows a buyer to reduce the price it pays for non-conforming goods in proportion to the reduced value of the non-conforming goods at the time of delivery. In other words, if the goods received were worth only 50% of what they should have been worth, then the buyer needs only pay 50% of the contract price. Article 74 provides an alternative remedy.

Damages under Article 74 include an amount equal to the difference between the value of what was ordered under the contract and the value of what was actually delivered. Where the buyer receives non-conforming goods that are worth only 50% of what they would have been worth, the buyer could claim damages for the amount of money that it would take to restore the goods to what they should have been, or to replace the goods with the goods originally expected.

If the goods have increased in value since the time the contract price was made, the measure of damages under Article 74 will be greater than the remedy provided for in Article 50. On the other hand, if the goods have decreased in value since the time of the contract, then the buyer will be better off using Article 50 and being forgiven from paying a portion of the contract price. Buyer could then use that savings to purchase the goods involved at the then lower market price.[14]

---

[13] *See e.g.* Franco Ferrari *Comparative Ruminations on the Foreseeability of Damages in Contract Law,* 53 La. L. Rev. 1257, 1266 (1993).

[14] John O. Honnold, *Uniform Law for International Sales under the 1980 United Nations Convention* 310–312 (3d ed., Kluwer L. Intl. 1999).

Example 6-2

A buyer of a shipment of insulated copper wire complained to the seller that the wire was not conforming because of the insulation used. The buyer claimed that the wire that was sent was only worth 60% of the wire that was ordered. Under Article 50 of the CISG, the buyer could opt to accept the goods and reduce the purchase price in proportion to the reduced value of the goods and thereby only pay 60% of the purchase price.

Alternatively, under Article 74 of the CISG, the buyer could claim damages in an amount equal to the amount it would take to either fix the non-conformity or purchase replacement goods. If the market price of the insulated copper wire had increased, then the Article 74 remedy for damages will be more advantageous than the Article 50 remedy of paying a fractional portion of the original price. If the market price of insulated copper wire had decreased, then the buyer will be better off paying a reduce price under Article 50 and using the money saved to buy more conforming goods.

B. DAMAGES IN A SUBSTITUTE TRANSACTION

Notice that Article 74's general formulation for damages applies whether the contract has been declared avoided or not. Articles 75 and 76, on the other hand, can be applied only when the injured party has gone as far as to declare the contract avoided (though actual notice of avoidance is sometimes not required). [15] As was explained in Chapter 5, avoidance means that the buyer is no longer obligated to accept and pay for the goods that were the subject of the contract; and the seller is no longer obligated to deliver those goods.

Article 75 addresses the situation in which one of the parties has declared the contract avoided and has entered into a substitute transaction. A substitute transaction for the buyer is where the buyer purchases goods in replacement of the goods it would have gotten from the seller. A substitute transaction for the seller is a re-sale of the goods that would have been delivered to buyer. In either case, damages may be calculated as the difference between the contract price for the goods involved and the substitute transaction price. Note that the language of this section includes the word "may" indicating that this calculation of damages

---

[15] See example 6-2, below for a case where notice of avoidance was not expressly required. But for a case that barred damage recovery based on a substitute transaction because the buyer had never avoided the transaction, see *D.B. GmbH v. C.N.H. (Ger. v. Pol.),* http://www.unilex.info/case .cfm?pid=1&do=case&id=1129&step=Abstract (Supreme Court of Poland 2006).

is one option, but is not mandatory. So, for example, a buyer that has entered into a substitute transaction might not seek this calculation of damages, but instead might calculate its damages solely with reference to other losses.

> **Article 75**
>
> If the contract is avoided and if, in a reasonable manner and within a reasonable time after avoidance, the buyer has bought goods in replacement or the seller has resold the goods, the party claiming damages may recover the difference between the contract price and the price in the substitute transaction as well as any further damages recoverable under article 74.

For the buyer purchasing substitute goods on the market,[16] the damages calculated under Article 75 should equal the substitute transaction price minus the original contract price. If the market price for the goods has decreased then this difference would be negative and the buyer would not be allowed a recovery under Article 75. The buyer would actually be in a better situation than it would have if the contract had been performed. Note, however, that the buyer might still recover damages under Article 74 for any other losses suffered as a result of seller's breach (such as costs involved with arranging the substitute transaction or costs attributable to the delay in getting the goods). However, those losses could be offset by any gains achieved in the substitute transaction.

However, for the seller attempting to resell goods that the buyer wrongfully rejected, the damages should equal the contract price minus the substitute transaction price. So, if the market price of the goods has increased and the seller earns more from the substitute transaction, then the damage amount would be a negative and the seller would not be allowed a recovery under Article 75. The seller in this case would be in a better situation than if the contract had been performed. Again, though, the seller can still recover damages under Article 74 for any other losses suffered as a result of the buyer's breach. But, once again, those losses could be offset by any gains achieved from the resale.

Note that whether it is the seller or the buyer entering into the substitute transaction, the substitute transaction must be reasonable and conducted within a reasonable amount of time after the avoidance (Article 75). As always, what is reasonable is frequently difficult to determine and will depend on the facts and circumstances of each case. Cases typically assert that a substitute transaction is reasonable if the party entering the transaction "behaves as a careful and prudent

---

[16] The UCC refers to the purchase of substitute goods as a "cover" transaction. *See* UCC §2-712.

businessman."[17] Further, the party entering the substitute transaction need not "conduct a deep investigation in order to get the most advantageous [deal]."[18]

Example 6-3

An English buyer had contracted with a German seller for the purchase of a large quantity of iron molybdenum from China. When the seller did not deliver by the original due date, the buyer gave the seller a *Nachfrist* notice under Article 47. When the seller did not deliver by the extended delivery date, the buyer ultimately declared that it was going to have to enter into a substitute transaction. The buyer then did enter into a substitute transaction at a price that was three times higher than the original contract price.

The court found that the buyer had the right to declare the contact avoided under both Articles 49(1)(a) (in that the breach by seller was fundamental since time had been made of the essence) and 49(1)(b) (in that the buyer had delivered a *Nachfrist* notice and the seller still did not perform). Although the buyer never expressly notified the seller of its avoidance, such notice was not necessary here where the seller had declared that it could not perform.

The court then reasoned that in accordance with Article 75 since the contract was avoided, the buyer had the right to enter into the substitute transaction and recover the difference between the price paid in that transaction and the original contract price. With regard to the price for the substitute transaction being three times greater than the original contract price, the court stated that there was no evidence that the transaction was conducted on anything but ordinary business principles. Thus, the substitute transaction was reasonable.[19]

C. DAMAGES WHEN NO SUBSTITUTE TRANSACTION

In cases where the injured party declares the contract avoided but does not engage in a substitute transaction, Article 76 outlines how damages can be

---

[17] A*ustrian Seller v. Swiss Buyer* (*Chemical fertilizer case*), ICC Arbitration Case No. 8128 (1995) (available at http://cisgw3.law.pace.edu/cases/958128i1.html).

[18] *Id.*

[19] *English Buyer v. German Seller*, Oberlandesgericht Hamburg Case 1 U 167/95 (Germany Feb. 28, 1997) (available at http://cisgw3.law.pace.edu/cases/970228g1.html).

calculated with reference to the prevailing market price for the goods involved.[20] Like Article 75, this article is permissive and simply states that damages "may" be calculated in this manner. Like Article 75, Article 76 also allows the injured party to potentially recover any additional damages (like lost profits) under Article 74. Article 76 may be most relevant when, for whatever reason, there is no possibility of a substitute transaction. In that case, damages would be calculated as (i) the difference between the current market price of the goods involved and the contract price plus (ii) any other losses, including lost profits.

Article 76

(1) If the contract is avoided and there is a current price for the goods, the party claiming damages may, if he has not made a purchase or resale under article 75, recover the difference between the price fixed by the contract and the current price at the time of avoidance as well as any further damages recoverable under article 74. If, however, the party claiming damages has avoided the contract after taking over the goods, the current price at the time of such taking over shall be applied instead of the current price at the time of avoidance.

(2) For the purposes of the preceding paragraph, the current price is the price prevailing at the place where delivery of the goods should have been made or, if there is no current price at that place, the price at such other place as serves as a reasonable substitute, making due allowance for differences in the cost of transporting the goods.

The market price to be used is the price prevailing at the time of avoidance. Accordingly, in the case of the seller breaching, the buyer can recover the market price of the goods prevailing at the time the buyer declares the contract avoided. However, if the buyer has taken the goods, then the market price is determined at the time the buyer took the goods. In either of these cases, the market price is

---

[20] Article 75 and 76 are sometimes referred to as being concrete (Article 75) and abstract (Article 76) measures of damages. *See* Lookofsky, *supra* n. 6, at 157. This terminology was used in *Chinese Seller v. German Buyer*, Schiedsgericht der Handelskammer Hamburg Partial Arbitral Award (Germany Mar. 21, 1996) (available at http://cisgw3.law.pace.edu/cases/960321g1.html#14) (where the tribunal ruled that a "concrete determination of the damages prevails over an abstract calculation made on the basis of market prices according to Art. 76 CISG").

calculated at the time when the buyer should know that it will need to cover and could indeed purchase substitute goods at that time.

In the case of the buyer breaching, where the seller does not or cannot re-sell the goods, the seller may demand damages based on the difference between the contract price and the market price at the time of avoidance. Again, this time is used because it is at that time that the seller could re-sell the goods and recover the market value then prevailing for the goods.

Article 76 goes on to specify that when calculating the market price, one should use the price prevailing in the place where the delivery would have taken place.[21] If no such place can be determined, then a reasonable substitute place can be used (Article 76). As always, what is reasonable will depend on the circumstances of the case and the judgment of the tribunal involved.

Example 6-4

A German seller agreed to sell PVC materials to a Swiss buyer. When the seller failed to deliver the goods, the buyer declared the contract avoided. It did not enter into a substitute transaction and therefore damages were calculated in accordance with CISG Article 76. In accordance with that section damages were measured by the difference between the contract price and the average market price for the goods at the time of avoidance.[22]

D.   MITIGATION

Perhaps the most important qualification on an injured party's recovery of damages is Article 77's requirement that the injured party mitigate any losses caused by a breach. Article 77 states that the injured party "must" mitigate. This is in stark contrast to Articles 75 and 76, which each state that damages may be calculated with reference to a substitute transaction or market price. Those sections are permissive. It is possible to calculate damages in accordance with those sections but not necessary and, in any event, damages are not limited to the

---

[21] *See Dutch Buyer v. Vietnamese Seller (Rice case)*, ICC Arbitration 8502 (November 1996) (available at http://www.unilex.info/case.cfm?pid=1&do=case&id=395&step=FullText) (delivery of the goods involved was F.O.B. Ho Chi Minh City and therefore the ICC tribunal ruled that market price should be calculated based on the price prevailing there).

[22] *See Swiss Buyer v. German Seller (PVC and Other Synthetic Materials case)*, Kantonsgericht Zug Case A3 1997 61 (Switzerland Oct. 21, 1999) (available at http://cisgw3.law.pace.edu/cases/991021s1.html). For a case where the buyer refused delivery and the seller avoided and therefore could consider damages under Article 75, see *Italian Seller v. German Buyer*, Oberlandesgericht Düsseldorf Case 17 U 146/93 (Germany Jan. 14, 1994) (available at http://www.cisg.law.pace.edu/cisg/wais/db/cases2/940114g1.html).

amounts calculated pursuant to those sections. Article 77, by contrast, demands that the injured party take action to minimize the losses caused by a breach. The injured party cannot simply do nothing in the aftermath of a breach and expect the breaching party to pay for any and all losses that ensue.

> **Article 77**
>
> A party who relies on a breach of contract must take such measures as are reasonable in the circumstances to mitigate the loss, including loss of profit, resulting from the breach. If he fails to take such measures, the party in breach may claim a reduction in the damages in the amount by which the loss should have been mitigated.

One difficulty in applying Article 77's mitigation requirement comes in assessing what steps are "reasonable" for an injured party to take in minimizing the losses caused by the breaching party. Mitigation of losses, in fact, directly helps the breaching party, assuming the breaching party ultimately compensates the injured party for its losses. It seems ironic to demand that the injured party help the very party that caused the injury. From this perspective, it is perhaps unreasonable to expect the injured party to take any extreme measures to minimize the losses caused by the counterparty's breach. It may even be unreasonable to expect the injured party to take anything but the most obvious and convenient steps to mitigate its losses.[23]

Other sections of the CISG might buttress this interpretation. Articles 34, 37, and 48 allow the seller to cure its own breach only when the seller does not cause the buyer any unreasonable inconvenience or expense. This standard seems to indicate some sympathy for the injured party and an expectation that the injured party not be caused any unreasonable inconvenience or expense in any case. Ultimately, of course, what is "reasonable" will be a function of the specific facts involved and the discretion of the tribunal involved.

---

[23] Professors Enderlein and Maskow further explain what is expected of an aggrieved party:
> No exceptional efforts are required from that party; he only has to take such measures as are reasonable under the circumstances. Such measures may frequently include a cover purchase or sale. It can also include the possibility that the buyer himself remedies defective goods delivered to the buyer.

Fritz Enderlein & Dietrich Maskow, *International Sales Law* 308 (Oceana Publications 1992).

Example 6–5

An Italian buyer refused to take delivery of goods from a Swiss seller. The seller mitigated its losses by selling the goods at a reduced price to a Filipino buyer. The tribunal determined the seller's actions were consistent with Article 77 on mitigation. Further, the seller was entitled to damages under Article 75 as the difference between the price of the original contract and the price received from the resale.[24]

Minimizing Losses and Maximizing Wealth

The necessity to mitigate damages under Article 77 underscores a general principle upon which, it can fairly be argued, the CISG rests—minimizing losses. Said differently, this principle might also be referred to as maximizing wealth. By minimizing the losses involved, the parties' collective wealth will be greater, regardless of how any disputes are ultimately resolved.

This principle is also reflected in the articles promoting communication between the parties and encouraging breaching parties to cure. For example, Articles 47, 48, and 49, taken together, create a regime where it is difficult for the buyer to declare its contract avoided unless the party communicates with the other party and provides an opportunity to cure. Recall that Article 49(1)(b) allows the buyer to avoid the contract if it has given the seller a *Nachfrist* notice under Article 47, extending the time during which the seller can perform. Article 49(1)(a) allows the buyer to avoid a contract when there is a fundamental breach, but the term fundamental is determined, in part, by reference to whether the seller has had an opportunity to cure under Article 48.

By encouraging parties to solve their own disputes quickly and to avoid formal dispute resolution, the CISG also attempts to minimize any losses caused by an initial breach. Likewise, Article 85 through 88 requiring preservation of goods, discussed in Chapter 5, reinforce the principle of minimizing losses.

---
[24] *ICC Arbitration Case 10329 (Switz. v. Italy)*, 29 Yearbook Commercial Arbitration (2004) 108–132 (ICC 2000).

II.   INTEREST

The CISG provides for interest on any amounts due and owing from one party to another.   Thus, damages are subject to interest being added to any amount due. Recall that Article 84 also specifically required the seller to add interest to any purchase price amounts that it must return to the buyer. Including interest to any amounts due under the CISG reinforces the notion of full compensation reflected in Article 74's formulation of damages (and further explained in the Advisory Council Opinion on damages set out above).   If a party owes another party $1,000,000 for a year, that money could have been earning interest.   Even at a relatively modest interest rate of 5%, the interest earned would be $50,000.   The interest provisions reflect the idea that allowing the breaching party to keep that sum from the injured party would be unjust.

Article 78

If a party fails to pay the price or any other sum that is in arrears, the other party is entitled to interest on it, without prejudice to any claim for damages recoverable under article 74.

However, this seemingly basic notion is complicated by its application.   The mandate that interest be paid overlooks the necessary question of what rate of interest should be applied.   Indeed, many cases decided under the CISG have involved controversies over what rate of interest should be paid to the injured party. Recall here, again, Article 7's mandate that where an issue is covered by the CISG but not settled in it, the issue should be resolved with reference to the general principles underlying the CISG. Article 7 itself set as a goal of the CISG the promotion of international uniformity in the application of the CISG. In that light, the rate of interest used should perhaps be an average of interest rates prevailing in major world markets.[25]   Cases have also applied Article 9 as a way of setting an interest rate that is consistent with general trade practices in a

---

[25] Professor Honnold surveys some of the legislative history of this provision and concludes that there was no general agreement on how to arrive at an interest calculation. He also, however, describes Article 78 as a general provision that was meant to remove the issue of interest from "the vagaries of domestic law." Honnold, *supra* n. 14, at 465. Professor Honnold goes on to suggest that the question of interest seems well suited for application of Article 7(2)'s mandate that questions covered by the CISG but not settled in it should be resolved with reference to the general principles underlying the CISG. *Id.*

particular area.[26] Nonetheless, scholars and courts grappling with this issue have frequently deferred to applicable domestic law rules on applicable interest rates.[27]

Example 6-6

A Canadian food supplier delivered spoiled pork ribs to an American meat company. The court determined the meat company was entitled to damages and prejudgment interest as authorized by Article 78. Because Article 78 does not specify an interest rate and the parties' agreement was silent on the issue, the court applied Illinois state law to calculate the interest component. [28]

In addition to the complication about what rate of interest to apply, there is the prohibition on interest in certain countries of the world. For example, many Islamic nations prohibit interest from being charged. This presents a conundrum where the CISG mandates that interest be included in any award, but then such an award would likely not be enforceable in an Islamic country. In cases where enforcement is likely to be in an Islamic country, therefore, a tribunal should be careful to indicate that the award consists of a certain amount where interest is not included, and a different amount if interest is allowed. In that case, perhaps, the award (not including interest) might indeed be enforced.

Example 6-7

In a case between two Saudi Arabian parties, an ICC tribunal considered the question of whether interest could be included in an award for damages under the Shari'a doctrine of riba. The tribunal ruled and reasoned as follows:

"Defendant also contends that any claim based upon these matters is a disguised claim for interest which is barred in Saudi

---

[26] Bermatex s.r.l. v. Valentin Rius Clapers S.A. v. Sbrojovka Vsetin S.A., Juzgado Nacional de Primera Instancia en lo Comercial No. 10 Case 56.179 (Argentina Oct. 6, 1994) (applying a rate of interest "generally recognized in international trade" based upon Article 9 of the CISG).

[27] For example, Schlechtriem argued that "the details of the obligation to pay interest - in particular, the amount - are governed by the applicable domestic law chosen by conflicts rules." http://www.cisg.law.pace.edu/cisg/biblio/schlechtriem-78.html; *see also Chicago Prime Packers, Inc. v. Northam Food Trading Co.*, 320 F. Supp. 2d 702 (N.D. Ill. 2004), *aff'd*, 408 F. 2d 894 (7th Cir. 2005).

[28] *Id.*

law by the doctrine of *riba*, and that this bar applies directly, and even more clearly, to the matters referred to above."

"In connection with the scope of the doctrine of *riba* we have carefully studied the diverging opinions of the parties' expert witnesses.... In the result, we do not agree that, in the circumstances of this case, some additional award for financial damages is precluded under the doctrine of *riba*."

"We agree, of course, that anything in the nature of usury or unjust taking of interest, as well as compound interest, are barred by this doctrine under Shari'a law. But we do not accept that it also bars all awards of compensation for financial loss due to a party not having had the use of a sum of money to which it would have otherwise been entitled, e.g. as the result of late payment. This conclusion is reflected in modern commercial life in Saudi Arabia in the same way as anywhere else. Thus, commercial banks take and charge interest for loans, and there is nothing in the Saudi banking code which prohibits this. The Saudi Government has issued bonds which are repayable at maturity in a larger amount than their original cost, and which therefore earn interest."[29]

III. EXEMPTIONS

The CISG contains exemptions from liability for two situations. The first exempts a party from liability for damages where an uncontrollable impediment has prevented the party's performance. The second allows a party to avoid liability where its conduct was caused by some act or omission of the party making the claim.

A. UNCONTROLLABLE IMPEDIMENTS

Article 79 exempts a party from liability for damages where an uncontrollable impediment has prevented its performance. This provision is frequently compared to the "force majeure" provisions found in many domestic legal system's law of contracts. However, the CISG's formulation of this impediment is unique and is subject to a set of very specific qualifications. Accordingly, an occurrence that may represent a force majeure event under certain domestic legal systems might not qualify as an impediment under Article 79.

---

[29] Final award in ICC case no. 7063 of 1993.

Article 79's exemption from liability is not triggered unless the impediment involved is: (i) beyond the party's control, *and* (ii) unforeseeable, *and* (iii) unavoidable. Furthermore, the exemption applies only for as long as the impediment lasts (Article 79(3)) and only to claims for damages (Article 79(5)).

Article 79

(1) A party is not liable for a failure to perform any of his obligations if he proves that the failure was due to an impediment beyond his control and that he could not reasonably be expected to have taken the impediment into account at the time of the conclusion of the contract or to have avoided or overcome it or its consequences.

(2) If the party's failure is due to the failure by a third person whom he has engaged to perform the whole or a part of the contract, that party is exempt from liability only if:

(a) he is exempt under the preceding paragraph; and

(b) the person whom he has so engaged would be so exempt if the provisions of that paragraph were applied to him.

(3) The exemption provided by this article has effect for the period during which the impediment exists.

(4) The party who fails to perform must give notice to the other party of the impediment and its effect on his ability to perform. If the notice is not received by the other party within a reasonable time after the party who fails to perform knew or ought to have known of the impediment, he is liable for damages resulting from such non-receipt.

(5) Nothing in this article prevents either party from exercising any right other than to claim damages under this Convention.

Examples of impediments that are beyond a party's control include extreme weather, acts of war, labor strikes, and potentially political, legal, or economic changes. However, not only does the impediment need to be beyond the party's control, it also must be something that the party could not reasonably be expected to take into account when planning its transaction. Again, there is a reasonability standard here so the circumstances of the transaction will need to be considered and the judgment of the tribunal will control this determination. So, for example, it is possible that a labor strike could be considered an impediment beyond a party's control. However, depending on the frequency of such strikes in the industry and region involved, it might be reasonable for a party to take the possibility of a strike into consideration when planning a transaction. Thus, a strike might not qualify a party for an exemption from liability under this article.

Example 6-8

A Belgian buyer had agreed to purchase a shipment of frozen raspberries from a Chilean seller. When the world price for raspberries declined, the Belgian buyer attempted to re-negotiate the price it had agreed to for the raspberries. The Chilean party declared the contract avoided and the Belgian court ruled that even the sharp decline in the world price of strawberries was not an impediment under Article 79 since the buyer should have foreseen fluctuations in price as an ordinary business occurrence.[30]

In addition, the impediment must be the type that the party could not be expected to avoid or overcome. Continuing with the example of a labor strike, if the labor could be outsourced to another factory or even another country where the labor force was not on strike, then this third requirement may not be met.

Example 6-9

A hurricane devastated the cocoa bean crop. As a result, a commodity exporter was unable to fulfill its contract obligations to several confectionaries. A tribunal could find that the exporter was exempt from liability to the confectionaries because the hurricane created an impediment that was uncontrollable, unforeseeable, and unavoidable.

However, the tribunal could find that the exporter should have anticipated potential weather problems that may affect its crop and could be expected to avoid or overcome the consequences of bad weather. For example, the exporter could have purchased

---

[30] *Vital Berry Marketing NV [Chile] v. Dira-Frost NV [Belgium]*, Rechtbank van Koophandel Hasselt Case A.R. 1849/94, 4205/94 (Belgium May 2, 1995) (available at http://www.unilex.info/case.cfm?pid=1&do=case&id=263&step=Abstract).

> beans from another supplier that was unaffected by the hurricane and delivered those beans to its counterparty.[31]

Article 79(2) provides an exemption from liability for non-performance for a party that is prevented from performing due to a third party's failure to perform. However, for this provision to apply, both the primary party and the third party must fit into the criteria outlined in Article 79(1), namely that each was prevented from performing by an event that was beyond its control, was unreasonable to contemplate in planning the transaction, and could not have been avoided or overcome. For the primary party, the event beyond its control is the inability of the third party to perform.[32]

Example 6-10
As in the case described in Example 6-3, an English buyer had arranged to purchase iron molybdenum from a Belgian seller who in turn was procuring the goods from a supplier in China. When the time for delivery arrived the Belgian seller did not perform. It argued, among other things that its Chinese supplier did not perform and that therefore it should be excused under Article 79. The Belgian court ruled that the failure of a third party to perform only amounts to an impediment under Article 79(2) for the seller where the third party had a qualifying impediment under Article 79(1). Since there was no evidence of that being the case, the Belgian seller was not entitled to rely on the Article 79 exemption. Note that from the time the parties had concluded their contract to the time of the breach, the price for the iron molybdenum had approximately tripled.[33]

Any party wishing to take advantage of the exemption contained in Article 79 must notify its counterparty in a timely manner once the impediment becomes known to it (Article 79(4)). The timing standard is one that is familiar throughout the CISG: "within a reasonable time after the party who fails to perform knew or ought to have known of the impediment" (Article 79(4)). In the event, if the party does not so notify its counterparty, the party will be liable for

---

[31] See problem from the 12th Annual Willem C. Vis Commercial Arbitration Moot at http://www.cisg.law.pace.edu/cisg/moot/moot12.pdf.

[32] See Comment above.

[33] *English Buyer v. German Seller (Iron molybdenum case)*, Oberlandesgericht Hamburg Case 1 U 167/95 (Germany Feb. 28, 1997) (available at http://cisgw3.law.pace.edu/cases/970228g1.html).

any damages that the failure to notify causes. Notice this qualification. The failure to notify does not eliminate the exemption entirely, it merely limits the exemption and makes the breaching party liable for damages that the failure to notify caused. In fact, those damages could be zero even where damages for the non-performance were great.

In addition to the restrictions and qualifications on Article 79 outlined above, it is also instructive to consider Article 50's interaction with this article. Article 79 exempts a party from paying damages, but it does not prevent a party from pursuing any other remedy (Article 79(5)). Article 50 can provide an effective alternative remedy for an injured buyer even where Article 79 applies. Article 50 is available where the seller has delivered goods that do not conform to its contract with buyer. If Article 79 applies to exempt the seller from paying Article 74 damages, the buyer may pursue a reduction in the price it owes to the seller under Article 50.[34]

B.   EXCUSE WHEN FAILURE TO PERFORM IS CAUSED BY COUNTERPARTY

The second exemption from liability for a party that does not perform is found in Article 80. In accordance with that Article, a party is not liable for its non-performance where that non-performance is caused by the counterparty's conduct.

Article 80

A party may not rely on a failure of the other party to perform, to the extent that such failure was caused by the first party's act or omission.

This exemption seems to reflect the notion of comparative fault. If the party seeking a remedy was indeed to blame in some meaningful way for the loss, then that party should not be allowed to recover.

---

[34] Secretariat Commentary Art. 46 [draft counterpart CISG Art. 50] para. 5 ("[E]ven if the seller is excused from paying damages for his failure to perform the contract by virtue of article 65 *[draft counterpart of CISG article 79]*, the buyer may still reduce the price if the goods do not conform with the contract."). Professor Honnold also provides an explanation and example of this phenomenon in his treatise. *See* Honnold, *supra* n. 14, at 334–336.

```
┌─────────────────────────────────────────────────┐
│                  Example 6-11                     │
│ A real estate developer contracted with an electrical supply │
│ company for the fabrication of fuse boxes containing X type │
│ fuses. Despite a no oral modifications clause, the commercial │
│ developer agreed to allow for Y fuses instead of X fuses during a │
│ phone conversation. Unfortunately, the electrical company in │
│ the buyer's country would not connect fuse boxes containing Y │
│ fuses. Subsequently, the buyer claimed damages from the seller │
│ for shipping the goods that did not conform to the parties' │
│ original contract. A tribunal could find that the seller is exempt │
│ because it shipped the fuse boxes containing JS fuses as a result │
│ of the buyer agreeing that such a substitution was acceptable.[35] │
└─────────────────────────────────────────────────┘
```

PROBLEMS

Problem 6-1: J&G delivers 9,000 of 10,000 razors required by its contract with NNM. What remedies are available to NNM under the CISG? Is any one of them preferable? What if J&G had not delivered at all? How does that change your analysis? What if J&G had delivered all 10,000 razors, but they were not the late model, MAK X. Instead they were an earlier model, the MAK V. What then?

Problem 6-2: An American importer orders chocolates from a Belgian confectioner for $25,000. The Belgian seller took responsibility for shipping. The chocolates melt during shipment, reducing their quality and value to $10,000. What damages can the importer recover?

Problem 6-3: Out Front Steak House, a well known American restaurant corporation, purchased beef sirloin from a Canadian supplier for $50,000, without any explanation of how the beef was to be used. The restaurant had intended to serve the beef as steaks but found the meat to be too tough for its standards. Instead, the restaurant spent a further $5,000 to convert the sirloin into ground sirloin to be used for hamburgers, and an additional $2,000 printing up menus that contained the sirloin burgers as an option. It turns out the restaurant prints up menus every month in any event but did have to change its menu listings. In the end, the restaurant recognized only $35,000 in profits from the sale of the burgers, instead of the $200,000 it would have realized if it had been able to sell the beef as steaks. What damages is the restaurant entitled to?

Problem 6-4: An Irish potato farmer's crop is completely destroyed by a parasite. The farmer had entered a contract with an American food company for the sale of

---

[35] See problem from the 14th Annual Willem C. Vis Commercial Arbitration Moot, at
http://www.cisg.law.pace.edu/cisg/moot/moot14.pdf

his crop. Will the farmer breach the contract by failing to deliver the potatoes? Will the farmer be able to claim an exemption from damages under Article 79? Is there any recourse for the buyer in this case? Might there be in some cases?

Problem 6-5: The terrorist attacks of September 11, 2001 caused a New York company to miss delivery deadlines imposed by a contract with a French business. Would the seller be eligible for an exemption under Article 79?

Problem 6-6: Now that the material on the CISG has been presented, review Problem 1-1 and see how your perspective and answers may have changed.

Part III | DISPUTE RESOLUTION

Arbitration of international contract disputes is, in and of itself, a product of *contract*. Parties agree to a binding *procedure* for the resolution of certain disputes—as an *alternative to court adjudication*—ultimately leading to an *enforceable award*. One can quickly see from this description that a complete conception of arbitration requires an examination from multiple perspectives. Arbitration, like the proverbial "Elephant" examined by the "Blind Men,"[1] includes a variety of different attributes and can take on a multitude of appearances, depending on the lens through which it is examined.

To begin with, arbitration is one of a number of forms of *alternative dispute resolution*, by which parties attempt to resolve their disputes without resort to national courts. From this perspective, **Chapter 7** considers the pros and cons of arbitration compared to national court adjudication, as well as a variety of issues parties might consider in drafting an arbitration agreement. Parties will often address these issues by designating a particular set of arbitration rules, and a variety of available sets of rules are introduced. The chapter concludes with a discussion of governing law and the interaction of that law with any designated rules in defining the parties' dispute resolution regime.

Assuming that the parties have agreed to arbitration as a means to decide their disputes, **Chapter 8** next considers the parties' agreement as a matter of *contract*. As in the case of any contract, the parties may disagree on issues relating to the formation, interpretation, or enforceability of their purported agreement to submit their disputes to binding arbitration. In evaluating these questions, one must also consider who should decide them—the courts or the arbitrators—and how and when they should be addressed. As an integral part of this same set of questions,

---

[1] *See* John Godfrey Saxe, *The Blind Men and the Elephant*, in *The Poems of John Godfrey Saxe* 135 (J.R. Osgood ed. 1873) (each of six learned, but sightless, men having come to believe he had a clear idea of the nature of an elephant, when in fact each had only come into contact with a single—and very different—part of the elephant, thereby having a different—and very incomplete—conception of the elephant as a whole). The parable of the blind men and the elephant is generally thought to have originated in India and has been attributed to the Buddha, as well as others. Coincidentally, Professor Park has used this same analogy in reference to arbitration, albeit for the purpose of drawing somewhat different distinctions. *See* William W. Park, *The Specificity of International Arbitration: The Case for FAA Reform*, 36 Vand. J. Transnatl. L. 1241, 1242 n. 1 (2003); William W. Park, *Arbitration of International Business Disputes* 222 n. 1 (Oxford U. Press 2006) (pointing out a broad variety of different types of legal disputes that might be resolved through arbitration).

one must consider the process of constituting the tribunal—again, largely a matter of contract—but a process that must be completed before the arbitrators can decide any of the relevant questions (thus occasionally necessitating resort to the courts for early interim measures). One can quickly begin to see some of the challenges of circularity, which are explored in some depth. Issues involving the separability of the arbitration agreement from the main contract are also considered, as well as any governmental limits on the arbitrability of certain kinds of disputes.

Once the tribunal has been constituted and has decided any threshold questions involving the parties' agreement (including any jurisdictional issues), the parties' focus, and that of **Chapter 9**, shifts to the *procedure* by which the parties' substantive dispute is actually decided. While the procedural issues, like other elements of arbitration, are largely a matter of party intent, the focus here is on the more mechanical elements of these issues. Such elements include, for example, the nature of written submissions, default proceedings, exchanges of information, oral hearings, experts, and the ultimate decision making process of the tribunal.

Finally, **Chapter 10** concludes with questions relating to the legal viability of the arbitrators' decision as an *enforceable and preclusive award* resolving the parties' dispute. Often, parties will voluntarily pay any monetary award. However, to the extent that one or both of the parties may be unhappy with the decision of the arbitrators, they may want to consider two different potential means for rendering the award ineffective. First, a disappointed party may seek to have the award set aside in the courts of the place of arbitration. Second, a disappointed party may seek to avoid enforcement of the award in the courts of the country of attempted enforcement. Both options, as well as their interrelationship, are explored fully.

Each of the above described perspectives on arbitration is of course important and a full understanding of arbitration requires a substantial understanding of all of them—just as a full understanding of the proverbial elephant requires an understanding of all of its parts. The materials that follow will address each in turn.

7 | ARBITRATION AS AN ALTERNATIVE TO NATIONAL COURTS

> Gentlemen, I fervently trust that before long the principle
> of arbitration may win such confidence as to justify its
> extension to a wider field of international differences.
>
> - Henry Campbell-Bannerman (1906)[1]

These materials will address dispute resolution in the context of an international sale of goods.[2] In an international transaction, the seller and buyer of goods are located in different countries and may come from very different business cultures. They may be unfamiliar with each other's legal systems and may even fear potential bias in having disputes adjudicated in each other's national courts. They may be concerned that their respective legal counsel may not be able to represent them in courts outside of their own jurisdictions, and they may be concerned about uncertainties involving jurisdiction, parallel adjudication, or enforceability issues that may arise in the absence of an effective provision for dispute resolution. These uncertainties, coupled with the desire of the parties for a fair and efficient means of resolving their business disputes, will often lead the parties to consider binding arbitration as an alternative to national court adjudication.

A brief reconsideration of the hypothetical first introduced in Chapter 1 provides a useful context as one considers the materials that follow.

---

[1] From "The Duma Is Dead: Long Live the Duma." This speech, on the subject of international peace and conflict resolution among nations, was given by Sir Henry Campbell-Bannerman MP, British Prime Minister, to the 1906 Interparliamentary Conference. It was given from the Royal Gallery of the House of Lords on July 23, 1906 in the French language and translated into English by the author.

[2] International commercial arbitration encompasses a much wider range of disputes, including most business-to-business contracts between private parties and many contracts involving a private party and a State party. For example, the 1966 Convention on the Settlement of Investment Disputes between States and Nationals of Other States (the "Washington Convention" providing for "ICSID" arbitration) allows a foreign investor to bring a claim against a State for governmental actions allegedly depriving the investor of the value of her investment. However, this casebook is primarily focused on the international sale of goods, so our treatment of arbitration will focus on the resolution of commercial disputes involving the international sale of goods.

Example 7-1

Johnson & Gamble ("J&G") is a diversified multi-national consumer products company headquartered in the United States. Its shares are publicly owned and listed on the New York Stock Exchange. NizhnyNorilskMagnetogorsk ("NNM") is a huge Russian conglomerate that manufactures steel, aluminum and nickel. It is partly state owned (75%), and partly privatized (25%). J&G are interested in purchasing steel from NNM in order to make their new MAK X disposable razor blades.

Each of the parties is excited about the opportunity to profit from their proposed business relationship, and their primary focus is on these positive prospects. However, the parties also know that sometimes—despite the best of intentions—disputes may arise in a business relationship. The challenge of resolving such disputes may be particularly acute in international transactions.

In times past—before the end of the "Cold War"—dispute resolution presented significant challenges in transactions involving U.S. and Soviet business parties. These are explored briefly in the historical materials below. Today, Russian legal institutions and business culture have arguably become somewhat more westernized. However, a Russian partially state owned business remains very different from an American multi-national corporation, and the Russian legal and business culture is still very different from that of the United States. These differences present significant challenges in constructing an effective dispute resolution regime. One thing that has remained constant is the parties' frequent choice of arbitration as an effective means of overcoming these differences.

This chapter begins with (I) a brief historical overview and the role of UNCITRAL in the development of modern arbitration, followed by (II) a discussion of the pros and cons of arbitration, generally. Assuming one has decided in favor of arbitration, the next item to consider is (III) the negotiation and drafting of an effective arbitration agreement. As an integral part of this consideration, one must also consider (IV) various bodies of private arbitration "rules," which the parties may incorporate into their agreement by reference, as well as (V) the law governing the arbitration. The chapter concludes with a discussion of the manner in which the parties may, with relative ease, combine the use of private rules with the governing law in constructing an effective arbitration regime.

I.   THE WORK OF UNCITRAL AND THE DEVELOPMENT OF
      MODERN ARBITRATION

While a complete history of arbitration is beyond the scope of this casebook, a brief historical introduction is useful—particularly in understanding the role of UNCITRAL in promoting the development of international commercial arbitration. This introduction begins with (A) a description of the evolution of the UNCITRAL Rules, as well as a useful contextual history that accompanies it. This is followed by (B) a brief description of the work of UNCITRAL in the development and promotion of the two most important bodies of law governing international commercial arbitration—the UNCITRAL Model Law and the New York Convention.

A.   A BRIEF HISTORICAL PERSPECTIVE AND THE DEVELOPMENT OF THE
      UNCITRAL RULES

The use of arbitration for private resolution of individual disputes dates back to early Roman law, which recognized the parties' rights to refer their disputes to an *arbiter* or arbitrator for resolution. This voluntary and consensual reference (a *compromissum*) to a private decision maker was in many ways quite similar to modern arbitration. Modern international commercial arbitration also first began to develop in continental Europe. Likely the most significant early international commercial institution was the International Chamber of Commerce (the "ICC"), which created its International Court of Arbitration in 1923.

The following historical perspective comes from the unique viewpoint of Professor Eric Bergsten, the former Secretary of UNCITRAL:

> Although the ICC is headquartered in Paris, it is not a French institution. Nevertheless, the location of its headquarters impacted the development of the ICC. France, Germany, Switzerland, and other continental parties primarily used the ICC's arbitral facilities while no common-law states, (including the United States and England) participated in the ICC during this period. The ICC became a civil law operation. Lawyers approach arbitration with knowledge of their own legal system, and the ICC rules developed under this premise. In other words, international commercial arbitration developed essentially as an adaptation of the civil law rules of procedure, and not those of the common law known in the United States and England.
>
> International commercial arbitration has undergone a radical change in the past fifty years. At present, both the United States

and England are heavily involved in international commercial arbitration.   International commercial arbitration was first adopted in the United States; it became popular in England later. The initial change in the American attitude toward international commercial arbitration resulted from the major political and economic developments beginning in the 1950s.

. . .

[*As part of the decolonization trend following the Second World War, many of the former colonies began asserting their newly acquired sovereignty by, among other things, nationalizing various private assets (often petroleum reserves) that had been subject to less than favorable agreements negotiated during the prior colonial periods. Many of the resulting disputes ended up in arbitration, and large American law firms were often hired to represent the parties on one or both sides of these substantial and often complex cases.*]

. . .

American lawyers participating in international commercial arbitration brought and used American litigation skills.   The Americans utilized a more aggressive form of advocacy than the continental Europeans were used to in international commercial arbitration.   The European arbitrators tended to be the "Grand Old Men" of the European legal community.   While this is a broad generalization, it is accurate.   The American attorneys tended to be fact-oriented while European attorneys tended to be law-oriented, and wanted to hear more about the appropriate legal theories relevant to the dispute.   A group of American lawyers once had copies of transcripts prepared, at great expense, for the arbitrators.   The arbitrators were not interested in the transcripts and never looked at them.   This exemplified the tremendous differences in legal style and advocacy between the Americans and the Europeans.

One concern since the 1960s has been a perception that the judgments of American courts are not enforced by foreign courts to the extent that the judgments of foreign courts are enforced in the United States.   One solution offered by the American Arbitration Association was that commercial parties should include arbitration clauses in their international contracts. This became more feasible in 1970, after the United States ratified the New York Convention on the Recognition and Enforcement of

Foreign Arbitral Awards (hereinafter New York Convention). The New York Convention assured that an arbitral award would be enforced in other Contracting States, an assurance that was not, and is not, available in regard to the judgments of the courts of the United States. Nevertheless, American participation in international arbitrations continued to be relatively rare.

In the 1970s, the United States increased trade with the Soviet Union and other state-trading countries. The American party was usually a private corporation that required an acceptable, predetermined dispute settlement mechanism. Although disputes over international trade contracts arose in only a small percent of the contracts, it was important for the parties to know how they would be settled. It was obvious that the Soviets would not participate in the American courts, and conversely that the Americans would not participate in the courts in Moscow. The Soviets did not submit trade disputes to their courts, and instead used an arbitral tribunal in Moscow that decided international commercial disputes. The Americans refused to participate in the Soviet arbitral tribunal, and the Soviets refused to participate in ICC arbitration, mainly because they considered the ICC to be the symbol of big-business capitalism.

As a result of evolving international trade affairs between major powers who did not trust each other, a new forum was needed to settle international contract disputes. Arbitration appeared to be the answer. The Soviets were used to the arbitration of trade disputes and the United States had ratified the New York Convention a few years earlier. Furthermore, the Final Act of the Conference on Security and Co-operation in Europe, signed at Helsinki on August 1, 1975, recommended that the participating states suggest "where appropriate, to organizations, enterprises and firms in their countries, to include arbitration clauses in commercial contracts . . . and that the provisions on arbitration should provide for arbitration under a mutually acceptable set of arbitration rules. . . ." The only problem that remained was for the Soviets and Americans to find a mutually acceptable set of arbitration rules. It may not have been a coincidence that the United Nations Commission on International Trade Law (UNCITRAL) was already engaged in drafting recommended rules for *ad hoc*[3] arbitrations. The draft

---

[3] "*Ad hoc*" arbitration does not involve the assistance of a private arbitral institution. In effect, all that is required for *ad hoc* arbitration is an agreement to arbitrate and an arbitrator or arbitrators.

rules were adopted by the UNCITRAL in 1976 as the UNCITRAL Arbitration Rules.

. . .

. . . The agreement in January 1977 between the Soviet Chamber of Commerce and Industry, the American Arbitration Association, and the Stockholm Chamber of Commerce, which provided for the arbitration of U.S.-Soviet trade disputes in Stockholm under the Rules, had a more significant impact on American involvement in international arbitration. While the agreement was made by the arbitration organizations of the three countries, the governmental bodies of each were actively consulted. Sweden modified its existing law to accommodate the anticipated U.S.-Soviet arbitrations.

The Soviet-American agreement was the first of a series of agreements between the American Arbitration Association and foreign arbitral organizations in Central and Eastern European countries. . . .

By the end of the 1970s the United States government had become a strong supporter of international commercial arbitration, and this played a key role when the American-Iranian dispute arose in 1979. . . . [O]n November 4, 1979, the American embassy was seized by radical students and embassy personnel were held hostage. Though some of the hostages were released relatively quickly, fifty-two were held for four hundred-forty four days. This assault on the American embassy became known in the United States as the Iran Hostage Crisis.

There was an important economic element affected by the Iran Hostage Crisis. Iran had approximately $8 billion on deposit in the United States, which were frozen soon after the embassy was seized. On the other hand, there were thousands of American companies that claimed that contracts with Iranian public and private entities had been improperly terminated. . . .

[a tribunal was established to address all of these claims, largely in accordance with the UNCITRAL Arbitration Rules]

While most "rules" are provided by arbitral institutions that also assist in facilitating the arbitration, the UNCITRAL Rules were specifically developed for *ad hoc* arbitration. Of course, they can also be used with institutional arbitration, as long as permitted by the institution (many institutions allow this). The distinction between institutional and *ad hoc* arbitration is explained in more detail in Section IV below, and will be further developed throughout these material on arbitration, generally.

. . . As a result . . . , lawyers representing the private claimants became intimately involved in the arbitration proceedings, and thousands of American lawyers were exposed to the international arbitration of commercial disputes under the Rules. Following this exposure, American lawyers gained an appreciation for international commercial arbitration, viewing it as a way of settling not only ordinary commercial disputes, but also highly contentious disputes with commercial elements.

During the 1960s and 1970s, the American Arbitration Association (AAA) actively promoted international commercial arbitration in the United States, although its principal focus remained labor and other forms of domestic arbitration. By 1986, the AAA had adopted Supplementary Procedures for International Disputes to its Commercial Arbitration Rules. As the American Arbitration Association became more prominent in the field of international commercial arbitration, it created a new division, the International Center for Dispute Resolution (ICDR). The new division took the word "American" out of the title to increase the appearance of neutrality.

By 2005, the American business and legal communities accepted arbitration as the preferred method of settlement of international commercial disputes. Consequently, American lawyers and parties have become significant actors in international arbitration. For example, about one-fourth of the cases heard before the ICC involve an American party. While it may be too much to claim that international commercial arbitration has been Americanized, as the title of this session suggests, the American presence has had an important impact on it.

American lawyers tend to see the courts and arbitration as two different forums for the litigation of commercial disputes, but often they use the same litigation techniques in both. On the other hand, the Europeans tend to litigate before the courts and arbitrate before an arbitrator. While the European "Grand Old Men's" approach to arbitration from fifty years ago is no longer prevalent, there is a general feeling that litigation techniques, in particular procedural disputes, do not belong in arbitration. Nevertheless, the trend in international arbitration is to move towards the American style of litigation. For example, procedural disputes have multiplied, jurisdictional objections are common, and cross-examination is prevalent. While American style discovery remains anathema, the limited discovery procedure discussed in Article 3 of the International Bar Association Rules of Evidence has become commonplace. International commercial arbitrations also permit the interviewing of witnesses, which was traditionally considered unethical. Furthermore, there are many additional procedural issues that have been introduced by American lawyers into international commercial arbitration in recent years.

The international commercial arbitration experience during the last fifty years is analogous to the experience of immigration into a country. Immigrants must adjust to their new country, but the country will also change to accommodate them. This is what happened to international commercial arbitration when the Americans arrived, and things have been evolving ever since.

The foregoing was excerpted from: Eric Bergsten, *The Americanization of International Arbitration*, 18 Pace Intl. L. Rev. 289 (2005) (footnotes, including citations, are omitted).

* * * * *

B.   THE DEVELOPMENT OF THE UNCITRAL MODEL LAW AND THE PROMOTION OF THE NEW YORK CONVENTION

As indicated above, the development of the UNCITRAL Arbitration Rules represented a significant milestone in the historical development of international commercial arbitration. However, these private rules were not, by any means, the only contribution. UNCITRAL was also instrumental in the development of the law governing international commercial arbitration—both in the drafting of the UNCITRAL Model Law and in the active promotion of the New York Convention.

The following is from a presentation by Howard Holtzmann, a delegate of the United States at each of the UNCITRAL sessions described:

UNCITRAL was established by the United Nations in 1966. At that time, the General Assembly, to use the words of one United Nations source, "recognized that disparities in national laws [and practices] created obstacles to the free flow of trade" and assigned to UNCITRAL the goal of removing, or at least lessening, those obstacles. Over the years, to again quote the same United Nations source, UNCITRAL "has come to be the core legal body in the United Nations system" devoted to facilitating international trade.

UNCITRAL's latest activities in the field of dispute resolution are closely related to its earlier projects for improving the laws, procedures and practices for resolving disputes that may arise in international trade transactions. It may, therefore, be useful to review briefly those earlier activities.

The first UNCITRAL project in the field of dispute resolution was the preparation of the UNCITRAL Arbitration Rules, which were completed in 1976. The Rules are widely used by agreement of parties, but even when the parties agree to arbitrate under institutional rules, the UNCITRAL Rules have a major influence because most modern institutional rules resonate with strong echoes of the UNCITRAL Rules, and some, indeed, include key provisions identical to the UNCITRAL text. Further, some new arbitration centers adopt the UNCITRAL text as their institutional rules.

. . .

UNCITRAL's most ambitious program in the field of dispute resolution and perhaps its most influential, was drafting the Model Law on International Commercial Arbitration, which was completed in 1985. It was prepared to assist legislators in reforming and modernizing arbitration laws, and has been enacted both in developed and developing nations, including several states of the United States. In some jurisdictions, the UNCITRAL text has been adopted with almost no changes, while elsewhere its principles and some of its wording have been enacted with modifications to reflect local legal preferences. In any event, the UNCITRAL Model Law is the yardstick by which all arbitration laws are measured.

You may have noticed that I have not mentioned the New York Convention on the Recognition and Enforcement of Foreign Arbitral Awards that is the foundation on which the legal structure of effective international arbitration has been built. The task of drafting the Convention was completed in 1958 before UNCITRAL was born, but since UNCITRAL has come into existence the promotion of the Convention has been an integral part of UNCITRAL's work and all of its texts relating to dispute resolution have been carefully written to take account of the New York Convention.

. . .

> Every one of the UNCITRAL texts that I have mentioned was recommended by the United Nations General Assembly by consensus, without a single voice or vote raised against it by any nation. That is, indeed, remarkable evidence of the broad acceptance that UNCITRAL's work has achieved in this field.

The foregoing was excerpted from Howard M. Holtzmann, *Recent Work on Dispute Resolution by the United Nations Commission on International Trade Law*, 5 J. Intl. & Comp. L. 425 (1999).

* * * * *

Notes and Questions

Note 1: The arbitration materials that follow will focus, in particular, on two important bodies of law: (1) the New York Convention on the Recognition and Enforcement of Arbitral Awards (1958); and (2) the UNCITRAL Model Law on International Commercial Arbitration (1985, as revised 2006).[4] While each represents an important source of law governing international commercial arbitration, it is worthwhile to draw a few distinctions between the two.

The New York Convention is an international treaty that has been ratified by over 140 countries and therefore amounts to binding law in almost every important trading nation around the world. Although the New York Convention was prepared by the United Nations prior to the establishment of UNCITRAL, the promotion of the Convention has been an integral part of the Commission's work.

The Model Law, however, is a model for national legislation, which may be adopted by individual countries (sometimes with minor changes) as national law governing international commercial arbitration. The Model Law has been so adopted in over fifty countries[5] and in seven U.S. states.[6] The Model Law also represents a typical modern arbitration statute and, as such, provides an excellent

---

[4] A number of significant provisions of these two legal instruments are included within the textual materials that follow. However, a complete copy of each instrument is essential to understanding the interrelationships between the various provisions and the legal instrument as a whole. Copies of each can each be found at: http://www.uncitral.org/uncitral/en/uncitral_texts/arbitration.html.

[5] *See* app. A (for a list of jurisdictions, by geographic region).

[6] California, Connecticut, Illinois, Louisiana, North Carolina, Oregon, and Texas have all adopted state laws governing international commercial arbitration based on the Model Law. However, the Federal Arbitration Act, governing arbitration in the United States, generally, is not typical of modern arbitration statutes and is quite different from the Model Law. Questions involving the application of federal versus state law in international arbitrations conducted within the United States raise some interesting and sometimes challenging issues. However, these issues are largely beyond the scope of this book, which is focused primarily on modern legal regimes governing international commercial arbitration rather than the somewhat arcane Federal Arbitration Act.

focal point for consideration of various legal issues arising in the context of arbitration. Thus, while occasionally addressing national variations, these materials will focus primarily on the Model Law, as if enacted and controlling authority for purposes of the issues to be considered.[7]

Note 2: Various sets of arbitration "Rules" are also considered, beginning in section IV below. While not technically necessary for the resolution of a dispute through arbitration (the governing law will typically provide for a basic set of default legal rules), the majority of arbitrations are conducted pursuant to a set of pre-established private rules expressly chosen by the parties.

Law versus Rules

The distinction between the "law" governing the arbitration and the "rules" chosen by the parties is an important one and is more fully developed below. However, the distinction is worth noting here at the outset. For example, one must distinguish between the UNCITRAL Model Law and the UNCITRAL Rules each introduced above. The Model Law is a model for legislation to be adopted by a state sovereign; whereas, the Rules are one of many available bodies of private arbitration rules that may be adopted by the parties to an arbitration agreement. This distinction is developed further in sections IV and V below.

Today, the natural effects of cross-cultural interaction and exchanges have given rise to an international arbitration practice reflecting elements of common and civil law traditions, as well as differing national legal perspectives. The efforts of UNCITRAL have helped to channel these evolving practical norms into more consistent and unified international standards applicable to the drafting, enforcement, application, and recognition of agreements to resolve international commercial disputes through arbitration. The materials that follow will explore the content of these standards.

---

[7] To facilitate analysis of the Model Law—particularly in the presentation of Problems—this casebook will sometimes employ the mythical city and country of Vindobona, Danubia, as the parties' chosen place of arbitration. Danubia has adopted—exactly as written—the UNCITRAL Model Law on International Commercial Arbitration (1985, as revised 2006), selecting Article 7, *Option 1*, and designating the Commercial Court of Vindobona, Danubia under Article 6. Those familiar with the Vis International Commercial Arbitration Moot will recognize Vindobona as the mythical jurisdiction in which the Moot is held each year.

II. EVALUATING THE PROS AND CONS OF ARBITRATION

The popularity of arbitration as a means of resolving international business disputes continues to grow, and it has in many circumstances displaced national courts as the preeminent means of binding dispute resolution. However, arbitration is not a panacea without any challenges of its own. Under certain circumstances, national court adjudication may in fact be preferable to arbitration. An attorney must, therefore, understand both (A) the reasons in favor of choosing arbitration and (B) the reasons against choosing arbitration. Lastly, one should recognize that (C) considerations of cost may cut both directions—either favoring arbitration or not—depending on the circumstances and depending on one's focus.

A. REASONS FOR CHOOSING ARBITRATION

In international business transactions, the parties are often particularly interested in arbitration (1) for its perceived neutrality. Unlike national courts, the members of an arbitral panel do not necessarily have ties to any particular country, and a panel of three arbitrators is often chosen from multiple countries. Arbitration awards are also typically (2) much easier to enforce in a country other than that in which the award is rendered based on the wide acceptance of the New York Convention. The parties might choose arbitration for a variety of additional reasons, including, but not limited to, (3) confidentiality, (4) the expeditiousness of the decision making process, and/or (5) the expertise of the decision makers.

1. Neutrality

In an international transaction, the parties may fear that they will not receive fair treatment if disputes are resolved in the other party's national courts. While many national courts are likely quite fair in adjudicating disputes involving foreign parties, instances of bias and unfair treatment certainly exist. Moreover, the parties' concerns are quite real and, therefore, provide the impetus to seek a neutral alternative. Arbitration provides just such a neutral alternative.

The parties may choose a neutral place of arbitration, a neutral set of rules and/or institution to administer the arbitration, and a neutral arbitrator or arbitrators. Through a combination of these choices, the parties can construct a dispute resolution mechanism that provides each with the confidence that any dispute will be decided in a cultural neutral and unbiased forum. Moreover, the place of arbitration need not be in the expected place of enforcement (often the home country of one of the parties).

2.   Enforceability

A judicial decision by a national court may or may not be enforceable outside of the country from which the decision originates, and, even if enforceable, the process may be time consuming, costly, and uncertain. By contrast, the New York Convention provides for relatively simple and predictable enforcement of arbitration awards in any of each of the Convention's many member States. Thus, an award made in France will be easily enforceable in China, subject only to a very narrow set of exceptions under Convention Article V.

In many instances, a party to an arbitration agreement will promptly and voluntarily pay any award rendered by the tribunal against the party. However, if a party refuses to pay an award, then the prevailing party will need to ask a court to issue a judicial order requiring payment by the recalcitrant losing party. If the award is issued within a country in which the losing party has sufficient assets to satisfy the obligation, then enforcement will be quite easy (as would enforcement of an original decision by a national court). However, if the losing party's assets are all located in countries other than the one in which the dispute is decided (this will often be the case), then the international enforcement of the award becomes crucial.

This symbiotic combination of the neutrality of an arbitral forum and international enforceability of arbitration awards is arguably the single most important factor favoring arbitration of international commercial disputes.[8] A neutral and enforceable dispute resolution mechanism goes a long way towards reducing many of the inherent risks of international business. When one considers the substantial benefits of an effective dispute resolution mechanism, along with the benefits of uniform substantive law, such as the CISG, the importance of the work of UNCITRAL comes into very clear focus.

3.   Confidentiality

Commercial parties will also frequently place a high premium on confidentiality in their business dealings—especially in the event of a dispute. For example, a seller of goods would typically like to avoid the publicity of a claim by one of its

---

[8] The Hague Convention on Choice of Court Agreements, 20th Diplomatic Session, adopted June 30, 2005 may provide similar opportunities for the parties to choose courts they perceive as neutral and enforce the resulting judgments internationally. *See* Ronald Brand, Presentation, *The New Hague Convention on Choice of Court Agreements*, ASIL Insights, American Society of International Law (Am. Socy. Intl. L., Washington, D.C., July 26, 2005). If this convention achieves wide acceptance, it will be interesting to see how it may affect the parties' choices of dispute resolution forums in various kinds of contracts.

customers that its products are "defective."[9] Or, from the opposite perspective, a buyer might prefer to avoid public claims that it is not meeting its payment obligations, perhaps leading others to wonder if buyer's claims of non-conforming products are real or are merely an excuse offered by a financially troubled buyer. As a result, many businesses will prefer to resolve their contract disputes privately and confidentially, outside of the public eye. Arbitration can provide a significant measure of confidentiality, whereas court proceedings are typically quite public.[10]

4.   Speed/Efficiency

For business parties, in particular, time and energy spent in dispute resolution is generally time spent away from the profit making activities of the business. Time spent engaging in a dispute with a business partner is also generally time spent damaging a business relationship rather than building and benefiting from that relationship. As a result, the parties to a commercial agreement will almost always prefer a dispute resolution mechanism that quickly and efficiently resolves their dispute and allows them to get back to business. Arbitration provides such a streamlined process, resolving the parties' dispute fully and finally, without many of the protracted procedural battles, crowded dockets, and protracted appeals more typical of national court systems.

Like confidentiality, the degree of speed and efficiency may vary with the parties' agreement, including any choice of institution and or rules. For example, some institutions expressly provide for fast track arbitration with shortened procedural time frames. Conversely, the parties may, in their agreement, attempt to provide for expanded appellate review.[11] The benefits of speed and efficiency may also be lost, to at least some degree, if one of the parties challenges the validity of the arbitration agreement.

---

[9] While CISG Article 35 uses the less disparaging term, "non-conformity" to address breach of the seller's obligations to deliver proper goods, the parties' own characterizations will often be a bit more inflammatory.

[10] As noted below, however, the degree of confidentiality varies, depending on the parties' agreement, including any choice of arbitration rules. In any case, some degree of confidentiality may be lost if the parties to an arbitration agreement end up seeking redress in national courts.

[11] The effectiveness of such a provision is currently an open question under the American Federal Arbitration Act. *See Hall Street Associates, L.L.C. v. Mattel, Inc.,* 127 S. Ct. 2875 (2007) (granting petition for certiorari on issue of parties' right to contract for expanded appellate review in the context of arbitration).

5.   Expertise

In many national court systems, judges are expected to hear a wide range of legal disputes, often including both civil and criminal matters. In such circumstances, it is probably unreasonable to expect a high degree of expertise from a judge in any particular legal area, much less any particular trade or factual context.[12] Parties may, however, choose arbitrators based precisely on relevant legal or factual expertise. While parties will often choose arbitrators from the legal profession, they may also choose non-lawyers, focusing instead on expertise in a particular trade or profession. Whatever the parties' focus and whatever the nature of the dispute, arbitration offers the parties far greater opportunities to choose a decision maker possessing a high degree of expertise related to the particular sort of dispute at issue.

B.   Reasons for Not Choosing Arbitration

Notwithstanding all of the benefits described above, arbitration also presents certain risks and challenges, which may, under certain circumstances, dictate a different choice. The parties to an arbitration agreement (1) will sometimes be unable to join additional claims, and third parties cannot be required to participate in arbitration without express consent; (2) court involvement may be required during the arbitral process; and (3) an erroneous decision by the arbitrators is not generally subject to appeal. All of these factors must be considered by the parties in deciding whether or not arbitration is appropriate for the transaction in question.

1.   Inability to Join Additional Parties or Claims

Many business contracts are simply elements of a larger series of transactions. For example, a buyer in one transaction may resell the goods in the next, or a buyer may purchase raw materials from a variety of sellers in order to manufacture goods for its own buyers. In many such transactions, a dispute between the parties to one contract may necessarily implicate issues arising from other contracts, some of which may involve the same parties and some of which may not. However, where each individual dispute is a part of a larger case or controversy (potentially involving multiple relationships), such disputes are typically best resolved on a global basis in order to avoid inconsistent decisions involving the same overall dispute.

---

[12] Whatever their merits in certain circumstances, juries common in the United States are even less likely to possess any particularized legal or relevant factual expertise.

In legal actions before national courts, such issues involving complex cases can often be addressed through a court's inherent powers to join claims and/or parties under certain circumstances. However, arbitration is based entirely on the consent of the parties, thereby dramatically limiting the potential for joining parties and claims absent consent. Of course, such consent becomes far more difficult to obtain once a dispute has arisen. While the issue can sometimes be addressed in advance with common arbitration provisions in separate contracts, parties often fail to address it in advance—either for lack of foresight or lack of agreement.

2.   Potential Need for Court Involvement

In an ideal world, parties to an arbitration agreement would never need to set foot in a national court. Unfortunately, the world of arbitration is not an ideal world, and even a well drafted arbitration agreement will not always avoid at least some level of involvement by the courts. For example, one of the parties may attempt to bring a court action—irrespective of the agreement to arbitrate. If so, the parties may be required to engage in litigation over the arbitration agreement, either in a parallel proceeding, or perhaps before a panel of arbitrators is even formed to address their substantive dispute on the merits.

Even if neither party contests the arbitration agreement, a party seeking specific relief or preservation of evidence may need to do so before the tribunal is formed, in which case resort to a court may be necessary. And even if the tribunal is available for such relief, its interim award is not likely enforceable without converting it to a court order in the jurisdiction of enforcement. Moreover, a final award is subject to court review, albeit limited, and court assistance is needed for enforcement, unless the award is paid voluntarily. Thus, an arbitration agreement may—notwithstanding other elements of efficiency— require a certain level of inconvenience and redundancy in involving national courts in issues that are otherwise subject to arbitration.

3.   Lack of a Right to Appeal

One of the benefits of arbitration is its relatively quick progress to a final and binding conclusion. A significant element of this benefit is the non-appealability (except on very limited grounds) of the tribunal's final award. However, this benefit necessarily carries with it a corresponding burden. A disappointed party will typically be stuck with the tribunal's decision—even where that decision is clearly wrong on the law, the facts, or both.[13]

There is also a perception among some that arbitrators may be more inclined to render compromise decisions (e.g., the Solomonic notion of "splitting the baby"), perhaps without complete regard for controlling legal authority.[14] Whether such solutions are better or worse than those more closely adhering to a legalistic approach will often depend on one's perspective.

In effect, an agreement to final resolution of disputes through arbitration to at least some degree places a higher value on speed, efficiency, and finality than on reaching an absolutely correct decision on the application of controlling law to the facts. Under certain circumstances, this balance between prompt finality and getting the "right result" may militate against arbitration.

C.   THE QUESTION OF COST

The cost of arbitration may favor or disfavor arbitration, depending on the circumstances of the dispute. In view of its somewhat mixed effect, the question of cost is treated here separately.

In terms of the cost of the tribunal itself, arbitration will almost always be more expensive because the parties must pay the arbitrators. National court judges, by comparison, are typically paid for by local taxpayers. In the case of institutional arbitration, the parties must also pay the institution for its services. Thus, one begins from the perspective that arbitration is more costly than court adjudication. Arbitration, however, will very often result in other cost savings that will more than offset the additional costs of the tribunal.

While arbitration may increase the cost of the tribunal, it will often reduce the cost of attorneys' fees by virtue of its streamlined procedures. Arbitration provides at least the opportunity for a less adversarial and less protracted process of presenting and advocating the respective claims defenses of the parties. To the

---

[13] As an exception to this general rule, the United States Supreme Court has added a judicially created doctrine under the Federal Arbitration Act allowing for vacation of a tribunal's decision "in manifest disregard of the law." *See Wilco v. Swan,* 346 U.S. 427 (1953) (first suggesting the potential application of the standard as a basis for vacating an arbitration award). Interestingly, the international arbitration community views this exception far more negatively than positively. *See* William Park, *The Specificity of International Arbitration: The Case for FAA Reform,* 36 Vand. J. Transnatl. L. 1241 (2003) (explaining that the international arbitration community is generally very wary of the "manifest disregard" standard applied by American courts).

[14] Such an approach may be entirely appropriate if the parties have expressly provided that the arbitrators shall decide the issue *ex aequo et bono* (as a matter of equity), but the parties more typically expect the arbitrators to make their decision by applying the relevant substantive law to the facts of the case.

extent that such opportunities are realized, the cost of the parties' legal counsel may be substantially reduced.

Perhaps even more importantly, time is money to a business party. To the extent that the parties are able to bring their dispute to a final resolution more quickly and efficiently, they will undoubtedly save substantial costs in terms of the lost employee time and lost business focus that are often associated with legal actions brought in court. For most business parties, this will likely make arbitration substantially more cost effective, overall, than national court adjudication.

Of course these time and cost savings will often require at least some degree of cooperation between the parties after the dispute has arisen. Either of the parties, or their counsel, may engage in tactics intended to delay or otherwise obstruct the prompt completion of the dispute resolution process. If so, much of the anticipated savings of both time and money may be lost.

In deciding whether arbitration is the most appropriate dispute resolution mechanism for any particular transaction or commercial relationship, the parties and their counsel will need to consider all of the above issues carefully. There is no single correct answer for all commercial disputes.

Tipping the Balance in International Transactions: Neutrality and Enforceability

Most of the above pros and cons would apply with equal force in the context of arbitration of commercial disputes between business parties from the same country. However, neutrality and enforceability—each of which have little relevance in domestic arbitration—arguably serve as "super factors" in often tipping the balance strongly in favor of arbitration in international transactions.

PROBLEMS

Problem 7-1: What sorts of international commercial transactions might be most suitable for arbitration? Why?

Problem 7-2: What sorts of transactions might be least suitable for arbitration? Why? In these latter transactions, is there some way a party might be able to avoid any potential pitfalls of arbitration in the context of these transactions, while maintaining its benefits?

III.   NEGOTIATING AND DRAFTING AN EFFECTIVE ARBITRATION
        AGREEMENT

In considering the construction of an effective arbitration regime, this section first considers the contextual differences between (A) arbitration agreements concluded before a dispute arises and those concluded after a dispute has already arisen. This is followed by consideration of (B) the content of an arbitration agreement concluded as part of the main contract.

A.   DECIDING ON ARBITRATION—BEFORE OR AFTER A DISPUTE ARISES

Arbitration agreements are generally divided into two basic groups: those concluded before a dispute arises; and those concluded after a dispute has already arisen. The first, a pre-dispute arbitration agreement, is often referred to as an *ex ante* agreement or a *clause compromissiore*. It is often found in a dispute resolution clause (or section) within the parties' broader commercial agreement—*e.g.*, a contract for the sale of goods. Parties to a series of transactions may also draft a master dispute resolution agreement applicable to all of their transactions, or may simply adopt by reference the provision of an earlier agreement.

Alternatively, the parties may decide, after a dispute has already arisen, to submit their dispute to arbitration. This post-dispute arbitration agreement is often referred to as an *ex post* agreement or a *compromise*. In many ways, this sort of arbitration agreement is much easier to construct, because the parties will likely know a good deal about the nature of their dispute. Presumably, they can structure the arbitration accordingly, in a manner that is ideally suited for this dispute. Having done so, the parties are likely to proceed directly to the merits of their dispute under the agreed upon procedures. The challenge, of course, is reaching any such agreement to arbitrate after the dispute has arisen. Once a dispute arises that the parties cannot resolve through negotiation, it is often difficult for them to reach agreement on anything else, and the dispute frequently ends up in a court or courts. In view of these challenges, pre-dispute arbitration provisions are far more typical, and this casebook will focus on arbitration provisions included within the parties' basic contract for the sale of goods.

While a post-dispute arbitration agreement may be difficult to agree upon, at least the parties each understand the nature of the dispute they are seeking to resolve. In the case of the typical pre-dispute arbitration agreement, the parties are likely attempting to provide for a broad range of potential disputes that may arise in relation to their broader agreement. As such, these pre-dispute arbitration clauses may be somewhat more challenging as exercises in clairvoyance. Perhaps even more importantly, the parties to a commercial agreement have little interest in talking about dispute resolution when negotiating their broader agreement.

The seller and buyer in a typical sale of goods are far more interested in the prospects of a successful and profitable business relationship than in dealing with the vague possibility—one they would often rather not even acknowledge—that some sort of irreconcilable dispute may later arise between them. A contracting partner that wants to talk about the details of a dispute resolution clause might well be viewed as someone who is difficult to work with and has a propensity towards legal actions when problems arise. If so, the negotiation of an arbitration provision might be seen as detrimental to the business relationship before it even begins—perhaps even effectively killing the overall deal. As a result, the development of an effective pre-dispute agreement to arbitrate presents a unique set of challenges. These challenges are addressed below.

B.   CONSIDERING THE CONTENT OF THE ARBITRATION AGREEMENT

In thinking about an effective arbitration agreement, one is generally trying to anticipate and address issues that might arise in the event arbitration is required. In this sense, an arbitration agreement is similar to any other contract. However, an arbitration agreement is a unique form of contract and, as such, will often raise a unique set of issues. The following materials address some of these issues and also provide a useful preview of many of the questions that will be addressed in the remainder of the arbitration materials in Part III.

The following excerpt comes from "Drafting Arbitration Clauses in International Agreements – a guide for European lawyers,"

Edward Lestrade

Introduction

Increasingly, in Europe, the parties to international commercial agreements are specifying arbitration as the primary means of dispute resolution. . . .

. . .

In that regard, this paper intends to provide a background summary and a checklist for drafters to assist them in the construction of the desirable and effective contents of arbitration clauses in agreements that primarily concern international commerce.

. . .

Constructing the Arbitration Clause

Enforceability

Firstly, the parties must also ensure that the award granted by the tribunal will be enforceable. Therefore checks should be made that the country where enforcement is likely to be sought is a contracting state to the New York Convention, or other treaty which provides for the enforcement of foreign arbitral awards.

Arbitration Clause to be in Writing

The Convention and most arbitration courts require that the arbitration agreement is to be contained in a written document signed by the parties. As such oral arbitration clauses are not effective.

Choice of Law

In international commercial agreements, there will be at least 2 jurisdictions involved. . . . . As the parties are in different jurisdictions, they are free to choose which law will govern their agreement. . . . Where the parties do not specify a choice of law, then this matter will be left to the arbitrator who will have regard to the default rules of the arbitration court/ institution where this applies and of the applicable treaty in force.

Provisions could also be made in the agreement to allow the arbitrator to make such interlocutory decisions relating, say to the giving of security to cover the expected costs of either of the parties.

Extent of Court Intervention

It may become necessary for a party, or the parties to approach a court within the territory of the seat of the arbitration for the purposes of obtaining an interlocutory, or interim order. Therefore, the extent to which this is permitted should be specified in the agreement. However, it should be noted that the rules of most arbitral institutions provide for the circumstances where such a national court may intervene, but these standard provisions may not suit the parties and the drafter is encouraged to examine such rules prior to accepting them as the as the default rules.[15]

Choice of Procedural Rules [Ad Hoc or Institutional Arbitration]

Generally, the parties will need to decide whether the arbitration procedure will be 'Ad hoc', or 'Institutional'. Where the arbitration is 'Ad hoc', the parties themselves decide on the procedure of arbitration proceedings.[16] Where institutional arbitration is chosen, the procedure [is] set by the [rules of the] relevant institution. However, the parties are free to vary them where the institution is agreeable. Where the parties have chosen institutional arbitration, the place of arbitration is usually the seat of the institution.[17] However, in *ad hoc* arbitration, the parties are able to decide that the arbitral proceedings may be conducted wherever they wish. The parties may choose from a wide selection of rules of procedure, including those of the national jurisdiction.[18] The rules of the arbitral institution can be used either specifically, or by default (depending on the provisions of the agreement for arbitration services), or in amended form by the parties.

The drafter of the rules clause should be a lawyer familiar with the rules of the more reputable arbitral courts/ or institutions and also the procedural rules of the national courts which may have review jurisdiction over the dispute, and the procedural rules of the place/ country where the arbitration is seated.

---

[15] Casebook Authors' Note: One might also consider the law governing the arbitration, or *lex arbitri*, on the issue of interim relief. See e.g., Model Law Article 9, as well as the new provisions included in Model Law Article 17 as a part of the 2006 revisions.

[16] Casebook Authors' Note: The parties may do this by developing their own procedure, or they may adopt a set of rules designed for *ad hoc* arbitration, such as the UNCITRAL Rules. *See supra* sec. IV.

[17] Casebook Authors' Note: This is not necessarily true with respect to most major institutions. For example, parties will often choose institutional arbitration with the ICC, but will establish the place of arbitration outside of France. However, this concern remains noteworthy inasmuch as there are still a few institutions that will only administer cases choosing the institution's home country as the place of arbitration.

[18] Casebook Authors' Note: Again, it is important to distinguish between legal rules (positive law of the sovereign, even if only a legal default rule) and private rules (solely invoked by way of party consent). It is not entirely clear which the author is speaking of here, perhaps because he may be referencing rules of former State institutions in Eastern Europe. In many of those institutions, the lines between private and State "rules" were somewhat blurred, as most arbitral institutions were organs of the State.

Language of the proceedings

It is important to specify the language of the proceedings. This is especially important in international settings so as to provide for coherence in the proceedings.

Specification of the Place and Nature of the Arbitration

An arbitration clause should be certain where and how disputes will be resolved.

Where the arbitration clause is valid, and the ensuing dispute is within its scope and determinable by arbitration, then either party is able to obtain the intervention of a national court to stay any proceedings initiated by the opposing party in contradiction of the arbitration agreement. If the parties fail to agree on a place of arbitration, then the arbitrator is able to choose the seat on their behalf, but will need to consider: the implied intention of the parties, convenience of the parties, choice of law by the parties, and other similar factors.

Generally, the procedural rules of the place of arbitration dictate the procedure of the arbitration and collateral issues. As such, the drafter should ensure that the seat of the arbitration is specific in the arbitration clause as failure to do so, often causes delays in the start of the arbitration process. It could also be used by a party reluctant to the arbitration, to stall and delay the arbitration process.

Upon specifying the seat, it is crucial to determine what assistance the local courts would be prepared to give to the arbitral tribunal, by way of securing evidence, issuing subpoenas for witnesses if required, granting orders for the inspection of property, and other such matters relevant to the settlement of the dispute.

The drafter should be aware that confidentiality issues should be addressed in the agreement as the procedural rules regarding proceedings generally do not automatically cover this issue.

Parties to be aware of 'No Appeal' from Arbitrator's Decision

The drafter should ensure that the parties are aware that the arbitrator's award will be final and binding on them, with a very limited right of appeal or review. However, different national legal systems do have differing views in this regard. However, those states that have signed the New York Convention, have very little scope to review international arbitration awards, and are compelled to order a stay of all proceedings contravening the provisions of international arbitration clauses.

Appointment of the Arbitrator

The various arbitration institutions provide for the procedures for the appointment of arbitrators. As such, the drafter must be familiar with the appointment procedures these institutions. The default scenario is that where this is not specified in the arbitration clause, the rules of the institution will prevail. However, the parties are also free to select the arbitrators by specifying their own procedures provided, where an institution is engaged, the institution is amenable to that.

The parties should also agree on the number of arbitrators, as certain institutions provide that in the absence of such agreement, the parties will be assumed to have chosen three arbitrators and of course, the more arbitrators, generally, the more costly the proceedings are.

Costs of Arbitration

The costs of the arbitration are largely dependent on the type of arbitration procedure selected and on the institution chosen. So the drafter should make some price comparisons prior to the selection of an institution.

Scope of Arbitral Clause in respect of the Parties Concerned with the Agreement

In agreements where there is likely to be more than one party to a transaction, for example, where sub-contractors are concerned, it will be useful to provide for all parties to the agreement to be the arbitration clause. The drafter should also provide for multiple arbitrations concerning the same cause of action or to the same subject matter, to be able to be consolidated into a single hearing.

Eisemann's Arbitration Clause Drafting Criteria

Frederic Eisemann who served as Secretary General of the ICC International Court of Arbitration proposed certain criteria as essential in respect of the functions of an arbitration clause.

The first should specify compulsory consequences for the parties with regard to the procedure for dispute resolution within their agreement. These consequences would include the obligation to submit the dispute to arbitration, the procedures for so doing and to regard the arbitrator's award as final and binding.

The second criterion excludes the intervention of a state's court in the settlement of a dispute, prior to the decision of the arbitrator. However, it may be useful to provide for a certain level of state court's intervention where, for example, interlocutory relief is required and its award is beyond the authority of the arbitrator, or arbitration court. This could refer to: the issuing of subpoenas; searching, or freezing orders, etc.

The third criterion provides to give the arbitrators authority to resolve the disputes under the agreement. These powers could include the authority to make various procedural and interim orders.

The fourth envisages the putting in place of a system that provides of the optimum conditions for effective and speedy determination of the arbitration which can be enforced by a state's court.

Eisemann's 'Pathological Clauses'

According to Eisemann, bad clauses are "pathological". For example, often the description of the seat of the arbitration is incorrect. The effect of this clause may result in a collateral dispute regarding the seat of the arbitration which would need to be resolved by the arbitrator or by a court – all this will certainly add to the costs of the arbitration. Other frequent errors are the failure of the arbitral clause to specify issues concerning the applicable procedural rules, the number of arbitrators and the applicable substantive law. The 'pathologens' can be used by a defaulting party to delay the arbitral process.

Care should be taken in limiting the application or the scope of the arbitration unnecessarily. For example: 'issues arising out of the performance of the agreement are to be referred to arbitration' – this would have the effect of specifying only 'performance' issues for arbitration, whereas: 'all disputes arising in connection with the agreement', would have a wider and more complete scope.

When an appointing authority (for the arbitration court, or arbitrator) care must be taken to ensure that the appointing authority is able (and willing) to make the appointment. Again, it is important to determine whether the appointing authority will require and receive any fees for its appointment role and in that case how the fees will be met. Such defects would mean that the parties would need to have the issues decided by a state court – again adding unnecessary costs to the arbitral clause.

Generally, pathogens can be resolved upon application to a state court; however, there are costs and delays which will normally lessen the efficacy of the choice of dispute resolution via arbitration.

Finally, it is important for drafters to appreciate that arbitration agreements need to contain detailed and clear provisions about how the dispute will be resolved. Failure to do so can result in significant delays where a party is reluctant to cooperate in the dispute-resolution process.

Summary

Drafters of arbitration clauses should bear in mind Eisemann's principles. Imprecision and any ambiguity should be scrupulously avoided. Clauses should be kept simple without being vague. The place of the arbitration should be chosen carefully. . . .

. . .

In order for arbitration clause to serve its purpose, the parties themselves should pay adequate attention to the wording of the arbitration clause. The arbitration clauses should be drafted depending on the type, scale and complexity of the possible dispute, the location, language and culture of the parties, the advantages and disadvantages of the respective substantive and procedural laws.

Generally, it is very difficult to specify which of the particular elements of the arbitration clause the most important one is. Each of them compliment each other and is dependent on others, however, it is hoped that this article will give drafters a wider perspective for the efficiency of arbitration clauses in international commercial agreements.

Drafting Arbitration Clauses in International Agreements—A Guide for European lawyers, Dr Edward Lestrade, K.OSt.J, LLB, MA, DrJurSc, Associate Director & Lead Counsel, Lestrade Law Associates LLC.

* * * * *

A Checklist for an Arbitration Agreement
____ Clear and unequivocal commitment to final and binding arbitration[19]
____ Scope of the range of disputes subject to arbitration
____ Place or seat of arbitration
____ Applicable procedural law (*lex arbitri*)[20]
____ Applicable substantive law (law governing main contract)
____ Language of arbitration
____ Name of administering institution (or *ad hoc* arbitration)
____ Arbitration rules
____ Number of arbitrators
____ Method of choosing arbitrators
____ Arbitrator qualifications, including any neutrality requirements[21]
____ Designation of an appointing authority to assist in constituting the tribunal if the parties fail
____ Arbitrator compensation arrangements
____ Confidentiality requirements (including award publication)
____ Discovery and other procedural issues (e.g., evidentiary rules, expert testimony, examination of fact witnesses)
____ Availability of interim measures
____ Multi-party and multi-claim consolidation

---

[19] Arbitration is sometimes confused by lay persons with other private means of dispute resolution such as meditation or conciliation. However, true arbitration is different from all of these other forms of dispute resolution in one crucial respect. In arbitration, the parties agree in advance (typically in advance of the dispute itself, and always in advance of the tribunal's decision) to be bound by the tribunal's decision, while in other forms of dispute resolution, the parties retain at least some level of autonomy in accepting or rejecting any proposed resolution.

[20] The *lex arbitri* is distinguished here from the place of arbitration, or *lex loci arbitri*, simply for analytical purposes. As further explained below, however, these will almost always be the same, and any decision by the parties to the contrary may give rise to significant complications.

[21] While international practice has moved strongly towards a model requiring neutrality of all arbitrations, some systems, including the American one, may in some circumstances still contemplate party appointed arbitrators that are not subject to a strict requirement of neutrality. This issue is further addressed in Chapter 8.

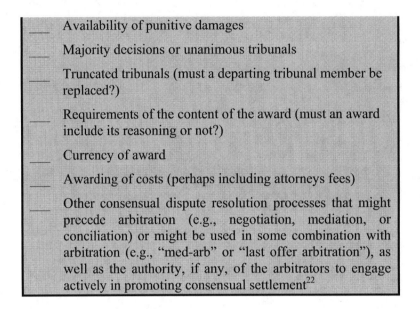

____ Availability of punitive damages

____ Majority decisions or unanimous tribunals

____ Truncated tribunals (must a departing tribunal member be replaced?)

____ Requirements of the content of the award (must an award include its reasoning or not?)

____ Currency of award

____ Awarding of costs (perhaps including attorneys fees)

____ Other consensual dispute resolution processes that might precede arbitration (e.g., negotiation, mediation, or conciliation) or might be used in some combination with arbitration (e.g., "med-arb" or "last offer arbitration"), as well as the authority, if any, of the arbitrators to engage actively in promoting consensual settlement[22]

Notes and Questions

Note 1: The above list represents the authors' own suggested checklist of issues that one might, at least theoretically, want to consider in drafting an arbitration agreement. This list includes many of the raised in the previous article, and includes additional items as well. While quite lengthy, it is not necessarily comprehensive in view of the broad ranges of issues that might, perhaps, arise in the arbitration of an international commercial dispute

Note 2: Having read the previous article and examined the above list, one may be thinking that an arbitration clause must be a lengthy and complex agreement all by itself—in addition to whatever complexities exist within the main contract. Is it realistic to expect the parties (or even their counsel) to negotiate terms addressing all of these issues, while simultaneously negotiating their main contract? Perhaps surprisingly (or perhaps not), most arbitration agreement are in practice quite short. Consider the recommended arbitration clauses that follow in the next section.

---

[22] The potential combination of arbitration with other consensual forms of dispute resolution is, itself, a substantial and important topic, but one that is beyond the scope of this casebook. For more complete treatment of the subject, *see* Alan Redfern and Martin Hunter, *Law and Practice of International Commercial Arbitration* §§ 1-69 to 1-96 (4th ed., 2004).

IV.   INSTITUTIONAL AND *AD HOC* ARBITRATION RULES

Rather than drafting a long and complex arbitration agreement, the parties can instead simply designate and incorporate a "pre-drafted" body of procedural "rules." As explained earlier, these are private rules are employed only if chosen by the parties. In this respect, private "rules" are different from the "law" or "legal rules," which are enacted by a sovereign state. The relationship between the arbitration rules and law is very much like the relationship between Incoterms and the CISG discussed earlier in Chapter 4.[23] The materials that follow begin with (A) an introduction to private rules and institutions and then provide (B) a variety of sample arbitration clauses.

A.   PRIVATE RULES AND ARBITRAL INSTITUTIONS

With the growth of international commercial arbitration, the number of institutional providers of arbitration has grown as well. Virtually every major trading country serves as the home to one or more major arbitral institutions that organize and provide rules for international commercial arbitration. These institutions assist the parties in facilitating the arbitration in a variety of ways, many of which are discussed in Chapters 8 and 9. In addition, an institution will provide a pre-drafted set of rules that address many of the issues raised in section III above. The rules of different arbitral institutions may be similar in some respects and quite different in others. Thus, the choice of an institution and its rules may ultimately have a significant effect on the content of the parties' arbitration agreement.[24]

Throughout the arbitration materials in Part III, frequent reference will be made to various institutional rules. Specific rules will be used to highlight and compare the resolution of certain issues often arising in arbitration. For these comparative purposes, the rules of five different arbitral institutions have been selected: the American Arbitration Association / International Centre for Dispute Resolution ("AAA/ICDR Rules"); the International Chamber of Commerce ("ICC Rules"); the London Court of International Arbitration ("LCIA Rules"); Singapore International Arbitration Centre ("SIAC Rules"); and the Swiss Chambers of Commerce of Basel, Berne, Geneva, Lausanne, Lugano and Zurich ("Swiss Rules").[25]

---

[23] *See* Appendix B for further development of this relationship.

[24] There are a variety of publications available that provide detailed comparisons of various sets of arbitration rules. Such a complete comparison is far beyond the scope of this casebook. However, the materials that follow will often make reference to various sets of rules, as examples of the manner in which the issues in question might be addressed.

[25] Copies of each of these sets of rules will be helpful in understanding some of the issues addressed by institutional rules and some of the differences in the way in which these issues are

While many parties choose institutional arbitration, they are not required to do so. Under most modern arbitration laws, all that is required is a writing (or writings) signed by the parties and agreeing to final and binding arbitration. An arbitration agreement that does not designate an arbitral institution is characterized as an agreement for "*ad hoc*" arbitration. In effect, it is up to the parties to structure and facilitate the resolution of their own dispute. This can often, of course, present challenges when the parties are already engaged in a dispute they have been unable to resolve between themselves.

The parties may choose *ad hoc* arbitration for a variety of reasons. They may do so inadvertently by simply failing to designate an institution. Or they may do so in hopes of saving money. An institution will charge fees for its services, in addition to the cost of the arbitrators themselves. Or perhaps the parties may not be able to agree on an institution in advance. If the parties, for any reason, consciously choose *ad hoc* arbitration, they may wish to choose the UNCITRAL Arbitration Rules, which were specifically adopted for that purpose.[26] In addition to the five sets of institutional rules listed above, the UNCITRAL Rules will also sometimes be used for comparative purposes.[27]

B.   RECOMMENDED MODEL ARBITRATION CLAUSES

The following model clauses are provided for use with particular bodies of arbitration rules. The first provides for *ad hoc* arbitration under the UNCITRAL Rules, while the remainder provide for institutional arbitration administered under the rules of the designated institution.

UNCITRAL Rules (1976)

Any dispute, controversy or claim arising out of or relating to this contract, or the breach, termination or invalidity thereof, shall be settled by arbitration in accordance with the UNCITRAL Arbitration Rules as at present in force.

{Note - Parties may wish to consider adding}

---

addressed. The AAA/ICDR Rules (2007) are available at: http://www.adr.org/sp.asp?id =28144#Intl_Arb_Rules. The ICC Rules (1998) are available at: http://www.iccwbo.org/ court/arbitration/id4199/index.html. The LCIA Rules (1998) are available at: http://www.lcia-arbitration.com. The SIAC Rules (2007) are available at: http://www.siac.org.sg/rules-siac.htm. The Swiss Rules (2006) are available at http://www.swissarbitration.ch/rules.php.

[26] The UNCITRAL Rules may, in many cases, also be used in institutional arbitration.

[27] The UNCITRAL Rules are available at: http://www.uncitral.org/uncitral/en/uncitral_texts/ arbitration/1976Arbitration_rules.html.

(a) The appointing authority shall be . . . (name of institution or person);

(b) The number of arbitrators shall be . . . (one or three);

(c) The place of arbitration shall be . . . (town or country);

(d) The language(s) to be used in the arbitral proceedings shall be . . .

AAA/ICDR Rules (2007)

Any controversy or claim arising out of or relating to this contract, or the breach thereof, shall be determined by arbitration administered by the American Arbitration Association [or International Centre for Dispute Resolution] in accordance with its International Arbitration Rules.

The parties should consider adding:

(a) The number of arbitrators shall be (one or three);

(b) The place of arbitration shall be (city and/or country); or

(c) The language(s) of the arbitration shall be _____.

ICC Rules (1998)

All disputes arising out of or in connection with the present contract shall be finally settled under the Rules of Arbitration of the International Chamber of Commerce by one or more arbitrators appointed in accordance with the said Rules.

LCIA Rules (1998)

Any dispute arising out of or in connection with this contract, including any question regarding its existence, validity or termination, shall be referred to and finally resolved by arbitration under the LCIA Rules, which Rules are deemed to be incorporated by reference into this clause.

The number of arbitrators shall be [one/three].

The seat, or legal place, of arbitration shall be [City and/or Country].

The language to be used in the arbitral proceedings shall be
[   ].

The governing law of the contract shall be the substantive law of
[   ].

SIAC Rules (2007)

Any dispute arising out of or in connection with this contract, including any question regarding its existence, validity or termination, shall be referred to and finally resolved by arbitration in Singapore in accordance with the Arbitration Rules of the Singapore International Arbitration Centre ("SIAC Rules") for the time being in force, which rules are deemed to be incorporated by reference in this clause.

The Tribunal shall consist of _____ (one or three) arbitrator(s) to be appointed by the Chairman of the SIAC.

The language of the arbitration shall be _____.

Swiss Rules (2006)

Any dispute, controversy or claim arising out of or in relation to this contract, including the validity, invalidity, breach or termination thereof, shall be settled by arbitration in accordance with the Swiss Rules of International Arbitration of the Swiss Chambers of Commerce in force on the date when the Notice of Arbitration is submitted in accordance with these Rules.

The number of arbitrators shall be ... (one or three);

The seat of the arbitration shall be in ... (city in Switzerland, unless the parties agree on a city abroad);

The arbitral proceedings shall be conducted in ... (insert desired language).

* * * * *

Notes and Questions

Note 1: Compare the six different recommended arbitration clauses. Consider both the similarities and any differences. What sort of considerations might give rise to the differences?

Note 2: In thinking about how best to construct an arbitration agreement, reconsider some the issues addressed above: the context of a pre-dispute agreement to arbitrate, as a part of a broader commercial agreement; the range of potential issues to be addressed by such an agreement; and potential external sources available to address these issues. Consider also the hierarchy presented in "Source of Contracting Parties' Rights and Obligations" in Appendix B. Can the parties construct an arbitration clause that is both short and effective? Part of the answer to this question involves the law governing the arbitration, or *lex arbitri*.

V. THE IMPORTANCE OF THE *LEX ARBITRI* AND THE INTERACTION OF EXPRESS TERMS, RULES, AND LAW

The law governing the arbitration, as a unique set of contractual obligations, is most often called the "*lex arbitri*." The *lex arbitri* is sometimes characterized as the "procedural" law governing the arbitration, and it's true that it will often address procedural issues. However, the *lex arbitri* may also address other issues, such as formal validity. There are in fact a variety of different legal issues that may arise in the context of arbitration, and some may be governed by law other than the *lex arbitri*. [28] These issues, and the law governing them, will be addressed in detail in Chapters 8, 9, and 10. For now, however, it is sufficient to recognize that the *lex arbitri* will serve as governing law with respect to the vast majority of issues arising under the parties' agreement to resolve their disputes through arbitration. To the extent that the parties fail to designate any specific arbitration rules, the *lex arbitri* will effectively define the content of their agreement to arbitrate. Understanding the importance of the *lex arbitri* as governing law, one must next (A) understand how the *lex arbitri* is determined and (B) how the parties' express terms, any chosen rules, and the *lex arbitri* interact to define the parties' arbitration agreement.

A. DETERMINATION OF THE *LEX ARBITRI*

The *lex arbitri* will normally be the *lex loci arbitri*, or the arbitration law of the place of arbitration. Thus, an arbitration agreement designating Paris as the place of arbitration will normally be governed by the French Code of Civil Procedure,

---

[28] An agreement to arbitrate may raise a variety of different legal issues, which may be governed by different bodies of law. While some of these issues may be resolved by reference to the law of the same State, each must be considered independently. For a brief overview, the reader may wish to refer to the chart in Appendix C. This chart provides an overview of various conflicts of law issues, as well as the interaction between governing law, any chosen rules, and the parties' own specific terms of agreement. All of this material will, however, be covered in turn throughout the remainder of this chapter, as well as Chapters 8, 9, and 10.

Book IV, Arbitration, while an arbitration agreement designating London as the place of arbitration will normally be governed by the English Arbitration Act of 1996. If the parties choose a place of arbitration in a state that has adopted the Model Law, such as Germany, Mexico, or Japan, their arbitration will be governed by that state's enactment of the Model Law. In effect, the parties' choice of a place of arbitration will normally amount to a choice of law governing the arbitration as well.

Article 20

Place of arbitration

(1) The parties are free to agree on the place of arbitration. Failing such agreement, the place of arbitration shall be determined by the arbitral tribunal having regard to the circumstances of the case, including the convenience of the parties.

(2) Notwithstanding the provisions of paragraph (1) of this article, the arbitral tribunal may, unless otherwise agreed by the parties, meet at any place it considers appropriate for consultation among its members, for hearing witnesses, experts or the parties, or for inspection of goods, other property or documents.

In theory, the parties may be able to choose a *lex arbitri* other than the law of the place of arbitration.[29] However, this is a choice that has been increasingly restricted under modern law, and, even where allowed, should not be made without a great deal of thought (thought that the authors suggest will rarely lead one to choose a place of arbitration divorced from its own local arbitration law). While arbitration is largely a matter of contract, the parties may, for various reasons that will be addressed throughout these materials, need recourse to courts in relation to arbitration, and the assistance of such national courts is often tied to

---

[29] In fact, some commentators have also argued for a supranational approach to arbitration, effectively foregoing any national governing law. However, the practical problems with this approach are sufficiently significant that a thorough discussion of this topic is beyond the scope of this casebook.

state arbitration law.[30] Moreover, many arbitration laws limit their effectiveness to arbitration in which the place of arbitration is within the state in question.[31]

The "place" of arbitration is of much more than simply theoretical importance, because this law will affect many aspects of the enforceability of the arbitration agreement, as well as the ability of a disappointed party to challenge the award after it is issued. Moreover, a modern fully developed arbitration law, such as the Model Law, will provide a variety of default legal rules, thus addressing many of the most important arbitration issues in the event the parties' agreement does not otherwise address them.[32]

It is also important to note at this stage that the tribunal may conduct the proceedings or varies elements of such proceedings at any convenient location, which need not necessarily be the same as the place of arbitration.[33] In other words, the physical location of various arbitration events is largely a matter of convenience, whereas the choice of the "place of arbitration" will have significant legal consequences.[34] The following article more fully develops the relationship between the place of arbitration, the place of hearings, and the *lex arbitri*.

---

[30] *See e.g.* Model Law Article 6.

[31] *See e.g.* Model Law Article 1(2) (The only provisions effective if the place of arbitration is elsewhere are those deferring to the foreign arbitration or those relating to enforcement of a foreign arbitration award.); Federal Statute of Private International Law, Chapter 12, Article 176 (1988).

[32] As discussed supra in Chapter 7, the l*ex arbitri* provides a potential set of legal rules in the event the parties do not address important issues directly or, more typically, by adopting a well developed set of private rules. While most modern arbitration regimes include a full set of default legal rules, some do not. Perhaps the most notable exception in this regard is the Federal Arbitration Act, a 1925 enactment still governing arbitration in the United States. While the FAA, as interpreted by the United States Supreme Court, provides for a very pro-arbitration legal regime, it provides very little by way of default legal rules. *See* Jack Graves, *Arbitration as Contract: The Need for a Fully Developed and Systematic Set of Statutory Default Legal Rules* (to be published 2008).

[33] *See e.g.* Model Law Art. 20(2).

[34] *See e.g.* Model Law Art. 31(3) (explaining that the award will be deemed made in the place of arbitration, which, as we will later see, has effects on actions to vacate or enforce an award).

**Identifying and Applying the Law Governing the Arbitration Procedure –
The Role of the Law of the Place of Arbitration,**

Gabrielle Kaufmann-Kohler

II. Identifying the Law Governing the Arbitral Proceedings

*1. The Alternatives: The Law of the Place of Arbitration or the
Law Chosen by the Parties?*

What law governs the proceedings before the arbitrators? An
easy answer, and in practice often a sufficient one, would be: the
rules chosen by the parties, for instance, institutional arbitration
rules, or the rules set by the arbitrators. But this is not the answer
we are looking for. We are looking for the national law,
sometimes called *lex arbitri*, which grants the parties or the
arbitrators the freedom to set the rules, which may also impose
some restrictions on them, and which – even more importantly –
will control the use of that freedom and sanction any abuses by
setting aside the award.

To find the law governing the arbitration proceedings we must
first identify the possible connecting factors pointing to that law.
Conceptually, there are two primary connecting factors
available: the place of arbitration and the parties' intent. The first
factor emphasizes the procedural nature of arbitration (like a
court, the arbitration has its closest connection to the State of its
location), while the second factor reflects the consensual or
contractual aspect of arbitration (like a contract, the arbitration is
governed by the law chosen by the parties).

Even when the connecting factor is the place of arbitration, the
parties are often said to be authorized to choose a foreign
arbitration law to govern the proceedings. However, unlike the
situation when the connecting factor is the intent, such a choice
remains within the limits of the mandatory rules of the place of
arbitration, the application of which is subject to the control of
the courts at the same place. It is no different in this respect from
a mere reference to institutional rules.

*2. The Solution: Predominantly, the Law of the Place of
Arbitration*

Bearing in mind this opposition between the place of arbitration
and the parties' intent, a traveller engaging today on a world tour
of international commercial arbitration is likely to observe that a
majority of recently enacted statutes adopts the principle of

territoriality, i.e., gives the preference to the connecting factor of the place of arbitration. Among the more recent arbitration texts, the UNCITRAL Model Law on International Commercial Arbitration (the Model Law) is an inescapable first stop on this tour. It has adopted the territoriality principle as the sole connecting factor in its Art. 1(2), which reads as follows: "The provisions of this Law, except Arts. 8, 9, 35 and 36 [none of which introduces the connecting factor of the parties' intent], apply only if the place of arbitration is in the territory of this State".

Not surprisingly, the issue of the Model Law's territorial scope arose in the course of the discussion on the jurisdiction of the courts in aid and control of arbitration. Should the parties be entitled to opt out of the Model Law being the law of the place of arbitration by agreeing on a foreign procedural law? The main reason for deciding against this possibility was the risk of conflicts between the jurisdiction of the courts of the State whose law had been chosen and that of the courts at the place of arbitration. Moreover, most national laws on arbitration did not contain this possibility and, where it was provided, it was seldom used. Finally, allowing such a choice would not have served much of a purpose, since the Model Law grants the parties broad procedural autonomy in any event.

. . .

Numerous other recent statutes, which are not shaped after the Model Law, also follow the territoriality principle. So, for instance, the provisions of Chapter 12 of the Swiss Private International Law Act of 1987 apply "if the seat of the arbitral tribunal is in Switzerland". Wording of similar import is found in the Dutch, the English, the Italian, the Portuguese, the Austrian Arbitration Acts, as well as the Swedish Draft Act. Further away, China's first arbitration statute enacted in 1994 shows a particularly strong inclination to territoriality.

Compared to these statutes, French and Belgian law are often said to be exceptions. This is true only in part. Let us first look to France. Art. 1494(1) of the New French Code of Civil Procedure provides that the parties may "define the procedure to be followed in the arbitral proceedings", including by submitting it "to a given procedural law". This rule is a restatement of well-settled case law, which accepted that an arbitration held in France be submitted to a foreign law and vice versa. This court practice culminated when the Paris Court of Appeal decided in GNMTC v. Götaverken handed down in 1980(31) that an ICC award in an arbitration held in France was not subject to setting aside proceedings in France, because the arbitration was not governed by French arbitration law, neither the parties nor the arbitrators having expressed such an intention.

Although this solution was a consistent implementation of the connecting factor based on the parties' intent, the drafters of the new arbitration provisions enacted the following year did not adopt it. On the contrary, they provided for the jurisdiction of the French courts over setting aside actions, whenever the award was rendered in France. This implies that, whatever the foreign law governing the proceedings, the parties and the arbitrators must comply with mandatory French rules of procedure as they are reflected in the grounds for setting aside awards. In other words, even in France, the law of the place of arbitration submits the procedure before the arbitrators to certain minimum requirements: a situation in which the end result is identical to the one found in many jurisdictions applying the territorial principle.

The same does not hold true in connection with Belgian law. Art. 1717 of the Judicial Code – the future of which is at present uncertain – rules out any action for setting aside awards in Belgian courts, unless at least one of the parties is "either a physical person having Belgian nationality or residing in Belgium, or a legal person formed in Belgium or having a branch or other seat of operation there".

As a consequence, an arbitral tribunal sitting in Belgium does not need to take into account even the minimum procedural requirements embodied in the local grounds for annulling awards. The arbitration here is truly unbound. This does not mean that the arbitrators' whims are equally so. A party still has the right to resist enforcement of the award. Indeed, despite eminent views to the contrary, there appears to be no compelling reason to remove stateless or anational awards from the scope of the New York Convention. The result is that the arbitral tribunal will have to comply with the minimum requirements under the Convention (which in certain cases will in turn be measured by the standards of the country of origin!).

. . .

3. What Is the Place of Arbitration?

So arbitrations are generally governed by the law of the place where they are held. But is the place a legal connection or a physical, geographical location? How is it selected? Can part or even all procedural steps be carried out elsewhere?

Pursuant to Art. 20(1) of the Model Law, the parties are free to select the place of arbitration. They may do so directly or by delegation to an institution. In the absence of an agreement by the parties, the arbitrators have the power to choose the place, which they must do taking into account "the circumstances of the case, including the convenience of the parties". This latter phrase refers to the legal convenience as well, especially to the suitability of the applicable procedural law. Indeed, in addition to its factual significance (the arbitration is in principle expected to be held there), the choice of the place has legal consequences under the Model Law: it determines the applicability of the Model Law and the place of origin of the award for enforcement purposes.

According to the second paragraph of Art. 20, subject to the parties' contrary agreement, the arbitral tribunal may meet at any place it considers appropriate "for consultation among its members, for hearing witnesses, experts or the parties, or for inspection of goods, other property or documents". As opposed to this, early drafts followed the UNCITRAL Arbitration Rules, which limit the meetings held elsewhere to hearing witnesses, inspecting goods, and consulting among arbitrators. To meet practical needs, the drafters later broadened the formula to add hearing experts and parties, with the result that all stages of the arbitration are covered in the final version. Therefore, an arbitration may take place in its entirety outside the place of arbitration, which is reduced to "nothing but a fiction".

. . . This makes sense: the constructive place is often chosen for its neutrality, i.e., for its absence of connection to either party, while the actual place may be chosen precisely for the opposite reason, because it shows a link to a party due, for instance, to the presence of witnesses.

. . .

Recent non-Model Law legislations provide the same rules. Among these, English law calls for a particular comment. Sect. 3 of the English Arbitration Act 1996 expressly states that the seat in the meaning of the Act is a legal, juridical connection. In Naviera Amazonica Peruana SA v. Compañia Internacional de Seguros del Peru, Lord Justice Kerr for the English Court of Appeal had emphasized the "distinction between the legal localisation of an arbitration on the one hand and the appropriate or convenient geographical locality for hearings of arbitration on the other hand". This distinction is confirmed by Sects. 43 and 2(3)(a) of the Act, which permit a court to secure attendance of witnesses present in the United Kingdom, provided the hearing takes place there, even though the seat of the arbitration is located abroad.

Similarly, the Swiss Supreme Court has recently stressed the same distinction, as well as the legal nature of the place or seat: "By choosing a Swiss legal domicile [ein schweizerisches Rechtsdomizil] for the arbitral tribunal, the parties manifestly intended to submit their dispute to Swiss arbitration law, not to provide for an exclusive location for meetings among arbitrators at the place of arbitration.... [T]he determination of a given place of arbitration is of significance to the extent that the award is deemed to be rendered at such place. It is irrelevant that a hearing was effectively held or that the award was effectively issued there". Indeed, although there is no statutory provision to this effect, it is generally accepted that hearings and meetings in a Swiss arbitration may take place outside of Switzerland.

. . .

[*Sports arbitration involving the Olympics (the place of arbitration is Switzerland, but hearings are held wherever the Olympics are being held), as well as online arbitration (with hearings held in cyberspace), are offered as further examples of arbitration in which the physical place of arbitration may be completely divorced from the legal place of arbitration and its governing law.*]

. . .

6. A Paradox which Fosters Uniformity

Having returned from his trip, the traveler tells of two main evolutions. First, the territorial connection nowadays prevails, primarily because it is easy to handle and provides certainty. In other words, to identify the law applicable to the arbitration procedure, one must define the place of arbitration. Second, that place is increasingly viewed as a fiction which has no necessary connection to the physical location of the proceedings. This trend is evident, even if in the great majority of cases the legal place still coincides with the physical location. With the continuing globalization of the world and the changes brought about by the technological revolution, this evolution cannot but gain in importance.

These two paradoxical evolutions bridge the gap between the intent-based territorial connections. The choice of a place ends up being nothing but a choice of the law governing the arbitration. It delocalizes the arbitration proceedings, removing the authority of the local *lex arbitri* and the powers of the local courts to supervise the proceedings and set aside the award.

Delocalization, denationalization, deterritorialization gave rise to passionate arguments a number of years ago. Will the once-heated debate be revived by phenomena such as online, Olympic or similar delocalized arbitrations?

If it is accepted that the (legal) place may be a fiction, then the issue of delocalization becomes moot, because delocalization is in fact achieved, though indirectly. One of the main purposes of delocalization as it was once discussed was to eliminate the unintended effects of peculiarities of the law of the place where the arbitration happened to be held. By the choice of an arbitration-friendly fictional place of arbitration, that goal is fully met. It is not threatened by uncertainties or conflicts about competent courts, if courts consistently apply the concept of a legal place or seat and accept jurisdiction in aid and control of arbitration only at that place.

A different question remains, which is whether an arbitration can be detached of any national law. It would go beyond the limits of this Report to address it in any detail. Suffice it to say that denationalization in this sense would certainly mirror the transnational nature of disputes which arise out of genuinely global activities. However, at least at this stage of the development of arbitration law, it is likely to raise more problems than it would solve. Moreover, if by way of the choice of a place, one can avoid inhospitable features of the law where the dispute is physically heard, then denationalization loses much of its practical interest. Not to speak of the fact that the increasing uniformity of arbitration laws makes the search for hospitable fora less of a necessity.

. . .

ICCA Congress Series No. 9 (Paris/1999), pp. 336–365.

* * * * *

Notes and Questions

Note 1: The selection of the place of arbitration is not merely the selection of a place of convenience, but also amounts to a selection of the law that will govern many of the issues that may arise in the context of the arbitration.[35] Along with the selection of the arbitrators, it might well be the most important decision the parties make. Chapter 8 will also address additional issues in which the law of the place of arbitration, as well as the law of any potential place of enforcement, may have a significant effect on the jurisdiction of the tribunal to consider the parties' dispute.

Note 2: As suggested in the preceding article, the "place" or "seat" of arbitration and physical location of any hearings need not necessarily be the same. Consider the following example.

> ### Example 7-2
> A Canadian seller and a German buyer of goods may wish to provide for arbitration in New York City, as the location most convenient for the parties, each of whom has a branch office there. However, the parties may prefer a more modern arbitration law than the American Federal Arbitration Act, which would govern if they designated New York as the "place of arbitration." They might, instead, select Dublin, Ireland as the place of arbitration, thus effectively choosing Ireland's enactment of the UNCITRAL Model Law as the *lex arbitri* governing their arbitration hearings to be held in New York. Of course, this means that any court assistance might require the parties to appear before Irish courts.

---

[35] In cases in which the parties fail to choose a place of arbitration, the choice of a set of institutional rules will often address this on a default basis. *See e.g.* SIAC Rules Article 18.1 (choosing Singapore in the absence of any express party choice).

B.   THE *LEX ARBITRI*, THE RULES, AND THE ARBITRATION CLAUSE: PUTTING
         THEM ALL TOGETHER TO BUILD AN ARBITRATION REGIME

It should by now be apparent that, in constructing an arbitration regime for resolution of their disputes, the parties need not engage in a lengthy drafting exercise or detailed negotiations over its provisions. The necessary elements of such a regime may, instead, be assembled through the use of a relatively brief arbitration clause, adopting a set of well established rules, providing for arbitration in a place with a well developed, modern *lex arbitri*, and addressing any particular nuances desired by the parties in the clause itself.

Many of the most significant issues likely to arise during the constitution of the tribunal and the conduct of arbitration proceedings are addressed in both the law governing the arbitration, as well as various *ad hoc* or institutional rules the parties might adopt. For example, the Model Law, as a typical modern *lex arbitri*, and virtually all modern rules each address the question of the number of arbitrators who will decide the parties' dispute.[36]

Some arbitral institutions may also include specific rules not necessarily addressed by the *lex arbitri*. For example, Article 27 of the ICC Rules contains a somewhat unique provision for scrutiny of all awards by the International Court of Arbitration[37] of the ICC.[38] While the Court is not entitled to modify the decision of the tribunal, it may "draw its attention to points of substance." In effect, this provides a unique form "peer review." While is not binding, it might potentially influence a tribunal to, itself, reconsider an award that is clearly flawed in its substantive analysis. Confidentiality is another matter that is addressed in differing fashions under different sets of arbitration rules[39]—some providing greater degrees of confidentiality than others.[40] Many rules also

---

[36] *See e.g.* Model Law Article 10; UNCITRAL Rules Article 5; AAA/ICDR Rules Article 5; ICC Rules Article 8(2); LCIA Article 5.4; SIAC Rules Article 5.1; Swiss Rules Article 6(1) (providing a variety of approaches to determining the number of arbitrators).

[37] The International Court of Arbitration of the ICC should not be confused with a national court established by a sovereign. The International Court of Arbitration is a private arbitration body appointed by the Council of the ICC. *See* ICC Rules Article 1(1). Nor are all arbitral "courts" the same. *See e.g.* LCIA Rules Article 3 (describing the LCIA "Court").

[38] The SIAC Rules also provide for somewhat similar process under Article 27.1.

[39] *See e.g.* UNCITRAL Rules Article 25(4); AAA/ICDR Rules Articles 20(4) and 34; ICC Rules Article 21(3) and Appendix II, Article 1; Swiss Rules Article 25(4) (all providing relatively typical levels of confidentiality, focusing primarily on the closed nature of the proceedings and the obligations of the arbitrators and institution to maintain confidentiality).

[40] *See e.g.* LCIA Rules Article 19.4 and 30; SIAC Rules Articles 21.4 and 34 (providing a significantly greater degree of confidentiality than most rules assigning obligations of confidentiality to the parties, subject only to relatively narrow exceptions.

expressly provide for expedited procedures under certain circumstances.[41] All of these issues are addressed more fully in Chapter 9.

Lastly, of course, to the extent that the parties may wish to provide for any specific issues in a manner not addressed by the *lex arbitri* or an available set of rules, they may do so within the language of the arbitration clause itself. The parties may address an issue to which the *lex arbitri* or rules do not speak, or they may address an issue differently than it is addressed in the *lex arbitri* or rules. The parties' specific expressions of intent will always take precedence over their adopted rules, and both specific expressions of intent and adopted rules will take precedence over the default (though not mandatory) legal rules of the *lex arbitri*.[42]

For example, the Canadian seller and a German buyer of goods referenced earlier in Example 7-2 might choose to include the following arbitration clause in their contract.

Example 7-3

Any controversy or claim arising out of or relating to this contract, or the breach thereof, shall be determined by arbitration administered by the International Centre for Dispute Resolution in accordance with its International Arbitration Rules.

(a) The number of arbitrators shall be one;

(b) The place of arbitration shall be Dublin, Ireland;

(c) All hearings requiring the presence of the parties or their counsel shall be held in New York City, USA;

(d) The language of the arbitration shall be English; and

(e) The substantive law governing the contract shall be the law of Canada, including the UN Convention Governing the International Sale of Goods.

The parties in the above example have chosen Canadian law—not as an alternative to the CISG, but simply to address any issues not governed by the CISG. They have also chosen the AAA/ICDR Rules. Thus, if the buyer wished to bring a claim against seller for non-conforming goods under CISG Article 35,

---

[41] *See e.g.* AAA/ICDR Rules Article 37 (expedited emergency measures); LCIA Rules Article 9 (expedited formation of the tribunal); Swiss Rules Article 42 (expedited proceedings).
[42] *See* app. B.

it would be required to commence arbitration pursuant to the AAA/ICDR Rules. In addition to the substantive law, the actual language of the contract would determine the number of arbitrators, the place of arbitration, the location of any hearings, and the language of arbitration. The choice of Dublin Ireland, as the place of arbitration, would also effectively designate Ireland's adoption of the Model Law as the *lex arbitri*. All remaining issues would be governed by the chosen AAA/ICDR Rules, unless a particular Rule was inconsistent with Ireland's adoption of the Model Law.[43] To the extent these Rules failed to address any issue involving the parties' arbitration, Ireland's Model Law default provisions would govern the issue.

PROBLEMS

The problems here and in the remaining chapters will often incorporate the mythical city and country of Vindobona, Danubia, which will serve as a potential place of arbitration. Danubia has adopted the UNCITRAL Model Law on International Commercial Arbitration (1985, as revised 2006), selecting Article 7, *Option 1*, and designating the Commercial Court of Vindobona, Danubia under Article 6.

Problem 7-3: Chi-Tek, a Chinese manufacturer of multi-function web access devices, is interested in selling its products through T-Mart, a multi-state retailer headquartered in Texas. T-Mart sells a broad variety of retail goods and is interested in the Chi-Tek product because it represents cutting edge technology. T-Mart typically makes very large purchases and sometimes has trouble with suppliers who make more sales commitments than they are capable of meeting. When T-Mart has problems with its suppliers, it is primarily interested in getting the dispute resolve with minimum hassle and cost, and it particularly likes for its counsel to move quickly to secure any rights to goods that might be lost through delay. Chi-Tek doesn't really want to talk much about dispute resolution, as it seems to carry negative implications (that a dispute might actually arise), but its primary concern is to avoid bad publicity if there are any problems with its products or its deliveries. What would an ideal dispute resolution look like if you represented Chi-Tek? How about T-Mart? How, if at all, are they different and how might you accommodate any differences?

Problem 7-4: Pablo, a Peruvian sweater maker, imports wool from Nancy, a New Zealand sheep farmer, and uses it to produce sweaters, which he sells to Günther, a retail distributor in Germany. Each transaction is rather small (typically less than € 100,000), but it is important to Pablo that he has an

---

[43] This is very unlikely. Most modern arbitration rules are drafted to ensure that they are fully consistent with any mandatory legal rules contained in any modern arbitration statutes.

effective means of dispute resolution. He would prefer a relatively quick and simple, but nonetheless easily enforceable, means of dispute resolution. He is also concerned about any claims by Günther that might be attributable to the wool supplied by Nancy. What sort of arbitration clause should Pablo use and with whom?

Problem 7-5: NNM is planning a steel shipment from Moscow to J&G in New York and wishes to include an arbitration clause in the agreement. What kind of provision should NNM propose if it does not wish to pay anyone to administer any arbitration that might occur, but would like a well defined set of arbitration rules? Suppose NNM includes a minimal clause providing only for "binding arbitration of any and all disputes related in any way to the sale of steel, such arbitration to be held in Vindobona, Danubia." Is this enforceable? Where are the parties' rights and obligations found under this arbitration agreement?

8 | ARBITRATION AS A CONTRACT BETWEEN THE PARTIES

> Good people do not need laws to tell them to act responsibly,
> while bad people will find a way around the laws.
>
> - Plato (427–347 B.C.)

The focus changes in this chapter from the selection of an arbitration regime to the implementation of the parties' agreement to arbitrate. The following materials assume that the parties have included some sort of arbitration agreement within the structure of their overall business relationship as a buyer and seller of goods, and further assume that a dispute has now arisen that is at least arguably related in some fashion to that business relationship.

Example 8-1

J&G has concluded a contract with NNM in which NNM has agreed to sell steel to J&G for use in its new MAK X disposable razor blades. Within their contract for the sale of steel (sometimes called the "main" or "container" contract with reference to arbitration issues), the parties have also included a provision stating that: "any dispute, controversy or claim arising out of or in relation to this contract, including the validity, invalidity, breach or termination thereof, shall be settled by final and binding arbitration."

Unfortunately, a dispute has arisen over the quality of the steel delivered by NNM. J&G asserts that the steel does not conform to the parties' agreement and has refused to pay for it. NNM asserts that the steel is fully conforming, and J&G is in breach of its obligation to pay for the steel. Each of the parties is contemplating legal action.

An arbitration agreement is, in effect, a conditional contract because the parties' contractual obligations are not typically triggered until a dispute arises. Once a dispute does arise, however, the parties' performance obligations come due, just as they do in any other conditional contract in which the condition of performance is satisfied. This chapter will address the parties' obligations in the sequence in which they typically arise, from the initiation of the arbitration by a claimant, through the ultimate decision of the arbitral panel to exercise jurisdiction over the dispute (or not). While the tribunal's exercise of jurisdiction does not end the parties' contractual obligations, it does change the nature of those obligations in view of the increased role played by the tribunal in bringing the arbitration process to completion.

It is also useful to remember that the performance of the arbitration agreement actually gives rise to one or more additional contracts. The parties, in what might be characterized as something akin to a joint venture in dispute resolution, will contract with an arbitrator or arbitrators to decide their dispute. The arbitrators will promise to render an award consistent with the parties' agreement in exchange for the parties' promise to pay the arbitrators. This arbitral procedure in which the tribunal actually decides the substantive issues submitted by the parties is addressed in Chapter 9. In the case of institutional arbitration, the parties will also contract with the institution to assist in establishing the arbitral tribunal and administering the resolution of the dispute. This chapter focuses on the parties' performance of the arbitration agreement between themselves—the agreement to forego national courts and set in motion a process resulting in the constitution of an arbitral panel—while the next focuses on the performance by the arbitrators of their promise to the parties to decide the parties' dispute and render an enforceable award.

The chapter begins with (I) a claimant's decision to seek legal relief and commence arbitration, followed by (II) an overview of the options available to the other contracting party in response. If neither party challenges the validity of the arbitration agreement, there is normally no need for court intervention. However, (III) even parties to a valid arbitration agreement will typically have a right—if necessary—to seek certain interim relief in an appropriate court. Once the arbitration has been commenced, (IV) the first order of business in the arbitration proceedings is the selection of the arbitrator or arbitrators. If neither party contests the jurisdiction of the arbitral tribunal, then one could move directly to consideration of the procedure for deciding the merits of the parties' dispute. However, a jurisdictional challenge by one of the parties may raise complex questions that must be addressed before any consideration of the merits of the parties' dispute. These jurisdictional issues are addressed in two discrete parts: (V) the question of who decides any jurisdictional issues; and (VI) the substance or content of various jurisdictional issues that may need to be decided.

I.   THE DECISION TO COMMENCE ARBITRATION PROCEEDINGS

The parties to a contract dispute will often settle the matter between themselves, without the need to resort to any external assistance. They may also engage a neutral third party to assist them in reaching a fully consensual settlement through mediation or conciliation.[1] In many instances, these sorts of "win-win" resolutions will offer the parties the best overall solution, as a whole. Mediation or conciliation may be invoked prior to arbitration based on a contractual provision requiring a "multi-tiered" approach,[2] or the parties may agree to mediation or conciliation after the dispute has already arisen. A brief comparison between arbitration and meditation or conciliation may be useful here.

An arbitral tribunal is often faced with a choice in which one party must necessarily win, and one party must necessarily lose. The arbitrators may also feel constrained by the nature of the parties' claims and defenses under the applicable substantive law. In contrast, a mediator or conciliator has far greater creative latitude in helping the parties to craft a mutually beneficial solution to their dispute that may have little, if any, relationship to their formal legal positions relating to the dispute in question.[3] Unfortunately, however, such consensual resolutions cannot always be achieved, and when they fail, the need for binding arbitration arises.[4]

Once a party decides to seek resolution of a dispute through binding arbitration, it must "commence" the process. This commencement has at least two substantial effects: (1) it triggers a number of additional obligations of each party, and (2) it tolls the applicable period of limitations within which any claim must be made.

---

[1] The term "conciliation" is more often used in an international context, *see, e.g.*, UNCITRAL Model Law on International Commercial Conciliation (2002), while mediation is more often used in the United States. The two terms are generally used interchangeably, though some commentators suggest a continuing distinction, with conciliators taking a somewhat more proactive role than mediators. *See generally* Harold I. Abramson, *International Mediation Basics*, in Rufus von Thulen Roades, Daniel M. Kolkey & Richard Chernick, *Practitioner's Handbook on International Arbitration and Mediation* § 1.01 (Juris Publg. 2005).

[2] The inclusion of such a clause was mentioned at the end of the Arbitration Agreement Checklist provided in Chapter 7.

[3] *See generally* Roger Fisher, William Ury & Bruce Patton, *Getting to Yes: Negotiating Agreement without Giving In* (2d ed., Penguin Bks. 1991) (in particular, Chapter 4, "Invent Options for Mutual Gain" addresses the idea of finding solutions that avoid the "zero sum" problem). Of course, this same sort of creative latitude may be granted to arbitrators if the parties expressly authorize the tribunal to decide the dispute *ex aequo et bono* or as *amiable compositeur*. *See* Model Law Article 28(3). However, the risks of such authority are somewhat greater in arbitration. While either party can always reject a solution suggested by a mediator or conciliator, the arbitrator's mandated solution is binding.

[4] Parties may also sometimes combine mediation and arbitration in an almost countless variety of ways. Perhaps the most common is to begin with mediation and then proceed to arbitration only on issues the parties are unable to resolve. This is commonly referred to as med-arb. Multiple dispute resolution processes may also be connected in various fashions. For example, in "last offer" arbitration (often call "baseball arbitration," the arbitrators may be limited to choosing between the parties' respective final settlement offers in negotiations or mediation. *See generally* Alan Redfern & Martin Hunter, *Law and Practice of International Commercial Arbitration* §§ 1-69 to 1-84 (4th ed., Sweet & Maxwell 2004).

> **Article 21**
>
> **Commencement of arbitral proceedings**
>
> Unless otherwise agreed by the parties, the arbitral proceedings in respect of a particular dispute commence on the date on which a request for that dispute to be referred to arbitration is received by the respondent.

Of course the Model Law provision on commencement is simply a default rule ("unless otherwise agreed"). Thus, the details of commencement may ultimately depend on the parties' agreement. For example, the parties have included the following clause in their contract.

> **Example 8-2**
>
> Any controversy or claim arising out of or relating to this contract, or the breach thereof, shall be determined by arbitration in Dublin, Ireland, to be administered by the International Centre for Dispute Resolution in accordance with its International Arbitration Rules.

This arbitration clause provides for institutional arbitration administered by the ICDR (the international arm of the AAA). Thus, the details of commencement would be found in Article 2 of the AAA/ICDR Rules.[5] Subsection (1) of Article 2 explains that the claimant commencing the arbitration must provide written notice to both the administering institution and to the other party, the respondent. Subsection (2) states that the arbitration is deemed "commenced" when the notice is received by the administrator, and subsection (3) provides the details as to the content of the required notice. Article 16 of the Rules provides further detailed requirements of any "notice," including a notice of commencement.

With institutional arbitration, such as that described here, the claimant will also typically be required to make a financial deposit, either with its claim or upon request by the administrator.[6] The claimant may also be expected to provide any required arbitrator designation along with its initial request for arbitration.[7] Thus,

---

[5] In Chapter 7, six different sets of arbitration rules were introduced in section IV, and some of these rules will be referenced with respect to various issues in this chapter addressed by the rules.

[6] *Compare* Article 33 of the AAA/ICDR Rules (deposit required upon request), *with* Article 4(4) of the ICC Rules (requiring an advance party with claimant's initial request for arbitration).

[7] *See* Article 1, 1.1(e) of the LCIA Rules (requiring that, if the agreement calls for party appointed arbitrators, claimant provide the details of its nominee).

the chosen institutional rules provide all of the necessary details. These rules are also fully consistent with any mandatory provisions of the law of the designated place of arbitration—Ireland's enactment of the UNCITRAL Model Law.

Or the parties might have agreed the following.

Example 8-3

Any controversy or claim arising out of or relating to this contract, or the breach thereof, shall be determined by binding arbitration in Geneva, Switzerland, in accordance with the UNCITRAL Arbitration Rules.

If so, the details of commencement would be found in Article 3 of the UNCITRAL Rules, providing details for the required notice to the respondent and stating that commencement occurs upon receipt of such notice by the respondent. Note that there is no provision for notice to any administering institution. This is because the UNCITRAL Rules were specifically intended to accommodate *ad hoc* arbitration.[8] Article 2 provides the particulars as to notice, generally. The Swiss Federal Statue of Private International Law, Chapter 12 (1988) does not speak directly to the issue of commencement, so the Rules would fully control the issue.

Lastly, the parties' agreement might simply provide the following.

Example 8-4

Any controversy or claim arising out of or relating to this contract, or the breach thereof, shall be determined by binding arbitration in Vindobona, Danubia.[9]

---

[8] While the UNCITRAL Rules were designed for *ad hoc* arbitration, there use is certainly not limited as such. For example, the Hong Kong International Arbitration Centre uses the UNCITRAL Rules as its own default (as referenced in its model clause), while other institutions, such as the Inter-American Commercial Arbitration Commission have used the UNCITRAL Rules as a model for their own. In addition, many institutions, such as the Singapore International Arbitration Centre, allow the parties to choose the UNCITRAL Rules in lieu of the institution's own rules.

[9] The reader will recall Vindobona, Danubia, as the mythical jurisdiction sometimes referenced in these materials that has adopted the UNCITRAL Model Law verbatim.

Under most governing law, such a provision is entirely enforceable, as it meets the minimal requirements of a written agreement to binding arbitration within its defined scope.[10] However, the agreement neither provides any details of its own, nor incorporates any rules—institutional or otherwise. Thus, the parties must turn to the governing law of the place of arbitration, the *lex arbitri*, for guidance. In this case, Model Law Article 21 (included above) provides that the arbitration commences on the date that the respondent receives notice thereof. While the Model Law does not address the content of such notice in the same sort of detail as the rules addressed above, some guidance might be found in Article 18 and its mandate that each party be given a full opportunity to present its case. In order to present its case effectively, respondent must obviously learn from claimant the nature and extent of the dispute.

In each case above, commencement requires—at an absolute minimum—notification to the other party that arbitration proceedings have been initiated. As one can see, these three arbitration clauses also provide examples of: institutional administered arbitration; *ad hoc* arbitration under a designated set of rules; and *ad hoc* arbitration without any designated rules.[11] Of course, the parties could have addressed all of the details required for commencing an arbitration proceeding by individually providing for them in their arbitration agreement. As noted in the last chapter, however, such level of detail in an arbitration agreement, itself, is rarely practical or even desirable.

II.   RESPONDENT'S OBLIGATIONS AND OPTIONS

The respondent has now received the claimant's notice of arbitration, and the arbitration has been formally commenced. Of course, a respondent could simply ignore the notice, but various legal provisions and arbitration rules regarding waiver, as well as the ability of the tribunal to move forward in the respondent's absence,[12] would suggest that would likely be a poor course to follow. Respondent does, however, often have a few options, and these are explored below—beginning with (A) the arbitral process and followed by (B) the options for court action.

---

[10] However, the provision would not likely be enforceable under French domestic law, which requires that the agreement provide a means for selecting the arbitrators. *See* Code of Civil Procedure, Book IV, Arbitration, Article 1443 (1981). French law governing international commercial arbitration does, however, provide for appointment of arbitrators in the absence any party agreement by submitted the matter of appointment to the *President of the Tribunal de Grande Instance* of Paris.

[11] Such a clause is rarely, if ever, to be recommended, but may nonetheless appear in an agreement—particularly one drafted without assistance of competent counsel.

[12] Default proceedings are addressed in Chapter 9.

A.   RESPONDENT'S OBLIGATIONS TRIGGERED BY COMMENCEMENT

The respondent must consider at least two additional items in addition to the responding to the claims brought by the claimant. First, (1) in addition to answering any claim against it, does respondent wish to bring any of its own claims in this same proceeding? Second, (2) does respondent wish to challenge the tribunal's jurisdiction?

1.   Answering the Claim and Bringing Any Counter-Claim

As with the claimant's commencement of the arbitration, the requirements of respondent will vary to some extent depending on the content of the arbitration agreement. For example, the parties might have included the following clause providing for institutional arbitration under the SIAC Rules.

Example 8-5

Any dispute arising out of or in connection with this contract, including any question regarding its existence, validity or termination, shall be referred to and finally resolved by arbitration in Singapore in accordance with the Arbitration Rules of the Singapore International Arbitration Centre ("SIAC Rules") for the time being in force, which rules are deemed to be incorporated by reference in this clause.

Article 4 of these Rules explains that the respondent must, within 14 days, provide to both the SIAC Registrar and the claimant its answer, including any counterclaims, as well as any comments on the claimant's proposed conduct arbitration and any comments on or nominations of proposed arbitrators. Article 2 provides the details for notices and other communications required of either party.

If the respondent is making its own counter-claims, it must also advance the required deposit associated with the institutional cost of bringing the claims. While each party will generally be required to advance the institutional cost of its own claims, as an initial matter, the parties will generally share the costs of the arbitrators themselves.[13] Each of these costs is potentially subject to an award shifting some or all of them to the other party when the proceedings are closed.[14]

---

[13] *See* Article 26 of the SIAC Rules.
[14] The shifting of costs and fees is addressed in Chapter 9.

Alternatively, the parties might choose *ad hoc* arbitration under the UNCITRAL Rules,[15] in which case the respondent's only initial obligations relate to the constitution of the tribunal, a subject addressed below. The respondent's first obligation to reply to the substance of the claims contained in the notice of arbitration does not arise under Article 19 until after the appointment of the arbitrators.[16] Without institutional administration, the rules tend to minimize any requirements on the parties until such time as the tribunal has been convened.

Lastly, *ad hoc* arbitration under a minimalist clause—one failing to provide any details or designate any institution or body of rules[17]—must rely to a large degree on the cooperation of the parties. The Model Law does not provide for any affirmative obligations of respondent prior to the appointment of the arbitrators. *Ad hoc* arbitration is somewhat more dependent on the parties' cooperation and, therefore, somewhat more vulnerable to a lack thereof. In particular, a party's refusal to participate in the selection of the arbitrators presents significant challenges in *ad hoc* arbitration, which are addressed below in section IV. Statements of defense, counter-claims, and additional joinder issues are more fully addressed in Chapter 9.

2.   Challenging Jurisdiction

As part of its initial response, the respondent may also challenge jurisdiction. Such a challenge should typically be raised at the earliest possible juncture, though it may generally be raised in a subsequent statement of defense.[18] If the initial response includes the respondent's statement of defense, then any jurisdictional challenge must be made at that time, or it may be deemed waived.[19] The complete nature of jurisdictional challenges is more fully addressed in section VI below.

B.   CAN RESPONDENT GO TO COURT INSTEAD OF PARTICIPATING IN THE ARBITRATION?

If the respondent provides an appropriate and timely answer under any applicable rules and/or *lex arbitri*, and the respondent timely raises any jurisdictional challenge with the arbitral tribunal itself, the process will typically proceed in a

---

[15] *See* Example 8-3 above.
[16] *See* Article 19(1) of the UNCITRAL Rules (stating that the arbitral panel shall determine when respondent's statement of defense is due).
[17] *See* Example 8-4 above.
[18] *See e.g.* Swiss Rules Article 21(3).
[19] *See* Model Law Article 16(2).

relatively straightforward manner. In most modern legal systems,[20] the tribunal is constituted with a clear understanding that the respondent has not waived any jurisdictional challenge, and the constituted tribunal decides the jurisdictional question itself.

However, a recalcitrant party may sometimes decide to ignore the arbitral process and bring its claims or defenses in court—either before or after the arbitral process has been commenced. This party may also go to court to challenge the tribunal's jurisdiction, even if it is simultaneously challenging jurisdiction before the tribunal, itself. This of course significantly complicates matters. What should the court do? The court certainly should not proceed immediately to decide the parties' dispute on the merits without any consideration of the parties' purported arbitration agreement. However, there is a much wider divergence of approaches as to an appropriate level of jurisdictional inquiry by the court at this stage of the proceedings.

In some instances, one of the parties may have instituted court proceedings before the arbitration has been commenced. If so, the party seeking to enforce the arbitration agreement must affirmatively raise the issue of the arbitration agreement with the court, in which case the court must refer the parties to arbitration, unless it finds the arbitration agreement "null and void, inoperative or incapable of being performed."[21] This request to stay or dismiss court proceedings and refer the parties to arbitration must generally be made no later than the party's first statement on the substance of the dispute, or the right to arbitration is deemed waived.[22]

Of course, the court should retain jurisdiction in the absence of an arbitration agreement. And it should certainly send the parties to arbitration if that is what they have agreed upon. But how much time and effort should the court spend—and how much time and money should the parties spend in court—addressing the jurisdictional issue before the tribunal has even been constituted or considered the issue itself? These questions are thoroughly addressed below in Part V, but they are important questions to consider as one continues through the process of constituting the tribunal pursuant to the parties' agreement to arbitrate. First, however, there is one additional issue that may give rise to early court action.

---

[20] This is not necessarily the case under the American Federal Arbitration Act, which provides that a court will make most jurisdictional decisions absent the parties' agreement to the contrary.

[21] Model Law Article 8(1); New York Convention Article II.3. This particular language in the two instruments is identical.

[22] *See* Model Law Article 8(1). However, the United States Federal Arbitration Act contains no such limitation, and courts will often refer parties to arbitration after the court proceedings are well underway if a party subsequently realizes it has a right to arbitration. Under the German adoption of Model Law Article 8(1), the right to arbitration must be raised any time prior to the beginning of the first oral hearing on the dispute.

III. THE POTENTIAL NEED FOR IMMEDIATE INTERIM RELIEF

As indicated above, the first step in the arbitration process normally involves the filing of a notice and a statement of claim by the claimant, followed by an answer by the respondent, perhaps also including a jurisdictional challenge. At this early stage, these statements are simply transmitted to the other parties and/or any institution administering the arbitration. However, an arbitral panel has not yet been constituted. This lack of an arbitral decision maker could present a problem for a party in need of immediate interim relief.

For example, consider the following dispute between a Mexican buyer and Spanish seller of goods.

> **Example 8-6**
>
> The Spanish seller is refusing to deliver the goods, and the Mexican buyer has commenced arbitration seeking, among other things, specific performance by the Spanish seller. The buyer has asserted its right to specific performance under CISG Article 46, but the buyer believes that the seller may sell the goods to someone else before the tribunal can even be constituted, in which case an award of specific performance will be of little value to the buyer. What the buyer really needs is immediate temporary legal relief precluding or enjoining the seller from selling the goods to anyone until the tribunal has decided on buyer's right to specific performance. Moreover, the buyer may ultimately need an order from a Spanish court in any case if an enforcement action is required.

In instances such as these, the effectiveness of the relief sought may be entirely dependent on its promptness. However, a party seeking relief from a court might be deemed to have waived its right to arbitrate,[23] absent some sort of provision expressly allowing resort to the courts under these circumstances.

Another example of a potential need for immediate relief arises when a party is concerned that it must have access to crucial evidence in possession of the other party. If so, the party seeking access to the evidence may want an order that such evidence be preserved for later use in the arbitration. Again, the party may need

---

[23] This doctrine applies differently in differently under different arbitration laws. In some cases, the filing of a party's basic claim in court may be deemed a waiver of the right to arbitrate (particularly once the other party relies on that waiver and, itself, begins to engage in court proceedings). In other cases, such as in United States courts, a court will often allow a party to assert its right to arbitrate a dispute even after substantial proceedings have transpired in court.

to take immediate action in order to obtain effective relief, but does not want to do anything to jeopardize its right to bring its claims in arbitration.

Modern arbitration rules and laws resolve this issue by expressly allowing a party to seek interim measures of protection from an appropriate court. The Model Law provides an excellent example.

Article 9

Arbitration agreement and interim measures by court

It is not incompatible with an arbitration agreement for a party to request, before or during arbitral proceedings, from a court an interim measure of protection and for a court to grant such measure.

By seeking immediate interim relief in court, a party is able to protect its rights pending a later decision on the issue by the arbitral tribunal. Such relief is not limited, however, to that which a party might seek before a panel has been formed, because there is an additional issue beyond the timing problem discussed above. To the extent that a party may want court assistance in actually enforcing the interim order, going straight to court instead of first seeking interim measures from the arbitrators eliminates one step in the process and may avoid other enforcement challenges. These issues are discussed more fully in Chapter 9.

PROBLEM

Problem 8-1: Assuming that buyer in State A is bringing an action against seller in State B and wants an order enjoining buyer from selling or otherwise disposing of the allegedly promised goods. The place of arbitration is State C. In the courts of which State should buyer seek an injunction? Suppose the buyer is negotiating the original contract and prefers to try not to involve courts at all in the event interim relief is required (even before the arbitral panel is formed). Is there any simple way to provide for this? *Hint: You might want to consider either the LCIA Rules (expedited formation) or the AAA/ICDR Rules (emergency measures of protection).*[24]

---

[24] Each of the relevant rules was mentioned in section V at the end of the Chapter 7.

IV.   CONSTITUTION OF THE ARBITRAL TRIBUNAL

As indicated earlier, the performance of the parties' arbitration agreement will typically involve a series of additional agreements between the parties and others. In institutional arbitration, for example, the parties will contract with the institution for the provision of certain administrative services in exchange for the parties' agreement to pay for such services. The parties will also contract with the arbitrator or arbitrators who will actually decide the parties' dispute, again in exchange for the parties' agreement to pay for such services. One of the significant differences between *ad hoc* and institutional arbitration is that a designated institution will typically serve as the parties' agent in contracting with the arbitrators.   This difference may have a variety affects with respect to different aspects of the constitution of the tribunal.

This section begins with a discussion of (A) various methods by which arbitrators are chosen. Sometimes, however, (B) these methods will fail because one or both of the parties cannot or will not make a required choice, thus requiring an alternative means of arbitrator selection. However selected, (C) an arbitrator is held to strict standards of disclosure and neutrality, and (D) a party may challenge the appointment of an arbitrator for failure to meet such standards.

A.   CHOOSING THE ARBITRATORS

The choice of arbitrators is often said to be the single most important choice made in an arbitration proceeding.[25] This of course makes the methodology for choosing the arbitrators quite important as well. The method for choosing the arbitrators is largely up to the parties, who may exercise this choice through specific provisions in their agreement or by choosing a particular set of rules. In the absence of such a choice, the *lex arbitri* will dictate the method.

Typically, the parties will either provide for a single arbitrator, to be selected in a cooperative fashion between them, or they will provide for three arbitrators, with each party to select one arbitrator and the two party appointees to select a presiding arbitrator. Such provisions may be written into the arbitration clause itself or adopted by choosing a particular set of rules adopting the same approach by default.[26] Some institutional rules may, however, provide for default selection of arbitrators by the institution,[27] particularly the choice of the presiding arbitrator.[28] Again, it should be remembered that the parties may overcome these defaults by agreement, but such agreement may be difficult to achieve after a

---

[25] *See* Redfern & Hunter, *supra* n. 4, at § 4-12.
[26] *See e.g.* UNCITRAL Rules Articles 6 & 7.
[27] *See e.g.* LCIA Rules Article 5
[28] *See* ICC Rules Article 8.

dispute has arise. Moreover, a few institutions may not allow the parties complete freedom in choosing arbitrators under any circumstances. Thus, the choice of a particular set of institutional rules is often significant in the ultimate selection of arbitrators.

A set of rules will also provide defaults with respect to the number of arbitrators in the event the parties fail to agree on this. Most provide for a sole arbitrator as the standard default, but allow for institutional discretion to appoint a three-member panel if the circumstances warrant it.[29] However, the UNCITRAL Rules simply provide for a three-member panel as the standard default.[30]

In the absence of any specific provision in the parties' agreement or any choice of rules, the constitution of the tribunal will be governed by the *lex arbitri.* Under the UNCITRAL Model Law, the default is a three-member tribunal,[31] with each party to choose one arbitrator, and the two party appointees to choose the presiding arbitrator.[32]

Assuming that the parties are entitled to choose the arbitrator or arbitrators, one might reasonably ask how such a choice is made. Most institutions typically have lists of well established arbitrators, though the parties are not typically limited to such lists.[33] But how should a party decide on one arbitrator over another? May a party or its counsel interview potential arbitrators? Historically, the European answer was that the party and its counsel must make any choice from whatever information is available, such as the general reputation the arbitrator within the trade or legal community, or any publications by the arbitrator or other publicly available information. However, the party or its counsel could not typically interview a prospective arbitrator directly—not even a party appointed arbitrator. This is one of the many practices that have begun to change in response to increased American involvement in international commercial arbitration.

Generally, a party may not engage in *ex parte* contact with an arbitrator regarding the matter in dispute—either before or after the arbitrator's appointment. Such rules are obviously intended to preserve the required impartiality and independence of the arbitrators, and the rule is near absolute with respect to sole arbitrators. However, it has begun to soften somewhat with respect to party appointed arbitrators. In recent years, the American practice of interviewing prospective party appointed arbitrators has begun to make its way into European

---

[29] *See e.g.* ICC Rules Article 8(2); AAA/ICDR Rules Article 5.

[30] UNCITRAL Rules Article 5.

[31] Article 10(2).

[32] Article 11(3)(a).

[33] *But see* Arbitration Rules of China International Economic and Trade Arbitration Commission (CIETAC) Article 24 (limiting any arbitrator choices to the Panel of Arbitrators of the Arbitration Commission).

practice. The nature and content of such interviews is, however, severely constrained and often subject to full disclosure to the opposing party (both as to the occurrence and content of the interview).[34]

The AAA/ICDR Rules are somewhat unique in specifically allowing party contact with a prospective party appointed arbitrator regarding an unusually broad range of subjects, among other things, the "general nature of the controversy," the "anticipated proceedings," and the "suitability of candidates for selection as a third arbitrator."[35] The right to such *ex parte* contact with a potential arbitrator may come as a surprise to some European parties, but it is likely to make American parties somewhat more comfortable with this important choice. This rule is undoubtedly reflection of the former American practice in which party appointed arbitrators were not expected to be neutral, but were seen as a sort of advocate within the tribunal. The trend in the United States has moved significantly towards requiring neutrality of all arbitrators, and the AAA/ICDR Rules themselves provide for such neutrality.[36] However, this rule reflects a continuing American belief in the idea that the parties are entitled to a high degree of trust and confidence that their arguments will receive a particularly fair airing before any arbitrator they appoint.

In contrast, the LCIA Rules maintain an absolute ban on contact between parties and prospective arbitrators prior to the formation of the tribunal.[37] All communications must be made through the institution. Other rules often don't speak specifically to the issue.

Limits on *ex parte* contact between the parties and the arbitrators can present particularly significant challenges in *ad hoc* arbitration, where the parties must, to a large degree, accomplish the selection and engagement of an arbitral panel (including issues such as fees) without any institutional assistance in communicating with the arbitrator.

B.   ARBITRATOR SELECTION WHEN THE PARTIES CANNOT OR WILL NOT

If each of the parties performs all of its obligations under the arbitration agreement, then the selection of arbitrators is typically a reasonably simple process. However, if the parties are unable to reach agreement on a consensual selection, or if a party fails in its obligation to select a party appointed arbitrator, the constitution of the tribunal comes to an abrupt halt. Inasmuch as the tribunal

---

[34] *See* Redfern & Hunter, *supra* n. 4, at § 4-50, 235 (describing both the recent trend and a list of recommended limitations).
[35] *See* AAA/ICDR Rules Article 7(2). Even these rules do not, however, allow for *ex parte* contact with a sole arbitrator. *Id.*
[36] *See* AAA/ICDR Rules Article 7(1).
[37] *See* LCIA Rules Article 13.1.

has not yet been formed, there is a potential vacuum in terms of authority to move the appointment process forward. There are a variety of means of filling this vacuum, with varying levels of efficiency.

The simplest and most efficient method is found in institutional arbitration allowing the administering institution or a designated appointed authority simply to make the necessary appointment if either or both parties fail to do so.[38] The availability of this remedy is one of the single most significant advantages of institutional arbitration[39] and also serves to discourage a recalcitrant party from failing to make a necessary selection in hopes of delaying the process.

Example 8-7

The parties' arbitration agreement provides for arbitration in Geneva under the Swiss Rules. If the parties have agreed to a sole arbitrator, but are unable to reach agreement within the applicable time-limit, then Article 7(3) authorizes the Swiss "Chambers" (through its Arbitration Committee) to make the appointment itself. Similarly, if the parties have agreed to a three-member tribunal, and one of the parties fails to designate an arbitrator as required, the Chambers may make the appointment itself under Article 8(2).

Where parties agree to *ad hoc* arbitration, the issue of a stalled appointment process becomes considerably more challenging. If the parties have adopted the UNCITRAL Rules, they do provide, however, at least a reasonably workable solution. Article 6(2) provides that any party to the arbitration "may request the Secretary-General of the Permanent Court of Arbitration at the Hague ("PCA") to designate an appointing authority." Typically, the PCA will designate an arbitration institution located in the place of arbitration of the place in which the dispute arose. That institution shall have the same authority to appoint arbitrators as if the parties had chosen it themselves.

If, however, the parties agree to *ad hoc* arbitration without designating any rules providing for an appointing authority or such a designation, then the parties are left with only the option of petitioning a court for assistance. For example, Model Law Article 11 provides that the court designated in Article 6 shall appoint arbitrators when the parties are unable to do so pursuant to their

---

[38] *See e.g.* SIAC Rules Articles 6 & 7; Swiss Rules Articles 7 & 8.
[39] After the tribunal has been constituted, the importance of institutional assistance is somewhat lessened.

agreement.[40]   In the selection of arbitrators, the importance of selecting an effective set of rules and, typically, an administering institution cannot be overstated if the parties hope to minimize recourse to the courts.

C.   ARBITRATOR DISCLOSURES AND STANDARDS OF NEUTRALITY

Arbitrator selections by the parties are not of course the last word on the issue. The arbitrators selected by the parties (or, for that matter, the institution) must accept their appointment.   One issue will of course involve the arbitrator's current workload and schedule. However, assuming the arbitrator is interested in the engagement and has sufficient time available, the arbitrator must first determine if he or she would have any ethical conflicts of interest that would preclude service as an arbitrator in this dispute.[41]

Article 12

Grounds for challenge

(1) When a person is approached in connection with his possible appointment as an arbitrator, he shall disclose any circumstances likely to give rise to justifiable doubts as to his impartiality or independence. An arbitrator, from the time of his appointment and throughout the arbitral proceedings, shall without delay disclose any such circumstances to the parties unless they have already been informed of them by him.

(2) An arbitrator may be challenged only if circumstances exist that give rise to justifiable doubts as to his impartiality or independence, or if he does not possess qualifications agreed to by the parties. A party may challenge an arbitrator appointed by him, or in whose appointment he has participated, only for reasons of which he becomes aware after the appointment has been made.

---

[40] The American Federal Arbitration Act also provides to court appointment in section 5. In contrast, however to the three-member tribunal default under the Model Law, FAA section 5 provides for a single arbitrator—one of the few default rules in the FAA.
[41] This analysis is similar, in many respects, to the sort of conflicts analysis a lawyer would undertake before agreeing to represent a new client.

All arbitrators—whether party appointed or otherwise—are expected to be entirely impartial and independent.[42] A prospective arbitrator "shall disclose any circumstances likely to give rise to justifiable doubts as to his impartiality or independence."[43] This duty of disclosure is a continuing obligation to the extent that circumstances may change or new information may arise.[44]

While often considered to be two parts of the same package, impartiality and independence may be distinguished in the manner in which each is evaluated. An arbitrator's independence might be questioned where he has some sort of financial or other relationship with one of the parties. This is generally considered to be an objective test based on whether a particular relationship would give rise to justifiable doubts in a reasonable person.

In contrast an arbitrator's impartiality might be questioned where she has an actual bias in favor of one of the parties. This is generally considered to be a subjective test, focused on the arbitrator's actual state of mind. Of course, one of the sources of proving such bias would be an objectively shown lack of independence, and a subjective lack of impartiality will often arise out of a relationship drawing one's independence into question. In short, these two elements are analytically distinct, but are often fully intertwined.

D.   CHALLENGING THE APPOINTMENT OF AN ARBITRATOR

A party that is not satisfied with the independence or impartiality of an arbitrator may challenge that arbitrator, typically within a limited time period after the arbitrator's appointment, or after the learning the facts giving rise to any justifiable doubts.[45] In fact, a party may typically even challenge an arbitrator it selected, itself, provided that the grounds for the challenge arose after the selection.[46]

---

[42] *See* IBA Guidelines on Conflicts of Interest in International Arbitration (International Bar Association 2004). As indicated above, the American practice historically provided for non-neutral party appointed arbitrators. While such party advocates are still common in domestic arbitration, the practice in international arbitration now fully embraces the neutrality requirement for all arbitrators.

[43] Model Law Article 12(1); *see also* UNCITRAL Rules Article 9 (each providing the same); AAA/ICDR Rules Article 7(1) (same); *but see* ICC Rules Articles 9 & 11(1) (the latter providing for a challenge based on the arbitrator's lack of independence *or otherwise*).

[44] Model Law Article 12(1).

[45] *See e.g.* Model Law Article 13(2) (allowing only fifteen days for any challenge).

[46] *See e.g.* Model Law Article 12(2).

Article 13

Challenge procedure

(1) The parties are free to agree on a procedure for challenging an arbitrator, subject to the provisions of paragraph (3) of this article.

(2) Failing such agreement, a party who intends to challenge an arbitrator shall, within fifteen days after becoming aware of the constitution of the arbitral tribunal or after becoming aware of any circumstance referred to in article 12(2), send a written statement of the reasons for the challenge to the arbitral tribunal. Unless the challenged arbitrator withdraws from his office or the other party agrees to the challenge, the arbitral tribunal shall decide on the challenge.

(3) If a challenge under any procedure agreed upon by the parties or under the procedure of paragraph (2) of this article is not successful, the challenging party may request, within thirty days after having received notice of the decision rejecting the challenge, the court or other authority specified in article 6 to decide on the challenge, which decision shall be subject to no appeal; while such a request is pending, the arbitral tribunal, including the challenged arbitrator, may continue the arbitral proceedings and make an award.

The arbitrator may, if challenged, decide to withdraw from the tribunal, in which case a replacement arbitrator shall be appointed.[47] An arbitrator may, under some rules, also be required to withdraw if the challenge is accepted by the opposing party.[48] However, if the arbitrator does not withdraw in some manner, then the challenge must be determined by an appropriate decision maker.

The Model Law default legal rule and a few institutional rules provide that any challenge shall be determined by the arbitral tribunal, including the challenged arbitrator.[49] However, most institutional arbitration rules provide that a challenge

---

[47] *See e.g.* Model Law Article 15. In the event of a prompt challenge and withdrawal or a decisional removal an arbitrator will almost always be replaced, as long as arbitrator withdraws or is removed before the proceedings begin. However, if an arbitrator's service is terminated some time after the proceedings have begun, the proceedings may be continued in some circumstances without replacement. This issue is addressed in Chapter 9.

[48] AAA/ICDR Rules Article 8(3).

[49] *See* Model Law Article 13(2); DIS Arbitration Rules (1998) Article 18.2.

shall be determined by the institution rather than the arbitrators.[50] Again, various legal or private rules may provide differing means of deciding any challenge. While neither approach is unreasonable, a party may want to consider the differences in constructing an arbitration regime.

V. JURISDICTION PART I: THE QUESTION OF WHO DECIDES ANY JURISDICTIONAL CHALLENGE

In deciding the jurisdiction of the tribunal to arbitrate the parties' dispute, two levels of threshold questions must be considered initially. First, who decides the ultimate jurisdictional question—national courts or arbitrators? Second, to the extent that each may have a role in making this decision, what sort of decision making sequence is appropriate? The doctrine of competence-competence addresses each of these questions.

In answering these questions, one must also ask if the same approach is appropriate for all jurisdictional issues. In particular, who should decide issues relating to the validity of the parties' overall sale of goods contract (sometimes called the "main" or "container" agreement inasmuch as it "contains" the subject arbitration clause). For reasons explained below, this particular issue is almost uniformly assigned to the arbitrators under the doctrine of separability. The doctrine of separability also protects the viability of the arbitration process in the event the tribunal finds the contract containing the arbitration clause to be null and void. Without separability, the tribunal would, under such circumstances, be required to decline jurisdiction without issuing any sort of award. Separability, however, allows the tribunal to decide on the validity of the container agreement by issuing a fully preclusive and enforceable award.

Model Law Article 16(1) provides an excellent example of a statute addressing both competence-competence and separability.

> ### Article 16(1)
> ### Competence of arbitral tribunal to rule on its jurisdiction
>
> (1) The arbitral tribunal may rule on its own jurisdiction, including any objections with respect to the existence or validity of the arbitration agreement. For that purpose, an arbitration clause which forms part of a contract shall be treated as an

---

[50] *See e.g.* ICC Rules Article 11; LCIA Rules Article 10.4; AAA/ICDR Rules Article 9; Swiss Rules Article 11.1; SIAC Rules Article 12.1; *see also* UNCITRAL Rules Article 12(1) (providing for any challenge to be decided by an appointing authority even in the absence of institutional arbitration).

> agreement independent of the other terms of the contract. A decision by the arbitral tribunal that the contract is null and void shall not entail *ipso jure* the invalidity of the arbitration clause.

These questions of "who decides," including the doctrine of separability are addressed below, while the issues to be addressed in making the actual jurisdictional decision (whether made by the tribunal or national courts) are addressed in section VI. The following excerpted article helps to introduce each of the issues in this section.

Who Decides the Arbitrators' Jurisdiction? Separability and Competence-Competence in Transnational Perspective,

John J. Barceló

. . .

II. The "Who Decides?" Question at Different Stages of the Court-Arbitration Process

For purposes of analysis, this comment divides the court-arbitration process into three stages. Stage 1 encompasses litigation, generally at the outset of the dispute, over whether the court should hear the dispute or send the parties to arbitration. Stage 2 encompasses decision making by arbitrators concerning whether to hear the dispute or decline jurisdiction. Stage 3 encompasses court review of an award (set-aside or recognition and enforcement) respecting whether the arbitrators had good jurisdiction. The parties may bypass Stage 1 altogether and go directly to Stage 2. Or Stage 1 and Stage 2 may proceed concurrently, with one party urging a court to take jurisdiction and the other, an arbitral tribunal.

Stage 1 is generally the point at which judges and scholars ask the "who decides" question. Who decides—court or arbitrator—whether a dispute goes to arbitration or stays in court? If the parties go directly to Stage 2, but one of them nevertheless challenges the jurisdiction of the arbitral tribunal, the arbitrators will decide whether they have jurisdiction. This, at a minimum, is what is meant by competence-competence: the arbitrators are authorized to decide their own jurisdiction, at least as an initial matter.

Sometimes the "who decides" question arises at Stage 3. The

arbitrators have decided they have jurisdiction, either in a preliminary award or in the final award itself. When a court reviews that award, in either a set-aside or a recognition and enforcement proceeding, the court must decide how much weight to give the arbitrators' decision upholding arbitral jurisdiction. They may give it no weight at all (de novo review) or various levels of deference (from affirming if the arbitrators' award is reasonable, to affirming if there is any colorable justification for it, to affirming without second guessing the arbitrators at all). . . .

Stage 1 is crucial concerning whether arbitration is allowed to go forward efficaciously or is obstructed by court intervention. At Stage 1, a party opposing arbitration may raise any of a series of legal issues requiring court, rather than arbitrator, decision. These may include any or all of the following claims: (1) the container contract is invalid (for a reason that would not directly invalidate the arbitration clause); (2) no arbitration agreement came into existence between the parties; (3) an existing arbitration agreement is either formally invalid (for example, not in writing) or materially invalid (for example, violative of mandatory law); (4) a disputed issue is not within the scope of the arbitration agreement; (5) mandatory law prohibits a disputed issue, though within the scope of the parties' arbitration agreement, to be arbitrated (a special type of material invalidity respecting a specific issue fraught with public policy concerns, such as (formerly) antitrust or securities fraud); (6) some precondition for permissible arbitration has not been met (for example, a time-limit on initiating arbitration); (7) the party seeking arbitration has waived its right to arbitrate or is estopped from claiming that right.

The greater the number of these claims required to be fully litigated at Stage 1, the greater the potential for disruption of the arbitration process-or, in other words, the greater the potential for an obstructing party to frustrate a genuine agreement to arbitrate. Thus at Stage 1, an extremely proarbitration legal order might send all of these questions to the arbitrators, with no, or perhaps minimal (prima facie), judicial scrutiny. But of course arbitration is not the holy grail. Not all parties resisting arbitration are obstructionists. A party should be entitled to its day in court unless it has agreed to arbitrate. That is the competing value. A legal order must decide what weight to give to these competing values and how to structure the process to maximize overall value by reducing opportunities for obstructionism while preserving legitimate claims for reasonably prompt judicial decision. The doctrines of separability and competence-competence operate at this tension point in a legal order.

. . .

36 VAND. J. TRANSNAT'L L. 1115 (2003).

* * * * *

Notes and Questions

Note 1: Note the seven potential bases for a jurisdictional challenge listed by the author above. Reasons 2 through 7 each specifically address the viability of the arbitration agreement, itself, or a party's right to bring a claim pursuant to that specific agreement. As such, one must consider the relative competence of courts and arbitral tribunals to address each of these jurisdictional challenges, as well as any potential required sequence for such decisions. Reason 1, however, focuses solely on the "main" or "container" contract within which the arbitration provision is included. For the reasons explained below, the doctrine of separability essentially excludes entirely from court review issues involving reason 1—a challenge to the container contract that does not specifically relate to the arbitration clause.

The doctrine of separability avoids the entire "sequence" issue with respect to challenges within its scope, because a court is not empowered to address such issues at all. The (A) separability paradigm is, therefore, addressed first below. It is followed by a complete discussion of the interaction between courts and arbitral tribunals on all of the remaining jurisdictional challenges (those not subject to separability) in the (B) competence-competence paradigm.

A.   THE SEPARABILITY PARADIGM

The doctrine of separability serves to protect the viability of the arbitration process in the event the agreement containing the arbitration clause is ultimately found to be "null and void."[51] Defenses to contract validity (*e.g.*, mistake, fraud or duress/threat) are often wrapped up in the merits of the parties' dispute. As

---

[51] These are the terms used in Model Law Article 16(1), and they are typical among arbitration statutes, though there is some variation. *See e.g.* English Arbitration Act, section 7 (providing an arbitration clause is not affected by a decision that the container "agreement is invalid, or did not come into existence or has become ineffective"). In contrast, the United States Federal Arbitration Act does not address separability at all in the statute itself.

such, a tribunal may not decide on such defenses until it renders a final award. If the arbitrators ultimately determine that the agreement containing the arbitration clause is invalid, then one might reasonably ask whether the arbitration clause within it is rendered invalid as well. The doctrine of separability provides that the invalidity of the container agreement does not, in and of itself, invalidate the arbitration agreement, thereby preserving the arbitrators' jurisdiction to render an award—even an award finding the container agreement invalid.

From a theoretical perspective, it is not obvious that any element of an invalid agreement would normally survive such invalidity—*i.e.*, something cannot come from nothing.[52] One might suggest that an arbitration agreement within a container agreement later found invalid has at least a moment of validity. For example, an agreement rendered invalid based on duress is said to be voidable and, therefore, enjoys at least a theoretical moment of validity. If the duress defense does not directly touch upon the arbitration clause within the container agreement, then one might perhaps explain that such an already existent and fully autonomous arbitration clause is saved by its separability from the container contract, because the defense itself only touches upon the container contract. Of course this theoretical justification becomes much more difficult to maintain as one moves from voidable to void contracts,[53] and from void contracts to questions of whether a contract ever came into existence in the first instance.[54] However, reasons of pure practicality provide additional support of the doctrine of separability.

If a finding that the overall agreement is invalid would also invalidate the arbitration clause within, the very existence of arbitration as an effective means of dispute resolution would be undermined. In effect, an award in favor of a defense against the validity of the overall agreement would itself be made invalid at the moment it was issued. The award invalidating the container agreement would effectively destroy the very basis upon which the jurisdiction of its issuing tribunal was based. Inasmuch as such an award would have no preclusive effect, the arbitrators would, instead, be required to decline jurisdiction—arguably a decision without any preclusive effect. The parties would have, thereby, wasted their time and money in presenting the issue to the tribunal in the first instance. The losing party in arbitration could then, presumably, bring the issue before a

---

[52] *See Prima Paint Corp. v. Flood & Conklin Mfg. Co.*, 388 U.S. 395, 407–425 (Black, J., dissenting) (addressing the basic analytical flaws in separability as a matter of contract theory and consent—inasmuch as fraud vitiates the entire contract, leaving nothing).

[53] *See Buckeye Check Cashing, Inc. v. Cardegna*, 546 U.S. 440 (2006). In *Buckeye*, the United States Supreme Court rejected any distinction between voidable and void contracts in holding that a validity issue involving illegality (thus rendering the container agreement void) is for the arbitrators.

[54] *See e.g.* English Arbitration Act of 1996, Article 7 (extending separability to circumstances in which the arbitration agreement "did not come into existence").

court of competent jurisdiction, which could reach a different conclusion on the merits of the defense decided earlier by the arbitrators. That decision of course would indicate that the arbitrators actually had jurisdiction.

The problem is obviously one of circularity. There are really only two basic solutions to break the circularity: (1) allow a court to decide in advance all issues in any way affecting the enforceability of the container contract based on the potential effect of such issues on the jurisdiction of the arbitrators; or (2) the doctrine of separability. The problem with the former is that enforceability issues will almost always involve the merits of the parties' overall dispute, and the court's decision on these issues in the context of a decision on jurisdiction will often effectively deprive the parties' of their original bargain—arbitration of the merits of their dispute. Even to the extent the court's decision left undecided issues for the arbitrators, the parties would virtually have to put on their case again, thus losing much of the efficiency they sought from arbitration in the first instance.

In short, the doctrine of separability is, at the very least, a necessary fiction that allows a tribunal to decide all claims and defenses relating to the main contract, together, and preserves the jurisdiction of the tribunal—however it might ultimately decide such claims and defenses. The doctrine of separability is a fundamental necessity of any effective arbitration regime.[55]

However, the doctrine of separability is not necessarily without limits. For example, almost all would agree that if the signature on the written container contract is a forgery, this invalidates the container agreement, as well as the arbitration clause within.[56] A validity defense that specifically addresses the arbitration agreement itself will also invalidate the arbitration agreement. For example, a party might assert that the arbitration clause, itself, was only added to the contract after its initial conclusion and was specifically done so under circumstances involving duress or improper threat. In such cases, a finding of forgery, or a finding of duress or improper threat involving the arbitration clause, itself, would require that the arbitrators simply decline jurisdiction as a threshold matter, without any formal award, because any tribunal award would be rendered invalid based on a finding invalidating the arbitration clause itself.

At the extremes, the reach of separability is relatively consistent. The doctrine will almost certainly preserve the tribunal's jurisdiction to rule in favor of an

---

[55] Separability operates in a similar fashion with respect to choice-of-law issues avoiding the same sort of problems of circularity. As mentioned earlier in Chapter 5, CISG Article 81(1) also operates in a somewhat similar vein. Article 81(1) protects the viability of the arbitration agreement (or any other dispute resolution provision) in the event one of the parties exercises its right to avoid the main contract.

[56] This approach is also dictated by the requirement of a signed writing for any arbitration agreement under New York Convention Article II(2).

invalidity defense relating to the container contract, while it will not preserve the tribunal's jurisdiction to rule that the signature on the container contract was forged. Between these extremes, the reach of separability is less consistent or less clear. On one hand, many jurisdictions limit the doctrine to invalidity defenses,[57] while, on the other hand, some jurisdictions extend separability to non-existence of the container contract.[58] The UNCITRAL Model Law is less clear on the issue. While the tribunal's jurisdiction to determine its own jurisdiction (*see* competence-competence below) definitely extends to issues involving the existence of the agreement, the doctrine of separability extends only to contracts deemed "null and void." Whether the words "null and void" include "non-existent" container agreements may in fact have significant ramifications for an arbitration regime.

If the words "null and void" are interpreted as limited to invalidity, then a tribunal has the jurisdiction to determine whether or not the parties ever formed the container contract (i.e., its existence), but may not issue an award if it determines they did not. Instead, the tribunal would simply have to decline jurisdiction. If, however, the words "null and void" are interpreted broadly to include non-existence as well as invalidity, then a tribunal might be empowered to issue an award determining that the parties never formed an agreement. Inasmuch as questions of formation (e.g., offer, acceptance, withdrawal, revocation) are often inextricably intertwined with the merits of the parties' dispute, it would seem far more efficient, as a practical matter, to extend separability to such issues of formation.[59] However, such an extension might be seen by many as going too far beyond the bounds of party consent upon which arbitration is based. The trend is nonetheless in the direction of extending rather than contracting the doctrine of separability.

Thus, the doctrine of separability almost uniformly allows the tribunal to decide at least one jurisdictional issue—the validity of the agreement containing the arbitration clause—and has also been extended under some arbitration law to issues involving the existence of the container agreement. However, other issues of jurisdiction may be allocated in a variety of ways between courts and arbitrators. This is the larger "who decides" question.

---

[57] *See Buckeye Check Cashing, Inc. v. Cardegna*, 546 U.S. 440 (2006).

[58] *See e.g.* English Arbitration Act of 1996, Article 7 (extending separability to circumstances in which the arbitration agreement "did not come into existence").

[59] *See* Stewart Shackleton, *Arbitration without Contract*, 17 Mealey's Intl. Arb. Rep. (Sept. 2002) (suggesting that section 7 of the English Arbitration Act extends separability to reach a failure in the formation of the underlying contract). The issue is particularly important in arbitration clauses expressly including contract "formation" within the scope of issues to be arbitrated. *See e.g.* JAMS International Arbitration Rules and WIPO Arbitration Rules. Unless separability extends to formation, the tribunal could not decide in an award that the parties had failed to form a contract without eliminating the source of its jurisdiction in the process.

B.   THE COMPETENCE-COMPETENCE PARADIGM

On a relatively simplistic level, the question of "who decides" jurisdiction is answered easily under most governing laws. For example, Model Law Article 16(1) states quite clearly and unequivocally that the tribunal itself "may rule on its own jurisdiction, including any objections with respect to the existence or validity of the arbitration agreement."[60] Articles 16(3) and 34, together, provide that the tribunal's decision is subject to review by the appropriate court—whether decided as a preliminary matter or as part of the ultimate award. Indeed, this same result obtains under most modern arbitration laws. Even under the American Federal Arbitration Act, which does not itself grant the tribunal authority to rule on its own jurisdiction, the parties may do so[61] and are generally deemed by courts to have done so by incorporating a set of rules granting the tribunal such authority.[62]

However, a careful reader will also note that Model Law Article 8(1), as well as New York Convention Article II(3), provide in almost identical language that a court before which an action subject to arbitration is brought shall, upon request, refer the parties to arbitration, unless it finds the arbitration agreement is "null and void, inoperative or incapable of being performed."

Article 8 (Model Law)

Arbitration agreement and substantive claim before court

(1) A court before which an action is brought in a matter which is the subject of an arbitration agreement shall, if a party so requests not later than when submitting his first statement on the substance of the dispute, refer the parties to arbitration

---

[60] The entire text of Article 16 was provided at the beginning of section V.

[61] *See First Options of Chicago v. Kaplan*, 514 U.S. 938, 944–945 (1995) (holding that the parties may grant the tribunal the right to rule on its own jurisdiction, but may only do so based on *"clear and unmistakable"* evidence of such intent, so as to overcome the normative presumption under the FAA that this question of who decides is for the courts (emphasis in original)).

[62] *See e.g.* Article 15 of the AAA/ICDR Rules (providing that the tribunal "shall have the power to rule on its own jurisdiction, including any objections with respect to the existence, scope or validity of the arbitration agreement"). While one might reasonably question whether the adoption of a set of rules by incorporation is sufficient to establish the requisite "clear and unmistakable" intent required under *First Options, see e.g.* Richard C. Reuben, *First Options, Consent to Arbitration, and the Demise of Separability: Restoring Access to Justice for Contracts with Arbitration Provisions*, 56 S.M.U. L. Rev. 819, 869 (2003), the majority of courts addressing the issue continue to find that it does, though a few decline to do so. *See* Joseph L. Franco, Comment, *Casually Finding the Clear and Unmistakable: A Re-Evaluation of* First Options *in Light of Recent Lower Court Decisions*, 10 Lewis & Clark L. Rev. 443 (2006).

> unless it finds that the agreement is null and void,
> inoperative or incapable of being performed.
>
> (2) Where an action referred to in paragraph (1) of this article
> has been brought, arbitral proceedings may nevertheless be
> commenced or continued, and an award may be made, while
> the issue is pending before the court.

> **Article II (New York Convention)**
>
> . . .
>
> (3) The court of a Contracting State, when seized of an action in
> a matter in respect of which the parties have made [an
> agreement in writing to submit their dispute to arbitration],
> shall, at the request of one of the parties, refer the parties to
> arbitration, unless it finds that the agreement is null and
> void, inoperative or incapable of being performed.

Neither Model Law Article 8(1), nor New York Convention Article II provides much express guidance with respect to the extent of any court review prior to a jurisdictional decision by the tribunal under Model Law Article 16.[63] Moreover, Model Law Article 8(2) expressly provides for the possibility of parallel proceedings on jurisdiction, as between the court and arbitral tribunal. This raises a variety of questions regarding the relationship between the court's authority under Model Law Article 8 and New York Convention Article II(3) on one hand, and the arbitral tribunal's authority under Model Law Article 16 on the other—as well as similar issues arising under other national laws governing arbitration. Professor Barceló's article, excerpted above, continues below with an excellent comparative analysis of various approaches to "competence-competence."

---

[63] At least one commentator has, however, suggested that New York Convention Article II(3) (using the same language as Model Law Article 8(1)) was intended to provide only for narrow court review and should be limited to "manifest" failures to agree to arbitration. *See* Albert Jan van den Berg, *The New York Convention of 1958: Towards a Uniform Judicial Interpretation* 155 (Kluwer L. & Taxation 1981).

Who Decides the Arbitrators' Jurisdiction? Separability and Competence-Competence in Transnational Perspective,

John J. Barceló *(continued from above)*

. . .

IV. Competence-Competence

Whereas separability sends only [*issues limited to the invalidity of the container contract as a whole*][64] to the arbitrators, competence-competence may send [*the remaining jurisdictional issues*][65] to them as well, following no, or only prima facie, judicial scrutiny. Under a robust competence-competence doctrine even issues of the existence and validity of the arbitration agreement may go initially to the arbitrators. Competence-competence thus addresses the "who decides" question on a broader scale and is more central to resolving the policy tension between protecting arbitration from obstruction, on one hand, and preserving legitimate disputes over arbitrator jurisdiction for a prompt court hearing, on the other. Competence-competence is also the more controversial of the two "who decides" doctrines. Whereas separability is universally accepted, competence-competence is controversial and has spawned a range of different national responses.

. . .

[W]hether courts or arbitrators are the preferred decision makers at Stage 1 impacts the effectiveness of arbitration. To the extent that courts are preferred outright and without qualification, parties opposing arbitration have an incentive to raise as many of these Stage 1 judicial questions as possible. This can tie up arbitration significantly and charge courts with decisions that may preempt the merits. Moreover, the availability of de novo judicial review at Stage 3 does not truly undercut a number of consequences that flow from early arbitrator decision making. First, if the arbitrators' award is convincing, there may never be a Stage 3. The losing party may prefer to pay or negotiate a settlement. Second, even if Stage 3 review is de novo, a court will not confront a tabula rasa. A well-reasoned award can

---

[64] Authors' Note: As indicated in the text in section A *supra*, one might also extend separability to the non-existence of the container contract.

[65] Authors' Note: The remainder of the jurisdictional issues are perhaps somewhat less likely to be bound up with the merits of the dispute and, therefore, less problematic to be decided as threshold matters by either a court or arbitrators.

strongly influence the judicial outcome. Third, and perhaps most important, in international arbitration an award set aside at the seat may nevertheless be enforced in another jurisdiction. Thus, it matters whether courts stay their hand at Stage 1 and allow arbitrators to proceed to an award.

A. Positive and Negative Competence-Competence

Most discussions of competence-competence, especially in U.S. literature, treat only the positive aspect of the doctrine, which is a simple and uncontroversial notion. It means that, at Stage 2, arbitrators are empowered to rule on their own jurisdiction; they are not required to stay the proceeding to seek judicial guidance.

The doctrine has another, much more consequential aspect, known as the negative effect of competence-competence. It originated in French law, which is well known for its proarbitration character. The negative effect doctrine holds that in order to allow arbitrators to rule on their own jurisdiction at Stage 2 as an initial matter, court jurisdiction at Stage 1 should be constrained.

The core challenge underlying the doctrine is to find the right amount of and context for court restraint. A legal order needs the right balance between avoiding arbitration-obstructing tactics at Stage 1 and protecting parties from being forced to arbitrate without their legitimate and genuine consent. Because this is a complex issue, a number of procedural permutations have surfaced in different countries—primarily in Europe. The next subsection first discusses the leading approaches and the justifications for them and then closes with an assessment of where U.S. law stands on these issues.

B. The Negative Effect Doctrine in Transnational Law

1. The French Approach

The negative competence-competence principle was codified in French law with the 1981 enactment of Article 1458 of French New Code of Civil Procedure:

Whenever a dispute submitted to an arbitral tribunal by virtue of an arbitration agreement is brought before the court of the state, such court shall decline jurisdiction. If the arbitral tribunal has not yet been seized of the matter, the court should also decline jurisdiction unless the arbitration agreement is manifestly null. Although Article 1458 concerns domestic arbitration in France, the principle has been extended by court decision to international arbitration.

The French approach turns on two principal considerations. First, if an arbitration tribunal has already been seized of the matter, the French court will refuse jurisdiction and leave questions respecting the arbitration agreement's existence, validity and scope to the arbitrators. Second, if an arbitration tribunal has not been seized, the court will undertake a limited scrutiny of those questions and will retain jurisdiction only if the arbitration agreement is manifestly null. Thus, if the court finds prima facie existence, validity and scope, it will refer the parties to arbitration. After an award is rendered—that is, at Stage 3— French courts will review the arbitrators' jurisdiction de novo.

The primary policy justification for this approach is to prevent a party from obstructing or delaying arbitration. The French doctrine allows greater court scrutiny if a party goes to court before the case has been presented to arbitrators, on the theory that such a party is more likely to be acting in good faith with legitimate concerns about the arbitrators' jurisdiction. But even here, initial court review is only to establish a prima facie case for arbitration. If this prima facie test is met, or if an arbitral tribunal is already seized, the arbitrators themselves must be the first to give full consideration to jurisdictional challenges. Since most arbitration statutes and institutional rules provide for the arbitrators to render a preliminary award on jurisdiction, in most cases such a preliminary award will not be long in coming. Such an early award on jurisdiction can then be the subject of annulment proceedings at the seat of arbitration. If the seat is in France, the annulment review will be de novo.

Thus, in the vast majority of cases the arbitral process will go forward, but parties with a legitimate basis for objecting to the arbitrators' jurisdiction will have an opportunity, after only moderate delay, to make their case to a judge. Presumably those with principally obstructionist motives, who might consider such jurisdictional challenges at Stage 1 cost-justified, could reach a different conclusion at Stage 3—especially in the face of a well-reasoned award.

A problem arises, however, where the arbitrators take advantage of the discretion arbitration statutes and institutional rules generally accord them and delay their decision on jurisdiction until the final award. They might do so, for example, either out of lack of sensitivity to the consequences of delaying judicial review or because the questions involved are so intertwined with the merits that a full proceeding is needed to resolve them. Even considering the possibility that the arbitrators might not rule on jurisdiction until the final award, one might still prefer the French solution. In the first place, such cases presumably will not be plentiful. But even where they arise, the party resisting arbitration for sound reasons presumably will ultimately prevail before a court most of the time. In many legal systems the prevailing party will be able to recoup the arbitration and litigation costs against the losing party. (A special rule allowing this result would seem appropriate in legal systems that would not normally allow it.) The party preferring arbitration who ultimately loses will of course suffer the wasted cost of the arbitral proceeding, but one might argue that this is the concomitant risk of proceeding with arbitration in the face of a strong jurisdictional challenge.

. . .

3. The UNCITRAL Model Law

Two different provisions of the Model Law are relevant to the negative competence-competence doctrine-Article 8(1) and Article 16. Article 8(1) deals directly with a judicial decision at Stage 1 respecting the existence of a valid arbitration agreement:

A court before which an action is brought in a matter which is the subject of an arbitration agreement shall, if a party so requests not later than when submitting his first statement of the substance of the dispute, refer the parties to arbitration unless it finds that the agreement is null and void, inoperative or incapable of being performed.

On its face the language "unless it finds that the agreement is null and void, inoperative or incapable of being performed" could be read to authorize a full judicial determination of the arbitration agreement's existence and validity. The legislative history significantly buttresses that view. During the early 1980s, after enactment of the 1981 revision of the French Code of Civil Procedure, the Model Law drafters specifically refused to add the word "manifestly" before "null and void." The intent of that proposed addition was to limit the court to a prima facie finding that a valid arbitration agreement exists. The drafters apparently preferred, however, for the court to "settle" the issue before referring the parties to arbitration.

One consideration cuts the other way and introduces the possibility of ambiguity. It is the way in which Article 8(1) tracks identically the wording of the New York Convention, Article II(3): "unless [the court] finds that the said [arbitration] agreement is null and void, inoperative, or incapable of being performed." One of the leading commentators on the drafting of the New York Convention has observed that the pro-enforcement bias of the Convention should lead courts construing Article II(3) to accept the arbitration agreement's invalidity " in manifest cases only." Indeed, Swiss courts have apparently interpreted language in the 1987 Swiss Private International Law Act, virtually identical to New York Convention Article II(3), as requiring only a prima facie verification of the arbitration agreement's existence and validity at Stage 1.

Model Law Article 16 deals more directly with the competence-competence principle. Whereas, Article 16(1) codifies the positive competence-competence concept, Articles 16(3) and 8(2) go further and adopt at least a partial negative competence-competence doctrine. Article 16(3) reads:

> The arbitral tribunal may rule on a plea . . . [that it does not have jurisdiction] either as a preliminary question or in an award on the merits. If the arbitral tribunal rules as a preliminary question that it has jurisdiction, any party may request, within thirty days after having received notice of that ruling, the court specified in article 6 to decide the matter, which decision shall be subject to no appeal; while such a request is pending, the arbitral tribunal may continue the arbitral proceedings and make an award.

Article 8(2) reads: "Where an action . . . [in a matter that is subject to an arbitration agreement] has been brought, arbitral proceedings may nevertheless be commenced or continued, and an award may be made, while the issue is pending before the court."

These provisions certainly do not codify a French-version, negative competence-competence doctrine. At the same time, however, they clearly accommodate it. The legislative history shows that the doctrine was controversial. The adopted text was a compromise. Article 8(2) allows arbitral proceedings to go forward, despite court consideration of the arbitrators' jurisdiction. Thus, the court might be encouraged to defer to the arbitrators entirely or to give the arbitration agreement only prima facie scrutiny at Stage 1. Article 16(3) further encourages this outcome by allowing, even encouraging, arbitrators to rule on their jurisdiction as a preliminary question and providing for rapid, unappealable judicial review of that decision. Indeed, in jurisdictions that have adopted the Model Law, some courts seem to have read the negative competence-competence principle into Article 16.

4. The British Variation on the Model Law

The British Arbitration Act of 1996, which is based on the Model Law,[66] contains the standard Model Law Article 8(1) provision requiring a court to stay legal proceedings "unless satisfied that the arbitration agreement is null and void, inoperative, or incapable of being performed." The negative competence-competence issue here concerns whether "unless satisfied" entails only a prima facie review. Indeed, it seems arguable that "unless satisfied" is closer to "unless it is manifest" than is the Model Law terminology "unless it finds."

The true innovation in the British Act occurs in Sections 30-32. Like the Model Law, the British Act allows the arbitrators to render a decision on jurisdiction either in a preliminary award or in the final award. To deal with the difficulty noted above concerning the possibility that arbitrators might abuse that discretion and refuse to render a preliminary award, and thus delay judicial review, the British Act allows the parties by agreement to force the arbitrators to decide jurisdiction preliminarily. The party opposing arbitration could have no objection to such a procedure. Thus, the party favoring arbitration but concerned about wasteful proceedings would control, in effect, whether to insist on an early arbitrator decision on jurisdiction followed by rapid court review.

The British Act also protects the legitimate interests of the party

---

[66] Authors' Note: While this article is correct in suggesting that the British Arbitration Act has adopted much of the philosophy of the Model Law, UNCITRAL does not list the United Kingdom as an enacting state. For this reason, the casebook Authors have not to included the United Kingdom in Appendix A.

opposing arbitration. Even before the arbitrators render a decision on jurisdiction, a party may petition a court for an immediate determination of the jurisdictional issues. The court must render a decision if the arbitrators agree to the petition (or alternatively if all the parties agree). The arbitrators will presumably agree only if they conclude that dilatory tactics are not involved and the issue is truly a close question. If only the arbitrators have agreed, but not the other party or parties, then the court itself must also be satisfied that there are good reasons for it to intervene.

5. The German Variation on the Model Law

The German law of Kompetenz-Kompetenz prior to the new 1998 German Arbitration Act was relatively unique, or at least arguably so. Some commentators maintain that during the pre-1998 period if the parties expressly provided in the arbitration clause that the arbitrators had the power to decide their own jurisdiction, then this provision would exclude all judicial scrutiny of the question, even at Stage 3. Whether or not this was ever an accurate description of German law, it is certainly not an accurate description today because the 1998 German Arbitration Act is now based on the Model Law.

The new German statute's major variation from the Model Law respecting negative Kompetenz-Kompetenz arises in Section 1032(2), which is the German equivalent of Model Law Article 8. Under 1032(2) a German court may only decide the arbitrators' jurisdiction if requested to do so before "the arbitral tribunal is constituted." In this respect it follows the French approach. On the other hand, at least one commentator has maintained that when a court is properly seized of the jurisdictional issue, it is to make a full determination, not merely a prima facie one, as required in French law.

Section 1040 of the new German statute essentially follows the provisions of Model Law Article 16. One difference is that the German law expressly states a preference for the arbitrators to decide their jurisdiction in an interim award. That award would of course be subject to immediate set-aside proceedings.

6. The American Approach to Negative Competence-Competence

a. Domestic Arbitration

. . .

In sum, U.S. domestic arbitration law does not contain a robust negative competence-competence doctrine. Questions of the existence and validity of an arbitration agreement are for full, non-truncated decision by courts at Stage 1, whether or not arbitrators have been previously seized of the dispute. Would this conclusion be different if the dispute involved international arbitration subject to the New York Convention?

b. International Arbitration

[The above analysis of controlling United States Supreme Court case law involved domestic arbitration arising under Chapter 1 of the Federal Arbitration Act, sections 3 and 4, which have been interpreted as requiring a complete trial on Stage 1 issues to the extent there may be genuine issues of material fact.]

. . .

If the suit involves international arbitration subject to the New York Convention, however, then Chapter 2 of the FAA would apply. An agreement to arbitrate would fall under the New York Convention for the purposes of a U.S. proceeding, if (1) the agreement contemplates an award in a New York Convention country other than the United States or (2) although the seat of arbitration is within the United States, the United States does not regard the arbitration as domestic.

Though these provisions raise complex questions, case (1) is relatively straightforward. If the arbitration is to take place in a Convention country other than the United States the New York Convention applies. In such a case, the "who decides" question technically turns on interpretation of New York Convention Article II(3). This is because FAA Section 201 incorporates the Convention into U.S. law, and Section 208 provides that FAA Chapter 1 applies only to the extent that it is not inconsistent with the Convention. In other words, the Convention has priority.

The relevant language of the New York Convention Article II(3) is as follows:

The court of a Contracting State, when seized of an action in a matter in respect of which the parties have made an agreement within the meaning of this article, shall, at the request of one of the parties, refer the parties to arbitration, unless it finds that the said agreement is null and void, inoperative, or incapable of being performed.

How should a U.S. court interpret the language "unless it finds that the said agreement is null and void, inoperative or incapable of being performed"? Recall that at least one leading commentator has argued that this language should be understood as calling for only a prima facie determination of the existence and validity of an arbitration agreement. If the Supreme Court accepts that interpretation in a future case, the U.S. law of negative competence-competence would approach that of the French, at least respecting international arbitration.

Such an outcome is not impossible to imagine. The U.S. Supreme Court has frequently been more receptive to proarbitration arguments respecting international, as opposed to domestic, agreements. An important consideration is that these agreements are commercial and involve sophisticated, generally well-advised parties. The desire for uniformity of interpretation under the New York Convention could also influence the Court, but perhaps only if more countries than at present subscribe to the prima facie interpretation.

36 VAND. J. TRANSNAT'L L. 1115 (2003).

* * * * *

Notes and Questions

Note 1: The preceding article suggests that a pro-arbitration legal regime will minimize any court involvement prior to the tribunal's own decision on any jurisdictional issues. When one considers the nature of an agreement to arbitrate as an agreement to avoid national courts to the extent possible, this logic is quite compelling. Assuming the parties chose arbitration for its speed and efficiency, the less resort to courts, the more effective the choice.[67]

---

[67] This is not of course to suggest the absence of any contrary view. One could also argue that the court, as the final decision-maker on the issue of jurisdiction, ought in the interests of efficiency, simply make its determination first, thereby saving the parties the unnecessary expense of convening an arbitral tribunal.

Note 2: Governing law is not, however, the only way in which parties might seek to minimize court actions by recalcitrant parties and insure that the tribunal will have the "first word" on jurisdiction. For example, the parties might expressly agree in their contract "not to apply to any state court or other judicial authority for any relief regarding the Arbitral Tribunal's jurisdiction or authority, except with the agreement in writing of all parties to the arbitration or the prior authorization of the Arbitral Tribunal or following the latter's award ruling on the objection to its jurisdiction or authority." This essentially amounts to a contractual version of "negative competence-competence." Or the parties might simply adopt the LCIA Rules, from which the preceding quotation is drawn.[68] In either case, if one of the parties brought a premature court action, such action would likely be deemed a breach of contract subject to a claim for damages based on the costs incurred in the premature court action.[69]

VI. JURISDICTION PART II: THE SUBSTANTIVE JURISDICTIONAL ISSUES TO BE DECIDED—IT'S ALMOST ALL ABOUT CONSENT

Either party may challenge the jurisdiction of the tribunal. A respondent may challenge the tribunal's jurisdiction with respect to the original claims brought by the claimant, and the claimant may challenge the tribunal's jurisdiction with respect to any counter-claims or claims for setoff brought by the respondent. Such a plea challenging the jurisdiction of the tribunal must be made not later than the party's responsive pleading to the claim giving rise to its challenge. Absent good cause, an untimely challenge is deemed waived.[70]

Challenges to the jurisdiction generally involve questions of the parties' intent. Inasmuch as arbitration is entirely a consensual process, the parties intentions—to the extent they can be ascertained—will almost always control. Thus, a challenge will often focus on (A) whether the parties in fact agreed to arbitrate anything, (B) whether any such agreement is valid, and, if so, (C) whether the dispute in question is within its scope. However, party autonomy to arbitrate is not necessarily limitless. Some disputes, based on their subject matter, may be deemed inarbitrable as a matter of public policy—based on either (D) inarbitrability of the subject matter of the dispute or (E) other public policy

---

[68] *See* LCIA Rules Article 23.4; *see also* LCIA Rules Article 22.2 (similarly precluding resort to court regarding the resolution of various procedural issues allocated to the arbitrators).

[69] A request for an interim measure requiring specific performance of the promise might raise other issues often arising in anti-suit injunctions. These can be quite controversial when they involve a court in one country attempting to bar suit in another or when an arbitral tribunal is attempting to bar suit in court.

[70] *See e.g.* Model Law Article 16(2); LCIA Rules Article 23.2.

precluding arbitration of the dispute. If so, then the tribunal may be said to lack jurisdiction over the parties' dispute, irrespective of the parties' consent.[71]

A tribunal may render its decision on jurisdiction as a preliminary matter, or it may reserve the jurisdictional decision until its final award on the merits.[72] To the extent its jurisdictional decision can be made as a preliminary matter, this is typically desirable, because a disappointed party may promptly seek review of the decision in an appropriate court.[73] While the arbitration need not be stayed during the pendency of any such court review,[74] a prompt review may nonetheless save needless time and expense.[75] However, in some circumstances any jurisdictional issues may be inextricably intertwined with the dispute on the merits, or there may be other reasons that a preliminary decision on jurisdiction is not appropriate.

A.   DID THE PARTIES AGREE TO ARBITRATE ANYTHING?

If a party challenges the jurisdiction of the tribunal based on the lack of an arbitration agreement, this will present a threshold question as explained above, often involving some level of engagement in the merits of the parties' alleged contractual relationship. When such challenges initially take place in court, the court must determine to what extent it should delve into the merits of a dispute potentially assigned to the arbitrators. This issue was discussed above in the materials addressing competence-competence, but it is somewhat easier to see the challenges presented in the context of an actual case in which the court is

---

[71] The reader may recall a similar "list" of jurisdictional issues initially introduced in Professor Barceló's article excerpted in the introduction to section V. These are essentially the same issues (excluding of course invalidity of the container agreement, which is subject to separability), albeit with a few minor variations. Professor Barceló combines arbitrability and public in his reason number 5, and he also adds reasons number 6 and 7 not addressed in this section. His reasons number 6 and 7 address what are essentially basic contract issues. First, an arbitration agreement may be subject to a condition precedent (e.g., mediation or conciliation before arbitration). If such condition precedent has not yet occurred, then the parties' obligation to arbitrate has not yet arisen. Second, after the parties' arbitration agreement has arisen, one of the parties may waive its right to arbitrate (e.g., by bring its claims in court and proceeding to a hearing on the merits) or otherwise act in a manner that serves as an estoppel precluding the party from asserting its right to arbitrate. While not unimportant, these two issues are generally left to basic contract principles and are not specifically addressed herein.

[72] *See* Model Law Article 16(3).

[73] *See* Model Law Article 16(3). In the mythical jurisdiction of Danubia, this would be the Commercial Court of Vindobona, Danubia, designated in Article 6, whose decision on jurisdiction would be final and subject to no appeal. See also

[74] See Model Law Article 16(3).

[75] In an effort to promote such efficiency, the Swiss Federal Statute of Private International Law, Chapter 12 (1988), provides in Article 186(3) that "[t]he arbitral tribunal shall, as a rule, decide its jurisdiction by preliminary award."

attempting to answer the question of whether the parties agreed to arbitrate, but has trouble avoiding the merits of the dispute. The *Filanto v. Chilewich* case from Chapter 3 is again addressed below—this time focusing on the arbitration issues.[76] When reading this portion of the case, you might consider the various approaches to competence-competence discussed earlier.

FILANTO, S.p.A., v. CHILEWICH INT'L CORP.

789 F. Supp. 1229 (S.D.N.Y. 1992)

MEMORANDUM & ORDER

BRIEANT, Chief Judge.

. . .

[for factual background, see earlier case excerpt in Chapter 3 at _____.]

. . .

Jurisdiction/Applicable Law

Plaintiff bases subject matter jurisdiction in this action on diversity of citizenship, as Filanto is an Italian corporation with its principal place of business in Italy, while Chilewich is a New York corporation with its principal place of business in New York, thereby invoking New York law and choice of law rules, under *Erie R. Co. v. Tompkins,* 304 U.S. 64, 58 S.Ct. 817, 82 L.Ed. 1188 (1938).

This Court, however, finds another overriding basis for subject matter jurisdiction which will affect our choice of law: chapter 2 of the Federal Arbitration Act, which comprises the Convention on the Recognition and Enforcement of Foreign Arbitral Awards and its implementing legislation, *codified at* 9 U.S.C. § 201 *et seq.* (West Supp.1991). The United States, Italy and the USSR are all signatories to this Convention, and its implementing legislation makes clear that the Arbitration Convention governs disputes regarding arbitration agreements between parties to international commercial transactions:

"An arbitration agreement or arbitral award arising out of a legal relationship, whether contractual or not, which is considered as

---

[76] The reader may want to refer back to the original case presentation for the basic facts, as those are not reproduced here.

commercial, including a transaction, contract, or agreement described in section 2 of this title, falls under the Convention. An agreement or award arising out of such a relationship which is entirely between citizens of the United States should be deemed not to fall under the Convention ..." 9 U.S.C. § 202 (West Supp.1991).

The Arbitration Convention specifically requires courts to recognize any "agreement in writing under which the parties undertake to submit to arbitration...." Convention on the Recognition and Enforcement of Foreign Arbitral Awards Article II(1). The term "agreement in writing" is defined as " an arbitral clause in a contract or an arbitration agreement, signed by the parties or contained in an exchange of letters or telegrams" . Convention on the Recognition and Enforcement Of Foreign Arbitral Awards Article II(2).

. . .

[*The court goes on to explain that Chapter 2 of the Federal Arbitration Act provides federal subject matter jurisdiction over the parties' dispute.*]

. . .

However, . . . the threshold question is whether these parties actually agreed to arbitrate their disputes at all. In such a situation, where the issue is whether there is any arbitration agreement between the parties, there is authority for the proposition that state, rather than federal law, should be applied. . . . Indeed, the Supreme Court has recently indicated that this analysis is correct, at least with respect to cases controlled by chapter 1 of the Arbitration Act: "Thus, state law, whether of legislative or judicial origin, is applicable *if* that law arose to govern issues concerning the validity, revocability, and enforceability of contracts generally." *Perry v. Thomas,* 482 U.S. 483, 492 n. 9, 107 S.Ct. 2520, 2527, 96 L.Ed.2d 426 (1987) (emphasis in original). . . .

Plaintiff at one point did contend that state law applied, for an understandable reason: New York law arguably imposes a heavier burden on a party seeking to compel arbitration than does its federal counterpart. . . . There is, however, some authority in this Circuit that federal law applies to contract formation issues when the existence of an agreement to arbitrate is in issue. *David L. Threlkeld & Co., Inc., v. Metallgesellschaft*

Ltd., 923 F.2d 245, 249 (2d Cir.) (applying federal law of contracts to dispute regarding existence of agreement to arbitrate), *cert. dismissed,* 501 U.S. 1267, 112 S.Ct. 17, 115 L.Ed.2d 1094 (1991); . . .

This Court concludes that the question of whether these parties agreed to arbitrate their disputes is governed by the Arbitration Convention and its implementing legislation. That Convention, as a treaty, is the supreme law of the land, U.S. Const. art. VI cl. 2, and controls *any* case in any American court falling within its sphere of application. Thus, any dispute involving international commercial arbitration which meets the Convention's jurisdictional requirements, whether brought in state or federal court, must be resolved with reference to that instrument. . . .

Accordingly, the Court will apply federal law to the issue of whether an "agreement in writing" to arbitrate disputes exists between these parties.

Courts confronted by cases governed by the Arbitration Convention must conduct a limited, four-part inquiry:

> (1) Is there an agreement in writing to arbitrate the subject of the dispute? Convention, Articles II(1), II(2). (2) Does the agreement provide for arbitration in the territory of a signatory country? Convention, Articles I(1), I(3); 9 U.S.C. § 206; . . . . (3) Does the agreement arise out of a legal relationship, whether contractual or not, which is considered as commercial? Convention, Article I(3); 9 U.S.C. § 202. (4) Is a party to the contract not an American citizen, or does the commercial relationship have some reasonable relation with one or more foreign states? 9 U.S.C. § 202.

[Citations omitted.]

In this case, the second, third and fourth criteria are clearly satisfied, as the purported agreement provides for arbitration in Moscow, the Chilewich-Filanto relationship is a "commercial" relationship, and Filanto is an Italian corporation. The central disputed issue, therefore, is whether the correspondence between the parties, viewed in light of their business relationship, constitutes an "agreement in writing."

Courts interpreting this "agreement in writing" requirement have generally started their analysis with the plain language of the Convention, which requires "an arbitral clause in a contract or an arbitration agreement, signed by the parties or contained in an exchange of letters or telegrams," Article I(1), . . .

. . . [A]s plaintiff correctly notes, the "general principles of contract law" relevant to this action, [are] found in the United Nations Convention on Contracts for the International Sale of Goods (the "Sale of Goods Convention"), *codified at* 15 U.S.C. Appendix (West Supp.1991).[77] . . . [S]ince both the United States and Italy are signatories to the Convention, the Court will interpret the "agreement in writing" requirement of the Arbitration Convention in light of, and with reference to, the substantive international law of contracts embodied in the Sale of Goods Convention.

Not surprisingly, the parties offer varying interpretations of the numerous letters and documents exchanged between them. . . .

. . .

[*the court goes on to describe the parties' arguments with respect to contract formation, as such arguments may relate to the inclusion (or not) of an arbitration agreement—see earlier case excerpt in Chapter 3.*]

. . .

More generally, both parties seem to have lost sight of the narrow scope of the inquiry required by the Arbitration Convention. *Ledee, supra,* at 186. All that this Court need do is to determine if a sufficient "agreement in writing" to arbitrate disputes exists between these parties. *Cf. United Steelworkers of America v. Warrior & Gulf Co.,* 363 U.S. 574, 582, 80 S.Ct. 1347, 1352-53, 40 L.Ed.2d 1409 (1960) (party cannot be required to submit to arbitration absent agreement). Although that inquiry is informed by the provisions of the Sale of Goods Convention, the Court lacks the authority on this motion to resolve all outstanding issues between the parties. Indeed, contracts and the arbitration clauses included therein are

---

[77] [Footnote 5 in original] Of course, as with the Arbitration Convention, the Sale of Goods Convention is also "state law." U.S. Const. art. VI, cl. 2; *Hauenstein v. Lynham,* 100 U.S. 483, 490 (1880) ("[T]he Constitution, laws, and treaties of the United States are as much a part of the law of every state as its own local laws and Constitution.").

considered to be "severable," a rule that the Sale of Goods Convention itself adopts with respect to avoidance of contracts generally. Sale of Goods Convention Article 81(1). There is therefore authority for the proposition that issues relating to existence of the contract, as opposed to the existence of the arbitration clause, are issues for the arbitrators: "The district court reasoned that an arbitrator can derive his or her power only from a contract, so that when there is a challenge to the existence of the contract itself, the court must first decide whether there is a valid contract between the parties. Although this appears logical, it goes beyond the requirements of the statute and violates the clear directive of *Prima Paint,* 388 U.S. at 404, 87 S.Ct. at 1806 ..." *Republic of Nicaragua v. Standard Fruit Co.,* 937 F.2d 469, 476 n. 9 (9th Cir.1991), *cert. denied,* 503 U.S. 919, 112 S.Ct. 1294, 117 L.Ed.2d 516 (1992).

The *Standard Fruit* court is technically correct in its interpretation of the *Prima Paint* case, which drew a distinction between a challenge to the validity of the contract itself and a challenge to the validity of the arbitration clause; the former, in the Court's view, was a question for the arbitrators, while the latter was a question for the court. *Prima Paint, supra,* 388 U.S. at 404, 87 S.Ct. at 1806.

However, there are often limits to how many angels can dance on the head of a pin-even when the performance is choreographed by the distinguished courts just cited. There seems, for example, to be some confusion in the Ninth Circuit itself about the proper application of the Prima Paint rule, as a case decided six months prior to Standard Fruit shows. *See* Three Valleys Municipal Water District v. E.F. Hutton & Co. Inc., 925 F.2d 1136, 1138-42 (9th Cir. 1991) (holding whether contract containing arbitration clause formed initially question for court). [*The court goes on to describe additional cases in which courts have declined to find an agreement to arbitrate based on findings that the parties failed to reach agreement on the purported contract containing the arbitration clause*].

Since the issue of whether and how a contract between these parties was formed is obviously related to the issue of whether Chilewich breached any contractual obligations, the Court will direct its analysis to whether there was objective conduct evidencing an intent to be bound with respect to the arbitration provision. *Cf. Matterhorn, Inc., v. NCR Corp.,* 763 F.2d 866,

871-73 (7th Cir.1985) (Posner, J.) (discussing cases). *See also Teledyne, Inc. v. Kone Corp.,* 892 F.2d 1404, 1410 (9th Cir.1990) (arbitration clause enforceable despite later finding by arbitrator that contract itself invalid).

The Court is satisfied on this record that there *was* indeed an agreement to arbitrate between these parties.

There is simply no satisfactory explanation as to why Filanto failed to object to the incorporation by reference of the Russian Contract in a timely fashion. As noted above, Chilewich had in the meantime commenced its performance under the Agreement, and the Letter of Credit it furnished Filanto on May 11 *itself* mentioned the Russian Contract. An offeree who, knowing that the offeror has commenced performance, fails to notify the offeror of its objection to the terms of the contract within a reasonable time will, under certain circumstances, be deemed to have assented to those terms. Restatement (Second) of Contracts § 69 (1981); *Graniteville v. Star Knits of California, Inc.,* 680 F.Supp. 587, 589-90 (S.D.N.Y.1988) (compelling arbitration since party who failed timely to object to salesnote containing arbitration clause deemed to have accepted its terms); *Imptex International Corp. v. Lorprint, Inc.,* 625 F.Supp. 1572, 1572 (S.D.N.Y.1986) (Weinfeld, J.) (party who failed to object to inclusion of arbitration clause in sales confirmation agreement bound to arbitrate). The Sale of Goods Convention itself recognizes this rule: Article 18(1), provides that "A statement made by or other conduct of the offeree indicating assent to an offer is an acceptance." Although mere "silence or inactivity" does not constitute acceptance, Sale of Goods Convention Article 18(1), the Court may consider previous relations between the parties in assessing whether a party's conduct constituted acceptance, Sale of Goods Convention Article 8(3). In this case, in light of the extensive course of prior dealing between these parties, Filanto was certainly under a duty to alert Chilewich in timely fashion to its objections to the terms of the March 13 Memorandum Agreement-particularly since Chilewich had repeatedly referred it to the Russian Contract and Filanto had had a copy of that document for some time.

There are three other convincing manifestations of Filanto's true understanding of the terms of this agreement. First, Filanto's Complaint in this action, as well as affidavits subsequently submitted to the Court by Mr. Filograna, refer to the *March 13* contract: the Complaint, for example, states that "On or about March 13, 1990, Filanto entered into a contract with Chilewich . . ." Complaint at ¶ 5. These statements clearly belie Filanto's *post hoc* assertion that the contract was actually formed at some point after that date. Indeed, Filanto finds itself in an awkward position: it has sued on a contract whose terms it must now question, in light of the defendant's assertion that the contract contains an arbitration provision. This situation is hardly unknown in the context of arbitration agreements. *See Tepper Realty Co., v. Mosaic Tile Co.,* 259 F.Supp. 688, 692 (S.D.N.Y.1966) ("In short, the plaintiffs cannot have it both ways. They cannot relay on the contract, when it works to their advantage, and repudiate it when it works to their disadvantage").

Second, Filanto *did* sign the March 13 Memorandum Agreement. That Agreement, as noted above, specifically referred to the incorporation by reference of the arbitration provision in the Russian Contract; although Filanto, in its August 7 letter, did purport to "have to respect" only a small part of the Russian Contract, Filanto in that very letter noted that it was returning the March 13 Memorandum Agreement *"signed for acceptance."* Exhibit A to November 28 Filograna Affidavit (emphasis added). In light of Filanto's knowledge that Chilewich had already performed its part of the bargain by furnishing it the Letter of Credit, Filanto's characterization of this action as a rejection and a counteroffer is almost frivolous.

Third, and most important, Filanto, in a letter to Byerly Johnson dated June 21, 1991, explicitly stated that "[t]he April Shipment and the September shipment are governed by the Master Purchase Contract of February 28, 1989 [the Russian Contract]." Exhibit H to December 4 Simon Chilewich Affidavit. Furthermore, the letter, which responds to claims by Johnson that some of the boots that *were* supplied were defective, expressly relies on section 9 of the Russian Contract-another section which Filanto had in its earlier correspondence purported to exclude. The Sale of Goods Convention specifically directs that "[i]n determining the intent of a party . . . due consideration is to be given to . . . any subsequent conduct of the parties," Sale of Goods Convention Article 8(3). In this case, as the letter post-dates the partial performance of the contract, it is particularly strong evidence that Filanto recognized itself to be bound by *all* the terms of the Russian Contract.

In light of these factors, and heeding the presumption in favor of arbitration, *Moses H. Cone, supra,* at 24-26, 103 S.Ct. at 941-42, which is even stronger in the context of international commercial transactions, *Mitsubishi Motors Corp. v. Soler Chrysler-Plymouth, Inc.,* 473 U.S. 614, 631, 105 S.Ct. 3346, 3356, 87 L.Ed.2d 444 (1985), the Court holds that Filanto is bound by the terms of the March 13 Memorandum Agreement, and so must arbitrate its dispute in Moscow.

. . .

* * * * *

Notes and Questions

Note 1: This court was addressing choice of law issues in the context of American federalism and was attempting to determine whether state or federal law governed the formation of any arbitration agreement. The difficulty with this question is that the law governing arbitration is federal, but contract law is typically state law (the CISG is exceptional in that it is federal law). Ultimately, the court decides on U.S. federal law. Was this the proper analysis, or should the court have applied some other national law to determine whether the parties had agreed to arbitrate?

One might consider Article II(3) of the New York Convention, adopted in Chapter 2 of the Federal Arbitration Act. It initially governs the court's analysis here, but does not directly state what law the court should look to in determining whether the parties agreed to arbitrate. Does New York Convention Article V(1)(a) answer this question? If so, should the court have been looking to Russian contract law, or should the court simply test the purported arbitration agreement for formal validity (i.e., requiring "an agreement in writing")? If so, what about the requirement of substantive validity? Formal and substantive validity are each addressed in the next section. In reading about substantive validity, consider again the issue of separability discussed in section V.A. above. Should questions of formation, such as those addressed in the instant case, be treated in the same manner as invalidity defenses when looking at substantive validity?

Note 2: Why is the court discussing the CISG? Is it applying the CISG to the question of whether the parties agreed to arbitrate, or to the merits of the dispute, or both?

Note 3: In this case, the court is not only trying to avoid the merits of the dispute (which is of course subject to arbitration), but is also attempting to avoid any questions as to the validity of the overall contract. U.S. Law provides that courts must answer the question of the validity of the arbitration agreement, but leaves for the arbitral tribunal issues of validity of the overall contract under the doctrine of separability. The court discusses apparently conflicting authority as to whether the same sort of separability analysis is appropriate when considering whether the parties ever agreed to a contract in the first place. Is the distinction between validity and formation realistic or appropriate in the context of a case like this?

Note 4: How easy is it for a national court to apply foreign law governing arbitration, particularly when such analysis may also implicate the dispute on the merits, which may be governed by another body of law? Does this suggest an appropriate level of court review under New York Convention Article II(3) and Model Law Article 8(1)?

Note 5: All things considered, did the court "get it right" in the end? How much might it have cost the parties to get that answer (which of course said nothing about the merits of the original dispute)?

B.   IS THE ARBITRATION AGREEMENT VALID?

The validity of the arbitration agreement, including the capacity of the parties, may implicate the law of the place of arbitration, the law of the place of enforcement, and/or any law to which the parties have subjected it,[78] as further illustrated in Appendix C. This analysis will typically implicate the *lex arbitri* and the law of the place of enforcement on issues of *formal validity* (*i.e.*, the writing requirement). Unless the parties provide otherwise, the contract law of the place of arbitration will likely govern issues of capacity and other issues of *substantive validity*, absent specific provisions of the *lex arbitri* addressing these issues in the context of an arbitration agreement. The materials that follow begin with consideration of (1) formal validity and follow with consideration of (2) substantive validity.

1.   Formal validity

The most typical formal validity requirement of arbitration agreements is the writing requirement found in most national arbitration laws[79] and the New York

---

[78] *See e.g.* Model Law Articles 7 and 34(2)(a)(i); New York Convention Articles II & V(1)(a).

[79] *See e.g.* Model Law Article 7 (Option 1); *but see* Model Law Article 7 (Option 2) (which would eliminate the writing requirement to the extent adopted). While the adoption of Option 2 under the Model Law would have little effect today (the New York Convention would still require a writing for enforcement), it is indicative of a movement away from past formalistic requirements and towards an approach more consistent with CISG Article 11. This also reflects the increasing

Convention.[80] However, the definition of such an "agreement in writing" has not been without controversy. The New York Convention, completed in 1958, included a relatively narrow definition of an "agreement in writing."

Article II (New York Convention)

(1) Each Contracting State shall recognize an agreement in writing under which the parties undertake to submit to arbitration all or any differences which have arisen or which may arise between them in respect of a defined legal relationship, whether contractual or not, concerning a subject matter capable of settlement by arbitration.

(2) The term "agreement in writing" shall include an arbitral clause in a contract or an arbitration agreement, signed by the parties or contained in an exchange of letters and telegrams.

. . .

In contrast, the UNCITRAL Model Law, completed 27 years later, in 1985, used a somewhat broader definition.

Article 7 (Model Law – 1985)

Definition and form of arbitration agreement

(1) "Arbitration agreement" is an agreement by the parties to submit to arbitration all or certain disputes which have arisen or which may arise between them in respect of a defined legal relationship, whether contractual or not. An arbitration agreement may be in the form of an arbitration clause in a contract or in the form of a separate agreement.

(2) The arbitration agreement shall be in writing. An agreement is in writing if it is contained in a document signed by the parties or in an exchange of letters, telex, telegrams or other means of telecommunication which provide a record of the agreement, or in an exchange of statements of claim and

---

acceptance of arbitration as the norm, rather than the exception, in resolving international commercial disputes.
[80] New York Convention Article II.

> defence in which the existence of an agreement is alleged by one party and not denied by another. The reference in a contract to a document containing an arbitration clause constitutes an arbitration agreement provided that the contract is in writing and the reference is such as to make that clause part of the contract.

While the broadened language of the Model Law was generally welcomed, it was of questionable value if the Model Law might deem an agreement to arbitrate enforceable, but the standards of the New York Convention would deny the resulting award's enforcement based on the narrower requirements of the Convention.[81]

Over time, as arbitration has continued to gain favor as the norm for dispute resolution in international commerce, and as modern means of business communication have evolved, the application of this writing requirement has been even further relaxed, and Model Law Article 7 has recently been revised to allow even a broader range of the parties, communications to satisfy the writing requirement.

> ### Article 7 (Model Law – 2006 revision)[82]
>
> ### Definition and form of arbitration agreement
>
> (1) "Arbitration agreement" is an agreement by the parties to submit to arbitration all or certain disputes which have arisen or which may arise between them in respect of a defined legal relationship, whether contractual or not. An arbitration agreement may be in the form of an arbitration clause in a contract or in the form of a separate agreement.
>
> (2) The arbitration agreement shall be in writing.
>
> (3) An arbitration agreement is in writing if its content is recorded in any form, whether or not the arbitration

---

[81] For a thorough treatment of many of the issues involving the requirement of a signed writing under the New York Convention, *see* Toby Landau, *The Requirement of a Written Form for an Arbitration Agreement When "Written" Means "Oral,"* ICCA Congress Series No. 11 (2003).

[82] *See* UNCITRAL Model Law Article 7 (Option 1) (as amended in 2006). Article 7 also provides an Option 2, which would drop the writing requirement altogether. Again, however, this elimination of the writing requirement would be of little help in attempting to enforce any resulting award under the New York Convention.

agreement or contract has been concluded orally, by conduct, or by other means.

(4) The requirement that an arbitration agreement be in writing is met by an electronic communication if the information contained therein is accessible so as to be useable for subsequent reference; "electronic communication" means any communication that he parties make by means of data messages; "data message" means information generated, sent, received or stored by electronic, magnetic, optical or similar means, including, but not limited to, electronic data interchange (EDI), electronic mail, telegram, telex or telecopy.

(5) Furthermore, an arbitration agreement is in writing if it is contained in an exchange of statements of claim and defence in which the existence of an agreement is alleged by one party and not denied by the other.

(6) The reference in a contract to any document containing an arbitration clause constitutes an arbitration agreement in writing, provided that the reference is such as to make that clause part of the contract.

Unfortunately, amending the writing requirement of Article II of the New York Convention would likely be considerably more difficult in view of the large number of signatories and other potential issues that might arise in the context of the amendment process. However, in conjunction with the revisions of Article 7 of the Model Law, UNCITRAL and the U.N. General Assembly adopted the resolution endorsing the following recommendation:

Recommendation regarding the interpretation of article II, paragraph 2, and article VII, paragraph 1, of the Convention on the Recognition and Enforcement of Foreign Arbitral Awards, done in New York, 10 June 1958, adopted by the United Nations Commission on International Trade Law on 7 July 2006 at its thirty-ninth session

The United Nations Commission on International Trade Law,

> *Recalling* General Assembly resolution 2205 (XXI) of 17 December 1966, which established the United Nations Commission on International Trade Law with the object of promoting the progressive harmonization and unification of the

law of international trade by, inter alia, promoting ways and means of ensuring a uniform interpretation and application of international conventions and uniform laws in the field of the law of international trade,

Conscious of the fact that the different legal, social and economic systems of the world, together with different levels of development, are represented in the Commission,

Recalling successive resolutions of the General Assembly reaffirming the mandate of the Commission as the core legal body within the United Nations system in the field of international trade law to coordinate legal activities in this field,

Convinced that the wide adoption of the Convention on the Recognition and Enforcement of Foreign Arbitral Awards, done in New York on 10 June 1958, has been a significant achievement in the promotion of the rule of law, particularly in the field of international trade,

Recalling that the Conference of Plenipotentiaries which prepared and opened the Convention for signature adopted a resolution, which states, inter alia, that the Conference "considers that greater uniformity of national laws on arbitration would further the effectiveness of arbitration in the settlement of private law disputes,"

Bearing in mind differing interpretations of the form requirements under the Convention that result in part from differences of expression as between the five equally authentic texts of the Convention,

Taking into account article VII, paragraph 1, of the Convention, a purpose of which is to enable the enforcement of foreign arbitral awards to the greatest extent, in particular by recognizing the right of any interested party to avail itself of law or treaties of the country where the award is sought to be relied upon, including where such law or treaties offer a regime more favourable than the Convention,

Considering the wide use of electronic commerce,

Taking into account international legal instruments, such as the 1985 UNCITRAL Model Law on International Commercial Arbitration, as subsequently revised, particularly with respect to article 7, the UNCITRAL Model Law on Electronic Commerce, the UNCITRAL Model Law on Electronic Signatures and the

United Nations Convention on the Use of Electronic Communications in International Contracts,

Taking into account also enactments of domestic legislation, as well as case law, more favourable than the Convention in respect of form requirement governing arbitration agreements, arbitration proceedings and the enforcement of arbitral awards,

Considering that, in interpreting the Convention, regard is to be had to the need to promote recognition and enforcement of arbitral awards,

1. *Recommends* that article II, paragraph 2, of the Convention on the Recognition and Enforcement of Foreign Arbitral Awards, done in New York, 10 June 1958, be applied recognizing that the circumstances described therein are not exhaustive;

2. *Recommends* also that article VII, paragraph 1, of the Convention on the Recognition and Enforcement of Foreign Arbitral Awards, done in New York, 10 June 1958, should be applied to allow any interested party to avail itself of rights it may have, under the law or treaties of the country where an arbitration agreement is sought to be relied upon, to seek recognition of the validity of such an arbitration agreement.

Report of the United Nations Commission on International Trade Law on the work of its thirty-ninth session, U.N. GAOR, 61st Sess., Supplement No. 17, U.N. Doc. A/61/17 (19 Jun-7 Jul 2006).

* * * * *

Notes and Questions

Note 1: In combination, the revision of Article 7 of the Model Law and the new recommendations for interpretation and application of Article II of the New York Convention go a long way towards modernizing formal validity requirements to reflect both modern commercial practices and modern attitudes towards international commercial arbitration.

Note 2: Of course, it must be remembered that revised Article 7 of the Model Law is simply that—a revision of the model provision. It is not the law of any jurisdiction until and unless it is actually adopted. However, a tribunal *may* nonetheless consider both the revision of the Model Law and the above recommended interpretation as persuasive authority guiding its interpretation of current enactments of Model Law Article 7, as well as the New York Convention.

2.   Substantive validity

In one of the most common limitations on substantive validity, many national laws render *ex ante* arbitration agreements involving consumers or employees invalid.[83]   However, specific limitations on substantive validity of arbitration agreements involving commercial parties are rare. Standard contractual validity defenses, such as fraud, mistake, or duress would of course invalidate an arbitration clause—provided the defense related specifically to the arbitration agreement, as distinguished from the broader agreement containing the arbitration clause.[84]   Again, however, the instances in which such defenses relate specifically to the arbitration agreement are rare.

Example 8-8

A U.S. seller and Croatian buyer conclude an agreement for the sale of goods, but do not include an arbitration clause. After the conclusion of the contract, the seller proposes that the parties modify their agreement to include an arbitration clause, but the buyer refuses. Knowing that the buyer must have immediate and timely delivery of seller's goods and has no other source of supply for these goods, seller threatens to withhold delivery unless buyer agrees to add the proposed arbitration clause to their contract. With no realistic alternative, and no time to seek an order of specific performance, buyer agrees.

Later, buyer sues seller in a New York federal court claiming that the goods are subject to a third-party security interest allegedly held by a New York bank, and that seller has therefore breached its obligations under CISG Article 41. Seller moves for dismissal and asks the court to refer the parties to arbitration pursuant to New Convention Article II(3). However, the court will likely find the alleged arbitration agreement invalid based on buyer's defense of duress, which relates specifically to the arbitration agreement, thereby rendering it substantively invalid.

---

[83] The American Federal Arbitration Act is somewhat unique in that it has been interpreted by the United States Supreme Court as making *ex ante* arbitration agreements involving consumers and employees fully enforceable.

[84] This distinction between defenses to the validity of the overall agreement, as distinct from defenses specifically involving the arbitration clause alone, involves the doctrine of separability discussed *supra* in section V.

Perhaps the most frequent validity challenge relates to arbitration clauses that are particularly vague or ambiguous. If the arbitration agreement is so unclear that a tribunal cannot reasonable ascertain the objective intent of the parties, the arbitration clause may be deemed unenforceable as "inoperative or incapable of being performed."[85]   Such a clause is often called "pathological"[86] inasmuch as its effect is to raise a new dispute over its interpretation instead of providing the parties with prompt resolution of their original dispute. While such pathological clauses appear more frequently than one might expect, the pro-arbitration bias of most modern arbitration regimes generally leads to enforcement of the clauses, as long as the parties' intent to arbitrate (in some fashion) seems clear. Of course, there are always exceptions, as illustrated by the following case—one that gives particularly illustrative meaning to the term "pathological," as applied to an arbitration clause.

Marks 3-Zet-Ernst Marks Gmbh & Co. KG v. Presstek, Inc.,

455 F.3d 7

(1st Cir. 2006)

[The following uncontested factual and procedural background really tells the whole story here, as the legal analysis that follows is all but a foregone conclusion]

. . . Presstek [*a Delaware corporation, with its principle place of business in New Hampshire*] and Marks [*a German company*] supply products for the printing industry. In December 2000, Presstek and Marks entered into a contract whereby Marks agreed to market Presstek's products in parts of Europe. Under the contract, neither party was permitted to terminate the contract for three years, except under certain conditions.

Under Section 10(g) of the contract, the parties agreed to submit disputes to arbitration:

> ***Applicable Law and Jurisdiction.*** Any dispute ... between the Parties arising out of or relating to this Agreement which cannot be settled amicably shall be referred to and determined by ***arbitration in the Hague under the***

---

[85] *See* Model Law Article 8(1); New York Convention Article II(3).

[86] *See* Frédéric Eisemann, *La clause d'arbitrage pathologique*, in *Commercial Arbitration: Essays in Memorium Eugenio Minoli* 129 (Unione tipografico-editrice torinese 1974); Benjamin G. Davis, *Pathological Clauses: Frederic Eisemann's Still Vital Criteria*, 7 Arb. Intl. 365 (1991).

> ***International Arbitration rules*** [*emphasis
> supplied by casebook authors*]. The ruling by
> the arbitration court shall be final and binding
> and the Parties undertake to abide by and to
> carry out the award immediately and voluntarily.
> In the event that such award is not immediately
> abided by and carried out, the award of whatever
> nature may be enforced without review in any
> court of competent jurisdiction. The arbitration
> award shall determine which Party shall bear the
> expenses of the arbitration or the portion thereof
> which each Party shall bear.

On April 4, 2002, Presstek provided notice that it wished to
terminate the contract. According to Marks, this termination
constituted a breach of contract. Marks thereafter attempted to
have Presstek agree to arbitrate the dispute, but to no avail.
Marks first asked Presstek to arbitrate the dispute under the
UNCITRAL Arbitration Rules on November 29, 2002. This
request led to negotiations, which were ultimately unsuccessful.

Marks made a second request for arbitration to Presstek on
March 27, 2003, but Presstek did not respond. The record does
not contain either the November 2002 or March 2003 requests by
Marks, and does not reveal whether Marks asked Presstek to
arbitrate their dispute before a particular forum. When Presstek
did not respond, Marks did not go to court to seek to compel
arbitration or alternatively to sue for breach of contract.

The arbitration clause was poorly drafted: First, the clause does
not identify the specific arbitral body at The Hague that would
adjudicate any dispute. Second, the contract language ("the
International Arbitration rules") suggests that a *particular* set of
arbitration rules would govern the dispute; but, as it turns out,
there are no rules called the "International Arbitration rules."

A. Proceedings Before the PCA

[*the Permanent Court of Arbitration in The Hague, Netherlands*]

After Presstek did not respond to its March 2003 arbitration
request, Marks sent letters to the PCA, on June 4 and July 31,
2003, asking the PCA to designate an "Appointing Authority"
that would initiate arbitration proceedings and appoint
arbitrators. In its application, Marks asserted to the PCA that
under the arbitration clause "[i]t is evident from the choice of

The Hague as the forum for the arbitration that the 'International Arbitration Rules' referred to in the clause are those formulated by UNCITRAL, since these authorize the Secretary-General of the PCA based in The Hague to appoint members to the tribunal or to nominate a so-called Appointing Authority."

On August 4, 2003, after receipt of Marks' request, an Assistant Legal Counsel of the PCA sent a letter to Presstek, with a copy to Marks, informing Presstek of the arbitration request by Marks. The letter raised questions about the competence of the PCA to act as an arbitrator in the case:

> Prior to acting . . . , the Secretary-General [of the PCA] first satisfies himself, on the basis of a prima facie screening of the documentation submitted by the parties, that he is competent to act. The Secretary-General's competence may derive from the parties' agreement to the application of the UNCITRAL Arbitration Rules, Articles 6 and 7 of which describe his role, or from any other agreement that calls for him to act.

The PCA letter noted that the language in the parties' arbitration agreement referred only to "the International Arbitration rules" and "The Hague as the place of arbitration." The PCA letter asked Presstek to provide its comments with respect to Marks' application, after which the matter would be submitted to the Secretary-General of the PCA for consideration.

Presstek, in an August 14, 2003 letter to the PCA requesting an extension of time, noted that its basic position was that a clear agreement to apply UNCITRAL Arbitration Rules was required before the PCA could exercise jurisdiction over the arbitration, that there was no such clear agreement, and that the reference to "International Arbitration rules" in the parties' contract was too vague on the point.

The PCA granted Presstek's request for an extension, in a letter on August 18, 2003, and noted Presstek's objection. The letter reiterated the PCA's policy that "before acting in matters such as this, the Secretary-General of the PCA first satisfies himself, on the basis of a prima facie screening of the documents submitted to him, that he is competent to act." The letter also noted that "[w]hen the Secretary-General is not satisfied of his competence to act, parties may, of course, seek implementation of their arbitration agreement elsewhere or before the appropriate national courts." The PCA invited Presstek "to comment on whether it wished to agree to the application of the UNCITRAL Arbitration Rules in the present dispute."

On October 20, 2003, Presstek filed its comments with the PCA. It refused to stipulate to application of the UNCITRAL Arbitration Rules and reiterated its position that the contract was not sufficiently clear as to whether the UNCITRAL rules would apply and that the PCA should therefore decline jurisdiction. Presstek argued that only a court, and not the PCA, could resolve the ambiguities and concluded that the PCA should decline to arbitrate the matter "until such time as a . . . court indicates that it may." The record does not contain any reply by Marks.

On October 21, 2003, the PCA, in a letter to the parties, stated that the Secretary-General had considered the parties' submissions and concluded that it did not have the competence to act because, based on its interpretation of the arbitration agreement, the parties had not agreed to the application of UNCITRAL rules:

> The Secretary-General considers that he may designate an Appointing Authority pursuant to the UNCITRAL Arbitration Rules only when the parties to a contract have agreed that disputes in relation to that contract shall be referred to arbitration under the UNCITRAL Arbitration Rules. With respect to the dispute arising from the parties' [contract], the Secretary-General is not satisfied, on the basis of a prima facie screening of the documentation submitted by the parties, that he is competent to act in this matter.

The letter concluded, however, by inviting the parties "to seek the interpretation of their arbitration agreement from any court having jurisdiction." It noted that arbitration at the PCA might be possible, "[g]iven that paragraph 10(g) of the Agreement specifies The Hague as the place of arbitration."

On March 25, 2004, Marks requested Presstek to arbitrate the dispute again, this time under the Netherlands Arbitration Act. Again, the record does not contain this request, or reveal whether

Marks had asked for arbitration at a particular forum, either the PCA or elsewhere. Presstek did not respond to this request.

B. Proceedings before the District Court

Marks did not challenge the PCA's refusal to hear the case, either at the PCA itself or in a court in the Netherlands, or attempt to arbitrate the dispute in any other forum at The Hague. It did not immediately seek an interpretation of the agreement by a court of competent jurisdiction, as the PCA had invited it to do. Instead, it waited nearly eighteen months, until April 5, 2005, to file a motion to compel arbitration in U.S. District Court in New Hampshire under the New York Convention, as implemented by 9 U.S.C. §§ 4 and 206.

. . .

In its petition to compel arbitration, Marks asked for an order "direct[ing] that arbitration proceed in the manner set forth in the Agreement: in *The Hague*, and that the Court order such arbitration to proceed under the *American Arbitration Act's International Rules*" (emphases added). Marks also requested that the court order Presstek to submit to arbitration; hold a hearing on Marks' petition under Section 4 of the FAA; and award "costs, interest, attorneys' fees and such other and further relief as the Court deems appropriate and just." As to the proceedings before the PCA, Marks stated only that "[t]he President of the PCA ... concluded that the application of the [UNCITRAL] Rules to the Agreement was not appropriate and gave no further opinion with respect to the Agreement."

There were a number of problems with Marks' petition. Although Marks stated that it wanted arbitration at "The Hague" (where a number of groups provide arbitration), the only arbitral body mentioned in the petition was the PCA. Furthermore, there is no set of rules called "the American Arbitration Act's International Rules." It was not until its motion for reconsideration that Marks clarified that it "intended to reference the American Arbitration Association's international rules." But whatever rules Marks intended to reference, Marks' petition did not take the position that the parties' arbitration clause contemplated application of the UNCITRAL Arbitration Rules, which, based on the PCA letters, were the only rules which would give the PCA the competence to act in the parties' dispute.

Thus, a natural reading of the complaint was that Marks was seeking arbitration of the dispute at the PCA under rules which the Secretary-General of the PCA had already stated could not give the PCA the competence to act. The district court, in an August 9, 2005 order, gave fair warning of its concern that it would be unable to grant the relief Marks was seeking, using the language of mootness. It ordered Marks to show cause why its petition to compel arbitration should not be dismissed.[87]

Marks filed a memorandum in response on September 1, 2005. Marks stated that "[t]he order sought from this court by Marks . . . will address and resolve the PCA's uncertainty" as to "whether it has the authority to act." Marks relied on the statement in the PCA letter that "the parties are invited to inform the PCA should they wish to utilize the services of the PCA in the administration of the case." Based on its reading of the PCA letter, Marks argued that it was in truth only seeking the interpretation of the agreement which the PCA had invited-an interpretation as to which arbitral rules to apply-and that a dispute about that very question could not render the case moot or preclude the relief Marks sought. Marks did not seek to amend its claims for relief in the petition to compel arbitration.

The district court dismissed Marks' petition on September 20, 2005, on the grounds that "the relief Marks seeks, an order requiring Presstek to arbitrate their dispute at the PCA under the American Arbitration Act's International Rules, is unavailable." The district court read the PCA letter to say that the PCA will "proceed with arbitration *only* if the parties have agreed to arbitrate under the UNCITRAL Arbitration Rules." The court observed that Marks "did not plead a claim seeking to interpret the agreement to determine which arbitration rules would apply," did not "include any allegations as to the meaning of the parties' agreement with respect to which arbitration rules would apply," nor "even suggest[ed] that the parties agreed to the UNCITRAL Arbitration Rules."

---

[87] [Footnote 2 in original] The August 9, 2005 order also denied an earlier motion by Presstek to dismiss the petition. Presstek had argued that the PCA's decision not to hear the case was an "award" within the meaning of the FAA, that the only court with the competence to overturn that award under the New York Convention was a court in the Netherlands, and that Marks' petition, properly construed as a motion to vacate an arbitral award, was untimely. The district court rejected these arguments, finding that the PCA's refusal to arbitrate the dispute was not an "award" under the New York Convention and that Marks' petition was timely under the FAA. Presstek does not appeal these determinations.

Marks moved for reconsideration on October 4, 2005, under Fed.R.Civ.P. 59(e).   It argued that the district court was misreading the PCA letter, and that the PCA would "assist parties . . . pursuant to the order of any court with jurisdiction" even if the parties did not agree to apply the UNCITRAL Arbitration Rules.

For the first time, Marks clarified that the PCA letter was immaterial. It was immaterial because arbitration could be had in either a different forum or under a different set of arbitration rules:

Marks has prayed that, following the required hearing or trial, the AAA International Rules apply, given that they are closest to the expressed intent of the parties in their agreement. . . . However, Marks has also asked in its Petition for the Court to grant whatever "relief it deems just and appropriate" consistent with the parties' agreement to arbitrate, the New York Convention and the strong state and federal policies in favor of arbitration. *It is certainly possible that, following a hearing and trial if necessary, the Court may find an alternative location in The Hague, and/or rules, appropriate in order to effectuate the parties' agreement to arbitration* (emphasis added and citation omitted). Marks noted that there were other arbitral bodies at The Hague besides the PCA that could hear the case, and argued that the district court was obligated under the New York Convention and Section 4 of the FAA to hold a hearing or a trial to determine "the nature of the parties' arbitration agreement as it relates to any ambiguous terms, including but not limited [to] which rules to apply and the agency and organization to preside or supervise."

This was not the relief clearly sought in the original complaint. Nor was this relief sought after the district court warned Marks of the problems with how it had framed this case. This theory was clearly articulated for the first time some three-and-a-half years after the contract dispute arose, two years after the PCA had declined to accept competence over the arbitration, and six months after Marks had filed its federal court petition to compel arbitration.

The district court denied Marks' motion for reconsideration. Marks appeals, arguing (1) that the district court erred in its initial conclusion that it could not grant the relief requested, and (2) that the district court should, nonetheless, have held a hearing to find a different forum at which to order the arbitration, under perhaps a different set of rules.

. . .

[*Marks' arguments on appeal, including arguments based on the strong policy bias in favor of arbitration under the FAA and the New York Convention, were predictably rejected, and the decisions of the trial court were affirmed*]

. . .

* * * * *

Notes and Questions

Note 1: It is worth walking through the factual background leading up to the appeal to ask what counsel for Marks might have done differently. First, what is the basic problem with the arbitration agreement? Is it valid under the relevant provisions of the Model Law and the New York Convention?

Note 2: What exactly was Marks requesting from the PCA? Why did the Secretary General of the PCA decline to designate an "appointing authority" in this matter? What is the effect of its decision? Read footnote 2 from the original case. Actions to set aside or vacate an award will be addressed more fully in Chapter 10. What should Marks have done next? How should Marks have argued its position? Consider the potential alternative arguments Marks might have made to an appropriate court. Might the case have turned out differently?

Note 3: What might have motivated Marks to bring the action to compel in a New Hampshire federal court instead? Was this a sound decision? What was Marks' initial theory in this action to compel? Was this a sound theory? Do you see any estoppel concerns, or is Marks simply making reasonable alternative arguments?

Note 4: Consider the final theory articulated by Marks in its motion for reconsideration. When, and before whom, should this theory have been advanced in the first instance?

C.   IS THE PARTIES' DISPUTE WITHIN THE SCOPE OF THE ARBITRATION
       AGREEMENT?

Even if the parties validly concluded an arbitration agreement, a given dispute may or may not fall within its scope. The issue of scope is typically one of basic contract interpretation. Did the parties intend to submit the specific dispute in question to binding arbitration under the terms of their arbitration agreement? For example, the following provision would arguably provide for a relatively broad scope, though it would nonetheless be limited to issues touching in some manner upon the contract within which it was included.

> **Example 8-9**
> Any dispute, controversy, or claim arising out of, relating to, or concerning this contract, including the negotiation, formation, performance, breach, validity, or termination thereof, shall be determined by final and binding arbitration.

The choice of law governing the interpretation of the arbitration agreement may also be important inasmuch as a court or tribunal may be required to interpret the scope or other provisions of the arbitration agreement.   As illustrated in Appendix C, the interpretation of the arbitration agreement will typically invoke the law of the place of arbitration, unless the parties have chosen a different law. Unfortunately, however, there is no single approach to determining whether the parties have in fact made such a choice with respect to the arbitration agreement.

On one hand, the arbitration agreement is part of the main contract, and one might reasonably urge that it be interpreted under the law applicable to the main contract, especially if it is subject to an express choice of law governing the main contract.[88] On the other hand, the arbitration agreement is, for many purposes, considered separable from the main contract, and one might reasonably consider it separable for choice of law purposes. The parties might, by virtue of their choice of a place of arbitration, be deemed to have impliedly chosen the general contract law of the place of arbitration for the interpretation of the arbitration agreement, inasmuch as this law would likely have the closest connection to the arbitration in the absence of any express choice.[89]

Of course, if the parties specifically choose the law governing the interpretation of the arbitration agreement (as distinct from the main contract) this choice would likely be given effect. Alternatively, in the absence of any express choice by the parties, one might—in addition to the approaches discussed above—look to international rules of general contract interpretation, such as the Unidroit

---

[88] While most would agree that a broad choice of law clause reaches only the substantive contract law—and has no effect on the *lex arbitri*—this is a much closer question when dealing with the substantive interpretation of the arbitration agreement.

[89] Most choice of law rules in fact allow for such dépeçage, wherein parties may choose different laws for different elements of their contract.

Principles, in interpreting the parties agreement to arbitrate an international dispute.[90]

In many cases, the above discussion may have little more than theoretical relevance because many jurisdictions employ a reasonably similar methodology in determining the objectively viewed intent of the parties, including relevant practices and usages, and the terms of the agreement may be clear. However, the interpretation of an ambiguous or poorly drafted arbitration agreement may very well determine the jurisdiction of the tribunal—as it may determine whether or not the parties made an enforceable agreement to arbitrate anything, and, if so, whether the dispute in question falls within the scope of that agreement. If the tribunal exercises jurisdiction in a manner inconsistent with the parties' agreement, then it may be subject to vacation or non-enforcement.[91]

The parties' arbitration agreement determines the scope of disputes subject to arbitration.[92] Normally, parties preferring arbitration will want to write this provision quite broadly to encompass any possible dispute in any way touching upon the formation, performance, breach, termination, or validity of their contractual relationship. To the extent the parties wish to provide for a narrower scope, they must arguably be even more precise in their drafting. Assuming that the parties wish to provide for a broad arbitration agreement, the standard arbitration clauses provided along with various rules are particularly useful in that most have been carefully drafted and have stood the test of time and challenge.

D.   IS THE PARTIES' DISPUTE ARBITRABLE?

A final source of jurisdictional challenges is found not in the parties' agreement, but in the regulatory law of a relevant jurisdiction. This is the question of "arbitrability." This term has, unfortunately been used by different people to mean a variety of different things. In particular, the United States Supreme Court has used it in reference to virtually any question relating to the arbitrators' jurisdiction.[93] However, the term remains useful in a narrow sense, and this

---

[90] One might also look to CISG Article 8 as an interpretive rule. However, the CISG contains no indication that it purports to govern dispute resolution agreements.

[91] *See e.g.* Model Law Article 34(2)(a)(iii); New York Convention Article V(1)(c).

[92] It might be helpful to refer back to the recommended arbitration clauses contained in Chapter 7, section III.C.

[93] *See* First Options of Chicago, Inc. v. Kaplan, 514 U.S. 938 (1995); *see also* Alan Scott Rau, *Federal Common Law and Arbitral Power*, __ NEV. L.J. __ (forthcoming) (criticizing the Court's broad use of the term in a manner that has arguably deprived it of any specific meaning).

casebook will use it narrowly to address the specific question of whether the particular subject matter of any given dispute is subject to arbitration.[94]

For example, a State might reasonably determine, as a matter of public policy, that certain issues involving third party rights, such as antitrust or competition laws, might not be appropriately decided in private arbitration. As further explained in the final section of this chapter, most disputes are arbitrable under most legal regimes. However, the issue is nonetheless a potentially important one, because an attempt to arbitrate an inarbitrable dispute will likely result in the setting aside or non-enforcement of the resulting award. Moreover, as illustrated in Appendix C, one must consider the laws governing arbitrability of both the place of arbitration[95] and potential places of enforcement.[96]

Of course such a regulatory challenge is typically raised by one of the parties who, having initially agreed to arbitration, later has second thoughts about the decision. The following is the seminal American case on subject matter arbitrability in the context of international commercial arbitration.

MITSUBISHI MOTORS CORP. v.
SOLER CHRYSLER-PLYMOUTH, INC.
473 U.S. 614 (1985)

JUSTICE BLACKMUN delivered the opinion of the Court.

The principal question presented by these cases is the arbitrability, pursuant to the Federal Arbitration Act, 9 U.S.C. 1 et seq., and the Convention on the Recognition and Enforcement of Foreign Arbitral Awards (Convention), 1970. 21 U.S. T. 2517, T. I. A. S. No. 6997, of claims arising under the Sherman Act, 15 U.S.C. 1 et seq., and encompassed within a valid arbitration clause in an agreement embodying an international commercial transaction.

. . .

[The *Court first determined that the language of the parties' agreement to arbitrate was sufficient to reach the statutory antitrust claims in question.*]

---

[94] *See* FOUCHARD, GAILLARD, GOLDMAN ON INTERNATIONAL COMMERCIAL ARBITRATION ¶ 532 (Emmanuel Gaillard and John Savage, eds., 1999) (also noting broad and confusing use of the term by the United States Supreme Court and also adopting the same narrow definition consistent with more typical international usage).

[95] *See, e.g.*, Model Law Article 34(2)(b)(i) (focusing on the law of the place of arbitration).

[96] *See* New York Convention Article V(2)(a) (focusing on the law of the enforcing State).

. . .

III

We now turn to consider whether Soler's antitrust claims are nonarbitrable even though it has agreed to arbitrate them. In holding that they are not, the Court of Appeals followed the decision of the Second Circuit in *American Safety Equipment Corp. v. J. P. Maguire & Co.*, 391 F.2d 821 (1968). Notwithstanding the absence of any explicit for such an exception in either the Sherman Act or the Federal Arbitration Act, the Second Circuit there reasoned that "the pervasive public interest in enforcement of the antitrust laws, and the nature of the claims that arise in such cases, combine to make . . . antitrust claims . . . inappropriate for arbitration." *Id.*, at 827-828. We find it unnecessary to assess the legitimacy of the American Safety doctrine as applied to agreements to arbitrate arising from domestic transactions. As in *Scherk v. Alberto-Culver Co.*, 417 U.S. 506 (1974), we conclude that concerns of international comity, respect for the capacities of foreign and transnational tribunals, and sensitivity to the need of the international commercial system for predictability in the resolution of disputes require that we enforce the parties' agreement, even assuming that a contrary result would be forthcoming in a domestic context.

Even before *Scherk*, this Court had recognized the utility of forum-selection clauses in international transactions. In [*The Bremen v. Zapata Off-Shore Co.* 407 U.S. 1 (1972)], an American oil company, seeking to evade a contractual choice of an English forum and, by implication, English law, filed a suit in admiralty in a United States District Court against the German corporation which had contracted to tow its rig to a location in the Adriatic Sea. Notwithstanding the possibility that the English court would enforce provisions in the towage contract exculpating the German party which an American court would refuse to enforce, this Court gave effect to the choice-of-forum clause. It observed:

> The expansion of American business and industry will hardly be encouraged if, notwithstanding solemn contracts, we insist on a parochial concept that all disputes must be resolved under our laws and in our courts. . . . We cannot have trade and commerce in world

> markets and international waters exclusively on
> our terms, governed by our laws, and resolved in
> our courts.

407 U.S., at 9.

Recognizing that "agreeing in advance on a forum acceptable to both parties is an indispensable element in international trade, commerce, and contracting," *id.*, at 13-14, the decision in *The Bremen* clearly eschewed a provincial solicitude for the jurisdiction of domestic forums.

Identical considerations governed the Court's decision in *Scherk*, which categorized "[a]n agreement to arbitrate before a specified tribunal [as], in effect, a specialized kind of forum-selection clause that posits not only the situs of suit but also the procedure to be used in resolving the dispute." 417 U.S., at 519. In *Scherk*, the American company Alberto-Culver purchased several interrelated business enterprises, organized under the laws of Germany and Liechtenstein, as well as the rights held by those enterprises in certain trademarks, from a German citizen who at the time of trial resided in Switzerland. Although the contract of sale contained a clause providing for arbitration before the International Chamber of Commerce in Paris of "any controversy or claim [arising] out of this agreement or the breach thereof," Alberto-Culver subsequently brought suit against Scherk in a Federal District Court in Illinois, alleging that Scherk had violated 10(b) of the Securities Exchange Act of 1934 by fraudulently misrepresenting the status of the trade-marks as unencumbered. The District Court denied a motion to stay the proceedings before it and enjoined the parties from going forward before the arbitral tribunal in Paris. The Court of Appeals for the Seventh Circuit affirmed, relying on this Court's holding in *Wilko v. Swan*, 346 U.S. 427 (1953), that agreements to arbitrate disputes arising under the Securities Act of 1933 are nonarbitrable. This Court reversed, enforcing the arbitration agreement even while assuming for purposes of the decision that the controversy would be nonarbitrable under the holding of *Wilko* had it arisen out of a domestic transaction. Again, the Court emphasized:

> A contractual provision specifying in advance
> the forum in which disputes shall be litigated
> and the law to be applied is . . . an almost
> indispensable precondition to achievement of the

orderliness and predictability essential to any
international business transaction. . . .

A parochial refusal by the courts of one country
to enforce an international arbitration agreement
would not only frustrate these purposes, but
would invite unseemly and mutually destructive
jockeying by the parties to secure tactical
litigation advantages. . . . [It would] damage the
fabric of international commerce and trade, and
imperil the willingness and ability of
businessmen to enter into international
commercial agreements.

417 U.S., at 516-517. Accordingly, the Court held Alberto-
Culver to its bargain, sending it to the international arbitral
tribunal before which it had agreed to seek its remedies.

The Bremen and *Scherk* establish a strong presumption in favor
of enforcement of freely negotiated contractual choice-of-forum
provisions. Here, as in *Scherk*, that presumption is reinforced by
the emphatic federal policy in favor of arbitral dispute resolution.
And at least since this Nation's accession in 1970 to the
Convention, see 1970. 21 U.S. T. 2517, T. I. A. S. 6997, and the
implementation of the Convention in the same year by
amendment of the Federal Arbitration Act, that federal policy
applies with special force in the field of international commerce.
Thus, we must weigh the concerns of American Safety against a
strong belief in the efficacy of arbitral procedures for the
resolution of international commercial disputes and an equal
commitment to the enforcement of freely negotiated choice-of-
forum clauses.

At the outset, we confess to some skepticism of certain aspects
of the *American Safety* doctrine. As distilled by the First Circuit,
723 F.2d, at 162, the doctrine comprises four ingredients. First,
private parties play a pivotal role in aiding governmental
enforcement of the antitrust laws by means of the private action
for treble damages. Second, "the strong possibility that contracts
which generate antitrust disputes may be contracts of adhesion
militates against automatic forum determination by contract."
Third, antitrust issues, prone to complication, require
sophisticated legal and economic analysis, and thus are "ill-
adapted to strengths of the arbitral process, i. e., expedition,
minimal requirements of written rationale, simplicity, resort to

basic concepts of common sense and simple equity." Finally, just as "issues of war and peace are too important to be vested in the generals, . . . decisions as to antitrust regulation of business are too important to be lodged in arbitrators chosen from the business community - particularly those from a foreign community that has had no experience with or exposure to our law and values." See *American Safety*, 391 F.2d, at 826-827.

Initially, we find the second concern unjustified. The mere appearance of an antitrust dispute does not alone warrant invalidation of the selected forum on the undemonstrated assumption that the arbitration clause is tainted. A party resisting arbitration of course may attack directly the validity of the agreement to arbitrate. See *Prima Paint Corp. v. Flood & Conklin Mfg. Co.*, 388 U.S. 395 (1967). Moreover, the party may attempt to make a showing that would warrant setting aside the forum-selection clause - that the agreement was "[a]ffected by fraud, undue influence, or overweening bargaining power"; that "enforcement would be unreasonable and unjust"; or that proceedings "in the contractual forum will be so gravely difficult and inconvenient that [the resisting party] will for all practical purposes be deprived of his day in court." *The Bremen*, 407 U.S., at 12, 15, 18. But absent such a showing - and none was attempted here - there is no basis for assuming the forum inadequate or its selection unfair.

Next, potential complexity should not suffice to ward off arbitration. We might well have some doubt that even the courts following *American Safety* subscribe fully to the view that antitrust matters are inherently insusceptible to resolution by arbitration, as these same courts have agreed that an undertaking to arbitrate antitrust claims entered into after the dispute arises is acceptable. [citations omitted] See also, in the present cases, 723 F.2d, at 168, n. 12 (leaving question open). And the vertical restraints which most frequently give birth to antitrust claims covered by an arbitration agreement will not often occasion the monstrous proceedings that have given antitrust litigation an image of intractability. In any event, adaptability and access to expertise are hallmarks of arbitration. The anticipated subject matter of the dispute may be taken into account when the arbitrators are appointed, and arbitral rules typically provide for the participation of experts either employed by the parties or appointed by the tribunal. Moreover, it is often a judgment that streamlined proceedings and expeditious results will best serve their needs that causes parties to agree to arbitrate their disputes; it is typically a desire to keep the effort and expense required to resolve a dispute within manageable bounds that prompts them mutually to forgo access to judicial remedies. In sum, the factor of potential complexity alone does not persuade us that an arbitral tribunal could not properly handle an antitrust matter.

For similar reasons, we also reject the proposition that an arbitration panel will pose too great a danger of innate hostility to the constraints on business conduct that antitrust law imposes. International arbitrators frequently are drawn from the legal as well as the business community; where the dispute has an important legal component, the parties and the arbitral body with whose assistance they have agreed to settle their dispute can be expected to select arbitrators accordingly.[18] We decline to indulge the presumption that the parties and arbitral body conducting a proceeding will be unable or unwilling to retain competent, conscientious, and impartial arbitrators.

We are left, then, with the core of the *American Safety* doctrine - the fundamental importance to American democratic capitalism of the regime of the antitrust laws. [citations omitted] Without doubt, the private cause of action plays a central role in enforcing this regime. [citations omitted] As the Court of Appeals pointed out:

> A claim under the antitrust laws is not merely a private matter. The Sherman Act is designed to promote the national interest in a competitive economy; thus, the plaintiff asserting his rights

---

[18] [in original] See Craig, Park, & Paulsson, supra, 12.03, p. 28; Sanders, Commentary on UNCITRAL Arbitration Rules 15.1, in 2 Yearbook Commercial Arbitration, supra, at 203. We are advised by Mitsubishi and *amicus* International Chamber of Commerce, without contradiction by Soler, that the arbitration panel selected to hear the parties' claims here is composed of three Japanese lawyers, one a former law school dean, another a former judge, and the third a practicing attorney with American legal training who has written on Japanese antitrust law. Brief for Petitioner in No. 83-1569, p. 26; Brief for International Chamber of Commerce as *Amicus Curiae* 16, n. 28. The Court of Appeals was concerned that international arbitrators would lack "experience with or exposure to our law and values." 723 F.2d, at 162. The obstacles confronted by the arbitration panel in this case, however, should be no greater than those confronted by any judicial or arbitral tribunal required to determine foreign law. See, *e. g.*, Fed. Rule Civ. Proc. 44.1. Moreover, while our attachment to the antitrust laws may be stronger than most, many other countries, including Japan, have similar bodies of competition law. See, e. g., 1 Law of Transnational Business Transactions, ch. 9 (Banks, Antitrust Aspects of International Business Operations), 9.037. (V. Nanda ed. 1984); H. Iyori & A. Uesugi, The Antimonopoly Laws of Japan (1983).

> under the Act has been likened to a private attorney-general who protects the public's interest.

723 F.2d, at 168, quoting *American Safety*, 391 F.2d, at 826.

The treble-damages provision wielded by the private litigant is a chief tool in the antitrust enforcement scheme, posing a crucial deterrent to potential violators. [*citations omitted*] The importance of the private damages remedy, however, does not compel the conclusion that it may not be sought outside an American court. Notwithstanding its important incidental policing function, the treble-damages cause of action conferred on private parties by 4 of the Clayton Act, 15 U.S.C. 15, and pursued by Soler here by way of its third counterclaim, seeks primarily to enable an injured competitor to gain compensation for that injury.

> Section 4 . . . is in essence a remedial provision. It provides treble damages to `[a]ny person who shall be injured in his business or property by reason of anything forbidden in the antitrust laws . . . .' Of course, treble damages also play an important role in penalizing wrongdoers and deterring wrongdoing, as we also have frequently observed. . . . It nevertheless is true that the treble-damages provision, which makes awards available only to injured parties, and measures the awards by a multiple of the injury actually proved, is designed primarily as a remedy.

Brunswick Corp. v. Pueblo Bowl-O-Mat, Inc., 429 U.S. 477, 485-486 (1977).

After examining the respective legislative histories, the Court in *Brunswick* recognized that when first enacted in 1890 as 7 of the Sherman Act, 26 Stat. 210, the treble-damages provision "was conceived of primarily as a remedy for `[t]he people of the United States as individuals,'" 429 U.S., at 486, n. 10, quoting 21 Cong. Rec. 1767-1768 (1890) (remarks of Sen. George); when reenacted in 1914 as 4 of the Clayton Act, 38 Stat. 731, it was still "conceived primarily as `open[ing] the door of justice to every man, whenever he may be injured by those who violate the antitrust laws, and giv[ing] the injured party ample damages for the wrong suffered.'" 429 U.S., at 486, n. 10, quoting 51 Cong. Rec. 9073 (1914) (remarks of Rep. Webb). And, of course, the antitrust cause of action remains at all times under the control of the individual litigant: no citizen is under an obligation to bring an antitrust suit, [citations omitted], and the private antitrust plaintiff needs no executive or judicial approval before settling one. It follows that, at least where the international cast of a transaction would otherwise add an element of uncertainty to dispute resolution, the prospective litigant may provide in advance for a mutually agreeable procedure whereby he would seek his antitrust recovery as well as settle other controversies.

There is no reason to assume at the outset of the dispute that international arbitration will not provide an adequate mechanism. To be sure, the international arbitral tribunal owes no prior allegiance to the legal norms of particular states; hence, it has no direct obligation to vindicate their statutory dictates. The tribunal, however, is bound to effectuate the intentions of the parties. Where the parties have agreed that the arbitral body is to decide a defined set of claims which includes, as in these cases, those arising from the application of American antitrust law, the tribunal therefore should be bound to decide that dispute in accord with the national law giving rise to the claim. Cf. *Wilko v. Swan*, 346 U.S., at 433-434.[19] And so long as the prospective

---

[19] [in original] In addition to the clause providing for arbitration before the Japan Commercial Arbitration Association, the Sales Agreement includes a choice-of-law clause which reads: "This Agreement is made in, and will be governed by and construed in all respects according to the laws of the Swiss Confederation as if entirely performed therein." App. 56. The United States raises the possibility that the arbitral panel will read this provision not simply to govern interpretation of the contract terms, but wholly to displace American law even where it otherwise would apply. Brief for United States as *Amicus Curiae* 20. The International Chamber of Commerce opines that it is "[c]onceivabl[e], although we believe it unlikely, [that] the arbitrators could consider Soler's affirmative claim of anti-competitive conduct by CISA and Mitsubishi to fall within the purview of this choice-of-law provision, with the result that it would be decided under Swiss law rather than the U.S. Sherman Act." Brief for International Chamber of Commerce as *Amicus Curiae* 25. At oral argument, however, counsel for Mitsubishi conceded that American law applied to the antitrust claims and represented that the claims had been submitted to the arbitration panel in Japan on that basis. Tr. of Oral. Arg. 18. The record confirms that before the decision of the Court of Appeals the arbitral panel had taken these claims under submission. See District Court Order of May 25, 1984, pp. 2–3. We therefore have no occasion to speculate on this matter at this stage in the proceedings, when Mitsubishi seeks to enforce the agreement to arbitrate, not to enforce an award. Nor need we consider now the effect of an arbitral tribunal's failure to take cognizance of the statutory cause of action on the claimant's capacity to reinitiate suit in federal court. We merely note that in the event the choice-of-forum and choice-of-law clauses operated in tandem as a prospective waiver of a party's right to pursue statutory remedies for antitrust violations, we would have little hesitation in condemning the agreement as against public policy. [citations omitted]

litigant effectively may vindicate its statutory cause of action in the arbitral forum, the statute will continue to serve both its remedial and deterrent function.

Having permitted the arbitration to go forward, the national courts of the United States will have the opportunity at the award-enforcement stage to ensure that the legitimate interest in the enforcement of the antitrust laws has been addressed. The Convention reserves to each signatory country the right to refuse enforcement of an award where the "recognition or enforcement of the award would be contrary to the public policy of that country." Art. V(2)(b), 21 U.S. T., at 2520; see *Scherk*, 417 U.S., at 519, n. 14. While the efficacy of the arbitral process requires that substantive review at the award-enforcement stage remain minimal, it would not require intrusive inquiry to ascertain that the tribunal took cognizance of the antitrust claims and actually decided them.

As international trade has expanded in recent decades, so too has the use of international arbitration to resolve disputes arising in the course of that trade. The controversies that international arbitral institutions are called upon to resolve have increased in diversity as well as in complexity. Yet the potential of these tribunals for efficient disposition of legal disagreements arising from commercial relations has not yet been tested. If they are to take a central place in the international legal order, national courts will need to "shake off the old judicial hostility to arbitration," *Kulukundis Shipping Co. v. Amtorg Trading Corp.*, 126 F.2d 978, 985 (CA2 1942), and also their customary and understandable unwillingness to cede jurisdiction of a claim arising under domestic law to a foreign or transnational tribunal. To this extent, at least, it will be necessary for national courts to subordinate domestic notions of arbitrability to the international policy favoring commercial arbitration. See *Scherk, supra*.

Accordingly, we "require this representative of the American business community to honor its bargain," *Alberto-Culver Co. v. Scherk*, 484 F.2d 611, 620 (CA7 1973) (Stevens, J., dissenting), by holding this agreement to arbitrate "enforce[able] . . . in accord with the explicit provisions of the Arbitration Act." *Scherk*, 417 U.S., at 520.

The judgment of the Court of Appeals is affirmed in part and reversed in part, and the cases are remanded for further proceedings consistent with this opinion.

. . .

[dissenting opinions of JUSTICES STEVENS, BRENNAN, and
POWELL are omitted]

* * * * *

Notes and Questions

Note 1: Under the Court's logic, is there any sort of commercial dispute that it
might find inarbitrable?

Note 2: Today, virtually all commercial disputes are deemed arbitrable under
most national laws. In addition to antitrust actions, patent, copyright, and
securities claims, for example, are all considered arbitrable under American law.
Swiss law simply states that "[a]ny dispute of financial interest may be the
subject of an arbitration."[97] It is hard to image what, if any, sort of dispute might
fall outside of such a broad definition.

Note 3: In short, arbitrability is rarely an issue today in most countries. However,
one must still consider the issue. In some countries, private autonomous ordering
remains subject to significant government regulation. If such a country provides
the place of arbitration or a potential place of enforcement, then a more thorough
examination of the relevant law governing arbitrability may be necessary.

E.   DOES PUBLIC POLICY PRECLUDE ARBITRATION OF THE PARTIES' DISPUTE?

Lastly, a tribunal may decline jurisdiction over any matter in which a resulting
award would likely be unenforceable based on public policy of a relevant
jurisdiction.[98] In addressing such an issue, the tribunal will need to consider any
applicable public policies that might invalidate an award, whether contained in
the law of the place of arbitration[99] or in the law of a likely place of
enforcement.[100] For example, the arbitration of a dispute arising from a contract
deemed not only illegal, but also contrary to basic notions of morality and justice
may be deemed contrary to public policy. A tribunal must consider such public
policy issues in advance of exercising jurisdiction, because the tribunal has a
duty to the parties to render an enforceable award. However, these issues are

---

[97] Federal Statute of Private International Law, Chapter 12, Article 177(1) (1988).
[98] A tribunal has a duty to render an enforceable award or decline jurisdiction if this is not possible.
[99] *See e.g.* Model Law Article 34(2)(b)(ii).
[100] *See* New York Convention Article V(2)(b).

somewhat more easily understood in the context of actions to set aside or enforce an award and will, therefore be addressed more fully in Chapter 10.

Concluding Notes and Questions on Chapter 8

Note 1: Parties to an arbitration agreement presumably prefer to arbitrate their contract disputes—at least at the time they conclude the contract at issue. Of course that preference often changes for one of the parties after the dispute has arisen. Thus, one might reasonably ask "what are the most important elements of an arbitration regime, assuming the parties genuinely wish at the time of their agreement to stay out of court—even if one of the parties later seeks to disregard the agreement to arbitrate?"

Note 2: The first requirement is a strong competence-competence regime. This is the best way to prevent a recalcitrant party from bringing a court action intended to obstruct, delay, or even avoid the agreed upon arbitration proceedings. The second requirement is a mechanism for constituting the tribunal when one of the parties refuses to participate—and doing so without going to court. This will generally require the adoption of a set of rules providing for such an appointment mechanism. Such mechanisms are found in most institutional rules and are also found in the UNCITRAL Rules for use in *ad hoc* arbitration. The third requirement is a broad scope provision encompassing any potential dispute that might arise in connection with the contract at issue, thus minimizing the likelihood of jurisdictional challenges, at whatever point in time they may occur. The last requirement is a strongly pro-arbitration legal regime, which of course also minimizes likely challenges before, during, or after the completion of the arbitration proceedings.

Note 3: Consider again the questions posed Chapter 7, section III.B regarding the content of the arbitration agreement. Are there any more important elements in an arbitration clause than the scope provision, the choice of place, and the choice of rules?[101] Do those necessarily take more than a single paragraph? What then must an attorney know in drafting an appropriate arbitration agreement?

---

[101] This question is not intended to suggest that a choice of substantive law provision is necessarily any more or less important than any of these. However, the choice of law provision is to some degree a part of the substantive agreement rather than the arbitration clause, even though it is often included within an overall dispute resolution section.

PROBLEMS

Problem 8-2: Consider again the case of *Filanto v. Chilewich* presented above. Assuming that Chilewich was seeking dismissal of Filanto's court action so as to require Filanto to bring any claims against Chilewich in arbitration proceedings in Moscow, how might Chilewich have argued its case in an effort to focus the court's attention on the key issues and minimize the litigation of issues purportedly committed to arbitration.

Problem 8-3: A Ukrainian seller and a Korean buyer engage in negotiations over a potential sale of goods contract. The buyer submits an offer in the form of a signed purchase order, which seller counter-signs and purports to accept. However, buyer refuses to perform. Buyer asserts that it learned the goods were not suitable for its intended purpose and effectively revoked the offer under CISG Article 16 before seller's acceptance was dispatched. Buyer's offer included an arbitration clause with the following scope provision and place of arbitration:

> Any dispute, controversy, or claim arising out of, relating to, or concerning this contract, including the negotiation, formation, performance, breach, validity, or termination thereof, shall be determined by final and binding arbitration in Vindobona, Danubia.

When seller commences arbitration seeking damages for breach of contract, buyer challenges the jurisdiction of any arbitral tribunal to decide seller's claims. Buyer asserts that it revoked its offer and, therefore, never agreed to any contract with seller (for arbitration or anything else). Assuming that an arbitral tribunal is properly constituted, can the tribunal hear the merits of seller's claim? If the tribunal does so and decides that buyer's offer was effectively revoked, how does this affect the tribunal's jurisdiction? If the tribunal must decline jurisdiction in the event that it determines that buyer revoked its offer, how does this affect the scope of the arbitration clause contained in buyer's offer?

Suppose that buyer had not attempted to revoke its offer. However, seller had sent its own signed letter (instead of counter-signing the offer) purporting to accept buyer's offer, but reducing the quantity of goods from that contained in buyer's offer. Everything else in seller's purported acceptance, including the arbitration clause is identical to buyer's offer. Again, buyer refuses to perform, claiming no contract was ever formed, and seller commences arbitration seeking to enforce. Have the parties concluded a contract for the sale of goods? Can an arbitral tribunal answer this question for the parties by deciding their case on the merits?

Problem 8-4: Consider again Problems 7-3, 7-4 and 7-5 at the end of the previous chapter. Do any of the materials covered in the current chapter affect the analysis?

9 | ARBITRATION AS A PROCEDURE TO DECIDE THE PARTIES' DISPUTE

> In theory, there is no difference between theory and practice.
> But in practice, there is.
>
> - Yogi Berra[1]

The previous chapter began with the commencement of the arbitration and followed with an exploration of threshold issues involving the constitution of tribunal, jurisdictional questions, and the potential involvement of the courts. This chapter assumes the tribunal has been formed and has accepted jurisdiction over the parties' dispute.[2] As such, the focus shifts to the procedures by which the tribunal conducts the arbitration, and the parties present their respective cases.

Example 9-1

J&G has concluded a contract with NNM in which NNM has agreed to sell steel to J&G for use in its new MAK X disposable razor blades, and their contract included an arbitration clause. A dispute has arisen over the quality of the steel delivered by NNM, and J&G has commenced arbitration. The panel has been constituted, and any jurisdictional challenges have been resolved. J&G is asserting that the steel delivered by NNM is non-conforming under CISG Article 35. NNM is considering counter-claims of its own that J&G failed to pay for the steel as required by the contract and CISG Article 53. NNM is also wondering if it might be able to assert certain other claims arising out of separate agreements under which J&G contracted to sell consumer goods to NNM.

---

[1] Yogi Berra is a former baseball player for the New York Yankees and former manager of both the New York Yankees and New York Mets. While he has absolutely no connection with international commercial arbitration (at least as far as the authors are aware), he is one of the few managers to have won league championships in both the National and American baseball leagues.

[2] Alternatively, a tribunal could defer its jurisdictional decision pending its consideration of the merits. *See e.g.* Model Law Article 16(3). In such a case, the tribunal would again find itself at the threshold of a proceeding on the merits.

The reader will likely recall the introduction to Chapter 8, which pointed out that the performance of an arbitration agreement between the parties actually gives rise to one or more additional contracts. The parties contract with an arbitrator or arbitrators to decide their dispute. The arbitrators promise to render an award consistent with the parties' agreement in exchange for the parties' promise to pay the arbitrators for their services. If the parties' agreement provides for institutional arbitration, they will also contract with the institution to provide administrative services, often including assistance in establishing the parties' relationship with the arbitrators. The current chapter focuses on the performance of each of these additional agreements, consistent with the parties' original agreement to resolve their disputes by arbitration. One of the things the reader may notice is that, once the tribunal has been constituted, the differences between *ad hoc* and institutional arbitration are often much less significant.

The process will typically begin with (I) an exchange of statements of claim and defense between the parties, the establishment of a structured plan for the proceedings, and may also include various other preliminary matters. If, however, a party (II) defaults or fails to participate, the proceedings may nonetheless continue in the party's absence. Once preliminary matters have been completed, (III) the parties will be afforded an opportunity to present their respective cases, generally including oral hearings on the merits of their respective claims and defenses. The process will typically conclude with (IV) the issuance of a final award by the arbitrators.

I.   PLEADINGS, PLANNING AND OTHER PRELIMINARY MATTERS

Under most arbitration regimes, the proceedings will begin with (A) an exchange of statements of claim and defense, as well as any counter-claims, claims for setoff, or requests for joinder. The parties' exchange of pleadings is typically followed by (B) a meeting or meetings between the parties and the arbitrators in an effort to establish a plan and a schedule for conducting the arbitration process, and often to delineate the specific substantive issues to be decided by the tribunal. Before deciding these substantive issues, the tribunal must (C) determine the law applicable to the merits of the parties' dispute, (D) address any requests for interim relief, and (E) address any issues involving discovery.

A.   STATEMENTS OF CLAIM AND DEFENSE, COUNTERCLAIMS, SET-OFF, AND JOINDER

The parties' statements of claim and defense, including any amendments, essentially lay out the facts and law supporting their respective claims, defenses, and requests for relief.

Article 23

Statements of claim and defence

(1) Within the period of time agreed by the parties or
determined by the arbitral tribunal, the claimant shall state
the facts supporting his claim, the points at issue and the
relief or remedy sought, and the respondent shall state his
defence in respect of these particulars, unless the parties
have otherwise agreed as to the required elements of such
statements. The parties may submit with their statements all
documents they consider to be relevant or may add a
reference to the documents or other evidence they will
submit.

(2) Unless otherwise agreed by the parties, either party may
amend or supplement his claim or defence during the course
of the arbitral proceedings, unless the arbitral tribunal
considers it inappropriate to allow such amendment having
regard to the delay in making it.

These pleadings may be included with the claimant's initial request to commence arbitration and the respondent's initial answer,[3] or they may be submitted later upon the request of the tribunal after it has been formed.[4]

In either case, these statements of the parties' respective positions will typically frame the issues ultimately to be decided by the arbitral tribunal in the award. Virtually all rules provide some allowance for the parties to amend their claims or defense. However, such amendments are typically constrained by certain limits.

As shown in subsection (2) above, the Model Law default provides for liberal amendment or supplementation of claims or defenses. In contrast, the ICC Rules provide that, after the Terms of Reference have been approved (based on the parties' statements of claim and defense—*see* below), "no party shall make new claims or counterclaims which fall outside the limits of the Terms of Reference unless it has been authorised to do so by the Arbitral Tribunal."[5] The decision of whether to allow amendment will often come down to the same issue—the reasons for the need to amend and any potential prejudice to the other party.

---

[3] *See e.g.* ICC Rules Articles 4 & 5.
[4] *See e.g.* UNCITRAL Rules Articles; LCIA Rules Article 15 (providing for specific time limits after the formation of the tribunal for submission of statements of claim and defense).
[5] ICC Rules Article 19.

However, these two provisions exemplify two different approaches to the issue—a rule allowing amendment, subject to exception, and a rule precluding amendment, subject to exception.

This presumption regarding amendment is subject to two competing concerns. On one hand, one of the major reasons the parties likely choose arbitration is speed and efficiency, and liberal amendment will often delay the proceedings to allow the other party to address new claims or defenses. On the other, it is important to allow each party to present its case fully.[6] Most law and rules attempt to strike a balance between these concerns, but all will not necessarily strike the balance in quite the same manner.

Another issue that often comes up at the pleading stage is the availability of counterclaims or claims of set-off.[7] Under many rules, both are strictly limited to those arising out of the same contract as the original claim.[8] In contrast, the Swiss Rules somewhat uniquely provide for very broad jurisdiction over setoff claims, even where such claims arise out of an agreement with a different arbitration agreement or forum-selection clause.[9] While unquestionably promoting efficiency in resolving all of the parties' disputes in a single forum, some might suggest that this rule pushes the tribunal's jurisdiction beyond the bounds of party consent.[10]

As indicated in Chapter 7, one of the potential shortcomings of arbitration is the frequent inability to join third parties or unrelated claims.[11] When multiple parties are implicated in a single disputed transaction, efficiency concerns would suggest that all of their claims and defenses be addressed in a single proceeding. A single proceeding will also avoid the possibility of inconsistent decisions by different tribunals or courts. Multiple claims between the same parties may also

---

[6] Model Law Article 18.

[7] Generally, a counter-claim will arise out of the same legal relationship as the original claim; whereas, a claim of setoff may potentially arise from any alleged financial obligation of the claiming party to the responding party—irrespective of whether or not such financial obligation arises from the same contractual relationship. Thus, the applicable rules may have a significant effect on the extent of set-off defenses available in the arbitration. For example, Article 8.1 of the UNIDROIT Principles (2004) provides for set-off of any obligation arising out of the same contract, Article 8.1(2), but limits obligations arising from other contracts to those that are both due and liquidated (determined as to both existence and amount), Article 8.1(1).

[8] *See, e.g.* UNCITRAL Rules Article 19(3).

[9] *See* Swiss Rule Article 21.5.

[10] Of course, one might argue that, by agreeing to the Swiss Rules, a party agrees to override any prior expressions of intent, but what of a subsequent agreement involving a different arbitration clause. The provision is not, however, without controversy, as it seems to push the boundaries of consent to the extent it reaches relationships not directly subject to arbitration before the instant tribunal.

[11] Even Swiss Rules Article 21(5) is limited to claims of setoff, which by no means fully encompasses the broad range of potential claims two parties engaged in a legal dispute may have against each other.

be more efficient to decide together, particularly when such claims may result in offsetting financial obligations.[12]

Multi-party arbitration is perhaps the most problematic in the absence of consent by all of the parties. A party who has not agreed to arbitrate pursuant to the agreement at issue can hardly be said to have consented in any fashion to participate in the instant arbitration. If all of the parties executed the same arbitration agreement, and it allows for joinder, then the there is no issue. Likewise, the original parties to an arbitration agreement and any third-parties implicated in the dispute may consent to joinder after the dispute has arisen. The LCIA Rules go even further in providing that, if a third-party consents to participate in the arbitration, then one of the original parties may petition the tribunal to require joinder, irrespective of the opposition of the other original party.[13] However, all means of party joinder to arbitration require, at a bare minimum, the consent of the party to be joined.

The issue of joinder of claims is somewhat different to the extent that each of the parties has at least agreed to arbitration of some of its disputes before the instant tribunal. Thus, the question is one of extent of the parties' consent rather than its bare existence. For example, the ICC Rules provide for consolidation of claims under certain circumstances in which the parties to a newly commenced arbitration already have another arbitration proceeding pending before the ICC.[14] There is also some authority supporting consolidation of claims under circumstance in which all of the claims between the parties to an arbitration agreement are part of the same group or series of contracts, such as to constitute an economic unity or ensemble.[15]

Ultimately, the most effective means of joinder of parties or claims lies with national courts, and some have urged national legislation allowing for court ordered joinder in arbitration. However, this concept has gained little traction. While the courts could overcome any lack of party consent (based on sovereign power instead of private consent), any resulting awards would not be enforceable under the New York Convention.[16]

---

[12] Indeed, this is one of the justifications in support of Swiss Rules Article 21(5).

[13] LCIA Rules Article 22.1(h).

[14] ICC Rules Article 4(6).

[15] *See Fouchard, Gaillard, Goldman on International Commercial Arbitration* 518–524 (Emmanuel Gaillard & John Savage eds., Kluwer L. Intl. 1999) (thoroughly examining the various circumstances in which the application of the doctrine may or may not be appropriate).

[16] Enforcement under the Convention is based entirely on notions of consent, as discussed further in Chapter 10.

B.   PLANNING THE ARBITRATION

At some point early in the proceedings, either before or after the exchange of statements of claim and defense, the parties and one or more of the arbitrators will likely meet to address planning issues relating to the proceedings.[17]   Such issues may include delineating the issues (to the extent not already addressed), any requests for interim relief, the extent of any discovery, the schedule and nature of hearings on the merits, as well as any of the other issues that might come up in the course of the arbitration—many of which are addressed below.

This sort of planning conference will often include only the presiding arbitrator, even in the event of a three-member tribunal. In such instances, the presiding arbitrator will be empowered to act for the tribunal as a whole,[18] and efficiency and cost savings are enhanced without the need to have all of the arbitrators present. If, however, one of the parties is seeking interim relief at this time, then all arbitrators may be more likely to attend.

Under some institutional rules, this process of delineating the issues is quite formal. In particular, the ICC Rules require the drafting and agreement upon specific "Terms of Reference" before the arbitration can proceed.[19] On the basis of the claimant's request for arbitration and the respondent's answer, as well as any other relevant documents, the tribunal will draw up these terms of reference, including the nature of the claims and relief sought, the issues to be determined, the place of arbitration, the particulars of any procedural rules, and contact information for all of the relevant participants. This is typically drafted in consultation with the parties, who must sign it when completed. The signed, completed terms of reference are then submitted to the ICC Court for final approval.[20] Only then can the arbitration proceed. Separate from the terms of reference, a provisional timetable for the arbitration is established.[21] A somewhat similar process occurs under the SIAC Rules.[22]

---

[17] Such conferences will typically occur by phone or teleconference, as there is no need to have everyone present in the same physical room, unless of course one of the parties is also seeking interim relief requiring some sort of evidentiary hearing.

[18] *See e.g.* LCIA Rules Article 14.3.

[19] *See* ICC Rules Article 18.

[20] These terms of reference strictly limit the claims, relief, and issues to be addressed by the arbitrators in the eventual award, unless expressly modified.

[21] ICC Rules Article 18(4).

[22] *See e.g.* SIAC Rules Article 17 (providing for the preparation by the tribunal, in consultation with the parties who must ultimately sign it, of a memorandum of issues to be decided in the award.)

C.   CHOICE OF SUBSTANTIVE LAW GOVERNING THE MERITS OF THE DISPUTE

Consistent with its contractual roots, the arbitration process provides the parties with complete autonomy to choose the substantive law governing their agreement, subject only to relevant public policy limitations of the *lex arbitri* or any likely state of enforcement.[23]

Article 28

Rules applicable to substance of dispute

(1) The arbitral tribunal shall decide the dispute in accordance with such rules of law as are chosen by the parties as applicable to the substance of the dispute. Any designation of the law or legal system of a given State shall be construed, unless otherwise expressed, as directly referring to the substantive law of that State and not to its conflict of laws rules.

(2) Failing any designation by the parties, the arbitral tribunal shall apply the law determined by the conflict of laws rules which it considers applicable.

(3) The arbitral tribunal shall decide ex aequo et bono or as amiable compositeur only if the parties have expressly authorized it to do so.

(4) In all cases, the arbitral tribunal shall decide in accordance with the terms of the contract and shall take into account the usages of the trade applicable to the transaction.

---

[23] The application of substantive law contrary to public policy of the *lex arbitri* or an enforcing state could lead to setting aside of the award or render it unenforceable, and the arbitrators have a duty to render an enforceable award. As explained in Chapter 10, *infra*, this public policy exception to party autonomy is typically quite narrow.

This respect for party autonomy is reflected in most modern arbitration laws,[24] including Model Law Article 28(1) above. It is also reflected in most modern arbitration rules.[25] The parties' ability to choose substantive law also includes the right to choose private rules of law, which have not been adopted by any sovereign state.[26] For example, the parties might choose the UNIDROIT Principles of International Contracts (2004)[27] to govern their agreement—either in total or to the extent that an issue is not governed by the CISG.[28] However, the parties will sometimes fail to include a choice of substantive law, in which case the arbitrators' task becomes somewhat more interesting.

A national court sitting in the place of arbitration would be required to follow its own conflict of laws rules.[29] However, an arbitral tribunal may typically apply whatever conflict of laws rules it deems appropriate under the circumstances.[30] The parties' choice of a *lex arbitri* or choice of rules may of course limit some of the arbitrators' discretion by, for example, providing a conflict of laws rule within the arbitration law or rules.[31] Or the chosen *lex arbitri* or arbitration rules may expand the arbitrators' discretion by allowing for *voie direct*, or direct

---

[24] *See e.g.* Swiss Statute of Private International Law, Chapter 12, Article 187(1) (1988); *but see generally* Federal Arbitration Act Chapter 1 (failing to address choice of substantive law). In the case of choice of law under the Federal Arbitration Act governing arbitration in the United States, there is some question whether or not the arbitrators must follow the relevant state conflict of laws rules. *See* Jack Graves, *Party Autonomy in the Choice of Commercial Law: The Failure of Revised U.C.C. § 1-301 and a Proposal for Broader Reform*, 36 Seton Hall L. Rev. 59, 80 n. 129 (2005) (suggesting that the arbitrators are not required to follow such rules, but also citing a contrary view).

[25] *See e.g.* UNCITRAL Rules Article 33(1).

[26] *See* Model Law Article 28(1) (providing that the tribunal shall decide according to the "rules of law" designated by the parties); *see also e.g.* LCIA Rules Article 22.3 (providing that the tribunal shall decide according to the "law(s) or rules of law" designated by the parties). The Model Law and most modern institutional rules are almost universally interpreted as allowing for the choice of non-national rules of law, as well as national law.

[27] The choice of the UNIDROIT Principles as governing substantive law is expressly addressed in official comment 4(a) to the Preamble to the Principles, and arbitration is suggested as a means of insuring respect for such a choice. *See supra* Chapter 1.

[28] For example, the UNIDROIT Principles address many of the validity issues not governed by the CISG (*see* Article 4), include a statute of limitations, which the CISG does not, and are perfectly suitable for contracts for services or other transactions not governed by the CISG at all.

[29] As indicated earlier, conflict of law rules are also sometimes called rules of private international law.

[30] *See* Model Law Article 28(2); UNCITRAL Rules Article 33(1). Some institutional rules may also omit provisions on the selection of substantive law, *see e.g.* SIAC Rules, relying instead on the default provisions of the *lex arbitri*, *see* Singapore Arbitration Act (2002 ed.), section 32(2) (providing a similar rule to Model Law Article 28(2)).

[31] *See* Swiss Statute of Private International Law, Chapter 12, Article 187(1); Swiss Rules Article 33(1) (expressly providing for a "closest connection" conflict of laws rule).

choice, without reference to any conflict of laws rules whatsoever.[32] Most rules allowing for direct choice by the arbitrators allow a choice of private rules of law, such as the UNIDROIT Principles, as well as the law of a sovereign state.

> **Example 9-2**
> J&G and NNM have agreed to arbitration under the UNCITRAL Rules, but have failed to include a choice of substantive law. Article 33(1) provides that the tribunal must determine the substantive law by applying conflict of laws rules (those it deems appropriate). In contrast, if the parties had agreed to arbitration under the ICC Rules, Article 17 provides for direct choice of substantive law by the tribunal. Unconstrained by conflict of laws rules, an ICC tribunal could even choose non-national law, such as the UNIDROIT Principles.

Alternatively, the parties may decide—in lieu of any specific substantive law—to authorize the tribunal to decide their dispute *ex aequo et bono* (according to what is right and good) or as *amiable compositeur*.[33] Essentially, such a designation authorizes the tribunal to decide the dispute as a matter of fairness and equity, without regard to substantive law.[34]

Lastly, Model Law Article 28(4) makes clear that the terms of the parties' agreement are to be given priority, as are any relevant usages of trade. This is of

---

[32] *See* French Code of Civil Procedure Article 1496; ICC Rules Article 17(1); AAA/ICDR Rules Article 17(1); LCIA Rules Article 22.3. While each of these rules is fully consistent with French law, and the American Federal Arbitration Act does not speak to the issue, the applicability of either of these rules might present an interesting issue in a Model Law jurisdiction in that the Model Law provides for the use of conflict of laws rules rather than direct choice. Of course, one might suggest that if the parties have the right to choose the substantive law themselves (which they of course do under Model Law Article 28(1)), then they certainly must have the right to provide for the arbitrators to make this choice instead. However, this is expressly excluded by Model Law Article 2, which allows the parties to effective delegate any choice—except for those choices allocated to the parties under Article 28. The English Arbitration Act (1996), Article 46(3), also provides for the use of applicable conflict of laws rules, like the Model Law, but does not include the sort of express limitation included in Model Law Article 2. Thus, the parties' choice of LCIA Rules Article 22.3 providing for direct choice would seem to simply take precedence over the English Arbitration Act's provision for the use of conflict of laws rules.
[33] *See e.g.* Model Law Article 28(3); UNCITRAL Rules Article 33(2); Swiss Rules Article 33(2).
[34] One might distinguish between *ex aequo et bono* and *amiable compositeur*, the former allowing an arbitrator to entirely ignore law in favor of equity, with the latter limited to more of a softening effect on the strict rules of law. However, in modern practice these distinctions seem to have little significance.

course fully consistent with CISG Articles 8 and 9, under which the terms of the parties' agreement and any relevant usage will often be determined.

D.   INTERIM MEASURES AND PRELIMINARY ORDERS

Early in an arbitration proceeding, a party may wish to seek interim or temporary relief in order to preserve the *status quo*, pending the final outcome of the arbitration. Such relief is generally characterized as "interim measures." For example, one buyer may seek an order barring a seller from disposing of goods subject to a claim for performance by seller under CISG Article 46, or a party may seek an interim measure requiring a party to preserve evidence until it can be examined by the party or the tribunal.

Chapter 8 addressed concerns relating to the need for interim relief before the tribunal had been formed and explained the availability of direct relief through national courts, as well as expedited relief available under some rules. Even after the tribunal has been formed, a party may apply directly to national courts in seeking interim relief.[35] However, a party may sometimes prefer to seek such relief through the tribunal once it has been constituted. Such requests to a tribunal for interim measures may nonetheless present a variety of challenges in the context of arbitration.

To begin with, interim measures ordered by the tribunal may or may not be enforceable in national courts. Many court decisions have limited the applicability of the New York Convention to final awards, though others have granted enforcement of interim awards.[36] Even where enforceability in courts is unclear, a party may nonetheless deem it prudent to comply with a measure ordered by the tribunal that has been entrusted with deciding its dispute. For example, a party disregarding an order to preserve evidence might find the tribunal deciding to draw all inferences relating to the lost evidence against the party who ignored its preservation order. Or a seller ignoring an order to preserve goods subject to a claim for performance under CISG Article 46 might find the tribunal inclined to rule in favor of buyer on any close questions relating to the amount or availability of damages under CISG Article 74. Of course, parties will in many instances simply follow any orders of the tribunal as a matter of course, but enforcement is often uncertain when they do not.

The parties have also historically been precluded from seeking such relief through *ex parte* application to the tribunal. Often, the mere notice of application

---

[35] *See* Model Law Article 9 (allowing resort to national courts before or during arbitral proceedings).
[36] *See* Alan Redfern & Martin Hunter, *Law and Practice of International Commercial Arbitration* § 7-16 (4th ed., Sweet & Maxwell 2004) (providing examples of both approaches).

for interim relief may cause the party against whom such relief is sought to take immediate action thereby making moot any interim order (*e.g.*, disposing of potentially relevant evidence before being ordered to preserve it).

Thus, the provisions of the original 1985 version of the Model Law, as well as various bodies of private rules provided minimal guidance and even less certainty as to the availability and effectiveness of interim measures through the tribunal.[37] The recent 2006 amendments to the Model Law have attempted to address these challenges.

Newly revised Model Law Article 17 begins by defining in detail the nature of interim relief available from the tribunal.

Article 17

Power of arbitral tribunal to order interim measures

(1) Unless otherwise agreed by the parties, the arbitral tribunal may, at the request of a party, grant interim measures.

(2) An interim measure is any temporary measure, whether in the form of an award or in another form, by which, at any time prior to the issuance of the award by which the dispute is finally decided, the arbitral tribunal orders a party to:

(a) Maintain or restore the status quo pending determination of the dispute;

(b) Take action that would prevent, or refrain from taking action that is likely to cause, current or imminent harm or prejudice to the arbitral process itself;

(c) Provide a means of preserving assets out of which a subsequent award may be satisfied; or

(d) Preserve evidence that may be relevant and material to the resolution of the dispute.

Article 17A then goes on to specify the standards by which the tribunal shall decide any request for interim measures.

---

[37] *See* Model Law Article 17 (1985) (providing that: "[u]nless otherwise agreed by the parties, the arbitral tribunal may, at the request of a party, order any party to take such interim measure of protections as the arbitral tribunal may consider necessary in respect of the subject-matter of the dispute. The arbitral tribunal may require any party to provide appropriate security in connection with such measure."); *see also* UNCITRAL Rules Article 26 (also providing minimal guidance).

Article 17 A

Conditions for granting interim measures

(1) The party requesting an interim measure under article 17, paragraph 2 (a), (b) and (c) shall satisfy the arbitral tribunal that:

(a) Harm not adequately reparable by an award of damages is likely to result if the measure is not ordered, and such harm substantially outweighs the harm that is likely to result to the party against whom the measure is directed if the measure is granted; and

(b) There is a reasonable possibility that the requesting party will succeed on the merits of the claim. The determination on this possibility shall not affect the discretion of the arbitral tribunal in making any subsequent determination.

(2) With regard to a request for an interim measure under article 17, paragraph 2 (d), the requirements in paragraph 1 (a) and (b) of this article shall apply only to the extent the arbitral tribunal considers appropriate.

Articles 17B and 17C address the mechanics of seeking "preliminary" orders (preliminary even to "interim" relief, which itself precedes final relief in any final award) on an *ex parte* basis, as well as the means for a prompt hearing with parties present, after which a preliminary order may or may not be converted into an "interim measure." In reading this provision, one should take care to distinguish between "preliminary" and "interim" relief and might also note the balance the provision is seeking to achieve in attempting to protect each of the parties' rights. Lastly, note the final provision in Article 17C(5) and compare it to Article 17H(1) below.

Article 17 B

Applications for preliminary orders and conditions for granting preliminary orders

(1) Unless otherwise agreed by the parties, a party may, without notice to any other party, make a request for an interim measure together with an application for a preliminary order directing a party not to frustrate the purpose of the interim measure requested.

(2) The arbitral tribunal may grant a preliminary order provided it considers that prior disclosure of the request for the interim measure to the party against whom it is directed risks frustrating the purpose of the measure.

(3) The conditions defined under article 17 A apply to any preliminary order, provided that the harm to be assessed under article 17 A, paragraph 1 (a), is the harm likely to result from the order being granted or not.

Article 17 C

Specific regime for preliminary orders

(1) Immediately after the arbitral tribunal has made a determination in respect of an application for a preliminary order, the arbitral tribunal shall give notice to all parties of the request for the interim measure, the application for the preliminary order, the preliminary order, if any, and all other communications, including by indicating the content of any oral communication, between any party and the arbitral tribunal in relation thereto.

(2) At the same time, the arbitral tribunal shall give an opportunity to any party against whom a preliminary order is directed to present its case at the earliest practicable time.

(3) The arbitral tribunal shall decide promptly on any objection to the preliminary order.

(4) A preliminary order shall expire after twenty days from the date on which it was issued by the arbitral tribunal. However, the arbitral tribunal may issue an interim measure adopting or modifying the preliminary order, after the party against whom the preliminary order is directed has been given notice and an opportunity to present its case.

(5) A preliminary order shall be binding on the parties but shall not be subject to enforcement by a court. Such a preliminary order does not constitute an award.

Article 17F requires continuing disclosure by the parties of any changes in relevant circumstances, and Article 17D provides that the tribunal may, under appropriate circumstances, modify, suspend, or terminate an interim measure or preliminary order. Article 17G provides for an award of costs expended or damages suffered by a party as a result of the other party's improvident request for interim or preliminary relief, and Article 17E allows the tribunal to require a party seeking an interim measure or preliminary order to provide security (including a default presumption of the requirement in the case of a preliminary order).

Article 17H provides for recognition and enforcement of interim measures (recall that preliminary orders are not enforceable in court). The limited grounds for non-enforcement listed in Article 17I are virtually identical to those found in New York Convention Article V, along with a few additional grounds unique to interim measures.

Article 17 H

Recognition and enforcement

(1) An interim measure issued by an arbitral tribunal shall be recognized as binding and, unless otherwise provided by the arbitral tribunal, enforced upon application to the competent court, irrespective of the country in which it was issued, subject to the provisions of article 17 I.

(2) The party who is seeking or has obtained recognition or enforcement of an interim measure shall promptly inform the court of any termination, suspension or modification of that interim measure.

(3) The court of the State where recognition or enforcement is sought may, if it considers it proper, order the requesting party to provide appropriate security if the arbitral tribunal has not already made a determination with respect to security or where such a decision is necessary to protect the rights of third parties.

Article 17 I

Grounds for refusing recognition or enforcement[*]

(1) Recognition or enforcement of an interim measure may be refused only:

(a) At the request of the party against whom it is invoked if the court is satisfied that:

(i) Such refusal is warranted on the grounds set forth in article 36, paragraph 1 (a)(i), (ii), (iii) or (iv); or

(ii) The arbitral tribunal's decision with respect to the provision of security in connection with the interim measure issued by the arbitral tribunal has not been complied with; or

(iii) The interim measure has been terminated or suspended by the arbitral tribunal or, where so empowered, by the court of the State in which the arbitration takes place or under the law of which that interim measure was granted; or

(b) If the court finds that:

(i) The interim measure is incompatible with the powers conferred upon the court unless the court decides to reformulate the interim measure to the extent necessary to adapt it to its own powers and procedures for the purposes of enforcing that interim measure and without modifying its substance; or

(ii) Any of the grounds set forth in article 36, paragraph 1 (b)(i) or (ii), apply to the recognition and enforcement of the interim measure.

(2) Any determination made by the court on any ground in paragraph 1 of this article shall be effective only for the purposes of the application to recognize and enforce the interim measure. The court where recognition or enforcement is sought shall not, in making that determination, undertake a review of the substance of the interim measure.

---

[*] The conditions set forth in article 17I are intended to limit the number of circumstances in which the court may refuse to enforce an interim measure. It would not be contrary to the level of harmonization sought to be achieved by these model provisions if a State were to adopt fewer circumstances in which enforcement may be refused.

Lastly, Article 17J confirms that a national court, whether in the place of arbitration or otherwise, shall have whatever powers regarding arbitration proceedings as it would have in judicial proceedings. Thus, the provisions of Article 17 are directed at requests for interim relief directed to the arbitral tribunal. Article 17J does, however, suggest that a court shall exercise its own powers in a manner mindful of the specific features of international commercial arbitration.

The revisions reflected in Article 17 are of course simply revisions to the "Model Law." Absent and until adoption by national legislatures, they do not carry the force of national law. However, they do represent modern perspectives on interim measures within the international arbitration community and, as such, may serve as an excellent source of persuasive authority in addressing issues involving interim measures that are not expressly addressed by applicable rules or law. Institutional rules adopted by the parties may also provide some guidance with respect to the availability of interim relief.[38]

Notes and Questions

Note 1: Consider the revised Model Law requirements for issuance of an interim measure by the tribunal. Are these necessarily the same as the requirements for specific performance under the CISG? Under what circumstances might they be different?

Note 2: Under the revised Model Law, what are the differences between interim measures and preliminary orders? When might an initial request for an interim measure be preferable? When might an initial request for a preliminary order be preferable?

PROBLEMS

Problem 9-1: A buyer of goods has already commenced arbitration seeking performance by the seller under CISG Article 46. However, the buyer is worried that seller might sell the goods—which are unique and irreplaceable—to someone else before the tribunal can issue a final award. The buyer wants some sort of directive from the tribunal precluding the seller from disposing of the goods until the tribunal can determine whether buyer is ultimately entitled to relief under Article 46. Which provisions of revised Article 17 should the buyer invoke, and how should it frame its arguments under those provisions.

---

[38] *See e.g.* SIAC Rules Article 24(f)–24(n) (providing the tribunal with the power to provide various forms of interim relief).

Problem 9-2: A seller of goods has commenced arbitration against a purported buyer for breach of an alleged contract. Seller hopes to obtain relevant evidence regarding e-mail exchanges from buyer's electronic records. However, the seller is worried that the buyer may dispose of any such records if it becomes aware of seller's interest. The seller wants some sort of directive from the tribunal precluding the buyer from disposing of the records until the tribunal can determine whether seller is entitled to production of these records (production of evidence is discussed further below). Which provisions of revised Article 17 should the seller invoke, and how should it frame its arguments under those provisions.

E.   DISCOVERY AND PRODUCTION OF EVIDENCE

Once the parties' written pleadings have been exchanged, the nature of the issues has been delineated, and any additional preliminary issues have been addressed, the parties will likely begin preparing for the actual arbitration. In virtually all modern arbitration, each party is required to disclose in advance the general nature and content of the evidence upon which each party intends to rely in supporting its claims and defenses.[39] In this respect, global discovery principles are quite consistent. However, the extent of discovery beyond that upon which a party itself intends to rely (i.e., potentially negative evidence in a party's control), as well as the right to prepare friendly witnesses or conduct recorded depositions of adverse witnesses prior to any hearing, vary considerably in different legal systems.

In the United States, extensive discovery is allowed in court proceedings, including very liberal rights to require the production of documents and other evidence from the other party, without any specific showing of actual relevance prior to such production.[40] A party, through its counsel, is also allowed to conduction depositions in which a third party or opposing party witness is examined under oath, and the examination recorded, prior to and solely in preparation for a hearing or trial.[41] Lastly, a party's counsel will typically spend considerable time "preparing" a witness before any hearing or trial, thoroughly reviewing and often rehearsing the subject matter of the witness's expected testimony in advance. In American litigation practice, such techniques are not

---

[39] Model Law Article 18 provides that each party shall have a full and fair opportunity to present its case, and a minimal notice of the essential nature of the opposing party's evidence would seem to be a basic prerequisite for such an opportunity.

[40] By detractors, such broad discovery requests are often referred to as "fishing expeditions" in that one seemingly tosses one's hook and line into a large body of water in hopes of netting a fish that might, or might not, be found there.

[41] The process of depositions for purposes of preserving testimony of a witness unable to appear at a trial or hearing presents an entirely different set of issues.

only allowed, but an attorney might well fail his or her ethical obligations to a client by failing to take full advantage of these opportunities.

In stark contrast, many civil law systems provide much stricter limits on discovery. Depositions are rare, except to the extent absolutely necessary to preserve and provide testimony of an otherwise unavailable witness, and witness preparation is often considered unethical. The search for standards in international commercial arbitration is, therefore, to some degree an attempt to find common and neutral ground among differing national legal systems.

Subject only to mandatory law and any procedure agreed on by the parties, arbitrators have considerable discretion with respect to deciding procedural issues arising in the context of arbitration. This discretion is reflected in Model Law Article 19.

Article 19

Determination of rules of procedure

(1) Subject to the provisions of this Law, the parties are free to agree on the procedure to be followed by the arbitral tribunal in conducting the proceedings.

(2) Failing such agreement, the arbitral tribunal may, subject to the provisions of this Law, conduct the arbitration in such manner as it considers appropriate. The power conferred upon the arbitral tribunal includes the power to determine the admissibility, relevance, materiality and weight of any evidence.

Many rules simply echo this same sort of discretion in the absence of more specific provisions adopted by the parties.[42] The rules will often provide the tribunal with the authority to order one party to provide evidence requested by another party seeking discovery.[43] However, enforcement of such orders may raise additional issues. Unless the *lex arbitri* provides for enforcement of such orders, they may not be enforceable in a court of law. However, orders involving discovery or production of evidence may be effectively enforced by the tribunal itself. If a party refuses to comply, the tribunal might simply exercise its

---

[42] *See e.g.* UNCITRAL Rules Articles 15 & 24.
[43] *See e.g.* AAA/ICDR Rules Article 19.

discretion to draw an inference that the evidence in question would have been adverse to the obstructing party's case, and decide any issues accordingly.[44]

Arbitral rules typically do not provide much specificity as to how a tribunal should decide what is or is not discoverable.[45] In view of divergent national practices, as well as significant discretion provided by arbitral law and practice, the need for some sort of international standards is evident. Fortunately, the IBA Rules on the Taking of Evidence in International Commercial Arbitration ("IBA Rules")[46] provide one such source of standards.

Summary of IBA Rules Regarding Discovery Issues

1) A party shall timely submit to the tribunal and other parties a list of witnesses and copies of all documents (except those provided by the other party) upon which it expects to rely in supporting its claims and defenses.[47]

2) For any listed witness upon whose testimony a party expects to rely, the tribunal may require each party to supply a witness statement, including a complete and detailed description of the witness's proposed testimony, fully sufficient to serve as the evidence provided in support of this witness in support of the parties' case. The witness statement shall be affirmed, signed, and dated.[48] When such witness statements are provided, discovery depositions are less necessary and rarely allowed.[49]

3) A party may interview witnesses or potential witnesses.[50]

---

[44] *See e.g.* UNCITRAL Rules Article 28(3) (providing that, in the event of a party's failure without good cause to produce required evidence, the "arbitral tribunal may make the award on the evidence before it"—seemingly inviting such an adverse inference). The JAMS International Arbitration Rules are somewhat more explicit in providing that, under such circumstances "the tribunal may draw the inferences that it considers appropriate." Article 27.3

[45] *See e.g.* UNCITRAL Rules Article 24.3; *but see* LCIA Rules Article 22.1(e) (providing the tribunal with the power to order "relevant" discovery).

[46] The IBA Rules may be found at: http://www.ibanet.org/images/downloads/IBA%20rules%20on %20the%20taking%20of%20Evidence.pdf.

[47] *See* IBA Rules Articles 3.1 & 4.1. See Articles 5 and 6 for details on disclosure of expected expert testimony.

[48] *See* IBA Rules Article 4.4 & 4.5. See Articles 5 and 6 for details on required reports by expert witnesses.

[49] The witness will, however, typically be required to appear in person for cross-examination, as described below.

[50] *See* IBA Rules Article 4.3. Actual witness "prep" is somewhat less relevant in the context of witness statements, though the mechanisms for generating the statements themselves may be

> 4) A party may ask the assistance of the tribunal in requiring another party to use its best efforts to cause the attendance of a witness within its control or in otherwise seeking the attendance of the third party. The party must describe with particularity the information it believes the witness possesses and must establish that this information is both **relevant** and **material** to the outcome of the case.[51]
>
> 5) A party may ask the tribunal to require another party to produce documents under its control. The party must describe with particularity the nature of the document and must establish that this document is both **relevant** and **material** to the outcome of the case.[52]

These rules are intended to attempt to strike a balance between the virtues of speedy and efficient dispute resolution and the requirement that each party have a full and fair opportunity to present its case. Again, the IBA Rules are simply representative of international norms (unless expressly adopted by the parties), but nonetheless serve to guide the discretion of the arbitrators in addressing various procedural issues.

Most modern arbitration laws also provide for court assistance, as needed, in the taking of evidence.

Article 27

Court assistance in taking evidence

The arbitral tribunal or a party with the approval of the arbitral tribunal may request from a competent court of this State assistance in taking evidence. The court may execute the request within its competence and according to its rules on taking evidence.

This is particularly useful in seeking important fact testimony, and perhaps even documents, from third-parties not directly involved in the dispute. Such parties

---

subject to dramatically different approaches. Presumably, the nature of the process of preparing such statements will be subject to cross-examination (unless privileged) thereby potentially affecting the weight to be afforded the written testimony.

[51] *See* IBA Rules Articles 4.10 and 4.11.

[52] *See* IBA Rules Articles 3.3.

are often unwilling to provide such evidence absent judicial compulsion. Under some arbitration laws, the arbitrators themselves may even be given such subpoena power to compel third-parties to provide testimony or documents.[53]

As one can readily see, the availability of discovery varies to some extent between different jurisdictions and arbitration rules. In the absence of clearly articulated standards, discovery is subject to substantial discretion on the part of the arbitrators. In view of the significant differences between American-style discovery and that practiced in much of the rest of the world, this can often be an important factor in choosing a particular set of arbitration rules.

II.   DEFAULT PROCEEDINGS

Sometimes one of the parties will simply refuse to participate in the arbitration. Chapter 8 addressed the challenges in appointing the arbitrators when one of the parties refuses to participate. If a party declines to participate after the tribunal has been constituted, then the question arises as to whether the proceedings can be conducted in that party's absence and, if so, how the arbitration should proceed.

Article 25

Default of a party

Unless otherwise agreed by the parties, if, without showing sufficient cause,

(a) the claimant fails to communicate his statement of claim in accordance with article 23(1), the arbitral tribunal shall terminate the proceedings;

(b) the respondent fails to communicate his statement of defence in accordance with article 23(1), the arbitral tribunal shall continue the proceedings without treating such failure in itself as an admission of the claimant's allegations;

(c) any party fails to appear at a hearing or to produce documentary evidence, the arbitral tribunal may continue the proceedings and make the award on the evidence before it.

---

[53] *See* U.S. Federal Arbitration Act 9 U.S.C. § 7 (providing the arbitrators with subpoena power essentially equivalent to the courts).

Subsection (a) provides that, where the claimant is in default, the proceedings are simply terminated. Subsection (c) provides for continuation of the proceedings in the face of a more limited default of a party. Perhaps the most typical default occurs, however, when the party against whom the claims have been brought—the respondent—simply declines to participate at all. The following arbitration award provides an example of how this process works under subsection (b).

8 July 2003 - Ad Hoc Award - UNCITRAL Model Law[54]

E, a BVI Company, and T, and Irish Company, entered into a contract whereby E purchased 10,000 tonnes of crude oil from T. The contract was dawn up in both English and Russian. E transferred money to T in advance of the delivery of the oil, however the oil was never delivered. T repaid less than half of the money which had been advanced to it.

The arbitration clause in the contract stated "[A]ll disputes or differences, which arise out of this Contract or in connection with it, will be settled by negotiations. In case of unreaching agreement in defendant's Arbitration Court." No choice of law clause was present in the contract. The tribunal interpreted this clause as meaning that the seat of any eventual arbitration shall be in either Ireland or the BVI depending on which party happens to be the Respondent. As T was the Respondent, the seat of the arbitration was held to be in Ireland. The consequence of that decision was that the lex loci arbitri was governed by Ireland's Arbitration (International Commercial) Act, 1998, which, in effect, is the UNCITRAL Model Law. Further, the Tribunal held that the requirement for negotiations to settled disputes or differences imposes an obligation to make a bona fide attempt to reach a settlement of any dispute by negotiation, applying Cable & Wireless v IBM [2002] All ER 277, and Poire c/ Tripier Cour de cassation 14 February, 2003.

T failed to respond to requests to negotiate, or the subsequent initiation of the arbitration proceedings. An application was made to the Irish High Court to have an arbitrator appointed on behalf of T.

---

[54] Available on the Kluwer International Arbitration web site at http://www.kluwerarbitration.com. Institute for Transnational Arbitration (formerly InternationalADR), by Klaus Reichert, ITA Board of Reporters.

E then delivered its Statement of Claim together with supporting documentation. T failed to respond in any way, and the Tribunal requested that E verify its claim by way of affidavit. The Tribunal decided, in accordance with Article 25 of the Model Law, that the dispute had to be judged on its merits based on all the available materials. In the exercise of its discretion under Articles 19 and 24 of the Model Law, and having taken into account all the circumstances of the case, the Tribunal elected to make its decision from the written materials submitted without an oral hearing.

The contract failed to specify a law governing the substance. The Tribunal decided to apply the Rome Convention on Applicable Law, as Ireland is a signatory to that Convention, and Article 28 of the Model Law allowed it to apply the law determined by the conflict of laws rules which it considered appropriate. The Tribunal found that it was impossible to identify with certainty as to what law the parties might have chosen, there being numerous countries associated with the parties and the contract. The Tribunal decided that Article 4 of the Rome Convention was the appropriate method by which to ascertain the applicable law. The Tribunal then decided that the law of the country with which the contract was most closely connected (Article 4(1)) (itself being determined by the country where the party who is to effect the performance which is characteristic of the contract has its central administration). The Tribunal decided where there was contract for the sale of oil, the characteristic performance was the obligation in respect of which the money is payable, namely the delivery of the oil. This was held to be the seller, and hence the applicable law was held to be Irish Law.

The Tribunal then determined that the contract was validly concluded, that an initial payment was made by E, T did not deliver the oil, and that E was now entitled to its money back. In respect of interest, the Tribunal found that oil should have been received by E on 31 December, 1999, and therefore interest ran from 1 January, 2000. Compound interest was awarded as this was a commercial matter. Awarding simple interest would have been commercially unfair to E, and have provided an unwarranted advantage to T. The currency concerned was US Dollars, and the interest rate was an average over the 42 months from 1 January, 2000, to the date of the award, of the mean of the US Prime Rate and LIBOR. This was held to be 3.75% compounded at three-monthly rests. Costs were awarded, but not the costs incurred by E in making the application to the Irish High Court to have an arbitrator appointed on T's behalf.

* * * * *

Notes and Questions

Note 1: Did this tribunal find a threshold agreement to negotiate enforceable? What was the substance of the parties' arbitration agreement? Did the parties select an institution? Did they select any rules? Where did the tribunal find guidance in conducting the arbitration proceedings?

Note 2: Did the completion of the arbitration require court assistance? How, if at all, might that have been avoided? How were the costs of court assistance awarded? Why might it have reached this decision?

Note 3: Did Respondent's failure to participate preclude the tribunal from issuing a final award? Explain how the tribunal addressed this failure and its authority for doing so.

Note 4: As a result of the tribunal's analysis of governing law under Model Law Article 28, what substantive law governed the parties' agreement? Why?

Many institutional rules provide for similar mechanisms for completing the arbitration in the event one of the parties declines to participate.[55] Others provide for the same result by simply allowing the proceedings to go forward in the defaulting party's absence, but without including a specific section addressing default.[56] In summary, a party's refusal to participate will rarely, if ever, preclude the tribunal from deciding the parties' dispute and rendering an enforceable award, as long as the party is given proper notice and a meaningful opportunity to present its case.[57]

III.   HEARING THE PARTIES' CASE ON THE MERITS

If the parties agree, a tribunal could decide a dispute solely by reference to documentary evidence and written submissions. However, most arbitration proceedings will involve at least one oral hearing on the merits.

---

[55] *See e.g.* Swiss Rules Article 28; AAA/ICDR Rules Article 23.

[56] *See e.g.* ICC Rules Article 18(3) (providing for completion of the terms of reference without a defaulting party's signature) and Article 20(3) and 21(2) (providing for hearings either in the parties' presence, *or in their absence*, provided they have been summoned).

[57] *See* Model Law Article 34(2)(a)(ii); New York Convention Article V(1)(b).

Article 24

Hearings and written proceedings

(1) Subject to any contrary agreement by the parties, the arbitral tribunal shall decide whether to hold oral hearings for the presentation of evidence or for oral argument, or whether the proceedings shall be conducted on the basis of documents and other materials. However, unless the parties have agreed that no hearings shall be held, the arbitral tribunal shall hold such hearings at an appropriate stage of the proceedings, if so requested by a party.

(2) The parties shall be given sufficient advance notice of any hearing and of any meeting of the arbitral tribunal for the purposes of inspection of goods, other property or documents.

(3) All statements, documents or other information supplied to the arbitral tribunal by one party shall be communicated to the other party. Also any expert report or evidentiary document on which the arbitral tribunal may rely in making its decision shall be communicated to the parties.

As with pre-hearing discovery, the tribunal is generally afforded a broad degree of discretion in its control of any hearing on the merits.[58] This discretion is of course subject to any agreements of the parties, but most rules provide little direction beyond basic mandatory legal requirements that each of the parties be treated equally and be given a full opportunity to present its case.[59]

Article 18

Equal treatment of parties

The parties shall be treated with equality and each party shall be given a full opportunity of presenting his case.

---

[58] *See e.g.* ICC Rules Article 21.3. Alternatively, the tribunal may decide the case solely on the parties' pleadings and submitted documents, unless any party expressly requests a hearing. ICC Rules Article 20(6).

[59] *See e.g.* ICC Rules Articles 20 & 21.

Not surprisingly, national courts in different countries with different legal systems take significantly different approaches in conducting a hearing on the merits. In common law systems, the parties largely control proceedings based on an adversary system in which each party presents its case and the judge (and perhaps jury) is largely a passive observer, except to the extent necessary to serve as a referee if the parties disagree over procedural or evidentiary issues. In contrast, a civil law judge will often take a much more active role in both directing the sequence of the proceedings, questioning witnesses, and designating any necessary expert witnesses needed to decide the issues.

Again, the arbitrators must attempt to strike a balance between prompt and efficient completion of the arbitral process and the need to give each party the chance to present its case. And again, the IBA Rules on the Taking of Evidence in International Commercial Arbitration provide an excellent point of reference in the way of international standards.

In addition to relevant documentary evidence, hearings may include testimony of both (A) fact witnesses and (B) experts. Hearings (C) are typically closed to protect confidentiality. The parties may of course continue to consider (D) settlement during the pendency of the arbitration proceedings. Absent such settlement, the arbitration will proceed to completion (E) at which time they are deemed closed.

A.   TESTIMONY OF FACT WITNESSES

Direct testimony of witnesses is often provided by way of a witness statement rather than live testimony.[60] This effectively eliminates (or at least minimizes) any need for a pre-hearing deposition. The witness is, however, typically subject to live cross-examination, unless otherwise agreed by the parties.[61] The tribunal may also question the witness as it deems necessary.[62] This combination of pre-written direct testimony and live cross-examination (including any examination by the tribunal) is thought by many to present the best balance of efficiency and fairness.

---

[60] Of course the parties can agree upon direct live testimony, but this can be quite expensive when one considers the cost of the time of counsel, the arbitrators, and the parties themselves.

[61] If a witness fails to show up at the hearing, the tribunal may disallow the use of the witness statement, unless the parties agreed otherwise in advance. *See* IBA Rules Articles 4.8 & 4.9.

[62] *See e.g.* LCIA Rules Article 22.1(c).

B.   EXPERTS

The Model Law and some rules provide, primarily, for appointment of experts by the tribunal, only allowing parties to then appoint their own experts as needed to address any points raised by the expert appointed by the tribunal.[63]

Article 26

Expert appointed by arbitral tribunal

(1) Unless otherwise agreed by the parties, the arbitral tribunal

(a) may appoint one or more experts to report to it on specific issues to be determined by the arbitral tribunal;

(b) may require a party to give the expert any relevant information or to produce, or to provide access to, any relevant documents, goods or other property for his inspection.

(2) Unless otherwise agreed by the parties, if a party so requests or if the arbitral tribunal considers it necessary, the expert shall, after delivery of his written or oral report, participate in a hearing where the parties have the opportunity to put questions to him and to present expert witnesses in order to testify on the points at issue.

The IBA Rules provide for the appointment or party experts, as well as experts designated by the tribunal.[64] To a large extent, the number of experts employed will be driven by the cost issues. Experts can be quite expensive,[65] so parties may decide not to appoint their own experts if the dispute involves a relatively modest amount of money. On the other hand, in a dispute involving very large sums, the tribunal and each of the parties may each employ their own experts.

---

[63] Model Law Article 26; *see e.g.* Swiss Rules Article 27.

[64] *See* IBA Rules Articles 4.8 & 4.9.

[65] The parties of course pay for their own, respective experts, as well as a share of any expert appointed by the tribunal, and the losing party may in fact pay for all of the experts, depending on any allocation of costs.

C. CONFIDENTIALITY OF THE PROCEEDINGS

All proceedings are typically conducted *in camera*,[66] thus preserving the confidential nature of the arbitration. In addition, arbitrators are expected to maintain the confidentiality and information learned over the course of the proceedings based on both standard practice and various rules.[67] Institutions are also expected to maintain the confidentiality of the proceedings subject to limited rights to publish appropriately redacted awards.[68] In particular, numerous ICC awards are published. While all identifying information is eliminated, the awards are available for guidance in future international business transactions and arbitration.

Most arbitration regimes provide little in the way of express confidentiality restrictions on the parties. However, there are at least two notable exceptions. The LCIA and SIAC Rules provide substantial restriction on the parties' right to divulge information related in the arbitration, subject to a relatively narrow set of exceptions.[69] Of course, much of the benefit of any of these confidentiality provisions may be lost in subsequent public court proceedings to set aside or enforce an otherwise confidential award.

D. SETTLEMENT

In some instances, the parties may decide before, during, or even after a hearing[70] to settle a matter they have subjected to arbitration. This sort of settlement between the parties themselves is common in any dispute resolution environment, and arbitration is no exception. However, settlement is often aided by the facilitation of a third party mediator or conciliator. The beginning of Chapter 8 raised the possibility of mediation, as a preliminary effort at dispute resolution, to be followed by arbitration only if mediation was unsuccessful (i.e., "med-arb"). Here, the sequence is reversed, as the parties may decide to engage in mediation after the arbitration has already been commenced (i.e., "arb-med").

In the case of arb-med, a question may arise as to whether it is appropriate for the arbitrators, themselves, to actively attempt to facilitate settlement during the arbitration process. Historically, this dual role of arbitrator-mediator was generally thought inappropriate in that the sort of open style "give-and-take" in consensual dispute resolution may sometimes be inconsistent with the nature of zealous advocacy required in a "zero-sum" dispute resolution regime such as

---

[66] *See e.g.* UNCITRAL Rules Article 25(4); AAA/ICDR Rules Articles 20(4); SIAC Rules Articles 21.4.

[67] *See e.g.* AAA/ICDR Rules Article 34 (binds arbitrators and administrators)

[68] *See e.g.* ICC Rules Appendix II, Article 1.

[69] LCIA Rules Article 30; SIAC Rules Article 34.

[70] There is often some time between the closure of hearings and the issuance of the award.

binding arbitration. The arbitrator's role as decision maker in the latter process might serve to "chill" open dialogue in the former. However, over time, the process has begun to gain a more significant level of acceptance under certain circumstances.[71]

While active involvement by the arbitrators, as mediators, remains somewhat controversial, the general concept of arb-med is much less so. To the extent the parties mutually wish to recess proceedings in pursuit of settlement efforts, a tribunal is likely to attempt to accommodate the parties' request.

Article 30

Settlement

(1) If, during arbitral proceedings, the parties settle the dispute, the arbitral tribunal shall terminate the proceedings and, if requested by the parties and not objected to by the arbitral tribunal, record the settlement in the form of an arbitral award on agreed terms.

(2) An award on agreed terms shall be made in accordance with the provisions of article 31 and shall state that it is an award. Such an award has the same status and effect as any other award on the merits of the case.

If the parties are successful in reaching a consensual settlement, the Model Law and many rules allow the parties to memorialize the settlement in the form of an award issued by the arbitrators.[72] This may be useful in the event one of the parties later has second thoughts about compliance. Once turned into an award, the settlement is easily enforced, as in the case of any arbitral award.[73]

E.   CLOSURE OF THE HEARINGS ON THE MERITS

When the tribunal is satisfied that each of the parties has had a reasonable opportunity to present its case, the tribunal shall declare the proceedings closed.

---

[71] *See generally The Role of Arbitrators as Settlement Facilitators*, in *New Horizons in International Commercial Arbitration,* ICCA Congress Series No. 12 (Albert J. van den Berg ed., Kluwer 2004); *see also* Harold I. Abramson, *Protocols for International Arbitrators Who Dare to Settle Cases*, 10 Am. Rev. Intl. Arb. 1 (1999).

[72] *See* Model Law Article 30(1); *see also e.g.* AAA/ICDR Rules Article 29(1) (tribunal to issue award without reasons at request of parties).

[73] *See* Model Law Article 30(2).

Thereafter, no further evidence shall be received absent extraordinary circumstances justifying the reopening of the proceedings on the merits.[74] Upon closure of the hearings on the merits, the tribunal shall begin the final stage of the arbitration—deliberation leading to a final award.

IV.   THE FINAL AWARD

The final award is the ultimate work product promised by the arbitrators in exchange for the parties' payment for the arbitrators' service. Without an enforceable award, the entire process is for naught. As such, one of the most fundamental and important duties of the arbitrators is to render an enforceable award. Further details regarding enforceability will be addressed in Chapter 10.

The (A) final award must meet certain requirements and must designate the place of its issue, and (B) must fix and make any allocation of costs. The award may be subject to timely (C) correction and interpretation, after which the arbitration proceedings are deemed (D) terminated.

A.   REQUIREMENTS OF THE AWARD AND DESIGNATION OF PLACE

An arbitration award is subject to certain requirements with respect to form and content.

Article 31

Form and contents of award

(1) The award shall be made in writing and shall be signed by the arbitrator or arbitrators. In arbitral proceedings with more than one arbitrator, the signatures of the majority of all members of the arbitral tribunal shall suffice, provided that the reason for any omitted signature is stated.

(2) The award shall state the reasons upon which it is based, unless the parties have agreed that no reasons are to be given or the award is an award on agreed terms under article 30.

(3) The award shall state its date and the place of arbitration as determined in accordance with article 20(1). The award shall be deemed to have been made at that place.

---

[74] *See e.g.* UNCITRAL Rules Article 29; ICC Rules Article 22(1).

> **(4)** After the award is made, a copy signed by the arbitrators in accordance with paragraph (1) of this article shall be delivered to each party.

Much like the parties' arbitration agreement, the arbitrators' award must be in writing and must be signed by the arbitrator or arbitrators.[75] The award must also state the reasons upon which it is based, unless the parties have otherwise agreed.[76] The primary risk in requiring the tribunal to state reasons would seem to be that this could invite excessive scrutiny by a court during any action to set aside or enforce the award. However, courts in most legal systems today are sufficiently respectful of the arbitrators' decision on the merits[77] that this concern would seem to be minimal. Moreover, there are some significant benefits in stating the reasons for the award.

First, the parties are likely to be somewhat more satisfied with the award—even a losing party—to the extent the arbitrators explain how they arrived at their decision. Second, the award is likely to have a greater preclusive effect if reasons are stated. While all enforceable awards will have a claim preclusive or *res judicata* effect, an award with specific reasons or findings may also have an issue preclusive or collateral estoppel effect, thus avoiding future disputes over any issues necessarily decided by the tribunal, as reflected in the award.

An award must also state its date and the place of arbitration.[78] The date of the award will trigger the running of various time limits relating to actions to set aside or enforce the award. The place of arbitration will determine certain applicable laws in any action to set aside or enforce the award, and will also determine which courts have jurisdiction in any action to set aside the award.

Where the parties' dispute is heard by a sole arbitrator, that arbitrator will decide the case and draft the award. In the case of a three-member tribunal, the Model Law and almost all rules allow a final award to be made based on a majority decision of the arbitrators.[79]

---

[75] *See* Model Law Article 31(1).

[76] *See* Model Law Article 31(2); Swiss Rules Article 32(3).

[77] One of the more significant exceptions is of course the "manifest disregard" standard applicable under United States law.

[78] Model Law Article 31(3).

[79] *See*, Model Law Article 29; *see also e.g.* AAA/ICDR Rules Article 26(1).

> **Article 29**
>
> **Decision making by panel of arbitrators**
>
> In arbitral proceedings with more than one arbitrator, any decision of the arbitral tribunal shall be made, unless otherwise agreed by the parties, by a majority of all its members. However, questions of procedure may be decided by a presiding arbitrator, if so authorized by the parties or all members of the arbitral tribunal.

Dissenting opinions are not typical, but are sometimes included. If a three-member panel cannot even reach a majority decision, some rules provide for a decision by the presiding arbitrator, acting as a sole arbitrator.[80]

B.   FIXING AND ALLOCATING COSTS

In addition to its final award on the merits, the arbitral tribunal is responsible for fixing or determining the costs of the arbitration. These costs include the arbitrators' fees and expenses, the costs and expenses of any experts appointed by the tribunal, any institutional fees and expenses, and any other expenses reasonably incurred in the conduct of the arbitration.[81] Such costs also typically include the reasonable costs of legal representation incurred by the prevailing party.[82] In principle, the losing party typically must bear the entire costs of the arbitration.[83] However, various rules provide the tribunal with varying degrees of discretion in awarding such costs.[84] If the parties want to insure that costs, including attorney fees, will be divided in any particular way, this may be best addressed in the arbitration agreement itself.

The parties will often be required to deposit in advance an amount sufficient to cover the expected costs of the arbitration.[85] Thus, the arbitrators' determination

---

[80] *See e.g.* SIAC Rules Article 27.4; ICC Rules Article 25(1).

[81] *See e.g.* UNCITRAL Rules Article 38; AAA/ICDR Rules Article 31.

[82] *See e.g.* UNCITRAL Rules Article 38(e); AAA/ICDR Rules Article 31(d). This essentially rejects the American rule (each party bears its own cost of legal representation) as a default rule in international commercial arbitration. Unless otherwise agreed, the losing party will generally be liable for the other party's attorney fees.

[83] *See* UNCITRAL Rules Article 40.

[84] *Compare* AAA/ICDR Rules Article 31 (simply providing for "reasonable" apportionment of all costs, including the prevailing party's cost of legal representation); *with* Swiss Rules Article 40 (providing that costs, other than attorney fees, are to be paid by the losing party, but granting the tribunal complete discretion as to apportionment of attorney fees).

[85] *See* UNCITRAL Rules Article 41; AAA/ICDR Rules Article 33.

simply serves as a final accounting and division of liability for those costs, as between the parties themselves. The parties, however, will typically be liable jointly and severally for any and all amounts payable to the tribunal and institution.[86] As a result the prevailing party could end up paying the entire cost of the arbitration, notwithstanding a decision by the tribunal to charge the costs to the losing party. In recognition of this possibility, most rules allow a party, at the outset of the arbitration, to seek security for costs from a party that appears unlikely to be able to pay any final liability for costs.[87]

C.   CORRECTION AND INTERPRETATION OF AWARD

A final award is generally subject to a request to the tribunal for correction or clarification of the award. However, such requests typically must be made within a certain time period after receipt of the award, and corrections are typically limited to typographical, clerical, or computational errors.[88]

Article 33

Correction and interpretation of award; additional award

(1) Within thirty days of receipt of the award, unless another period of time has been agreed upon by the parties:

(a) a party, with notice to the other party, may request the arbitral tribunal to correct in the award any errors in computation, any clerical or typographical errors or any errors of similar nature;

(b) if so agreed by the parties, a party, with notice to the other party, may request the arbitral tribunal to give an interpretation of a specific point or part of the award.

If the arbitral tribunal considers the request to be justified, it shall make the correction or give the interpretation within thirty days of receipt of the request. The interpretation shall form part of the award.

(2) The arbitral tribunal may correct any error of the type referred to in paragraph (1)(a) of this article on its own initiative within thirty days of the date of the award.

---

[86] *See e.g.* SIAC Rules Article 26.7.
[87] *See e.g.* SIAC Rules Article 24(m).
[88] *See* Model Law Article 33.

(3) Unless otherwise agreed by the parties, a party, with notice to the other party, may request, within thirty days of receipt of the award, the arbitral tribunal to make an additional award as to claims presented in the arbitral proceedings but omitted from the award. If the arbitral tribunal considers the request to be justified, it shall make the additional award within sixty days.

(4) The arbitral tribunal may extend, if necessary, the period of time within which it shall make a correction, interpretation or an additional award under paragraph (1) or (3) of this article.

(5) The provisions of article 31 shall apply to a correction or interpretation of the award or to an additional award.

Various rules also address corrections, interpretations, or clarifications.[89] While also subject to requests for correction or clarification,[90] an ICC award is also subject to a more unique form of scrutiny, while still in draft form.[91] The ICC International Court of Arbitration is charged with scrutinizing the form of the award and making any necessary modifications as to such form. In addition, the Court may draw the tribunal's attention to matters of substance, though it is ultimately up to the tribunal to decide whether to address any such substantive concerns. This provision for a sort of non-binding "peer review" is unique to ICC arbitration.

D.   TERMINATION OF ARBITRAL PROCEEDINGS

The arbitral proceedings are deemed fully terminated when the arbitral tribunal issues its final award.[92]

---

[89] *See e.g.* UNCITRAL Rules Articles 35, 36 & 37.
[90] ICC Rules Article 29.
[91] ICC Rules Article 27.
[92] *See* Model Law Article 32(1).

Article 32

Termination of proceedings

(1) The arbitral proceedings are terminated by the final award or by an order of the arbitral tribunal in accordance with paragraph (2) of this article.

(2) The arbitral tribunal shall issue an order for the termination of the arbitral proceedings when:

(a) the claimant withdraws his claim, unless the respondent objects thereto and the arbitral tribunal recognizes a legitimate interest on his part in obtaining a final settlement of the dispute;

(b) the parties agree on the termination of the proceedings;

(c) the arbitral tribunal finds that the continuation of the proceedings has for any other reason become unnecessary or impossible.

(3) The mandate of the arbitral tribunal terminates with the termination of the arbitral proceedings, subject to the provisions of articles 33 and 34(4).

Alternatively, the tribunal may prematurely terminate the proceedings if the parties agree to such discontinuance or the tribunal otherwise finds their continuation unnecessary or impossible.[93]

PROBLEM

Problem 9-3: Consider again Problems 7-3, 7-4, and 7-5 at the end of Chapter 7. Do any of the materials covered in the current chapter affect the analysis?

---

[93] *See* Model Law Article 32(2).

10 | ARBITRATION AS A FINAL AWARD: CHALLENGES AND ENFORCEMENT

. . .
Money, it's a gas.
Grab that cash with both hands and make a stash.
New car, caviar, four star daydream,
Think I'll buy me a football team.

. . .
Huhuh! I was in the right!
Yes, absolutely in the right!
I certainly was in the right!

- Pink Floyd[1]

The tribunal has now issued a final award, thus terminating the arbitration proceedings. All of the contracts regarding the arbitration have now been largely performed, though certain obligations, such as confidentiality, will obviously continue. The award will often entitle one of the parties to a sum of money, providing damages pursuant to a claim or counterclaim. Or the award may deny all of the parties' claims, but nonetheless award one of the parties a right to recover various costs associated with the arbitration. In some instances, an award may deny any recovery at all if the tribunal denies all claims and does not make any award related to costs—thus leaving each party as it found itself at the conclusion of the arbitration. However, even the latter award may be the subject of recognition for its *res judicata* effect in a subsequent legal proceeding between the parties.[2] The law regarding recognition and enforcement of arbitral awards applies to both enforcement of rights to money and recognition of the award, itself, in other proceedings.

> **Example 10-1**
>
> A contract dispute has arisen over a contract for the sale of steel between NNM and J&G. J&G originally commenced arbitration. However, the arbitral panel ultimately determined that the steel delivered by NNM was fully conformed under

---

[1] From the song, *Money*, on the album *Dark Side of the Moon*, by Pink Floyd (1973).
[2] The term *res judicata* is used here in its broad sense, including, in at least some legal systems, both claim and issue preclusive effects. The nuances of issue preclusive effects of arbitral awards are, however, beyond the scope of this casebook.

> Article 35, and J&G had therefore breached the parties' agreement by failing to pay for the steel as required under Article 53. The panel has, therefore, issued a final award requiring J&G to pay NNM for the steel, and further requiring J&G to pay the entire cost of the arbitral proceedings.

In many instances, a party obligated by the final award to pay money will simply do so, as its final obligation under the arbitration agreement. However, a party may also decline to pay the award. This failure to pay the award may be based on a genuine belief that the award is in some way flawed, or it may simply be a matter of obstinacy or inability to pay. In either case, court action regarding the award is likely.

If the party obligated to pay money under the award has assets in the place of arbitration, then the process of converting the award into an enforceable money judgment in court is probably a relatively simple one governed by a the law of a single jurisdiction—the law of the place of arbitration, which is also law of the place of enforcement. As such, there will likely be only one forum in which any issues as to the legal viability of the award will be fully and finally determined. However, in international sales transactions, the place of arbitration (often chosen for its neutrality and/or its *lex arbitri*) will often be different from the place of enforcement (likely to be the place in which one of the parties has its business headquarters or substantial assets). Thus, a party's decision to resist the effects of an award involving an international sales transaction will typically lead to one or both of two distinct categories of court proceedings that may affect the award.

One must begin by (I) distinguishing between the basic nature of actions to set aside an award and actions to enforce an award. A party seeking to attack the award offensively will bring (II) an action to set aside the award. A party may also (III) defend against enforcement of the award in any place in which judicial enforcement is sought by the party entitled to relief under the award.

I.   INTRODUCTION TO COURT ACTIONS TO CHALLENGE OR ENFORCE THE ARBITRATORS' FINAL AWARD

First, either party may challenge the arbitrators' decision in an appropriate court in the place or arbitration.[3] While challenges are most often brought by the party required by the award to pay money, either party is entitled to challenge the award if it believes it has a valid basis to do so. An action to challenge the award

---

[3] The Model Law designates such a court in Article 6. As indicated earlier, this is the City Court of Vindobona in Danubia, our mythical place of arbitration.

in the place of arbitration is called an action to "set aside"[4] or "vacate" the award. If the challenge is successful, and the award is set aside, it will no longer have any legal force and effect in the place of arbitration.[5]

Second, a party entitled to a remedy under the final award may bring an action to enforce the award in the courts of the intended place of enforcement. Typically, the party entitled to receive money under the award will bring an enforcement action in a jurisdiction in which it believes the party obligated to pay money under the award has assets that can be seized or liquidated in payment of the award.[6] Such an action to enforce the award may be brought before, or after, or irrespective of whether there has been any action by the other party to set aside or vacate the award in the place of arbitration. If one party brings an action to enforce the award, the party against whom enforcement is sought may seek to defend against enforcement, irrespective of whether this party has sought to have the award set aside or vacated in the place of arbitration.

In summary, the legal viability of an arbitration award may be addressed in: (1) a court action to set aside or vacate the award in the place of arbitration; (2) a court action to enforce the award in the place of enforcement; or (3) both. In view of these two alternative, and potentially cumulative, forums in which the viability of the award might be addressed, one might reasonably ask whether the legal standards in each forum are the same or different. If they are different, then these differences could make the choice of forum for any challenge outcome determinative or could lead to inconsistent results in multiple forums. Is this a desirable effect?

One example of such differences is found in the American Federal Arbitration Act. FAA Chapter 2 formally adopts the New York Convention and its standards of enforceability with respect to international[7] awards. However, American courts typically apply the standards contained in Section 10[8] of FAA Chapter 1,

---

[4] *See* Model Law Article 34.

[5] It may in some circumstances, however, continue to have legal force and effect in other jurisdictions outside the place of arbitration. This is addressed more fully below.

[6] The precise nature of enforcement—i.e., creditor's remedies and debtor's rights—in various jurisdictions is beyond the scope of these materials. These issues will typically be governed by national laws attempting to balance the right of creditors to be paid any monies legally owing and the rights of debtors to be free of certain unreasonable seizures of their assets. Enforcement actions may also involve insolvency proceedings, which are again primarily subject to national laws. However, UNCITRAL has made some progress in the area of uniform law proposals governing cross-border insolvency. *See* UNCITRAL Model Law on Cross-Border Insolvency (1997).

[7] The FAA actually adopts a broad definition of "non-domestic" awards, as provided for under Article 1 of the New York Convention. *See* 9 U.S.C. § 207 (2000).

[8] There are other differences between section 10 of the FAA and Article V of the New York Convention beyond the "manifest disregard" standard (which is not found in the New York Convention or other modern arbitration law). The others may or may not have a significant

including the court created "manifest disregard" standard when addressing an action to set aside an award. Thus, the standards in the United States for setting aside an award are different from the standards for enforcement. The potential for conflict and confusion should be evident. In contrast to the FAA approach, consider the following description of the drafting of the standards for actions to set aside or enforce an award included in the UNCITRAL Model Law.

The History of the New York Convention,

Pieter Sander

. . .

III. Harmonizing Effect of the Convention

. . . I would like to draw attention to the harmonizing effect the New York Convention has had on national arbitration legislation. This development was not foreseen in 1958. It is thanks to the UNCITRAL Model Law of 1985 which virtually repeats the grounds for refusal of enforcement of the New York Convention in its model for national arbitration legislation. This was done not only for the grounds for the refusal of enforcement of an award but virtually the same grounds apply as grounds for the setting aside of an award. The Model Law has by now been adopted by [many] States of which [some] also did so for domestic arbitration. Therefore, the impact of the New York Convention on the Model Law has been considerable.

. . .

ICCA Congress Series No. 9 (Paris/1999), pp. 11 – 14.

* * * * *

The following discussion focuses primarily on the Model Law and the New York Convention. As such, the emphasis in each of the two parts that follow—actions to set aside and actions to enforce—will focus on differences in the context of the two actions instead of differences in standards of legal viability. Because the standards for legal viability are essentially identical, these standards can be fully addressed in a largely interchangeable fashion in each of the two parts that follow.

---

substantive effect, depending on how each is interpreted and applied. However, the significant differences in language certainly give rise to a potential for significant interpretive differences.

II.   DIRECT CHALLENGES BY THE DISAPPOINTED PARTY: OFFENSIVELY ATTACKING THE AWARD IN THE PLACE OF ARBITRATION

In earlier chapters addressing arbitration as dispute resolution, contract, and procedure, the *lex arbitri* has been paramount. Once again, in an action to set aside an arbitration award, the law of the place of arbitration, or *lex arbitri*, takes center stage. The only country in which an arbitration award may be rendered invalid is the place of arbitration.[9] While a party may resist enforcement in another country, any court judgment in the place of enforcement is without legal effect outside of that country. However, a decision to set aside the award may, at least, render the award invalid and unenforceable in all countries.[10] As such, the reviewing court in the place of arbitration has considerable power over the ultimate enforceability of the award.[11]

Most jurisdictions provide strict time limits for any action to set aside an award. The Model Law generally requires that such actions be brought within three months of the receipt or the award.[12] The (A) grounds for setting aside an award are quite limited. If, however, an award is set aside, (B) this will generally render the award without legal force and effect, subject to one rather significant exception.

A.   GROUNDS FOR SETTING ASIDE AN AWARD

The sole and exclusive grounds for setting aside an award under the Model Law are listed in subsection 2 of Article 34. The statute provides six distinct grounds upon which an award may be set aside.

---

[9] *See* Model Law Article 34(1).

[10] This general proposition is, however, subject to exceptions addressed in section I.B. *infra*.

[11] Under the Model Law, this is the court (or courts) designated in Article 6.

[12] *See* Model Law Article 34(3) (providing, in the alternative, that the action be brought within three months of any decision disposing of any request to correct or clarify an award). A failure to bring a timely action to set aside an award will not prevent a party from resisting enforcement in another county, but, again, a successful enforcement defense generally has a much narrower effect than a successful action to set aside the award.

Article 34

Application for setting aside as exclusive recourse against arbitral award

. . .

(2) An arbitral award may be set aside by the court specified in article 6 only if:

(a) the party making the application furnishes proof that:

(i) a party to the arbitration agreement referred to in article 7 was under some incapacity; or the said agreement is not valid under the law to which the parties have subjected it or, failing any indication thereon, under the law of this State; or

(ii) the party making the application was not given proper notice of the appointment of an arbitrator or of the arbitral proceedings or was otherwise unable to present his case; or

(iii) the award deals with a dispute not contemplated by or not falling within the terms of the submission to arbitration, or contains decisions on matters beyond the scope of the submission to arbitration, provided that, if the decisions on matters submitted to arbitration can be separated from those not so submitted, only that part of the award which contains decisions on matters not submitted to arbitration may be set aside; or

(iv) the composition of the arbitral tribunal or the arbitral procedure was not in accordance with the agreement of the parties, unless such agreement was in conflict with a provision of this Law from which the parties cannot derogate, or, failing such agreement, was not in accordance with this Law; or

(b) the court finds that:

(i) the subject-matter of the dispute is not capable of settlement by arbitration under the law of this State; or

(ii) the award is in conflict with the public policy of this State.

Subsection (2)(a)(i) addresses the validity of the arbitration agreement. These are the same issues addressed earlier in the discussions of governing law and issues involving any decision on the tribunal's jurisdiction. In those discussions, as well as the chart in Appendix C, it was suggested that validity issues must be addressed under the law of the place of arbitration, or *lex arbitri*, unless parties subject these issues to a different law. If another law were applied to issues of validity, then the award might be subject to being set aside. In effect, the tribunal's decision as to whether the parties validly concluded an arbitration agreement is subject to a full court review under this provision. Remember, however, the effect of separability under Model Law Article 16. An award finding the container agreement invalid (or perhaps even never concluded) will not, by itself, render the arbitration agreement invalid.

Example 10-2

The Peruvian buyer of wool and maker of sweaters assigned to a Paraguayan party his contract with the New Zealand seller of wool. The contract contained a provision calling for arbitration in Vindobona, Danubia. If a dispute subsequently arose between the New Zealand seller and Peruvian buyer (as assignee), the Peruvian buyer might assert that she did not validly consent to the arbitration clause as an assignee. In addressing this issue, a court hearing an action to set aside the award would likely need to look to the law of Danubia (absent any contrary party intent) in determining what effect, if any, the assignment on the contract had on the arbitration clause within it.

Subsection (2)(a)(ii) addresses basic notice and due process requirements. In essence, this provision ensures that each party was provided a full and fair opportunity to present its case, as required under Model Law Article 18. While issues could arise under this provision in a variety of contexts, one of the most common is in the case of a default proceeding, as allowed under Model Law Article 25. If an award is made in the absence of one of the parties, the reasonableness of attempts to notify the party failing to appear will often be determinative. Note that this is, essentially, the only ground related to the actual procedure on the merits of the dispute upon which an award may be vacated, other than public policy grounds. This further exemplifies the extent of discretion afforded the tribunal in determining the arbitral procedures, as long as each party is given a full and fair opportunity to present its case.[13]

---

[13] A failed attempt to challenge the appointment of an arbitrator for partiality or a lack of independence might also be raised here as affecting a party's opportunity to present its case.

Example 10-3

At respondent's request, the tribunal appointed experts to inspect and examine the quality and production capacity of certain equipment at issue. The inspection was attended by the experts, the president of the tribunal, and the claimant. However, respondent did not receive notice of or attend the inspection. In the award, the arbitrators relied on the expert report and concluded in favor of claimant. The award likely would have been subject to being set aside because respondent was unable to present its case. However, respondent had a full and fair opportunity to read the experts' report and never objected to its content or asked for a re-inspection, thereby waiving its right to challenge the report as a basis to set aside the award.[14]

Subsection (2)(a)(iii) focuses on the scope of the parties' arbitration agreement or any formal submission or agreement as to the issues to be decided. In an arbitration in which the issues are formally delineated early in the proceedings, such as the Terms of Reference in an arbitration proceeding under the ICC Rules,[15] such formal specifications of the issues to be determined will likely be controlling under this provision. In less formal proceedings, the parties' original arbitration agreement may define the scope of issues submitted to arbitration. In either case, any decision in the award beyond the mandate of the arbitrators will be set aside. If possible, the court may set aside only an offending portion of the award. If not, the whole award may be set aside.

Example 10-4

A buyer of rubber failed to open a letter of credit in favor of seller, and seller commenced arbitration proceedings ultimately leading to an award in its favor. However, the award was set aside because any award based on buyer's failure to open a letter of credit was deemed outside the scope of an arbitration clause providing for arbitration of "all disputes as to quality or condition of rubber or other dispute arising under these contract regulations shall be settled by arbitration."[16]

---

[14] *Hebei Import & Export Corp. v. Polytek Engineering Co. Ltd.,* 2 HKC 205, High Court of Hong Kong, Court of Final Appeal, Hong Kong, Feb. 9, 1999, UNCITRAL CLOUT Case 599.

[15] ICC Rules Article 18.

[16] *Tiong Huat Rubber Factory (SDN) BHN v. Wah Chang International (China) Co. Ltd. & ANOR,* Supreme Court of Hong Kong, Hong, Kong, Jan. 18, 1991, UNCITRAL CLOUT Case 675.

Which "contract regulations" did the court believe the parties intended in the arbitration clause above? Might the court have interpreted it differently? Should a tribunals and courts read arbitration clauses narrowly or broadly?

Subsection (2)(a)(iv) focuses on the constitution of the arbitral panel. This issue is governed by the parties' agreement, including any rules adopted, and, in the absence of any party agreement, by the default rules of the *lex arbitri*. If the actual constitution of the tribunal was contrary to agreement or default legal rules, then the tribunal's award may be set aside. For example, if a party is inappropriately precluded from exercising its right to choose an arbitrator, then the award might be set aside.

Example 10-5

The arbitration clause provided for three arbitrators—one appointed by each party and a third appointed by these two. The award was set aside because the arbitrators did not act in accordance with the parties' agreement when the two party-appointed arbitrators appointed a third, but then fully delegated their responsibilities and requested that the third arbitrator solely decide the dispute.[17]

While subsection (2)(a) requires the party seeking to set aside the award to "furnish proof" of the relevant grounds, subsection (2)(b) does not. While a party will likely raise any ground for setting aside the award under subsection (2)(b), the grounds under these latter provisions typically involve matters of pure law and policy, as applied to the substance of the award itself, rather than factual allegations to be proven under the applicable law.

Subsection (2)(b)(i) addresses the arbitrability question discussed earlier in Chapter 8. Like subsection (2)(a)(i) above, this was a necessary element of any jurisdictional decision. As indicated earlier, the general trend favors increasing arbitrability of almost any international commercial financial dispute. This is particularly true in major arbitral centers. However, this issue may arise later if an award is to be enforced in a country that has not embraced this trend and still considers various disputes implicating certain public interests to be inarbitrable.

Subsection (2)(b)(ii) addresses public policy issues other than arbitrability (which is itself a particularized public policy issue). Public policy must be distinguished from simply mandatory rules of law, most of which do not rise to the sort of

---

[17] *Fleming v. Space Homes, Ltd.,* Queens Bench, Alberta, Jan. 15, 1985, UNCITRAL CLOUT Case 628.

fundamental or essential nature of policies of sufficient public importance to justify setting aside an award. Again, this distinction is typically quite well developed in most arbitral centers, and the grounds for setting aside an award based on public policy are extremely narrow. Again, however, the issue may arise later if an award is to be enforced in a country that might not interpret "public policy" quite so narrowly.

Notes and Questions

Note 1: The reader will note that in subsection (2)(b), the focus is on the law of the place of arbitration. When the context shifts from an action to set aside to an action for enforcement, these same two standards will reappear, but each will instead look to the law of the place of enforcement in determining whether the standard is satisfied.

Note 2: One should also note that **none** of the six above described grounds for setting aside an arbitration award provides any basis for a review of the tribunal's decision on the merits. In fact, such a review on the merits would be inconsistent with the parties' express agreement for final and binding arbitration.[18] Nonetheless, a party asking that an award be set aside (or seeking to avoid enforcement, as discussed below) may assert that the tribunal's allegedly erroneous decision on the merits amounted to a "decision on matters beyond the scope of the submission to arbitration," thereby falling under subsection (2)(a)(iii).[19] Such arguments should be rejected, except where the award has decided issues that are unequivocally beyond the scope of any submission to arbitration. An award should not be set aside simply because the tribunal decided submitted issues in a manner that has left one of the parties disappointed, as this would effectively make all awards subject to judicial review on the merits.

Note 3: In some circumstances in which a party has brought an action to set aside an award, and it appears likely that the award is defective in some manner that is subject to correction, it may be possible to reconvene the tribunal. If so, it may be most efficient to allow the tribunal to attempt to remedy any defect before completing the action to set aside the award. Model Law Article 34(4) provides for such a possibility. The court may, if requested by a party, suspend the setting aside proceedings for a time in order to give the arbitral tribunal an opportunity

---

[18] The importance of this point is another reason to use the specific words "final and binding" in any arbitration agreement.

[19] A disappointed party may argue that the parties did not give the arbitrators the "powers" to decide the issue in a manner that is inconsistent with settled law under Article 34(2). Alternatively, a party may argue that an award inconsistent with settled law is contrary to public policy under subsection (2)(b)(ii). Fortunately, the argument has met with little success. Even the unique United States "manifest disregard of the law" standard is rarely employed to vacate an award.

to resume the arbitral proceedings or take such other action as may eliminate any grounds for setting aside the award.[20]

PROBLEM

Problem 10-1: A and B (from Argentina and Brazil, respectively) agree to arbitration of a sale of goods dispute. The agreement provides that "the tribunal shall make an award allowing the prevailing party to recover all of its costs incurred in the arbitration, including its reasonable attorney fees." In the final award, the tribunal grants to A the full amount of its claim, but expressly declines to make any award of costs or attorney fees. Does B have grounds to have the award set aside? What if the agreement expressly precluded the tribunal from making any award of costs or fees and it did so anyway. Would this provide grounds for setting aside the award? If so, does this mandate that the entire award be set aside?

B.   THE EFFECT OF A SUCCESSFUL ACTION TO SET ASIDE—OR IS THE AWARD STILL ENFORCEABLE?

If an award is set aside by a court of appropriate jurisdiction in the place of arbitration, then the award will no longer have any legal force and effect in that country. This primary proposition is clear and is subject to few, if any, exceptions. Under normal circumstances, the award will also be rendered unenforceable in any jurisdiction, including those outside of the place of arbitration. This second proposition is, however, subject to potential exception under certain circumstances. One might reasonably question how an award set aside in one state could possibly have any effect in another state. The answer to this question lies in the character of an international arbitration award and the language of Article VII of the New York Convention.

While an arbitration agreement and any proceedings under that agreement are subject to the law of the place of arbitration, the award nonetheless possesses an international character.[21] Moreover, the New York Convention provides only minimum requirements for enforcement, as Article VII.1 expressly leaves open the potential for broader enforcement under more favorable national law.[22]

---

[20] Model Law Article 34(4).

[21] *Cf. Mitsubishi v. Soler Chrysler-Plymouth, Inc.,* 473 U.S. 614 (1985) (emphasizing the international nature of the transaction and, thereby, taking a strong pro-arbitration view in determining that an action was arbitrable notwithstanding potential statutory anti-trust issues).

[22] "The provisions of the present Convention shall not . . . deprive any interested party of any right he may have to avail himself of an arbitral award in the manner and to the extent allowed by the law . . . of the treaties of the country where such award is sought to be relied upon." New York Convention Article VII.

Article V also makes clear that a competent court ruling setting aside an award allows an enforcing court to decline enforcement, but does not mandate such a result.[23] As such, an enforcing court outside of the place of arbitration may choose not to give effect to a court decision setting aside the award to the extent that such decision is inconsistent with international norms of commercial arbitration and is enforceable under applicable national law.

In the *Chromalloy* cases, this approach was employed by both U.S. and French courts to justify enforcement of an arbitration award set aside by the courts of Egypt, the place of arbitration.[24] This idea of recognizing vacated awards is not, of course, without controversy. In particular, it is important to recognize the right of a court in the place of arbitration to set aside an award that is inconsistent with its own public policy,[25] and failing to respect such a decision is arguably contrary to general notions of comity.

In Part III.B, below, the materials explore a more recent case in which a U.S. court declines to enforce an award that had been set aside by the courts of Columbia, the place of arbitration. The court purported to distinguish *Chromalloy*, but there is also a very different tenor to the opinion. Nonetheless, where a court in the place of arbitration sets aside an international award in a manner that is clearly inconsistent with well established international norms, there remains at least a possibility that a foreign court will decide to enforce the award—notwithstanding the fact that it has been set aside.

III.   WAITING FOR ENFORCEMENT: DEFENSIVELY RESISTING ENFORCEMENT ON ONE'S OWN TURF

In 1895, the U.S. Supreme Court described and generally endorsed the idea of comity, or respect for the judicial pronouncements of other legal systems, as a basis for enforcing judgments rendered by foreign courts.[26] As long as the proceedings leading up to such foreign judgments respected basic commonly held notions of fairness and due process, they should generally be afforded the same sort of deference as those of one's own jurisdiction. Unfortunately, not all

---

[23] "Recognition and enforcement *may* be refused" under the enumerated grounds in subsections (a) through (e) (the latter addressing awards set aside in the place of arbitration). New York Convention Article V (emphasis in original).

[24] *See The Arab Republic of Egypt v. Chromalloy Aeroservices, Inc.,* Cour d'Appel, Paris, Jan. 14 1997 (*published in* 12 International Arbitration Report (1997, no. 4) pp. B-1 to B-4 (in English and French)) (enforcing the award based on French law); *Matter of Chromalloy Aeroservices v. The Arab Republic of Egypt,* 939 F. Supp. 907 (D.D.C. 1996) (enforcing the award based on the U.S. Federal Arbitration Act).

[25] *See* Model Law Article 34(2)(b).

[26] *See Hilton v. Guyot,* 159 U.S. 113 (1895).

national courts share these views, and even those that purport to often apply the principle of comity in ways that are inconsistent and unpredictable at best.[27]

If all courts followed the dictates of *Hilton v. Guyot*, the impact of the New York Convention might have been somewhat less dramatic. As it is, however, the New York Convention, almost uniformly, makes the enforcement of foreign arbitration awards simpler, quicker, and considerably more certain than the enforcement of foreign judgments. While actions to enforce foreign judgments often require state involvement and/or the preparation of "letters rogatory," a sometimes complicated and lengthy process, an action to enforce an arbitration award is quite simple as further described below. As such, the issue of enforcement provides arbitration with one of its greatest advantages over court adjudication.[28]

Under the New York Convention, (A) the judicial enforcement of foreign arbitration awards is a relatively simple and straightforward process. However, even under the Convention, there remain limited (B) grounds for refusing to enforce an award. Perhaps the most important, and the most troublesome, ground for non-enforcement is (C) public policy of the country in which enforcement is sought.

A.   ENFORCEMENT UNDER THE NEW YORK CONVENTION

The centerpiece of the New York Convention, as the primary international instrument mandating enforcement of arbitration awards, is Article III.

Article III

Each Contracting State shall recognize arbitral awards as binding and enforce them in accordance with the rules of procedure of the territory where the award is relied upon, under the conditions

---

[27] *Hilton* is not even necessarily followed in the United States, as the issue of enforcement of a foreign judgment may be governed by state law. While many states have adopted uniform law generally allowing for enforcement of foreign judgments, others have taken a more restrictive approach, and many only enforce judgments from jurisdictions offering reciprocity in enforcement.

[28] The importance (more or less) of this single particular distinction between arbitration and court adjudication may become somewhat clearer in the near future. In 2005, the Geneva Convention of Choice of Court Agreements was completed. Under this Convention, forum selection clauses choosing specific courts would generally be treated in a manner similar to arbitration agreements, and judgments issued by the selected courts would be enforceable in foreign courts in much the same manner as arbitration awards. The Convention has not yet entered into force, but, if widely adopted, it could provide parties with some interesting choices between national courts and private arbitrators.

> laid down in the following articles. There shall not be imposed
> substantially more onerous conditions or higher fees or charges
> on the recognition or enforcement of arbitral awards to which
> this Convention applies than are imposed on the recognition or
> enforcement of domestic arbitral awards.

Note the specific language of Article III. International awards are enforceable, limited only to the terms of the Convention. Moreover, the Convention bars an enforcing court from imposing any greater burden on enforcement of international awards than domestic awards. Thus, an international award may be enforceable even under circumstances in which a domestic award is not. However, the mechanism for enforcement of an international award cannot be burdened to any greater extent than an enforceable domestic award.

The Convention's requirements for enforcement are relatively simple. First, Article II requires a signed writing, the requirements of which were addressed in Chapter 8 in reference to formal validity. Remember, in Chapter 8, the issue was formal validity under the *lex arbitri*, as a threshold jurisdictional issue. Here the issue is enforceability. The importance of UNCITRAL's efforts to bring about uniform standards of interpretation of the writing requirements of Model Law Article 7 and New York Convention Article II should now be much clearer.

Assuming that the formal validity requirements of Article II have been met, the enforcing party must simply comply with the procedural requirements of Article IV.

> **Article IV**
>
> 1. To obtain the recognition and enforcement mentioned in the preceding article, the party applying for recognition and enforcement shall, at the time of the application, supply:
>
> (a) The duly authenticated original award or a duly certified copy thereof;
>
> (b) The original agreement referred to in article II or a duly certified copy thereof.
>
> 2. If the said award or agreement is not made in an official language of the country in which the award is relied upon, the party applying for recognition and enforcement of the award shall produce a translation of these documents into such language. The translation shall be certified by an

> official or sworn translator or by a diplomatic or consular
> agent.

Once the enforcing party has complied with the above procedural requirements, the enforcing court must issue a court decree making the arbitration award fully enforceable as a money judgment, unless the party opposing enforcement can prove one or more of the limited grounds for refusing enforcement.

B.   GROUNDS FOR REFUSING ENFORCEMENT

The New York Convention provides for presumptive enforcement of arbitral awards, subject to a very limited set of grounds. You will note in the text of New York Convention Article V below, that the grounds for refusing enforcement under the New York Convention are virtually identical to the grounds for setting aside an award under the Model Law.[29]   There are only two significant differences, each of which is quite logical in view of the differing context. Take particular note of the ground provided in subsection 1(e), as well as the applicable law in each of the provisions of subsection 2.

> **Article V**
>
> 1. Recognition and enforcement of the award may be refused, at the request of the party against whom it is invoked, only if that party furnishes to the competent authority where the recognition and enforcement is sought, proof that:
>
> (a) The parties to the agreement referred to in article II were, under the law applicable to them, under some incapacity, or the said agreement is not valid under the law to which the parties have subjected it or, failing any indication thereon, under the law of the country where the award was made; or
>
> (b) The party against whom the award is invoked was not given proper notice of the appointment of the arbitrator or of the arbitration proceedings or was otherwise unable to present his case; or

---

[29] The Model Law also addresses actions for enforcement in Article 36. While the provisions of Article 36 are functionally identical to Article V of the New York Convention, these materials will make reference to the New York Convention and Article V in view of the much wider acceptance of the New York Convention on issues governing enforcement.

> (c) The award deals with a difference not contemplated by or not falling within the terms of the submission to arbitration, or it contains decisions on matters beyond the scope of the submission to arbitration, provided that, if the decisions on matters submitted to arbitration can be separated from those not so submitted, that part of the award which contains decisions on matters submitted to arbitration may be recognized and enforced; or
>
> (d) The composition of the arbitral authority or the arbitral procedure was not in accordance with the agreement of the parties, or, failing such agreement, was not in accordance with the law of the country where the arbitration took place; or
>
> (e) The award has not yet become binding on the parties, or has been set aside or suspended by a competent authority of the country in which, or under the law of which, that award was made.
>
> 2. Recognition and enforcement of an arbitral award may also be refused if the competent authority in the country where recognition and enforcement is sought finds that:
>
> (a) The subject matter of the difference is not capable of settlement by arbitration under the law of that country; or
>
> (b) The recognition or enforcement of the award would be contrary to the public policy of that country.

The provisions of subsections 1(a) through 1(d) are obviously the same as those provided under Model Law Article 34. Both the articulation of the relevant standard and the designation of the applicable law are, essentially, identical. Thus, any of the issues addressed in these provisions ought to result in the same decision—irrespective of whether determined in an action to set aside the award or an action to enforce the award.[30]

Subsection 1(e) is the one additional provision of Article V, and its addition is entirely contextual. If a competent court in the place of arbitration has set aside the award, then an enforcing court may decline to enforce it. As explained above, a court is not required to refuse enforcement simply because the

---

[30] In fact, one might even suggest that any decision of one court should have a preclusive effect on the decision of another court. However, the differing nature of the two actions may provide a court with a basis to rule otherwise.

subsection 1(e) has been satisfied. The enforcing court is, essentially, confronted with two competing values: (1) respect for international arbitration awards, and (2) respect for the judgment of a competent foreign court. In the *Chromalloy* case, the former value prevailed. In the case explored in the following example, the latter was arguably paramount.

Example 10-6

TermoRio contracted to sell energy to Electranta, an electrical supplier owned by the Columbian government, and the parties also agreed to arbitrate any disputes under the ICC Rules. Columbia subsequently decided to privatize Electranta and, in doing so, sold all of its assets without requiring the purchasers to assume its contractual obligations. Without any remaining assets, Electranta refused to perform its contractual obligations, and TermoRio successfully obtained a $60 million award against Electranta in the arbitration proceedings. Electranta then sought relief in the Columbian courts, which set aside the award because Columbian law did not at that time expressly permit the use of ICC arbitration rules. TermoRio then attempted to enforce the award in U.S. courts relying on the same theory that had succeeded in the *Chromalloy* case. This court rejected the reasoning of *Chromalloy* and, instead, on notions of comity to the courts of the place of arbitration. In effect, the court stated that, unless the court decision, itself, violated international public policy, an enforcing court should refuse to enforce the award under New York Convention Article V.1.(e). Inasmuch as the Columbian court's decision was not, on its face, improper, the court declined to enforce the award.[31]

The reader will recall the discussion of the *Chromalloy* case in Part I.B, in which the court enforced the award in favor of Chromalloy, notwithstanding the fact that it had been set aside by the government of Egypt. The entire tenor of the *Chromalloy* and *TermoRio* decisions is different.[32] *Chromalloy* focuses entirely on the importance of international commercial arbitration—particularly in

---

[31] *TermoRio S.A. E.S.P. v. Electranta S.P.,* 487 F.3d 928 (D.C. Cir. 2007).

[32] *Compare TermoRio S.A. E.S.P.,* 487 F.3d 928, *with Matter of Chromalloy Aeroservices,* 939 F. Supp. 907. The court attempts, in *TermoRio,* to distinguish *Chromalloy* based on a contractual promise by the award debtor not to seek to set aside the award in Egyptian courts. However, the *Chromalloy* case does not address this issue at all, and such a promise might well be ineffective as an ex-ante waiver of a right to judicial review. In short, this distinction is hardly compelling.

circumstances in which the court sets aside an award against its own government. The Court methodically walked through the discretionary provisions in New York Convention Articles V and VII and then applied the Federal Arbitration Act as a more pro-enforcement regime than the New York Convention under the circumstances of the case. Under remarkably similar circumstances, the *TermoRio* court suggested, with little specific support from the text, that the spirit of the New York Convention required substantial deference to courts in the place of enforcement.

While the *TermoRio* court did not expressly overrule the *Chromalloy* case, it certainly casts doubt upon the continuing vitality of its rationale. The two cases also provide excellent examples of two very different approaches to the question of enforcing international arbitration awards set aside in the place of arbitration. In the case of an international commercial arbitration award, to whom do foreign enforcing courts owe the greatest degree of comity—the arbitration tribunal or the courts in the place of arbitration? One might also ask if the nationality of the enforcing party is significant.[33]

A court seized of an enforcement action may take note of a pending action to set aside the award in the place of arbitration. The court in which the enforcement action is pending may, if it deems it proper, decide to adjourn or temporarily suspend the enforcement action, pending the outcome of the action to set aside the award. If the award is set aside in the place of arbitration, then the enforcing court may decline to enforce it under subsection 1(e), perhaps avoiding a potentially inconsistent decision of its own. Any such adjournment or suspension may, however, delay enforcement. A court may, therefore, require the party opposing enforcement to provide adequate security in view of any potential delay in enforcement.[34]

Subsection 1(e) also provides that a court need not enforce an award that is not yet binding in the place of arbitration.

Example 10-7

Claimant applied to enforce an award under Canada's adoption of Model Law Article 35(1). However, respondent has properly applied to the tribunal for correction of the award, and that request to the tribunal remained pending. As such, the award was not yet final and binding because the tribunal remained

---

[33] In *Chromalloy*, a United States corporation successfully enforced an award against the Egyptian government, even though it had been set aside by the Egyptian courts. In *TermoRio*, a foreign corporation was denied enforcement against former assets of Electranta sold by the Columbian government and then located in the United States.
[34] New York Convention Article VI.

> seized of the matter, and the award was not yet enforceable under Article 36(1)(a)(v) (same as NYC V.1.(e)).[35]

The provisions of subsections 2(a) and 2(b) include the same grounds for non-enforcement as those provided by Model Law Article 34 for setting aside an award. However, the applicable law in each is different. In an action to set aside an award, these provisions focus on the place of arbitration. In an action to enforce the award, these provisions instead focus on the place of enforcement.

In view of the fact that the party is seeking aid in enforcement of the award by the courts of place of enforcement, it would seem appropriate to consider issues of arbitrability and public policy under the law of that state. However, there is also much opportunity for the mischief of protectionism here, which is precisely one of the problems that the New York Convention was intended to remedy. The courts in the place of enforcement are also addressing issues under an applicable body of law that may not have been considered by the court in any earlier action to set aside—that court having considered these issues under its own law. Thus, issues of public policy, generally, deserve special attention when it comes to questions of enforcement.

C.   THE PUBLIC POLICY EXCEPTION: ITS USE AND ABUSE

The public policy exception to enforcement provides perhaps the most fertile grounds for court disputes. On one hand, the exception is important in recognizing that a state court should not be required to enforce an award that "would violate the forum state's most basic notions of morality and justice."[36] On the other hand, it can sometimes be quite difficult to determine whether an important mandatory rule of law may rise to the level of such fundamental notions of public policy. The following case addresses this question, as well as a question involving the validity of the arbitration clause.

---

[35] *Relais Nordik Inc. v. Secunda Marine Services Limited and Anor,* Federal Court, Trial Division, Canada, Apr. 12, 1990, UNCITRAL CLOUT Case 625.
[36] *Parsons & Whittemore Overseas Co., Inc. v. Société Générale de l'Industrie du Papier RAKTA and Bank of America,* 508 F.2d 969 (2d Cir. 1974).

Supreme Court of Korea
Case No. 93Da53054
14 February 1995
(from KluwerArbitration.com)[37]

Facts

Following a dispute between Adviso N.V. and Korea Overseas Construction Corp., an arbitral award was rendered in Zürich awarding damages to Adviso. . . . Adviso sought enforcement of the award in Korea. . . .

[*An excerpt of the decision of the Korean Supreme Court (reviewing the decision of the Seoul Court of Appeals) is presented below*]

I. On the First Argument

Art. IV(1) and (2) of the [1958 New York Convention] (hereinafter the ['New York Convention']) to which Korea became a party on 8 February 1973, prescribes that the party applying for recognition and enforcement of a foreign arbitral award has to meet the burden of proof by submitting (1) the duly authenticated original awards or a duly certified copy thereof and (2) the original arbitration agreement or a duly certified copy thereof and that, in the event that the said award or agreement is not made in an official language of the country in which the award is to be enforced, the party applying for recognition and enforcement of the award must produce a translation of these documents into such official language, certified by an official or sworn translator or by a diplomatic or consular agent.

The requirement [that] the translation of the arbitral award be certified by an official or sworn translator or by a diplomatic or consular agent under Art. IV(2) of the New York Convention does not go so far as to require that such translation be done personally by any of said persons. This requirement is met if anyone of them duly certifies that the translation is the translation of the arbitral awards concerned, even though the text of the arbitral awards is not translated personally by any one of said persons. Thus, an affixation of the signature of a diplomatic or consular agent is not necessarily required; nor does the

---

[37] KluwerArbitration.com, from the *Yearbook Commercial Arbitration,* vol. XXI, 612-616 (Albert J. van den Berg ed., 1996).

meaning of the term 'certified' encompass the certification of the accuracy of the translations.

The Court below held that where the plaintiff-respondent [hereinafter 'plaintiff'] had submitted, as shown by plaintiff Evidence Numbers 1, 2, 7-1 and 7-2, the duly certified copy of the arbitration agreement and the duly certified copy of the arbitral award as well as the translations which had been duly certified by diplomatic agents concerned, the arbitral award was enforceable in Korea in the absence of the reasons for refusal as provided under Art. V(1) and (2) of the New York Convention. We are persuaded that the decision of the Court below is correct and do not agree that the Court below erred in its interpretation of said provision. We reject this argument.

. . .

[*The second argument is omitted*]

. . .

III. On the Third Argument

The Court below noted that in this case the defendant did not argue that the arbitration agreement was void ad initio, but that, since the contract incorporating the arbitration agreement clause had been assigned to a third party, the assignor forfeited its right as a party to the arbitration, or the arbitration clause in the agreement was not valid between the original parties. The Court held that, in such cases, the validity of the arbitration agreement was to be judged by the arbitral tribunal, since such an issue was unavoidably tied to the merits of the arbitration.

Upon review of the award, the Court below found that the arbitration tribunal had decided in its majority opinion that, recognizing that the governing law of the alleged assignment should be the law of the Kingdom of Saudi Arabia which was most closely related to that assignment, the assignment was not valid under the law of Saudi Arabia in consideration of the views of the Committee for Settlement of Commercial Disputes of the Ministry of Justice of the Kingdom of Saudi Arabia and the Saudi Arabian National Center for Science and Technology. Then, the Court below rejected this defendant's argument because, since there were some ambiguities in the choice of the governing law and fact-findings, the arbitration award should be respected and not be reviewed by the courts of the country in which the enforcement is sought, unless accepting the interpretations of the arbitral tribunal was contrary to the fundamental moral principles and concept of justice in Korea.

On review of the records, we conclude that the findings and holdings of the Court below were reasonable and do not agree that the Court below failed to fully try this case in violation of the rules of evidence or that the Court below incorrectly interpreted Art. V(1)(a) of the New York Convention. We reject this argument.

IV. On the Fourth Argument

Art. V(2)(b) of the New York Convention provides that the competent court in the country where recognition and enforcement of an arbitral award is sought may refuse such recognition and enforcement if such court finds that the recognition or enforcement of the award would be contrary to the public policy of that country. The basic tenet of this provision is to protect the fundamental moral beliefs and social order of the country where recognition and enforcement of the award is sought from being harmed by such recognition and enforcement. As due regard should be paid to the stability of international commercial order, as well as domestic concerns, this provision should be interpreted narrowly. (citation omitted). When foreign legal rules applied in an arbitral award are in violation of mandatory provisions of Korean law, such a violation does not necessarily constitute a reason for refusal. Only when the concrete outcome of recognizing such an award is contrary to the good morality and other social order of Korea, will its recognition and enforcement be refused.

The Court below held firstly, that the fact that the period of statute of limitations under the law of the Netherlands Antilles applied in this arbitral award was thirty years and this period was longer than that under the mandatory provisions of the Korean law, did not necessarily render the enforcement of this award in violation of the public order of Korea; secondly, that the determination of the arbitral tribunal that it had jurisdiction because the right of the plaintiff to the defendant on the know-how contract made on 8 November 1978 was not assigned to SECRC, was not in violation of the principle of estoppel or the public order of Korea; thirdly, that the allegation that the plaintiff blackmailed and exercised undue influence on the defendant was not supported by evidence (defendant's Evidence

Numbers 7-1 and 2, and Number 8, submitted in support of this claim, were only letters from the plaintiff or its representatives demanding royalty payments). Also the Court below added that the contract was not unfair even if the contract was biased against the defendant and that the plaintiff's delay in asserting its right did not amount to an abuse. Thereby, the Court below rejected all the arguments claiming violations of the public order.

On review of the records, we conclude that these findings and holdings of the Court below are reasonable and do not agree that the Court below erred in applying Art. V(2)(b) of the New York Convention. We reject this argument.

. . .

* * * * *

Notes and Questions

Note 1: Note the context of the case. The Korean party is the one opposing enforcement. This will often be the case, as a party is attempting to avoid enforcement in its home jurisdiction. The possible temptations for protectionism by the courts are of course obvious. This court appears to do an admirable job of avoiding such temptations.

Note 2: Note the court's statement that the public policy exception must be interpreted narrowly in order to achieve the stability in international commercial transactions intended under the New York Convention. The court goes on to say that a mandatory rule of law does not necessarily rise to the level of a public policy justifying non-enforcement. Instead, only harm to the fundamental moral beliefs and social order of the enforcing state will justify non-enforcement under the Convention's public policy exception. What sort of elements of an award might violate a state's fundamental moral beliefs and social order?

Private international law generally draws a distinction between mandatory legal rules and issues involving *ordre public*. "Mandatory rules" are generally considered to be those legal rules of a state whose law would unequivocally govern a given transaction in the absence of party choice, from which the parties cannot derogate, either by choosing their own terms or by choosing the rules of another legal system.[38] Mandatory rules of another closely connected state,

---

[38] *See e.g.* Rome Convention Article 3. The choice of a given law will also likely subordinate any of the parties' own specific terms to any "mandatory rules" within the chosen body of law.

including the forum, may also be given effect depending on the circumstances.[39] However, a judicial forum may always give effect to its public policy (or *ordre public*) where any otherwise applicable rule is "manifestly incompatible with" that public policy.[40]

Even public policy may be subject to its own gradations. For example, domestic public policy is often distinguished from international public policy, the latter of which is considerably more limited than the former.[41] While such international public policy continues to find its source in the relevant domestic legal order, it is interpreted far more narrowly in view of its application to an international transaction. One could even further narrow the content of public policy by looking to transnational or "truly international public policy" as that having virtually universal application.[42] Such a public policy definition would be comparable to that of *jus cogens* in public international law. Most national courts interpret the public policy exception under the New York Convention based on the middle definition above—"international public policy" or "international *ordre public*" as a very narrow interpretation of domestic public policy concerns, as applied to international business transactions.

While the various national determinations of international public policy are often difficult to define with any precision, they are relegated to a very narrow and limited range of issues. Recognizing legitimate international public policy exceptions is perhaps a bit like recognizing pornography. While U.S. Supreme Court Justice Potter Stewart admitted he could not quite define it precisely, he stated with assurance that "I know it when I see it."[43]

Example 10-8

Parties submitted disputes arising from a contract for the sale of steel wire to the ICC for arbitration. The arbitrators determined the seller was entitled to damages and further determined in accord with French law that the interest rate on the award should increase by 5% two months after the award was issued. Under Article V(2)(b) of the New York Convention, a United States

---

[39] *See e.g.* Rome Convention Article 7. Certain mandatory rules of the forum may also be given particular deference to the extent that a state is being asked to serve as a forum for resolution of the dispute in question.

[40] *See e.g.* Rome Convention Article 16.

[41] *See e.g. Scherk v. Alberto-Culver Co.,* 417 U.S. 506 (1974).

[42] Audley Sheppard, *Interim Report on Public Policy as a Bar to Enforcement of International Arbitration Awards* (2003) (available at kluwerarbitration.com).

[43] *Jacobellis v. Ohio,* 378 U.S. 184 (1964). A similar analogy has been used by Professor Park in addressing abusive practices in arbitration, generally. *See* William W. Park, *Arbitration of International Business Disputes* 222 n. 1 (Oxford U. Press 2006).

> court refused to enforce interest on the award—to the extent of
> the 5% increase. The court ruled that the increased interest was
> penal rather than compensatory and, therefore, violated public
> policy.[44]

Did U.S. District Court above determine "public policy" under Article V(2)(b) in
the same manner as the Korean Supreme Court in the case above? If not, is there
some distinction that might be drawn between the two cases in justifying the
different approach by the U.S. court, or is this simply a case of protectionism?

Example 10-9

A party resisting enforcement of an award in Hong Kong
claimed that a key witness had been kidnapped by the other party
and was only released when he agreed to alter his testimony
before the tribunal. The Hong Kong High Court determined that,
if proven, these factual allegations would preclude enforcement
of the award under Article V(2)(b). The court stated that the
enforcement of an award made on basis of such fraudulently
procured testimony would be a violation of public policy.[45]

Did the Hong Kong High Court above give an appropriately narrow construction
to "public policy" in reaching its decision? Presumably, almost any state would
reach a similar decision on these facts. However, could the court have grounded
its decision on any other provisions of Article V?

Perhaps both the challenges and potential value of the public policy exception are
best expressed by the statements of two different English judges.[46] On one hand,
public policy is "a very unruly horse, and when you get astride it you never know
where it will carry you. It may lead you from sound law [and] it is never argued
at all, but when other points fail."[47] On the other hand, "with a good man [or
woman] in the saddle, the unruly horse can be kept in control."[48] When properly
and narrowly directed, the public policy exception to enforceability under the

---

[44] *See Laminoires-Trefileries-Cableries de Lens S.A. v. Southwire Co.,* 484 F. Supp. 1065 (N.D. Ga. 1980).

[45] *JJ. Agro Industries Ltd., v. Texuna Intl. Ltd.,* [1994] 1 HKLR 89, High Court, Hong Kong, May 29, 1992.

[46] This comparison is drawn from Audley Sheppard, Interim Report on Public Policy as a Bar to Enforcement of International Arbitration Awards (2003) (kluwerarbitration.com).

[47] *Richardson v. Mellish,* 2 Bing. 228 (1824).

[48] *Enderby Town Football Club Ltd v. The Football Association Ltd.,* [1971] Ch. 591 at 606.

New York Convention prevents an appropriate safety valve to avoid the use of public courts in a manner that is truly contrary to a nation's most basic and fundamental notions of morality and justice.

PROBLEMS

Problem 10-2: A U.S. seller obtained an arbitration award against a U.S. consumer (pursuant to an arbitration clause in a contract of sale) and sought to enforce the award in France where the consumer had significant assets. The law of France includes a mandatory rule making such *ex ante* arbitration clauses unenforceable.[49] Should a French court decline enforcement of the award as a matter of "public policy"?

Problem 10-3: A Chinese seller of goods brought an arbitration action against a Saudi buyer in Geneva, under the Swiss Rules. The tribunal issued an award, first determining that the CISG governed the transaction, and further determining that buyer's asserted grounds for avoidance under Article 49(1)(a) did not amount to a fundamental breach under Article 25. The tribunal, therefore, granted the Chinese seller's claim for the unpaid price of the goods (buyer proved no damages) under Article 74 and also awarded interest under Article 78. Interest is considered "*riba*" under the *Shari'a*, Saudi Islamic law, and is barred by the Koran to the extent that it is based on payment of money by one person for the use of the money of another.[50] First, is Saudi Arabia a CISG contracting state? Why would the tribunal apply CISG Article 78 here? Is the award enforceable in Saudi Arabia (Saudi Arabia is a New York Convention contracting state). If a tribunal is uncertain as to whether an award might be enforced under such circumstance, how might any claim of interest be addressed in the award?

---

[49] *See France*, in *International Handbook on Commercial Arbitration* 7 n. 6. (Albert J. van den Berg & Jan Paulsson eds., Kluwer L. Intl. & Intl. Council Commercial Arb., updated through Apr. 2007).

[50] *But see* ICC Case 7063 of 1993. In a case between two Saudi parties, the majority of a split ICC panel awarded an amount calculated only to compensate the party entitled to damages for losses caused by effects of inflation between the time of the harm and the time of the award (i.e., no compensation was awarded as a charge for the use of the money). While the majority of the panel thought that such an additional award solely intended to offset inflation did not violate the doctrine of *riba*, the dissenting panel member did not agree.

APPENDIX A: UNCITRAL MODEL LAW JURISDICTIONS

Jurisdictions with laws based on the UNCITRAL Model Law (1985)

Europe
Austria
Belarus
Bulgaria
Croatia
Denmark
Germany*
Greece
Hungary
Ireland
Lithuania
Malta
Northern Ireland
Norway
Poland
Russia
Scotland
Spain
Ukraine

North America
Bermuda
Canada
Mexico
    (*within U.S.*,
    California,
    Connecticut,
    Illinois, Louisiana,
    North Carolina,
    Oregon, and Texas)

South America
Chile
Guatemala
Nicaragua
Paraguay
Peru

Africa
Egypt
Kenya
Madagascar
Nigeria
Tunisia
Zambia
Zimbabwe

Asia
Bangladesh
Cambodia
India
Japan*
Korea
Philippines
Singapore
Sri Lanka
Thailand
    (*within China*, Hong
    Kong and Macau)

Eurasia
Azerbaijan
Bahrain
Cyprus
Iran
Jordan
Oman
Turkey

Australia
Australia
New Zealand

Examples of Significant National Arbitration Laws *not* Based on the Model Law (though many of these reflect a number of the same principles found in the Model Law)**

China
England
France

Netherlands
Switzerland
Sweden

United States

* This same body of law also governs domestic commercial arbitration.
** While these states have not adopted the Model Law, all have adopted the New York Convention, as have all of the states adopting the Model Law. The English Arbitration Act, in particular, has also adopted much of the approach of the Model Law. However, UNCITRAL does not list the United Kingdom as an enacting state.

APPENDIX B: SOURCES OF CONTRACTING PARTIES' RIGHTS AND OBLIGATIONS

I.   Mandatory Legal Rules[1]

II.   The Parties' Own Terms

    A.   Express Terms

        1.   Terms Specifically Included in the Agreement Itself[2]

        2.   Terms by Reference or Incorporation[3]

    B.   Implied Terms

        1.   Based on the Parties' Past Practices[4]

        2.   Based on Usages within the Relevant Trade[5]

        3.   Based on Other Relevant Circumstances of the Agreement[6]

III. Default Legal Rules[7]

The parties' rights and obligations are typically determined by reference to the content of highest listed item in the hierarchy in which an issue is resolved.

---

[1] Mandatory legal rules cannot be overcome by the express or implied intent of the parties. For example, CISG Article 12 mandatory in that "[t]he parties may not derogate from or vary the effect of this article." Model Law Article 18 is mandatory in requiring that "[t]he parties *shall* be treated with equality and each party *shall* be given a full opportunity of presenting his case" (emphasis supplied).

[2] "Provisions of a specific character prevail over provisions laying down more general rules." UNIDROIT Principle 4.4 (cmt. 2). Individually negotiated terms also prevail over standard terms in a pre-printed form agreement. *See* UNIDROIT Principle 2.1.21.

[3] The parties will often use a variety of terms within their agreement to incorporate, by reference, certain external terms—achieving a thorough treatment of a particular set of issues by using a very brief term included in the agreement itself. For example, parties to a sale of goods contract may use Incoterms 2000 to address issues related to carriage of goods and passage of risk. In a similar vein, parties may include in their arbitration clause an *ad hoc* or institutional body of arbitration rules.

[4] *See, e.g.*, CISG Article 9(1); UNIDROIT Principle 4.3.

[5] *See, e.g.*, CISG Article 9(2); UNIDROIT Principle 4.3.

[6] *See, e.g.*, CISG Article 8(3); UNIDROIT Principle 4.3.

[7] Like mandatory legal rules, default legal rules are also found in the governing law. However, unlike mandatory legal rules, default legal rules may be overcome by the express or implied intent of the parties. For example, CISG Article 35(2) provides default legal rules defining "conforming" goods, while Model Law Article 11 provides default legal rules for appointing arbitrators. In each case, the parties' intent is given priority if it has been expressed or may be factually implied. If not, then the default legal rule will control. In common law legal systems, default legal rules are often said to be "implied-in-law," (in contrast to parties' own "implied-in-fact" terms). In civil law legal systems, default legal rules are said to arise naturally, as standard incidents of certain types of contracts, based on the character of agreement itself (*e.g.*, *lois supplétives* under the French Civil Code).

APPENDIX C: SOURCES OF LAW AND PARTY INTENT APPLICABLE IN INTERNATIONAL COMMERCIAL ARBITRATION

Arbitration Agreement		
Formal Validity	Substantive Validity	Interpretation & Scope
Lex Arbitri **and** State of Enforcement	Law of Place* **or** Chosen by Parties	Law of Place* **or** Chosen by Parties

Arbitrability and Public Policy
Law of Place* **and** State of Enforcement

Arbitration Procedure**	Substantive Claims & Defenses
Lex Arbitri (mandatory rules)	Substantive Law (mandatory rules)
Specific Party Terms	Parties' Substantive Agreement
Arbitration Rules (if any)	Parties' Substantive Agreement
Lex Arbitri (default rules)	Substantive Law (default rules)

Action to Set Aside Award	Action to Enforce Award
Lex Arbitri	New York Convention (1958)

*   The law of the place regarding substantive validity, interpretation of the arbitration agreement, arbitrability or other public policy may be the *lex arbitri* or may be other local law of the place of arbitration.

**   The arbitration procedure includes issues involving the authority to decide jurisdiction, separability, the constitution of the tribunal, and the actual procedure employed in deciding the merits of the parties' dispute.

APPENDIX D: GROUNDS TO SET ASIDE OR REFUSE ENFORCEMENT OF AN ARBITRATION AWARD

Action to Set Aside the Award in the Courts of the Place of Arbitration		Action to Enforce the Award in the Courts of the Place of Enforcement
Model Law Article 34	Bases for Setting Aside or Refusing to Enforce an Award	**New York Convention Article V**[1]
(2)(a)(i)	No Valid Arbitration Agreement (including lack of capacity and both formal and substantive invalidity)	1(a)
(2)(a)(ii)	Party Did Not Receive Proper Notice or Full and Fair Opportunity to Present Case (i.e., Due Process)	1(b)
(2)(a)(iii)	Award is Outside Scope of Submission to Arbitration—Based on Arbitration Agreement or Terms of Reference	1(c)
(2)(a)(iv)	Constitution of the Arbitral Tribunal Not in Accord with Parties' Agreement or the *Lex Arbitri* Default Legal Rules	1(d)
If set aside or not binding in place of arbitration →		1(e)
(2)(b)(i)[*]	Arbitrability of the Subject Matter of the Dispute	2(a)[**]
(2)(b)(ii)[*]	Public Policy	2(b)[**]

---

[1] These same grounds for non-enforcement are also found in Model Law Article 36. However, the New York Convention has been more widely ratified than the Model Law has been enacted, so the Convention provides a preferred point of reference.

[*] This standard is applied under the law of the place of arbitration.

[**] This standard is applied under the law of the place of enforcement.

INDEX